MACROECONOMICS

TENTH EDITION

MICHAEL PARKIN
University of Western Ontario

Addison-Wesley
Boston Columbus Indianapolis New York San Francisco Upper Saddle River
Amsterdam Cape Town Dubai London Madrid Milan Munich Paris Montréal Toronto
Delhi Mexico City São Paulo Sydney Hong Kong Seoul Singapore Taipei Tokyo

Editor in Chief	Donna Battista
Senior Acquisitions Editor	Adrienne D'Ambrosio
Development Editor	Deepa Chungi
Managing Editor	Nancy Fenton
Assistant Editor	Jill Kolongowski
Photo Researcher	Angel Chavez
Production Coordinator	Alison Eusden
Director of Media	Susan Schoenberg
Senior Media Producer	Melissa Honig
Executive Marketing Manager	Lori DeShazo
Rights and Permissions Advisor	Jill Dougan
Senior Manufacturing Buyer	Carol Melville
Senior Media Buyer	Ginny Michaud
Copyeditor	Catherine Baum
Art Director and Cover Designer	Jonathan Boylan
Technical Illustrator	Richard Parkin
Text Design, Project Management and Page Make-up	Integra Software Services, Inc.

Cover Image: Medioimages/PhotoDisc/Getty Images

Photo credits appear on page C-1, which constitutes a continuation of the copyright page.

Library of Congress Cataloging-in-Publication Data
Parkin, Michael, 1939–
Macroeconomics/Michael Parkin. — 10th ed.
p. cm.
Includes index.
ISBN 978-0-13-139445-2 (alk. paper)
1. Economics. I. Title.
HB171.5.P313 2010
330—dc22 2010045760

2 3 4 5 6 7 8 10—CRK—14 13 12 11

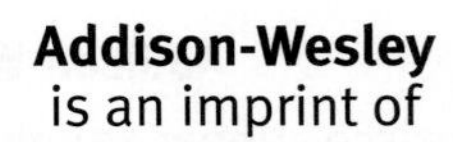

www.pearsonhighered.com

ISBN 10: 0-13-139445-2
ISBN 13: 978-0-13-139445-2

TO ROBIN

ABOUT THE AUTHOR

Michael Parkin is Professor Emeritus in the Department of Economics at the University of Western Ontario, Canada. Professor Parkin has held faculty appointments at Brown University, the University of Manchester, the University of Essex, and Bond University. He is a past president of the Canadian Economics Association and has served on the editorial boards of the *American Economic Review* and the *Journal of Monetary Economics* and as managing editor of the *Canadian Journal of Economics*. Professor Parkin's research on macroeconomics, monetary economics, and international economics has resulted in over 160 publications in journals and edited volumes, including the *American Economic Review*, the *Journal of Political Economy*, the *Review of Economic Studies*, the *Journal of Monetary Economics*, and the *Journal of Money, Credit and Banking*. He became most visible to the public with his work on inflation that discredited the use of wage and price controls. Michael Parkin also spearheaded the movement toward European monetary union. Professor Parkin is an experienced and dedicated teacher of introductory economics.

BRIEF CONTENTS

ALTERNATIVE PATHWAYS THROUGH THE CHAPTERS

Macro Flexibility

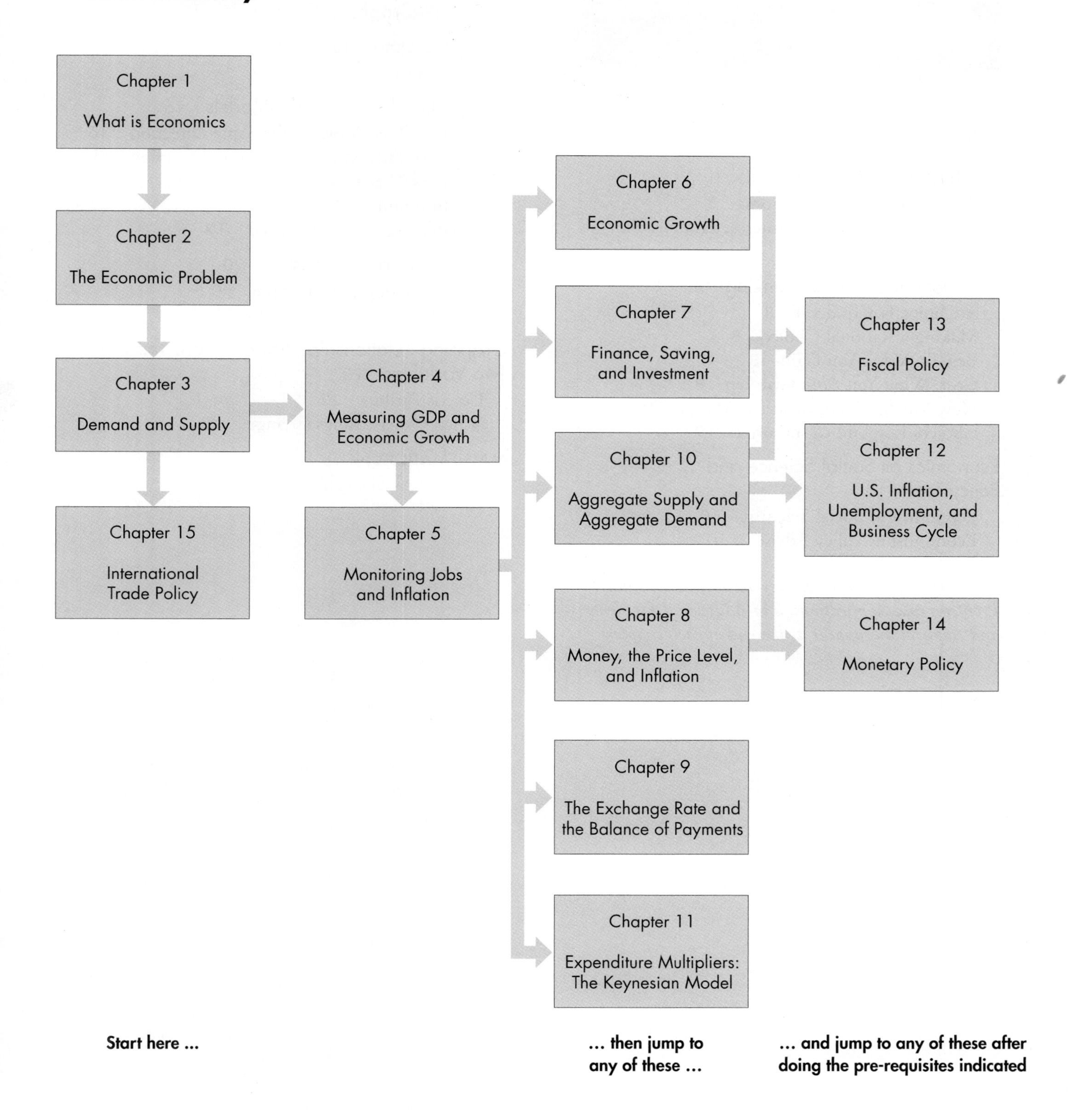

Start here ...

... then jump to any of these ...

... and jump to any of these after doing the pre-requisites indicated

TABLE OF CONTENTS

PART ONE INTRODUCTION 1

PART TWO
MONITORING MACROECONOMIC
PERFORMANCE 83

PART THREE MACROECONOMIC TRENDS 133

PART FOUR
MACROECONOMIC FLUCTUATIONS 241

The future is always uncertain. But at some times, and now is one such time, the range of possible near-future events is enormous. The major source of this great uncertainty is economic policy. There is uncertainty about the way in which international trade policy will evolve as protectionism is returning to the political agenda. There is uncertainty about exchange rate policy as competitive devaluation rears its head. There is extraordinary uncertainty about monetary policy with the Fed having doubled the quantity of bank reserves and continuing to create more money in an attempt to stimulate a flagging economy. And there is uncertainty about fiscal policy as a trillion dollar deficit interacts with an aging population to create a national debt time bomb.

Since the subprime mortgage crisis of August 2007 moved economics from the business report to the front page, justified fear has gripped producers, consumers, financial institutions, and governments.

Even the *idea* that the market is an efficient mechanism for allocating scarce resources came into question as some political leaders trumpeted the end of capitalism and the dawn of a new economic order in which tighter regulation reigned in unfettered greed.

Rarely do teachers of economics have such a rich feast on which to draw. And rarely are the principles of economics more surely needed to provide the solid foundation on which to think about economic events and navigate the turbulence of economic life.

Although thinking like an economist can bring a clearer perspective to and deeper understanding of today's events, students don't find the economic way of thinking easy or natural. *Macroeconomics* seeks to put clarity and understanding in the grasp of the student through its careful and vivid exploration of the tension between self-interest and the social interest, the role and power of incentives—of opportunity cost and marginal benefit—and demonstrating the possibility that markets supplemented by other mechanisms might allocate resources efficiently.

Parkin students begin to think about issues the way real economists do and learn how to explore difficult policy problems and make more informed decisions in their own economic lives.

The Tenth Edition Revision

Simpler where possible, stripped of some technical detail, more copiously illustrated with well-chosen photographs, reinforced with improved chapter summaries and problem sets, and even more tightly integrated with MyEconLab: These are the hallmarks of this tenth edition of *Macroeconomics*.

This comprehensive revision also incorporates and responds to the detailed suggestions for improvements made by reviewers and users, both in the broad architecture of the text and each chapter.

The revision builds on the improvements achieved in previous editions and retains its thorough and detailed presentation of the principles of economics, its emphasis on real-world examples and applications, its development of critical thinking skills, its diagrams renowned for pedagogy and precision, and its path-breaking technology.

Most chapters have been fine-tuned to achieve even greater clarity and to present the material in a more straightforward, visual, and intuitive way. Some chapters have been thoroughly reworked to cover new issues, particularly those that involve current policy problems. These changes are aimed at better enabling students to learn how to use the economic toolkit to analyze their own decisions and understand the events and issues they are confronted with in the media and at the ballot box.

Current issues organize each chapter. News stories about today's major economic events tie each chapter together, from new chapter-opening vignettes to end-of-chapter problems and online practice. Each chapter includes a discussion of a critical issue of our time to demonstrate how economic theory can be applied to explore a particular debate or question. Among the many issues covered are

- The gains from trade, globalization, and protectionism in Chapters 2 and 15 and an updated conversation with Jagdish Bhagwati in the first part closer
- How ethanol competes with food and drives its price up in Chapter 2
- The Fed's extraordinary actions and their impact on the balance sheets of banks in Chapter 8
- Stubbornly high unemployment in Chapters 5, 10, and 12

- Currency fluctuations and the managed Chinese yuan in Chapter 9
- Fiscal stimulus and the debate about the fiscal stimulus multipliers in Chapter 13
- Monetary stimulus in Chapter 14 and the dangers of targeting unemployment in an updated conversation with Stephanie Schmitt-Grohé
- Real-world examples and applications appear in the body of each chapter and in the end-of-chapter problems and applications

A selection of questions that appear daily in MyEconLab in *Economics in the News* are also available for assignment as homework, quizzes, or tests.

Highpoints of the Revision

All the chapters have been updated to incorporate data through the second quarter of 2010 (later for some variables) and the news and policy situation through the fall of 2010. Beyond these general updates, the chapters feature the following eight notable revisions:

1. ***What Is Economics?*** (Chapter 1): I have reworked the explanation of the economic way of thinking around six key ideas, all illustrated with student-relevant choices. The graphing appendix to this chapter has an increased focus on scatter diagrams and their interpretation and on understanding shifts of curves.
2. ***Measuring GDP and Economic Growth*** (Chapter 4): I have revised the section on cross-country comparisons and the limitations of GDP to make the material clearer and added photo illustrations of *PPP* and items omitted from GDP. This chapter now has a graphing appendix which focuses on time-series and ratio scale graphs.
3. ***Monitoring Jobs and Inflation*** (Chapter 5): This chapter now includes a discussion and illustration of the alternative measures of unemployment reported by the BLS and the costs of different types of unemployment. I have rewritten the section on full employment and the influences on the natural unemployment rate and illustrated this discussion with a box on structural unemployment in Michigan. The coverage of the price level has been expanded to define and explain the costs of deflation as well as inflation.
4. ***Economic Growth*** (Chapter 6): I have simplified this chapter by omitting the technical details on growth accounting and replacing them with an intuitive discussion of the crucial role of human capital and intellectual property rights. I illustrate the role played by these key factors in Britain's *Industrial Revolution.* I have made the chapter more relevant and empirical by including a summary of the correlations between the growth rate and the positive and negative influences on it.
5. ***Money, the Price Level, and Inflation*** (Chapter 8): This chapter records and explains the Fed's extraordinary injection of monetary base following the financial panic of 2008. In revising this chapter, I have redrawn the line between this chapter, the "money and banking" chapter, and the later "monetary policy" chapter by including in this chapter a complete explanation of how an open-market operation works. I have also provided clearer and more thorough explanations of the money multiplier and money market equilibrium in the short and the long run and in the transition to the long run.
6. ***The Exchange Rate and the Balance of Payments*** (Chapter 9): I have revised this chapter to better explain the distinction between the fundamentals and the role of expectations. I have also included an explanation of how arbitrage works in the foreign exchange market and the temporary and risky nature of seeking to profit from the so-called "carry trade."
7. ***Fiscal Policy*** (Chapter 13): The topic of this chapter is front-page news almost every day and is likely to remain so. The revision describes the deficit and the accumulating debt and explains the consequences of the uncertainty they engender. An entirely new section examines the fiscal stimulus measures taken over the past year, channels through which stimulus works, its unwanted side-effects, its potentially limited power, and its shortcomings. The controversy about and range of views on the magnitude of fiscal stimulus multiplier is examined.
8. ***Monetary Policy*** (Chapter 14): This chapter describes and explains the dramatic monetary policy responses to the 2008–2009 recession and the persistently high unemployment of 2010. It also contains an improved description of the FOMC's decision-making process. Technical details about alternative monetary policy strategies have been replaced with a shorter and more focused discussion of inflation targeting as a tool for bringing clarity to monetary policy and anchoring inflation expectations.

Features to Enhance Teaching and Learning

Reading Between the Lines

This Parkin hallmark helps students think like economists by connecting chapter tools and concepts to the world around them. In *Reading Between the Lines*, which appears at the end of each chapter, students apply the tools they have just learned by analyzing an article from a newspaper or news Web site. Each article sheds additional light on the questions first raised in the Chapter Opener. Questions about the article also appear with the end-of-chapter problems and applications.

READING BETWEEN THE LINES

Demand and Supply: The Price of Coffee

Coffee Surges on Poor Colombian Harvests

FT.com
July 30, 2010

Coffee prices hit a 12-year high on Friday on the back of low supplies of premium Arabica coffee from Colombia after a string of poor crops in the Latin American country.

The strong fundamental picture has also encouraged hedge funds to reverse their previous bearish views on coffee prices.

In New York, ICE September Arabica coffee jumped 3.2 percent to 178.75 cents per pound, the highest since February 1998. It traded later at 177.25 cents, up 6.8 percent on the week.

The London-based International Coffee Organization on Friday warned that the "current tight demand and supply situation" was "likely to persist in the near to medium term."

Coffee industry executives believe prices could rise toward 200 cents per pound in New York before the arrival of the new Brazilian crop later this year.

"Until October it is going to be tight on high quality coffee," said a senior executive at one of Europe's largest coffee roasters. He said: "The industry has been surprised by the scarcity of high quality beans."

ESSENCE OF THE STORY

- The price of premium Arabica coffee increased by 3.2 percent to almost 180 cents per pound in July 2010, the highest price since February 1998

ECONOMIC ANALYSIS

- This news article reports two sources of changes in supply and demand that changed the price of coffee.
- The first source of change is the sequence of poor harvests in Columbia. These events decreased the world supply of Arabica coffee. (Arabica is the type that Starbucks uses.)
- Before the reported events, the world production of Arabica was 120 million bags per year and its price was 174 cents per pound.
- The decrease in the Columbian harvest decreased world production to about 116 million bags, which is about 3 percent of world production.
- Figure 1 shows the situation before the poor Columbia harvests and the effects of those poor harvests. The demand curve is *D* and initially, the supply curve was S^0. The market equilibrium is at 120 million bags per year and a price of 174 cents per pound.

Decrease in Columbia crop ...
... raises price ...
... and decreases quantity
Price (cents per pound)
Quantity (millions of bags)

Figure 1 The effects of the Columbian crop

Economics in the News

31. After you have studied *Reading Between the Lines* on pp. 74–75 answer the following questions.
    a. What happened to the price of coffee in 2010?
    b. What substitutions do you expect might have been made to decrease the quantity of coffee demanded?
    c. What influenced the demand for coffee in 2010 and what influenced the quantity of coffee demanded?

Diagrams That Show the Action

Through the past nine editions, this book has set new standards of clarity in its diagrams; the tenth edition continues to uphold this tradition. My goal has always been to show "where the economic action is." The diagrams in this book continue to generate an enormously positive response, which confirms my view that graphical analysis is the most powerful tool available for teaching and learning economics.

Because many students find graphs hard to work with, I have developed the entire art program with the study and review needs of the student in mind.

The diagrams feature:

- Original curves consistently shown in blue
- Shifted curves, equilibrium points, and other important features highlighted in red
- Color-blended arrows to suggest movement
- Graphs paired with data tables
- Diagrams labeled with boxed notes
- Extended captions that make each diagram and its caption a self-contained object for study and review.

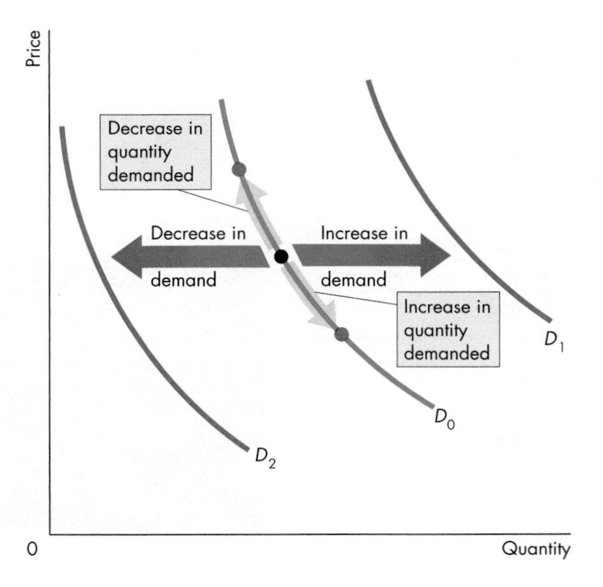

Economics in Action Boxes

This new feature uses boxes within the chapter to address current events and economic occurrences that highlight and amplify the topics covered in the chapter. Instead of simply reporting the current events, the material in the boxes applies the event to an economics lesson, enabling students to see how economics plays a part in the world around them as they read through the chapter.

Some of the many issues covered in these boxes include the global market for crude oil, the structural unemployment in Michigan, how loanable funds fuel a home price bubble, and the size of the fiscal stimulus multipliers. A complete list can be found on the inside back cover.

Economics in Action

The Global Market for Crude Oil

The demand and supply model provides insights into all competitive markets. Here, we'll apply what you've learned about the effects of an increase in demand to the global market for crude oil.

Crude oil is like the life-blood of the global economy. It is used to fuel our cars, airplanes, trains, and buses, to generate electricity, and to produce a wide range of plastics. When the price of crude oil rises, the cost of transportation, power, and materials all increase.

In 2001, the price of a barrel of oil was $20 (using the value of money in 2010). In 2008, before the global financial crisis ended a long period of economic expansion, the price peaked at $127 a barrel.

While the price of oil was rising, the quantity of oil produced and consumed also increased. In 2001, the world produced 65 million barrels of oil a day. By 2008, that quantity was 72 million barrels.

Who or what has been raising the price of oil? Is it the action of greedy oil producers? Oil producers might be greedy, and some of them might be big enough to withhold supply and raise the price, but it wouldn't be in their self-interest to do so. The higher price would bring forth a greater quantity supplied from other producers and the profit of the producer limiting supply would fall.

Oil producers could try to cooperate and jointly withhold supply. The Organization of Petroleum Exporting Countries, OPEC, is such a group of producers. But OPEC doesn't control the *world* supply and its members' self-interest is to produce the quantities that give them the maximum attainable profit.

So even though the global oil market has some big players, they don't fix the price. Instead, the actions of thousands of buyers and sellers and the forces of demand and supply determine the price of oil.

So how have demand and supply changed?

Because both the price and the quantity have increased, the demand for oil must have increased. Supply might have changed too, but here we'll suppose that supply has remained the same.

The global demand for oil has increased for one major reason: World income has increased. The increase has been particularly large in the emerging economies of Brazil, China, and India. Increased world income has increased the demand for oil-using goods such as electricity, gasoline, and plastics, which in turn has increased the demand for oil.

The figure illustrates the effects of the increase in demand on the global oil market. The supply of oil remained constant along supply curve *S*. The demand for oil in 2001 was D_{2001}, so in 2001 the price was $20 a barrel and the quantity was 65 million barrels per day. The demand for oil increased and by 2008 it had reached D_{2008}. The price of oil increased to $127 a barrel and the quantity increased to 72 million barrels a day. The increase in the quantity is an *increase in the quantity supplied*, not an increase in supply.

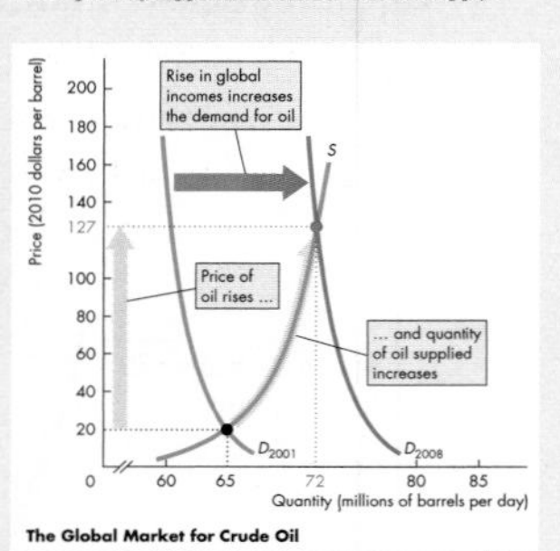

The Global Market for Crude Oil

Chapter Openers

Each chapter opens with a student-friendly vignette that raises questions to motivate the student and focus the chapter. This chapter-opening story is woven into the main body of the chapter and is explored in the *Reading Between the Lines* feature that ends each chapter.

Key Terms

Highlighted terms simplify the student's task of learning the vocabulary of economics. Each highlighted term appears in an end-of-chapter list with its page number, in an end-of-book glossary with its page number, boldfaced in the index, in MyEconLab, in the interactive glossary, and in the Flash Cards.

In-Text Review Quizzes

A review quiz at the end of each major section enables students to determine whether a topic needs further study before moving on. This feature includes a reference to the appropriate MyEconLab study plan to help students further test their understanding.

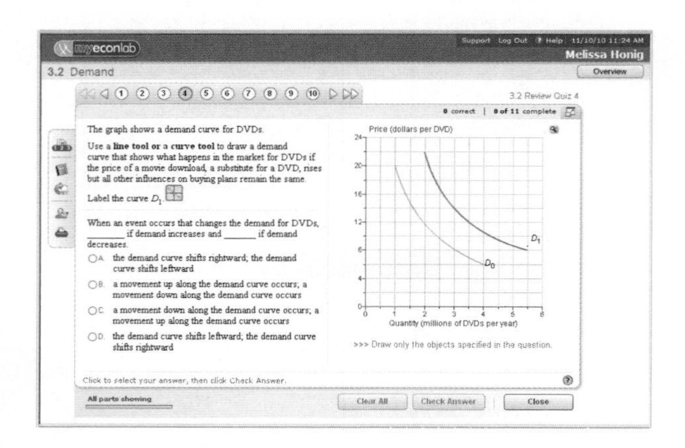

End-of-Chapter Study Material

Each chapter closes with a concise summary organized by major topics, lists of key terms with page references, and problems and applications. These learning tools provide students with a summary for review and exam preparation.

Interviews with Economists

Each major part of the text closes with a summary feature that includes an interview with a leading economist whose research and expertise correlates to what the student has just learned. These interviews explore the background, education, and research these prominent economists have conducted, as well as advice for those who want to continue the study of economics. I have returned to Jagdish Bhagwati, Stephanie Schmitt-Grohé, and Richard Clarida (all of Columbia University) and Ricardo Caballero (of the Massachusetts Institute of Technology) and included their more recent thoughts on our rapidly changing economic times.

For the Instructor

This book enables you to focus on the economic way of thinking and choose your own course structure in your principles course:

Focus on the Economic Way of Thinking

As an instructor, you know how hard it is to encourage a student to think like an economist. But that is your goal. Consistent with this goal, the text focuses on and repeatedly uses the central ideas: choice; tradeoff; opportunity cost; the margin; incentives; the gains from voluntary exchange; the forces of demand, supply, and equilibrium; the pursuit of economic rent; the tension between self-interest and the social interest; and the scope and limitations of government actions.

Flexible Structure

You have preferences for how you want to teach your course. I have organized this book to enable you to do so. The flexibility chart on p. vii illustrates the book's flexibility. By following the arrows through the charts you can select the path that best fits your preference for course structure. Whether you want to teach a traditional course that blends theory and policy, or one that takes a fast-track through either theory or policy issues, *Macroeconomics* gives you the choice.

Supplemental Resources

Instructor's Manual We have streamlined and reorganized the Instructor's Manual to reflect the focus and intuition of the tenth edition. The *Macroeconomics* Instructor's Manual written by Russ McCullough at Iowa State University, integrates the teaching and learning package and serves as a guide to all the supplements.

Each chapter contains

- A chapter overview
- A list of what's new in the tenth edition
- Ready-to-use lecture notes from each chapter enable a new user of Parkin to walk into a classroom armed to deliver a polished lecture. The lecture notes provide an outline of the chapter; concise statements of key material; alternative tables and figures; key terms and definitions; and boxes that highlight key concepts; provide an interesting anecdote, or suggest how to handle a difficult idea; and additional discussion questions. The PowerPoint® lecture notes incorporate the chapter outlines and teaching suggestions.

Solutions Manual For ease of use and instructor reference, a comprehensive solutions manual provides instructors with solutions to the Review Quizzes and the end-of-chapter Problems and Applications as well as additional problems and the solutions to these problems. Written by Mark Rush of the University of Florida and reviewed for accuracy by Jeannie Gillmore of the University of Western Ontario, the Solutions Manual is available in hard copy and electronically on the Instructor's Resource Center CD-ROM, in the Instructor's Resources section of MyEconLab, and on the Instructor's Resource Center.

Test Item File Three separate Test Item Files with nearly 7,000 questions, provide multiple-choice, true/false, numerical, fill-in-the-blank, short-answer, and essay questions. Mark Rush reviewed and edited all existing questions to ensure their clarity and consistency with the tenth edition and incorporated new questions into the thousands of existing Test Bank questions. The new questions, written by Barbara Moore at the University of Central Florida and Luke Armstrong at Lee College, follow the style and format of the end-of-chapter text problems and provide the instructor with a whole new set of testing opportunities and/or homework assignments. Additionally, end-of-part tests contain questions that cover all the chapters in the part and feature integrative questions that span more than one chapter.

Computerized Testbanks Fully networkable, the test banks are available for Windows® and Macintosh®. TestGen's graphical interface enables instructors to view, edit, and add questions; transfer questions to tests; and print different forms of tests. Tests can be formatted with varying fonts and styles, margins, and headers and footers, as in any word-processing document. Search and sort features let the instructor quickly locate questions and arrange them in a preferred order. QuizMaster, working with your school's computer network, automatically grades the exams, stores the results, and allows the instructor to view or print a variety of reports.

PowerPoint Resources Robin Bade has developed a full-color Microsoft® PowerPoint Lecture Presentation for each chapter that includes all the figures and tables from the text, animated graphs, and speaking notes. The lecture notes in the Instructor's Manual and the slide outlines are correlated, and the speaking notes are based on the Instructor's Manual teaching suggestions. A separate set of PowerPoint files containing large-scale versions of all the text's figures (most of them animated) and tables (some of which are animated) are also available. The presentations can be used electronically in the classroom or can be printed to create hard copy transparency masters. This item is available for Macintosh and Windows.

Clicker-Ready PowerPoint Resources This edition features the addition of clicker-ready PowerPoint slides for the Personal Response System you use. Each chapter of the text includes ten multiple-choice questions that test important concepts. Instructors can assign these as in-class assignments or review quizzes.

Instructor's Resource Center CD-ROM Fully compatible with Windows and Macintosh, this CD-ROM contains electronic files of every instructor supplement for the tenth edition. Files included are: Microsoft® Word and Adobe® PDF files of the Instructor's Manual, Test Item Files and Solutions Manual; PowerPoint resources; and the Computerized TestGen® Test Bank. Add this useful resource to your exam copy bookbag, or locate your local Pearson Education sales representative at www.pearsonhighered.educator to request a copy.

Instructors can download supplements from a secure, instructor-only source via the Pearson Higher Education Instructor Resource Center Web page (www.pearsonhighered.com/irc).

BlackBoard and WebCT BlackBoard and WebCT Course Cartridges are available for download from www.pearsonhighered.com/irc. These standard course cartridges contain the Instructor's Manual, Solutions Manual, TestGen Test Item Files, Instructor PowerPoints, Student Powerpoints and Student Data Files.

Study Guide The tenth edition Study Guide by Mark Rush is carefully coordinated with the text, MyEconLab, and the Test Item Files. Each chapter of the Study Guide contains

- Key concepts
- Helpful hints
- True/false/uncertain questions
- Multiple-choice questions
- Short-answer questions
- Common questions or misconceptions that the student explains as if he or she were the teacher
- Each part allows students to test their cumulative understanding with questions that go across chapters and to work a sample midterm examination.

MYECONLAB myeconlab

MyEconLab's powerful assessment and tutorial system works hand-in-hand with *Macroeconomics*. With comprehensive homework, quiz, test, and tutorial options, instructors can manage all assessment needs in one program.

- All of the Review Quiz questions and end-of-chapter Problems and Applications are assignable and automatically graded in MyEconLab.
- Students can work all the Review Quiz questions and end-of-chapter Study Plan Problems and Applications as part of the Study Plan in MyEconLab.
- Instructors can assign the end-of-chapter Additional Problems and Applications as auto-graded assignments. These Problems and Applications are not available to students in MyEconLab unless assigned by the instructor.
- Many of the problems and applications are algorithmic, draw-graph, and numerical exercises.
- Test Item File questions are available for assignment as homework.
- The Custom Exercise Builder allows instructors the flexibility of creating their own problems for assignment.
- The powerful Gradebook records each student's performance and time spent on Tests, the Study Plan, and homework and generates reports by student or by chapter.
- *Economics in the News* is a turn-key solution to bringing daily news into the classroom. Updated daily during the academic year, I upload two relevant articles (one micro, one macro) and provide links for further information and questions that may be assigned for homework or for classroom discussion.
- A comprehensive suite of ABC news videos, which address current topics such as education, energy, Federal Reserve policy, and business cycles, is available for classroom use. Video-specific exercises are available for instructor assignment.

Robin Bade and I, assisted by Jeannie Gillmore and Laurel Davies, author and oversee all of the MyEconLab content for *Macroeconomics*. Our peerless MyEconLab team has worked hard to ensure that it is tightly integrated with the book's content and vision. A more detailed walk-through of the student benefits and features of MyEconLab can be found on the inside front cover. Visit www.myeconlab.com for more information and an online demonstration of instructor and student features.

Experiments in MyEconLab

Experiments are a fun and engaging way to promote active learning and mastery of important economic concepts. Pearson's experiments program is flexible and easy for instructors and students to use.

- Single-player experiments allow your students to play against virtual players from anywhere at anytime with an Internet connection.
- Multiplayer experiments allow you to assign and manage a real-time experiment with your class.

Pre-and post-questions for each experiment are available for assignment in MyEconLab.

Economics Videos and Assignable Questions Featuring abcNEWS Economics videos featuring ABC news enliven your course with short news clips featuring real-world issues. These videos, available in MyEconLab, feature news footage and commentary by economists. Questions and problems for each video clip are available for assignment in MyEconLab.

Acknowledgments

I thank my current and former colleagues and friends at the University of Western Ontario who have taught me so much. They are Jim Davies, Jeremy Greenwood, Ig Horstmann, Peter Howitt, Greg Huffman, David Laidler, Phil Reny, Chris Robinson, John Whalley, and Ron Wonnacott. I also thank Doug McTaggart and Christopher Findlay, co-authors of the Australian edition, and Melanie Powell and Kent Matthews, coauthors of the European edition. Suggestions arising from their adaptations of earlier editions have been helpful to me in preparing this edition.

I thank the several thousand students whom I have been privileged to teach. The instant response that comes from the look of puzzlement or enlightenment has taught me how to teach economics.

It is a special joy to thank the many outstanding editors, media specialists, and others at Addison-Wesley who contributed to the concerted publishing effort that brought this edition to completion. Denise Clinton, Publisher of MyEconLab has played a major role in the evolution of this text since its third edition, and her insights and ideas can still be found in this new edition. Donna Battista, Editor-in-Chief for Economics and Finance, is hugely inspiring and has provided overall direction to the project. As ever, Adrienne D'Ambrosio, Senior Acquisitions Editor for Economics and my sponsoring editor, played a major role in shaping this revision and the many outstanding supplements that accompany it. Adrienne brings intelligence and insight to her work and is the unchallengeable pre-eminent economics editor. Deepa Chungi, Development Editor, brought a fresh eye to the development process, obtained outstanding reviews from equally outstanding reviewers, digested and summarized the reviews, and made many solid suggestions as she diligently worked through the drafts of this edition. Deepa also provided outstanding photo research. Nancy Fenton, Managing Editor, managed the entire production and design effort with her usual skill, played a major role in envisioning and implementing the cover design, and coped fearlessly with a tight production schedule. Susan Schoenberg, Director of Media, directed the development of MyEconLab; Noel Lotz, Content Lead for MyEconLab, managed a complex and thorough reviewing process for the content of MyEconLab; and Melissa Honig, Senior Media Producer ensured that all our media assets were correctly assembled. Lori Deshazo, Executive Marketing Manager, provided inspired marketing strategy and direction. Catherine Baum provided a careful, consistent, and intelligent copy edit and accuracy check. Jonathan Boylan designed the cover and package and yet again surpassed the challenge of ensuring that we meet the highest design standards. Joe Vetere provided endless technical help with the text and art files. Jill Kolongowski and Alison Eusden managed our immense supplements program. And Heather Johnson with the other members of an outstanding editorial and production team at Integra-Chicago kept the project on track on an impossibly tight schedule. I thank all of these wonderful people. It has been inspiring to work with them and to share in creating what I believe is a truly outstanding educational tool.

I thank our talented tenth edition supplements authors and contributors—Luke Armstrong, Jeannie Gillmore, Laurel Davies, Gary Hoover, Svitlana Maksymenko, Russ McCullough, Barbara Moore, Jim Self, and Laurie Wolff.

I especially thank Mark Rush, who yet again played a crucial role in creating another edition of this text and package. Mark has been a constant source of good advice and good humor.

I thank the many exceptional reviewers who have shared their insights through the various editions of this book. Their contribution has been invaluable.

I thank the people who work directly with me. Jeannie Gillmore provided outstanding research assistance on many topics, including the *Reading Between the Lines* news articles. Richard Parkin created the electronic art files and offered many ideas that improved the figures in this book. And Laurel Davies managed an ever-growing and ever more complex MyEconLab database.

As with the previous editions, this one owes an enormous debt to Robin Bade. I dedicate this book to her and again thank her for her work. I could not have written this book without the tireless and unselfish help she has given me. My thanks to her are unbounded.

Classroom experience will test the value of this book. I would appreciate hearing from instructors and students about how I can continue to improve it in future editions.

Michael Parkin
London, Ontario, Canada
michael.parkin@uwo.ca

Reviewers

Eric Abrams, Hawaii Pacific University
Christopher Adams, Federal Trade Commission
Tajudeen Adenekan, Bronx Community College
Syed Ahmed, Cameron University
Frank Albritton, Seminole Community College
Milton Alderfer, Miami-Dade Community College
William Aldridge, Shelton State Community College
Donald L. Alexander, Western Michigan University
Terence Alexander, Iowa State University
Stuart Allen, University of North Carolina, Greensboro
Sam Allgood, University of Nebraska, Lincoln
Neil Alper, Northeastern University
Alan Anderson, Fordham University
Lisa R. Anderson, College of William and Mary
Jeff Ankrom, Wittenberg University
Fatma Antar, Manchester Community Technical College
Kofi Apraku, University of North Carolina, Asheville
John Atkins, University of West Florida
Moshen Bahmani-Oskooee, University of Wisconsin, Milwaukee
Donald Balch, University of South Carolina
Mehmet Balcilar, Wayne State University
Paul Ballantyne, University of Colorado
Sue Bartlett, University of South Florida
Jose Juan Bautista, Xavier University of Louisiana
Valerie R. Bencivenga, University of Texas, Austin
Ben Bernanke, Chairman of Federal Reserve
Radha Bhattacharya, California State University, Fullerton
Margot Biery, Tarrant County College, South
John Bittorowitz, Ball State University
David Black, University of Toledo
Kelly Blanchard, Purdue University
S. Brock Blomberg, Claremont McKenna College
William T. Bogart, Case Western Reserve University
Giacomo Bonanno, University of California, Davis
Tan Khay Boon, Nanyard Technological University
Sunne Brandmeyer, University of South Florida
Audie Brewton, Northeastern Illinois University
Baird Brock, Central Missouri State University
Byron Brown, Michigan State University
Jeffrey Buser, Columbus State Community College
Alison Butler, Florida International University
Colleen Callahan, American University
Tania Carbiener, Southern Methodist University
Kevin Carey, American University
Scott Carrell, University of California at Davis
Kathleen A. Carroll, University of Maryland, Baltimore County
Michael Carter, University of Massachusetts, Lowell
Edward Castronova, California State University, Fullerton
Francis Chan, Fullerton College
Ming Chang, Dartmouth College
Subir Chakrabarti, Indiana University-Purdue University
Joni Charles, Texas State University
Adhip Chaudhuri, Georgetown University
Gopal Chengalath, Texas Tech University
Daniel Christiansen, Albion College
Kenneth Christianson, Binghamton University
John J. Clark, Community College of Allegheny County, Allegheny Campus
Cindy Clement, University of Maryland
Meredith Clement, Dartmouth College
Michael B. Cohn, U. S. Merchant Marine Academy
Robert Collinge, University of Texas, San Antonio
Carol Condon, Kean University
Doug Conway, Mesa Community College
Larry Cook, University of Toledo
Bobby Corcoran, retired, Middle Tennessee State University
Kevin Cotter, Wayne State University
James Peery Cover, University of Alabama, Tuscaloosa
Erik Craft, University of Richmond
Eleanor D. Craig, University of Delaware
Jim Craven, Clark College
Jeremy Cripps, American University of Kuwait
Elizabeth Crowell, University of Michigan, Dearborn
Stephen Cullenberg, University of California, Riverside
David Culp, Slippery Rock University
Norman V. Cure, Macomb Community College
Dan Dabney, University of Texas, Austin
Andrew Dane, Angelo State University
Joseph Daniels, Marquette University
Gregory DeFreitas, Hofstra University
David Denslow, University of Florida
Shatakshee Dhongde, Rochester Institute of Technology
Mark Dickie, University of Central Florida
James Dietz, California State University, Fullerton
Carol Dole, State University of West Georgia
Ronald Dorf, Inver Hills Community College
John Dorsey, University of Maryland, College Park
Eric Drabkin, Hawaii Pacific University
Amrik Singh Dua, Mt. San Antonio College
Thomas Duchesneau, University of Maine, Orono
Lucia Dunn, Ohio State University
Donald Dutkowsky, Syracuse University
John Edgren, Eastern Michigan University
David J. Eger, Alpena Community College
Harry Ellis, Jr., University of North Texas
Ibrahim Elsaify, Goldey-Beacom College
Kenneth G. Elzinga, University of Virginia

Patrick Emerson, Oregon State University
Tisha Emerson, Baylor University
Monica Escaleras, Florida Atlantic University
Antonina Espiritu, Hawaii Pacific University
Gwen Eudey, University of Pennsylvania
Barry Falk, Iowa State University
M. Fazeli, Hofstra University
Philip Fincher, Louisiana Tech University
F. Firoozi, University of Texas, San Antonio
Nancy Folbre, University of Massachusetts, Amherst
Kenneth Fong, Temasek Polytechnic (Singapore)
Steven Francis, Holy Cross College
David Franck, University of North Carolina, Charlotte
Mark Frank, Sam Houston State University
Roger Frantz, San Diego State University
Mark Frascatore, Clarkson University
Alwyn Fraser, Atlantic Union College
Marc Fusaro, East Carolina University
James Gale, Michigan Technological University
Susan Gale, New York University
Roy Gardner, Indiana University
Eugene Gentzel, Pensacola Junior College
Kirk Gifford, Brigham Young University-Idaho
Scott Gilbert, Southern Illinois University, Carbondale
Andrew Gill, California State University, Fullerton
Robert Giller, Virginia Polytechnic Institute and State University
Robert Gillette, University of Kentucky
James N. Giordano, Villanova University
Maria Giuili, Diablo College
Susan Glanz, St. John's University
Robert Gordon, San Diego State University
Richard Gosselin, Houston Community College
John Graham, Rutgers University
John Griffen, Worcester Polytechnic Institute
Wayne Grove, Syracuse University
Robert Guell, Indiana State University
William Gunther, University of Southern Mississippi
Jamie Haag, Pacific University, Oregon
Gail Heyne Hafer, Lindenwood University
Rik W. Hafer, Southern Illinois University, Edwardsville
Daniel Hagen, Western Washington University
David R. Hakes, University of Northern Iowa
Craig Hakkio, Federal Reserve Bank, Kansas City
Bridget Gleeson Hanna, Rochester Institute of Technology
Ann Hansen, Westminster College
Seid Hassan, Murray State University
Jonathan Haughton, Suffolk University
Randall Haydon, Wichita State University
Denise Hazlett, Whitman College
Julia Heath, University of Memphis
Jac Heckelman, Wake Forest University
Jolien A. Helsel, Kent State University
James Henderson, Baylor University
Doug Herman, Georgetown University
Jill Boylston Herndon, University of Florida
Gus Herring, Brookhaven College
John Herrmann, Rutgers University
John M. Hill, Delgado Community College
Jonathan Hill, Florida International University
Lewis Hill, Texas Tech University
Steve Hoagland, University of Akron
Tom Hoerger, Fellow, Research Triangle Institute
Calvin Hoerneman, Delta College
George Hoffer, Virginia Commonwealth University
Dennis L. Hoffman, Arizona State University
Paul Hohenberg, Rensselaer Polytechnic Institute
Jim H. Holcomb, University of Texas, El Paso
Robert Holland, Purdue University
Harry Holzer, Georgetown University
Gary Hoover, University of Alabama
Linda Hooks, Washington and Lee University
Jim Horner, Cameron University
Djehane Hosni, University of Central Florida
Harold Hotelling, Jr., Lawrence Technical University
Calvin Hoy, County College of Morris
Ing-Wei Huang, Assumption University, Thailand
Julie Hunsaker, Wayne State University
Beth Ingram, University of Iowa
Jayvanth Ishwaran, Stephen F. Austin State University
Michael Jacobs, Lehman College
S. Hussain Ali Jafri, Tarleton State University
Dennis Jansen, Texas A&M University
Andrea Jao, University of Pennsylvania
Barbara John, University of Dayton
Barry Jones, Binghamton University
Garrett Jones, Southern Florida University
Frederick Jungman, Northwestern Oklahoma State University
Paul Junk, University of Minnesota, Duluth
Leo Kahane, California State University, Hayward
Veronica Kalich, Baldwin-Wallace College
John Kane, State University of New York, Oswego
Eungmin Kang, St. Cloud State University
Arthur Kartman, San Diego State University
Gurmit Kaur, Universiti Teknologi (Malaysia)
Louise Keely, University of Wisconsin, Madison
Manfred W. Keil, Claremont McKenna College
Elizabeth Sawyer Kelly, University of Wisconsin, Madison
Rose Kilburn, Modesto Junior College
Amanda King, Georgia Southern University
John King, Georgia Southern University

Robert Kirk, Indiana University-Purdue University, Indianapolis
Norman Kleinberg, City University of New York, Baruch College
Robert Kleinhenz, California State University, Fullerton
John Krantz, University of Utah
Joseph Kreitzer, University of St. Thomas
Patricia Kuzyk, Washington State University
David Lages, Southwest Missouri State University
W. J. Lane, University of New Orleans
Leonard Lardaro, University of Rhode Island
Kathryn Larson, Elon College
Luther D. Lawson, University of North Carolina, Wilmington
Elroy M. Leach, Chicago State University
Jim Lee, Texas A & M, Corpus Christi
Sang Lee, Southeastern Louisiana University
Robert Lemke, Florida International University
Mary Lesser, Iona College
Jay Levin, Wayne State University
Arik Levinson, University of Wisconsin, Madison
Tony Lima, California State University, Hayward
William Lord, University of Maryland, Baltimore County
Nancy Lutz, Virginia Polytechnic Institute and State University
Brian Lynch, Lakeland Community College
Murugappa Madhavan, San Diego State University
K. T. Magnusson, Salt Lake Community College
Svitlana Maksymenko, University of Pittsburgh
Mark Maier, Glendale Community College
Jean Mangan, Staffordshire University Business School
Denton Marks, University of Wisconsin, Whitewater
Michael Marlow, California Polytechnic State University
Akbar Marvasti, University of Houston
Wolfgang Mayer, University of Cincinnati
John McArthur, Wofford College
Amy McCormick, Mary Baldwin College
Russ McCullough, Iowa State University
Catherine McDevitt, Central Michigan University
Gerald McDougall, Wichita State University
Stephen McGary, Brigham Young University-Idaho
Richard D. McGrath, Armstrong Atlantic State University
Richard McIntyre, University of Rhode Island
John McLeod, Georgia Institute of Technology
Mark McLeod, Virginia Polytechnic Institute and State University
B. Starr McMullen, Oregon State University
Mary Ruth McRae, Appalachian State University
Kimberly Merritt, Cameron University
Charles Meyer, Iowa State University
Peter Mieszkowski, Rice University
John Mijares, University of North Carolina, Asheville
Richard A. Miller, Wesleyan University
Judith W. Mills, Southern Connecticut State University
Glen Mitchell, Nassau Community College
Jeannette C. Mitchell, Rochester Institute of Technology
Khan Mohabbat, Northern Illinois University
Bagher Modjtahedi, University of California, Davis
Shahruz Mohtadi, Suffolk University
W. Douglas Morgan, University of California, Santa Barbara
William Morgan, University of Wyoming
James Morley, Washington University in St. Louis
William Mosher, Clark University
Joanne Moss, San Francisco State University
Nivedita Mukherji, Oakland University
Francis Mummery, Fullerton College
Edward Murphy, Southwest Texas State University
Kevin J. Murphy, Oakland University
Kathryn Nantz, Fairfield University
William S. Neilson, Texas A&M University
Bart C. Nemmers, University of Nebraska, Lincoln
Melinda Nish, Orange Coast College
Anthony O'Brien, Lehigh University
Norman Obst, Michigan State University
Constantin Ogloblin, Georgia Southern University
Neal Olitsky, University of Massachusetts, Dartmouth
Mary Olson, Tulane University
Terry Olson, Truman State University
James B. O'Neill, University of Delaware
Farley Ordovensky, University of the Pacific
Z. Edward O'Relley, North Dakota State University
Donald Oswald, California State University, Bakersfield
Jan Palmer, Ohio University
Michael Palumbo, Chief, Federal Reserve Board
Chris Papageorgiou, Louisiana State University
G. Hossein Parandvash, Western Oregon State College
Randall Parker, East Carolina University
Robert Parks, Washington University
David Pate, St. John Fisher College
James E. Payne, Illinois State University
Donald Pearson, Eastern Michigan University
Steven Peterson, University of Idaho
Mary Anne Pettit, Southern Illinois University, Edwardsville
William A. Phillips, University of Southern Maine
Dennis Placone, Clemson University
Charles Plot, California Institute of Technology, Pasadena
Mannie Poen, Houston Community College
Kathleen Possai, Wayne State University
Ulrika Praski-Stahlgren, University College in Gavle-Sandviken, Sweden
Edward Price, Oklahoma State University
Rula Qalyoubi, University of Wisconsin, Eau Claire
K. A. Quartey, Talladega College

Herman Quirmbach, Iowa State University
Jeffrey R. Racine, University of South Florida
Ramkishen Rajan, George Mason University
Peter Rangazas, Indiana University-Purdue University, Indianapolis
Vaman Rao, Western Illinois University
Laura Razzolini, University of Mississippi
Rob Rebelein, University of Cincinnati
J. David Reed, Bowling Green State University
Robert H. Renshaw, Northern Illinois University
Javier Reyes, University of Arkansas
Jeff Reynolds, Northern Illinois University
Rupert Rhodd, Florida Atlantic University
W. Gregory Rhodus, Bentley College
Jennifer Rice, Indiana University, Bloomington
John Robertson, Paducah Community College
Malcolm Robinson, University of North Carolina, Greensboro
Richard Roehl, University of Michigan, Dearborn
Carol Rogers, Georgetown University
William Rogers, University of Northern Colorado
Thomas Romans, State University of New York, Buffalo
David R. Ross, Bryn Mawr College
Thomas Ross, Baldwin Wallace College
Robert J. Rossana, Wayne State University
Jeffrey Rous, University of North Texas
Rochelle Ruffer, Youngstown State University
Mark Rush, University of Florida
Allen R. Sanderson, University of Chicago
Gary Santoni, Ball State University
Jeffrey Sarbaum, University of North Carolina at Chapel Hill
John Saussy, Harrisburg Area Community College
Don Schlagenhauf, Florida State University
David Schlow, Pennsylvania State University
Paul Schmitt, St. Clair County Community College
Jeremy Schwartz, Hampden-Sydney College
Martin Sefton, University of Nottingham
James Self, Indiana University
Esther-Mirjam Sent, University of Notre Dame
Rod Shadbegian, University of Massachusetts, Dartmouth
Neil Sheflin, Rutgers University
Gerald Shilling, Eastfield College
Dorothy R. Siden, Salem State College
Mark Siegler, California State University at Sacramento
Scott Simkins, North Carolina Agricultural and Technical State University
Jacek Siry, University of Georgia
Chuck Skoro, Boise State University
Phil Smith, DeKalb College
William Doyle Smith, University of Texas, El Paso
Sarah Stafford, College of William and Mary
Rebecca Stein, University of Pennsylvania
Frank Steindl, Oklahoma State University
Jeffrey Stewart, New York University
Allan Stone, Southwest Missouri State University
Courtenay Stone, Ball State University
Paul Storer, Western Washington University
Richard W. Stratton, University of Akron
Mark Strazicich, Ohio State University, Newark
Michael Stroup, Stephen F. Austin State University
Robert Stuart, Rutgers University
Della Lee Sue, Marist College
Abdulhamid Sukar, Cameron University
Terry Sutton, Southeast Missouri State University
Gilbert Suzawa, University of Rhode Island
David Swaine, Andrews University
Jason Taylor, Central Michigan University
Mark Thoma, University of Oregon
Janet Thomas, Bentley College
Kiril Tochkov, SUNY at Binghamton
Kay Unger, University of Montana
Anthony Uremovic, Joliet Junior College
David Vaughn, City University, Washington
Don Waldman, Colgate University
Francis Wambalaba, Portland State University
Sasiwimon Warunsiri, University of Colorado at Boulder
Rob Wassmer, California State University, Sacramento
Paul A. Weinstein, University of Maryland, College Park
Lee Weissert, St. Vincent College
Robert Whaples, Wake Forest University
David Wharton, Washington College
Mark Wheeler, Western Michigan University
Charles H. Whiteman, University of Iowa
Sandra Williamson, University of Pittsburgh
Brenda Wilson, Brookhaven Community College
Larry Wimmer, Brigham Young University
Mark Witte, Northwestern University
Willard E. Witte, Indiana University
Mark Wohar, University of Nebraska, Omaha
Laura Wolff, Southern Illinois University, Edwardsville
Cheonsik Woo, Vice President, Korea Development Institute
Douglas Wooley, Radford University
Arthur G. Woolf, University of Vermont
John T. Young, Riverside Community College
Michael Youngblood, Rock Valley College
Peter Zaleski, Villanova University
Jason Zimmerman, South Dakota State University
David Zucker, Martha Stewart Living Omnimedia

Supplements Authors

Luke Armstrong, Lee College
Sue Bartlett, University of South Florida
Kelly Blanchard, Purdue University
James Cobbe, Florida State University
Carol Dole, Jacksonville University
Karen Gebhardt, Colorado State University
John Graham, Rutgers University
Jill Herndon, University of Florida
Gary Hoover, University of Alabama
Patricia Kuzyk, Washington State University
Sang Lee, Southeastern Louisiana University
Svitlana Maksymenko, University of Pittsburgh
Russ McCullough, Iowa State University
Barbara Moore, University of Central Florida
James Morley, Washington University in St. Louis
William Mosher, Clark University
Constantin Ogloblin, Georgia Southern University
Edward Price, Oklahoma State University
Mark Rush, University of Florida
James K. Self, University of Indiana, Bloomington
Michael Stroup, Stephen F. Austin State University
Della Lee Sue, Marist College
Nora Underwood, University of Central Florida
Laura A. Wolff, Southern Illinois University, Edwardsville

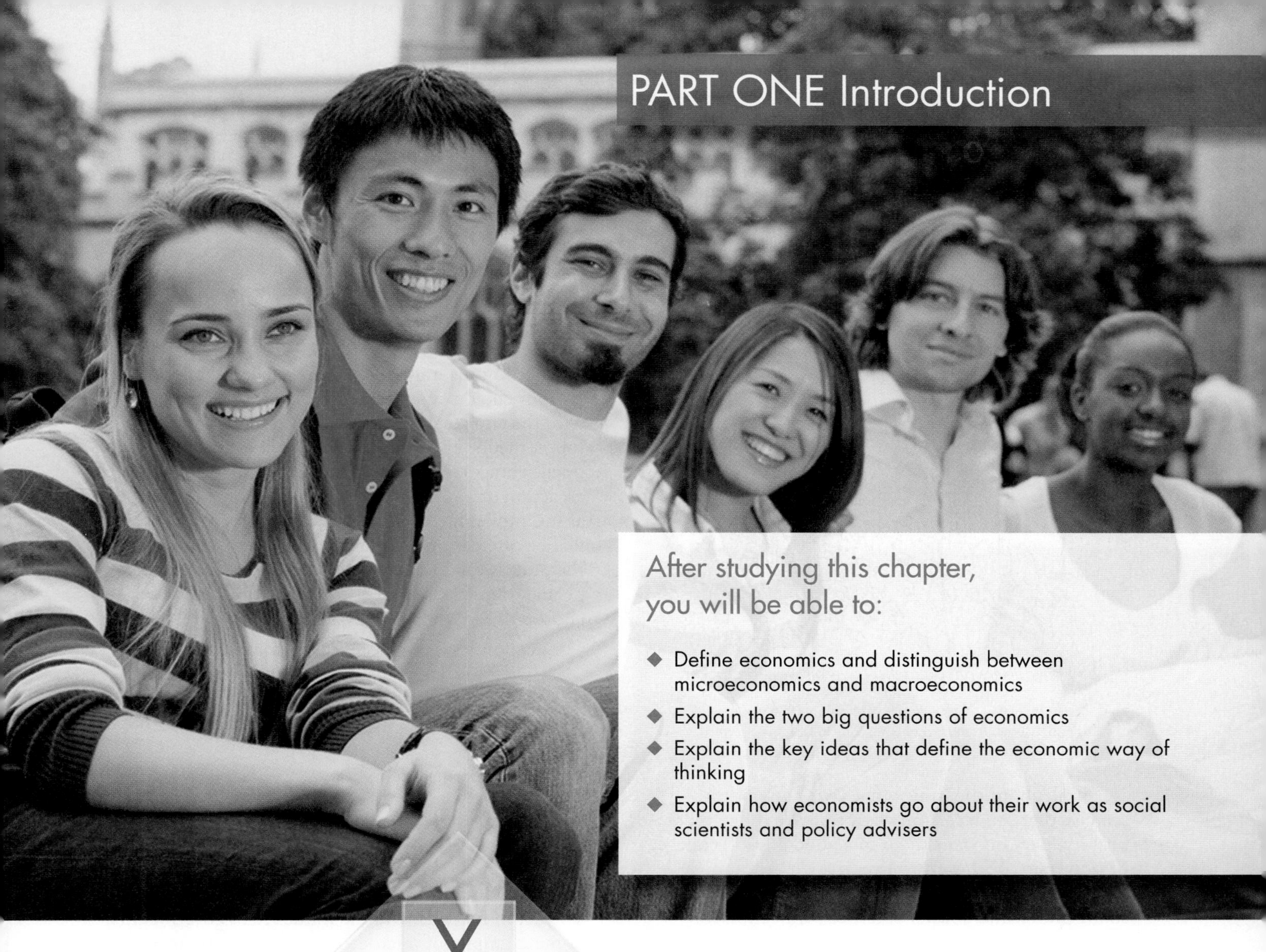

1 WHAT IS ECONOMICS?

You are studying economics at a time of extraordinary challenge and change. The United States, Europe, and Japan, the world's richest nations, are still not fully recovered from a deep recession in which incomes shrank and millions of jobs were lost. Brazil, China, India, and Russia, poorer nations with a combined population that dwarfs our own, are growing rapidly and playing ever-greater roles in an expanding global economy.

The economic events of the past few years stand as a stark reminder that we live in a changing and sometimes turbulent world. New businesses are born and old ones die. New jobs are created and old ones disappear. Nations, businesses, and individuals must find ways of coping with economic change.

Your life will be shaped by the challenges that *you* face and the opportunities that *you* create. But to face those challenges and seize the opportunities they present, you must understand the powerful forces at play. The economics that you're about to learn will become your most reliable guide. This chapter gets you started. It describes the questions that economists try to answer and the ways in which they think as they search for the answers.

Definition of Economics

A fundamental fact dominates our lives: We want more than we can get. Our inability to get everything we want is called **scarcity**. Scarcity is universal. It confronts all living things. Even parrots face scarcity!

Not only do I want a cracker—we all want a cracker!

Think about the things that *you* want and the scarcity that *you* face. You want to live a long and healthy life. You want to go to a good school, college, or university. You want to live in a well-equipped, spacious, and comfortable home. You want the latest smart phone and a faster Internet connection for your laptop or iPad. You want some sports and recreational gear—perhaps some new running shoes, or a new bike. And you want more time, much more than is available, to go to class, do your homework, play sports and games, read novels, go to the movies, listen to music, travel, and hang out with your friends.

What you can afford to buy is limited by your income and by the prices you must pay. And your time is limited by the fact that your day has 24 hours.

You want some other things that only governments provide. You want to live in a peaceful and secure world and safe neighborhood and enjoy the benefits of clean air, lakes, and rivers.

What governments can afford is limited by the taxes they collect. Taxes lower people's incomes and compete with the other things they want to buy.

What everyone can get—what *society* can get—is limited by the productive resources available. These resources are the gifts of nature, human labor and ingenuity, and all the previously produced tools and equipment.

Because we can't get everything we want, we must make *choices*. You can't afford *both* a laptop *and* an iPhone, so you must *choose* which one to buy. You can't spend tonight *both* studying for your next test *and* going to the movies, so again, you must *choose* which one to do. Governments can't spend a tax dollar on *both* national defense *and* environmental protection, so they must *choose* how to spend that dollar.

Your choices must somehow be made consistent with the choices of others. If you choose to buy a laptop, someone else must choose to sell it. Incentives reconcile choices. An **incentive** is a reward that encourages an action or a penalty that discourages one. Prices act as incentives. If the price of a laptop is too high, more will be offered for sale than people want to buy. And if the price is too low, fewer will be offered for sale than people want to buy. But there is a price at which choices to buy and sell are consistent.

> **Economics** is the social science that studies the *choices* that individuals, businesses, governments, and entire societies make as they cope with *scarcity* and the *incentives* that influence and reconcile those choices.

The subject has two parts:

- Microeconomics
- Macroeconomics

Microeconomics is the study of the choices that individuals and businesses make, the way these choices interact in markets, and the influence of governments. Some examples of microeconomic questions are: Why are people downloading more movies? How would a tax on e-commerce affect eBay?

Macroeconomics is the study of the performance of the national economy and the global economy. Some examples of macroeconomic questions are: Why is the U.S. unemployment rate so high? Can the Federal Reserve make our economy expand by cutting interest rates?

REVIEW QUIZ

1. List some examples of the scarcity that you face.
2. Find examples of scarcity in today's headlines.
3. Find an illustration of the distinction between microeconomics and macroeconomics in today's headlines.

You can work these questions in Study Plan 1.1 and get instant feedback.

Two Big Economic Questions

Two big questions summarize the scope of economics:

- How do choices end up determining *what, how,* and *for whom* goods and services are produced?
- Can the choices that people make in the pursuit of their own *self-interest* also promote the broader *social interest*?

What, How, and For Whom?

Goods and services are the objects that people value and produce to satisfy human wants. *Goods* are physical objects such as cell phones and automobiles. *Services* are tasks performed for people such as cell-phone service and auto-repair service.

What? What we produce varies across countries and changes over time. In the United States today, agriculture accounts for 1 percent of total production, manufactured goods for 22 percent, and services (retail and wholesale trade, health care, and education are the biggest ones) for 77 percent. In contrast, in China today, agriculture accounts for 11 percent of total production, manufactured goods for 49 percent, and services for 40 percent. Figure 1.1 shows these numbers and also the percentages for Brazil, which fall between those for the United States and China.

What determines these patterns of production? How do choices end up determining the quantities of cell phones, automobiles, cell-phone service, auto-repair service, and the millions of other items that are produced in the United States and around the world?

How? Goods and services are produced by using productive resources that economists call **factors of production**. Factors of production are grouped into four categories:

- Land
- Labor
- Capital
- Entrepreneurship

Land The "gifts of nature" that we use to produce goods and services are called **land**. In economics, land is what in everyday language we call *natural resources*. It includes land in the everyday sense

FIGURE 1.1 What Three Countries Produce

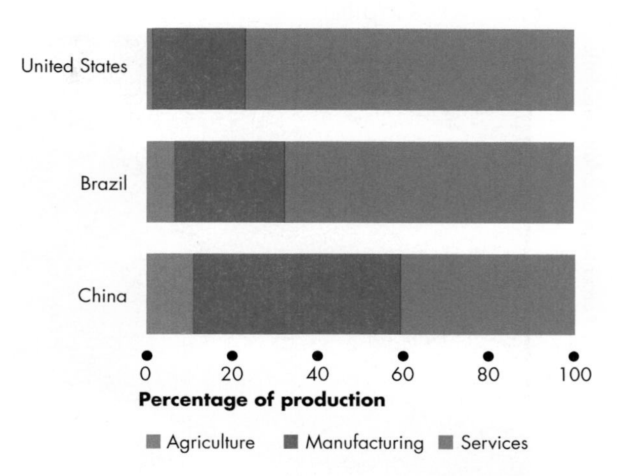

Agriculture and manufacturing is a small percentage of production in rich countries such as the United States and a large percentage of production in poorer countries such as China. Most of what is produced in the United States is services.

Source of data: CIA Factbook 2010, Central Intelligence Agency.

myeconlab animation

together with minerals, oil, gas, coal, water, air, forests, and fish.

Our land surface and water resources are renewable and some of our mineral resources can be recycled. But the resources that we use to create energy are nonrenewable—they can be used only once.

Labor The work time and work effort that people devote to producing goods and services is called **labor**. Labor includes the physical and mental efforts of all the people who work on farms and construction sites and in factories, shops, and offices.

The *quality* of labor depends on **human capital**, which is the knowledge and skill that people obtain from education, on-the-job training, and work experience. You are building your own human capital right now as you work on your economics course, and your human capital will continue to grow as you gain work experience.

Human capital expands over time. Today, 87 percent of the adult population of the United States have completed high school and 29 percent have a college or university degree. Figure 1.2 shows these measures of the growth of human capital in the United States over the past century.

FIGURE 1.2 A Measure of Human Capital

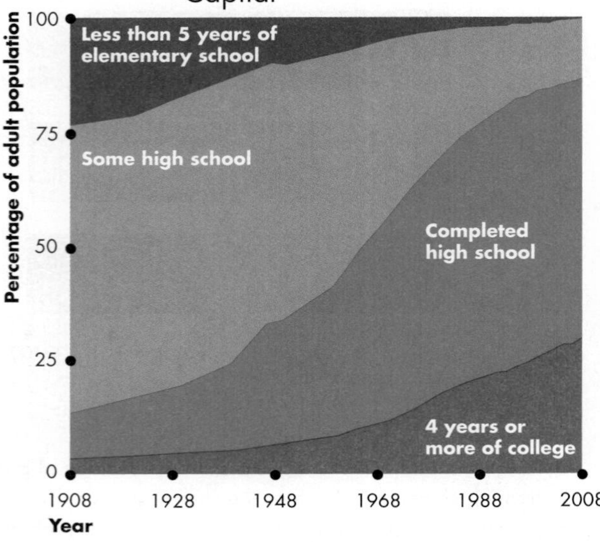

In 2008 (the most recent data), 29 percent of the population had 4 years or more of college, up from 2 percent in 1908. A further 58 percent had completed high school, up from 10 percent in 1908.

Source of data: U.S. Census Bureau, *Statistical Abstract of the United States*, 2010.

Capital The tools, instruments, machines, buildings, and other constructions that businesses use to produce goods and services are called **capital**.

In everyday language, we talk about money, stocks, and bonds as being "capital." These items are *financial* capital. Financial capital plays an important role in enabling businesses to borrow the funds that they use to buy physical capital. But because financial capital is not used to produce goods and services, it is not a productive resource.

Entrepreneurship The human resource that organizes labor, land, and capital is called **entrepreneurship**. Entrepreneurs come up with new ideas about what and how to produce, make business decisions, and bear the risks that arise from these decisions.

What determines the quantities of factors of production that are used to produce goods and services?

For Whom? Who consumes the goods and services that are produced depends on the incomes that people earn. People with large incomes can buy a wide range of goods and services. People with small incomes have fewer options and can afford a smaller range of goods and services.

People earn their incomes by selling the services of the factors of production they own:

- Land earns **rent**.
- Labor earns **wages**.
- Capital earns **interest**.
- Entrepreneurship earns **profit**.

Which factor of production earns the most income? The answer is labor. Wages and fringe benefits are around 70 percent of total income. Land, capital, and entrepreneurship share the rest. These percentages have been remarkably constant over time.

Knowing how income is shared among the factors of production doesn't tell us how it is shared among individuals. And the distribution of income among individuals is extremely unequal. You know of some people who earn very large incomes: Angelina Jolie earns $10 million per movie; and the New York Yankees pays Alex Rodriguez $27.5 million a year.

You know of even more people who earn very small incomes. Servers at McDonald's average around $7.25 an hour; checkout clerks, cleaners, and textile and leather workers all earn less than $10 an hour.

You probably know about other persistent differences in incomes. Men, on average, earn more than women; whites earn more than minorities; college graduates earn more than high-school graduates.

We can get a good sense of who consumes the goods and services produced by looking at the percentages of total income earned by different groups of people. The 20 percent of people with the lowest incomes earn about 5 percent of total income, while the richest 20 percent earn close to 50 percent of total income. So on average, people in the richest 20 percent earn more than 10 times the incomes of those in the poorest 20 percent.

Why is the distribution of income so unequal? Why do women and minorities earn less than white males?

Economics provides some answers to all these questions about what, how, and for whom goods and services are produced and much of the rest of this book will help you to understand those answers.

We're now going to look at the second big question of economics: Can the pursuit of self-interest promote the social interest? This question is a difficult one both to appreciate and to answer.

Can the Pursuit of Self-Interest Promote the Social Interest?

Every day, you and 311 million other Americans, along with 6.9 billion people in the rest of the world, make economic choices that result in *what*, *how*, and *for whom* goods and services are produced.

Self-Interest A choice is in your **self-interest** if you think that choice is the best one available for you. You make most of your choices in your self-interest. You use your time and other resources in the ways that make the most sense to you, and you don't think too much about how your choices affect other people. You order a home delivery pizza because you're hungry and want to eat. You don't order it thinking that the delivery person needs an income. And when the pizza delivery person shows up at your door, he's not doing you a favor. He's pursuing his self-interest and hoping for a good tip.

Social Interest A choice is in the **social interest** if it leads to an outcome that is the best for society as a whole. The social interest has two dimensions: efficiency and equity (or fairness). What is best for society is an efficient and fair use of resources.

Economists say that **efficiency** is achieved when the available resources are used to produce goods and services at the lowest possible cost and in the quantities that give the greatest possible value or benefit. We will make the concept of efficiency precise and clear in Chapter 2. For now, just think of efficiency as a situation in which resources are put to their best possible use.

Equity or fairness doesn't have a crisp definition. Reasonable people, both economists and others, have a variety of views about what is fair. There is always room for disagreement and a need to be careful and clear about the notion of fairness being used.

The Big Question Can we organize our economic lives so that when each one of us makes choices that are in our self-interest, we promote the social interest? Can trading in free markets achieve the social interest? Do we need government action to achieve the social interest? Do we need international cooperation and treaties to achieve the global social interest?

Questions about the social interest are hard ones to answer and they generate discussion, debate, and disagreement. Let's put a bit of flesh on these questions with four examples.

The examples are:

- Globalization
- The information-age economy
- Climate change
- Economic instability

Globalization The term *globalization* means the expansion of international trade, borrowing and lending, and investment.

Globalization is in the self-interest of those consumers who buy low-cost goods and services produced in other countries; and it is in the self-interest of the multinational firms that produce in low-cost regions and sell in high-price regions. But is globalization in the self-interest of the low-wage worker in Malaysia who sews your new running shoes and the displaced shoemaker in Atlanta? Is it in the social interest?

Economics in Action

Life in a Small and Ever-Shrinking World

When Nike produces sports shoes, people in Malaysia get work; and when China Airlines buys new airplanes, Americans who work at Boeing in Seattle build them. While globalization brings expanded production and job opportunities for some workers, it destroys many American jobs. Workers across the manufacturing industries must learn new skills, take service jobs, which are often lower-paid, or retire earlier than previously planned.

The Information-Age Economy The technological change of the past forty years has been called the *Information Revolution*.

The information revolution has clearly served your self-interest: It has provided your cell phone, laptop, loads of handy applications, and the Internet. It has also served the self-interest of Bill Gates of Microsoft and Gordon Moore of Intel, both of whom have seen their wealth soar.

But did the information revolution best serve the social interest? Did Microsoft produce the best possible Windows operating system and sell it at a price that was in the social interest? Did Intel make the right quality of chips and sell them in the right quantities for the right prices? Or was the quality too low and the price too high? Would the social interest have been better served if Microsoft and Intel had faced competition from other firms?

Climate Change Climate change is a huge political issue today. Every serious political leader is acutely aware of the problem and of the popularity of having proposals that might lower carbon emissions.

Every day, when you make self-interested choices to use electricity and gasoline, you contribute to carbon emissions; you leave your carbon footprint. You can lessen your carbon footprint by walking, riding a bike, taking a cold shower, or planting a tree.

But can each one of us be relied upon to make decisions that affect the Earth's carbon-dioxide concentration in the social interest? Must governments change the incentives we face so that our self-interested choices are also in the social interest? How can governments change incentives? How can we encourage the use of wind and solar power to replace the burning of fossil fuels that brings climate change?

Economics in Action

Chips and Windows

Gordon Moore, who founded the chip-maker Intel, and Bill Gates, a co-founder of Microsoft, held privileged positions in the *Information Revolution*.

For many years, Intel chips were the only available chips and Windows was the only available operating system for the original IBM PC and its clones. The PC and Apple's Mac competed, but the PC had a huge market share.

An absence of competition gave Intel and Microsoft the power and ability to sell their products at prices far above the cost of production. If the prices of chips and Windows had been lower, many more people would have been able to afford a computer and would have chosen to buy one.

Economics in Action

Greenhouse Gas Emissions

Burning fossil fuels to generate electricity and to power airplanes, automobiles, and trucks pours a staggering 28 billions tons—4 tons per person—of carbon dioxide into the atmosphere each year.

Two thirds of the world's carbon emissions comes from the United States, China, the European Union, Russia, and India. The fastest growing emissions are coming from India and China.

The amount of global warming caused by economic activity and its effects are uncertain, but the emissions continue to grow and pose huge risks.

Economic Instability The years between 1993 and 2007 were a period of remarkable economic stability, so much so that they've been called the *Great Moderation*. During those years, the U.S. and global economies were on a roll. Incomes in the United States increased by 30 percent and incomes in China tripled. Even the economic shockwaves of 9/11 brought only a small dip in the strong pace of U.S. and global economic growth.

But in August 2007, a period of financial stress began. A bank in France was the first to feel the pain that soon would grip the entire global financial system.

Banks take in people's deposits and get more funds by borrowing from each other and from other firms. Banks use these funds to make loans. All the banks' choices to borrow and lend and the choices of people and businesses to lend to and borrow from banks are made in self-interest. But does this lending and borrowing serve the social interest? Is there too much borrowing and lending that needs to be reined in, or is there too little and a need to stimulate more?

When the banks got into trouble, the Federal Reserve (the Fed) bailed them out with big loans backed by taxpayer dollars. Did the Fed's bailout of troubled banks serve the social interest? Or might the Fed's rescue action encourage banks to repeat their dangerous lending in the future?

Banks weren't the only recipients of public funds. General Motors was saved by a government bailout. GM makes its decisions in its self-interest. The government bailout of GM also served the firm's self-interest. Did the bailout also serve the social interest?

Economics in Action

A Credit Crunch

Flush with funds and offering record low interest rates, banks went on a lending spree to home buyers. Rapidly rising home prices made home owners feel well off and they were happy to borrow and spend. Home loans were bundled into securities that were sold and resold to banks around the world.

In 2006, as interest rates began to rise and the rate of rise in home prices slowed, borrowers defaulted on their loans. What started as a trickle became a flood. As more people defaulted, banks took losses that totaled billions of dollars by mid-2007.

Global credit markets stopped working, and people began to fear a prolonged slowdown in economic activity. Some even feared the return of the economic trauma of the *Great Depression* of the 1930s when more than 20 percent of the U.S. labor force was unemployed. The Federal Reserve, determined to avoid a catastrophe, started lending on a very large scale to the troubled banks.

REVIEW QUIZ

1. Describe the broad facts about *what*, *how*, and *for whom* goods and services are produced.
2. Use headlines from the recent news to illustrate the potential for conflict between self-interest and the social interest.

You can work these questions in Study Plan 1.2 and get instant feedback.

We've looked at four topics and asked many questions that illustrate the big question: Can choices made in the pursuit of self-interest also promote the social interest? We've asked questions but not answered them because we've not yet explained the economic principles needed to do so.

By working through this book, you will discover the economic principles that help economists figure out when the social interest is being served, when it is not, and what might be done when it is not being served. We will return to each of the unanswered questions in future chapters.

The Economic Way of Thinking

The questions that economics tries to answer tell us about the *scope of economics,* but they don't tell us how economists *think* and go about seeking answers to these questions. You're now going to see how economists go about their work.

We're going to look at six key ideas that define the *economic way of thinking.* These ideas are

- A choice is a *tradeoff.*
- People make *rational choices* by comparing *benefits* and *costs.*
- *Benefit* is what you gain from something.
- *Cost* is what you *must give up* to get something.
- Most choices are "*how-much*" choices made at the *margin.*
- Choices respond to *incentives.*

A Choice Is a Tradeoff

Because we face scarcity, we must make choices. And when we make a choice, we select from the available alternatives. For example, you can spend Saturday night studying for your next economics test or having fun with your friends, but you can't do both of these activities at the same time. You must choose how much time to devote to each. Whatever choice you make, you could have chosen something else.

You can think about your choices as tradeoffs. A **tradeoff** is an exchange—giving up one thing to get something else. When you choose how to spend your Saturday night, you face a tradeoff between studying and hanging out with your friends.

Making a Rational Choice

Economists view the choices that people make as rational. A **rational choice** is one that compares costs and benefits and achieves the greatest benefit over cost for the person making the choice.

Only the wants of the person making a choice are relevant to determine its rationality. For example, you might like your coffee black and strong but your friend prefers his milky and sweet. So it is rational for you to choose espresso and for your friend to choose cappuccino.

The idea of rational choice provides an answer to the first question: *What* goods and services will be produced and in what quantities? The answer is those that people rationally choose to buy!

But how do people choose rationally? Why do more people choose an iPod rather than a Zune? Why has the U.S. government chosen to build an interstate highway system and not an interstate high-speed railroad system? The answers turn on comparing benefits and costs.

Benefit: What You Gain

The **benefit** of something is the gain or pleasure that it brings and is determined by **preferences**—by what a person likes and dislikes and the intensity of those feelings. If you get a huge kick out of "Guitar Hero," that video game brings you a large benefit. And if you have little interest in listening to Yo Yo Ma playing a Vivaldi cello concerto, that activity brings you a small benefit.

Some benefits are large and easy to identify, such as the benefit that you get from being in school. A big piece of that benefit is the goods and services that you will be able to enjoy with the boost to your earning power when you graduate. Some benefits are small, such as the benefit you get from a slice of pizza.

Economists measure benefit as the most that a person is *willing to give up* to get something. You are willing to give up a lot to be in school. But you would give up only an iTunes download for a slice of pizza.

Cost: What You *Must* Give Up

The **opportunity cost** of something is the highest-valued alternative that must be given up to get it.

To make the idea of opportunity cost concrete, think about *your* opportunity cost of being in school. It has two components: the things you can't afford to buy and the things you can't do with your time.

Start with the things you can't afford to buy. You've spent all your income on tuition, residence fees, books, and a laptop. If you weren't in school, you would have spent this money on tickets to ball games and movies and all the other things that you enjoy. But that's only the start of your opportunity cost. You've also given up the opportunity to get a job. Suppose that the best job you could get if you weren't in school is working at Citibank as a teller earning $25,000 a year. Another part of your opportunity cost of being in school is all the things that you could buy with the extra $25,000 you would have.

As you well know, being a student eats up many hours in class time, doing homework assignments, preparing for tests, and so on. To do all these school activities, you must give up many hours of what would otherwise be leisure time spent with your friends.

So the opportunity cost of being in school is all the good things that you can't afford and don't have the spare time to enjoy. You might want to put a dollar value on that cost or you might just list all the items that make up the opportunity cost.

The examples of opportunity cost that we've just considered are all-or-nothing costs—you're either in school or not in school. Most situations are not like this one. They involve choosing *how much* of an activity to do.

How Much? Choosing at the Margin

You can allocate the next hour between studying and instant messaging your friends, but the choice is not all or nothing. You must decide how many minutes to allocate to each activity. To make this decision, you compare the benefit of a little bit more study time with its cost—you make your choice at the **margin**.

The benefit that arises from an increase in an activity is called **marginal benefit**. For example, your marginal benefit from one more night of study before a test is the boost it gives to your grade. Your marginal benefit doesn't include the grade you're already achieving without that extra night of work.

The *opportunity cost* of an *increase* in an activity is called **marginal cost**. For you, the marginal cost of studying one more night is the cost of not spending that night on your favorite leisure activity.

To make your decisions, you compare marginal benefit and marginal cost. If the marginal benefit from an extra night of study exceeds its marginal cost, you study the extra night. If the marginal cost exceeds the marginal benefit, you don't study the extra night.

Choices Respond to Incentives

Economists take human nature as given and view people as acting in their self-interest. All people—you, other consumers, producers, politicians, and public servants—pursue their self-interest.

Self-interested actions are not necessarily *selfish* actions. You might decide to use your resources in ways that bring pleasure to others as well as to yourself. But a self-interested act gets the most benefit for *you* based on *your* view about benefit.

The central idea of economics is that we can predict the self-interested choices that people make by looking at the *incentives* they face. People undertake those activities for which marginal benefit exceeds marginal cost; and they reject options for which marginal cost exceeds marginal benefit.

For example, your economics instructor gives you a problem set and tells you these problems will be on the next test. Your marginal benefit from working these problems is large, so you diligently work them. In contrast, your math instructor gives you a problem set on a topic that she says will never be on a test. You get little marginal benefit from working these problems, so you decide to skip most of them.

Economists see incentives as the key to reconciling self-interest and social interest. When our choices are *not* in the social interest, it is because of the incentives we face. One of the challenges for economists is to figure out the incentives that result in self-interested choices being in the social interest.

Economists emphasize the crucial role that institutions play in influencing the incentives that people face as they pursue their self-interest. Laws that protect private property and markets that enable voluntary exchange are the fundamental institutions. You will learn as you progress with your study of economics that where these institutions exist, self-interest can indeed promote the social interest.

REVIEW QUIZ

1. Explain the idea of a tradeoff and think of three tradeoffs that you have made today.
2. Explain what economists mean by rational choice and think of three choices that you've made today that are rational.
3. Explain why opportunity cost is the best forgone alternative and provide examples of some opportunity costs that you have faced today.
4. Explain what it means to choose at the margin and illustrate with three choices at the margin that you have made today.
5. Explain why choices respond to incentives and think of three incentives to which you have responded today.

You can work these questions in Study Plan 1.3 and get instant feedback.

Economics as Social Science and Policy Tool

Economics is both a social science and a toolkit for advising on policy decisions.

Economist as Social Scientist

As social scientists, economists seek to discover how the economic world works. In pursuit of this goal, like all scientists, economists distinguish between positive and normative statements.

Positive Statements A *positive* statement is about what *is*. It says what is currently believed about the way the world operates. A positive statement might be right or wrong, but we can test it by checking it against the facts. "Our planet is warming because of the amount of coal that we're burning" is a positive statement. We can test whether it is right or wrong.

A central task of economists is to test positive statements about how the economic world works and to weed out those that are wrong. Economics first got off the ground in the late 1700s, so it is a young science compared with, for example, physics, and much remains to be discovered.

Normative Statements A *normative* statement is about what *ought to be*. It depends on values and cannot be tested. Policy goals are normative statements. For example, "We ought to cut our use of coal by 50 percent" is a normative policy statement. You may agree or disagree with it, but you can't test it. It doesn't assert a fact that can be checked.

Unscrambling Cause and Effect Economists are particularly interested in positive statements about cause and effect. Are computers getting cheaper because people are buying them in greater quantities? Or are people buying computers in greater quantities because they are getting cheaper? Or is some third factor causing both the price of a computer to fall and the quantity of computers bought to increase?

To answer such questions, economists create and test economic models. An **economic model** is a description of some aspect of the economic world that includes only those features that are needed for the purpose at hand. For example, an economic model of a cell-phone network might include features such as the prices of calls, the number of cell-phone users, and the volume of calls. But the model would ignore cell-phone colors and ringtones.

A model is tested by comparing its predictions with the facts. But testing an economic model is difficult because we observe the outcomes of the simultaneous change of many factors. To cope with this problem, economists look for natural experiments (situations in the ordinary course of economic life in which the one factor of interest is different and other things are equal or similar); conduct statistical investigations to find correlations; and perform economic experiments by putting people in decision-making situations and varying the influence of one factor at a time to discover how they respond.

Economist as Policy Adviser

Economics is useful. It is a toolkit for advising governments and businesses and for making personal decisions. Some of the most famous economists work partly as policy advisers.

For example, Jagdish Bhagwati of Columbia University, whom you will meet on pp. 52–54, has advised governments and international organizations on trade and economic development issues.

Christina Romer of the University of California, Berkeley, is on leave and serving as the chief economic adviser to President Barack Obama and head of the President's Council of Economic Advisers.

All the policy questions on which economists provide advice involve a blend of the positive and the normative. Economics can't help with the normative part—the policy goal. But for a given goal, economics provides a method of evaluating alternative solutions—comparing marginal benefits and marginal costs and finding the solution that makes the best use of the available resources.

REVIEW QUIZ

1. Distinguish between a positive statement and a normative statement and provide examples.
2. What is a model? Can you think of a model that you might use in your everyday life?
3. How do economists try to disentangle cause and effect?
4. How is economics used as a policy tool?

You can work these questions in Study Plan 1.4 and get instant feedback.

SUMMARY

Key Points

Definition of Economics (p. 2)

- All economic questions arise from scarcity—from the fact that wants exceed the resources available to satisfy them.
- Economics is the social science that studies the choices that people make as they cope with scarcity.
- The subject divides into microeconomics and macroeconomics.

Working Problem 1 will give you a better understanding of the definition of economics.

Two Big Economic Questions (pp. 3–7)

- Two big questions summarize the scope of economics:
  1. How do choices end up determining *what*, *how*, and *for whom* goods and services are produced?
  2. When do choices made in the pursuit of *self-interest* also promote the *social interest*?

Working Problems 2 and 3 will give you a better understanding of the two big questions of economics.

The Economic Way of Thinking (pp. 8–9)

- Every choice is a tradeoff—exchanging more of something for less of something else.
- People make rational choices by comparing benefit and cost.
- Cost—*opportunity cost*—is what you must give up to get something.
- Most choices are "how much" choices made at the *margin* by comparing marginal benefit and marginal cost.
- Choices respond to incentives.

Working Problems 4 and 5 will give you a better understanding of the economic way of thinking.

Economics as Social Science and Policy Tool (p. 10)

- Economists distinguish between positive statements—what is—and normative statements—what ought to be.
- To explain the economic world, economists create and test economic models.
- Economics is a toolkit used to provide advice on government, business, and personal economic decisions.

Working Problem 6 will give you a better understanding of economics as social science and policy tool.

Key Terms

Benefit, 8
Capital, 4
Economic model, 10
Economics, 2
Efficiency, 5
Entrepreneurship, 4
Factors of production, 3
Goods and services, 3
Human capital, 3
Incentive, 2
Interest, 4
Labor, 3
Land, 3
Macroeconomics, 2
Margin, 9
Marginal benefit, 9
Marginal cost, 9
Microeconomics, 2
Opportunity cost, 8
Preferences, 8
Profit, 4
Rational choice, 8
Rent, 4
Scarcity, 2
Self-interest, 5
Social interest, 5
Tradeoff, 8
Wages, 4

STUDY PLAN PROBLEMS AND APPLICATIONS

myeconlab You can work Problems 1 to 6 in MyEconLab Chapter 1 Study Plan and get instant feedback.

Definition of Economics (Study Plan 1.1)

1. Apple Inc. decides to make iTunes freely available in unlimited quantities.
   a. Does Apple's decision change the incentives that people face?
   b. Is Apple's decision an example of a microeconomic or a macroeconomic issue?

Two Big Economic Questions (Study Plan 1.2)

2. Which of the following pairs does not match?
   a. Labor and wages
   b. Land and rent
   c. Entrepreneurship and profit
   d. Capital and profit
3. Explain how the following news headlines concern self-interest and the social interest.
   a. Starbucks Expands in China
   b. McDonald's Moves into Salads
   c. Food Must Be Labeled with Nutrition Data

The Economic Way of Thinking (Study Plan 1.3)

4. The night before an economics test, you decide to go to the movies instead of staying home and working your MyEconLab Study Plan. You get 50 percent on your test compared with the 70 percent that you normally score.
   a. Did you face a tradeoff?
   b. What was the opportunity cost of your evening at the movies?
5. **Costs Soar for London Olympics**
   The regeneration of East London, the site of the 2012 Olympic Games, is set to add extra £1.5 billion to taxpayers' bill.
   Source: *The Times*, London, July 6, 2006
   Is the cost of regenerating East London an opportunity cost of hosting the 2012 Olympic Games? Explain why or why not.

Economics as Social Science and Policy Tool (Study Plan 1.4)

6. Which of the following statements is positive, which is normative, and which can be tested?
   a. The United States should cut its imports.
   b. China is the largest trading partner of the United States.
   c. If the price of antiretroviral drugs increases, HIV/AIDS sufferers will decrease their consumption of the drugs.

ADDITIONAL PROBLEMS AND APPLICATIONS

myeconlab You can work these problems in MyEconLab if assigned by your instructor.

Definition of Economics

7. **Hundreds Line up for 5 p.m. Ticket Giveaway**
   By noon, hundreds of Eminem fans had lined up for a chance to score free tickets to the concert.
   Source: *Detroit Free Press*, May 18, 2009
   When Eminem gave away tickets, what was free and what was scarce? Explain your answer.

Two Big Economic Questions

8. How does the creation of a successful movie influence *what*, *how*, and *for whom* goods and services are produced?
9. How does a successful movie illustrate self-interested choices that are also in the social interest?

The Economic Way of Thinking

10. Before starring in *Iron Man*, Robert Downey Jr. had appeared in 45 movies that grossed an average of $5 million on the opening weekend. In contrast, *Iron Man* grossed $102 million.
    a. How do you expect the success of *Iron Man* to influence the opportunity cost of hiring Robert Downey Jr.?
    b. How have the incentives for a movie producer to hire Robert Downey Jr. changed?
11. What might be an incentive for you to take a class in summer school? List some of the benefits and costs involved in your decision. Would your choice be rational?

Economics as Social Science and Policy Tool

12. Look at today's *Wall Street Journal*. What is the leading economic news story? With which of the big economic questions does it deal and what tradeoffs does it discuss or imply?
13. Provide two microeconomic statements and two macroeconomic statements. Classify your statements as positive or normative. Explain why.

APPENDIX

Graphs in Economics

After studying this appendix, you will be able to:

- Make and interpret a scatter diagram
- Identify linear and nonlinear relationships and relationships that have a maximum and a minimum
- Define and calculate the slope of a line
- Graph relationships among more than two variables

Graphing Data

A graph represents a quantity as a distance on a line. In Fig. A1.1, a distance on the horizontal line represents temperature, measured in degrees Fahrenheit. A movement from left to right shows an increase in temperature. The point 0 represents zero degrees Fahrenheit. To the right of 0, the temperature is positive. To the left of 0 the temperature is negative (as indicated by the minus sign). A distance on the vertical line represents height, measured in thousands of feet. The point 0 represents sea level. Points above 0 represent feet above sea level. Points below 0 represent feet below sea level (indicated by a minus sign).

In Fig. A1.1, the two scale lines are perpendicular to each other and are called *axes*. The vertical line is the y-axis, and the horizontal line is the x-axis. Each axis has a zero point, which is shared by the two axes and called the *origin*.

To make a two-variable graph, we need two pieces of information: the value of the variable x and the value of the variable y. For example, off the coast of Alaska, the temperature is 32 degrees—the value of x. A fishing boat is located at 0 feet above sea level—the value of y. These two bits of information appear as point A in Fig. A1.1. A climber at the top of Mount McKinley on a cold day is 20,320 feet above sea level in a zero-degree gale. These two pieces of information appear as point B. On a warmer day, a climber might be at the peak of Mt. McKinley when the temperature is 32 degrees, at point C.

We can draw two lines, called *coordinates*, from point C. One, called the x-coordinate, runs from C to the vertical axis. This line is called "the x-coordinate" because its length is the same as the value marked off on the x-axis. The other, called the y-coordinate, runs from C to the horizontal axis. This line is called "the y-coordinate" because its length is the same as the value marked off on the y-axis.

FIGURE A1.1 Making a Graph

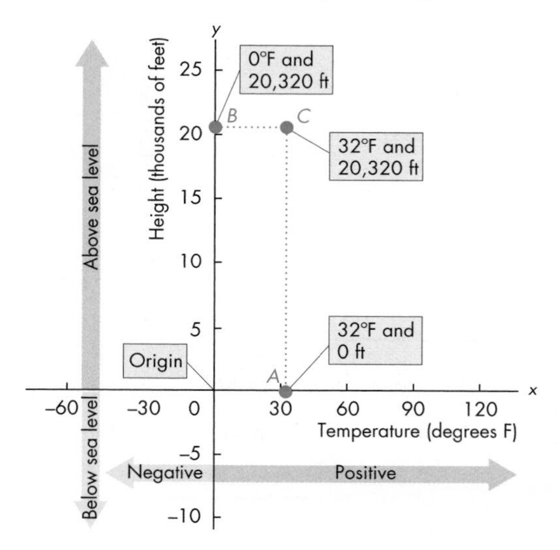

Graphs have axes that measure quantities as distances. Here, the horizontal axis (x-axis) measures temperature, and the vertical axis (y-axis) measures height. Point A represents a fishing boat at sea level (0 on the y-axis) on a day when the temperature is 32°F. Point B represents a climber at the top of Mt. McKinley, 20,320 feet above sea level at a temperature of 0°F. Point C represents a climber at the top of Mt. McKinley, 20,320 feet above sea level at a temperature of 32°F.

myeconlab animation

We describe a point on a graph by the values of its x-coordinate and its y-coordinate. For example, at point C, x is 32 degrees and y is 20,320 feet.

A graph like that in Fig. A1.1 can be made using any quantitative data on two variables. The graph can show just a few points, like Fig. A1.1, or many points. Before we look at graphs with many points, let's reinforce what you've just learned by looking at two graphs made with economic data.

Economists measure variables that describe *what*, *how*, and *for whom* goods and services are produced. These variables are quantities produced and prices. Figure A1.2 shows two examples of economic graphs.

FIGURE A1.2 Two Graphs of Economic Data

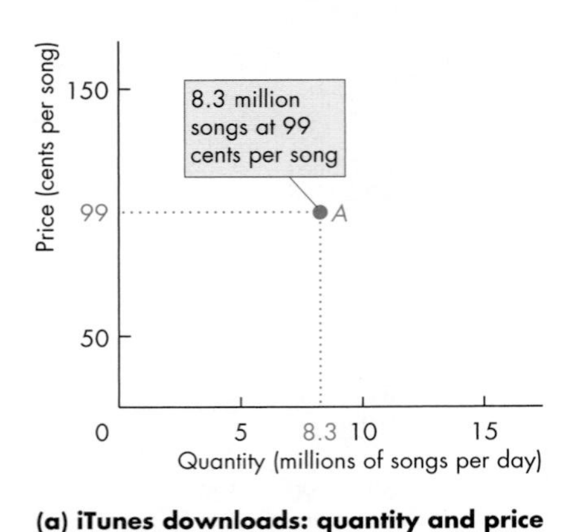

(a) iTunes downloads: quantity and price

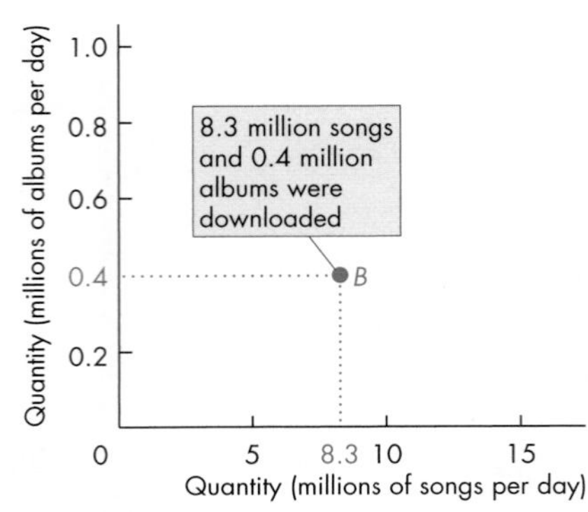

(b) iTunes downloads: songs and albums

The graph in part (a) tells us that in January 2010, 8.3 million songs per day were downloaded from the iTunes store at a price of 99 cents a song.

The graph in part (b) tells us that in January 2010, 8.3 million songs per day and 0.4 million albums per day were downloaded from the iTunes store.

myeconlab animation

Figure A1.2(a) is a graph about iTunes song downloads in January 2010. The *x*-axis measures the quantity of songs downloaded per day and the *y*-axis measures the price of a song. Point *A* tells us what the quantity and price were. You can "read" this graph as telling you that in January 2010, 8.3 million songs a day were downloaded at a price of 99¢ per song.

Figure A1.2(b) is a graph about iTunes song and album downloads in January 2010. The *x*-axis measures the quantity of songs downloaded per day and the *y*-axis measures the quantity of albums downloaded per day. Point *B* tells us what these quantities were. You can "read" this graph as telling you that in January 2010, 8.3 million songs a day and 0.4 million albums were downloaded.

The three graphs that you've just seen tell you how to make a graph and how to read a data point on a graph, but they don't improve on the raw data. Graphs become interesting and revealing when they contain a number of data points because then you can visualize the data.

Economists create graphs based on the principles in Figs. A1.1 and A1.2 to reveal, describe, and visualize the relationships among variables. We're now going to look at some examples. These graphs are called scatter diagrams.

Scatter Diagrams

A **scatter diagram** is a graph that plots the value of one variable against the value of another variable for a number of different values of each variable. Such a graph reveals whether a relationship exists between two variables and describes their relationship.

The table in Fig. A1.3 shows some data on two variables: the number of tickets sold at the box office and the number of DVDs sold for eight of the most popular movies in 2009.

What is the relationship between these two variables? Does a big box office success generate a large volume of DVD sales? Or does a box office success mean that fewer DVDs are sold?

We can answer these questions by making a scatter diagram. We do so by graphing the data in the table. In the graph in Fig. A1.3, each point shows the number of box office tickets sold (the *x* variable) and the number of DVDs sold (the *y* variable) of one of the movies. There are eight movies, so there are eight points "scattered" within the graph.

The point labeled *A* tells us that Star Trek sold 34 million tickets at the box office and 6 million DVDs. The points in the graph form a pattern, which reveals that larger box office sales are associated with larger DVD sales. But the points also tell us that this association is weak. You can't predict DVD sales with any confidence by knowing only the number of tickets sold at the box office.

Figure A1.4 shows two scatter diagrams of economic variables. Part (a) shows the relationship between income and expenditure, on average, during a ten-year period. Each point represents income and expenditure in a given year. For example, point *A* shows that in 2006, income was $31 thousand and expenditure was $30 thousand. This graph shows that as income increases, so does expenditure, and the relationship is a close one.

FIGURE A1.3 A Scatter Diagram

Movie	Tickets	DVDs
	(millions)	
Twilight	38	10
Transformers: Revenge of the Fallen	54	9
Up	39	8
Harry Potter and the Half-Blood Prince	40	7
Star Trek	34	6
The Hangover	37	6
Ice Age: Dawn of the Dinosaurs	26	5
The Proposal	22	5

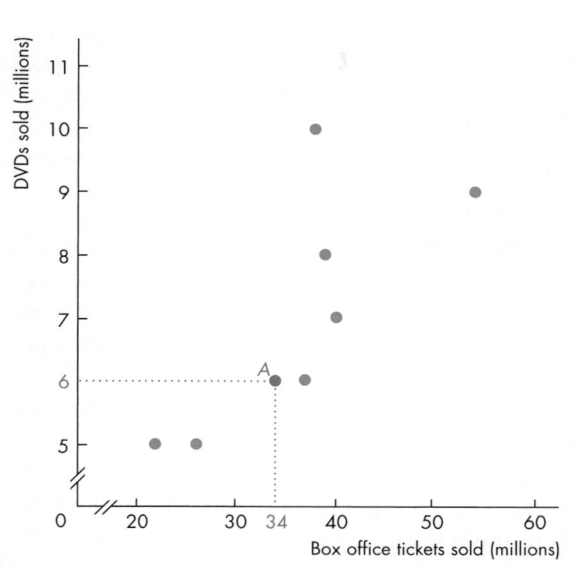

The table lists the number of tickets sold at the box office and the number of DVDs sold for eight popular movies. The scatter diagram reveals the relationship between these two variables. Each point shows the values of the two variables for a specific movie. For example, point *A* shows the point for *Star Trek*, which sold 34 million tickets at the box office and 6 million DVDs. The pattern formed by the points shows that there is a tendency for large box office sales to bring greater DVD sales. But you couldn't predict how many DVDs a movie would sell just by knowing its box office sales.

Figure A1.4(b) shows a scatter diagram of U.S. inflation and unemployment during the 2000s. Here, the points for 2000 to 2008 show no relationship between the two variables, but the high unemployment rate of 2009 brought a low inflation rate that year.

You can see that a scatter diagram conveys a wealth of information, and it does so in much less space than we have used to describe only some of its features. But you do have to "read" the graph to obtain all this information.

FIGURE A1.4 Two Economic Scatter Diagrams

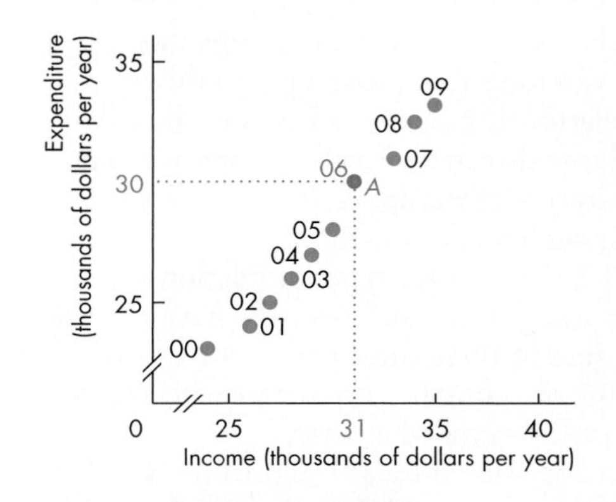

(a) Income and expenditure

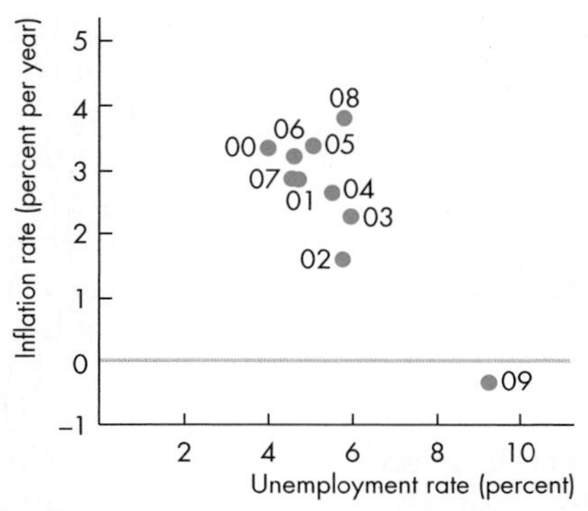

(b) Unemployment and inflation

The scatter diagram in part (a) shows the relationship between income and expenditure from 2000 to 2009. Point *A* shows that in 2006, income was \$31 (thousand) on the *x*-axis and expenditure was \$30 (thousand) on the *y*-axis. This graph shows that as income rises, so does expenditure and the relationship is a close one.

The scatter diagram in part (b) shows a weak relationship between unemployment and inflation in the United States during most of the 2000s.

myeconlab animation

Breaks in the Axes The graph in Fig. A1.4(a) has breaks in its axes, as shown by the small gaps. The breaks indicate that there are jumps from the origin, 0, to the first values recorded.

The breaks are used because the lowest values of income and expenditure exceed $20,000. If we made this graph with no breaks in its axes, there would be a lot of empty space, all the points would be crowded into the top right corner, and it would be difficult to see whether a relationship exists between these two variables. By breaking the axes, we are able to bring the relationship into view.

Putting a break in one or both axes is like using a zoom lens to bring the relationship into the center of the graph and magnify it so that the relationship fills the graph.

Misleading Graphs Breaks can be used to highlight a relationship, but they can also be used to mislead—to make a graph that lies. The most common way of making a graph lie is to put a break in the axis and either to stretch or compress the scale. For example, suppose that in Fig. A1.4(a), the *y*-axis that measures expenditure ran from zero to $35,000 while the *x*-axis was the same as the one shown. The graph would now create the impression that despite a huge increase in income, expenditure had barely changed.

To avoid being misled, it is a good idea to get into the habit of always looking closely at the values and the labels on the axes of a graph before you start to interpret it.

Correlation and Causation A scatter diagram that shows a clear relationship between two variables, such as Fig. A1.4(a), tells us that the two variables have a high correlation. When a high correlation is present, we can predict the value of one variable from the value of the other variable. But correlation does not imply causation.

Sometimes a high correlation is a coincidence, but sometimes it does arise from a causal relationship. It is likely, for example, that rising income causes rising expenditure (Fig. A1.4a) and that high unemployment makes for a slack economy in which prices don't rise quickly, so the inflation rate is low (Fig. A1.4b).

You've now seen how we can use graphs in economics to show economic data and to reveal relationships. Next, we'll learn how economists use graphs to construct and display economic models.

Graphs Used in Economic Models

The graphs used in economics are not always designed to show real-world data. Often they are used to show general relationships among the variables in an economic model.

An *economic model* is a stripped-down, simplified description of an economy or of a component of an economy such as a business or a household. It consists of statements about economic behavior that can be expressed as equations or as curves in a graph. Economists use models to explore the effects of different policies or other influences on the economy in ways that are similar to the use of model airplanes in wind tunnels and models of the climate.

You will encounter many different kinds of graphs in economic models, but there are some repeating patterns. Once you've learned to recognize these patterns, you will instantly understand the meaning of a graph. Here, we'll look at the different types of curves that are used in economic models, and we'll see some everyday examples of each type of curve. The patterns to look for in graphs are the four cases in which

- Variables move in the same direction.
- Variables move in opposite directions.
- Variables have a maximum or a minimum.
- Variables are unrelated.

Let's look at these four cases.

Variables That Move in the Same Direction

Figure A1.5 shows graphs of the relationships between two variables that move up and down together. A relationship between two variables that move in the same direction is called a **positive relationship** or a **direct relationship**. A line that slopes upward shows such a relationship.

Figure A1.5 shows three types of relationships: one that has a straight line and two that have curved lines. All the lines in these three graphs are called curves. Any line on a graph—no matter whether it is straight or curved—is called a *curve*.

A relationship shown by a straight line is called a **linear relationship**. Figure A1.5(a) shows a linear relationship between the number of miles traveled in

FIGURE A1.5 Positive (Direct) Relationships

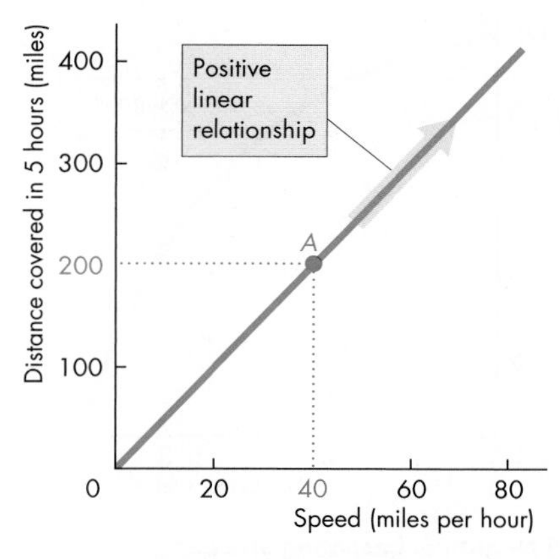

(a) Positive linear relationship

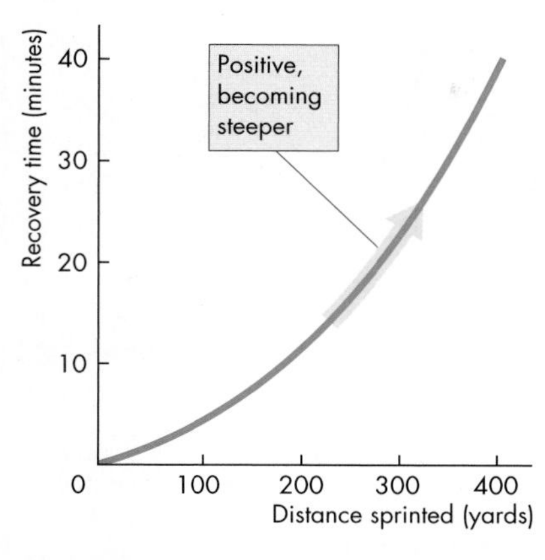

(b) Positive, becoming steeper

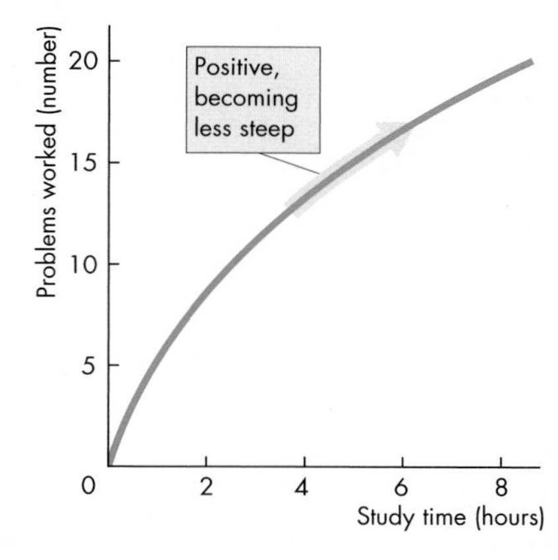

(c) Positive, becoming less steep

Each part shows a positive (direct) relationship between two variables. That is, as the value of the variable measured on the *x*-axis increases, so does the value of the variable measured on the *y*-axis. Part (a) shows a linear positive relationship—as the two variables increase together, we move along a straight line.

Part (b) shows a positive relationship such that as the two variables increase together, we move along a curve that becomes steeper.

Part (c) shows a positive relationship such that as the two variables increase together, we move along a curve that becomes flatter.

myeconlab animation

5 hours and speed. For example, point *A* shows that we will travel 200 miles in 5 hours if our speed is 40 miles an hour. If we double our speed to 80 miles an hour, we will travel 400 miles in 5 hours.

Figure A1.5(b) shows the relationship between distance sprinted and recovery time (the time it takes the heart rate to return to its normal resting rate). This relationship is an upward-sloping one that starts out quite flat but then becomes steeper as we move along the curve away from the origin. The reason this curve becomes steeper is that the additional recovery time needed from sprinting an additional 100 yards increases. It takes less than 5 minutes to recover from sprinting 100 yards but more than 10 minutes to recover from 200 yards.

Figure A1.5(c) shows the relationship between the number of problems worked by a student and the amount of study time. This relationship is an upward-sloping one that starts out quite steep and becomes flatter as we move along the curve away from the origin. Study time becomes less productive as the student spends more hours studying and becomes more tired.

Variables That Move in Opposite Directions

Figure A1.6 shows relationships between things that move in opposite directions. A relationship between variables that move in opposite directions is called a **negative relationship** or an **inverse relationship**.

Figure A1.6(a) shows the relationship between the hours spent playing squash and the hours spent playing tennis when the total time available is 5 hours. One extra hour spent playing tennis means one hour less spent playing squash and vice versa. This relationship is negative and linear.

Figure A1.6(b) shows the relationship between the cost per mile traveled and the length of a journey. The longer the journey, the lower is the cost per mile. But as the journey length increases, even though the cost per mile decreases, the fall in the cost is smaller the longer the journey. This feature of the relationship is shown by the fact that the curve slopes downward, starting out steep at a short journey length and then becoming flatter as the journey length increases. This relationship arises because some of the costs are fixed, such as auto insurance, and the fixed costs are spread over a longer journey.

FIGURE A1.6 Negative (Inverse) Relationships

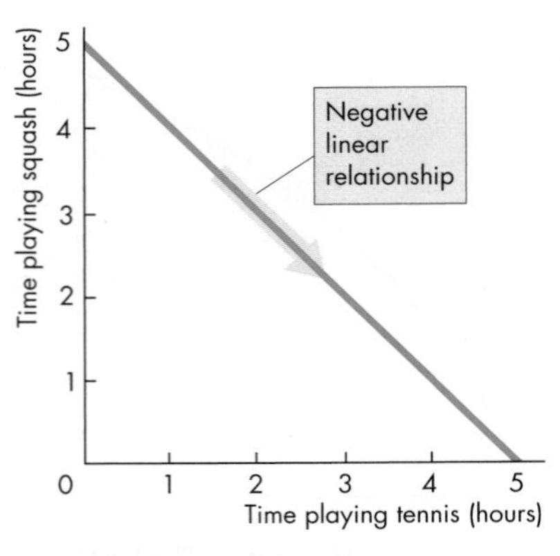

(a) Negative linear relationship

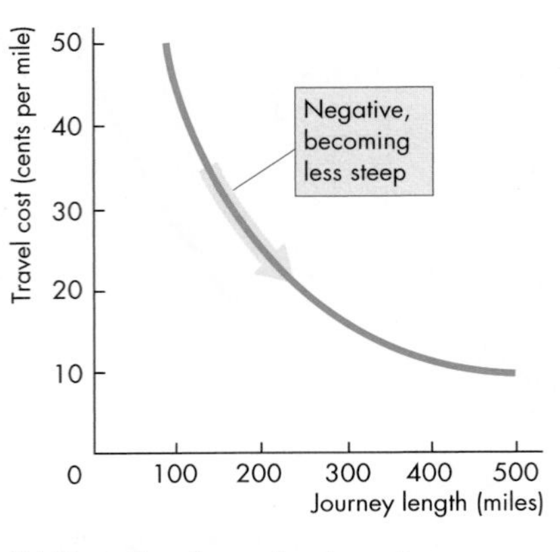

(b) Negative, becoming less steep

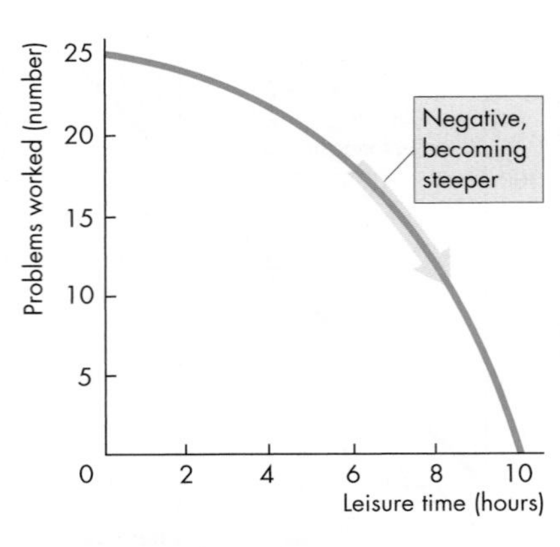

(c) Negative, becoming steeper

Each part shows a negative (inverse) relationship between two variables. Part (a) shows a linear negative relationship. The total time spent playing tennis and squash is 5 hours. As the time spent playing tennis increases, the time spent playing squash decreases, and we move along a straight line.

Part (b) shows a negative relationship such that as the journey length increases, the travel cost decreases as we move along a curve that becomes less steep.

Part (c) shows a negative relationship such that as leisure time increases, the number of problems worked decreases as we move along a curve that becomes steeper.

myeconlab animation

Figure A1.6(c) shows the relationship between the amount of leisure time and the number of problems worked by a student. Increasing leisure time produces an increasingly large reduction in the number of problems worked. This relationship is a negative one that starts out with a gentle slope at a small number of leisure hours and becomes steeper as the number of leisure hours increases. This relationship is a different view of the idea shown in Fig. A1.5(c).

Variables That Have a Maximum or a Minimum

Many relationships in economic models have a maximum or a minimum. For example, firms try to make the maximum possible profit and to produce at the lowest possible cost. Figure A1.7 shows relationships that have a maximum or a minimum.

Figure A1.7(a) shows the relationship between rainfall and wheat yield. When there is no rainfall, wheat will not grow, so the yield is zero. As the rainfall increases up to 10 days a month, the wheat yield increases. With 10 rainy days each month, the wheat yield reaches its maximum at 40 bushels an acre (point *A*). Rain in excess of 10 days a month starts to lower the yield of wheat. If every day is rainy, the wheat suffers from a lack of sunshine and the yield decreases to zero. This relationship is one that starts out sloping upward, reaches a maximum, and then slopes downward.

Figure A1.7(b) shows the reverse case—a relationship that begins sloping downward, falls to a minimum, and then slopes upward. Most economic costs are like this relationship. An example is the relationship between the cost per mile and speed for a car trip. At low speeds, the car is creeping in a traffic snarl-up. The number of miles per gallon is low, so the cost per mile is high. At high speeds, the car is traveling faster than its efficient speed, using a large quantity of gasoline, and again the number of miles per gallon is low and the cost per mile is high. At a speed of 55 miles an hour, the cost per mile is at its minimum (point *B*). This relationship is one that starts out sloping downward, reaches a minimum, and then slopes upward.

FIGURE A1.7 Maximum and Minimum Points

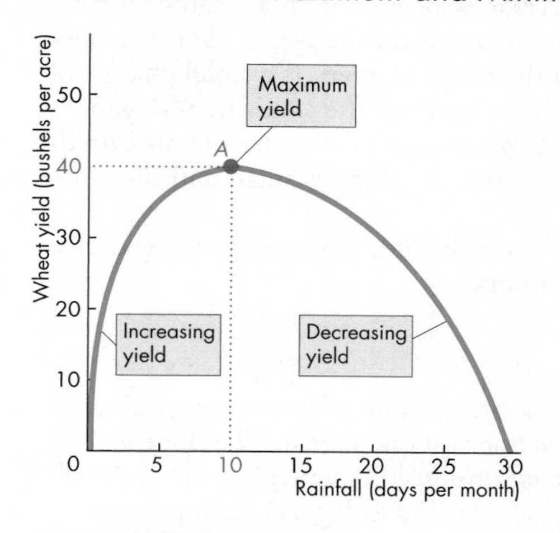

(a) Relationship with a maximum

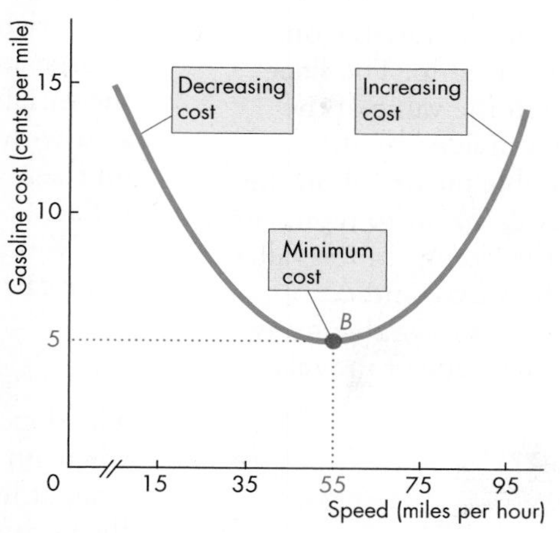

(b) Relationship with a minimum

Part (a) shows a relationship that has a maximum point, *A*. The curve slopes upward as it rises to its maximum point, is flat at its maximum, and then slopes downward.

Part (b) shows a relationship with a minimum point, *B*. The curve slopes downward as it falls to its minimum, is flat at its minimum, and then slopes upward.

myeconlab animation

Variables That Are Unrelated

There are many situations in which no matter what happens to the value of one variable, the other variable remains constant. Sometimes we want to show the independence between two variables in a graph, and Fig. A1.8 shows two ways of achieving this.

In describing the graphs in Fig. A1.5 through Fig. A1.7, we have talked about curves that slope upward or slope downward, and curves that become less steep or steeper. Let's spend a little time discussing exactly what we mean by *slope* and how we measure the slope of a curve.

FIGURE A1.8 Variables That Are Unrelated

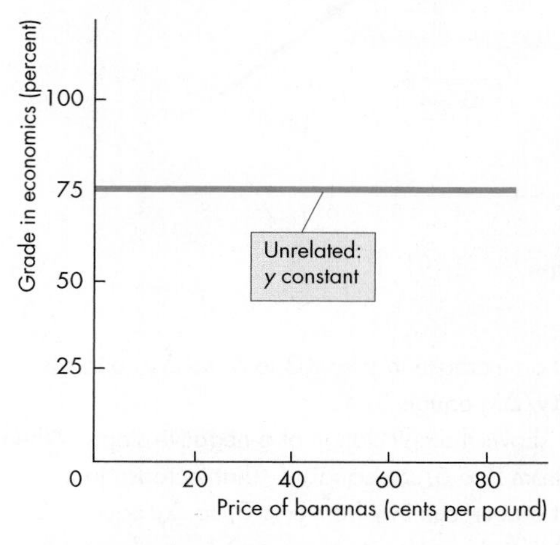

(a) Unrelated: *y* constant

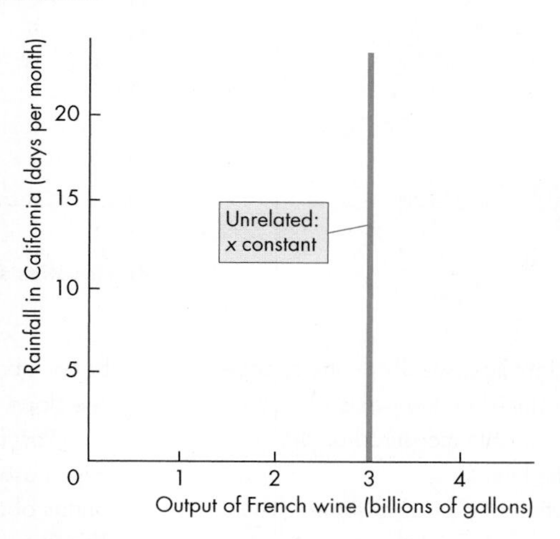

(b) Unrelated: *x* constant

This figure shows how we can graph two variables that are unrelated. In part (a), a student's grade in economics is plotted at 75 percent on the *y*-axis regardless of the price of bananas on the *x*-axis. The curve is horizontal.

In part (b), the output of the vineyards of France on the *x*-axis does not vary with the rainfall in California on the *y*-axis. The curve is vertical.

myeconlab animation

The Slope of a Relationship

We can measure the influence of one variable on another by the slope of the relationship. The **slope** of a relationship is the change in the value of the variable measured on the *y*-axis divided by the change in the value of the variable measured on the *x*-axis. We use the Greek letter Δ (*delta*) to represent "change in." Thus Δy means the change in the value of the variable measured on the *y*-axis, and Δx means the change in the value of the variable measured on the *x*-axis. Therefore the slope of the relationship is

$$\text{Slope} = \frac{\Delta y}{\Delta x}.$$

If a large change in the variable measured on the *y*-axis (Δy) is associated with a small change in the variable measured on the *x*-axis (Δx), the slope is large and the curve is steep. If a small change in the variable measured on the *y*-axis (Δy) is associated with a large change in the variable measured on the *x*-axis (Δx), the slope is small and the curve is flat.

We can make the idea of slope clearer by doing some calculations.

The Slope of a Straight Line

The slope of a straight line is the same regardless of where on the line you calculate it. The slope of a straight line is constant. Let's calculate the slope of the positive relationship in Fig. A1.9. In part (a),

FIGURE A1.9 The Slope of a Straight Line

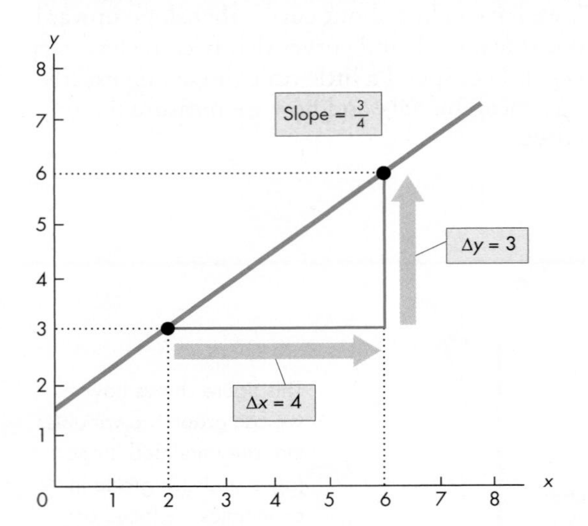

(a) Positive slope

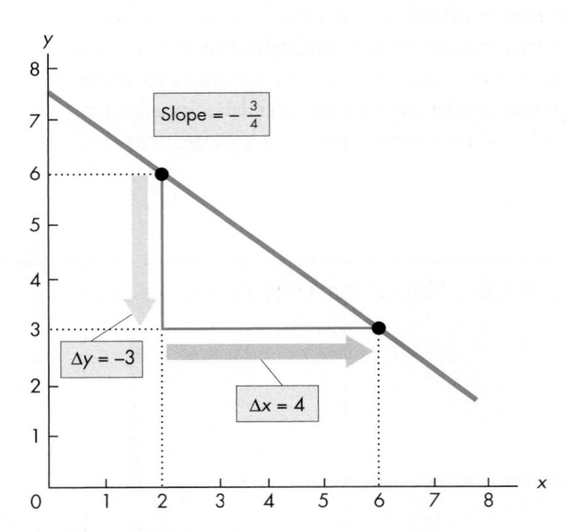

(b) Negative slope

To calculate the slope of a straight line, we divide the change in the value of the variable measured on the *y*-axis (Δy) by the change in the value of the variable measured on the *x*-axis (Δx) as we move along the line.

Part (a) shows the calculation of a positive slope. When *x* increases from 2 to 6, Δx equals 4. That change in *x* brings about an increase in *y* from 3 to 6, so Δy equals 3. The slope ($\Delta y/\Delta x$) equals 3/4.

Part (b) shows the calculation of a negative slope. When *x* increases from 2 to 6, Δx equals 4. That increase in *x* brings about a decrease in *y* from 6 to 3, so Δy equals –3. The slope ($\Delta y/\Delta x$) equals –3/4.

myeconlab animation

when x increases from 2 to 6, y increases from 3 to 6. The change in x is +4—that is, Δx is 4. The change in y is +3—that is, Δy is 3. The slope of that line is

$$\frac{\Delta y}{\Delta x} = \frac{3}{4}.$$

In part (b), when x increases from 2 to 6, y decreases from 6 to 3. The change in y is *minus* 3—that is, Δy is –3. The change in x is *plus* 4—that is, Δx is 4. The slope of the curve is

$$\frac{\Delta y}{\Delta x} = \frac{-3}{4}.$$

Notice that the two slopes have the same magnitude (3/4), but the slope of the line in part (a) is positive (+3/+4 = 3/4) while that in part (b) is negative (–3/+4 = –3/4). The slope of a positive relationship is positive; the slope of a negative relationship is negative.

The Slope of a Curved Line

The slope of a curved line is trickier. The slope of a curved line is not constant, so the slope depends on where on the curved line we calculate it. There are two ways to calculate the slope of a curved line: You can calculate the slope at a point, or you can calculate the slope across an arc of the curve. Let's look at the two alternatives.

Slope at a Point To calculate the slope at a point on a curve, you need to construct a straight line that has the same slope as the curve at the point in question. Figure A1.10 shows how this is done. Suppose you want to calculate the slope of the curve at point A. Place a ruler on the graph so that the ruler touches point A and no other point on the curve, then draw a straight line along the edge of the ruler. The straight red line is this line, and it is the tangent to the curve at point A. If the ruler touches the curve only at point A, then the slope of the curve at point A must be the same as the slope of the edge of the ruler. If the curve and the ruler do not have the same slope, the line along the edge of the ruler will cut the curve instead of just touching it.

Now that you have found a straight line with the same slope as the curve at point A, you can calculate the slope of the curve at point A by calculating the slope of the straight line. Along the straight line, as x increases from 0 to 4 (Δx is 4) y increases from 2 to 5 (Δy is 3). Therefore the slope of the straight line is

$$\frac{\Delta y}{\Delta x} = \frac{3}{4}.$$

So the slope of the curve at point A is 3/4.

Slope Across an Arc An arc of a curve is a piece of a curve. Fig. A1.11shows the same curve as in Fig. A1.10, but instead of calculating the slope at point A, we are now going to calculate the slope across the arc from point B to point C. You can see that the slope of the curve at point B is greater than at point C. When we calculate the slope across an arc, we are calculating the average slope between two points. As we move along the arc from B to C, x increases from 3 to 5 and y increases from 4.0 to 5.5. The change in x is 2 (Δx is 2), and the change in y is 1.5 (Δy is 1.5).

FIGURE A1.10 Slope at a Point

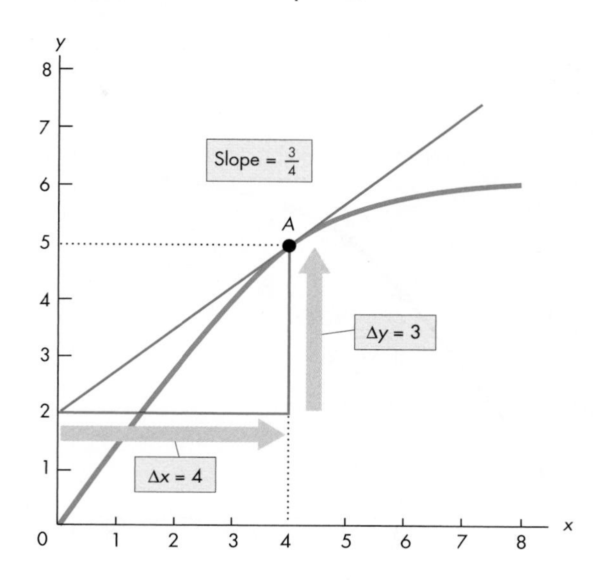

To calculate the slope of the curve at point A, draw the red line that just touches the curve at A—the tangent. The slope of this straight line is calculated by dividing the change in y by the change in x along the red line. When x increases from 0 to 4, Δx equals 4. That change in x is associated with an increase in y from 2 to 5, so Δy equals 3. The slope of the red line is 3/4, so the slope of the curve at point A is 3/4.

myeconlab animation

FIGURE A1.11 Slope Across an Arc

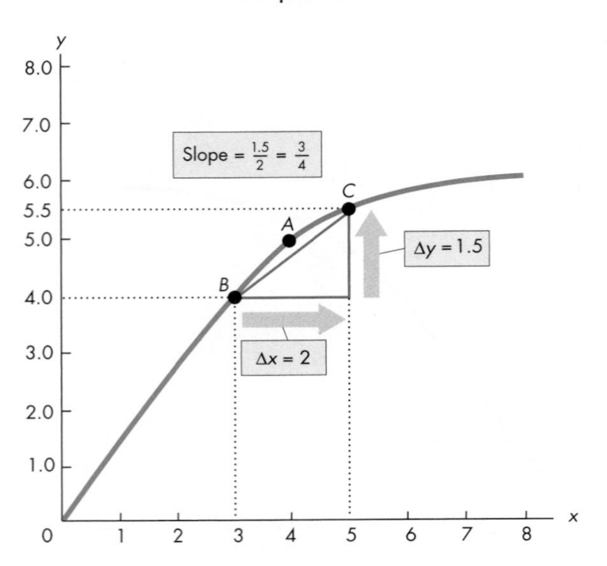

To calculate the average slope of the curve along the arc *BC*, draw a straight line from point *B* to point *C*. The slope of the line *BC* is calculated by dividing the change in *y* by the change in *x*. In moving from *B* to *C*, the increase in x is 2 (Δx equals 2) and the change in y is 1.5 (Δy equals 1.5). The slope of the line *BC* is 1.5 divided by 2, or 3/4. So the slope of the curve across the arc *BC* is 3/4.

Therefore the slope is

$$\frac{\Delta y}{\Delta x} = \frac{1.5}{2} = \frac{3}{4}.$$

So the slope of the curve across the arc *BC* is 3/4.

This calculation gives us the slope of the curve between points *B* and *C*. The actual slope calculated is the slope of the straight line from *B* to *C*. This slope approximates the average slope of the curve along the arc *BC*. In this particular example, the slope across the arc *BC* is identical to the slope of the curve at point *A*, but the calculation of the slope of a curve does not always work out so neatly. You might have fun constructing some more examples and a few counter examples.

You now know how to make and interpret a graph. So far, we've limited our attention to graphs of two variables. We're now going to learn how to graph more than two variables.

Graphing Relationships Among More Than Two Variables

We have seen that we can graph the relationship between two variables as a point formed by the *x*- and *y*-coordinates in a two-dimensional graph. You might be thinking that although a two-dimensional graph is informative, most of the things in which you are likely to be interested involve relationships among many variables, not just two. For example, the amount of ice cream consumed depends on the price of ice cream and the temperature. If ice cream is expensive and the temperature is low, people eat much less ice cream than when ice cream is inexpensive and the temperature is high. For any given price of ice cream, the quantity consumed varies with the temperature; and for any given temperature, the quantity of ice cream consumed varies with its price.

Figure A1.12 shows a relationship among three variables. The table shows the number of gallons of ice cream consumed each day at two different temperatures and at a number of different prices of ice cream. How can we graph these numbers?

To graph a relationship that involves more than two variables, we use the *ceteris paribus* assumption.

Ceteris Paribus

Ceteris paribus (often shortened to *cet par*) means "if all other relevant things remain the same." To isolate the relationship of interest in a laboratory experiment, a scientist holds everything constant except for the variable whose effect is being studied. Economists use the same method to graph a relationship that has more than two variables.

Figure A1.12 shows an example. There, you can see what happens to the quantity of ice cream consumed when the price of ice cream varies but the temperature is held constant.

The curve labeled 70°F shows the relationship between ice cream consumption and the price of ice cream if the temperature remains at 70°F. The numbers used to plot that curve are those in the first two columns of the table. For example, if the temperature is 70°F, 10 gallons are consumed when the price is $2.75 a scoop and 18 gallons are consumed when the price is $2.25 a scoop.

The curve labeled 90°F shows the relationship between ice cream consumption and the price of ice cream if the temperature remains at 90°F. The

FIGURE A1.12 Graphing a Relationship Among Three Variables

Price (dollars per scoop)	Ice cream consumption (gallons per day)	
	70°F	90°F
2.00	25	50
2.25	18	36
2.50	13	26
2.75	**10**	**20**
3.00	7	14
3.25	5	10
3.50	3	6

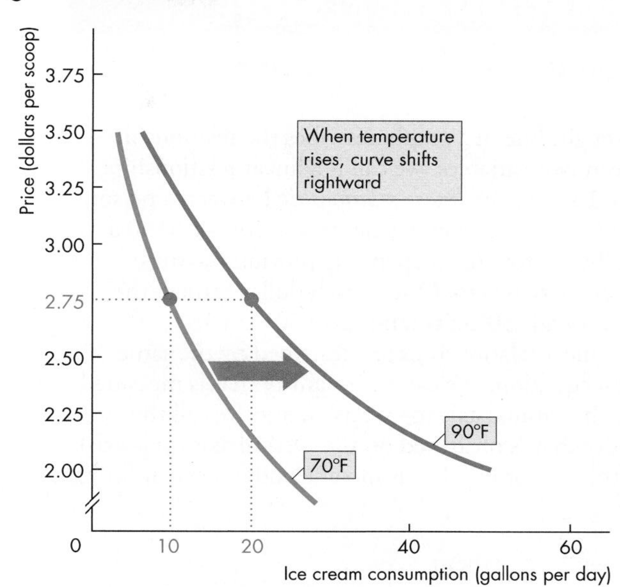

Ice cream consumption depends on its price and the temperature. The table tells us how many gallons of ice cream are consumed each day at different prices and two different temperatures. For example, if the price is $2.75 a scoop and the temperature is 70°F, 10 gallons of ice cream are consumed.

To graph a relationship among three variables, the value of one variable is held constant. The graph shows the relationship between price and consumption when temperature is held constant. One curve holds temperature at 70°F and the other holds it at 90°F.

A change in the price of ice cream brings a movement along one of the curves—along the blue curve at 70°F and along the red curve at 90°F.

When the temperature *rises* from 70°F to 90°F, the curve that shows the relationship between consumption and price *shifts* rightward from the blue curve to the red curve.

myeconlab animation

numbers used to plot that curve are those in the first and third columns of the table. For example, if the temperature is 90°F, 20 gallons are consumed when the price is $2.75 a scoop and 36 gallons are consumed when the price is $2.25 a scoop.

When the price of ice cream changes but the temperature is constant, you can think of what happens in the graph as a movement along one of the curves. At 70°F there is a movement along the blue curve and at 90°F there is a movement along the red curve.

When Other Things Change

The temperature is held constant along each of the curves in Fig. A1.12, but in reality the temperature changes. When that event occurs, you can think of what happens in the graph as a shift of the curve. When the temperature rises from 70°F to 90°F, the curve that shows the relationship between ice cream consumption and the price of ice cream shifts rightward from the blue curve to the red curve.

You will encounter these ideas of movements along and shifts of curves at many points in your study of economics. Think carefully about what you've just learned and make up some examples (with assumed numbers) about other relationships.

With what you have learned about graphs, you can move forward with your study of economics. There are no graphs in this book that are more complicated than those that have been explained in this appendix.

MATHEMATICAL NOTE

Equations of Straight Lines

If a straight line in a graph describes the relationship between two variables, we call it a linear relationship. Figure 1 shows the *linear relationship* between a person's expenditure and income. This person spends \$100 a week (by borrowing or spending previous savings) when income is zero. Out of each dollar earned, this person spends 50 cents (and saves 50 cents).

All linear relationships are described by the same general equation. We call the quantity that is measured on the horizontal axis (or x-axis) x, and we call the quantity that is measured on the vertical axis (or y-axis) y. In the case of Fig. 1, x is income and y is expenditure.

A Linear Equation

The equation that describes a straight-line relationship between x and y is

$$y = a + bx.$$

In this equation, a and b are fixed numbers and they are called *constants*. The values of x and y vary, so these numbers are called *variables*. Because the equation describes a straight line, the equation is called a *linear equation*.

The equation tells us that when the value of x is zero, the value of y is a. We call the constant a the y-axis intercept. The reason is that on the graph the straight line hits the y-axis at a value equal to a. Figure 1 illustrates the y-axis intercept.

For positive values of x, the value of y exceeds a. The constant b tells us by how much y increases above a as x increases. The constant b is the slope of the line.

Slope of Line

As we explain in the chapter, the *slope* of a relationship is the change in the value of y divided by the change in the value of x. We use the Greek letter Δ (delta) to represent "change in." So Δy means the change in the value of the variable measured on the y-axis, and Δx means the change in the value of the variable measured on the x-axis. Therefore the slope of the relationship is

$$\text{Slope} = \frac{\Delta y}{\Delta x}$$

To see why the slope is b, suppose that initially the value of x is x_1, or \$200 in Fig. 2. The corresponding value of y is y_1, also \$200 in Fig. 2. The equation of the line tells us that

$$y_1 = a + bx_1. \quad (1)$$

Now the value of x increases by Δx to $x_1 + \Delta x$ (or \$400 in Fig. 2). And the value of y increases by Δy to $y_1 + \Delta y$ (or \$300 in Fig. 2).

The equation of the line now tells us that

$$y_1 + \Delta y = a + b(x_1 + \Delta x). \quad (2)$$

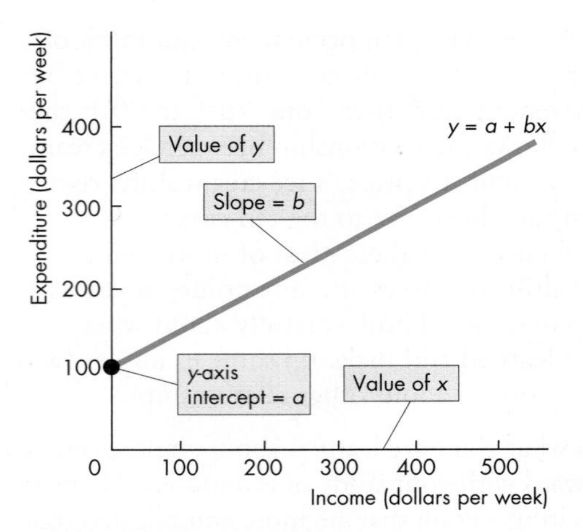

Figure 1 Linear relationship

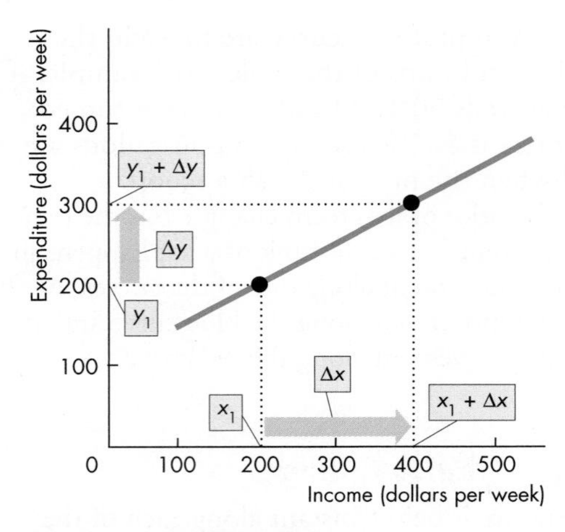

Figure 2 Calculating slope

To calculate the slope of the line, subtract equation (1) from equation (2) to obtain

$$\Delta y = b\Delta x \qquad (3)$$

and now divide equation (3) by Δx to obtain

$$\Delta y/\Delta x = b.$$

So the slope of the line is b.

Position of Line

The y-axis intercept determines the position of the line on the graph. Figure 3 illustrates the relationship between the y-axis intercept and the position of the line. In this graph, the y-axis measures saving and the x-axis measures income.

When the y-axis intercept, a, is positive, the line hits the y-axis at a positive value of y—as the blue line does. Its y-axis intercept is 100. When the y-axis intercept, a, is zero, the line hits the y-axis at the origin—as the purple line does. Its y-axis intercept is 0. When the y-axis intercept, a, is negative, the line hits the y-axis at a negative value of y—as the red line does. Its y-axis intercept is –100.

As the equations of the three lines show, the value of the y-axis intercept does not influence the slope of the line. All three lines have a slope equal to 0.5.

Positive Relationships

Figure 1 shows a positive relationship—the two variables x and y move in the same direction. All positive relationships have a slope that is positive. In the equation of the line, the constant b is positive. In this example, the y-axis intercept, a, is 100. The slope b equals $\Delta y/\Delta x$, which in Fig. 2 is 100/200 or 0.5. The equation of the line is

$$y = 100 + 0.5x.$$

Negative Relationships

Figure 4 shows a negative relationship—the two variables x and y move in the opposite direction. All negative relationships have a slope that is negative. In the equation of the line, the constant b is negative. In the example in Fig. 4, the y-axis intercept, a, is 30. The slope, b, equals $\Delta y/\Delta x$, which is –20/2 or –10. The equation of the line is

$$y = 30 + (-10)x$$

or

$$y = 30 - 10x.$$

Example

A straight line has a y-axis intercept of 50 and a slope of 2. What is the equation of this line?

The equation of a straight line is

$$y = a + bx$$

where a is the y-axis intercept and b is the slope.

So the equation is

$$y = 50 + 2x.$$

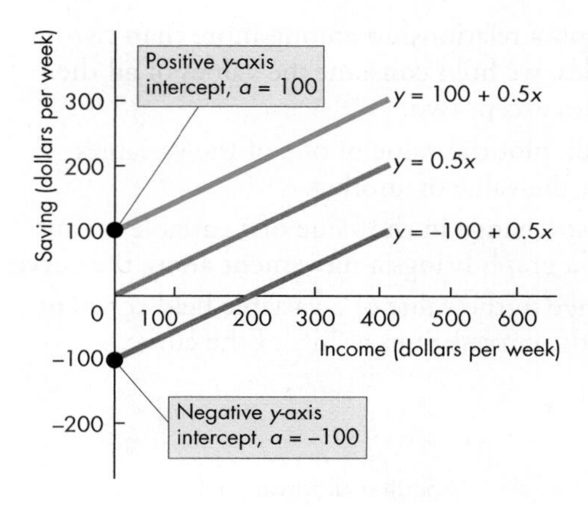

Figure 3 The y-axis intercept

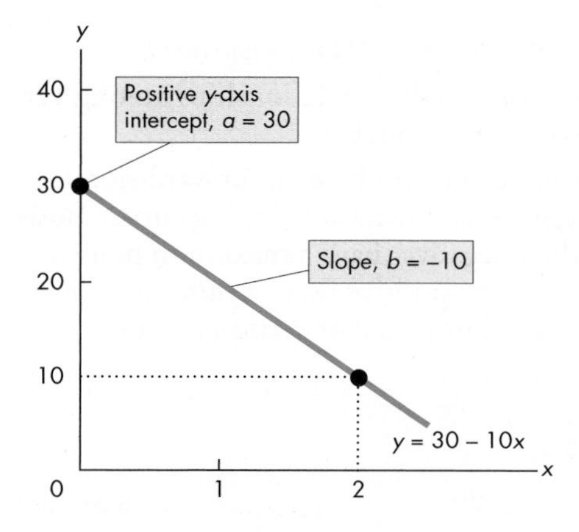

Figure 4 Negative relationship

REVIEW QUIZ

1. Explain how we "read" the three graphs in Figs A1.1 and A1.2.
2. Explain what scatter diagrams show and why we use them.
3. Explain how we "read" the three scatter diagrams in Figs A1.3 and A1.4.
4. Draw a graph to show the relationship between two variables that move in the same direction.
5. Draw a graph to show the relationship between two variables that move in opposite directions.
6. Draw a graph to show the relationship between two variables that have a maximum and a minimum.
7. Which of the relationships in Questions 4 and 5 is a positive relationship and which is a negative relationship?
8. What are the two ways of calculating the slope of a curved line?
9. How do we graph a relationship among more than two variables?
10. Explain what change will bring a *movement along* a curve.
11. Explain what change will bring a *shift* of a curve.

You can work these questions in Study Plan 1.A and get instant feedback.

SUMMARY

Key Points

Graphing Data (pp. 13–16)

- A graph is made by plotting the values of two variables x and y at a point that corresponds to their values measured along the x-axis and the y-axis.
- A scatter diagram is a graph that plots the values of two variables for a number of different values of each.
- A scatter diagram shows the relationship between the two variables. It shows whether they are positively related, negatively related, or unrelated.

Graphs Used in Economic Models (pp. 16–19)

- Graphs are used to show relationships among variables in economic models.
- Relationships can be positive (an upward-sloping curve), negative (a downward-sloping curve), positive and then negative (have a maximum point), negative and then positive (have a minimum point), or unrelated (a horizontal or vertical curve).

The Slope of a Relationship (pp. 20–22)

- The slope of a relationship is calculated as the change in the value of the variable measured on the y-axis divided by the change in the value of the variable measured on the x-axis—that is, $\Delta y/\Delta x$.
- A straight line has a constant slope.
- A curved line has a varying slope. To calculate the slope of a curved line, we calculate the slope at a point or across an arc.

Graphing Relationships Among More Than Two Variables (pp. 22–23)

- To graph a relationship among more than two variables, we hold constant the values of all the variables except two.
- We then plot the value of one of the variables against the value of another.
- A *cet par* change in the value of a variable on an axis of a graph brings a movement along the curve.
- A change in the value of a variable held constant along the curve brings a shift of the curve.

Key Terms

Ceteris paribus, 22
Direct relationship, 16
Inverse relationship, 17
Linear relationship, 16
Negative relationship, 17
Positive relationship, 16
Scatter diagram, 14
Slope, 20

STUDY PLAN PROBLEMS AND APPLICATIONS

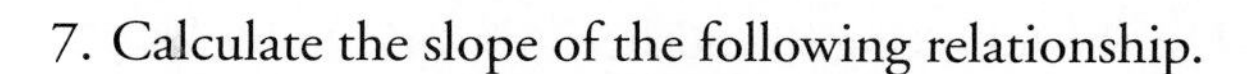

You can work Problems 1 to 11 in MyEconLab Chapter 1A Study Plan and get instant feedback.

Use the following spreadsheet to work Problems 1 to 3. The spreadsheet provides data on the U.S. economy: Column A is the year, column B is the inflation rate, column C is the interest rate, column D is the growth rate, and column E is the unemployment rate.

	A	B	C	D	E
1	1999	2.2	4.6	4.8	4.2
2	2000	3.4	5.8	4.1	4.0
3	2001	2.8	3.4	1.1	4.7
4	2002	1.6	1.6	1.8	5.8
5	2003	2.3	1.0	2.5	6.0
6	2004	2.7	1.4	3.6	5.5
7	2005	3.4	3.2	3.1	5.1
8	2006	3.2	4.7	2.7	4.6
9	2007	2.8	4.4	2.1	4.6
10	2008	3.8	1.4	0.4	5.8
11	2009	–0.4	0.2	–2.4	9.3

1. Draw a scatter diagram of the inflation rate and the interest rate. Describe the relationship.
2. Draw a scatter diagram of the growth rate and the unemployment rate. Describe the relationship.
3. Draw a scatter diagram of the interest rate and the unemployment rate. Describe the relationship.

Use the following news clip to work Problems 4 to 6.

***Clash of the Titans* Tops Box Office With Sales of $61.2 Million:**

Movie	Theaters (number)	Revenue (dollars per theater)
Clash of the Titans	3,777	16,213
Tyler Perry's Why Did I Get Married	2,155	13,591
How To Train Your Dragon	4,060	7,145
The Last Song	2,673	5,989

Source: Bloomberg.com, April 5, 2010

4. Draw a graph of the relationship between the revenue per theater on the y-axis and the number of theaters on the x-axis. Describe the relationship.
5. Calculate the slope of the relationship between 4,060 and 2,673 theaters.
6. Calculate the slope of the relationship between 2,155 and 4,060 theaters.
7. Calculate the slope of the following relationship.

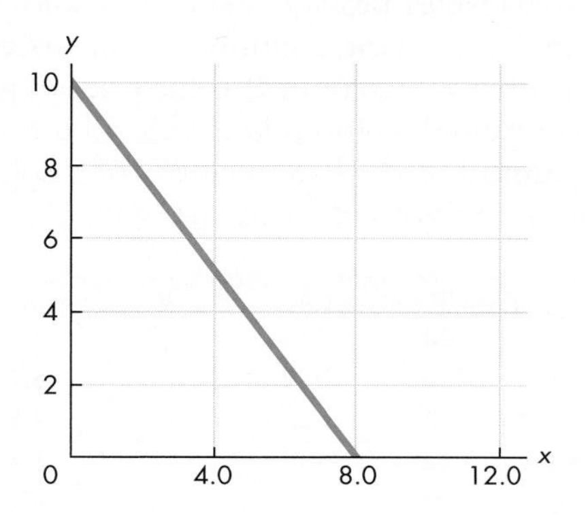

Use the following relationship to work Problems 8 and 9.

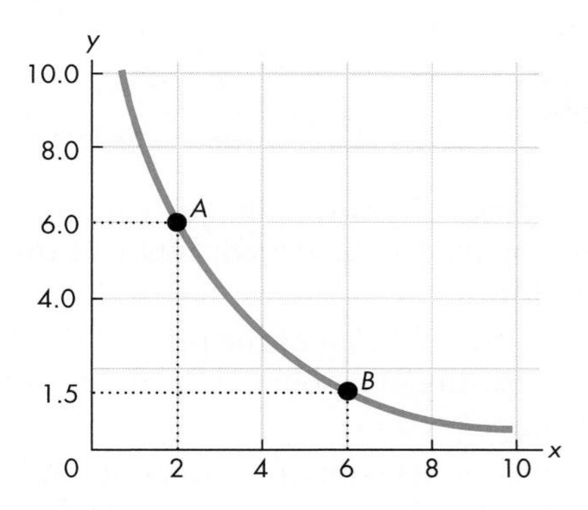

8. Calculate the slope of the relationship at point A and at point B.
9. Calculate the slope across the arc AB.

Use the following table to work Problems 10 and 11. The table gives the price of a balloon ride, the temperature, and the number of rides a day.

Price (dollars per ride)	Balloon rides (number per day)		
	50°F	70°F	90°F
5	32	40	50
10	27	32	40
15	18	27	32

10. Draw a graph to show the relationship between the price and the number of rides, when the temperature is 70°F. Describe this relationship.
11. What happens in the graph in Problem 10 if the temperature rises to 90°F?

ADDITIONAL ASSIGNABLE PROBLEMS AND APPLICATIONS

You can work these problems in MyEconLab if assigned by your instructor.

Use the following spreadsheet to work Problems 12 to 14. The spreadsheet provides data on oil and gasoline: Column A is the year, column B is the price of oil (dollars per barrel), column C is the price of gasoline (cents per gallon), column D is U.S. oil production, and column E is the U.S. quantity of gasoline refined (both in millions of barrels per day).

	A	B	C	D	E
1	1999	24	118	5.9	8.1
2	2000	30	152	5.8	8.2
3	2001	17	146	5.8	8.3
4	2002	24	139	5.7	8.4
5	2003	27	160	5.7	8.5
6	2004	37	190	5.4	8.7
7	2005	49	231	5.2	8.7
8	2006	56	262	5.1	8.9
9	2007	86	284	5.1	9.0
10	2008	43	330	5.0	8.9
11	2009	76	241	4.9	8.9

12. Draw a scatter diagram of the price of oil and the quantity of U.S. oil produced. Describe the relationship.
13. Draw a scatter diagram of the price of gasoline and the quantity of gasoline refined. Describe the relationship.
14. Draw a scatter diagram of the quantity of U.S. oil produced and the quantity of gasoline refined. Describe the relationship.

Use the following data to work Problems 15 to 17.

Draw a graph that shows the relationship between the two variables x and y:

x	0	1	2	3	4	5
y	25	24	22	18	12	0

15. a. Is the relationship positive or negative?
    b. Does the slope of the relationship become steeper or flatter as the value of x increases?
    c. Think of some economic relationships that might be similar to this one.
16. Calculate the slope of the relationship between x and y when x equals 3.
17. Calculate the slope of the relationship across the arc as x increases from 4 to 5.
18. Calculate the slope of the curve at point A.

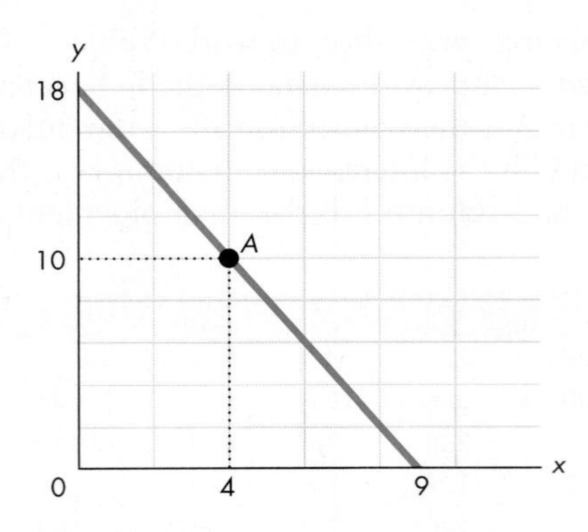

Use the following relationship to work Problems 19 and 20.

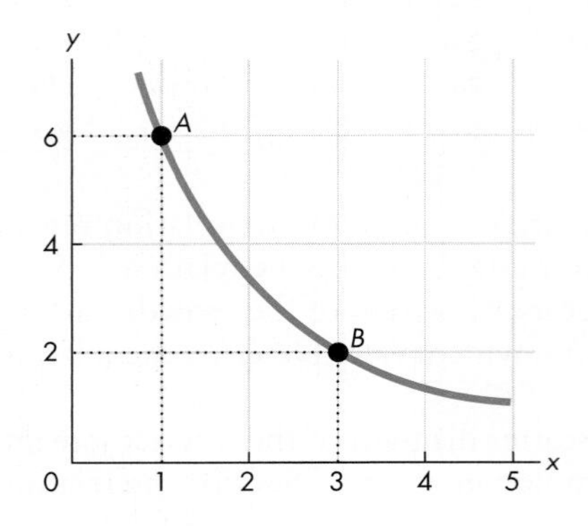

19. Calculate the slope at point A and at point B.
20. Calculate the slope across the arc *AB*.

Use the following table to work Problems 21 to 23. The table gives information about umbrellas: price, the number purchased, and rainfall in inches.

Price (dollars per umbrella)	Umbrellas (number purchased per day) 0 inches	1 inch	2 inches
20	4	7	8
30	2	4	7
40	1	2	4

21. Draw a graph to show the relationship between the price and the number of umbrellas purchased, holding the amount of rainfall constant at 1 inch. Describe this relationship.
22. What happens in the graph in Problem 21 if the price rises and rainfall is constant?
23. What happens in the graph in Problem 21 if the rainfall increases from 1 inch to 2 inches?

After studying this chapter, you will be able to:

- Define the production possibilities frontier and use it to calculate opportunity cost
- Distinguish between production possibilities and preferences and describe an efficient allocation of resources
- Explain how current production choices expand future production possibilities
- Explain how specialization and trade expand production possibilities
- Describe the economic institutions that coordinate decisions

2 THE ECONOMIC PROBLEM

Why does food cost much more today than it did a few years ago? One reason is that we now use part of our corn crop to produce ethanol, a clean biofuel substitute for gasoline. Another reason is that drought in some parts of the world has decreased global grain production. In this chapter, you will study an economic model—the production possibilities frontier—and you will learn why ethanol production and drought have increased the cost of producing food. You will also learn how to assess whether it is a good idea to increase corn production to produce fuel; how we can expand our production possibilities; and how we gain by trading with others.

At the end of the chapter, in *Reading Between the Lines*, we'll apply what you've learned to understanding why ethanol production is raising the cost of food.

Production Possibilities and Opportunity Cost

Every working day, in mines, factories, shops, and offices and on farms and construction sites across the United States, 138 million people produce a vast variety of goods and services valued at $50 billion. But the quantities of goods and services that we can produce are limited both by our available resources and by technology. And if we want to increase our production of one good, we must decrease our production of something else—we face a tradeoff. You are going to learn about the production possibilities frontier, which describes the limit to what we can produce and provides a neat way of thinking about and illustrating the idea of a tradeoff.

The **production possibilities frontier** (*PPF*) is the boundary between those combinations of goods and services that can be produced and those that cannot. To illustrate the *PPF*, we focus on two goods at a time and hold the quantities produced of all the other goods and services constant. That is, we look at a *model* economy in which everything remains the same except for the production of the two goods we are considering.

Let's look at the production possibilities frontier for cola and pizza, which represent *any* pair of goods or services.

Production Possibilities Frontier

The *production possibilities frontier* for cola and pizza shows the limits to the production of these two goods, given the total resources and technology available to produce them. Figure 2.1 shows this production possibilities frontier. The table lists some combinations of the quantities of pizza and cola that can be produced in a month given the resources available. The figure graphs these combinations. The *x*-axis shows the quantity of pizzas produced, and the *y*-axis shows the quantity of cola produced.

The *PPF* illustrates *scarcity* because we cannot attain the points outside the frontier. These points describe wants that can't be satisfied. We can produce at any point *inside* the *PPF* or *on* the *PPF*. These points are attainable. Suppose that in a typical month, we produce 4 million pizzas and 5 million cans of cola. Figure 2.1 shows this combination as point *E* and as possibility *E* in the table. The figure

FIGURE 2.1 Production Possibilities Frontier

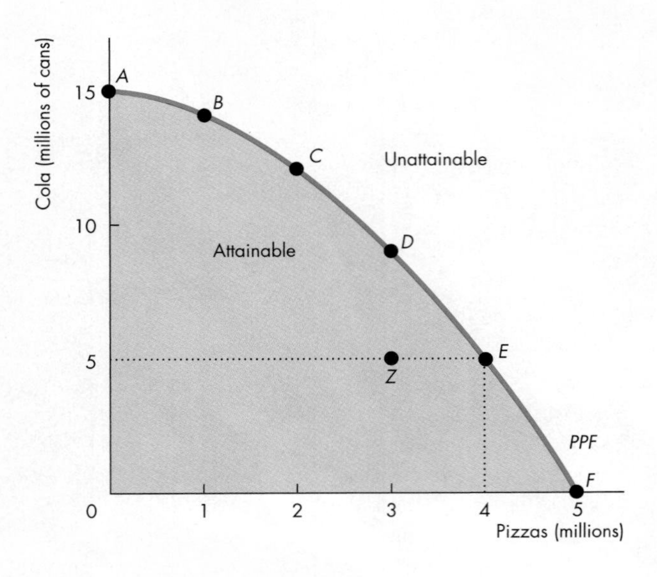

Possibility	Pizzas (millions)		Cola (millions of cans)
A	0	and	15
B	1	and	14
C	2	and	12
D	3	and	9
E	4	and	5
F	5	and	0

The table lists six production possibilities for cola and pizzas. Row *A* tells us that if we produce no pizzas, the maximum quantity of cola we can produce is 15 million cans. Points *A*, *B*, *C*, *D*, *E*, and *F* in the figure represent the rows of the table. The curve passing through these points is the production possibilities frontier (*PPF*).

The *PPF* separates the attainable from the unattainable. Production is possible at any point *inside* the orange area or *on* the frontier. Points outside the frontier are unattainable. Points inside the frontier, such as point *Z*, are inefficient because resources are wasted or misallocated. At such points, it is possible to use the available resources to produce more of either or both goods.

myeconlab animation

also shows other production possibilities. For example, we might stop producing pizza and move all the people who produce it into producing cola. Point *A* in the figure and possibility *A* in the table show this case. The quantity of cola produced increases to 15 million cans, and pizza production dries up. Alternatively, we might close the cola factories and switch all the resources into producing pizza. In this situation, we produce 5 million pizzas. Point *F* in the figure and possibility *F* in the table show this case.

Production Efficiency

We achieve **production efficiency** if we produce goods and services at the lowest possible cost. This outcome occurs at all the points *on* the *PPF.* At points *inside* the *PPF*, production is inefficient because we are giving up more than necessary of one good to produce a given quantity of the other good.

For example, at point *Z* in Fig. 2.1, we produce 3 million pizzas and 5 million cans of cola. But we have enough resources to produce 3 million pizzas and 9 million cans of cola. Our pizzas cost more cola than necessary. We can get them for a lower cost. Only when we produce *on* the *PPF* do we incur the lowest possible cost of production.

Production is *inefficient* inside the *PPF* because resources are either *unused* or *misallocated* or both.

Resources are *unused* when they are idle but could be working. For example, we might leave some of the factories idle or some workers unemployed.

Resources are *misallocated* when they are assigned to tasks for which they are not the best match. For example, we might assign skilled pizza chefs to work in a cola factory and skilled cola producers to work in a pizza shop. We could get more pizzas *and* more cola from these same workers if we reassigned them to the tasks that more closely match their skills.

Tradeoff Along the *PPF*

Every choice *along* the *PPF* involves a *tradeoff.* On the *PPF* in Fig. 2.1, we trade off cola for pizzas.

Tradeoffs arise in every imaginable real-world situation in which a choice must be made. At any given point in time, we have a fixed amount of labor, land, capital, and entrepreneurship. By using our available technologies, we can employ these resources to produce goods and services, but we are limited in what we can produce. This limit defines a boundary between what we can attain and what we cannot attain. This boundary is the real-world's production possibilities frontier, and it defines the tradeoffs that we must make. On our real-world *PPF*, we can produce more of any one good or service only if we produce less of some other goods or services.

When doctors want to spend more on AIDS and cancer research, they face a tradeoff: more medical research for less of some other things. When Congress wants to spend more on education and health care, it faces a tradeoff: more education and health care for less national defense or less homeland security. When an environmental group argues for less logging, it is suggesting a tradeoff: greater conservation of endangered wildlife for less paper. When you want to study more, you face a tradeoff: more study time for less leisure or sleep.

All tradeoffs involve a cost—an opportunity cost.

Opportunity Cost

The **opportunity cost** of an action is the highest-valued alternative forgone. The *PPF* makes this idea precise and enables us to calculate opportunity cost. Along the *PPF*, there are only two goods, so there is only one alternative forgone: some quantity of the other good. Given our current resources and technology, we can produce more pizzas only if we produce less cola. The opportunity cost of producing an additional pizza is the cola we *must* forgo. Similarly, the opportunity cost of producing an additional can of cola is the quantity of pizza we must forgo.

In Fig. 2.1, if we move from point *C* to point *D*, we get 1 million more pizzas but 3 million fewer cans of cola. The additional 1 million pizzas *cost* 3 million cans of cola. One pizza costs 3 cans of cola.

We can also work out the opportunity cost of moving in the opposite direction. In Fig. 2.1, if we move from point *D* to point *C*, the quantity of cola produced increases by 3 million cans and the quantity of pizzas produced decreases by 1 million. So if we choose point *C* over point *D*, the additional 3 million cans of cola *cost* 1 million pizzas. One can of cola costs 1/3 of a pizza.

Opportunity Cost Is a Ratio Opportunity cost is a ratio. It is the decrease in the quantity produced of one good divided by the increase in the quantity produced of another good as we move along the production possibilities frontier.

Because opportunity cost is a ratio, the opportunity cost of producing an additional can of cola is equal to the *inverse* of the opportunity cost of producing an additional pizza. Check this proposition by returning to the calculations we've just worked through. When we move along the *PPF* from *C* to *D*, the opportunity cost of a pizza is 3 cans of cola. The inverse of 3 is 1/3. If we decrease the production of pizza and increase the production of cola by moving from *D* to *C*, the opportunity cost of a can of cola must be 1/3 of a pizza. That is exactly the number that we calculated for the move from *D* to *C*.

Increasing Opportunity Cost The opportunity cost of a pizza increases as the quantity of pizzas produced increases. The outward-bowed shape of the *PPF* reflects increasing opportunity cost. When we produce a large quantity of cola and a small quantity of pizza—between points *A* and *B* in Fig. 2.1—the frontier has a gentle slope. An increase in the quantity of pizzas costs a small decrease in the quantity of cola—the opportunity cost of a pizza is a small quantity of cola.

When we produce a large quantity of pizzas and a small quantity of cola—between points *E* and *F* in Fig. 2.1—the frontier is steep. A given increase in the quantity of pizzas *costs* a large decrease in the quantity of cola, so the opportunity cost of a pizza is a large quantity of cola.

The *PPF* is bowed outward because resources are not all equally productive in all activities. People with many years of experience working for PepsiCo are good at producing cola but not very good at making pizzas. So if we move some of these people from PepsiCo to Domino's, we get a small increase in the quantity of pizzas but a large decrease in the quantity of cola.

Similarly, people who have spent years working at Domino's are good at producing pizzas, but they have no idea how to produce cola. So if we move some of these people from Domino's to PepsiCo, we get a small increase in the quantity of cola but a large decrease in the quantity of pizzas. The more of either good we try to produce, the less productive are the additional resources we use to produce that good and the larger is the opportunity cost of a unit of that good.

Economics in Action

Increasing Opportunity Cost on the Farm

Sanders Wright, a homesick Mississippi native, is growing cotton in Iowa. The growing season is short, so his commercial success is unlikely. Cotton does not grow well in Iowa, but corn does. A farm with irrigation can produce 300 bushels of corn per acre—twice the U.S. average.

Ronnie Gerik, a Texas cotton farmer, has started to grow corn. Ronnie doesn't have irrigation and instead relies on rainfall. That's not a problem for cotton, which just needs a few soakings a season. But it's a big problem for corn, which needs an inch of water a week. Also, corn can't take the heat like cotton, and if the temperature rises too much, Ronnie will be lucky to get 100 bushels an acre.

An Iowa corn farmer gives up almost no cotton to produce his 300 bushels of corn per acre—corn has a low opportunity cost. But Ronnie Gerick gives up a huge amount of cotton to produce his 100 bushels of corn per acre. By switching some land from cotton to corn, Ronnie has increased the production of corn, but the additional corn has a high opportunity cost.

"Deere worker makes 'cotton pickin' miracle happen," WCFCourier.com; and "Farmers stampede to corn," *USA Today*.

REVIEW QUIZ

1. How does the production possibilities frontier illustrate scarcity?
2. How does the production possibilities frontier illustrate production efficiency?
3. How does the production possibilities frontier show that every choice involves a tradeoff?
4. How does the production possibilities frontier illustrate opportunity cost?
5. Why is opportunity cost a ratio?
6. Why does the *PPF* bow outward and what does that imply about the relationship between opportunity cost and the quantity produced?

You can work these questions in Study Plan 2.1 and get instant feedback.

We've seen that what we can produce is limited by the production possibilities frontier. We've also seen that production on the *PPF* is efficient. But we can produce many different quantities on the *PPF*. How do we choose among them? How do we know which point on the *PPF* is the best one?

Using Resources Efficiently

We achieve *production efficiency* at every point on the *PPF*, but which point is best? The answer is the point on the *PPF* at which goods and services are produced in the quantities that provide the greatest possible benefit. When goods and services are produced at the lowest possible cost and in the quantities that provide the greatest possible benefit, we have achieved **allocative efficiency.**

The questions that we raised when we reviewed the four big issues in Chapter 1 are questions about allocative efficiency. To answer such questions, we must measure and compare costs and benefits.

The *PPF* and Marginal Cost

The **marginal cost** of a good is the opportunity cost of producing one more unit of it. We calculate marginal cost from the slope of the *PPF*. As the quantity of pizzas produced increases, the *PPF* gets steeper and the marginal cost of a pizza increases. Figure 2.2 illustrates the calculation of the marginal cost of a pizza.

Begin by finding the opportunity cost of pizza in blocks of 1 million pizzas. The cost of the first million pizzas is 1 million cans of cola; the cost of the second million pizzas is 2 million cans of cola; the cost of the third million pizzas is 3 million cans of cola, and so on. The bars in part (a) illustrate these calculations.

The bars in part (b) show the cost of an average pizza in each of the 1 million pizza blocks. Focus on the third million pizzas—the move from *C* to *D* in part (a). Over this range, because 1 million pizzas cost 3 million cans of cola, one of these pizzas, on average, costs 3 cans of cola—the height of the bar in part (b).

Next, find the opportunity cost of each additional pizza—the marginal cost of a pizza. The marginal cost of a pizza increases as the quantity of pizzas produced increases. The marginal cost at point *C* is less than it is at point *D*. On average over the range from *C* to *D*, the marginal cost of a pizza is 3 cans of cola. But it exactly equals 3 cans of cola only in the middle of the range between *C* and *D*.

The red dot in part (b) indicates that the marginal cost of a pizza is 3 cans of cola when 2.5 million pizzas are produced. Each black dot in part (b) is interpreted in the same way. The red curve that passes through these dots, labeled *MC*, is the marginal cost curve. It shows the marginal cost of a pizza at each quantity of pizzas as we move along the *PPF*.

FIGURE 2.2 The *PPF* and Marginal Cost

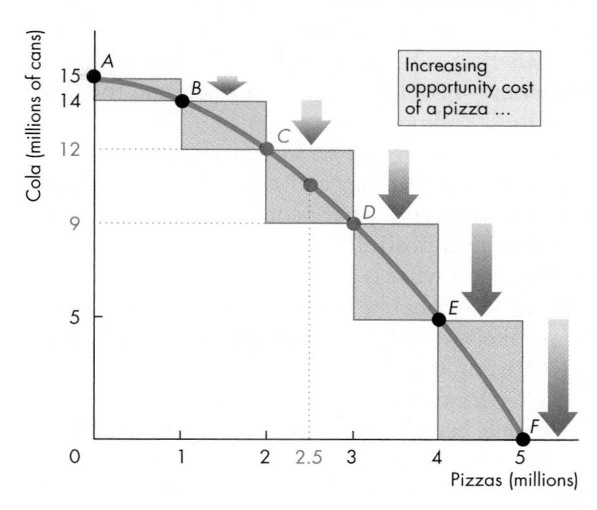

(a) *PPF* and opportunity cost

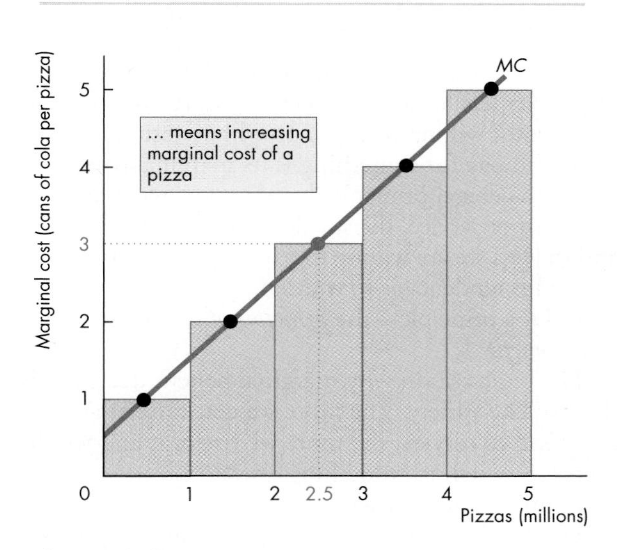

(b) Marginal cost

Marginal cost is calculated from the slope of the *PPF*. As the quantity of pizzas produced increases, the *PPF* gets steeper and the marginal cost of a pizza increases. The bars in part (a) show the opportunity cost of pizza in blocks of 1 million pizzas. The bars in part (b) show the cost of an average pizza in each of these 1 million blocks. The red curve, *MC*, shows the marginal cost of a pizza at each point along the *PPF*. This curve passes through the center of each of the bars in part (b).

myeconlab animation

Preferences and Marginal Benefit

The **marginal benefit** from a good or service is the benefit received from consuming one more unit of it. This benefit is subjective. It depends on people's **preferences**—people's likes and dislikes and the intensity of those feelings.

Marginal benefit and *preferences* stand in sharp contrast to *marginal cost* and *production possibilities.* Preferences describe what people like and want and the production possibilities describe the limits or constraints on what is feasible.

We need a concrete way of illustrating preferences that parallels the way we illustrate the limits to production using the *PPF.*

The device that we use to illustrate preferences is the **marginal benefit curve**, which is a curve that shows the relationship between the marginal benefit from a good and the quantity consumed of that good. Note that the *marginal benefit curve* is *unrelated* to the *PPF* and cannot be derived from it.

We measure the marginal benefit from a good or service by the most that people are *willing to pay* for an additional unit of it. The idea is that you are willing to pay less for a good than it is worth to you but you are not willing to pay more: The most you are willing to pay for something is its marginal benefit.

It is a general principle that the more we have of any good or service, the smaller is its marginal benefit and the less we are willing to pay for an additional unit of it. This tendency is so widespread and strong that we call it a principle—the *principle of decreasing marginal benefit.*

The basic reason why marginal benefit decreases is that we like variety. The more we consume of any one good or service, the more we tire of it and would prefer to switch to something else.

Think about your willingness to pay for a pizza. If pizza is hard to come by and you can buy only a few slices a year, you might be willing to pay a high price to get an additional slice. But if pizza is all you've eaten for the past few days, you are willing to pay almost nothing for another slice.

You've learned to think about cost as opportunity cost, not as a dollar cost. You can think about marginal benefit and willingness to pay in the same way. The marginal benefit, measured by what you are willing to pay for something, is the quantity of other goods and services that you are willing to forgo. Let's continue with the example of cola and pizza and illustrate preferences this way.

FIGURE 2.3 Preferences and the Marginal Benefit Curve

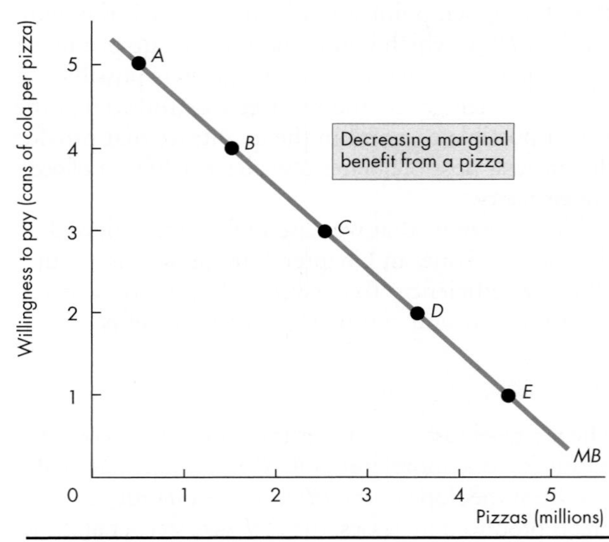

Possibility	Pizzas (millions)	Willingness to pay (cans of cola per pizza)
A	0.5	5
B	1.5	4
C	2.5	3
D	3.5	2
E	4.5	1

The smaller the quantity of pizzas available, the more cola people are willing to give up for an additional pizza. With 0.5 million pizzas available, people are willing to pay 5 cans of cola per pizza. But with 4.5 million pizzas, people are willing to pay only 1 can of cola per pizza. Willingness to pay measures marginal benefit. A universal feature of people's preferences is that marginal benefit decreases.

animation

Figure 2.3 illustrates preferences as the willingness to pay for pizza in terms of cola. In row *A*, with 0.5 million pizzas available, people are willing to pay 5 cans of cola per pizza. As the quantity of pizzas increases, the amount that people are willing to pay for a pizza falls. With 4.5 million pizzas available, people are willing to pay only 1 can of cola per pizza.

Let's now use the concepts of marginal cost and marginal benefit to describe allocative efficiency.

FIGURE 2.4 Efficient Use of Resources

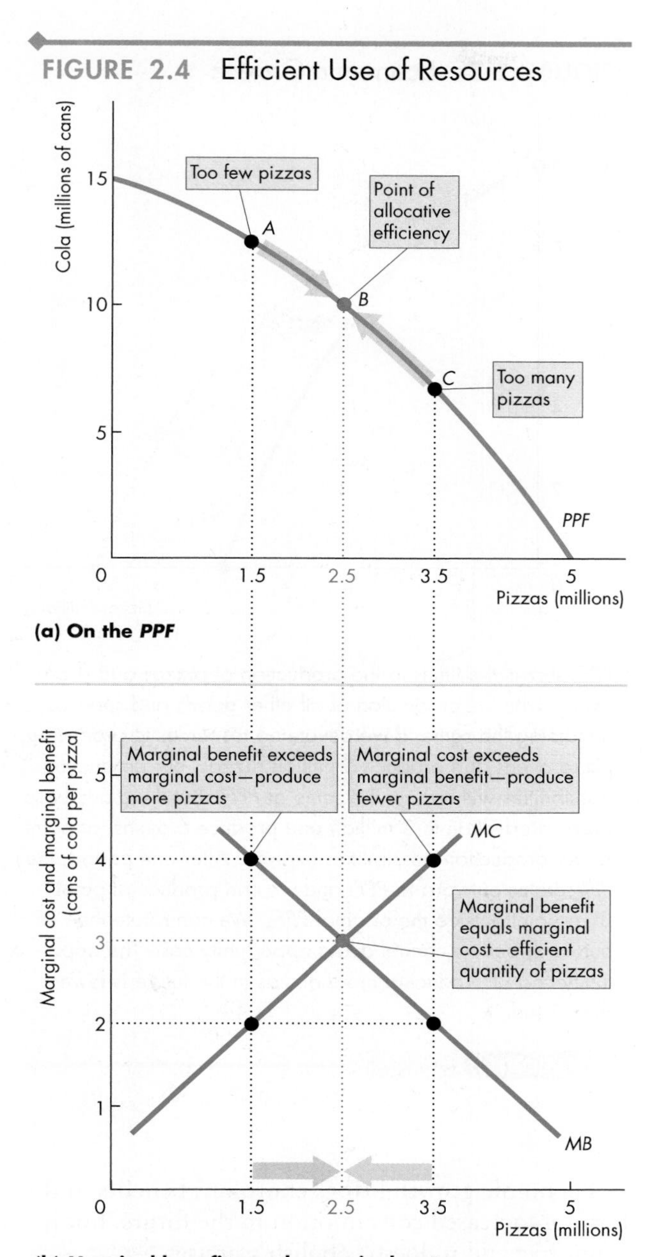

The greater the quantity of pizzas produced, the smaller is the marginal benefit (*MB*) from pizza—the less cola people are willing to give up to get an additional pizza. But the greater the quantity of pizzas produced, the greater is the marginal cost (*MC*) of a pizza—the more cola people must give up to get an additional pizza. When marginal benefit equals marginal cost, resources are being used efficiently.

Allocative Efficiency

At *any* point on the *PPF*, we cannot produce more of one good without giving up some other good. At the *best* point on the *PPF,* we cannot produce more of one good without giving up some other good that provides greater benefit. We are producing at the point of allocative efficiency—the point on the *PPF* that we prefer above all other points.

Suppose in Fig. 2.4, we produce 1.5 million pizzas. The marginal cost of a pizza is 2 cans of cola, and the marginal benefit from a pizza is 4 cans of cola. Because someone values an additional pizza more highly than it costs to produce, we can get more value from our resources by moving some of them out of producing cola and into producing pizza.

Now suppose we produce 3.5 million pizzas. The marginal cost of a pizza is now 4 cans of cola, but the marginal benefit from a pizza is only 2 cans of cola. Because the additional pizza costs more to produce than anyone thinks it is worth, we can get more value from our resources by moving some of them away from producing pizza and into producing cola.

Suppose we produce 2.5 million pizzas. Marginal cost and marginal benefit are now equal at 3 cans of cola. This allocation of resources between pizzas and cola is efficient. If more pizzas are produced, the forgone cola is worth more than the additional pizzas. If fewer pizzas are produced, the forgone pizzas are worth more than the additional cola.

REVIEW QUIZ

1. What is marginal cost? How is it measured?
2. What is marginal benefit? How is it measured?
3. How does the marginal benefit from a good change as the quantity produced of that good increases?
4. What is allocative efficiency and how does it relate to the production possibilities frontier?
5. What conditions must be satisfied if resources are used efficiently?

You can work these questions in Study Plan 2.2 and get instant feedback.

You now understand the limits to production and the conditions under which resources are used efficiently. Your next task is to study the expansion of production possibilities.

Economic Growth

During the past 30 years, production per person in the United States has doubled. The expansion of production possibilities is called **economic growth.** Economic growth increases our *standard of living,* but it doesn't overcome scarcity and avoid opportunity cost. To make our economy grow, we face a tradeoff—the faster we make production grow, the greater is the opportunity cost of economic growth.

The Cost of Economic Growth

Economic growth comes from technological change and capital accumulation. **Technological change** is the development of new goods and of better ways of producing goods and services. **Capital accumulation** is the growth of capital resources, including *human capital.*

Technological change and capital accumulation have vastly expanded our production possibilities. We can produce automobiles that provide us with more transportation than was available when we had only horses and carriages. We can produce satellites that provide global communications on a much larger scale than that available with the earlier cable technology. But if we use our resources to develop new technologies and produce capital, we must decrease our production of consumption goods and services. New technologies and new capital have an opportunity cost. Let's look at this opportunity cost.

Instead of studying the *PPF* of pizzas and cola, we'll hold the quantity of cola produced constant and examine the *PPF* for pizzas and pizza ovens. Figure 2.5 shows this *PPF* as the blue curve PPF_0. If we devote no resources to producing pizza ovens, we produce at point *A*. If we produce 3 million pizzas, we can produce 6 pizza ovens at point *B*. If we produce no pizza, we can produce 10 ovens at point *C*.

The amount by which our production possibilities expand depends on the resources we devote to technological change and capital accumulation. If we devote no resources to this activity (point *A*), our *PPF* remains the blue curve PPF_0 in Fig. 2.5. If we cut the current pizza production and produce 6 ovens (point *B*), then in the future, we'll have more capital and our *PPF* will rotate outward to the position shown by the red curve PPF_1. The fewer resources we use for producing pizza and the more resources we use for producing ovens, the greater is the expansion of our future production possibilities.

FIGURE 2.5 Economic Growth

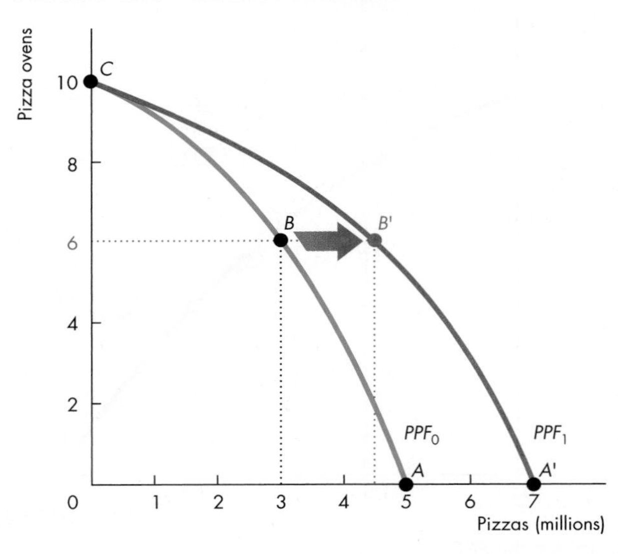

PPF_0 shows the limits to the production of pizzas and pizza ovens, with the production of all other goods and services remaining the same. If we devote no resources to producing pizza ovens and produce 5 million pizzas, our production possibilities will remain the same at PPF_0. But if we decrease pizza production to 3 million and produce 6 ovens, at point *B*, our production possibilities expand. After one period, the *PPF* rotates outward to PPF_1 and we can produce at point *B*', a point outside the original PPF_0. We can rotate the *PPF* outward, but we cannot avoid opportunity cost. The opportunity cost of producing more pizzas in the future is fewer pizzas today.

myeconlab animation

Economic growth brings enormous benefits in the form of increased consumption in the future, but it is not free and it doesn't abolish scarcity.

In Fig. 2.5, to make economic growth happen we must use some resources to produce new ovens, which leaves fewer resources to produce pizzas. To move to *B*' in the future, we must move from *A* to *B* today. The opportunity cost of more pizzas in the future is fewer pizzas today. Also, on the new *PPF*, we still face a tradeoff and opportunity cost.

The ideas about economic growth that we have explored in the setting of the pizza industry also apply to nations. Hong Kong and the United States provide a striking case study.

Economics in Action

Hong Kong Catching Up to the United States

In 1969, the production possibilities per person in the United States were more than four times those in Hong Kong (see the figure). The United States devotes one fifth of its resources to accumulating capital and in 1969 was at point *A* on its *PPF*. Hong Kong devotes one third of its resources to accumulating capital and in 1969, Hong Kong was at point *A* on its *PPF*.

Since 1969, both countries have experienced economic growth, but because Hong Kong devotes a bigger fraction of its resources to accumulating capital, its production possibilities have expanded more quickly.

By 2009, production possibilities per person in Hong Kong had reached 94 percent of those in the United States. If Hong Kong continues to devote more resources to accumulating capital than we do (at point *B* on its 2009 *PPF*), it will continue to grow more rapidly. But if Hong Kong decreases capital accumulation (moving to point *D* on its 2009 *PPF*), then its rate of economic growth will slow.

Hong Kong is typical of the fast-growing Asian economies, which include Taiwan, Thailand, South Korea, China, and India. Production possibilities expand in these countries by between 5 and almost 10 percent a year.

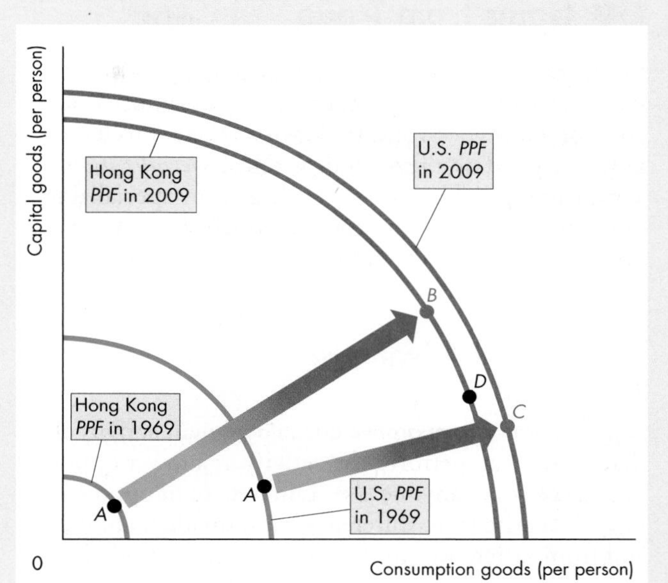

Economic Growth in the United States and Hong Kong

If such high economic growth rates are maintained, these other Asian countries will continue to close the gap between themselves and the United States, as Hong Kong is doing.

A Nation's Economic Growth

The experiences of the United States and Hong Kong make a striking example of the effects of our choices about consumption and capital goods on the rate of economic growth.

If a nation devotes all its factors of production to producing consumption goods and services and none to advancing technology and accumulating capital, its production possibilities in the future will be the same as they are today.

To expand production possibilities in the future, a nation must devote fewer resources to producing current consumption goods and services and some resources to accumulating capital and developing new technologies. As production possibilities expand, consumption in the future can increase. The decrease in today's consumption is the opportunity cost of tomorrow's increase in consumption.

REVIEW QUIZ

1. What generates economic growth?
2. How does economic growth influence the production possibilities frontier?
3. What is the opportunity cost of economic growth?
4. Why has Hong Kong experienced faster economic growth than the United States?
5. Does economic growth overcome scarcity?

You can work these questions in Study Plan 2.3 and get instant feedback.

Next, we're going to study another way in which we expand our production possibilities—the amazing fact that *both* buyers and sellers gain from specialization and trade.

Gains from Trade

People can produce for themselves all the goods and services that they consume, or they can produce one good or a few goods and trade with others. Producing only one good or a few goods is called *specialization.* We are going to learn how people gain by specializing in the production of the good in which they have a *comparative advantage* and trading with others.

Comparative Advantage and Absolute Advantage

A person has a **comparative advantage** in an activity if that person can perform the activity at a lower opportunity cost than anyone else. Differences in opportunity costs arise from differences in individual abilities and from differences in the characteristics of other resources.

No one excels at everything. One person is an outstanding pitcher but a poor catcher; another person is a brilliant lawyer but a poor teacher. In almost all human endeavors, what one person does easily, someone else finds difficult. The same applies to land and capital. One plot of land is fertile but has no mineral deposits; another plot of land has outstanding views but is infertile. One machine has great precision but is difficult to operate; another is fast but often breaks down.

Although no one excels at everything, some people excel and can outperform others in a large number of activities—perhaps even in all activities. A person who is more productive than others has an **absolute advantage.**

Absolute advantage involves comparing productivities—production per hour—whereas comparative advantage involves comparing opportunity costs.

A person who has an absolute advantage does not have a *comparative* advantage in every activity. John Grisham is a better lawyer and a better author of fast-paced thrillers than most people. He has an absolute advantage in these two activities. But compared to others, he is a better writer than lawyer, so his *comparative* advantage is in writing.

Because ability and resources vary from one person to another, people have different opportunity costs of producing various goods. These differences in opportunity cost are the source of comparative advantage.

Let's explore the idea of comparative advantage by looking at two smoothie bars: one operated by Liz and the other operated by Joe.

Liz's Smoothie Bar Liz produces smoothies and salads. In Liz's high-tech bar, she can turn out either a smoothie or a salad every 2 minutes—see Table 2.1. If Liz spends all her time making smoothies, she can produce 30 an hour. And if she spends all her time making salads, she can also produce 30 an hour. If she splits her time equally between the two, she can produce 15 smoothies and 15 salads an hour. For each additional smoothie Liz produces, she must decrease her production of salads by one, and for each additional salad she produces, she must decrease her production of smoothies by one. So

> Liz's opportunity cost of producing 1 smoothie is 1 salad,

and

> Liz's opportunity cost of producing 1 salad is 1 smoothie.

Liz's customers buy smoothies and salads in equal quantities, so she splits her time equally between the two items and produces 15 smoothies and 15 salads an hour.

Joe's Smoothie Bar Joe also produces smoothies and salads, but his bar is smaller than Liz's. Also, Joe has only one blender, and it's a slow, old machine. Even if Joe uses all his resources to produce smoothies, he can produce only 6 an hour—see Table 2.2. But Joe is good at making salads. If he uses all his resources to make salads, he can produce 30 an hour.

Joe's ability to make smoothies and salads is the same regardless of how he splits an hour between the two tasks. He can make a salad in 2 minutes or a smoothie in 10 minutes. For each additional smoothie

TABLE 2.1 Liz's Production Possibilities

Item	Minutes to produce 1	Quantity per hour
Smoothies	2	30
Salads	2	30

TABLE 2.2 Joe's Production Possibilities

Item	Minutes to produce 1	Quantity per hour
Smoothies	10	6
Salads	2	30

Joe produces, he must decrease his production of salads by 5. And for each additional salad he produces, he must decrease his production of smoothies by 1/5 of a smoothie. So

> Joe's opportunity cost of producing 1 smoothie is 5 salads,

and

> Joe's opportunity cost of producing 1 salad is 1/5 of a smoothie.

Joe's customers, like Liz's, buy smoothies and salads in equal quantities. So Joe spends 50 minutes of each hour making smoothies and 10 minutes of each hour making salads. With this division of his time, Joe produces 5 smoothies and 5 salads an hour.

Liz's Comparative Advantage In which of the two activities does Liz have a comparative advantage? Recall that comparative advantage is a situation in which one person's opportunity cost of producing a good is lower than another person's opportunity cost of producing that same good. Liz has a comparative advantage in producing smoothies. Her opportunity cost of a smoothie is 1 salad, whereas Joe's opportunity cost of a smoothie is 5 salads.

Joe's Comparative Advantage If Liz has a comparative advantage in producing smoothies, Joe must have a comparative advantage in producing salads. Joe's opportunity cost of a salad is 1/5 of a smoothie, whereas Liz's opportunity cost of a salad is 1 smoothie.

Achieving the Gains from Trade

Liz and Joe run into each other one evening in a singles bar. After a few minutes of getting acquainted, Liz tells Joe about her amazing smoothie business. Her only problem, she tells Joe, is that she would like to produce more because potential customers leave when her lines get too long.

Joe is hesitant to risk spoiling his chances by telling Liz about his own struggling business, but he takes the risk. Joe explains to Liz that he spends 50 minutes of every hour making 5 smoothies and 10 minutes making 5 salads. Liz's eyes pop. "Have I got a deal for you!" she exclaims.

Here's the deal that Liz sketches on a paper napkin. Joe stops making smoothies and allocates all his time to producing salads; Liz stops making salads and allocates all her time to producing smoothies. That is, they both specialize in producing the good in which they have a comparative advantage. Together they produce 30 smoothies and 30 salads—see Table 2.3(b).

They then trade. Liz sells Joe 10 smoothies and Joe sells Liz 20 salads—the price of a smoothie is 2 salads—see Table 2.3(c).

After the trade, Joe has 10 salads—the 30 he produces minus the 20 he sells to Liz. He also has the 10 smoothies that he buys from Liz. So Joe now has increased the quantities of smoothies and salads that he can sell to his customers—see Table 2.3(d).

TABLE 2.3 Liz and Joe Gain from Trade

(a) Before trade	**Liz**	**Joe**
Smoothies	15	5
Salads	15	5
(b) Specialization	**Liz**	**Joe**
Smoothies	30	0
Salads	0	30
(c) Trade	**Liz**	**Joe**
Smoothies	sell 10	buy 10
Salads	buy 20	sell 20
(d) After trade	**Liz**	**Joe**
Smoothies	20	10
Salads	20	10
(e) Gains from trade	**Liz**	**Joe**
Smoothies	+5	+5
Salads	+5	+5

Liz has 20 smoothies—the 30 she produces minus the 10 she sells to Joe. She also has the 20 salads that she buys from Joe. Liz has increased the quantities of smoothies and salads that she can sell to her customers—see Table 2.3(d). Liz and Joe both gain 5 smoothies and 5 salads an hour—see Table 2.3(e).

To illustrate her idea, Liz grabs a fresh napkin and draws the graphs in Fig. 2.6. The blue *PPF* in part (a) shows Joe's production possibilities. Before trade, he is producing 5 smoothies and 5 salads an hour at point *A*. The blue *PPF* in part (b) shows Liz's production possibilities. Before trade, she is producing 15 smoothies and 15 salads an hour at point *A*.

Liz's proposal is that they each specialize in producing the good in which they have a comparative advantage. Joe produces 30 salads and no smoothies at point *B* on his *PPF*. Liz produces 30 smoothies and no salads at point *B* on her *PPF*.

Liz and Joe then trade smoothies and salads at a price of 2 salads per smoothie or 1/2 a smoothie per salad. Joe gets smoothies for 2 salads each, which is less than the 5 salads it costs him to produce a smoothie. Liz gets salads for 1/2 a smoothie each, which is less than the 1 smoothie that it costs her to produce a salad.

With trade, Joe has 10 smoothies and 10 salads at point *C*—a gain of 5 smoothies and 5 salads. Joe moves to a point *outside* his *PPF*.

With trade, Liz has 20 smoothies and 20 salads at point *C*—a gain of 5 smoothies and 5 salads. Liz moves to a point *outside* her *PPF*.

Despite Liz being more productive than Joe, both of them gain from specializing—producing the good in which they have a comparative advantage—and trading.

FIGURE 2.6 The Gains from Trade

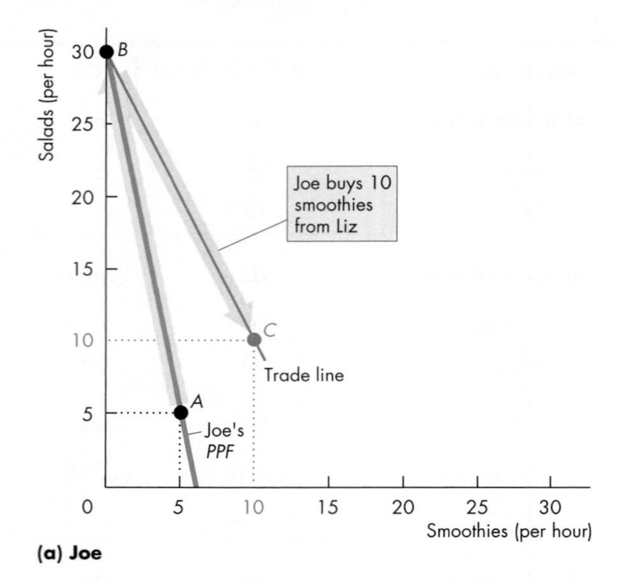

(a) Joe

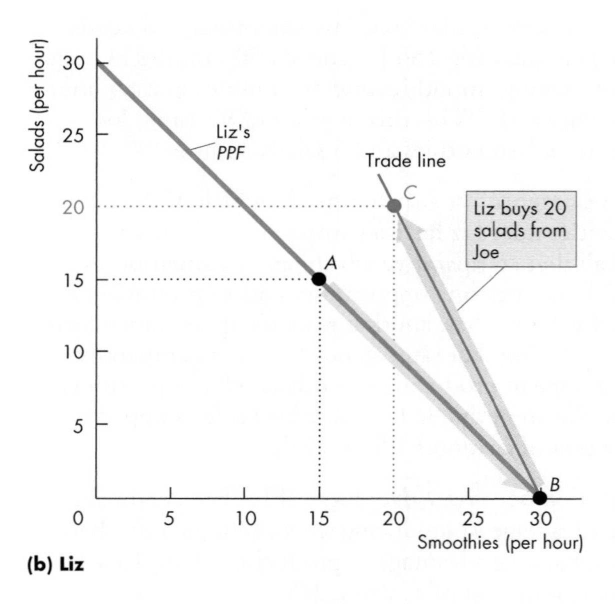

(b) Liz

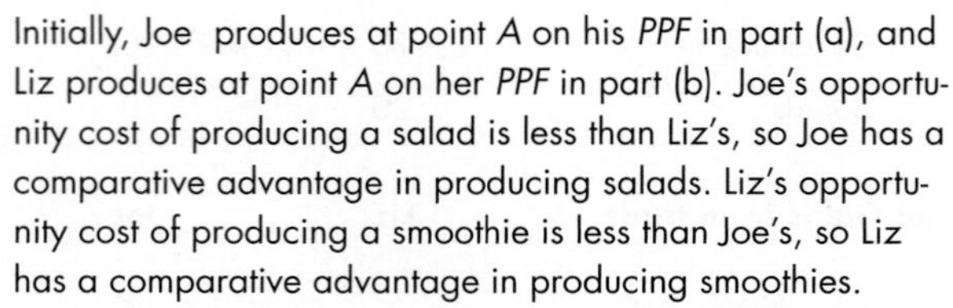

Initially, Joe produces at point *A* on his *PPF* in part (a), and Liz produces at point *A* on her *PPF* in part (b). Joe's opportunity cost of producing a salad is less than Liz's, so Joe has a comparative advantage in producing salads. Liz's opportunity cost of producing a smoothie is less than Joe's, so Liz has a comparative advantage in producing smoothies.

If Joe specializes in making salads, he produces 30 salads and no smoothies at point *B* on his *PPF*. If Liz specializes in making smoothies, she produces 30 smoothies and no salads at point *B* on her *PPF*. They exchange salads for smoothies along the red "Trade line." Liz buys salads from Joe for less than her opportunity cost of producing them. Joe buys smoothies from Liz for less than his opportunity cost of producing them. Each goes to point *C*—a point outside his or her *PPF*. With specialization and trade, Joe and Liz gain 5 smoothies and 5 salads each with no extra resources.

myeconlab animation

Economics in Action

The United States and China Gain From Trade

In Chapter 1 (see p. 5), we asked whether globalization is in the social interest. What you have just learned about the gains from trade provides a big part of the answer. We gain from specialization and trade.

The gains that we achieve from *international* trade are similar to those achieved by Joe and Liz. When Americans buy clothes that are manufactured in China and when China buys Boeing airplanes manufactured in the United States, the people of both countries gain.

We could slide along our *PPF* producing fewer airplanes and more jackets. Similarly, China could slide along its *PPF* producing more airplanes and fewer jackets. But everyone would lose. The opportunity cost of our jackets and China's opportunity cost of airplanes would rise.

By specializing in airplanes and trading with China, we get our jackets at a lower cost than that at which we can produce them, and China gets its aircraft at a lower cost than that at which it can produce them.

REVIEW QUIZ

1. What gives a person a comparative advantage?
2. Distinguish between comparative advantage and absolute advantage.
3. Why do people specialize and trade?
4. What are the gains from specialization and trade?
5. What is the source of the gains from trade?

You can work these questions in Study Plan 2.4 and get instant feedback.

Economic Coordination

People gain by specializing in the production of those goods and services in which they have a comparative advantage and then trading with each other. Liz and Joe, whose production of salads and smoothies we studied earlier in this chapter, can get together and make a deal that enables them to enjoy the gains from specialization and trade. But for billions of individuals to specialize and produce millions of different goods and services, their choices must somehow be coordinated.

Two competing economic coordination systems have been used: central economic planning and decentralized markets.

Central economic planning was tried in Russia and China and is still used in Cuba and North Korea. This system works badly because government economic planners don't know people's production possibilities and preferences. Resources get wasted, production ends up *inside* the *PPF*, and the wrong things get produced.

Decentralized coordination works best but to do so it needs four complementary social institutions. They are

- Firms
- Markets
- Property rights
- Money

Firms

A **firm** is an economic unit that hires factors of production and organizes those factors to produce and sell goods and services. Examples of firms are your local gas station, Wal-Mart, and General Motors.

Firms coordinate a huge amount of economic activity. For example, Wal-Mart buys or rents large buildings, equips them with storage shelves and checkout lanes, and hires labor. Wal-Mart directs the labor and decides what goods to buy and sell.

But Sam Walton would not have become one of the wealthiest people in the world if Wal-Mart produced all the goods that it sells. He became rich by specializing in providing retail services and buying from other firms that specialize in producing goods (just as Liz and Joe did). This trade between firms takes place in markets.

Markets

In ordinary speech, the word *market* means a place where people buy and sell goods such as fish, meat, fruits, and vegetables. In economics, a *market* has a more general meaning. A **market** is any arrangement that enables buyers and sellers to get information and to do business with each other. An example is the market in which oil is bought and sold—the world oil market. The world oil market is not a place. It is the network of oil producers, oil users, wholesalers, and brokers who buy and sell oil. In the world oil market, decision makers do not meet physically. They make deals by telephone, fax, and direct computer link.

Markets have evolved because they facilitate trade. Without organized markets, we would miss out on a substantial part of the potential gains from trade. Enterprising individuals and firms, each pursuing their own self-interest, have profited from making markets—standing ready to buy or sell the items in which they specialize. But markets can work only when property rights exist.

Property Rights

The social arrangements that govern the ownership, use, and disposal of anything that people value are called **property rights**. *Real property* includes land and buildings—the things we call property in ordinary speech—and durable goods such as plant and equipment. *Financial property* includes stocks and bonds and money in the bank. *Intellectual property* is the intangible product of creative effort. This type of property includes books, music, computer programs, and inventions of all kinds and is protected by copyrights and patents.

Where property rights are enforced, people have the incentive to specialize and produce the goods in which they have a comparative advantage. Where people can steal the production of others, resources are devoted not to production but to protecting possessions. Without property rights, we would still be hunting and gathering like our Stone Age ancestors.

Money

Money is any commodity or token that is generally acceptable as a means of payment. Liz and Joe didn't use money in the example above. They exchanged salads and smoothies. In principle, trade in markets can exchange any item for any other item. But you can perhaps imagine how complicated life would be if we exchanged goods for other goods. The "invention" of money makes trading in markets much more efficient.

Circular Flows Through Markets

Figure 2.7 shows the flows that result from the choices that households and firms make. Households specialize and choose the quantities of labor, land, capital, and entrepreneurial services to sell or rent to firms. Firms choose the quantities of factors of production to hire. These (red) flows go through the *factor markets*. Households choose the quantities of goods and services to buy, and firms choose the quantities to produce. These (red) flows go through the *goods markets*. Households receive incomes and make expenditures on goods and services (the green flows).

How do markets coordinate all these decisions?

Coordinating Decisions

Markets coordinate decisions through price adjustments. To see how, think about your local market for hamburgers. Suppose that too few hamburgers are available and some people who want to buy hamburgers are not able to do so. To make buying and selling plans the same, either more hamburgers must be offered for sale or buyers must scale down their appetites (or both). A rise in the price of a hamburger produces this outcome. A higher price encourages producers to offer more hamburgers for sale. It also encourages some people to change their lunch plans. Fewer people buy hamburgers, and more buy hot dogs. More hamburgers (and more hot dogs) are offered for sale.

Alternatively, suppose that more hamburgers are available than people want to buy. In this case, to make the choices of buyers and sellers compatible, more hamburgers must be bought or fewer hamburgers must be offered for sale (or both). A fall in the price of a hamburger achieves this outcome. A lower price encourages people to buy more hamburgers. It also encourages firms to produce a smaller quantity of hamburgers.

FIGURE 2.7 Circular Flows in the Market Economy

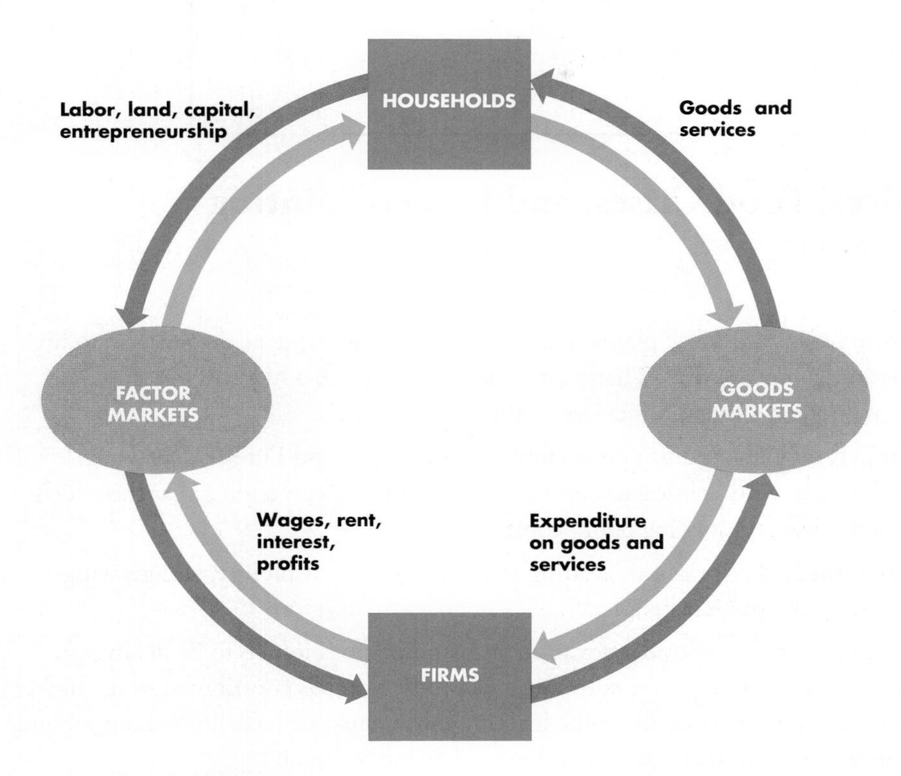

Households and firms make economic choices and markets coordinate these choices.

Households choose the quantities of labor, land, capital, and entrepreneurial services to sell or rent to firms in exchange for wages, rent, interest, and profits. Households also choose how to spend their incomes on the various types of goods and services available.

Firms choose the quantities of factors of production to hire and the quantities of goods and services to produce.

Goods markets and factor markets coordinate these choices of households and firms.

The counterclockwise red flows are real flows—the flow of factors of production from households to firms and the flow of goods and services from firms to households.

The clockwise green flows are the payments for the red flows. They are the flow of incomes from firms to households and the flow of expenditure on goods and services from households to firms.

REVIEW QUIZ

1. Why are social institutions such as firms, markets, property rights, and money necessary?
2. What are the main functions of markets?
3. What are the flows in the market economy that go from firms to households and the flows from households to firms?

You can work these questions in Study Plan 2.5 and get instant feedback.

You have now begun to see how economists approach economic questions. Scarcity, choice, and divergent opportunity costs explain why we specialize and trade and why firms, markets, property rights, and money have developed. You can see all around you the lessons you've learned in this chapter. *Reading Between the Lines* on pp. 44–45 provides an opportunity to apply the *PPF* model to deepen your understanding of the reasons for the increase in the cost of food associated with the increase in corn production.

The Rising Opportunity Cost of Food

Fuel Choices, Food Crises, and Finger-Pointing

http://www.nytimes.com

April 15, 2008

The idea of turning farms into fuel plants seemed, for a time, like one of the answers to high global oil prices and supply worries. That strategy seemed to reach a high point last year when Congress mandated a fivefold increase in the use of biofuels.

But now a reaction is building against policies in the United States and Europe to promote ethanol and similar fuels, with political leaders from poor countries contending that these fuels are driving up food prices and starving poor people. …

In some countries, the higher prices are leading to riots, political instability, and growing worries about feeding the poorest people. …

Many specialists in food policy consider government mandates for biofuels to be ill advised, agreeing that the diversion of crops like corn into fuel production has contributed to the higher prices. But other factors have played big roles, including droughts that have limited output and rapid global economic growth that has created higher demand for food.

That growth, much faster over the last four years than the historical norm, is lifting millions of people out of destitution and giving them access to better diets. But farmers are having trouble keeping up with the surge in demand.

While there is agreement that the growth of biofuels has contributed to higher food prices, the amount is disputed. …

C. Ford Runge, an economist at the University of Minnesota, said it is "extremely difficult to disentangle" the effect of biofuels on food costs. Nevertheless, he said there was little that could be done to mitigate the effect of droughts and the growing appetite for protein in developing countries.

"Ethanol is the one thing we can do something about," he said. "It's about the only lever we have to pull, but none of the politicians have the courage to pull the lever." …

ESSENCE OF THE STORY

- In 2007, Congress mandated a fivefold increase in the use of biofuels.
- Political leaders in poor countries and specialists in food policy say the biofuel mandate is ill advised and the diversion of corn into fuel production has raised the cost of food.
- Drought that has limited corn production and global economic growth that has increased the demand for protein have also raised the cost of food.
- An economist at the University of Minnesota says that while it is difficult to determine the effect of biofuels on food costs, it is the only factor under our control.

ECONOMIC ANALYSIS

- Ethanol is made from corn in the United States, so biofuel and food compete to use the same resources.
- To produce more ethanol and meet the Congress's mandate, farmers increased the number of acres devoted to corn production.
- In 2008, the amount of land devoted to corn production increased by 20 percent in the United States and by 2 percent in the rest of the world.
- Figure 1 shows the U.S. production possibilities frontier, *PPF*, for corn and other goods and services.
- The increase in the production of corn is illustrated by a movement along the *PPF* in Fig. 1 from point *A* in 2007 to point *B* in 2008.
- In moving from point *A* to point *B*, the United States incurs a higher opportunity cost of producing corn, as the greater slope of the *PPF* at point *B* indicates.
- In other regions of the world, despite the fact that more land was devoted to corn production, the amount of corn produced didn't change.
- The reason is that droughts in South America and Eastern Europe lowered the crop yield per acre in those regions.
- Figure 2 shows the rest of the world's *PPF* for corn and other goods and services in 2007 and 2008.
- The increase in the amount of land devoted to producing corn is illustrated by a movement along PPF_{07}.
- With a decrease in the crop yield, production possibilities decreased and the *PPF* rotated inward.
- The rotation from PPF_{07} to PPF_{08} illustrates this decrease in production possibilities.
- The opportunity cost of producing corn in the rest of the world increased for two reasons: the movement along its *PPF* and the inward rotation of the *PPF*.
- With a higher opportunity cost of producing corn, the cost of both biofuel and food increases.

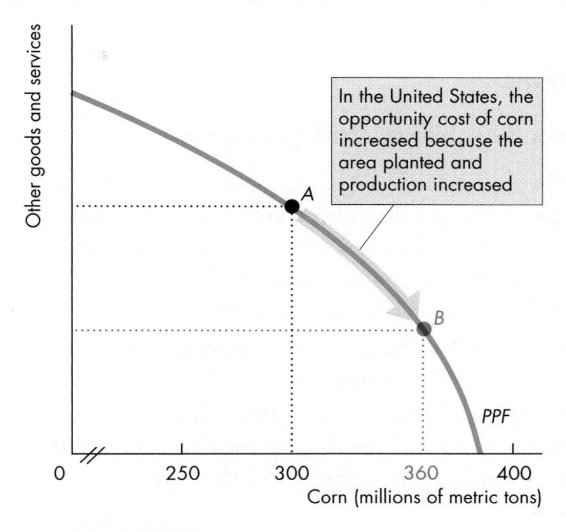

Figure 1 U.S. *PPF*

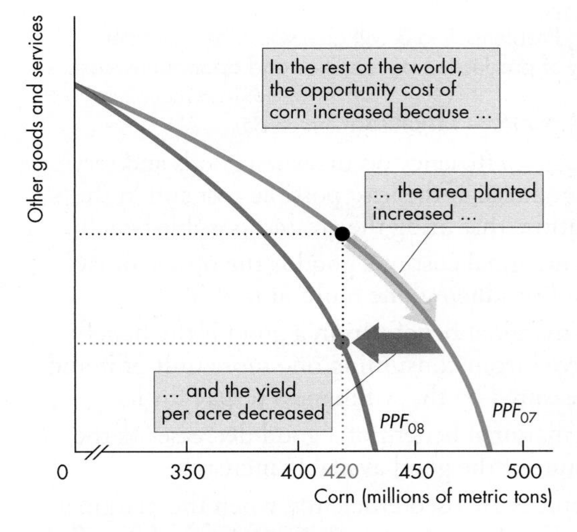

Figure 2 Rest of the World *PPF*

SUMMARY

Key Points

Production Possibilities and Opportunity Cost (pp. 30–32)

- The production possibilities frontier is the boundary between production levels that are attainable and those that are not attainable when all the available resources are used to their limit.
- Production efficiency occurs at points on the production possibilities frontier.
- Along the production possibilities frontier, the opportunity cost of producing more of one good is the amount of the other good that must be given up.
- The opportunity cost of all goods increases as the production of the good increases.

Working Problems 1 to 3 will give you a better understanding of production possibilities and opportunity cost.

Using Resources Efficiently (pp. 33–35)

- Allocative efficiency occurs when goods and services are produced at the least possible cost and in the quantities that bring the greatest possible benefit.
- The marginal cost of a good is the opportunity cost of producing one more unit of it.
- The marginal benefit from a good is the benefit received from consuming one more unit of it and is measured by the willingness to pay for it.
- The marginal benefit of a good decreases as the amount of the good available increases.
- Resources are used efficiently when the marginal cost of each good is equal to its marginal benefit.

Working Problems 4 to 10 will give you a better understanding of the efficient use of resources.

Economic Growth (pp. 36–37)

- Economic growth, which is the expansion of production possibilities, results from capital accumulation and technological change.
- The opportunity cost of economic growth is forgone current consumption.
- The benefit of economic growth is increased future consumption.

Working Problem 11 will give you a better understanding of economic growth.

Gains from Trade (pp. 38–41)

- A person has a comparative advantage in producing a good if that person can produce the good at a lower opportunity cost than everyone else.
- People gain by specializing in the activity in which they have a comparative advantage and trading with others.

Working Problems 12 and 13 will give you a better understanding of the gains from trade.

Economic Coordination (pp. 41–43)

- Firms coordinate a large amount of economic activity, but there is a limit to the efficient size of a firm.
- Markets coordinate the economic choices of people and firms.
- Markets can work efficiently only when property rights exist.
- Money makes trading in markets more efficient.

Working Problem 14 will give you a better understanding of economic coordination.

Key Terms

Absolute advantage, 38
Allocative efficiency, 33
Capital accumulation, 36
Comparative advantage, 38
Economic growth, 36
Firm, 41
Marginal benefit, 34
Marginal benefit curve, 34
Marginal cost, 33
Market, 42
Money, 42
Opportunity cost, 31
Preferences, 34
Production efficiency, 31
Production possibilities frontier, 30
Property rights, 42
Technological change, 36

STUDY PLAN PROBLEMS AND APPLICATIONS

myeconlab You can work Problems 1 to 20 in MyEconLab Chapter 2 Study Plan and get instant feedback.

Production Possibilities and Opportunity Cost

(Study Plan 2.1)

Use the following information to work Problems 1 to 3. Brazil produces ethanol from sugar, and the land used to grow sugar can be used to grow food crops. Suppose that Brazil's production possibilities for ethanol and food crops are as follows

Ethanol (barrels per day)		Food crops (tons per day)
70	and	0
64	and	1
54	and	2
40	and	3
22	and	4
0	and	5

1. a. Draw a graph of Brazil's PPF and explain how your graph illustrates scarcity.
   b. If Brazil produces 40 barrels of ethanol a day, how much food must it produce to achieve production efficiency?
   c. Why does Brazil face a tradeoff on its *PPF*?
2. a. If Brazil increases its production of ethanol from 40 barrels per day to 54 barrels per day, what is the opportunity cost of the additional ethanol?
   b. If Brazil increases its production of food crops from 2 tons per day to 3 tons per day, what is the opportunity cost of the additional food?
   c. What is the relationship between your answers to parts (a) and (b)?
3. Does Brazil face an increasing opportunity cost of ethanol? What feature of Brazil's *PPF* illustrates increasing opportunity cost?

Using Resources Efficiently (Study Plan 2.2)

Use the above table to work Problems 4 and 5.

4. Define marginal cost and calculate Brazil's marginal cost of producing a ton of food when the quantity produced is 2.5 tons per day.
5. Define marginal benefit, explain how it is measured, and explain why the data in the table does not enable you to calculate Brazil's marginal benefit from food.
6. Distinguish between *production efficiency* and *allocative efficiency.* Explain why many production possibilities achieve production efficiency but only one achieves allocative efficiency.

Use the following graphs to work Problems 7 to 10. Harry enjoys tennis but wants a high grade in his economics course. The graphs show his *PPF* for these two "goods" and his *MB* curve from tennis.

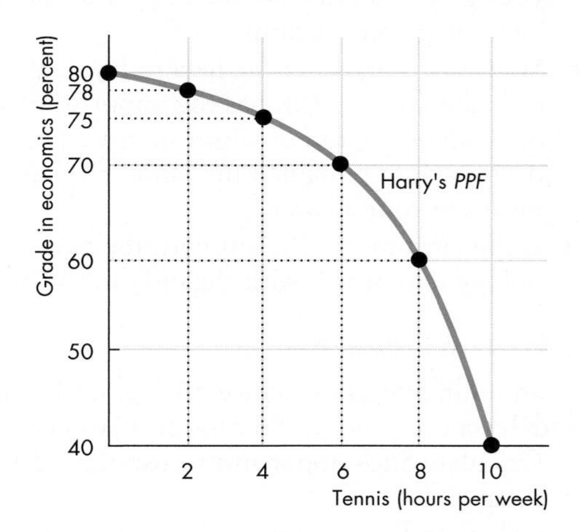

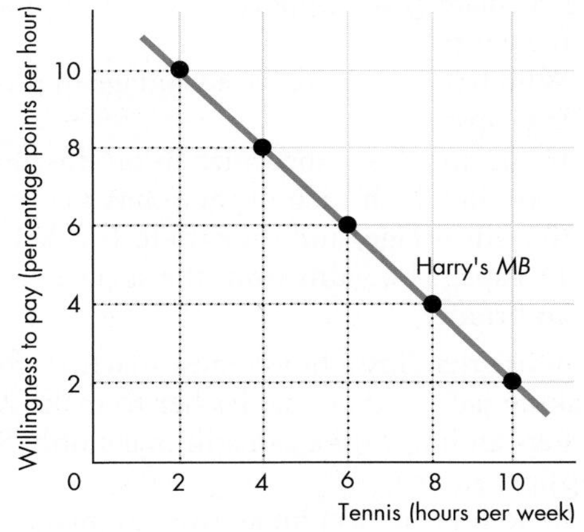

7. What is Harry's marginal cost of tennis if he plays for (i) 3 hours a week; (ii) 5 hours a week; and (iii) 7 hours a week?
8. a. If Harry uses his time to achieve allocative efficiency, what is his economics grade and how many hours of tennis does he play?
   b. Explain why Harry would be worse off getting a grade higher than your answer to part (a).
9. If Harry becomes a tennis superstar with big earnings from tennis, what happens to his *PPF*, *MB* curve, and his efficient time allocation?
10. If Harry suddenly finds high grades in economics easier to attain, what happens to his *PPF*, his *MB* curve, and his efficient time allocation?

Economic Growth (Study Plan 2.3)

11. A farm grows wheat and produces pork. The marginal cost of producing each of these products increases as more of it is produced.
    a. Make a graph that illustrates the farm's *PPF*.
    b. The farm adopts a new technology that allows it to use fewer resources to fatten pigs. Use your graph to illustrate the impact of the new technology on the farm's *PPF*.
    c. With the farm using the new technology described in part (b), has the opportunity cost of producing a ton of wheat increased, decreased, or remained the same? Explain and illustrate your answer.
    d. Is the farm more efficient with the new technology than it was with the old one? Why?

Gains from Trade (Study Plan 2.4)

12. In an hour, Sue can produce 40 caps or 4 jackets and Tessa can produce 80 caps or 4 jackets.
    a. Calculate Sue's opportunity cost of producing a cap.
    b. Calculate Tessa's opportunity cost of producing a cap.
    c. Who has a comparative advantage in producing caps?
    d. If Sue and Tessa specialize in producing the good in which each of them has a comparative advantage, and they trade 1 jacket for 15 caps, who gains from the specialization and trade?
13. Suppose that Tessa buys a new machine for making jackets that enables her to make 20 jackets an hour. (She can still make only 80 caps per hour.)
    a. Who now has a comparative advantage in producing jackets?
    b. Can Sue and Tessa still gain from trade?
    c. Would Sue and Tessa still be willing to trade 1 jacket for 15 caps? Explain your answer.

Economic Coordination (Study Plan 2.5)

14. For 50 years, Cuba has had a centrally planned economy in which the government makes the big decisions on how resources will be allocated.
    a. Why would you expect Cuba's production possibilities (per person) to be smaller than those of the United States?
    b. What are the social institutions that Cuba might lack that help the United States to achieve allocative efficiency?

Economics in the News (Study Plan 2.N)

Use the following data to work Problems 15 to 17.
Brazil produces ethanol from sugar at a cost of 83 cents per gallon. The United States produces ethanol from corn at a cost of $1.14 per gallon. Sugar grown on one acre of land produces twice the quantity of ethanol as the corn grown on an acre. The United States imports 5 percent of the ethanol it uses and produces the rest itself. Since 2003, U.S. ethanol production has more than doubled and U.S. corn production has increased by 45 percent.

15. a. Does Brazil or the United States have a comparative advantage in producing ethanol?
    b. Sketch the *PPF* for ethanol and other goods and services for the United States.
    c. Sketch the *PPF* for ethanol and other goods and services for Brazil.
16. a. Do you expect the opportunity cost of producing ethanol in the United States to have increased since 2003? Explain why.
    b. Do you think the United States has achieved production efficiency in its manufacture of ethanol? Explain why or why not.
    c. Do you think the United States has achieved allocative efficiency in its manufacture of ethanol? Explain why or why not.
17. Sketch a figure similar to Fig. 2.6 on p. 40 to show how both the United States and Brazil can gain from specialization and trade.

Use this news clip to work Problems 18 to 20.

Time For Tea

Americans are switching to loose-leaf tea for its health benefits. Tea could be grown in the United States, but picking tea leaves would be costly because it can only be done by workers and not by machine.

Source: *The Economist,* July 8, 2005

18. a. Sketch *PPF*s for the production of tea and other goods and services in India and in the United States.
    b. Sketch marginal cost curves for the production of tea in India and in the United States.
19. a. Sketch the marginal benefit curves for tea in the United States before and after Americans began to appreciate the health benefits of loose tea.
    b. Explain how the quantity of loose tea that achieves allocative efficiency has changed.
    c. Does the change in preferences toward tea affect the opportunity cost of producing tea?
20. Explain why the United States does not produce tea and instead imports it from India.

ADDITIONAL PROBLEMS AND APPLICATIONS

myeconlab You can work these problems in MyEconLab if assigned by your instructor.

Production Possibilities and Opportunity Cost

Use the following table to work Problems 21 to 22. Suppose that Yucatan's production possibilities are

Food (pounds per month)		Sunscreen (gallons per month)
300	and	0
200	and	50
100	and	100
0	and	150

21. a. Draw a graph of Yucatan's *PPF* and explain how your graph illustrates a tradeoff.
    b. If Yucatan produces 150 pounds of food per month, how much sunscreen must it produce if it achieves production efficiency?
    c. What is Yucatan's opportunity cost of producing 1 pound of food?
    d. What is Yucatan's opportunity cost of producing 1 gallon of sunscreen?
    e. What is the relationship between your answers to parts (c) and (d)?
22. What feature of a *PPF* illustrates increasing opportunity cost? Explain why Yucatan's opportunity cost does or does not increase.

Using Resources Efficiently

23. In problem 21, what is the marginal cost of a pound of food in Yucatan when the quantity produced is 150 pounds per day? What is special about the marginal cost of food in Yucatan?
24. The table describes the preferences in Yucatan.

Sunscreen (gallons per month)	Willingness to pay (pounds of food per gallon)
25	3
75	2
125	1

    a. What is the marginal benefit from sunscreen and how is it measured?
    b. Draw a graph of Yucatan's marginal benefit from sunscreen.

Economic Growth

25. Capital accumulation and technological change bring economic growth, which means that the *PPF* keeps shifting outward: Production that was unattainable yesterday becomes attainable today; production that is unattainable today will become attainable tomorrow. Why doesn't this process of economic growth mean that scarcity is being defeated and will one day be gone?

Gains from Trade

Use the following data to work Problems 26 and 27. Kim can produce 40 pies or 400 cakes an hour. Liam can produce 100 pies or 200 cakes an hour.

26. a. Calculate Kim's opportunity cost of a pie and Liam's opportunity cost of a pie.
    b. If each spends 30 minutes of each hour producing pies and 30 minutes producing cakes, how many pies and cakes does each produce?
    c. Who has a comparative advantage in producing pies? Who has a comparative advantage in producing cakes?
27. a. Draw a graph of Kim's *PPF* and Liam's *PPF*.
    b. On your graph, show the point at which each produces when they spend 30 minutes of each hour producing pies and 30 minutes producing cakes.
    c. On your graph, show what Kim produces and what does Liam produces when they specialize.
    d. When they specialize and trade, what are the total gains from trade?
    e. If Kim and Liam share the total gains equally, what trade takes place between them?

Economic Coordination

28. Indicate on a graph of the circular flows in the market economy, the real and money flows in which the following items belong:
    a. You buy an iPad from the Apple Store.
    b. Apple Inc. pays the designers of the iPad.
    c. Apple Inc. decides to expand and rents an adjacent building.
    d. You buy a new e-book from Amazon.
    e. Apple Inc. hires a student as an intern during the summer.

Economics in the News

29. After you have studied *Reading Between the Lines* on pp. 44–45, answer the following questions.
    a. How has an Act of the United States Congress increased U.S. production of corn?
    b. Why would you expect an increase in the quantity of corn produced to raise the opportunity cost of corn?

c. Why did the cost of producing corn increase in the rest of the world?

d. Is it possible that the increased quantity of corn produced, despite the higher cost of production, moves the United States closer to allocative efficiency?

30. **Malaria Eradication Back on the Table**

In response to the Gates Malaria Forum in October 2007, countries are debating the pros and cons of eradication. Dr. Arata Kochi of the World Health Organization believes that with enough money malaria cases could be cut by 90 percent, but he believes that it would be very expensive to eliminate the remaining 10 percent of cases. He concluded that countries should not strive to eradicate malaria.

Source: *The New York Times*, March 4, 2008

a. Is Dr. Kochi talking about *production efficiency* or *allocative efficiency* or both?

b. Make a graph with the percentage of malaria cases eliminated on the *x*-axis and the marginal cost and marginal benefit of driving down malaria cases on the *y*-axis. On your graph:

(i) Draw a marginal cost curve that is consistent with Dr. Kochi's opinion.

(ii) Draw a marginal benefit curve that is consistent with Dr. Kochi's opinion.

(iii) Identify the quantity of malaria eradicated that achieves allocative efficiency.

31. **Lots of Little Screens**

Inexpensive broadband access has created a generation of television producers for whom the Internet is their native medium. As they redirect the focus from TV to computers, cell phones, and iPods, the video market is developing into an open digital network.

Source: *The New York Times,* December 2, 2007

a. How has inexpensive broadband changed the production possibilities of video entertainment and other goods and services?

b. Sketch a *PPF* for video entertainment and other goods and services before broadband.

c. Show how the arrival of inexpensive broadband has changed the *PPF*.

d. Sketch a marginal benefit curve for video entertainment.

e. Show how the new generation of TV producers for whom the Internet is their native medium might have changed the marginal benefit from video entertainment.

f. Explain how the efficient quantity of video entertainment has changed.

Use the following information to work Problems 32 and 33.

Before the Civil War, the South traded with the North and with England. The South sold cotton and bought manufactured goods and food. During the war, one of President Lincoln's first actions was to blockade the ports and prevent this trade. The South increased its production of munitions and food.

32. In what did the South have a comparative advantage?

33. a. Draw a graph to illustrate production, consumption, and trade in the South before the Civil War.

b. Was the South consuming inside, on, or outside its *PPF*? Explain your answer.

c. Draw a graph to show the effects of the Civil War on consumption and production in the South.

d. Did the Civil War change any opportunity costs in the South? If so, did the opportunity cost of everything increase? Did the opportunity cost of any items decrease? Illustrate your answer with appropriate graphs.

Use the following information to work Problems 34 and 35.

He Shoots! He Scores! He Makes Movies!

NBA All-star Baron Davis and his school friend, Cash Warren, premiered their first movie *Made in America* at the Sundance Festival in January 2008. The movie, based on gang activity in South Central Los Angeles, received good reviews.

Source: *The New York Times,* February 24, 2008

34. a. Does Baron Davis have an absolute advantage in basketball and movie directing and is this the reason for his success in both activities?

b. Does Baron Davis have a comparative advantage in basketball or movie directing or both and is this the reason for his success in both activities?

35. a. Sketch a *PPF* between playing basketball and producing other goods and services for Baron Davis and for yourself.

b. How do you (and people like you) and Baron Davis (and people like him) gain from specialization and trade?

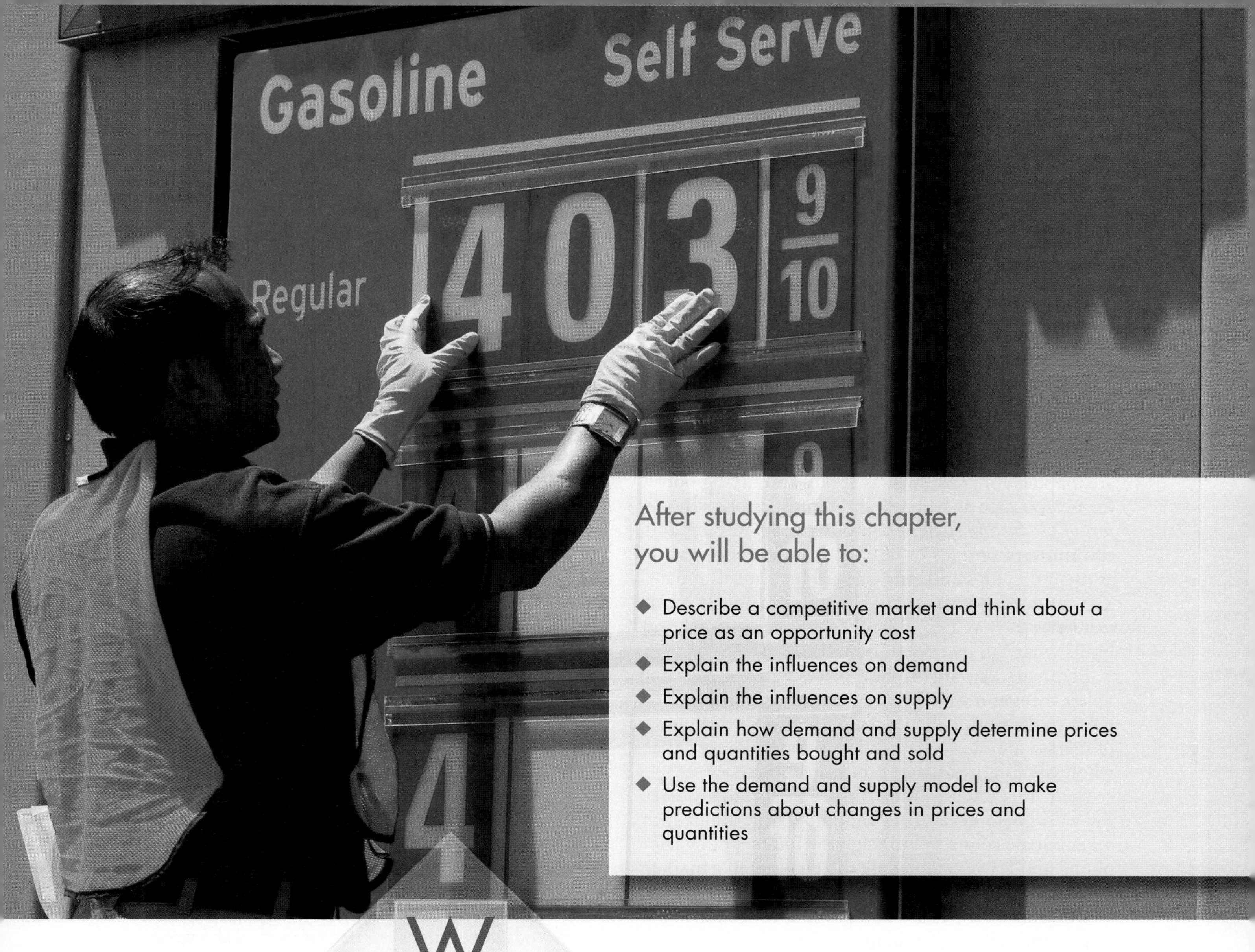

After studying this chapter, you will be able to:

- Describe a competitive market and think about a price as an opportunity cost
- Explain the influences on demand
- Explain the influences on supply
- Explain how demand and supply determine prices and quantities bought and sold
- Use the demand and supply model to make predictions about changes in prices and quantities

3 DEMAND AND SUPPLY

What makes the price of oil double and the price of gasoline almost double in just one year? Will these prices keep on rising? Are the oil companies taking advantage of people? This chapter enables you to answer these and similar questions about prices—prices that rise, prices that fall, and prices that fluctuate.

You already know that economics is about the choices people make to cope with scarcity and how those choices respond to incentives. Prices act as incentives. You're going to see how people respond to prices and how prices get determined by demand and supply. The demand and supply model that you study in this chapter is the main tool of economics. It helps us to answer the big economic question: What, how, and for whom goods and services are produced?

At the end of the chapter, in *Reading Between the Lines*, we'll apply the model to the market for coffee and explain why its price increased sharply in 2010 and why it was expected to rise again.

Markets and Prices

When you need a new pair of running shoes, want a bagel and a latte, plan to upgrade your cell phone, or need to fly home for Thanksgiving, you must find a place where people sell those items or offer those services. The place in which you find them is a *market.* You learned in Chapter 2 (p. 42) that a market is any arrangement that enables buyers and sellers to get information and to do business with each other.

A market has two sides: buyers and sellers. There are markets for *goods* such as apples and hiking boots, for *services* such as haircuts and tennis lessons, for *factors of production* such as computer programmers and earthmovers, and for other manufactured *inputs* such as memory chips and auto parts. There are also markets for money such as Japanese yen and for financial securities such as Yahoo! stock. Only our imagination limits what can be traded in markets.

Some markets are physical places where buyers and sellers meet and where an auctioneer or a broker helps to determine the prices. Examples of this type of market are the New York Stock Exchange and the wholesale fish, meat, and produce markets.

Some markets are groups of people spread around the world who never meet and know little about each other but are connected through the Internet or by telephone and fax. Examples are the e-commerce markets and the currency markets.

But most markets are unorganized collections of buyers and sellers. You do most of your trading in this type of market. An example is the market for basketball shoes. The buyers in this $3 billion-a-year market are the 45 million Americans who play basketball (or who want to make a fashion statement). The sellers are the tens of thousands of retail sports equipment and footwear stores. Each buyer can visit several different stores, and each seller knows that the buyer has a choice of stores.

Markets vary in the intensity of competition that buyers and sellers face. In this chapter, we're going to study a **competitive market**—a market that has many buyers and many sellers, so no single buyer or seller can influence the price.

Producers offer items for sale only if the price is high enough to cover their opportunity cost. And consumers respond to changing opportunity cost by seeking cheaper alternatives to expensive items.

We are going to study how people respond to *prices* and the forces that determine prices. But to pursue these tasks, we need to understand the relationship between a price and an opportunity cost.

In everyday life, the *price* of an object is the number of dollars that must be given up in exchange for it. Economists refer to this price as the **money price.**

The *opportunity cost* of an action is the highest-valued alternative forgone. If, when you buy a cup of coffee, the highest-valued thing you forgo is some gum, then the opportunity cost of the coffee is the *quantity* of gum forgone. We can calculate the quantity of gum forgone from the money prices of the coffee and the gum.

If the money price of coffee is $1 a cup and the money price of gum is 50¢ a pack, then the opportunity cost of one cup of coffee is two packs of gum. To calculate this opportunity cost, we divide the price of a cup of coffee by the price of a pack of gum and find the *ratio* of one price to the other. The ratio of one price to another is called a **relative price**, and a *relative price is an opportunity cost.*

We can express the relative price of coffee in terms of gum or any other good. The normal way of expressing a relative price is in terms of a "basket" of all goods and services. To calculate this relative price, we divide the money price of a good by the money price of a "basket" of all goods (called a *price index*). The resulting relative price tells us the opportunity cost of the good in terms of how much of the "basket" we must give up to buy it.

The demand and supply model that we are about to study determines *relative prices,* and the word "price" means *relative* price. When we predict that a price will fall, we do not mean that its *money* price will fall—although it might. We mean that its *relative* price will fall. That is, its price will fall *relative* to the average price of other goods and services.

REVIEW QUIZ

1. What is the distinction between a money price and a relative price?
2. Explain why a relative price is an opportunity cost.
3. Think of examples of goods whose relative price has risen or fallen by a large amount.

You can work these questions in Study Plan 3.1 and get instant feedback.

Let's begin our study of demand and supply, starting with demand.

Demand

If you demand something, then you

1. Want it,
2. Can afford it, and
3. Plan to buy it.

Wants are the unlimited desires or wishes that people have for goods and services. How many times have you thought that you would like something "if only you could afford it" or "if it weren't so expensive"? Scarcity guarantees that many—perhaps most—of our wants will never be satisfied. Demand reflects a decision about which wants to satisfy.

The **quantity demanded** of a good or service is the amount that consumers plan to buy during a given time period at a particular price. The quantity demanded is not necessarily the same as the quantity actually bought. Sometimes the quantity demanded exceeds the amount of goods available, so the quantity bought is less than the quantity demanded.

The quantity demanded is measured as an amount per unit of time. For example, suppose that you buy one cup of coffee a day. The quantity of coffee that you demand can be expressed as 1 cup per day, 7 cups per week, or 365 cups per year.

Many factors influence buying plans, and one of them is the price. We look first at the relationship between the quantity demanded of a good and its price. To study this relationship, we keep all other influences on buying plans the same and we ask: How, other things remaining the same, does the quantity demanded of a good change as its price changes?

The law of demand provides the answer.

The Law of Demand

The **law of demand** states

> Other things remaining the same, the higher the price of a good, the smaller is the quantity demanded; and the lower the price of a good, the greater is the quantity demanded.

Why does a higher price reduce the quantity demanded? For two reasons:

- Substitution effect
- Income effect

Substitution Effect When the price of a good rises, other things remaining the same, its *relative* price—its opportunity cost—rises. Although each good is unique, it has *substitutes*—other goods that can be used in its place. As the opportunity cost of a good rises, the incentive to economize on its use and switch to a substitute becomes stronger.

Income Effect When a price rises, other things remaining the same, the price rises *relative* to income. Faced with a higher price and an unchanged income, people cannot afford to buy all the things they previously bought. They must decrease the quantities demanded of at least some goods and services. Normally, the good whose price has increased will be one of the goods that people buy less of.

To see the substitution effect and the income effect at work, think about the effects of a change in the price of an energy bar. Several different goods are substitutes for an energy bar. For example, an energy drink could be consumed instead of an energy bar.

Suppose that an energy bar initially sells for $3 and then its price falls to $1.50. People now substitute energy bars for energy drinks—the substitution effect. And with a budget that now has some slack from the lower price of an energy bar, people buy even more energy bars—the income effect. The quantity of energy bars demanded increases for these two reasons.

Now suppose that an energy bar initially sells for $3 and then the price doubles to $6. People now buy fewer energy bars and more energy drinks—the substitution effect. And faced with a tighter budget, people buy even fewer energy bars—the income effect. The quantity of energy bars demanded decreases for these two reasons.

Demand Curve and Demand Schedule

You are now about to study one of the two most used curves in economics: the demand curve. You are also going to encounter one of the most critical distinctions: the distinction between *demand* and *quantity demanded.*

The term **demand** refers to the entire relationship between the price of a good and the quantity demanded of that good. Demand is illustrated by the demand curve and the demand schedule. The term *quantity demanded* refers to a point on a demand curve—the quantity demanded at a particular price.

Figure 3.1 shows the demand curve for energy bars. A **demand curve** shows the relationship between the quantity demanded of a good and its price when all other influences on consumers' planned purchases remain the same.

The table in Fig. 3.1 is the demand schedule for energy bars. A *demand schedule* lists the quantities demanded at each price when all the other influences on consumers' planned purchases remain the same. For example, if the price of a bar is 50¢, the quantity demanded is 22 million a week. If the price is $2.50, the quantity demanded is 5 million a week. The other rows of the table show the quantities demanded at prices of $1.00, $1.50, and $2.00.

We graph the demand schedule as a demand curve with the quantity demanded on the *x*-axis and the price on the *y*-axis. The points on the demand curve labeled *A* through *E* correspond to the rows of the demand schedule. For example, point *A* on the graph shows a quantity demanded of 22 million energy bars a week at a price of 50¢ a bar.

Willingness and Ability to Pay Another way of looking at the demand curve is as a willingness-and-ability-to-pay curve. The willingness and ability to pay is a measure of *marginal benefit.*

If a small quantity is available, the highest price that someone is willing and able to pay for one more unit is high. But as the quantity available increases, the marginal benefit of each additional unit falls and the highest price that someone is willing and able to pay also falls along the demand curve.

In Fig. 3.1, if only 5 million energy bars are available each week, the highest price that someone is willing to pay for the 5 millionth bar is $2.50. But if 22 million energy bars are available each week, someone is willing to pay 50¢ for the last bar bought.

A Change in Demand

When any factor that influences buying plans changes, other than the price of the good, there is a **change in demand.** Figure 3.2 illustrates an increase in demand. When demand increases, the demand curve shifts rightward and the quantity demanded at each price is greater. For example, at $2.50 a bar, the quantity demanded on the original (blue) demand curve is 5 million energy bars a week. On the new (red) demand curve, at $2.50 a bar, the quantity demanded is 15 million bars a week. Look closely at the numbers in the table and check that the quantity demanded at each price is greater.

FIGURE 3.1 The Demand Curve

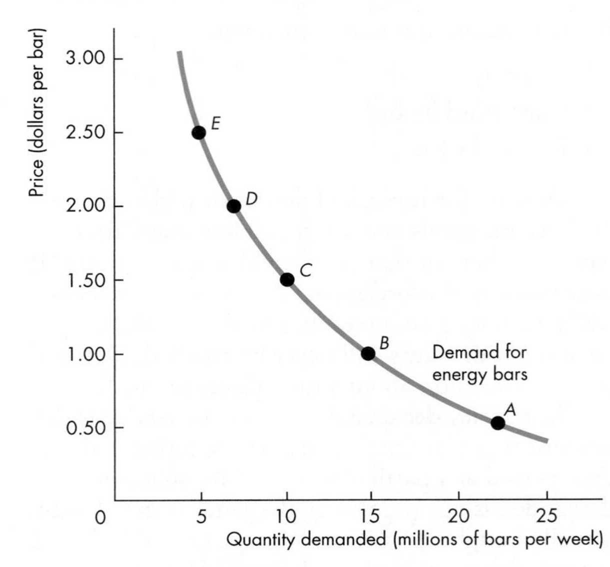

	Price (dollars per bar)	Quantity demanded (millions of bars per week)
A	0.50	22
B	1.00	15
C	1.50	10
D	2.00	7
E	2.50	5

The table shows a demand schedule for energy bars. At a price of 50¢ a bar, 22 million bars a week are demanded; at a price of $1.50 a bar, 10 million bars a week are demanded. The demand curve shows the relationship between quantity demanded and price, other things remaining the same. The demand curve slopes downward: As the price falls, the quantity demanded increases.

The demand curve can be read in two ways. For a given price, the demand curve tells us the quantity that people plan to buy. For example, at a price of $1.50 a bar, people plan to buy 10 million bars a week. For a given quantity, the demand curve tells us the maximum price that consumers are willing and able to pay for the last bar available. For example, the maximum price that consumers will pay for the 15 millionth bar is $1.00.

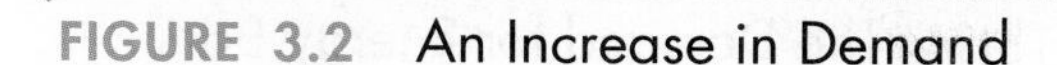

FIGURE 3.2 An Increase in Demand

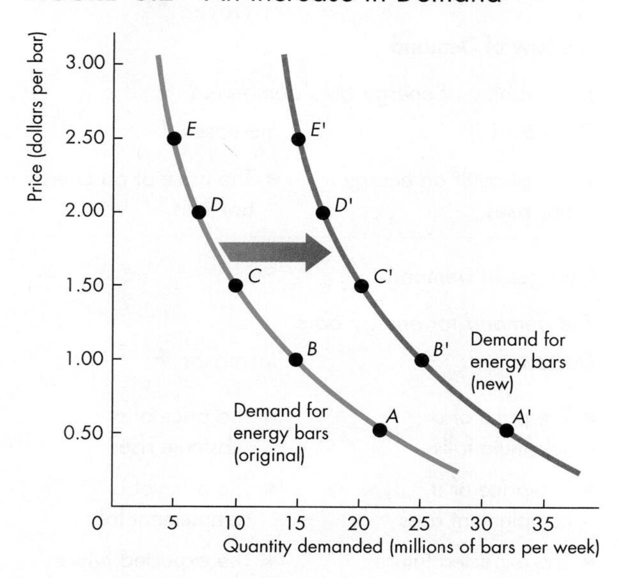

	Original demand schedule Original income			New demand schedule New higher income	
	Price (dollars per bar)	Quantity demanded (millions of bars per week)		Price (dollars per bar)	Quantity demanded (millions of bars per week)
A	0.50	22	A'	0.50	32
B	1.00	15	B'	1.00	25
C	1.50	10	C'	1.50	20
D	2.00	7	D'	2.00	17
E	2.50	5	E'	2.50	15

A change in any influence on buying plans other than the price of the good itself results in a new demand schedule and a shift of the demand curve. A change in income changes the demand for energy bars. At a price of $1.50 a bar, 10 million bars a week are demanded at the original income (row C of the table) and 20 million bars a week are demanded at the new higher income (row C'). A rise in income increases the demand for energy bars. The demand curve shifts *rightward*, as shown by the shift arrow and the resulting red curve.

myeconlab animation

Six main factors bring changes in demand. They are changes in

- The prices of related goods
- Expected future prices
- Income
- Expected future income and credit
- Population
- Preferences

Prices of Related Goods The quantity of energy bars that consumers plan to buy depends in part on the prices of substitutes for energy bars. A **substitute** is a good that can be used in place of another good. For example, a bus ride is a substitute for a train ride; a hamburger is a substitute for a hot dog; and an energy drink is a substitute for an energy bar. If the price of a substitute for an energy bar rises, people buy less of the substitute and more energy bars. For example, if the price of an energy drink rises, people buy fewer energy drinks and more energy bars. The demand for energy bars increases.

The quantity of energy bars that people plan to buy also depends on the prices of complements with energy bars. A **complement** is a good that is used in conjunction with another good. Hamburgers and fries are complements, and so are energy bars and exercise. If the price of an hour at the gym falls, people buy more gym time *and more* energy bars.

Expected Future Prices If the expected future price of a good rises and if the good can be stored, the opportunity cost of obtaining the good for future use is lower today than it will be in the future when people expect the price to be higher. So people retime their purchases—they substitute over time. They buy more of the good now before its price is expected to rise (and less afterward), so the demand for the good today increases.

For example, suppose that a Florida frost damages the season's orange crop. You expect the price of orange juice to rise, so you fill your freezer with enough frozen juice to get you through the next six months. Your current demand for frozen orange juice has increased, and your future demand has decreased.

Similarly, if the expected future price of a good falls, the opportunity cost of buying the good today is high relative to what it is expected to be in the future. So again, people retime their purchases. They buy less of the good now before its price is expected to fall, so the demand for the good decreases today and increases in the future.

Computer prices are constantly falling, and this fact poses a dilemma. Will you buy a new computer now, in time for the start of the school year, or will you wait until the price has fallen some more? Because people expect computer prices to keep falling, the current demand for computers is less (and the future demand is greater) than it otherwise would be.

Income Consumers' income influences demand. When income increases, consumers buy more of most goods; and when income decreases, consumers buy less of most goods. Although an increase in income leads to an increase in the demand for *most* goods, it does not lead to an increase in the demand for *all* goods. A **normal good** is one for which demand increases as income increases. An **inferior good** is one for which demand decreases as income increases. As incomes increase, the demand for air travel (a normal good) increases and the demand for long-distance bus trips (an inferior good) decreases.

Expected Future Income and Credit When expected future income increases or credit becomes easier to get, demand for the good might increase now. For example, a salesperson gets the news that she will receive a big bonus at the end of the year, so she goes into debt and buys a new car right now, rather than wait until she receives the bonus.

Population Demand also depends on the size and the age structure of the population. The larger the population, the greater is the demand for all goods and services; the smaller the population, the smaller is the demand for all goods and services.

For example, the demand for parking spaces or movies or just about anything that you can imagine is much greater in New York City (population 7.5 million) than it is in Boise, Idaho (population 150,000).

Also, the larger the proportion of the population in a given age group, the greater is the demand for the goods and services used by that age group.

For example, during the 1990s, a decrease in the college-age population decreased the demand for college places. During those same years, the number of Americans aged 85 years and over increased by more than 1 million. As a result, the demand for nursing home services increased.

TABLE 3.1 The Demand for Energy Bars

The Law of Demand

The quantity of energy bars demanded

Decreases if:	*Increases if:*
■ The price of an energy bar rises	■ The price of an energy bar falls

Changes in Demand

The demand for energy bars

Decreases if:	*Increases if:*
■ The price of a substitute falls	■ The price of a substitute rises
■ The price of a complement rises	■ The price of a complement falls
■ The expected future price of an energy bar falls	■ The expected future price of an energy bar rises
■ Income falls*	■ Income rises*
■ Expected future income falls or credit becomes harder to get*	■ Expected future income rises or credit becomes easier to get*
■ The population decreases	■ The population increases

*An energy bar is a normal good.

Preferences Demand depends on preferences. *Preferences* determine the value that people place on each good and service. Preferences depend on such things as the weather, information, and fashion. For example, greater health and fitness awareness has shifted preferences in favor of energy bars, so the demand for energy bars has increased.

Table 3.1 summarizes the influences on demand and the direction of those influences.

A Change in the Quantity Demanded Versus a Change in Demand

Changes in the influences on buying plans bring either a change in the quantity demanded or a change in demand. Equivalently, they bring either a movement along the demand curve or a shift of the demand curve. The distinction between a change in the quantity demanded and a change in demand is the same as that between a movement along the demand curve and a shift of the demand curve.

A point on the demand curve shows the quantity demanded at a given price, so a movement along the demand curve shows a **change in the quantity demanded.** The entire demand curve shows demand, so a shift of the demand curve shows a *change in demand.* Figure 3.3 illustrates these distinctions.

Movement Along the Demand Curve If the price of the good changes but no other influence on buying plans changes, we illustrate the effect as a movement along the demand curve.

A fall in the price of a good increases the quantity demanded of it. In Fig. 3.3, we illustrate the effect of a fall in price as a movement down along the demand curve D_0.

A rise in the price of a good decreases the quantity demanded of it. In Fig. 3.3, we illustrate the effect of a rise in price as a movement up along the demand curve D_0.

A Shift of the Demand Curve If the price of a good remains constant but some other influence on buying plans changes, there is a change in demand for that good. We illustrate a change in demand as a shift of the demand curve. For example, if more people work out at the gym, consumers buy more energy bars regardless of the price of a bar. That is what a rightward shift of the demand curve shows—more energy bars are demanded at each price.

In Fig. 3.3, there is a *change in demand* and the demand curve shifts when any influence on buying plans changes, other than the price of the good. Demand *increases* and the demand curve *shifts rightward* (to the red demand curve D_1) if the price of a substitute rises, the price of a complement falls, the expected future price of the good rises, income increases (for a normal good), expected future income or credit increases, or the population increases. Demand *decreases* and the demand curve *shifts leftward* (to the red demand curve D_2) if the price of a substitute falls, the price of a complement rises, the expected future price of the good falls, income decreases (for a normal good), expected future income or credit decreases, or the population decreases. (For an inferior good, the effects of changes in income are in the opposite direction to those described above.)

FIGURE 3.3 A Change in the Quantity Demanded Versus a Change in Demand

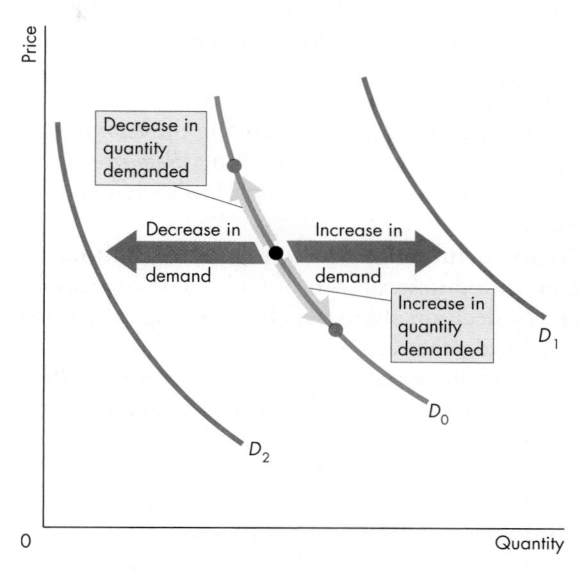

When the price of the good changes, there is a movement along the demand curve and *a change in the quantity demanded*, shown by the blue arrows on demand curve D_0. When any other influence on buying plans changes, there is a shift of the demand curve and a *change in demand*. An increase in demand shifts the demand curve rightward (from D_0 to D_1). A decrease in demand shifts the demand curve leftward (from D_0 to D_2).

myeconlab animation

REVIEW QUIZ

1 Define the quantity demanded of a good or service.
2 What is the law of demand and how do we illustrate it?
3 What does the demand curve tell us about the price that consumers are willing to pay?
4 List all the influences on buying plans that change demand, and for each influence, say whether it increases or decreases demand.
5 Why does demand not change when the price of a good changes with no change in the other influences on buying plans?

You can work these questions in Study Plan 3.2 and get instant feedback.

Supply

If a firm supplies a good or service, the firm

1. Has the resources and technology to produce it,
2. Can profit from producing it, and
3. Plans to produce it and sell it.

A supply is more than just having the *resources* and the *technology* to produce something. *Resources and technology* are the constraints that limit what is possible.

Many useful things can be produced, but they are not produced unless it is profitable to do so. Supply reflects a decision about which technologically feasible items to produce.

The **quantity supplied** of a good or service is the amount that producers plan to sell during a given time period at a particular price. The quantity supplied is not necessarily the same amount as the quantity actually sold. Sometimes the quantity supplied is greater than the quantity demanded, so the quantity sold is less than the quantity supplied.

Like the quantity demanded, the quantity supplied is measured as an amount per unit of time. For example, suppose that GM produces 1,000 cars a day. The quantity of cars supplied by GM can be expressed as 1,000 a day, 7,000 a week, or 365,000 a year. Without the time dimension, we cannot tell whether a particular quantity is large or small.

Many factors influence selling plans, and again one of them is the price of the good. We look first at the relationship between the quantity supplied of a good and its price. Just as we did when we studied demand, to isolate the relationship between the quantity supplied of a good and its price, we keep all other influences on selling plans the same and ask: How does the quantity supplied of a good change as its price changes when other things remain the same?

The law of supply provides the answer.

The Law of Supply

The **law of supply** states:

> Other things remaining the same, the higher the price of a good, the greater is the quantity supplied; and the lower the price of a good, the smaller is the quantity supplied.

Why does a higher price increase the quantity supplied? It is because *marginal cost increases.* As the quantity produced of any good increases, the marginal cost of producing the good increases. (See Chapter 2, p. 33 to review marginal cost.)

It is never worth producing a good if the price received for the good does not at least cover the marginal cost of producing it. When the price of a good rises, other things remaining the same, producers are willing to incur a higher marginal cost, so they increase production. The higher price brings forth an increase in the quantity supplied.

Let's now illustrate the law of supply with a supply curve and a supply schedule.

Supply Curve and Supply Schedule

You are now going to study the second of the two most used curves in economics: the supply curve. You're also going to learn about the critical distinction between *supply* and *quantity supplied.*

The term **supply** refers to the entire relationship between the price of a good and the quantity supplied of it. Supply is illustrated by the supply curve and the supply schedule. The term *quantity supplied* refers to a point on a supply curve—the quantity supplied at a particular price.

Figure 3.4 shows the supply curve of energy bars. A **supply curve** shows the relationship between the quantity supplied of a good and its price when all other influences on producers' planned sales remain the same. The supply curve is a graph of a supply schedule.

The table in Fig. 3.4 sets out the supply schedule for energy bars. A *supply schedule* lists the quantities supplied at each price when all the other influences on producers' planned sales remain the same. For example, if the price of an energy bar is 50¢, the quantity supplied is zero—in row *A* of the table. If the price of an energy bar is $1.00, the quantity supplied is 6 million energy bars a week—in row *B*. The other rows of the table show the quantities supplied at prices of $1.50, $2.00, and $2.50.

To make a supply curve, we graph the quantity supplied on the *x*-axis and the price on the *y*-axis. The points on the supply curve labeled *A* through *E* correspond to the rows of the supply schedule. For example, point *A* on the graph shows a quantity supplied of zero at a price of 50¢ an energy bar. Point *E* shows a quantity supplied of 15 million bars at $2.50 an energy bar.

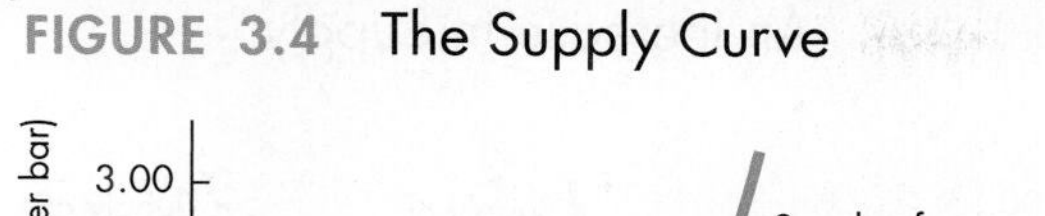

FIGURE 3.4 The Supply Curve

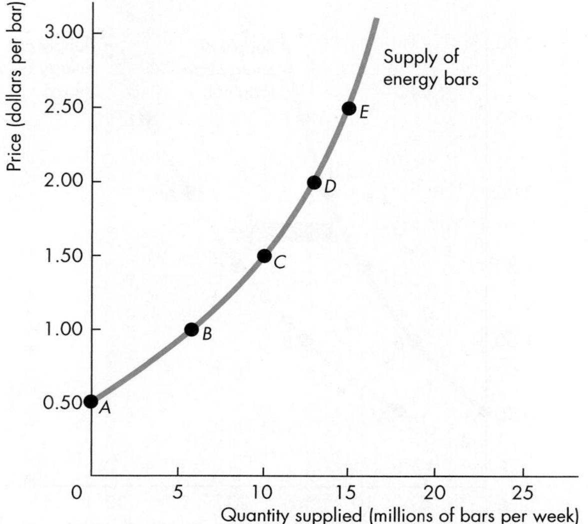

	Price (dollars per bar)	Quantity supplied (millions of bars per week)
A	0.50	0
B	1.00	6
C	1.50	10
D	2.00	13
E	2.50	15

The table shows the supply schedule of energy bars. For example, at a price of $1.00, 6 million bars a week are supplied; at a price of $2.50, 15 million bars a week are supplied. The supply curve shows the relationship between the quantity supplied and the price, other things remaining the same. The supply curve slopes upward: As the price of a good increases, the quantity supplied increases.

A supply curve can be read in two ways. For a given price, the supply curve tells us the quantity that producers plan to sell at that price. For example, at a price of $1.50 a bar, producers are planning to sell 10 million bars a week. For a given quantity, the supply curve tells us the minimum price at which producers are willing to sell one more bar. For example, if 15 million bars are produced each week, the lowest price at which a producer is willing to sell the 15 millionth bar is $2.50.

myeconlab animation

Minimum Supply Price The supply curve can be interpreted as a minimum-supply-price curve—a curve that shows the lowest price at which someone is willing to sell. This lowest price is the *marginal cost.*

If a small quantity is produced, the lowest price at which someone is willing to sell one more unit is low. But as the quantity produced increases, the marginal cost of each additional unit rises, so the lowest price at which someone is willing to sell an additional unit rises along the supply curve.

In Fig. 3.4, if 15 million bars are produced each week, the lowest price at which someone is willing to sell the 15 millionth bar is $2.50. But if 10 million bars are produced each week, someone is willing to accept $1.50 for the last bar produced.

A Change in Supply

When any factor that influences selling plans other than the price of the good changes, there is a **change in supply**. Six main factors bring changes in supply. They are changes in

- The prices of factors of production
- The prices of related goods produced
- Expected future prices
- The number of suppliers
- Technology
- The state of nature

Prices of Factors of Production The prices of the factors of production used to produce a good influence its supply. To see this influence, think about the supply curve as a minimum-supply-price curve. If the price of a factor of production rises, the lowest price that a producer is willing to accept for that good rises, so supply decreases. For example, during 2008, as the price of jet fuel increased, the supply of air travel decreased. Similarly, a rise in the minimum wage decreases the supply of hamburgers.

Prices of Related Goods Produced The prices of related goods that firms produce influence supply. For example, if the price of energy gel rises, firms switch production from bars to gel. The supply of energy bars decreases. Energy bars and energy gel are *substitutes in production*—goods that can be produced by using the same resources. If the price of beef rises, the supply of cowhide increases. Beef and cowhide are *complements in production*—goods that must be produced together.

Expected Future Prices If the expected future price of a good rises, the return from selling the good in the future increases and is higher than it is today. So supply decreases today and increases in the future.

The Number of Suppliers The larger the number of firms that produce a good, the greater is the supply of the good. As new firms enter an industry, the supply in that industry increases. As firms leave an industry, the supply in that industry decreases.

Technology The term "technology" is used broadly to mean the way that factors of production are used to produce a good. A technology change occurs when a new method is discovered that lowers the cost of producing a good. For example, new methods used in the factories that produce computer chips have lowered the cost and increased the supply of chips.

The State of Nature The state of nature includes all the natural forces that influence production. It includes the state of the weather and, more broadly, the natural environment. Good weather can increase the supply of many agricultural products and bad weather can decrease their supply. Extreme natural events such as earthquakes, tornadoes, and hurricanes can also influence supply.

Figure 3.5 illustrates an increase in supply. When supply increases, the supply curve shifts rightward and the quantity supplied at each price is larger. For example, at $1.00 per bar, on the original (blue) supply curve, the quantity supplied is 6 million bars a week. On the new (red) supply curve, the quantity supplied is 15 million bars a week. Look closely at the numbers in the table in Fig. 3.5 and check that the quantity supplied is larger at each price.

Table 3.2 summarizes the influences on supply and the directions of those influences.

A Change in the Quantity Supplied Versus a Change in Supply

Changes in the influences on selling plans bring either a change in the quantity supplied or a change in supply. Equivalently, they bring either a movement along the supply curve or a shift of the supply curve.

A point on the supply curve shows the quantity supplied at a given price. A movement along the supply curve shows a **change in the quantity supplied.** The entire supply curve shows supply. A shift of the supply curve shows a *change in supply.*

FIGURE 3.5 An Increase in Supply

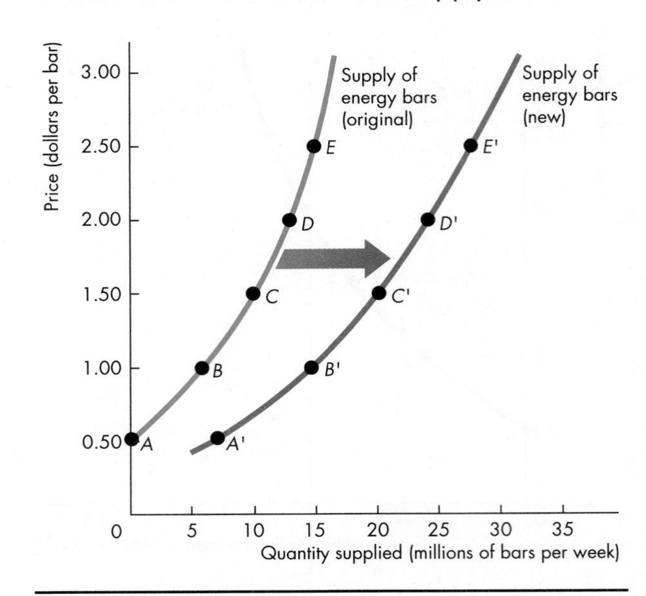

	Original supply schedule Old technology			New supply schedule New technology	
	Price (dollars per bar)	Quantity supplied (millions of bars per week)		Price (dollars per bar)	Quantity supplied (millions of bars per week)
A	0.50	0	*A'*	0.50	7
B	1.00	6	*B'*	1.00	15
C	1.50	10	*C'*	1.50	20
D	2.00	13	*D'*	2.00	25
E	2.50	15	*E'*	2.50	27

A change in any influence on selling plans other than the price of the good itself results in a new supply schedule and a shift of the supply curve. For example, a new, cost-saving technology for producing energy bars changes the supply of energy bars. At a price of $1.50 a bar, 10 million bars a week are supplied when producers use the old technology (row *C* of the table) and 20 million energy bars a week are supplied when producers use the new technology (row *C'*). An advance in technology *increases* the supply of energy bars. The supply curve shifts *rightward,* as shown by the shift arrow and the resulting red curve.

Figure 3.6 illustrates and summarizes these distinctions. If the price of the good changes and other things remain the same, there is a *change in the quantity supplied* of that good. If the price of the good falls, the quantity supplied decreases and there is a movement down along the supply curve S_0. If the price of the good rises, the quantity supplied increases and there is a movement up along the supply curve S_0. When any other influence on selling plans changes, the supply curve shifts and there is a *change in supply*. If supply increases, the supply curve shifts rightward to S_1. If supply decreases, the supply curve shifts leftward to S_2.

TABLE 3.2 The Supply of Energy Bars

The Law of Supply

The quantity of energy bars supplied

Decreases if:	*Increases if:*
■ The price of an energy bar falls	■ The price of an energy bar rises

Changes in Supply

The supply of energy bars

Decreases if:	*Increases if:*
■ The price of a factor of production used to produce energy bars rises	■ The price of a factor of production used to produce energy bars falls
■ The price of a substitute in production rises	■ The price of a substitute in production falls
■ The price of a complement in production falls	■ The price of a complement in production rises
■ The expected future price of an energy bar rises	■ The expected future price of an energy bar falls
■ The number of suppliers of bars decreases	■ The number of suppliers of bars increases
■ A technology change decreases energy bar production	■ A technology change increases energy bar production
■ A natural event decreases energy bar production	■ A natural event increases energy bar production

FIGURE 3.6 A Change in the Quantity Supplied Versus a Change in Supply

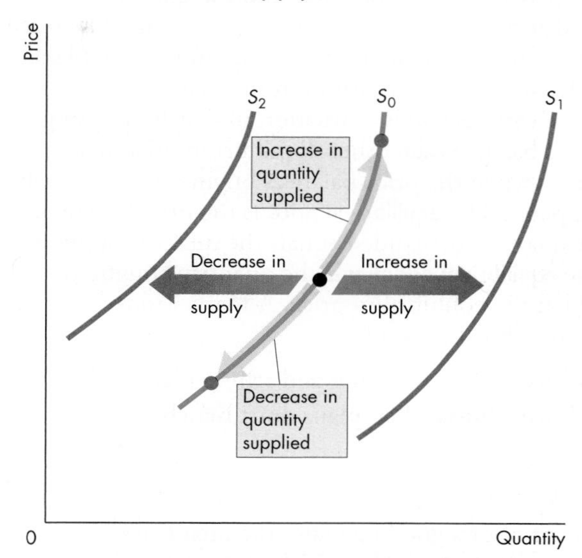

When the price of the good changes, there is a movement along the supply curve and *a change in the quantity supplied*, shown by the blue arrows on supply curve S_0. When any other influence on selling plans changes, there is a shift of the supply curve and a *change in supply*. An increase in supply shifts the supply curve rightward (from S_0 *to* S_1), and a decrease in supply shifts the supply curve leftward (from S_0 *to* S_2).

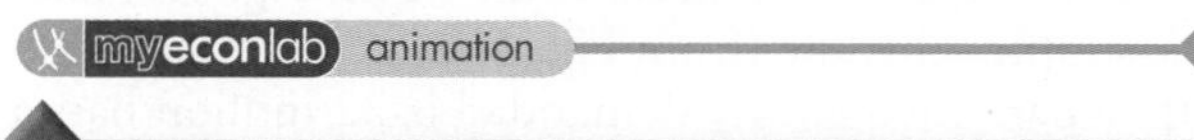

REVIEW QUIZ

1. Define the quantity supplied of a good or service.
2. What is the law of supply and how do we illustrate it?
3. What does the supply curve tell us about the producer's minimum supply price?
4. List all the influences on selling plans, and for each influence, say whether it changes supply.
5. What happens to the quantity of cell phones supplied and the supply of cell phones if the price of a cell phone falls?

You can work these questions in Study Plan 3.3 and get instant feedback.

Now we're going to combine demand and supply and see how prices and quantities are determined.

Market Equilibrium

We have seen that when the price of a good rises, the quantity demanded *decreases* and the quantity supplied *increases.* We are now going to see how the price adjusts to coordinate buying plans and selling plans and achieve an equilibrium in the market.

An *equilibrium* is a situation in which opposing forces balance each other. Equilibrium in a market occurs when the price balances buying plans and selling plans. The **equilibrium price** is the price at which the quantity demanded equals the quantity supplied. The **equilibrium quantity** is the quantity bought and sold at the equilibrium price. A market moves toward its equilibrium because

- Price regulates buying and selling plans.
- Price adjusts when plans don't match.

Price as a Regulator

The price of a good regulates the quantities demanded and supplied. If the price is too high, the quantity supplied exceeds the quantity demanded. If the price is too low, the quantity demanded exceeds the quantity supplied. There is one price at which the quantity demanded equals the quantity supplied. Let's work out what that price is.

Figure 3.7 shows the market for energy bars. The table shows the demand schedule (from Fig. 3.1) and the supply schedule (from Fig. 3.4). If the price is 50¢ a bar, the quantity demanded is 22 million bars a week but no bars are supplied. There is a shortage of 22 million bars a week. The final column of the table shows this shortage. At a price of $1.00 a bar, there is still a shortage but only of 9 million bars a week.

If the price is $2.50 a bar, the quantity supplied is 15 million bars a week but the quantity demanded is only 5 million. There is a surplus of 10 million bars a week.

The one price at which there is neither a shortage nor a surplus is $1.50 a bar. At that price, the quantity demanded equals the quantity supplied: 10 million bars a week. The equilibrium price is $1.50 a bar, and the equilibrium quantity is 10 million bars a week.

Figure 3.7 shows that the demand curve and the supply curve intersect at the equilibrium price of $1.50 a bar. At each price *above* $1.50 a bar, there is a surplus of bars. For example, at $2.00 a bar, the surplus is 6

FIGURE 3.7 Equilibrium

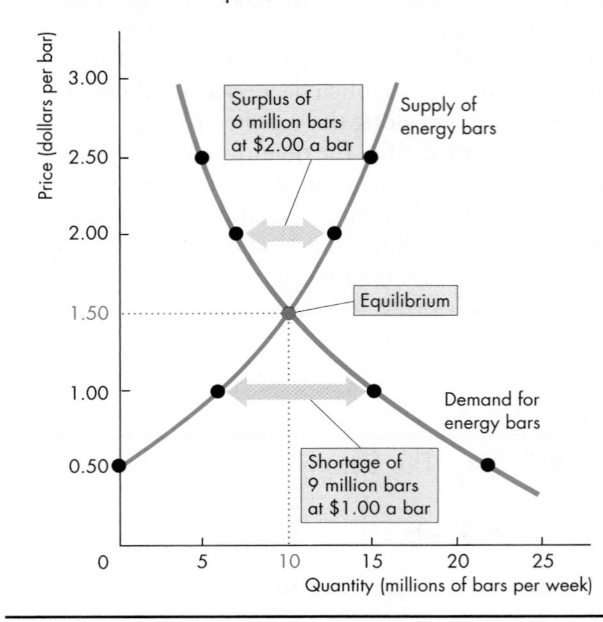

Price (dollars per bar)	Quantity demanded	Quantity supplied	Shortage (–) or surplus (+)
	(millions of bars per week)		
0.50	22	0	–22
1.00	15	6	–9
1.50	10	10	0
2.00	7	13	+6
2.50	5	15	+10

The table lists the quantity demanded and the quantity supplied as well as the shortage or surplus of bars at each price. If the price is $1.00 a bar, 15 million bars a week are demanded and 6 million bars are supplied. There is a shortage of 9 million bars a week, and the price rises.

If the price is $2.00 a bar, 7 million bars a week are demanded and 13 million bars are supplied. There is a surplus of 6 million bars a week, and the price falls.

If the price is $1.50 a bar, 10 million bars a week are demanded and 10 million bars are supplied. There is neither a shortage nor a surplus, and the price does not change. The price at which the quantity demanded equals the quantity supplied is the equilibrium price, and 10 million bars a week is the equilibrium quantity.

myeconlab animation

million bars a week, as shown by the blue arrow. At each price *below* $1.50 a bar, there is a shortage of bars. For example, at $1.00 a bar, the shortage is 9 million bars a week, as shown by the red arrow.

Price Adjustments

You've seen that if the price is below equilibrium, there is a shortage and that if the price is above equilibrium, there is a surplus. But can we count on the price to change and eliminate a shortage or a surplus? We can, because such price changes are beneficial to both buyers and sellers. Let's see why the price changes when there is a shortage or a surplus.

A Shortage Forces the Price Up Suppose the price of an energy bar is $1. Consumers plan to buy 15 million bars a week, and producers plan to sell 6 million bars a week. Consumers can't force producers to sell more than they plan, so the quantity that is actually offered for sale is 6 million bars a week. In this situation, powerful forces operate to increase the price and move it toward the equilibrium price. Some producers, noticing lines of unsatisfied consumers, raise the price. Some producers increase their output. As producers push the price up, the price rises toward its equilibrium. The rising price reduces the shortage because it decreases the quantity demanded and increases the quantity supplied. When the price has increased to the point at which there is no longer a shortage, the forces moving the price stop operating and the price comes to rest at its equilibrium.

A Surplus Forces the Price Down Suppose the price of a bar is $2. Producers plan to sell 13 million bars a week, and consumers plan to buy 7 million bars a week. Producers cannot force consumers to buy more than they plan, so the quantity that is actually bought is 7 million bars a week. In this situation, powerful forces operate to lower the price and move it toward the equilibrium price. Some producers, unable to sell the quantities of energy bars they planned to sell, cut their prices. In addition, some producers scale back production. As producers cut the price, the price falls toward its equilibrium. The falling price decreases the surplus because it increases the quantity demanded and decreases the quantity supplied. When the price has fallen to the point at which there is no longer a surplus, the forces moving the price stop operating and the price comes to rest at its equilibrium.

The Best Deal Available for Buyers and Sellers When the price is below equilibrium, it is forced upward. Why don't buyers resist the increase and refuse to buy at the higher price? The answer is because they value the good more highly than its current price and they can't satisfy their demand at the current price. In some markets—for example, the markets that operate on eBay—the buyers might even be the ones who force the price up by offering to pay a higher price.

When the price is above equilibrium, it is bid downward. Why don't sellers resist this decrease and refuse to sell at the lower price? The answer is because their minimum supply price is below the current price and they cannot sell all they would like to at the current price. Sellers willingly lower the price to gain market share.

At the price at which the quantity demanded and the quantity supplied are equal, neither buyers nor sellers can do business at a better price. Buyers pay the highest price they are willing to pay for the last unit bought, and sellers receive the lowest price at which they are willing to supply the last unit sold.

When people freely make offers to buy and sell and when demanders try to buy at the lowest possible price and suppliers try to sell at the highest possible price, the price at which trade takes place is the equilibrium price—the price at which the quantity demanded equals the quantity supplied. The price coordinates the plans of buyers and sellers, and no one has an incentive to change it.

REVIEW QUIZ

1. What is the equilibrium price of a good or service?
2. Over what range of prices does a shortage arise? What happens to the price when there is a shortage?
3. Over what range of prices does a surplus arise? What happens to the price when there is a surplus?
4. Why is the price at which the quantity demanded equals the quantity supplied the equilibrium price?
5. Why is the equilibrium price the best deal available for both buyers and sellers?

You can work these questions in Study Plan 3.4 and get instant feedback.

Predicting Changes in Price and Quantity

The demand and supply model that we have just studied provides us with a powerful way of analyzing influences on prices and the quantities bought and sold. According to the model, a change in price stems from a change in demand, a change in supply, or a change in both demand and supply. Let's look first at the effects of a change in demand.

An Increase in Demand

If more people join health clubs, the demand for energy bars increases. The table in Fig. 3.8 shows the original and new demand schedules for energy bars as well as the supply schedule of energy bars.

The increase in demand creates a shortage at the original price and to eliminate the shortage, the price must rise.

Figure 3.8 shows what happens. The figure shows the original demand for and supply of energy bars. The original equilibrium price is $1.50 an energy bar, and the equilibrium quantity is 10 million energy bars a week. When demand increases, the demand curve shifts rightward. The equilibrium price rises to $2.50 an energy bar, and the quantity supplied increases to 15 million energy bars a week, as highlighted in the figure. There is an *increase in the quantity supplied* but *no change in supply*—a movement along, but no shift of, the supply curve.

A Decrease in Demand

We can reverse this change in demand. Start at a price of $2.50 a bar with 15 million energy bars a week being bought and sold, and then work out what happens if demand decreases to its original level. Such a decrease in demand might arise if people switch to energy gel (a substitute for energy bars). The decrease in demand shifts the demand curve leftward. The equilibrium price falls to $1.50 a bar, the quantity supplied decreases, and the equilibrium quantity decreases to 10 million bars a week.

We can now make our first two predictions:

1. When demand increases, the price rises and the quantity increases.
2. When demand decreases, the price falls and the quantity decreases.

FIGURE 3.8 The Effects of a Change in Demand

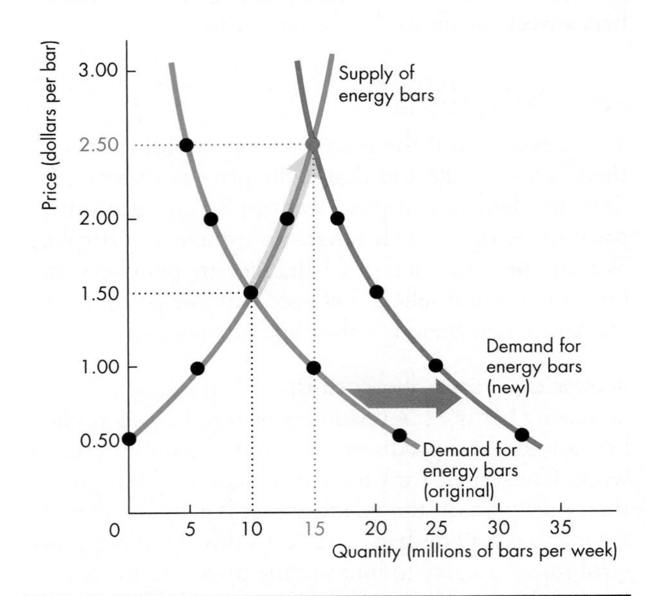

Price (dollars per bar)	Quantity demanded (millions of bars per week) Original	New	Quantity supplied (millions of bars per week)
0.50	22	32	0
1.00	15	25	6
1.50	**10**	20	**10**
2.00	7	17	13
2.50	5	15	15

Initially, the demand for energy bars is the blue demand curve. The equilibrium price is $1.50 a bar, and the equilibrium quantity is 10 million bars a week. When more health-conscious people do more exercise, the demand for energy bars increases and the demand curve shifts rightward to become the red curve.

At $1.50 a bar, there is now a shortage of 10 million bars a week. The price of a bar rises to a new equilibrium of $2.50. As the price rises to $2.50, the quantity supplied increases—shown by the blue arrow on the supply curve—to the new equilibrium quantity of 15 million bars a week. Following an increase in demand, the quantity supplied increases but supply does not change—the supply curve does not shift.

Economics in Action

The Global Market for Crude Oil

The demand and supply model provides insights into all competitive markets. Here, we'll apply what you've learned about the effects of an increase in demand to the global market for crude oil.

Crude oil is like the life-blood of the global economy. It is used to fuel our cars, airplanes, trains, and buses, to generate electricity, and to produce a wide range of plastics. When the price of crude oil rises, the cost of transportation, power, and materials all increase.

In 2001, the price of a barrel of oil was $20 (using the value of money in 2010). In 2008, before the global financial crisis ended a long period of economic expansion, the price peaked at $127 a barrel.

While the price of oil was rising, the quantity of oil produced and consumed also increased. In 2001, the world produced 65 million barrels of oil a day. By 2008, that quantity was 72 million barrels.

Who or what has been raising the price of oil? Is it the action of greedy oil producers? Oil producers might be greedy, and some of them might be big enough to withhold supply and raise the price, but it wouldn't be in their self-interest to do so. The higher price would bring forth a greater quantity supplied from other producers and the profit of the producer limiting supply would fall.

Oil producers could try to cooperate and jointly withhold supply. The Organization of Petroleum Exporting Countries, OPEC, is such a group of producers. But OPEC doesn't control the *world* supply and its members' self-interest is to produce the quantities that give them the maximum attainable profit.

So even though the global oil market has some big players, they don't fix the price. Instead, the actions of thousands of buyers and sellers and the forces of demand and supply determine the price of oil.

So how have demand and supply changed?

Because both the price and the quantity have increased, the demand for oil must have increased. Supply might have changed too, but here we'll suppose that supply has remained the same.

The global demand for oil has increased for one major reason: World income has increased. The increase has been particularly large in the emerging economies of Brazil, China, and India. Increased world income has increased the demand for oil-using goods such as electricity, gasoline, and plastics, which in turn has increased the demand for oil.

The figure illustrates the effects of the increase in demand on the global oil market. The supply of oil remained constant along supply curve S. The demand for oil in 2001 was D_{2001}, so in 2001 the price was $20 a barrel and the quantity was 65 million barrels per day. The demand for oil increased and by 2008 it had reached D_{2008}. The price of oil increased to $127 a barrel and the quantity increased to 72 million barrels a day. The increase in the quantity is an *increase in the quantity supplied*, not an increase in supply.

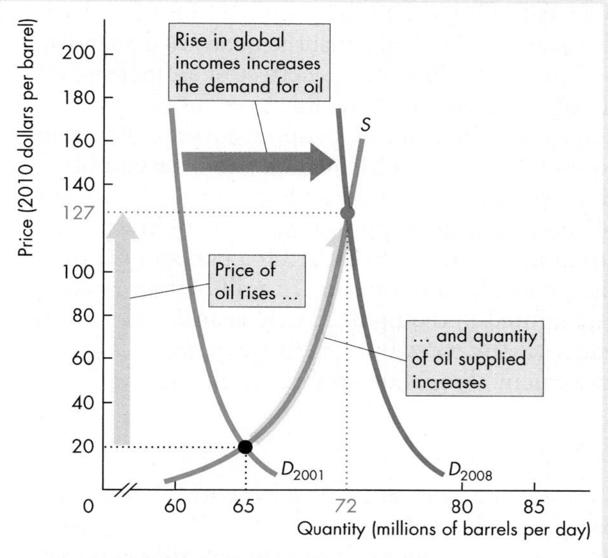

The Global Market for Crude Oil

An Increase in Supply

When Nestlé (the producer of PowerBar) and other energy bar producers switch to a new cost-saving technology, the supply of energy bars increases. Figure 3.9 shows the new supply schedule (the same one that was shown in Fig. 3.5). What are the new equilibrium price and quantity? The price falls to $1.00 a bar, and the quantity increases to 15 million bars a week. You can see why by looking at the quantities demanded and supplied at the old price of $1.50 a bar. The new quantity supplied at that price is 20 million bars a week, and there is a surplus. The price falls. Only when the price is $1.00 a bar does the quantity supplied equal the quantity demanded.

Figure 3.9 illustrates the effect of an increase in supply. It shows the demand curve for energy bars and the original and new supply curves. The initial equilibrium price is $1.50 a bar, and the equilibrium quantity is 10 million bars a week. When supply increases, the supply curve shifts rightward. The equilibrium price falls to $1.00 a bar, and the quantity demanded increases to 15 million bars a week, highlighted in the figure. There is an *increase in the quantity demanded* but *no change in demand*—a movement along, but no shift of, the demand curve.

A Decrease in Supply

Start out at a price of $1.00 a bar with 15 million bars a week being bought and sold. Then suppose that the cost of labor or raw materials rises and the supply of energy bars decreases. The decrease in supply shifts the supply curve leftward. The equilibrium price rises to $1.50 a bar, the quantity demanded decreases, and the equilibrium quantity decreases to 10 million bars a week.

We can now make two more predictions:

1. When supply increases, the price falls and the quantity increases.
2. When supply decreases, the price rises and the quantity decreases.

You've now seen what happens to the price and the quantity when either demand or supply changes while the other one remains unchanged. In real markets, both demand and supply can change together. When this happens, to predict the changes in price and quantity, we must combine the effects that you've just seen. That is your final task in this chapter.

FIGURE 3.9 The Effects of a Change in Supply

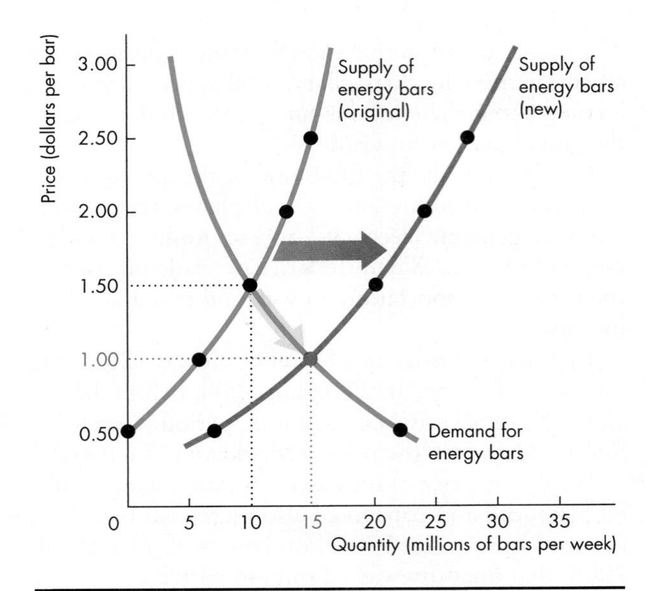

Price (dollars per bar)	Quantity demanded (millions of bars per week)	Quantity supplied (millions of bars per week)	
		Original	New
0.50	22	0	7
1.00	15	6	15
1.50	**10**	**10**	20
2.00	7	13	25
2.50	5	15	27

Initially, the supply of energy bars is shown by the blue supply curve. The equilibrium price is $1.50 a bar, and the equilibrium quantity is 10 million bars a week. When the new cost-saving technology is adopted, the supply of energy bars increases and the supply curve shifts rightward to become the red curve.

At $1.50 a bar, there is now a surplus of 10 million bars a week. The price of an energy bar falls to a new equilibrium of $1.00 a bar. As the price falls to $1.00, the quantity demanded increases—shown by the blue arrow on the demand curve—to the new equilibrium quantity of 15 million bars a week. Following an increase in supply, the quantity demanded increases but demand does not change—the demand curve does not shift.

Economics in Action

The Market for Strawberries

California produces 85 percent of the nation's strawberries and its crop, which starts to increase in March, is in top flight by April. During the winter months of January and February, Florida is the main strawberry producer.

In a normal year, the supplies from these two regions don't overlap much. As California's production steps up in March and April, Florida's production falls off. The result is a steady supply of strawberries and not much seasonal fluctuation in the price of strawberries.

But 2010 wasn't a normal year. Florida had exceptionally cold weather, which damaged the strawberry fields, lowered crop yields, and delayed the harvests. The result was unusually high strawberry prices.

With higher than normal prices, Florida farmers planted strawberry varieties that mature later than their normal crop and planned to harvest this fruit during the spring. Their plan worked perfectly and good growing conditions delivered a bumper crop by late March.

On the other side of the nation, while Florida was freezing, Southern California was drowning under unusually heavy rains. This wet weather put the strawberries to sleep and delayed their growth. But when the rains stopped and the temperature began to rise, California joined Florida with a super abundance of fruit.

With an abundance of strawberries, the price tumbled. Strawberry farmers in both regions couldn't hire enough labor to pick the super-sized crop, so some fruit was left in the fields to rot.

The figure explains what was happening in the market for strawberries.

Demand, shown by the demand curve, *D*, didn't change. In January, the failed Florida crop kept supply low and the supply curve was $S_{January}$. The price was high at $3.80 per pound and production was 5.0 million pounds per day.

In April, the bumper crops in both regions increased supply to S_{April}. This increase in supply lowered the price to $1.20 per pound and increased the quantity demanded—a movement along the demand curve—to 5.5 million pounds per day.

You can also see in the figure why farmers left fruit in the field to rot. At the January price of $3.80 a pound, farmers would have been paying top wages to hire the workers needed to pick fruit at the rate of 6.0 million pounds per day. This is the quantity on supply curve S_{April} at $3.80 a pound.

But with the fall in price to $1.20 a pound, growers were not able to earn a profit by picking more than 5.5 million pounds.

For some growers the price wasn't high enough to cover the cost of hiring labor, so they opened their fields to anyone who wanted to pick their own strawberries for free.

The events we've described here in the market for strawberries illustrate the effects of a change in supply with no change in demand.

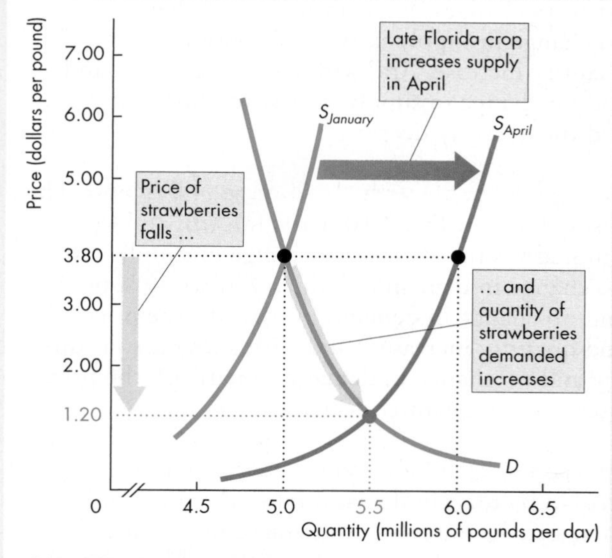

The Market for Strawberries

All the Possible Changes in Demand and Supply

Figure 3.10 brings together and summarizes the effects of all the possible changes in demand and supply. With what you've learned about the effects of a change in *either* demand or supply, you can predict what happens if *both* demand and supply change together. Let's begin by reviewing what you already know.

Change in Demand with No Change in Supply The first row of Fig. 3.10, parts (a), (b), and (c), summarizes the effects of a change in demand with no change in supply. In part (a), with no change in either demand or supply, neither the price nor the quantity changes. With an *increase* in demand and no change in supply in part (b), both the price and quantity increase. And with a *decrease* in demand and no change in supply in part (c), both the price and the quantity decrease.

Change in Supply with No Change in Demand The first column of Fig. 3.10, parts (a), (d), and (g), summarizes the effects of a change in supply with no change in demand. With an *increase* in supply and no change in demand in part (d), the price falls and quantity increases. And with a *decrease* in supply and no change in demand in part (g), the price rises and the quantity decreases.

Increase in Both Demand and Supply You've seen that an increase in demand raises the price and increases the quantity. And you've seen that an increase in supply lowers the price and increases the quantity. Fig. 3.10(e) combines these two changes. Because either an increase in demand or an increase in supply increases the quantity, the quantity also increases when both demand and supply increase. But the effect on the price is uncertain. An increase in demand raises the price and an increase in supply lowers the price, so we can't say whether the price will rise or fall when both demand and supply increase. We need to know the magnitudes of the changes in demand and supply to predict the effects on price. In the example in Fig. 3.10(e), the price does not change. But notice that if demand increases by slightly more than the amount shown in the figure, the price will rise. And if supply increases by slightly more than the amount shown in the figure, the price will fall.

Decrease in Both Demand and Supply Figure 3.10(i) shows the case in which demand and supply *both decrease*. For the same reasons as those we've just reviewed, when both demand and supply decrease, the quantity decreases, and again the direction of the price change is uncertain.

Decrease in Demand and Increase in Supply You've seen that a decrease in demand lowers the price and decreases the quantity. And you've seen that an increase in supply lowers the price and increases the quantity. Fig. 3.10(f) combines these two changes. Both the decrease in demand and the increase in supply lower the price, so the price falls. But a decrease in demand decreases the quantity and an increase in supply increases the quantity, so we can't predict the direction in which the quantity will change unless we know the magnitudes of the changes in demand and supply. In the example in Fig. 3.10(f), the quantity does not change. But notice that if demand decreases by slightly more than the amount shown in the figure, the quantity will decrease; if supply increases by slightly more than the amount shown in the figure, the quantity will increase.

Increase in Demand and Decrease in Supply Figure 3.10(h) shows the case in which demand increases and supply decreases. Now, the price rises, and again the direction of the quantity change is uncertain.

REVIEW QUIZ

What is the effect on the price and quantity of MP3 players (such as the iPod) if

1. The price of a PC falls or the price of an MP3 download rises? (Draw the diagrams!)
2. More firms produce MP3 players or electronics workers' wages rise? (Draw the diagrams!)
3. Any two of the events in questions 1 and 2 occur together? (Draw the diagrams!)

You can work these questions in Study Plan 3.5 and get instant feedback.

◆ To complete your study of demand and supply, take a look at *Reading Between the Lines* on pp. 70–71, which explains why the price of coffee increased in 2010. Try to get into the habit of using the demand and supply model to understand the movements in prices in your everyday life.

FIGURE 3.10 The Effects of All the Possible Changes in Demand and Supply

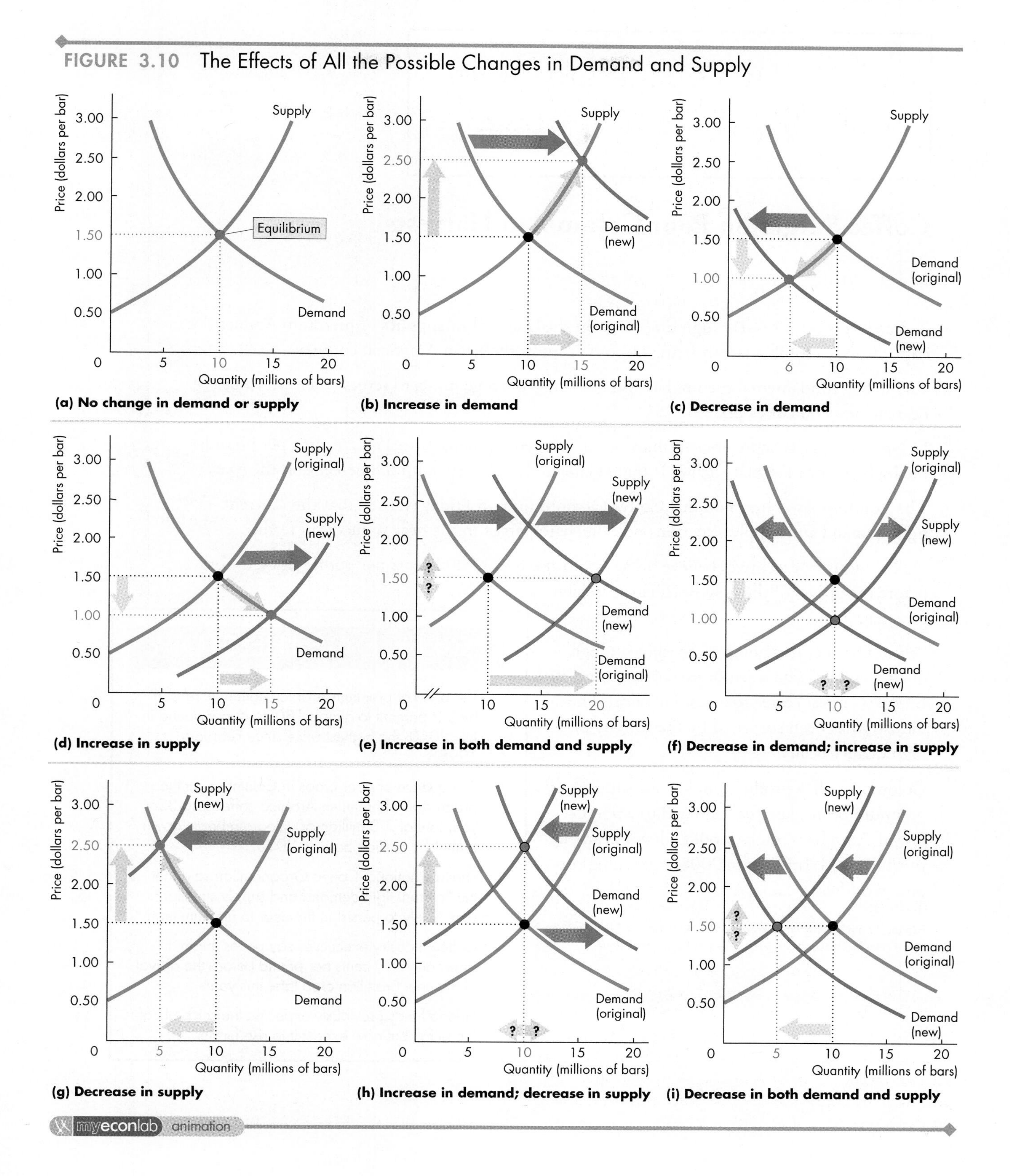

myeconlab animation

Demand and Supply: The Price of Coffee

Coffee Surges on Poor Colombian Harvests

FT.com
July 30, 2010

Coffee prices hit a 12-year high on Friday on the back of low supplies of premium Arabica coffee from Colombia after a string of poor crops in the Latin American country.

The strong fundamental picture has also encouraged hedge funds to reverse their previous bearish views on coffee prices.

In New York, ICE September Arabica coffee jumped 3.2 percent to 178.75 cents per pound, the highest since February 1998. It traded later at 177.25 cents, up 6.8 percent on the week.

The London-based International Coffee Organization on Friday warned that the "current tight demand and supply situation" was "likely to persist in the near to medium term."

Coffee industry executives believe prices could rise toward 200 cents per pound in New York before the arrival of the new Brazilian crop later this year.

"Until October it is going to be tight on high quality coffee," said a senior executive at one of Europe's largest coffee roasters. He said: "The industry has been surprised by the scarcity of high quality beans."

Colombia coffee production, key for supplies of premium beans, last year plunged to a 33-year low of 7.8m bags, each of 60kg, down nearly a third from 11.1m bags in 2008, tightening supplies worldwide. ...

ESSENCE OF THE STORY

- The price of premium Arabica coffee increased by 3.2 percent to almost 180 cents per pound in July 2010, the highest price since February 1998.
- A sequence of poor crops in Columbia cut the production of premium Arabica coffee to a 33-year low of 7.8 million 60 kilogram bags, down from 11.1 million bags in 2008.
- The International Coffee Organization said that the "current tight demand and supply situation" was "likely to persist in the near to medium term."
- Coffee industry executives say prices might approach 200 cents per pound before the arrival of the new Brazilian crop later this year.
- Hedge funds previously expected the price of coffee to fall but now expect it to rise further.

ECONOMIC ANALYSIS

- This news article reports two sources of changes in supply and demand that changed the price of coffee.
- The first source of change is the sequence of poor harvests in Columbia. These events decreased the world supply of Arabica coffee. (Arabica is the type that Starbucks uses.)
- Before the reported events, the world production of Arabica was 120 million bags per year and its price was 174 cents per pound.
- The decrease in the Columbian harvest decreased world production to about 116 million bags, which is about 3 percent of world production.
- Figure 1 shows the situation before the poor Columbia harvests and the effects of those poor harvests. The demand curve is *D* and initially, the supply curve was S^0. The market equilibrium is at 120 million bags per year and a price of 174 cents per pound.
- The poor Columbian harvests decreased supply and the supply curve shifted leftward to S^1. The price increased to 180 cents per pound and the quantity decreased to 116 million bags.
- The second source of change influenced both supply and demand. It is a change in the expected future price of coffee.
- The hedge funds referred to in the news article are speculators that try to profit from buying at a low price and selling at a high price.
- With the supply of coffee expected to remain low, the price was expected to rise further—a rise in the expected future price of coffee.
- When the expected future price of coffee rises, some people want to buy more coffee (so they can sell it later)—an increase in the demand today. And some people offer less coffee for sale (so they can sell it later for a higher price)—a decrease in the supply today.
- Figure 2 shows the effects of these changes in the demand and supply today.
- Demand increased and the demand curve shifted from D^0 to D^1. Supply decreased and the supply curve shifted from S^1 to S^2.
- Because demand increases and supply decreases, the price rises. In this example, it rises to 200 cents per pound.

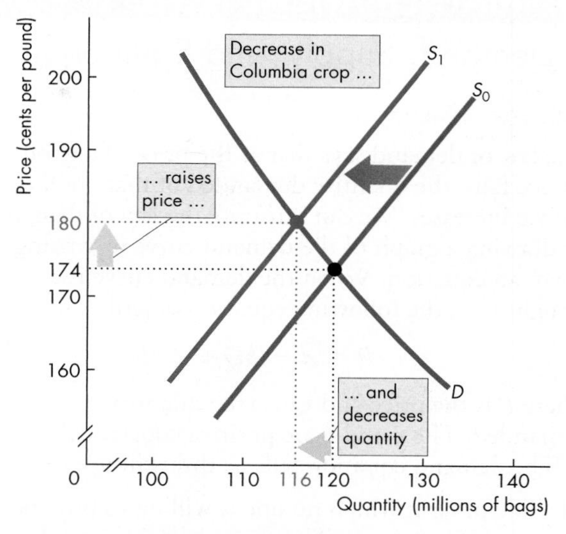

Figure 1 The effects of the Columbian crop

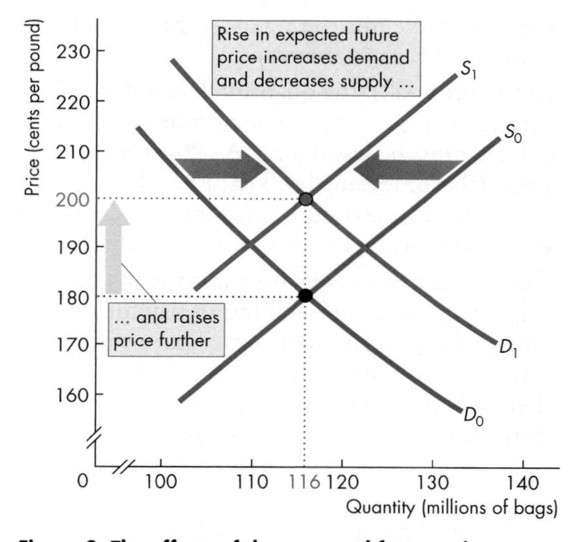

Figure 2 The effects of the expected future price

- Also, because demand increases and supply decreases, the change in the equilibrium quantity can go in either direction.
- In this example, the increase in demand equals the decrease in supply, so the equilibrium quantity remains constant at 116 million bags per year.

MATHEMATICAL NOTE

Demand, Supply, and Equilibrium

Demand Curve

The law of demand says that as the price of a good or service falls, the quantity demanded of that good or service increases. We can illustrate the law of demand by drawing a graph of the demand curve or writing down an equation. When the demand curve is a straight line, the following equation describes it:

$$P = a - bQ_D,$$

where P is the price and Q_D is the quantity demanded. The a and b are positive constants.

The demand equation tells us three things:

1. The price at which no one is willing to buy the good (Q_D is zero). That is, if the price is a, then the quantity demanded is zero. You can see the price a in Fig. 1. It is the price at which the demand curve hits the y-axis—what we call the demand curve's "y-intercept."
2. As the price falls, the quantity demanded increases. If Q_D is a positive number, then the price P must be less than a. As Q_D gets larger, the price P becomes smaller. That is, as the quantity increases, the maximum price that buyers are willing to pay for the last unit of the good falls.
3. The constant b tells us how fast the maximum price that someone is willing to pay for the good falls as the quantity increases. That is, the constant b tells us about the steepness of the demand curve. The equation tells us that the slope of the demand curve is $-b$.

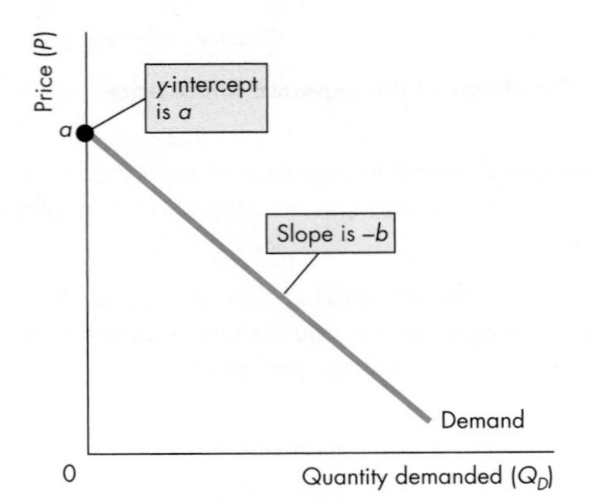

Figure 1 Demand curve

Supply Curve

The law of supply says that as the price of a good or service rises, the quantity supplied of that good or service increases. We can illustrate the law of supply by drawing a graph of the supply curve or writing down an equation. When the supply curve is a straight line, the following equation describes it:

$$P = c + dQ_S,$$

where P is the price and Q_S is the quantity supplied. The c and d are positive constants.

The supply equation tells us three things:

1. The price at which sellers are not willing to supply the good (Q_S is zero). That is, if the price is c, then no one is willing to sell the good. You can see the price c in Fig. 2. It is the price at which the supply curve hits the y-axis—what we call the supply curve's "y-intercept."
2. As the price rises, the quantity supplied increases. If Q_S is a positive number, then the price P must be greater than c. As Q_S increases, the price P becomes larger. That is, as the quantity increases, the minimum price that sellers are willing to accept for the last unit rises.
3. The constant d tells us how fast the minimum price at which someone is willing to sell the good rises as the quantity increases. That is, the constant d tells us about the steepness of the supply curve. The equation tells us that the slope of the supply curve is d.

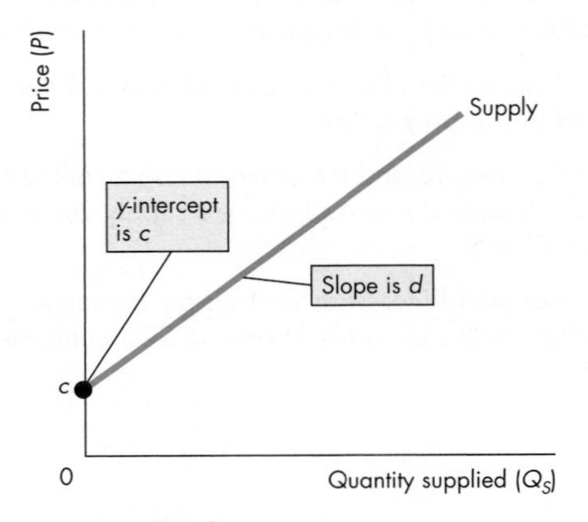

Figure 2 Supply curve

Market Equilibrium

Demand and supply determine market equilibrium. Figure 3 shows the equilibrium price (P^*) and equilibrium quantity (Q^*) at the intersection of the demand curve and the supply curve.

We can use the equations to find the equilibrium price and equilibrium quantity. The price of a good adjusts until the quantity demanded Q_D equals the quantity supplied Q_S. So at the equilibrium price (P^*) and equilibrium quantity (Q^*),

$$Q_D = Q_S = Q^*.$$

To find the equilibrium price and equilibrium quantity, substitute Q^* for Q_D in the demand equation and Q^* for Q_S in the supply equation. Then the price is the equilibrium price (P^*), which gives

$$P^* = a - bQ^*$$
$$P^* = c + dQ^*.$$

Notice that

$$a - bQ^* = c + dQ^*.$$

Now solve for Q^*:

$$a - c = bQ^* + dQ^*$$
$$a - c = (b + d)Q^*$$
$$Q^* = \frac{a - c}{b + d}.$$

To find the equilibrium price, (P^*), substitute for Q^* in either the demand equation or the supply equation.

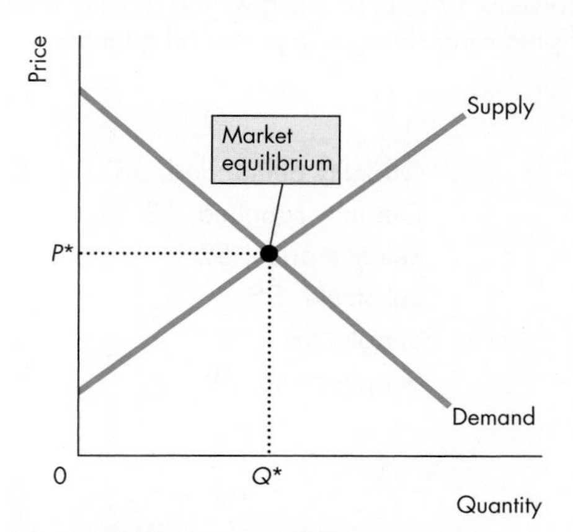

Figure 3 Market equilibrium

Using the demand equation, we have

$$P^* = a - b\left(\frac{a - c}{b + d}\right)$$
$$P^* = \frac{a(b + d) - b(a - c)}{b + d}$$
$$P^* = \frac{ad + bc}{b + d}.$$

Alternatively, using the supply equation, we have

$$P^* = c + d\left(\frac{a - c}{b + d}\right)$$
$$P^* = \frac{c(b + d) + d(a - c)}{b + d}$$
$$P^* = \frac{ad + bc}{b + d}.$$

An Example

The demand for ice-cream cones is

$$P = 800 - 2Q_D.$$

The supply of ice-cream cones is

$$P = 200 + 1Q_S.$$

The price of a cone is expressed in cents, and the quantities are expressed in cones per day.

To find the equilibrium price (P^*) and equilibrium quantity (Q^*), substitute Q^* for Q_D and Q_S and P^* for P. That is,

$$P^* = 800 - 2Q^*$$
$$P^* = 200 + 1Q^*.$$

Now solve for Q^*:

$$800 - 2Q^* = 200 + 1Q^*$$
$$600 = 3Q^*$$
$$Q^* = 200.$$

And

$$P^* = 800 - 2(200)$$
$$= 400.$$

The equilibrium price is \$4 a cone, and the equilibrium quantity is 200 cones per day.

SUMMARY

Key Points

Markets and Prices (p. 52)

- A competitive market is one that has so many buyers and sellers that no single buyer or seller can influence the price.
- Opportunity cost is a relative price.
- Demand and supply determine relative prices.

Working Problem 1 will give you a better understanding of markets and prices.

Demand (pp. 53–57)

- Demand is the relationship between the quantity demanded of a good and its price when all other influences on buying plans remain the same.
- The higher the price of a good, other things remaining the same, the smaller is the quantity demanded—the law of demand.
- Demand depends on the prices of related goods (substitutes and complements), expected future prices, income, expected future income and credit, the population, and preferences.

Working Problems 2 to 5 will give you a better understanding of demand.

Supply (pp. 58–61)

- Supply is the relationship between the quantity supplied of a good and its price when all other influences on selling plans remain the same.
- The higher the price of a good, other things remaining the same, the greater is the quantity supplied—the law of supply.
- Supply depends on the prices of factors of production used to produce a good, the prices of related goods produced, expected future prices, the number of suppliers, technology, and the state of nature.

Working Problems 6 to 9 will give you a better understanding of supply.

Market Equilibrium (pp. 62–63)

- At the equilibrium price, the quantity demanded equals the quantity supplied.
- At any price above the equilibrium price, there is a surplus and the price falls.
- At any price below the equilibrium price, there is a shortage and the price rises.

Working Problems 10 and 11 will give you a better understanding of market equilibrium

Predicting Changes in Price and Quantity (pp. 64–69)

- An increase in demand brings a rise in the price and an increase in the quantity supplied. A decrease in demand brings a fall in the price and a decrease in the quantity supplied.
- An increase in supply brings a fall in the price and an increase in the quantity demanded. A decrease in supply brings a rise in the price and a decrease in the quantity demanded.
- An increase in demand and an increase in supply bring an increased quantity but an uncertain price change. An increase in demand and a decrease in supply bring a higher price but an uncertain change in quantity.

Working Problems 12 and 13 will give you a better understanding of predicting changes in price and quantity.

Key Terms

STUDY PLAN PROBLEMS AND APPLICATIONS

myeconlab You can work Problems 1 to 17 in MyEconLab Chapter 3 Study Plan and get instant feedback.

Markets and Prices (Study Plan 3.1)

1. William Gregg owned a mill in South Carolina. In December 1862, he placed a notice in the *Edgehill Advertiser* announcing his willingness to exchange cloth for food and other items. Here is an extract:

   1 yard of cloth for 1 pound of bacon
   2 yards of cloth for 1 pound of butter
   4 yards of cloth for 1 pound of wool
   8 yards of cloth for 1 bushel of salt

   a. What is the relative price of butter in terms of wool?
   b. If the money price of bacon was 20¢ a pound, what do you predict was the money price of butter?
   c. If the money price of bacon was 20¢ a pound and the money price of salt was $2.00 a bushel, do you think anyone would accept Mr. Gregg's offer of cloth for salt?

Demand (Study Plan 3.2)

2. The price of food increased during the past year.
   a. Explain why the law of demand applies to food just as it does to all other goods and services.
   b. Explain how the substitution effect influences food purchases and provide some examples of substitutions that people might make when the price of food rises and other things remain the same.
   c. Explain how the income effect influences food purchases and provide some examples of the income effect that might occur when the price of food rises and other things remain the same.
3. Place the following goods and services into pairs of likely substitutes and pairs of likely complements. (You may use an item in more than one pair.) The goods and services are

   coal, oil, natural gas, wheat, corn, rye, pasta, pizza, sausage, skateboard, roller blades, video game, laptop, iPod, cell phone, text message, email, phone call, voice mail
4. During 2010, the average income in China increased by 10 percent. Compared to 2009, how do you expect the following would change:
   a. The demand for beef? Explain your answer.
   b. The demand for rice? Explain your answer.
5. In January 2010, the price of gasoline was $2.70 a gallon. By spring 2010, the price had increased to $3.00 a gallon. Assume that there were no changes in average income, population, or any other influence on buying plans. Explain how the rise in the price of gasoline would affect
   a. The demand for gasoline.
   b. The quantity of gasoline demanded.

Supply (Study Plan 3.3)

6. In 2008, the price of corn increased by 35 percent and some cotton farmers in Texas stopped growing cotton and started to grow corn.
   a. Does this fact illustrate the law of demand or the law of supply? Explain your answer.
   b. Why would a cotton farmer grow corn?

Use the following information to work Problems 7 to 9.

Dairies make low-fat milk from full-cream milk. In the process of making low-fat milk, the dairies produce cream, which is made into ice cream. In the market for low-fat milk, the following events occur one at a time:

(i) The wage rate of dairy workers rises.
(ii) The price of cream rises.
(iii) The price of low-fat milk rises.
(iv) With the period of low rainfall extending, dairies raise their expected price of low-fat milk next year.
(v) With advice from health-care experts, dairy farmers decide to switch from producing full-cream milk to growing vegetables.
(vi) A new technology lowers the cost of producing ice cream.

7. Explain the effect of each event on the supply of low-fat milk.
8. Use a graph to illustrate the effect of each event.
9. Does any event (or events) illustrate the law of supply?

Market Equilibrium (Study Plan 3.4)

10. "As more people buy computers, the demand for Internet service increases and the price of Internet service decreases. The fall in the price of Internet service decreases the supply of Internet service." Explain what is wrong with this statement.
11. The demand and supply schedules for gum are

Price (cents per pack)	Quantity demanded (millions of packs a week)	Quantity supplied (millions of packs a week)
20	180	60
40	140	100
60	100	140
80	60	180
100	20	220

   a. Draw a graph of the market for gum and mark in the equilibrium price and quantity.
   b. Suppose that the price of gum is 70¢ a pack. Describe the situation in the gum market and explain how the price adjusts.
   c. Suppose that the price of gum is 30¢ a pack. Describe the situation in the gum market and explain how the price adjusts.

Predicting Changes in Price and Quantity (Study Plan 3.5)

12. The following events occur one at a time:
    (i) The price of crude oil rises.
    (ii) The price of a car rises.
    (iii) All speed limits on highways are abolished.
    (iv) Robots cut car production costs.
    Which of these events will increase or decrease (state which occurs)
    a. The demand for gasoline?
    b. The supply of gasoline?
    c. The quantity of gasoline demanded?
    d. The quantity of gasoline supplied?
13. In Problem 11, a fire destroys some factories that produce gum and the quantity of gum supplied decreases by 40 million packs a week at each price.
    a. Explain what happens in the market for gum and draw a graph to illustrate the changes.
    b. If at the time the fire occurs there is an increase in the teenage population, which increases the quantity of gum demanded by 40 million packs a week at each price, what are the new equilibrium price and quantity of gum? Illustrate these changes on your graph.

Economics in the News (Study Plan 3.N)

14. **American to Cut Flights, Charge for Luggage**
    American Airlines announced yesterday that it will begin charging passengers $15 for their first piece of checked luggage, in addition to raising other fees and cutting domestic flights as it grapples with record-high fuel prices.
    Source: *Boston Herald*, May 22, 2008
    a. According to the news clip, what is the influence on the supply of American Airlines flights?
    b. Explain how supply changes.
15. **Of Gambling, Grannies, and Good Sense**
    Nevada has plenty of jobs for the over 50s and its elderly population is growing faster than that in other states.
    Source: *The Economist*, July 26, 2006
    Explain how grannies have influenced:
    a. The demand in some Las Vegas markets.
    b. The supply in other Las Vegas markets.
16. **Frigid Florida Winter is Bad News for Tomato Lovers**
    An unusually cold January in Florida destroyed entire fields of tomatoes and forced many farmers to delay their harvest. Florida's growers are shipping only a quarter of their usual 5 million pounds a week. The price has risen from $6.50 for a 25-pound box a year ago to $30 now.
    Source: *USA Today*, March 3, 2010
    a. Make a graph to illustrate the market for tomatoes in January 2009 and January 2010.
    b. On the graph, show how the events in the news clip influence the market for tomatoes.
    c. Why is the news "bad for tomato lovers"?
17. **Pump Prices on Pace to Top 2009 High by Weekend**
    The cost of filling up the car is rising as the crude oil price soars and pump prices may exceed the peak price of 2009.
    Source: *USA Today*, January 7, 2010
    a. Does demand for gasoline or the supply of gasoline or both change when the price of oil soars?
    b. Use a demand-supply graph to illustrate what happens to the equilibrium price of gasoline and the equilibrium quantity of gasoline bought when the price of oil soars.

ADDITIONAL PROBLEMS AND APPLICATIONS

myeconlab You can work these problems in MyEconLab if assigned by your instructor.

Markets and Prices

18. What features of the world market for crude oil make it a competitive market?
19. The money price of a textbook is $90 and the money price of the Wii game *Super Mario Galaxy* is $45.
    a. What is the opportunity cost of a textbook in terms of the Wii game?
    b. What is the relative price of the Wii game in terms of textbooks?

Demand

20. The price of gasoline has increased during the past year.
    a. Explain why the law of demand applies to gasoline just as it does to all other goods and services.
    b. Explain how the substitution effect influences gasoline purchases and provide some examples of substitutions that people might make when the price of gasoline rises and other things remain the same.
    c. Explain how the income effect influences gasoline purchases and provide some examples of the income effects that might occur when the price of gasoline rises and other things remain the same.
21. Think about the demand for the three game consoles: Xbox, PS3, and Wii. Explain the effect of the following events on the demand for Xbox games and the quantity of Xbox games demanded, other things remaining the same.
    a. The price of an Xbox falls.
    b. The prices of a PS3 and a Wii fall.
    c. The number of people writing and producing Xbox games increases.
    d. Consumers' incomes increase.
    e. Programmers who write code for Xbox games become more costly to hire.
    f. The expected future price of an Xbox game falls.
    g. A new game console that is a close substitute for Xbox comes onto the market.

Supply

22. Classify the following pairs of goods and services as substitutes in production, complements in production, or neither.
    a. Bottled water and health club memberships
    b. French fries and baked potatoes
    c. Leather purses and leather shoes
    d. Hybrids and SUVs
    e. Diet coke and regular coke
23. As the prices of homes fell across the United States in 2008, the number of homes offered for sale decreased.
    a. Does this fact illustrate the law of demand or the law of supply? Explain your answer.
    b. Why would home owners decide not to sell?
24. **G.M. Cuts Production for Quarter**
    General Motors cut its fourth-quarter production schedule by 10 percent because Ford Motor, Chrysler, and Toyota sales declined in August.
    Source: *The New York Times*, September 5, 2007
    Explain whether this news clip illustrates a change in the supply of cars or a change in the quantity supplied of cars.

Market Equilibrium

Use the following figure to work Problems 25 and 26.

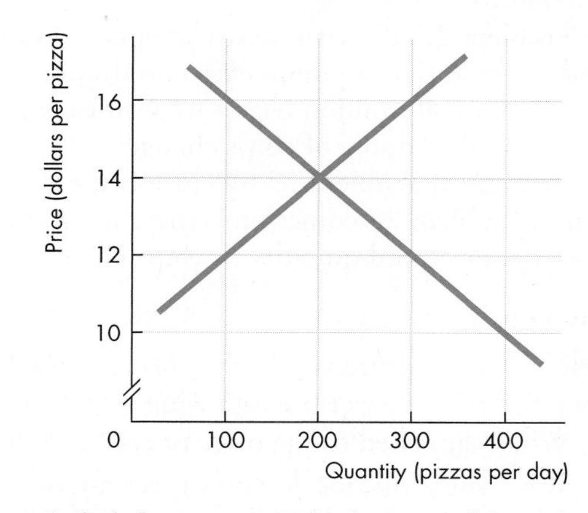

25. a. Label the curves. Which curve shows the willingness to pay for a pizza?
    b. If the price of a pizza is $16, is there a shortage or a surplus and does the price rise or fall?

c. Sellers want to receive the highest possible price, so why would they be willing to accept less than $16 a pizza?

26. a. If the price of a pizza is $12, is there a shortage or a surplus and does the price rise or fall?
b. Buyers want to pay the lowest possible price, so why would they be willing to pay more than $12 for a pizza?

27. The demand and supply schedules for potato chips are

Price (cents per bag)	Quantity demanded (millions of bags per week)	Quantity supplied (millions of bags per week)
50	160	130
60	150	140
70	140	150
80	130	160
90	120	170
100	110	180

a. Draw a graph of the potato chip market and mark in the equilibrium price and quantity.
b. If the price is 60¢ a bag, is there a shortage or a surplus, and how does the price adjust?

Predicting Changes in Price and Quantity

28. In Problem 27, a new dip increases the quantity of potato chips that people want to buy by 30 million bags per week at each price.
a. How does the demand and/or supply of chips change?
b. How does the price and quantity of chips change?

29. In Problem 27, if a virus destroys potato crops and the quantity of potato chips produced decreases by 40 million bags a week at each price, how does the supply of chips change?

30. If the virus in Problem 29 hits just as the new dip in Problem 28 comes onto the market, how does the price and quantity of chips change?

Economics in the News

31. After you have studied *Reading Between the Lines* on pp. 70–71 answer the following questions.
a. What happened to the price of coffee in 2010?
b. What substitutions do you expect might have been made to decrease the quantity of coffee demanded?
c. What influenced the demand for coffee in 2010 and what influenced the quantity of coffee demanded?
d. What influenced the supply of coffee during 2010 and how did the supply of coffee change?
e. How did the combination of the factors you have noted in parts (c) and (d) influence the price and quantity of coffee?
f. Was the change in quantity of coffee a change in the quantity demanded or a change in the quantity supplied?

32. **Strawberry Prices Drop as Late Harvest Hits Market**
Shoppers bought strawberries in March for $1.25 a pound rather than the $3.49 a pound they paid last year. With the price so low, some growers plowed over their strawberry plants to make way for spring melons; others froze their harvests and sold them to juice and jam makers.
Source: *USA Today*, April 5, 2010
a. Explain how the market for strawberries would have changed if growers had not plowed in their plants but offered locals "you pick for free."
b. Describe the changes in demand and supply in the market for strawberry jam.

33. **"Popcorn Movie" Experience Gets Pricier**
Cinemas are raising the price of popcorn. Demand for field corn, which is used for animal feed, corn syrup, and ethanol, has increased and its price has exploded. That's caused some farmers to shift from growing popcorn to easier-to-grow field corn.
Source: *USA Today*, May 24, 2008
Explain and illustrate graphically the events described in the news clip in the market for
a. Popcorn
b. Movie tickets

Use the following news clip to work Problems 34 and 35.

Sony's Blu-Ray Wins High-Definition War
Toshiba Corp. yesterday withdrew from the race to be the next-generation home movie format, leaving Sony Corp.'s Blu-ray technology the winner. The move could finally jump-start a high-definition home DVD market.
Source: *The Washington Times*, February 20, 2008

34. a. How would you expect the price of a used Toshiba player on eBay to change? Will the price change result from a change in demand, supply, or both, and in which directions?
b. How would you expect the price of a Blu-ray player to change?

35. Explain how the market for Blu-ray format movies will change.

PART ONE

UNDERSTANDING THE SCOPE OF ECONOMICS

Your Economic Revolution

Three periods in human history stand out as ones of economic revolution. The first, the *Agricultural Revolution,* occurred 10,000 years ago. In what is today Iraq, people learned to domesticate animals and plant crops. People stopped roaming in search of food and settled in villages, towns, and cities where they specialized in the activities in which they had a comparative advantage and developed markets in which to exchange their products. Wealth increased enormously.

You are studying economics at a time that future historians will call the *Information Revolution*. Over the entire world, people are embracing new information technologies and prospering on an unprecedented scale.

Economics was born during the *Industrial Revolution,* which began in England during the 1760s. For the first time, people began to apply science and create new technologies for the manufacture of textiles and iron, to create steam engines, and to boost the output of farms.

During all three economic revolutions, many have prospered but many have been left behind. It is the range of human progress that poses the greatest question for economics and the one that Adam Smith addressed in the first work of economic science: What causes the differences in wealth among nations?

Many people had written about economics before **Adam Smith**, *but he made economics a science. Born in 1723 in Kirkcaldy, a small fishing town near Edinburgh, Scotland, Smith was the only child of the town's customs officer. Lured from his professorship (he was a full professor at 28) by a wealthy Scottish duke who gave him a pension of £300 a year—ten times the average income at that time—Smith devoted ten years to writing his masterpiece:* An Inquiry into the Nature and Causes of the **Wealth of Nations**, *published in 1776.*

Why, Adam Smith asked , are some nations wealthy while others are poor? He was pondering these questions at the height of the Industrial Revolution, and he answered by emphasizing the role of the division of labor and free markets.

To illustrate his argument, Adam Smith described two pin factories. In the first, one person, using the hand tools available in the 1770s, could make 20 pins a day. In the other, by using those same hand tools but breaking the process into a number of individually small operations in which people specialize—by the division of labor*—ten people could make a staggering 48,000 pins a day. One draws out the wire, another straightens it, a third cuts it, a fourth points it, a fifth grinds it. Three specialists make the head, and a fourth attaches it. Finally, the pin is polished and packaged.*

But a large market is needed to support the division of labor: One factory employing ten workers would need to sell more than 15 million pins a year to stay in business!

"It is not from the benevolence of the butcher, the brewer, or the baker that we expect our dinner, but from their regard to their own interest."

ADAM SMITH
The Wealth of Nations

TALKING WITH **Jagdish Bhagwati**

Professor Bhagwati, what attracted you to economics?

When you come from India, where poverty hits the eye, it is easy to be attracted to economics, which can be used to bring prosperity and create jobs to pull up the poor into gainful employment.

I learned later that there are two broad types of economist: those who treat the subject as an arid mathematical toy and those who see it as a serious social science.

If Cambridge, where I went as an undergraduate, had been interested in esoteric mathematical economics, I would have opted for something else. But the Cambridge economists from whom I learned—many among the greatest figures in the discipline—saw economics as a social science. I therefore saw the power of economics as a tool to address India's poverty and was immediately hooked.

Who had the greatest impact on you at Cambridge?

Most of all, it was Harry Johnson, a young Canadian of immense energy and profound analytical gifts. Quite unlike the shy and reserved British dons, Johnson was friendly, effusive, and supportive of students who flocked around him. He would later move to Chicago, where he became one of the most influential members of the market-oriented Chicago school. Another was Joan Robinson, arguably the world's most impressive female economist.

When I left Cambridge for MIT, going from one Cambridge to the other, I was lucky to transition from one phenomenal set of economists to another. At MIT, I learned much from future Nobel laureates Paul Samuelson and Robert Solow. Both would later become great friends and colleagues when I joined the MIT faculty in 1968.

After Cambridge and MIT, you went to Oxford and then back to India. What did you do in India?

I joined the Planning Commission in New Delhi, where my first big job was to find ways of raising the bottom 30 percent of India's population out of poverty to a "minimum income" level.

And what did you prescribe?

My main prescription was to "grow the pie." My research suggested that the share of the bottom 30 percent of the pie did not seem to vary dramatically with differences in economic and political systems. So growth in the pie seemed to be the principal (but not the only) component of an anti-poverty strategy. To supplement growth's good effects on the poor, the Indian planners were also dedicated to education, health, social reforms, and land reforms. Also, the access of the lowest-income and socially disadvantaged groups to the growth process and its benefits was to be improved in many ways, such as extension of credit without collateral.

My main prescription was to "grow the pie" ... Much empirical work shows that where growth has occurred, poverty has lessened.

Today, this strategy has no rivals. Much empirical work shows that where growth has occurred, poverty has lessened. It is nice to know that one's basic take on an issue of such central importance to humanity's well-being has been borne out by experience!

You left India in 1968 to come to the United States and an academic job at MIT. Why?

While the decision to emigrate often reflects personal factors—and they were present in my case—the offer of a professorship from MIT certainly helped me

JAGDISH BHAGWATI is University Professor at Columbia University. Born in India in 1934, he studied at Cambridge University in England, MIT, and Oxford University before returning to India. He returned to teach at MIT in 1968 and moved to Columbia in 1980. A prolific scholar, Professor Bhagwati also writes in leading newspapers and magazines throughout the world. He has been much honored for both his scientific work and his impact on public policy. His greatest contributions are in international trade but extend also to developmental problems and the study of political economy.

Michael Parkin talked with Jagdish Bhagwati about his work and the progress that economists have made in understanding the benefits of economic growth and international trade since the pioneering work of Adam Smith.

make up my mind. At the time, it was easily the world's most celebrated department. Serendipitously, the highest-ranked departments at MIT were not in engineering and the sciences but in linguistics (which had Noam Chomsky) and economics (which had Paul Samuelson). Joining the MIT faculty was a dramatic breakthrough: I felt stimulated each year by several fantastic students and by several of the world's most creative economists.

We hear a lot in the popular press about fair trade and level playing fields. What's the distinction between free trade and fair trade? How can the playing field be unlevel?

Free trade simply means allowing no trade barriers such as tariffs, subsidies, and quotas. Trade barriers make domestic prices different from world prices for traded goods. When this happens, resources are not being used efficiently. Basic economics from the time of Adam Smith tells us why free trade is good for us and why barriers to trade harm us, though our understanding of this doctrine today is far more nuanced and profound than it was at its creation.

Fair trade, on the other hand, is almost always a sneaky way of objecting to free trade. If your rivals are hard to compete with, you are not likely to get protection simply by saying that you cannot hack it. But if you say that your rival is an "unfair" trader, that is an easier sell! As international competition has grown fiercer, cries of "unfair trade" have therefore multiplied. The lesser rogues among the protectionists ask for "free and fair trade," whereas the worst ones ask for "fair, not free, trade."

Fair trade ... is almost always a sneaky way of objecting to free trade.

At the end of World War II, the General Agreement on Tariffs and Trade (GATT) was established and there followed several rounds of multilateral trade negotiations and reductions in barriers to trade. How do you assess the contribution of GATT and its successor, the World Trade Organization (WTO)?

The GATT has made a huge contribution by overseeing massive trade liberalization in industrial goods among the developed countries. GATT rules, which "bind" tariffs to negotiated ceilings, prevent the raising of tariffs and have prevented tariff wars like those of the 1930s in which mutual and retaliatory tariff barriers were raised, to the detriment of everyone.

The GATT was folded into the WTO at the end of the Uruguay Round of trade negotiations, and the WTO is institutionally stronger. For instance, it has a binding dispute settlement mechanism, whereas the GATT had no such teeth. It is also more ambitious in its scope, extending to new areas such as the environment, intellectual property protection, and investment rules.

Running alongside the pursuit of multilateral free trade has been the emergence of bilateral trade agreements such as NAFTA and the European Union (EU). How do you view the bilateral free trade areas in today's world?

Unfortunately, there has been an explosion of bilateral free trade areas today. By some estimates, the ones in place and others being plotted approach 400! Each bilateral agreement gives preferential treatment to its trading partner over others. Because there are now so many bilateral agreements, such as those between the United States and Israel and between the United States and Jordan, the result is a chaotic pattern of different tariffs depending on where a product comes from. Also, "rules of origin" must be agreed upon to determine whether a product is, say, Jordanian or Taiwanese if Jordan qualifies for a preferential tariff but Taiwan does not and Taiwanese inputs enter the Jordanian manufacture of the product.

I have called the resulting crisscrossing of preferences and rules of origin the "spaghetti bowl" problem. The world trading system is choking under these proliferating bilateral deals. Contrast this complexity with the simplicity of a multilateral system with common tariffs for all WTO members.

We now have a world of uncoordinated and inefficient trade policies. The EU makes bilateral free trade agreements with different non-EU countries, so the United States follows with its own bilateral agreements; and with Europe and the United States doing it, the Asian countries, long wedded to multilateralism, have now succumbed to the mania.

We now have a world of uncoordinated and inefficient trade policies.

Instead, if the United States had provided leadership by rewriting rules to make the signing of such bilateral agreements extremely difficult, this plague on the trading system today might well have been averted.

Is the "spaghetti bowl" problem getting better or worse?

Unquestionably it is getting worse. Multilateralism is retreating and bilateralism is advancing. The 2010 G-20 meeting in Canada was a disappointment. At the insistence of the United States, a definite date for completing the Doha Round was dropped and instead, unwittingly rubbing salt into the wound, President Barack Obama announced his administration's willingness to see the U.S.-South Korea free trade agreement through. There are distressing recent reports that the U.S. Commerce Department is exploring ways to strengthen the bite of anti-dumping actions, which are now generally agreed to be a form of discriminatory protectionism aimed selectively at successful exporting nations and firms. Equally distressing is Obama's decision to sign a bill that raises fees on some temporary work visas in order to pay for higher border-enforcement expenditures.Further, it was asserted that a tax on foreign workers would reduce the numbers coming in and "taking jobs away" from U.S. citizens. Many supporters of the proposal claimed, incoherently, that it would simultaneously discourage foreign workers from entering the United States and increase revenues.Obama's surrender exemplified the doctrine that one retreat often leads to another, with new lobbyists following in others' footsteps. Perhaps the chief mistake, as with recent "Buy American" provisions in U.S. legislation, was to allow the Employ American Workers Act (EAWA) to be folded into the stimulus bill. This act makes it harder for companies to get govern-mental support to hire skilled immigrants with H1(b) visas: They must first show that they have not laid off or plan to lay off U.S. workers in similar occupations. Whatever the shortcomings of such measures in economic-policy terms, the visa-fee-enhancement provision is de facto discriminatory, and thus violates WTO rules against discrimination between domestic and foreign firms, or between foreign firms from different WTO countries. While the visa-fee legislation is what lawyers call "facially" non-discriminatory, its design confers an advantage on U.S. firms vis-à-vis foreign firms.Such acts of discrimination in trade policies find succor in the media and in some of America's prominent think tanks. For example, in the wake of the vast misery brought by flooding to the people of Pakistan, the U.S. and other governments have risen to the occasion with emergency aid. But there have also been proposals to grant duty-free access to Pakistan's exports. But this would be discriminatory toward developing countries that do not have duty-free access, helping Pakistan at their expense.

What advice do you have for a student who is just starting to study economics? Is economics a good subject in which to major?

I would say: enormously so. In particular, we economists bring three unique insights to good policy making.

First, economists look for second- and subsequent-round effects of actions.

Second, we correctly emphasize that a policy cannot be judged without using a counterfactual. It is a witticism that an economist, when asked how her husband was, said, "compared to what?"

Third, we uniquely and systematically bring the principle of social cost and social benefit to our policy analysis.

4

MEASURING GDP AND ECONOMIC GROWTH

Will our economy expand more rapidly in 2011 or will it sink into another recession—a "double-dip"? Many U.S. corporations wanted to know the answers to these questions at the beginning of 2011. Google wanted to know whether to expand its server network and introduce new services or hold off on any new launches. Amazon.com wanted to know whether to increase its warehousing facilities. To assess the state of the economy and to make big decisions about business expansion, firms such as Google and Amazon use forecasts of GDP. What exactly is GDP and what does it tell us about the state of the economy?

Some countries are rich while others are poor. How do we compare economic well-being in one country with that in another? How can we make international comparisons of production?

In this chapter, you will find out how economic statisticians at the Bureau of Economic Analysis measure GDP and the economic growth rate. You will also learn about the uses and the limitations of these measures. In *Reading Between the Lines* at the end of the chapter, we'll look at some future scenarios for the U.S. economy.

Gross Domestic Product

What exactly is GDP, how is it calculated, what does it mean, and why do we care about it? You are going to discover the answers to these questions in this chapter. First, what *is* GDP?

GDP Defined

GDP, or **gross domestic product**, is the market value of the final goods and services produced within a country in a given time period. This definition has four parts:

- Market value
- Final goods and services
- Produced within a country
- In a given time period

We'll examine each in turn.

Market Value To measure total production, we must add together the production of apples and oranges, computers and popcorn. Just counting the items doesn't get us very far. For example, which is the greater total production: 100 apples and 50 oranges or 50 apples and 100 oranges?

GDP answers this question by valuing items at their *market values*—the prices at which items are traded in markets. If the price of an apple is 10 cents, then the market value of 50 apples is $5. If the price of an orange is 20 cents, then the market value of 100 oranges is $20. By using market prices to value production, we can add the apples and oranges together. The market value of 50 apples and 100 oranges is $5 plus $20, or $25.

Final Goods and Services To calculate GDP, we value the *final goods and services* produced. A **final good** (or service) is an item that is bought by its final user during a specified time period. It contrasts with an **intermediate good** (or service), which is an item that is produced by one firm, bought by another firm, and used as a component of a final good or service.

For example, a Ford truck is a final good, but a Firestone tire on the truck is an intermediate good. A Dell computer is a final good, but an Intel Pentium chip inside it is an intermediate good.

If we were to add the value of intermediate goods and services produced to the value of final goods and services, we would count the same thing many times—a problem called *double counting*. The value of a truck already includes the value of the tires, and the value of a Dell PC already includes the value of the Pentium chip inside it.

Some goods can be an intermediate good in some situations and a final good in other situations. For example, the ice cream that you buy on a hot summer day is a final good, but the ice cream that a restaurant buys and uses to make sundaes is an intermediate good. The sundae is the final good. So whether a good is an intermediate good or a final good depends on what it is used for, not what it is.

Some items that people buy are neither final goods nor intermediate goods and they are not part of GDP. Examples of such items include financial assets—stocks and bonds—and secondhand goods—used cars or existing homes. A secondhand good was part of GDP in the year in which it was produced, but not in GDP this year.

Produced Within a Country Only goods and services that are produced *within a country* count as part of that country's GDP. Nike Corporation, a U.S. firm, produces sneakers in Vietnam, and the market value of those shoes is part of Vietnam's GDP, not part of U.S. GDP. Toyota, a Japanese firm, produces automobiles in Georgetown, Kentucky, and the value of this production is part of U.S. GDP, not part of Japan's GDP.

In a Given Time Period GDP measures the value of production *in a given time period*—normally either a quarter of a year—called the quarterly GDP data—or a year—called the annual GDP data.

GDP measures not only the value of total production but also total income and total expenditure. The equality between the value of total production and total income is important because it shows the direct link between productivity and living standards. Our standard of living rises when our incomes rise and we can afford to buy more goods and services. But we must produce more goods and services if we are to be able to buy more goods and services.

Rising incomes and a rising value of production go together. They are two aspects of the same phenomenon: increasing productivity. To see why, we study the circular flow of expenditure and income.

GDP and the Circular Flow of Expenditure and Income

Figure 4.1 illustrates the circular flow of expenditure and income. The economy consists of households, firms, governments, and the rest of the world (the rectangles), which trade in factor markets and goods (and services) markets. We focus first on households and firms.

Households and Firms Households sell and firms buy the services of labor, capital, and land in factor markets. For these factor services, firms pay income to households: wages for labor services, interest for the use of capital, and rent for the use of land. A fourth factor of production, entrepreneurship, receives profit.

Firms' retained earnings—profits that are not distributed to households—are part of the household sector's income. You can think of retained earnings as being income that households save and lend back to firms. Figure 4.1 shows the total income—*aggregate income*—received by households, including retained earnings, as the blue flow labeled *Y*.

Firms sell and households buy consumer goods and services—such as inline skates and haircuts—in the goods market. The total payment for these goods and services is **consumption expenditure**, shown by the red flow labeled *C*.

Firms buy and sell new capital equipment—such as computer systems, airplanes, trucks, and assembly line equipment—in the goods market. Some of what firms produce is not sold but is added to inventory. For example, if GM produces 1,000 cars and sells 950 of them, the other 50 cars remain in GM's inventory of unsold cars, which increases by 50 cars. When a firm adds unsold output to inventory, we can think of the firm as buying goods from itself. The

FIGURE 4.1 The Circular Flow of Expenditure and Income

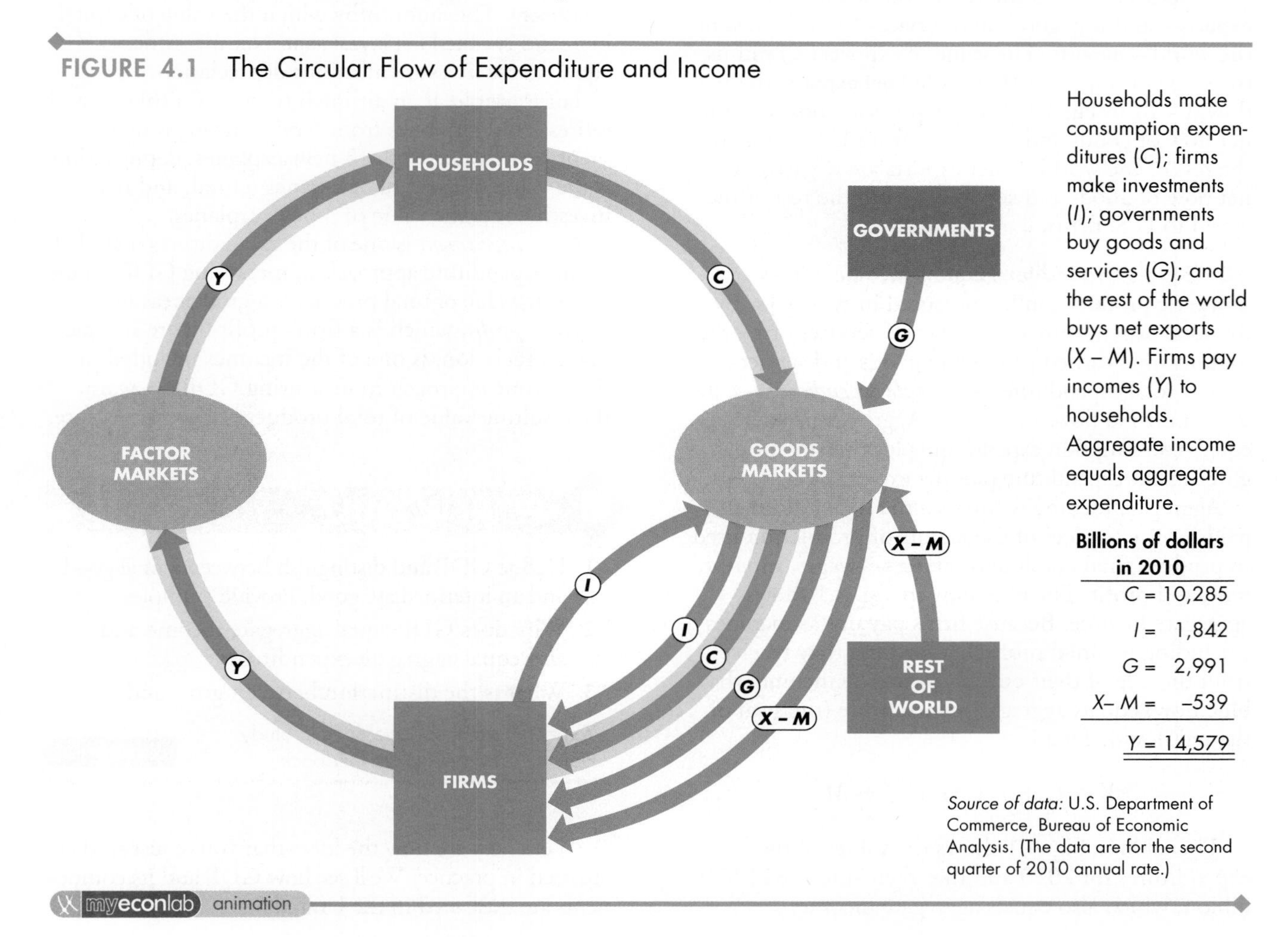

Households make consumption expenditures (*C*); firms make investments (*I*); governments buy goods and services (*G*); and the rest of the world buys net exports (*X* – *M*). Firms pay incomes (*Y*) to households. Aggregate income equals aggregate expenditure.

Billions of dollars in 2010	
C =	10,285
I =	1,842
G =	2,991
X – *M* =	–539
Y =	14,579

Source of data: U.S. Department of Commerce, Bureau of Economic Analysis. (The data are for the second quarter of 2010 annual rate.)

myeconlab animation

purchase of new plant, equipment, and buildings and the additions to inventories are **investment**, shown by the red flow labeled *I*.

Governments Governments buy goods and services from firms and their expenditure on goods and services is called **government expenditure**. In Fig. 4.1, government expenditure is shown as the red flow *G*.

Governments finance their expenditure with taxes. But taxes are not part of the circular flow of expenditure and income. Governments also make financial transfers to households, such as Social Security benefits and unemployment benefits, and pay subsidies to firms. These financial transfers, like taxes, are not part of the circular flow of expenditure and income.

Rest of the World Firms in the United States sell goods and services to the rest of the world—**exports**—and buy goods and services from the rest of the world—**imports**. The value of exports (X) minus the value of imports (M) is called **net exports**, the red flow $X - M$ in Fig 4.1. If net exports are positive, the net flow of goods and services is from U.S. firms to the rest of the world. If net exports are negative, the net flow of goods and services is from the rest of the world to U.S. firms.

GDP Equals Expenditure Equals Income Gross domestic product can be measured in two ways: By the total expenditure on goods and services or by the total income earned producing goods and services.

The total expenditure—*aggregate expenditure*—is the sum of the red flows in Fig. 4.1. Aggregate expenditure equals consumption expenditure plus investment plus government expenditure plus net exports.

Aggregate income is equal to the total amount paid for the services of the factors of production used to produce final goods and services—wages, interest, rent, and profit. The blue flow in Fig. 4.1 shows aggregate income. Because firms pay out as incomes (including retained profits) everything they receive from the sale of their output, aggregate income (the blue flow) equals aggregate expenditure (the sum of the red flows). That is,

$$Y = C + I + G + X - M.$$

The table in Fig. 4.1 shows the values of the expenditures for 2010 and that their sum is $14,579 billion, which also equals aggregate income.

Because aggregate expenditure equals aggregate income, the two methods of measuring GDP give the same answer. So

GDP equals aggregate expenditure and equals aggregate income.

The circular flow model is the foundation on which the national economic accounts are built.

Why Is Domestic Product "Gross"?

"Gross" means before subtracting the depreciation of capital. The opposite of "gross" is "net," which means after subtracting the depreciation of capital.

Depreciation is the decrease in the value of a firm's capital that results from wear and tear and obsolescence. The total amount spent both buying new capital and replacing depreciated capital is called **gross investment**. The amount by which the value of capital increases is called **net investment**. Net investment equals gross investment minus depreciation.

For example, if an airline buys 5 new airplanes and retires 2 old airplanes from service, its gross investment is the value of the 5 new airplanes, depreciation is the value of the 2 old airplanes retired, and net investment is the value of 3 new airplanes.

Gross investment is one of the expenditures included in the expenditure approach to measuring GDP. So the resulting value of total product is a gross measure.

Gross profit, which is a firm's profit before subtracting depreciation, is one of the incomes included in the income approach to measuring GDP. So again, the resulting value of total product is a gross measure.

REVIEW QUIZ

1. Define GDP and distinguish between a final good and an intermediate good. Provide examples.
2. Why does GDP equal aggregate income and also equal aggregate expenditure?
3. What is the distinction between gross and net?

You can work these questions in Study Plan 4.1 and get instant feedback.

Let's now see how the ideas that you've just studied are used in practice. We'll see how GDP and its components are measured in the United States today.

Measuring U.S. GDP

The Bureau of Economic Analysis (BEA) uses the concepts in the circular flow model to measure GDP and its components in the *National Income and Product Accounts.* Because the value of aggregate production equals aggregate expenditure and aggregate income, there are two approaches available for measuring GDP, and both are used. They are

- The expenditure approach
- The income approach

The Expenditure Approach

The *expenditure approach* measures GDP as the sum of consumption expenditure (C), investment (I), government expenditure on goods and services (G), and net exports of goods and services ($X - M$). These expenditures correspond to the red flows through the goods markets in the circular flow model in Fig. 4.1. Table 4.1 shows these expenditures and GDP for 2010. The table uses the terms in the *National Income and Product Accounts.*

Personal consumption expenditures are the expenditures by U.S. households on goods and services produced in the United States and in the rest of the world. They include goods such as soda and books and services such as banking and legal advice. They also include the purchase of consumer durable goods, such as TVs and microwave ovens. But they do *not* include the purchase of new homes, which the BEA counts as part of investment.

Gross private domestic investment is expenditure on capital equipment and buildings by firms and the additions to business inventories. It also includes expenditure on new homes by households.

Government expenditure on goods and services is the expenditure by all levels of government on goods and services, such as national defense and garbage collection. It does *not* include *transfer payments*, such as unemployment benefits, because they are not expenditures on goods and services.

Net exports of goods and services are the value of exports minus the value of imports. This item includes airplanes that Boeing sells to British Airways (a U.S. export), and Japanese DVD players that Circuit City buys from Sony (a U.S. import).

Table 4.1 shows the relative magnitudes of the four items of aggregate expenditure.

TABLE 4.1 GDP: The Expenditure Approach

Item	Symbol	Amount in 2010 (billions of dollars)	Percentage of GDP
Personal consumption expenditures	C	10,285	70.5
Gross private domestic investment	I	1,842	12.6
Government expenditure on goods and services	G	2,991	20.5
Net exports of goods and services	$X - M$	–539	–3.7
Gross domestic product	Y	**14,579**	**100.0**

The expenditure approach measures GDP as the sum of personal consumption expenditures (C), gross private domestic investment (I), government expenditure on goods and services (G), and net exports ($X - M$). In 2010, GDP measured by the expenditure approach was $14,579 billion. More than two thirds of aggregate expenditure is on personal consumption goods and services.

Source of data: U.S. Department of Commerce, Bureau of Economic Analysis.

The Income Approach

The *income approach* measures GDP by summing the incomes that firms pay households for the services of the factors of production they hire—wages for labor, interest for capital, rent for land, and profit for entrepreneurship. These incomes correspond to the blue flow through the factor markets in the circular flow model in Fig. 4.1.

The *National Income and Product Accounts* divide incomes into two big categories:

1. Compensation of employees
2. Net operating surplus

Compensation of employees is the payment for labor services. It includes net wages and salaries (called "take-home pay") that workers receive plus taxes withheld on earnings plus fringe benefits such as Social Security and pension fund contributions.

Net operating surplus is the sum of all other factor incomes. It has four components: *net interest, rental income*, *corporate profits*, and *proprietors' income*.

Net interest is the interest households receive on loans they make minus the interest households pay on their own borrowing.

Rental income is the payment for the use of land and other rented resources.

Corporate profits are the profits of corporations, some of which are paid to households in the form of dividends and some of which are retained by corporations as undistributed profits. They are all income.

Proprietors' income is the income earned by the owner-operator of a business, which includes compensation for the owner's labor, the use of the owner's capital, and profit.

Table 4.2 shows the two big categories of factor incomes and their relative magnitudes. You can see that compensation of employees—labor income—is approximately twice the magnitude of the other factor incomes that make up the net operating surplus.

The factor incomes sum to *net domestic income at factor cost.* The term "factor cost" is used because it is the cost of the factors of production used to produce final goods. When we sum the expenditures on final goods, we arrive at a total called *domestic product at market prices*. Market prices and factor cost diverge because of indirect taxes and subsidies.

An *indirect tax* is a tax paid by consumers when they buy goods and services. (In contrast, a *direct tax* is a tax on income.) State sales taxes and taxes on alcohol, gasoline, and tobacco products are indirect taxes. Because of indirect taxes, consumers pay more for some goods and services than producers receive. Market price exceeds factor cost. For example, if the sales tax is 7 percent, you pay $1.07 when you buy a $1 chocolate bar. The factor cost of the chocolate bar including profit is $1. The market price is $1.07.

A *subsidy* is a payment by the government to a producer. Payments made to grain growers and dairy farmers are subsidies. Because of subsidies, consumers pay less for some goods and services than producers receive. Factor cost exceeds market price.

To get from factor cost to market price, we add indirect taxes and subtract subsidies. Making this adjustment brings us to *net domestic income at market prices*. We still must get from a *net* to a *gross* measure.

Total expenditure is a *gross* number because it includes *gross* investment. Net domestic income at market prices is a net income measure because corporate profits are measured *after deducting depreciation*. They are a *net* income measure. To get from net income to gross income, we must *add depreciation*.

TABLE 4.2 GDP: The Income Approach

Item	Amount in 2010 (billions of dollars)	Percentage of GDP
Compensation of employees	7,929	54.4
Net interest	924	6.3
Rental income	299	2.1
Corporate profits	1,210	8.3
Proprietors' income	1,050	7.2
Net domestic income at factor cost	11,412	78.3
Indirect taxes *less* subsidies	1,127	7.7
Net domestic income at market prices	12,539	86.0
Depreciation	1,860	12.8
GDP (income approach)	**14,399**	**98.8**
Statistical discrepancy	180	1.2
GDP (expenditure approach)	**14,579**	**100.0**

The sum of factor incomes equals *net domestic income at factor cost*. GDP equals net domestic income at factor cost plus indirect taxes less subsidies plus depreciation.

In 2010, GDP measured by the income approach was $14,399 billion. This amount is $180 billion less than GDP measured by the expenditure approach—a statistical discrepancy of $151 billion or 1.2 percent of GDP.

Compensation of employees—labor income—is by far the largest part of aggregate income.

Source of data: U.S. Department of Commerce, Bureau of Economic Analysis.

We've now arrived at GDP using the income approach. This number is not exactly the same as GDP using the expenditure approach. For example, if a waiter doesn't report all his tips when he fills out his income tax return, they get missed in the income approach but they show up in the expenditure approach when he spends his income. So the sum of expenditures might exceed the sum of incomes. Also the sum of expenditures might exceed the sum of incomes because some expenditure items are estimated rather than directly measured.

The gap between the expenditure approach and the income approach is called the *statistical discrepancy* and it is calculated as the GDP expenditure total minus the GDP income total. The discrepancy is never large. In 2010, it was 1.2 percent of GDP.

Nominal GDP and Real GDP

Often, we want to *compare* GDP in two periods, say 2000 and 2010. In 2000, GDP was $9,952 billion and in 2010, it was $14,579 billion—46 percent higher than in 2000. This increase in GDP is a combination of an increase in production and a rise in prices. To isolate the increase in production from the rise in prices, we distinguish between *real* GDP and *nominal* GDP.

Real GDP is the value of final goods and services produced in a given year when *valued at the prices of a reference base year*. By comparing the value of production in the two years at the same prices, we reveal the change in production.

Currently, the reference base year is 2005 and we describe real GDP as measured in 2005 dollars—in terms of what the dollar would buy in 2005.

Nominal GDP is the value of final goods and services produced in a given year when valued at the prices of that year. Nominal GDP is just a more precise name for GDP.

Economists at the Bureau of Economic Analysis calculate real GDP using the method described in the Mathematical Note on pp. 100–101. Here, we'll explain the basic idea but not the technical details.

Calculating Real GDP

We'll calculate real GDP for an economy that produces one consumption good, one capital good, and one government service. Net exports are zero.

Table 4.3 shows the quantities produced and the prices in 2005 (the base year) and in 2010. In part (a), we calculate nominal GDP in 2005. For each item, we multiply the quantity produced in 2005 by its price in 2005 to find the total expenditure on the item. We sum the expenditures to find nominal GDP, which in 2005 is $100 million. Because 2005 is the base year, both real GDP and nominal GDP equal $100 million.

In Table 4.3(b), we calculate nominal GDP in 2010, which is $300 million. Nominal GDP in 2010 is three times its value in 2005. But by how much has production increased? Real GDP will tell us.

In Table 4.3(c), we calculate real GDP in 2010. The quantities of the goods and services produced are those of 2010, as in part (b). The prices are those in the reference base year—2005, as in part (a).

For each item, we multiply the quantity produced in 2010 by its price in 2005. We then sum these expenditures to find real GDP in 2010, which is $160 million. This number is what total expenditure would have been in 2010 if prices had remained the same as they were in 2005.

Nominal GDP in 2010 is three times its value in 2005, but real GDP in 2010 is only 1.6 times its 2005 value—a 60 percent increase in production.

TABLE 4.3 Calculating Nominal GDP and Real GDP

	Item	Quantity (millions)	Price (dollars)	Expenditure (millions of dollars)
(a) In 2005				
C	T-shirts	10	5	50
I	Computer chips	3	10	30
G	Security services	1	20	20
Y	Real and Nominal GDP in 2005			100
(b) In 2010				
C	T-shirts	4	5	20
I	Computer chips	2	20	40
G	Security services	6	40	240
Y	Nominal GDP in 2010			300
(c) Quantities of 2010 valued at prices of 2005				
C	T-shirts	4	5	20
I	Computer chips	2	10	20
G	Security services	6	20	120
Y	Real GDP in 2010			160

In 2005, the reference base year, real GDP equals nominal GDP and was $100 million. In 2010, nominal GDP increased to $300 million. But real GDP in 2010 in part (c), which is calculated by using the quantities of 2010 in part (b) and the prices of 2005 in part (a), was only $160 million—a 60 percent increase from 2005.

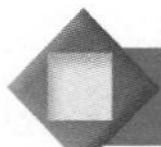

REVIEW QUIZ

1. What is the expenditure approach to measuring GDP?
2. What is the income approach to measuring GDP?
3. What adjustments must be made to total income to make it equal GDP?
4. What is the distinction between nominal GDP and real GDP?
5. How is real GDP calculated?

You can work these questions in Study Plan 4.2 and get instant feedback.

The Uses and Limitations of Real GDP

Economists use estimates of real GDP for two main purposes:

- To compare the standard of living over time
- To compare the standard of living across countries

The Standard of Living Over Time

One method of comparing the standard of living over time is to calculate real GDP per person in different years. **Real GDP per person** is real GDP divided by the population. Real GDP per person tells us the value of goods and services that the average person can enjoy. By using *real* GDP, we remove any influence that rising prices and a rising cost of living might have had on our comparison.

We're interested in both the long-term trends and the shorter-term cycles in the standard of living.

Long-Term Trend A handy way of comparing real GDP per person over time is to express it as a ratio of some reference year. For example, in 1960, real GDP per person was $15,850 and in 2010, it was $42,800. So real GDP per person in 2010 was 2.7 times its 1960 level—that is, $42,800 ÷ $15,850 = 2.7. To the extent that real GDP per person measures the standard of living, people were 2.7 times as well off in 2010 as their grandparents had been in 1960.

Figure 4.2 shows the path of U.S. real GDP per person for the 50 years from 1960 to 2010 and highlights two features of our expanding living standard:

- The growth of potential GDP per person
- Fluctuations of real GDP per person

The Growth of Potential GDP **Potential GDP** is the maximum level of real GDP that can be produced while avoiding shortages of labor, capital, land, and entrepreneurial ability that would bring rising inflation. Potential GDP per person, the smoother black line in Fig. 4.2, grows at a steady pace because the quantities of the factors of production and their productivities grow at a steady pace.

But potential GDP per person doesn't grow at a *constant* pace. During the 1960s, it grew at 2.8 percent per year but slowed to only 2.3 percent per year during the 1970s. This slowdown might seem small, but it had big consequences, as you'll soon see.

FIGURE 4.2 Rising Standard of Living in the United States

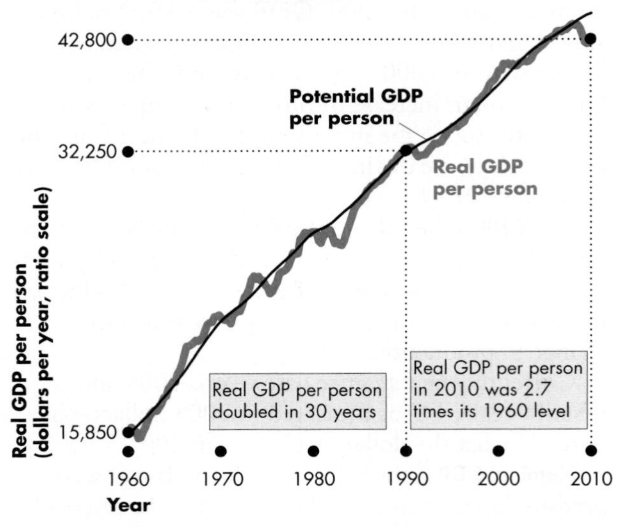

Real GDP per person in the United States doubled between 1960 and 1990. In 2010, real GDP per person was 2.7 times its 1960 level. Real GDP per person, the red line, fluctuates around potential GDP per person, the black line. (The *y*-axis is a ratio scale—see the Appendix, pp, 504–505.)

Sources of data: U.S. Department of Commerce, Bureau of Economic Analysis and Congressional Budget Office.

myeconlab animation

Fluctuations of Real GDP You can see that real GDP shown by the red line in Fig. 4.2 fluctuates around potential GDP, and sometimes real GDP shrinks.

Let's take a closer look at the two features of our expanding living standard that we've just outlined.

Productivity Growth Slowdown How costly was the slowdown in productivity growth after 1970? The answer is provided by the *Lucas wedge*, which is the dollar value of the accumulated gap between what real GDP per person would have been if the 1960s growth rate had persisted and what real GDP per person turned out to be. (Nobel Laureate Robert E. Lucas Jr. drew attention to this gap.)

Figure 4.3 illustrates the Lucas wedge. The wedge started out small during the 1970s, but by 2010 real GDP per person was $28,400 per year lower than it would have been with no growth slowdown, and the accumulated gap was an astonishing $380,000 per person.

FIGURE 4.3 The Cost of Slower Growth: The Lucas Wedge

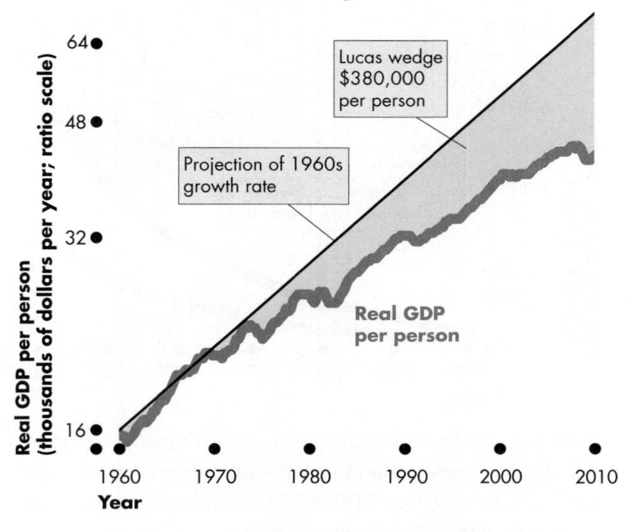

The black line projects the 1960s growth rate of real GDP per person to 2010. The Lucas wedge arises from the slowdown of productivity growth that began during the 1970s. The cost of the slowdown is $380,000 per person.

Sources of data: U.S. Department of Commerce Bureau of Economic Analysis, Congressional Budget Office, and author's calculations.

myeconlab animation

Real GDP Fluctuations—The Business Cycle We call the fluctuations in the pace of expansion of real GDP the business cycle. The **business cycle** is a periodic but irregular up-and-down movement of total production and other measures of economic activity. The business cycle isn't a regular predictable cycle like the phases of the moon, but every cycle has two phases:

1. Expansion
2. Recession

and two turning points:

1. Peak
2. Trough

Figure 4.4 shows these features of the most recent U.S. business cycle.

An **expansion** is a period during which real GDP increases. In the early stage of an expansion real GDP returns to potential GDP and as the expansion progresses, potential GDP grows and real GDP eventually exceeds potential GDP.

A common definition of **recession** is a period during which real GDP decreases—its growth rate is negative—for at least two successive quarters. The definition used by the National Bureau of Economic Research, which dates the U.S. business cycle phases and turning points, is "a period of significant decline in total output, income, employment, and trade, usually lasting from six months to a year, and marked by contractions in many sectors of the economy."

An expansion ends and recession begins at a business cycle *peak*, which is the highest level that real GDP has attained up to that time. A recession ends at a *trough*, when real GDP reaches a temporary low point and from which the next expansion begins.

In 2008, the U.S. economy went into an unusually severe recession. Starting from a long way below potential GDP, a new expansion began in mid-2009. But the outlook for the expansion in 2011 and beyond was very uncertain (see *Reading Between the Lines* on pp. 96–97).

FIGURE 4.4 The Most Recent U.S. Business Cycle

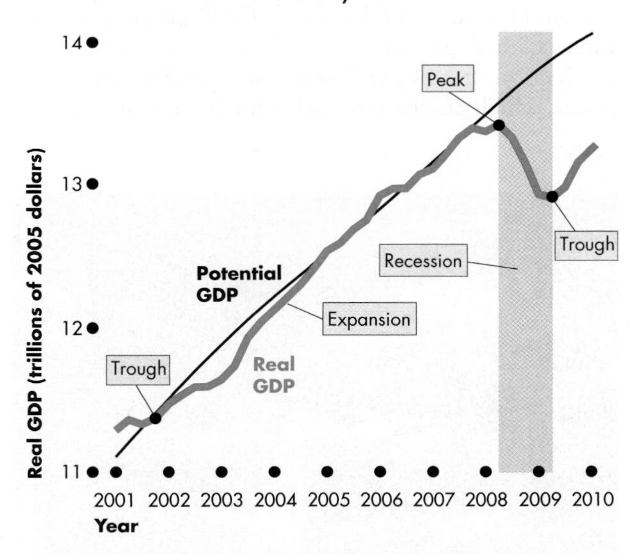

A business cycle expansion began from a trough in the fourth quarter of 2001 and ended at a peak in the second quarter of 2008. A deep and long recession followed the 2008 peak.

Sources of data: U.S. Department of Commerce Bureau of Economic Analysis, Congressional Budget Office, and National Bureau of Economic Research.

myeconlab animation

The Standard of Living Across Countries

Two problems arise in using real GDP to compare living standards across countries. First, the real GDP of one country must be converted into the same currency units as the real GDP of the other country. Second, the goods and services in both countries must be valued at the same prices. Comparing the United States and China provides a striking example of these two problems.

China and the United States in U.S. Dollars In 2010, real GDP per person in the United States was $42,800 and in China it was 23,400 yuan. The yuan is the currency of China and the price at which the dollar and the yuan exchanged, the *market exchange rate*, was 8.2 yuan per $1 U.S. Using this exchange rate, 23,400 yuan converts to $2,850. On these numbers, real GDP per person in the United States was 15 times that in China.

The red line in Fig. 4.5 shows real GDP per person in China from 1980 to 2010 when the market exchange rate is used to convert yuan to U.S. dollars.

China and the United States at PPP Figure 4.5 shows a second estimate of China's real GDP per person that values China's production on the same terms as U.S. production. It uses *purchasing power parity* or *PPP* prices, which are the *same prices* for both countries. The prices of some goods are higher in the United States than in China, so these items get a smaller weight in China's real GDP than they get in U.S. real GDP. An example is a Big Mac that costs $3.75 in Chicago. In Shanghai, a Big Mac costs 13.25 yuan which is the equivalent of $1.62. So in China's real GDP, a Big Mac gets less than half the weight that it gets in U.S. real GDP.

Some prices in China are higher than in the United States but more prices are lower, so Chinese prices put a lower value on China's production than do U.S. prices.

According to the PPP comparisons, real GDP per person in the United States in 2010 was 6.5 times that of China, not 15 times.

You've seen how real GDP is used to make standard of living comparisons over time and across countries. But real GDP isn't a perfect measure of the standard of living and we'll now examine its limitations.

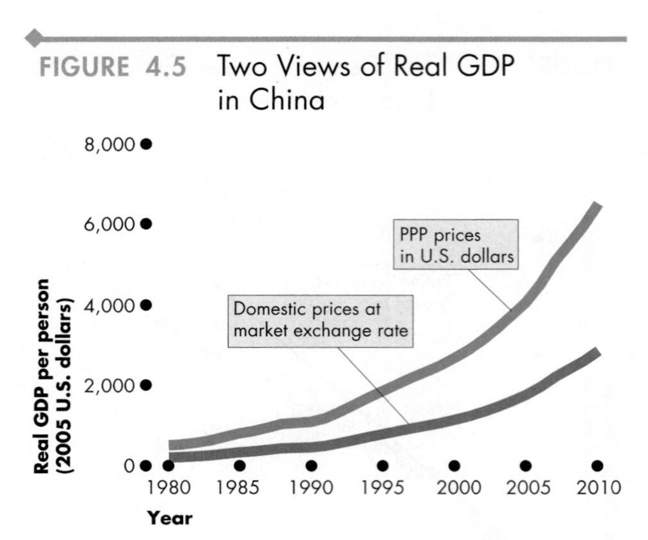

FIGURE 4.5 Two Views of Real GDP in China

Real GDP per person in China has grown rapidly. But how rapidly it has grown and to what level depends on how real GDP is valued. When GDP in 2010 is valued at the market exchange rate, U.S. income per person is 15 times that in China. China looks like a poor developing country. But the comparison is misleading. When GDP is valued at purchasing power parity prices, U.S. income per person is only 6.5 times that in China.

Source of data: International Monetary Fund, *World Economic Outlook database*, April 2010 .

myeconlab animation

A Big Mac costs $3.75 in Chicago and 13.25 yuan or $1.62 in Shanghai. To compare real GDP in China and the United States, we must value China's Big Macs at the $3.75 U.S. price—the PPP price.

Limitations of Real GDP

Real GDP measures the value of goods and services that are bought in markets. Some of the factors that influence the standard of living and that are not part of GDP are

- Household production
- Underground economic activity
- Health and life expectancy
- Leisure time
- Environmental quality
- Political freedom and social justice

Household Production An enormous amount of production takes place every day in our homes. Preparing meals, cleaning the kitchen, changing a light bulb, cutting grass, washing a car, and caring for a child are all examples of household production. Because these productive activities are not traded in markets, they are not included in GDP.

The omission of household production from GDP means that GDP *underestimates* total production. But it also means that the growth rate of GDP *overestimates* the growth rate of total production. The reason is that some of the growth rate of market production (included in GDP) is a replacement for home production. So part of the increase in GDP arises from a decrease in home production.

Two trends point in this direction. One is the number of women who have jobs, which increased from 38 percent in 1960 to 58 percent in 2010. The other is the trend in the market purchase of traditionally home-produced goods and services. For example, more and more families now eat in restaurants—one of the fastest-growing industries in the United States—and use day-care services. This trend means that an increasing proportion of food preparation and child care that were part of household production are now measured as part of GDP. So real GDP grows more rapidly than does real GDP plus home production.

Underground Economic Activity The *underground economy* is the part of the economy that is purposely hidden from the view of the government to avoid taxes and regulations or because the goods and services being produced are illegal. Because underground economic activity is unreported, it is omitted from GDP.

The underground economy is easy to describe, even if it is hard to measure. It includes the production and distribution of illegal drugs, production that uses illegal labor that is paid less than the minimum wage, and jobs done for cash to avoid paying income taxes. This last category might be quite large and includes tips earned by cab drivers, hairdressers, and hotel and restaurant workers.

Estimates of the scale of the underground economy in the United States range between 9 and 30 percent of GDP ($1,300 billion to $4,333 billion).

Provided that the underground economy is a stable proportion of the total economy, the growth rate of real GDP still gives a useful estimate of changes in economic well-being and the standard of living. But sometimes production shifts from the underground economy to the rest of the economy, and sometimes it shifts the other way. The underground economy expands relative to the rest of the economy if taxes

Whose production is more valuable: the chef's whose work gets counted in GDP ...

... or the busy mother's whose dinner preparation and child minding don't get counted?

become especially high or if regulations become especially restrictive. And the underground economy shrinks relative to the rest of the economy if the burdens of taxes and regulations are eased. During the 1980s, when tax rates were cut, there was an increase in the reporting of previously hidden income and tax revenues increased. So some part (but probably a very small part) of the expansion of real GDP during the 1980s represented a shift from the underground economy rather than an increase in production.

Health and Life Expectancy Good health and a long life—the hopes of everyone—do not show up in real GDP, at least not directly. A higher real GDP enables us to spend more on medical research, health care, a good diet, and exercise equipment. And as real GDP has increased, our life expectancy has lengthened—from 70 years at the end of World War II to approaching 80 years today.

But we face new health and life expectancy problems every year. AIDS and drug abuse are taking young lives at a rate that causes serious concern. When we take these negative influences into account, we see that real GDP growth overstates the improvements in the standard of living.

Leisure Time Leisure time is an economic good that adds to our economic well-being and the standard of living. Other things remaining the same, the more leisure we have, the better off we are. Our working time is valued as part of GDP, but our leisure time is not. Yet that leisure time must be at least as valuable to us as the wage that we earn for the last hour worked. If it were not, we would work instead of taking leisure. Over the years, leisure time has steadily increased. The workweek has become shorter, more people take early retirement, and the number of vacation days has increased. These improvements in economic well-being are not reflected in real GDP.

Environmental Quality Economic activity directly influences the quality of the environment. The burning of hydrocarbon fuels is the most visible activity that damages our environment. But it is not the only example. The depletion of nonrenewable natural resources, the mass clearing of forests, and the pollution of lakes and rivers are other major environmental consequences of industrial production.

Resources that are used to protect the environment are valued as part of GDP. For example, the value of catalytic converters that help to protect the atmosphere from automobile emissions is part of GDP. But if we did not use such pieces of equipment and instead polluted the atmosphere, we would not count the deteriorating air that we were breathing as a negative part of GDP.

An industrial society possibly produces more atmospheric pollution than an agricultural society does. But pollution does not always increase as we become wealthier. Wealthy people value a clean environment and are willing to pay for one. Compare the pollution in China today with pollution in the United States. China, a poor country, pollutes its rivers, lakes, and atmosphere in a way that is unimaginable in the United States.

Political Freedom and Social Justice Most people in the Western world value political freedoms such as those provided by the U.S. Constitution. And they value social justice—equality of opportunity and of access to social security safety nets that protect people from the extremes of misfortune.

A country might have a very large real GDP per person but have limited political freedom and social justice. For example, a small elite might enjoy political liberty and extreme wealth while the vast majority are effectively enslaved and live in abject poverty. Such an economy would generally be regarded as having a lower standard of living than one that had the same amount of real GDP but in which political freedoms were enjoyed by everyone. Today, China has rapid real GDP growth but limited political freedoms, while Poland and Ukraine have moderate real GDP growth but democratic political systems. Economists have no easy way to determine which of these countries is better off.

The Bottom Line Do we get the wrong message about the level and growth in economic well-being and the standard of living by looking at the growth of real GDP? The influences that are omitted from real GDP are probably important and could be large. Developing countries have a larger amount of household production and a larger underground economy than do developed countries so the gap between their living standards is exaggerated. Also, as real GDP grows, part of the measured growth might reflect a switch from home production to market production and underground to regular production. This measurement error overstates the growth in economic well-being and the improvement in the standard of living.

Economics in Action

A Broader Indicator of Economic Well-Being

The limitations of real GDP reviewed in this chapter affect the standard of living and general well-being of every country. So to make international comparisons of the general state of economic well-being, we must look at real GDP and other indicators.

The United Nations has constructed a broader measure called the Human Development Index (HDI), which combines real GDP, life expectancy and health, and education. Real GDP per person (measured on the PPP basis) is a major component of the HDI.

The dots in the figure show the relationship between real GDP per person and the HDI. The United States (along with a few other countries) has the highest real GDP per person, but the United States has the thirteenth highest HDI. (Norway has the highest HDI, and Australia, Canada, and Japan have a higher HDI than the United States.)

The HDI of the United States is lower than that of 12 other countries because the people of those countries live longer and have better access to health care and education than do Americans.

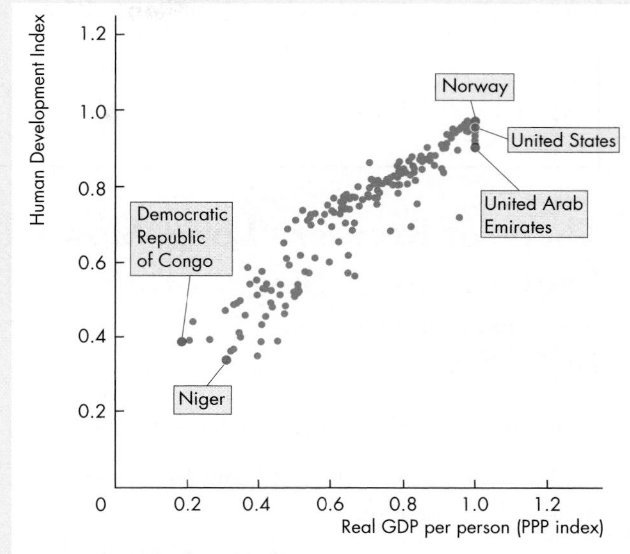

The Human Development Index

Source of data: United nations hdr.undp.org/en/statistics/data

African nations have the lowest levels of economic well-being. The Democratic Republic of Congo has the lowest real GDP per person and Niger has the lowest HDI.

Other influences on the standard of living include the amount of leisure time available, the quality of the environment, the security of jobs and homes, and the safety of city streets.

It is possible to construct broader measures that combine the many influences that contribute to human happiness. Real GDP will be one element in those broader measures, but it will by no means be the whole of those measures. The United Nation's Human Development Index (HDI) is one example of attempts to provide broader measures of economic well-being and the standard of living. This measure places a good deal of weight on real GDP.

Dozens of other measures have been proposed. One includes resource depletion and emissions in a Green GDP measure. Another emphasizes the enjoyment of life rather than the production of goods in a "genuine progress index" or GPI.

Despite all the alternatives, real GDP per person remains the most widely used indicator of economic well-being.

REVIEW QUIZ

1 Distinguish between real GDP and potential GDP and describe how each grows over time.
2 How does the growth rate of real GDP contribute to an improved standard of living?
3 What is a business cycle and what are its phases and turning points?
4 What is PPP and how does it help us to make valid international comparisons of real GDP?
5 Explain why real GDP might be an unreliable indicator of the standard of living.

You can work these questions in Study Plan 4.3 and get instant feedback.

You now know how economists measure GDP and what the GDP data tell us. *Reading Between the Lines* on pp. 96–97 uses GDP to describe some possible future paths as we emerge from recession.

Real GDP Forecasts in the Uncertain Economy of 2010

Shape of Recovery Long, Slow Growth … a "Square Root" Slog

http://www.denverpost.com
July 26, 2010

Hopes for a "V-shaped" recovery have shifted to fears of a "W-shaped" double dip.

William Greiner, president of Scout Investment Advisors, wants to add another symbol to the mix—the square root.

The square root represents a rebound, a smaller version of the V, followed by an extended period of below-average growth. No double dip, just a long, hard slog.

Greiner … predicts [a fall in] inflation-adjusted economic growth from 3.3 percent, the average in the post-war period, to about 2 percent, hence the square root.

No big deal? Think again.

"Potentially, the economic implications as to slow growth are monumental," Greiner said. "It is hard to overstate this issue."

Two percent real GDP growth will keep pace with U.S. population growth of 0.89 percent a year. But it won't leave much to form capital, fund research and development, and improve living standards.

Since World War II, the country has grown fast enough to double living standards every 29 years—translating into bigger homes, more cars and consumer goods, and more trips and meals out than previous generations enjoyed.

But at a 2 percent growth rate, living standards double every 64 years. Americans could be forced to shift their hopes for greater prosperity from their children to their grandchildren. …

What will make the slower growth feel even worse is that nominal economic growth, or GDP unadjusted for inflation, will run closer to 4 percent in the near term, far below its 7 percent average in recent decades. ...

ESSENCE OF THE STORY

- Investment advisor William Greiner says the recovery will be neither a V nor a W but the shape of the square root symbol.
- Greiner predicts real GDP growth of 2 percent a year, down from a 3.3 percent post-war average.
- A growth rate of 3.3 percent per year doubles the standard of living every 29 years, but at 2 percent a year the standard of living doubles every 64 years.
- The news article says that growth will feel even worse because nominal GDP will grow at only 4 percent a year, down from 7 percent a year in recent decades.

ECONOMIC ANALYSIS

- The 2008 recession was an unusually deep one and even by the middle of 2010, recovery was weak.
- Figure 1 illustrates the severity of the 2008 recession using the concepts of potential GDP and real GDP that you learned about in this chapter.
- At the *trough* in the second quarter of 2009, real GDP was almost $1 trillion below potential GDP.
- When real GDP is below potential GDP, the economy is operating *inside* the *PPF* (Chapter 2, pp. 30–31) and production is lost.
- To put the magnitude of the gap between potential GDP and real GDP into perspective, each person's share (*your* share) of the lost production in 2009 was about $3,250.
- The severity of the recession and the slow recovery led economists to speculate about the shape of the future recovery—about whether it will be V-shaped or W-shaped.
- A V-shaped recovery, illustrated in Fig. 2, would mean the resumption of rapid real GDP growth.
- A W-shaped recovery, also illustrated in Fig. 2, would be bad news. It means a "double-dip" recession. That is, there will be another downturn and recession before a recovery finally gets going.
- The news article speculates about a third shape—a "square-root" recovery. Figure 2 illustrates this possibility. A square root symbol has a flat top, which means zero real GDP growth. The real GDP path predicted in the news article is almost flat.
- The news article is correct to emphasize that a growth slowdown is a big deal. The Lucas wedge (p. 91) occurred because of a similar slowdown during the 1970s.
- But if real GDP growth does slow to 2 percent a year, the Lucas wedge will become extremely large.
- The news article is *not* correct that slow growth will feel even worse because nominal GDP will grow at only 4 percent a year, down from 7 percent a year in recent decades.
- The numbers are correct, but the reasoning is wrong. Growth will feel slow because (if the forecast is correct) it really will be slow.
- The point of calculating *real* GDP is to isolate the change in the quantity of goods and services produced—the real things on which the standard of living depends.
- A slowdown in *nominal* GDP growth combines the slowdown in real GDP growth and a slowdown in the inflation rate and obscures what is *really* happening to the standard of living.

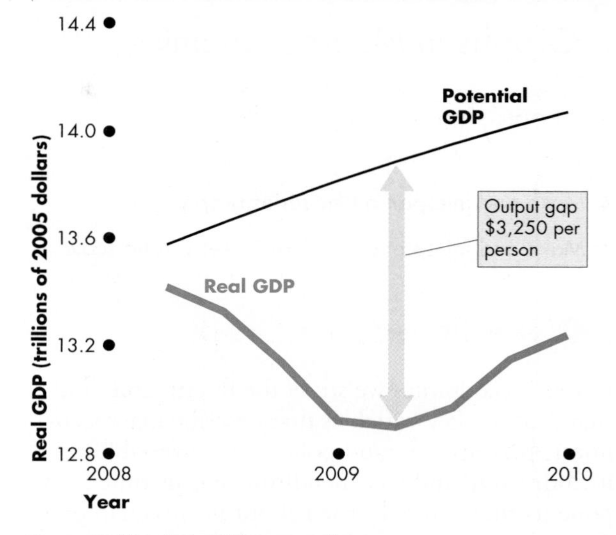

Figure 1 The deep 2008 recession

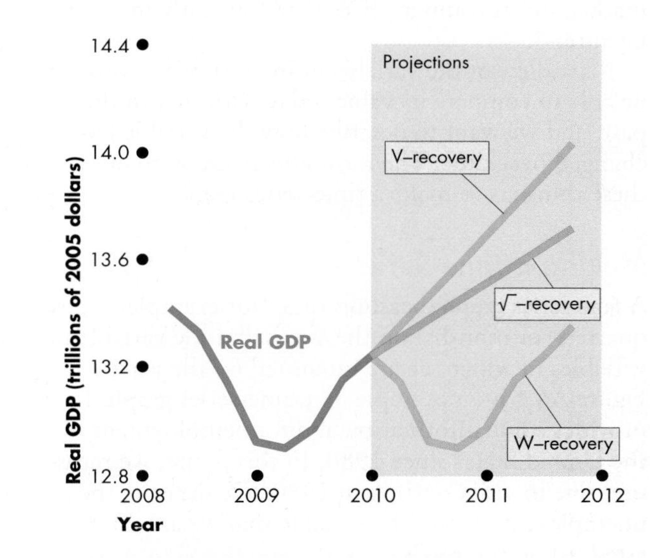

Figure 2 Some alternative recovery paths

APPENDIX

Graphs in Macroeconomics

After studying this appendix, you will be able to:

- Make and interpret a time-series graph
- Make and interpret a graph that uses a ratio scale

The Time-Series Graph

In macroeconomics we study the fluctuations and trends in the key variables that describe macroeconomic performance and policy. These variables include GDP and its expenditure and income components that you've learned about in this chapter. They also include variables that describe the labor market and consumer prices that you study in Chapter 5.

Regardless of the variable of interest, we want to be able to compare its value today with that in the past; and we want to describe how the variable has changed over time. The most effective way to do these things is to make a time-series graph.

Making a Time-Series Graph

A **time-series graph** measures time (for example, years, quarters, or months) on the *x*-axis and the variable or variables in which we are interested on the *y*-axis. Figure A4.1 is an example of a time-series graph. It provides some information about unemployment in the United States since 1980. In this figure, we measure time in years starting in 1980. We measure the unemployment rate (the variable that we are interested in) on the *y*-axis.

A time-series graph enables us to visualize how a variable has changed over time and how its value in one period relates to its value in another period. It conveys an enormous amount of information quickly and easily.

Let's see how to "read" a time-series graph.

Reading a Time-Series Graph

To practice reading a time-series graph, take a close look at Fig. A4.1. The graph shows the level, change and speed of change of the variable.

FIGURE A4.1 A Time-Series Graph

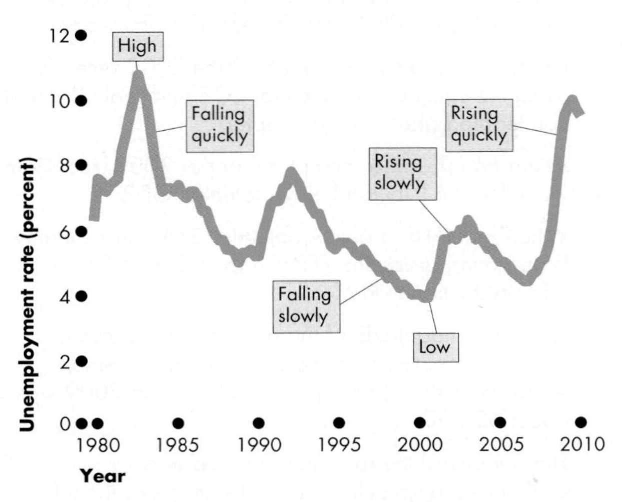

A time-series graph plots the level of a variable on the *y*-axis against time (here measured in years) on the *x*-axis. This graph shows the unemployment rate each year from 1980 to 2010. Its shows when unemployment was high, when it was low, when it increased, when it decreased and when it changed quickly and slowly.

myeconlab animation

- The *level* of the variable: It tells us when unemployment is *high* and *low*. When the line is a long distance above the *x*-axis, the unemployment rate is high, as it was, for example, in 1983 and again in 2009. When the line is close to the *x*-axis, the unemployment rate is low, as it was, for example, in 2001.
- The *change* in the variable: It tells us how unemployment *changes*—whether it *increases* or *decreases.* When the line slopes upward, as it did in 2008 and 2009, the unemployment rate is rising. When the line slopes downward, as it did in 1984 and 1997, the unemployment rate is falling.
- The *speed of change* in the variable: It tells us whether the unemployment rate is rising or falling *quickly* or *slowly*. If the line is very steep, then the unemployment rate increases or decreases quickly. If the line is not steep, the unemployment rate increases or decreases slowly. For example, the unemployment rate rose quickly in 2008 and slowly in 2003 and it fell quickly in 1984 and slowly in 1997.

Ratio Scale Reveals Trend

A time-series graph also reveals whether a variable has a **cycle**, which is a tendency for a variable to alternate between upward and downward movements, or a **trend**, which is a tendency for a variable to move in one general direction.

The unemployment rate in Fig. A4.1 has a cycle but no trend. When a trend is present, a special kind of time-series graph, one that uses a ratio scale on the *y*-axis, reveals the trend.

A Time-Series with a Trend

Many macroeconomics variables, among them GDP and the average level of prices, have an upward trend. Figure A4.2 shows an example of such a variable: the average prices paid by consumers.

In Fig. A4.2(a), consumer prices since 1970 are graphed on a normal scale. In 1970 the level is 100. In other years, the average level of prices is measured as a percentage of the 1970 level.

The graph clearly shows the upward trend of prices. But it doesn't tell us when prices were rising fastest or whether there was any change in the trend. Just looking at the upward-sloping line in Fig. A4.2(a) gives the impression that the pace of growth of consumer prices was constant.

Using a Ratio Scale

On a graph axis with a normal scale, the gap between 1 and 2 is the same as that between 3 and 4. On a graph axis with a ratio scale, the gap between 1 and 2 is the same as that between 2 and 4. The ratio 2 to 1 equals the ratio 4 to 2. By using a ratio scale, we can "see" when the growth rate (the percentage change per unit of time) changes.

Figure A4.2(b) shows an example of a ratio scale. Notice that the values on the *y*-axis get closer together but the gap between 400 and 200 equals the gap between 200 and 100: The ratio gaps are equal.

Graphing the data on a ratio scale reveals the trends. In the case of consumer prices, the trend is much steeper during the 1970s and early 1980s than in the later years. The steeper the line in the ratio-scale graph in part (b), the faster are prices rising. Prices rose rapidly during the 1970s and early 1980s and more slowly in the later 1980s and 1990s. The ratio-scale graph reveals this fact. We use ratio-scale graphs extensively in macroeconomics.

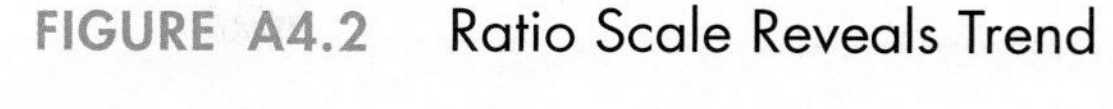

FIGURE A4.2 Ratio Scale Reveals Trend

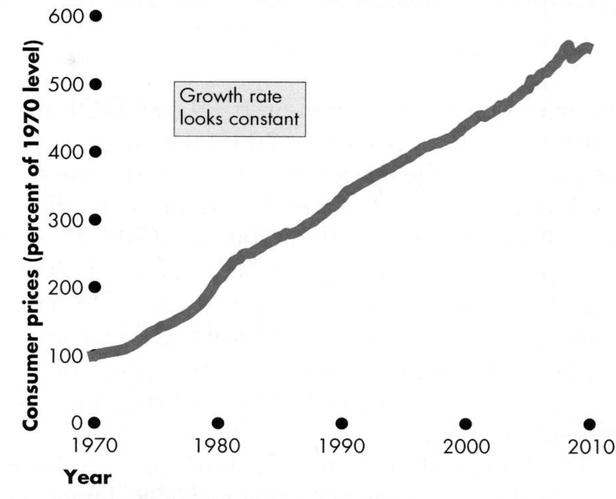

(a) Normal scale

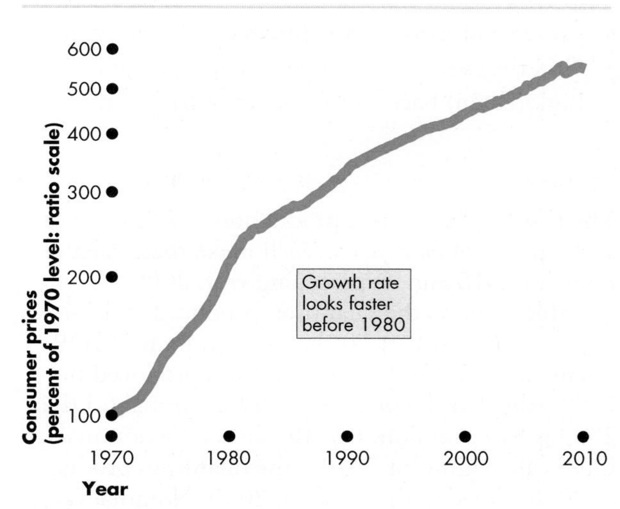

(b) Ratio scale

The graph shows the average of consumer prices from 1970 to 2010. The level is 100 in 1970 and the value for other years are percentages of the 1970 level. Consumer prices normally rise each year so the line slopes upward. In part (a), where the *y*-axis scale is normal, the rate of increase appears to be constant.

In part (b), where the y-axis is a ratio scale (the ratio of 400 to 200 equals the ratio 200 to 100), prices rose faster in the 1970s and early 1980s and slower in the later years. The ratio scale reveals this trend.

MATHEMATICAL NOTE

Chained-Dollar Real GDP

In the real GDP calculation on p. 89, real GDP in 2010 is 1.6 times its value in 2005. But suppose that we use 2010 as the reference base year and value real GDP in 2005 at 2010 prices. If you do the math, you will see that real GDP in 2005 is $150 million at 2010 prices. GDP in 2010 is $300 million (in 2010 prices), so now the numbers say that real GDP has doubled. Which is correct: Did real GDP increase 1.6 times or double? Should we use the prices of 2005 or 2010? The answer is that we need to use *both* sets of prices.

The Bureau of Economic Analysis uses a measure of real GDP called **chained-dollar real GDP**. Three steps are needed to calculate this measure:

- Value production in the prices of adjacent years
- Find the average of two percentage changes
- Link (chain) back to the reference base year

Value Production in Prices of Adjacent Years

The first step is to value production in *adjacent* years at the prices of *both* years. We'll make these calculations for 2010 and its preceding year, 2009.

Table 1 shows the quantities produced and prices in the two years. Part (a) shows the nominal GDP calculation for 2009—the quantities produced in 2009 valued at the prices of 2009. Nominal GDP in 2009 is $145 million. Part (b) shows the nominal GDP calculation for 2010—the quantities produced in 2010 valued at the prices of 2010. Nominal GDP in 2010 is $300 million. Part (c) shows the value of the quantities produced in 2010 at the prices of 2009. This total is $160 million. Finally, part (d) shows the value of the quantities produced in 2009 at the prices of 2010. This total is $275 million.

TABLE 1 Real GDP Calculation Step 1: Value Production in Adjacent Years at Prices of Both Years

	Item	Quantity (millions)	Price (dollars)	Expenditure (millions of dollars)
(a) In 2009				
C	T-shirts	3	5	15
I	Computer chips	3	10	30
G	Security services	5	20	100
Y	Real and Nominal GDP in 2009			**145**
(b) In 2010				
C	T-shirts	4	5	20
I	Computer chips	2	20	40
G	Security services	6	40	240
Y	Nominal GDP in 2010			**300**
(c) Quantities of 2010 valued at prices of 2009				
C	T-shirts	4	5	20
I	Computer chips	2	10	20
G	Security services	6	20	120
Y	2010 production at 2009 prices			**160**
(d) Quantities of 2009 valued at prices of 2010				
C	T-shirts	3	5	15
I	Computer chips	3	20	60
G	Security services	5	40	200
Y	2009 production at 2010 prices			**275**

Step 1 is to value the production of adjacent years at the prices of both years. Here, we value the production of 2009 and 2010 at the prices of both 2009 and 2010. The value of 2009 production at 2009 prices, in part (a), is nominal GDP in 2009. The value of 2010 production at 2010 prices, in part (b), is nominal GDP in 2010. Part (c) calculates the value of 2010 production at 2009 prices, and part (d) calculates the value of 2009 production at 2010 prices. We use these numbers in Step 2.

Find the Average of Two Percentage Changes

The second step is to find the percentage change in the value of production based on the prices in the two adjacent years. Table 2 summarizes these calculations.

Part (a) shows that, valued at the prices of 2009, production increased from $145 million in 2009 to $160 million in 2010, an increase of 10.3 percent.

Part (b) shows that, valued at the prices of 2010, production increased from $275 million in 2009 to $300 million in 2010, an increase of 9.1 percent. Part (c) shows that the average of these two percentage changes in the value of production is 9.7. That is, $(10.3 + 9.1) \div 2 = 9.7$.

By applying this average percentage change to real GDP, we can find the value of real GDP in 2010. Real GDP in 2009 is $145 million, so a 9.7 percent increase is $14 million. Then real GDP in 2010 is

TABLE 2 Real GDP Calculation Step 2: Find Average of Two Percentage Changes

Value of Production	Millions of dollars	
(a) At 2009 prices		
Nominal GDP in 2009	145	
2010 production at 2009 prices	160	
Percentage change in production at 2009 prices		10.3
(b) At 2010 prices		
2009 production at 2010 prices	275	
Nominal GDP in 2010	300	
Percentage change in production at 2010 prices		9.1
(c) Average percentage change in 2010		**9.7**

Using the numbers calculated in Step 1, the percentage change in production from 2009 to 2010 valued at 2009 prices is 10.3 percent, in part (a). The percentage change in production from 2009 to 2010 valued at 2010 prices is 9.1 percent, in part (b). The average of these two percentage changes is 9.7 percent, in part (c).

$145 million plus $14 million, which equals $159 million. Because real GDP in 2009 is in 2009 dollars, real GDP in 2010 is also in 2009 dollars.

Although the real GDP of $159 million is expressed in 2009 dollars, the calculation uses the average of the prices of the final goods and services that make up GDP in 2009 and 2010.

Link (Chain) to the Base Year

The third step is to express GDP in the prices of the reference base year. To do this, the BEA performs calculations like the ones that you've just worked through to find the percentage change in real GDP in *each* pair of years. It then selects a base year (currently 2005) in which, by definition, real GDP equals nominal GDP. Finally, it uses the percentage changes to calculate real GDP in 2005 prices starting from real GDP in 2005.

To illustrate this third step, we'll assume that the BEA has calculated the growth rates since 2004 shown in Table 3. The 2010 growth rate that we've just calculated is highlighted in the table. The other (assumed) growth rates are calculated in exactly the same way as that for 2010.

TABLE 3 Real GDP Calculation Step 3: Repeat Growth Rate Calculations

Year	**2005**	2006	2007	2008	2009	**2010**
Growth rate	7.0	8.0	6.0	7.0	8.0	**9.7**

Figure 1 illustrates the chain link calculations. In the reference base year, 2005, real GDP equals nominal GDP, which we'll assume is $125 million. Table 3 tells us that the growth rate in 2005 was 7 percent, so real GDP in 2005 is 7 percent higher than it was in 2004, which means that real GDP in 2004 is $117 million ($117 \times 1.07 = 125$).

Table 3 also tells us that the growth rate in 2006 was 8 percent, so real GDP in 2006 is 8 percent higher than it was in 2005, which means that real GDP in 2006 is $135 million ($125 \times 1.08 = 135$).

By repeating these calculations for each year, we obtain *chained-dollar real GDP* in 2005 dollars for each year. In 2009, *chained-dollar real GDP* in 2005 dollars is $165 million. So the 9.7 percent growth rate in 2010 that we calculated in Table 2 means that real GDP in 2010 is $181 million.

Notice that the growth rates are independent of the reference base year, so changing the reference base year does not change the growth rates.

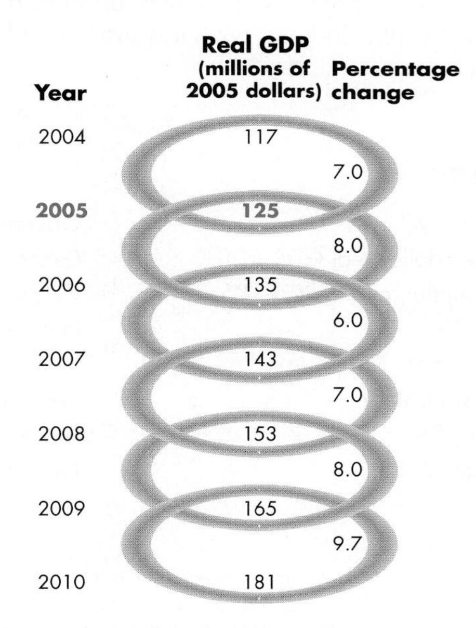

Figure 1 Real GDP calculation step 3: link (chain) back to base year

SUMMARY

Key Points

Gross Domestic Product (pp. 84–86)

- GDP, or gross domestic product, is the market value of all the final goods and services produced in a country during a given period.
- A final good is an item that is bought by its final user, and it contrasts with an intermediate good, which is a component of a final good.
- GDP is calculated by using either the expenditure or income totals in the circular flow model.
- Aggregate expenditure on goods and services equals aggregate income and GDP.

Working Problems 1 to 7 will give you a better understanding of gross domestic product.

Measuring U.S. GDP (pp. 87–89)

- Because aggregate expenditure, aggregate income, and the value of aggregate production are equal, we can measure GDP by using the expenditure approach or the income approach.
- The expenditure approach sums consumption expenditure, investment, government expenditure on goods and services, and net exports.
- The income approach sums wages, interest, rent, and profit (plus indirect taxes less subsidies plus depreciation).
- Real GDP is measured using a common set of prices to remove the effects of inflation from GDP.

Working Problems 8 to 15 will give you a better understanding of measuring U.S. GDP.

The Uses and Limitations of Real GDP (pp. 88–95)

- Real GDP is used to compare the standard of living over time and across countries.
- Real GDP per person grows and fluctuates around the more smoothly growing potential GDP.
- A slowing of the growth rate of real GDP per person during the 1970s has lowered incomes by a large amount.
- International real GDP comparisons use PPP prices.
- Real GDP is not a perfect measure of the standard of living because it excludes household production, the underground economy, health and life expectancy, leisure time, environmental quality, and political freedom and social justice.

Working Problem 16 will give you a better understanding of the uses and limitations of real GDP.

Key Terms

Business cycle, 91
Chained-dollar real GDP, 100
Consumption expenditure, 85
Cycle, 99
Depreciation, 86
Expansion, 91
Exports, 86
Final good, 84
Government expenditure, 86
Gross domestic product (GDP), 84
Gross investment, 86
Imports, 86
Intermediate good, 84
Investment, 86
Net exports, 86
Net investment, 86
Nominal GDP, 89
Potential GDP, 90
Real GDP, 89
Real GDP per person, 90
Recession, 91
Time-series graph, 98
Trend, 99

STUDY PLAN PROBLEMS AND APPLICATIONS

myeconlab You can work Problems 1 to 17 in MyEconLab Chapter 4 Study Plan and get instant feedback.

Gross Domestic Product (Study Plan 4.1)

1. Classify each of the following items as a final good or service or an intermediate good or service and identify which is a component of consumption expenditure, investment, or government expenditure on goods and services:
   - Banking services bought by a student.
   - New cars bought by Hertz, the car rental firm.
   - Newsprint bought by *USA Today* .
   - The purchase of a new limo for the president.
   - New house bought by Al Gore.
2. The firm that printed this textbook bought the paper from XYZ Paper Mills. Was this purchase of paper part of GDP? If not, how does the value of the paper get counted in GDP?

Use the following figure, which illustrates the circular flow model, to work Problems 3 and 4.

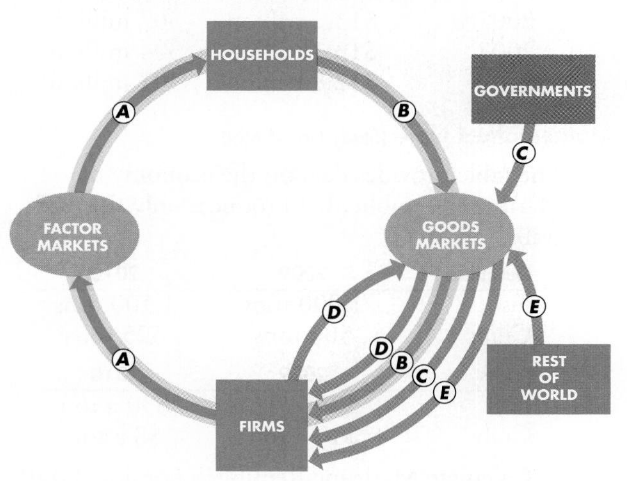

3. During 2008, in an economy:
   - Flow B was $9 trillion.
   - Flow C was $2 trillion.
   - Flow D was $3 trillion.
   - Flow E was –$0.7 trillion.

   Name the flows and calculate the value of
   a. Aggregate income.
   b. GDP.
4. During 2009, flow A was $13.0 trillion, flow B was $9.1 trillion, flow D was $3.3 trillion, and flow E was –$0.8 trillion.

   Calculate the 2009 values of
   a. GDP.
   b. Government expenditure.
5. Use the following data to calculate aggregate expenditure and imports of goods and services.
   - Government expenditure: $20 billion
   - Aggregate income: $100 billion
   - Consumption expenditure: $67 billion
   - Investment: $21 billion
   - Exports of goods and services: $30 billion
6. **U.S. Economy Shrinks Modestly**

   GDP fell 1 percent as businesses cut investment by 8.9 percent, consumers cut spending by 1.2 percent, purchases of new houses fell 38 percent, and exports fell 29.9 percent.

   Source: Reuters, July 31, 2009

   Use the letters on the figure in Problem 3 to indicate the flow in which each item in the news clip occurs. How can GDP have fallen by only 1.0 percent with the big expenditure cuts reported?
7. A U.S. market research firm deconstructed an Apple iPod and studied the manufacturers, costs, and profits of each of the parts and components. The final results are
   - An Apple iPod sells in the United States for $299.
   - A Japanese firm, Toshiba, makes the hard disk and display screen, which cost $93.
   - Other components produced in South Korea cost $25.
   - Other components produced in the United States cost $21.
   - The iPod is assembled in China at a cost of $5.
   - The costs and profits of retailers, advertisers, and transportation firms in the United States are $75.

   a. What is Apple's profit?
   b. Where in the national income and product accounts of the United States, Japan, South Korea, and China are these transactions recorded.
   c. What contribution does one iPod make to world GDP?

Measuring U.S. GDP (Study Plan 4.2)

Use the following data to work Problems 8 and 9.

The table lists some macroeconomic data for the United States in 2008.

Item	Billions of dollars
Wages paid to labor	8,000
Consumption expenditure	10,000
Net operating surplus	3,200
Investment	2,000
Government expenditure	2,800
Net exports	–700
Depreciation	1,800

8. Calculate U.S. GDP in 2008.
9. Explain the approach (expenditure or income) that you used to calculate GDP.

Use the following data to work Problems 10 and 11.

The national accounts of Parchment Paradise are kept on (you guessed it) parchment. A fire destroys the statistics office. The accounts are now incomplete but they contain the following data:

- GDP (income approach): $2,900
- Consumption expenditure: $2,000
- Indirect taxes less subsidies: $100
- Net operating surplus: $500
- Investment: $800
- Government expenditure: $400
- Wages: $2,000
- Net exports: –$200

10. Calculate GDP (expenditure approach) and depreciation.
11. Calculate net domestic income at factor cost and the statistical discrepancy.

Use the following data to work Problems 12 and 13.

Tropical Republic produces only bananas and coconuts. The base year is 2008, and the table gives the quantities produced and the prices.

Quantities	2008	2009
Bananas	800 bunches	900 bunches
Coconuts	400 bunches	500 bunches
Prices	**2008**	**2009**
Bananas	$2 a bunch	$4 a bunch
Coconuts	$10 a bunch	$5 a bunch

12. Calculate nominal GDP in 2008 and 2009.
13. Calculate real GDP in 2009 expressed in base-year prices.

Use the following news clip to work Problems 14 and 15.

Toyota to Shift U.S. Manufacturing Efforts

Toyota announced it planned to adjust its U.S. manufacturing operations to meet customer demands for smaller, more fuel-efficient vehicles. In 2008, Toyota started building a plant to produce the 2010 Prius for the U.S. market in Blue Springs, Mississippi. Earlier models of the Prius were produced in Asia.

Source: CNN, July 10, 2008

14. Explain how this change by Toyota will influence U.S. GDP and the components of aggregate expenditure.
15. Explain how this change by Toyota will influence the factor incomes that make up U.S. GDP.

The Uses and Limitations of Real GDP (Study Plan 4.3)

16. Use the following table to work out in which year the U.S. standard of living (i) increases and (ii) decreases? Explain your answer.

Year	Real GDP	Population
2006	$13.0 trillion	300 million
2007	$13.2 trillion	302 million
2008	$13.2 trillion	304 million
2009	$12.8 trillion	307 million

Mathematical Note (Study Plan 4.MN)

17. The table provides data on the economy of Maritime Republic that produces only fish and crabs.

Quantities	2009	2010
Fish	1,000 tons	1,100 tons
Crabs	500 tons	525 tons
Prices	**2009**	**2010**
Fish	$20 a ton	$30 a ton
Crabs	$10 a ton	$8 a ton

a. Calculate Maritime Republic's nominal GDP in 2009 and 2010.

b. Calculate Maritime Republic's chained-dollar real GDP in 2010 expressed in 2009 dollars.

Data Graphing

Use the *Data Grapher* in MyEconLab to work Problems 18 and 19.

18. In which country in 2009 was the growth rate of real GDP per person highest: Canada, Japan, or the United States?
19. In which country in 2009 was the growth rate of real GDP per person lowest: France, China, or the United States?

ADDITIONAL PROBLEMS AND APPLICATIONS

myeconlab You can work these problems in MyEconLab if assigned by your instructor.

Gross Domestic Product

20. Classify each of the following items as a final good or service or an intermediate good or service and identify which is a component of consumption expenditure, investment, or government expenditure on goods and services:
    - Banking services bought by Google.
    - Security system bought by the New York Stock Exchange.
    - Coffee beans bought by Starbucks.
    - New coffee grinders bought by Starbucks.
    - Starbuck's grande mocha frappuccino bought by a student.
    - New battle ship bought by the U.S. Navy.

Use the figure in Problem 3 to work Problems 21 and 22.

21. In 2009, flow A was \$1,000 billion, flow C was \$250 billion, flow B was \$650 billion, and flow E was \$50 billion. Calculate investment.
22. In 2010, flow D was \$2 trillion, flow E was –\$1 trillion, flow A was \$10 trillion, and flow C was \$4 trillion. Calculate consumption expenditure.

Use the following information to work Problems 23 and 24.

Mitsubishi Heavy Industries makes the wings of the new Boeing 787 Dreamliner in Japan. Toyota assembles cars for the U.S. market in Kentucky.

23. Explain where these activities appear in the U.S. National Income and Product Accounts.
24. Explain where these activities appear in Japan's National Income and Product Accounts.

Use the following news clip to work Problems 25 and 26, and use the circular flow model to illustrate your answers.

Boeing Bets the House

Boeing is producing some components of its new 787 Dreamliner in Japan and is assembling it in the United States. Much of the first year's production will be sold to ANA (All Nippon Airways), a Japanese airline.

Source: *The New York Times*, May 7, 2006

25. Explain how Boeing's activities and its transactions affect U.S. and Japanese GDP.
26. Explain how ANA's activities and its transactions affect U.S. and Japanese GDP.

Measuring U.S. GDP

Use the following data to work Problems 27 and 28.

The table lists some macroeconomic data for the United States in 2009.

Item	Billions of dollars
Wages paid to labor	8,000
Consumption expenditure	10,000
Net operating surplus	3,400
Investment	1,500
Government expenditure	2,900
Net exports	–340

27. Calculate U.S. GDP in 2009.
28. Explain the approach (expenditure or income) that you used to calculate GDP.

Use the following data to work Problems 29 to 31.

An economy produces only apples and oranges. The base year is 2009, and the table gives the quantities produced and the prices.

Quantities	2009	2010
Apples	60	160
Oranges	80	220

Prices	2009	2010
Apples	\$0.50	\$1.00
Oranges	\$0.25	\$2.00

29. Calculate nominal GDP in 2009 and 2010.
30. Calculate real GDP in 2009 and 2010 expressed in base-year prices.
31. **GDP Expands 11.4 Percent, Fastest in 13 Years**

    China's gross domestic product grew 11.4 percent last year and marked a fifth year of double-digit growth. The increase was especially remarkable given that the United States is experiencing a slowdown due to the sub-prime crisis and housing slump. Citigroup estimates that each 1 percent drop in the U.S. economy will shave 1.3 percent off China's growth, because Americans are heavy users of Chinese products. In spite of the uncertainties, China is expected to post its sixth year of double-digit growth next year.

    Source: *The China Daily*, January 24, 2008

    Use the expenditure approach for calculating China's GDP to explain why "each 1 percent drop in the U.S. economy will shave 1.3 percent off China's growth."

The Uses and Limitations of Real GDP

32. The United Nations' Human Development Index (HDI) is based on real GDP per person, life expectancy at birth, and indicators of the quality and quantity of education.
    a. Explain why the HDI might be better than real GDP as a measure of economic welfare.
    b. Which items in the HDI are part of real GDP and which items are not in real GDP?
    c. Do you think the HDI should be expanded to include items such as pollution, resource depletion, and political freedom? Explain.
    d. What other influences on economic welfare should be included in a comprehensive measure?
33. **U.K. Living Standards Outstrip U.S.**

    Oxford analysts report that living standards in Britain are set to rise above those in America for the first time since the nineteenth century. Real GDP per person in Britain will be £23,500 this year, compared with £23,250 in America, reflecting not only the strength of the pound against the dollar but also the UK economy's record run of growth since 2001. But the Oxford analysts also point out that Americans benefit from lower prices than those in Britain.

    Source: *The Sunday Times*, January 6, 2008

    If real GDP per person is more in the United Kingdom than in the United States but Americans benefit from lower prices, does this comparison of real GDP per person really tell us which country has the higher standard of living?
34. Use the news clip in Problem 31.
    a. Why might China's recent GDP growth rates overstate the actual increase in the level of production taking place in China?
    b. Explain the complications involved with attempting to compare the economic welfare in China and the United States by using the GDP for each country.
35. **Poor India Makes Millionaires at Fastest Pace**

    India, with the world's largest population of poor people created millionaires at the fastest pace in the world in 2007. India added another 23,000 more millionaires in 2007 to its 2006 tally of 100,000 millionaires measured in dollars. That is 1 millionaire for about 7,000 people living on less than $2 a day.

    Source: *The Times of India*, June 25, 2008

    a. Why might real GDP per person misrepresent the standard of living of the average Indian?
    b. Why might $2 a day underestimate the standard of living of the poorest Indians?

Economics in the News

36. After you have studied *Reading Between the Lines* on pp. 96–97 answer the following questions.
    a. Which measure of GDP would you use to describe the shape of the recovery from recession: real GDP or nominal GDP? Explain your answer.
    b. Which measure of GDP would you use to describe the rate of growth of the standard of living: real GDP or nominal GDP? Explain your answer.
    c. If the recovery was a precise "square-root" shape, what would the growth rate of real GDP be?
    d. Why is the news article wrong about the effect of a slowdown in nominal GDP growth on how slow the growth rate will "feel"?
37. **Totally Gross**

    GDP has proved useful in tracking both short-term fluctuations and long-run growth. Which isn't to say GDP doesn't miss some things. Amartya Sen, at Harvard, helped create the United Nations' Human Development Index, which combines health and education data with per capita GDP to give a better measure of the wealth of nations. Joseph Stiglitz, at Columbia, advocates a "green net national product" that takes into account the depletion of natural resources. Others want to include happiness in the measure. These alternative benchmarks have merit but can they be measured with anything like the frequency, reliability and impartiality of GDP?

    Source: *Time*, April 21, 2008

    a. Explain the factors that the news clip identifies as limiting the usefulness of GDP as a measure of economic welfare.
    b. What are the challenges involved in trying to incorporate measurements of those factors in an effort to better measure economic welfare?
    c. What does the ranking of the United States in the Human Development Index imply about the levels of health and education relative to other nations?

Mathematical Note

38. Use the information in Problem 29 to calculate the chained-dollar real GDP in 2010 expressed in 2009 dollars.

After studying this chapter, you will be able to:

- Explain why unemployment is a problem, define the unemployment rate, the employment-to-population ratio, and the labor force participation rate, and describe the trends and cycles in these labor market indicators
- Explain why unemployment is an imperfect measure of underutilized labor, why it is present even at full employment, and how unemployment and real GDP fluctuate together over a business cycle
- Explain why inflation is a problem, how we measure the price level and the inflation rate, and why the CPI measure of inflation might be biased

5 MONITORING JOBS AND INFLATION

Each month, we chart the course of employment and unemployment as measures of U.S. economic health. How do we count the number of people working and the number unemployed? What do the level of employment and the unemployment rate tell us? Are they reliable vital signs for the economy?

Having a good job that pays a decent wage is only half of the equation that translates into a good standard of living. The other half is the cost of living. We track the cost of the items that we buy with another number that is published every month, the Consumer Price Index, or CPI. What is the CPI? How is it calculated? And does it provide a reliable guide to the changes in our cost of living?

As the U.S. economy expanded after a recession in 2001, job growth was weak and questions about the health of the labor market became of vital importance to millions of American families. *Reading Between the Lines*, at the end of this chapter, puts the spotlight on the labor market during the expansion of the past few years and the slowdown of 2008.

We begin by looking at unemployment: What it is, why it matters, and how we measure it.

Employment and Unemployment

What kind of job market will you enter when you graduate? Will there be plenty of good jobs to choose among, or will jobs be so hard to find that you end up taking one that doesn't use your education and pays a low wage? The answer depends, to a large degree, on the total number of jobs available and on the number of people competing for them.

The class of 2009 had an unusually tough time in the jobs market. At the depth of recession in October 2009, 16.5 million American's wanted a job but couldn't find one. In a normal year, unemployment is less than half that level. And the U.S. economy is an incredible job-creating machine. Even in 2009 at the depths of recession, 139 million people had jobs—4 million more than in 1999 and 22 million more than in 1989. But in recent years, population growth has outstripped jobs growth, so unemployment is a serious problem.

Why Unemployment Is a Problem

Unemployment is a serious personal and social economic problem for two main reasons. It results in

- Lost incomes and production
- Lost human capital

Lost Incomes and Production The loss of a job brings a loss of income and lost production. These losses are devastating for the people who bear them and they make unemployment a frightening prospect for everyone. Unemployment benefits create a safety net, but they don't fully replace lost earnings.

Lost production means lower consumption and a lower investment in capital, which lowers the living standard in both the present and the future.

Lost Human Capital Prolonged unemployment permanently damages a person's job prospects by destroying human capital.

Economics in Action

What Keeps Ben Bernanke Awake at Night

The Great Depression began in October 1929, when the U.S. stock market crashed. It reached its deepest point in 1933, when 25 percent of the labor force was unemployed, and lasted until 1941, when the United States entered World War II. The depression quickly spread globally to envelop most nations.

The 1930s were and remain the longest and worst period of high unemployment in history. Failed banks, shops, farms, and factories left millions of Americans without jobs, homes, and food. Without the support of government and charities, millions would have starved.

The Great Depression was an enormous political event: It fostered the rise of the German and Japanese militarism that were to bring the most devastating war humans have ever fought. It also led to President Franklin D. Roosevelt's "New Deal," which enhanced the role of government in economic life and made government intervention in markets popular and the market economy unpopular.

The Great Depression also brought a revolution in economics. British economist John Maynard Keynes published his *General Theory of Employment, Interest, and Money* and created what we now call macroeconomics.

Many economists have studied the Great Depression and tried to determine why what started out as an ordinary recession became so devastating. Among them is Ben Bernanke, the Chairman of the Federal Reserve.

One of the reasons the Fed was so aggressive in cutting interest rates, saving Bear Stearns, and propping up Fannie Mae and Freddie Mac is because Ben Bernanke is so vividly aware of the horrors of total economic collapse and determined to avoid any risk of a repeat of the Great Depression.

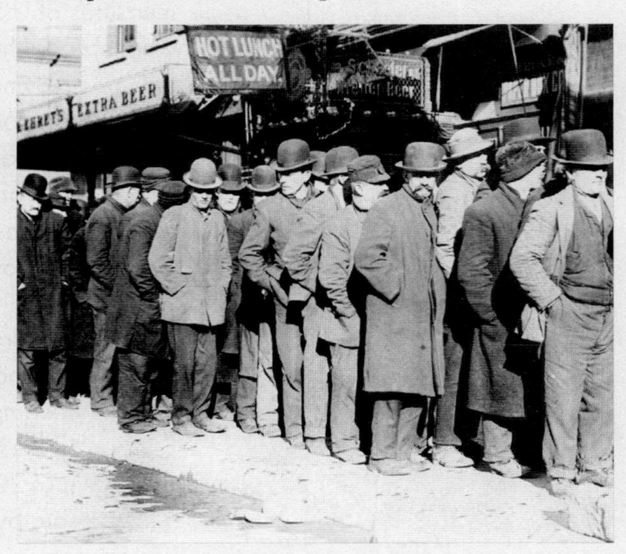

Think about a manager who loses his job when his employer downsizes. The only work he can find is driving a taxi. After a year in this work, he discovers that he can't compete with new MBA graduates. Eventually, he gets hired as a manager but in a small firm and at a lower wage than before. He has lost some of his human capital.

The cost of unemployment is spread unequally, which makes it a highly charged political problem as well as a serious economic problem.

Governments make strenuous efforts to measure unemployment accurately and to adopt policies to moderate its level and ease its pain. Here, we'll learn how the U.S. government monitors unemployment.

Current Population Survey

Every month, the U.S. Census Bureau surveys 60,000 households and asks a series of questions about the age and job market status of the members of each household. This survey is called the Current Population Survey. The Census Bureau uses the answers to describe the anatomy of the labor force.

Figure 5.1 shows the population categories used by the Census Bureau and the relationships among the categories.

The population divides into two broad groups: the working-age population and others who are too young to work or who live in institutions and are unable to work. The **working-age population** is the total number of people aged 16 years and over who are not in jail, hospital, or some other form of institutional care.

The Census Bureau divides the working-age population into two groups: those in the labor force and those not in the labor force. It also divides the labor force into two groups: the employed and the unemployed. So the **labor force** is the sum of the employed and the unemployed.

To be counted as employed in the Current Population Survey, a person must have either a full-time job or a part-time job. To be counted as *un*employed, a person must be available for work and must be in one of three categories:

1. Without work but has made specific efforts to find a job within the previous four weeks
2. Waiting to be called back to a job from which he or she has been laid off
3. Waiting to start a new job within 30 days

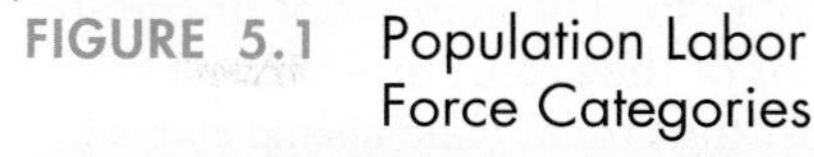

FIGURE 5.1 Population Labor Force Categories

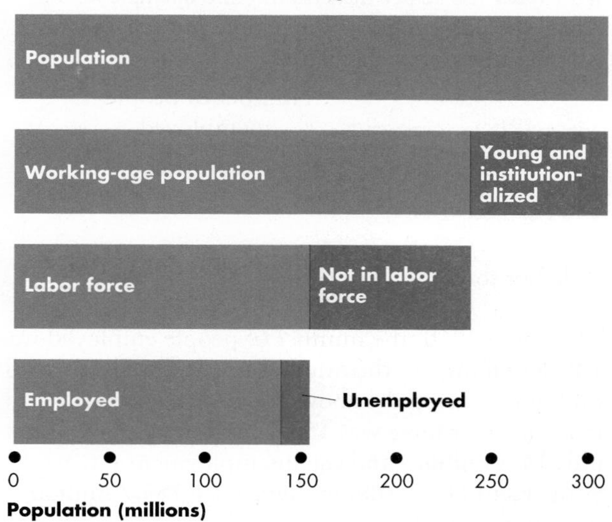

The total population is divided into the working-age population and the young and institutionalized. The working-age population is divided into those in the labor force and those not in the labor force. The labor force is divided into the employed and the unemployed.

Source of data: Bureau of Labor Statistics.

Anyone surveyed who satisfies one of these three criteria is counted as unemployed. People in the working-age population who are neither employed nor unemployed are classified as not in the labor force.

In June 2010, the population of the United States was 309.6 million; the working-age population was 237.7 million. Of this number, 84 million were not in the labor force. Most of these people were in school full time or had retired from work. The remaining 153.7 million people made up the U.S. labor force. Of these, 139.1 million were employed and 14.6 million were unemployed.

Three Labor Market Indicators

The Census Bureau calculates three indicators of the state of the labor market. They are

- The unemployment rate
- The employment-to-population ratio
- The labor force participation rate

The Unemployment Rate The amount of unemployment is an indicator of the extent to which people who want jobs can't find them. The **unemployment rate** is the percentage of the people in the labor force who are unemployed. That is,

$$\text{Unemployment rate} = \frac{\text{Number of people unemployed}}{\text{Labor force}} \times 100$$

and

$$\text{Labor force} = \begin{array}{l}\text{Number of people employed} + \\ \text{Number of people unemployed.}\end{array}$$

In June 2010, the number of people employed was 139.1 million and the number unemployed was 14.6 million. By using the above equations, you can verify that the labor force was 153.7 million (139.1 million plus 14.6 million) and the unemployment rate was 9.5 percent (14.6 million divided by 153.7 million, multiplied by 100).

Figure 5.2 shows the unemployment rate from 1980 to 2010. The average unemployment rate during this period is 6.2 percent—equivalent to 9.5 million people being unemployed in 2010.

The unemployment rate fluctuates over the business cycle and reaches a peak value after a recession ends.

Each peak unemployment rate in the recessions of 1982, 1990–1991, and 2001 was lower than the previous one. But the recession of 2008–2009 ended the downward trend.

The Employment-to-Population Ratio The number of people of working age who have jobs is an indicator of both the availability of jobs and the degree of match between people's skills and jobs. The **employment-to-population ratio** is the percentage of people of working age who have jobs. That is,

$$\text{Employment-to-population ratio} = \frac{\text{Number of people employed}}{\text{Working-age population}} \times 100.$$

In June 2010, the number of people employed was 139.1 million and the working-age population was 237.7 million. By using the above equation, you can verify that the employment-to-population ratio was 58.5 percent (139.1 million divided by 237.7 million, multiplied by 100).

Figure 5.3 shows the employment-to-population ratio. This indicator followed an upward trend before 2000 and then a downward trend. The increase before 2000 means that the U.S. economy created

FIGURE 5.2 The Unemployment Rate: 1980–2010

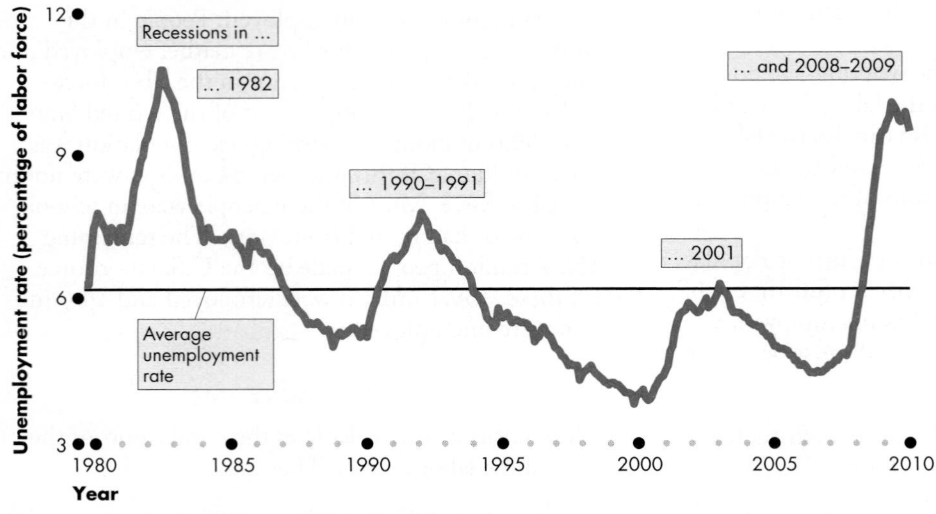

The average unemployment rate from 1980 to 2010 was 6.2 percent. The unemployment rate increases in a recession, peaks after the recession ends, and decreases in an expansion. The peak unemployment rate during a recession was on a downward trend before the 2008–2009 recession, with each successive recession having a lower unemployment rate. The severe recession of 2008–2009 broke this trend.

Source of data: Bureau of Labor Statistics.

myeconlab animation

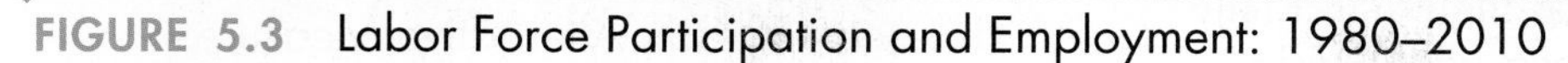

FIGURE 5.3 Labor Force Participation and Employment: 1980–2010

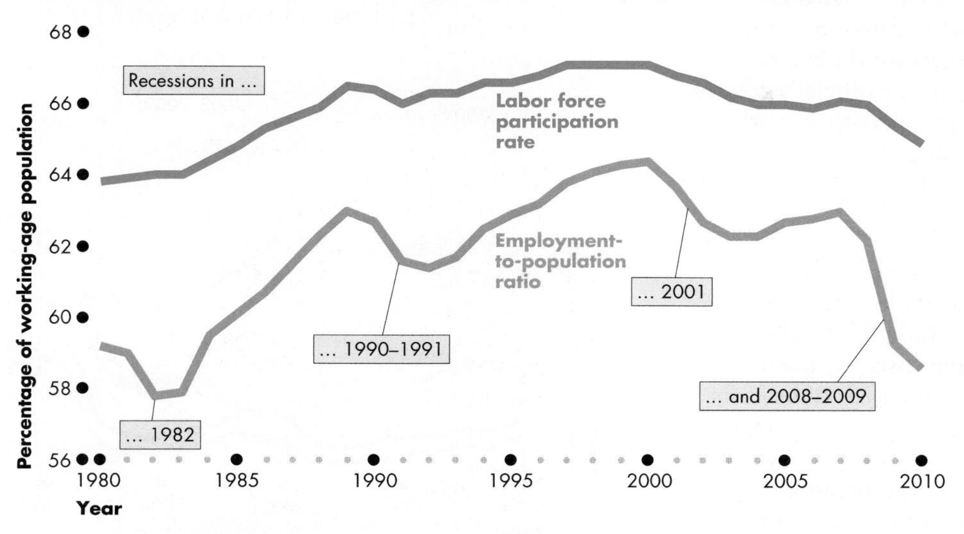

Source of data: Bureau of Labor Statistics.

The trend in the labor force participation rate and the employment-to-population ratio is upward before 2000 and downward after 2000.

The employment-to-population ratio fluctuates more than the labor force participation rate over the business cycle and reflects cyclical fluctuations in the unemployment rate.

myeconlab animation

jobs at a faster rate than the working-age population grew. This indicator also fluctuates: It falls during a recession and increases during an expansion.

The Labor Force Participation Rate The number of people in the labor force is an indicator of the willingness of people of working age to take jobs. The **labor force participation rate** is the percentage of the working-age population who are members of the labor force. That is,

$$\text{Labor force participation rate} = \frac{\text{Labor force}}{\text{Working-age population}} \times 100.$$

In June 2010, the labor force was 153.7 million and the working-age population was 237.7 million. By using the above equation, you can verify that the labor force participation rate was 64.7 percent (153.7 million divided by 237.7 million, multiplied by 100).

Figure 5.3 shows the labor force participation rate. Like the employment-to-population ratio, this indicator has an upward trend before 2000 and then a downward trend. It also has mild fluctuations around the trend. These fluctuations result from unsuccessful job seekers leaving the labor force during a recession and reentering during an expansion.

Other Definitions of Unemployment

Do fluctuations in the labor force participation rate over the business cycle mean that people who leave the labor force during a recession should be counted as unemployed? Or are they correctly counted as not-in-the-labor force?

The Bureau of Labor Statistics (BLS) believes that the official unemployment definition gives the correct measure of the unemployment rate. But the BLS provides data on two types of underutilized labor excluded from the official measure. They are

- Marginally attached workers
- Part-time workers who want full-time jobs

Marginally Attached Workers A **marginally attached worker** is a person who currently is neither working nor looking for work but has indicated that he or she wants and is available for a job and has looked for work sometime in the recent past. A marginally attached worker who has stopped looking for a job because of repeated failure to find one is called a **discouraged worker**.

The official unemployment measure excludes marginally attached workers because they haven't made specific efforts to find a job within the past four weeks. In all other respects, they are unemployed.

Part-Time Workers Who Want Full-Time Jobs Many part-time workers want to work part time. This arrangement fits in with the other demands on their time. But some part-time workers would like full-time jobs and can't find them. In the official statistics, these workers are called economic part-time workers and they are partly unemployed.

Most Costly Unemployment

All unemployment is costly, but the most costly is long-term unemployment that results from job loss.

People who are unemployed for a few weeks and then find another job bear some costs of unemployment. But these costs are low compared to the costs borne by people who remain unemployed for many weeks.

Also, people who are unemployed because they voluntarily quit their jobs to find better ones or because they have just entered or reentered the labor market bear some costs of unemployment. But these costs are lower than those borne by people who lose their job and are forced back into the job market.

The unemployment rate doesn't distinguish among these different categories of unemployment. If most of the unemployed are long-term job losers, the situation is much worse than if most are short-term voluntary job searchers.

Alternative Measures of Unemployment

To provide information about the aspects of unemployment that we've just discussed, the Bureau of Labor Statistics reports six alternative measures of the unemployment rate: two narrower than the official measure and three broader ones. The narrower measures focus on the personal cost of unemployment and the broader measures focus on assessing the full amount of unused labor resources.

Figure 5.4 shows these measures from 1994 (the first year for which they are available) to 2010. U–3 is the official unemployment rate. Long-term unemployment (U–1) and unemployed job losers (U–2) are about 40 percent of the unemployed on average but 60 percent in a deep recession. Adding discouraged workers (U–4) makes very little difference to the unemployment rate, but adding all marginally attached workers (U–5) adds one percentage point. A big difference is made by adding the economic part-time workers (U–6). In June 2010, after adding these workers the unemployment rate was 16 percent.

FIGURE 5.4 Six Alternative Measures of Unemployment

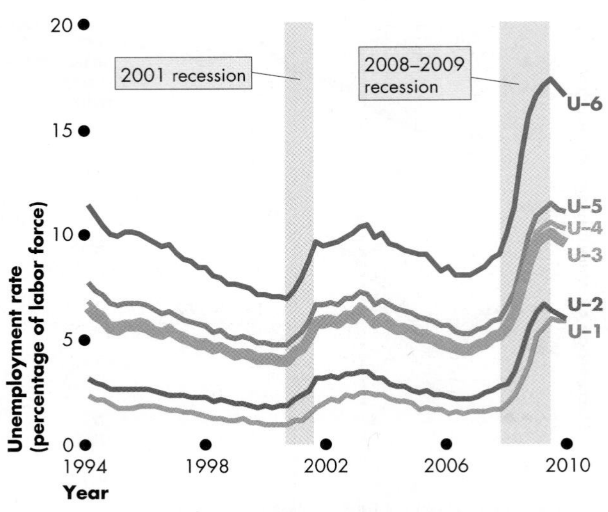

U–1 are those unemployed for 15 weeks or more, and U–2 are job losers. U–3 is the official unemployment rate. U–4 adds discouraged workers, and U–5 adds all marginally attached workers. The broadest measure, U–6, adds part-time workers who want full-time jobs. Fluctuations in all the alternative measures are similar to those in the official measure, U–3.

Source of data: Bureau of Labor Statistics.

REVIEW QUIZ

1. What determines if a person is in the labor force?
2. What distinguishes an unemployed person from one who is not in the labor force?
3. Describe the trends and fluctuations in the U.S. unemployment rate from 1980 to 2010.
4. Describe the trends and fluctuations in the U.S. employment-to-population ratio and labor force participation rate from 1980 to 2010.
5. Describe the alternative measures of unemployment.

You can work these questions in Study Plan 5.1 and get instant feedback.

You've seen how we measure employment and unemployment. Your next task is to see what we mean by full employment and how unemployment and real GDP fluctuate over the business cycle.

Unemployment and Full Employment

There is always someone without a job who is searching for one, so there is always some unemployment. The key reason is that the economy is a complex mechanism that is always changing—it experiences frictions, structural change, and cycles.

Frictional Unemployment

There is an unending flow of people into and out of the labor force as people move through the stages of life—from being in school to finding a job, to working, perhaps to becoming unhappy with a job and looking for a new one, and finally, to retiring from full-time work.

There is also an unending process of job creation and job destruction as new firms are born, firms expand or contract, and some firms fail and go out of business.

The flows into and out of the labor force and the processes of job creation and job destruction create the need for people to search for jobs and for businesses to search for workers. Businesses don't usually hire the first person who applies for a job, and unemployed people don't usually take the first job that comes their way. Instead, both firms and workers spend time searching for what they believe will be the best available match. By this process of search, people can match their own skills and interests with the available jobs and find a satisfying job and a good income.

The unemployment that arises from the normal labor turnover we've just described—from people entering and leaving the labor force and from the ongoing creation and destruction of jobs—is called **frictional unemployment**. Frictional unemployment is a permanent and healthy phenomenon in a dynamic, growing economy.

Structural Unemployment

The unemployment that arises when changes in technology or international competition change the skills needed to perform jobs or change the locations of jobs is called **structural unemployment**. Structural unemployment usually lasts longer than frictional unemployment because workers must retrain and possibly relocate to find a job. When a steel plant in Gary, Indiana, is automated, some jobs in that city disappear. Meanwhile, new jobs for security guards, retail clerks, and life-insurance salespeople are created in Chicago and Indianapolis. The unemployed former steelworkers remain unemployed for several months until they move, retrain, and get one of these jobs. Structural unemployment is painful, especially for older workers for whom the best available option might be to retire early or take a lower-skilled, lower-paying job.

Cyclical Unemployment

The higher than normal unemployment at a business cycle trough and the lower than normal unemployment at a business cycle peak is called **cyclical unemployment.** A worker who is laid off because the economy is in a recession and who gets rehired some months later when the expansion begins has experienced cyclical unemployment.

"Natural" Unemployment

Natural unemployment is the unemployment that arises from frictions and structural change when there is no cyclical unemployment—when all the unemployment is frictional and structural. Natural unemployment as a percentage of the labor force is called the **natural unemployment rate.**

Full employment is defined as a situation in which the unemployment rate equals the natural unemployment rate.

What determines the natural unemployment rate? Is it constant or does it change over time?

The natural unemployment rate is influenced by many factors but the most important ones are

- The age distribution of the population
- The scale of structural change
- The real wage rate
- Unemployment benefits

The Age Distribution of the Population An economy with a young population has a large number of new job seekers every year and has a high level of frictional unemployment. An economy with an aging population has fewer new job seekers and a low level of frictional unemployment.

The Scale of Structual Change The scale of structural change is sometimes small. The same jobs using the same machines remain in place for many years. But sometimes there is a technological upheaval. The old ways are swept aside and millions of jobs are lost and the skill to perform them loses value. The amount of structural unemployment fluctuates with the pace and volume of technological change and the change driven by fierce international competition, especially from fast-changing Asian economies. A high level of structural unemployment is present in many parts of the United States today (as you can see in *Economics in Action* below).

The Real Wage Rate The natural unemployment rate is influenced by the level of the real wage rate. Real wage rates that bring unemployment are a *minimum wage* and an *efficiency wage*. An *efficiency wage* is a wage set above the going market wage to enables firms to attract the most productive workers, get them to work hard, and discourage them from quitting.

Unemployment Benefits Unemployment benefits increase the natural unemployment rate by lowering the opportunity cost of job search. European countries have more generous unemployment benefits and higher natural unemployment rates than the United States. Extending unemployment benefits increases the natural unemployment rate.

There is no controversy about the existence of a natural unemployment rate. Nor is there disagreement that the natural unemployment rate changes. But economists don't know its exact size or the extent to which it fluctuates. The Congressional Budget Office estimates the natural unemployment rate and its estimate for 2010 was 4.8 percent—about a half of the unemployment in that year.

Real GDP and Unemployment Over the Cycle

The quantity of real GDP at full employment is *potential GDP* (p. 90). Over the business cycle, real GDP fluctuates around potential GDP. The gap between real GDP and potential GDP is called the **output gap**. As the output gap fluctuates over the business cycle, the unemployment rate fluctuates around the natural unemployment rate.

Economics in Action

Structural Unemployment and Labor Reallocation in Michigan

At 13.6 percent, Michigan had the nation's highest official unemployment rate in 2010. The long-term unemployment rate was 8.4 percent and when marginally attached workers and part-time workers who want full time jobs are added, almost 22 percent of the state's labor force was unemployed or underemployed.

Michigan's main problem is structural—a collapse of manufacturing jobs centered on the auto industry. These jobs had been disappearing steadily as robot technologies spread to do ever more of the tasks in the assembly of automobiles. The 2008–2009 recession accelerated this rate of job loss.

But the story is not all negative, and the outlook is not all bleak. Around 11,000 businesses in Michigan produce high-tech scientific instruments and components for defense equipment, energy plants, and medical equipment. These businesses employ almost 400,000 people, which is more than 10 percent of the state's labor force and two thirds of all manufacturing jobs. Workers in high-tech manufacturing enjoy incomes almost 60 percent higher than the state's average income. Although the recession hit these firms, they cut employment by only 10 percent, compared with a 24 percent cut in manufacturing jobs in the rest of the Michigan economy.

The structural unemployment rate remains high because job gains in new advanced-manufacturing firms are not yet enough to offset the job losses in the shrinking parts of manufacturing.

FIGURE 5.5 The Output Gap and the Unemployment Rate

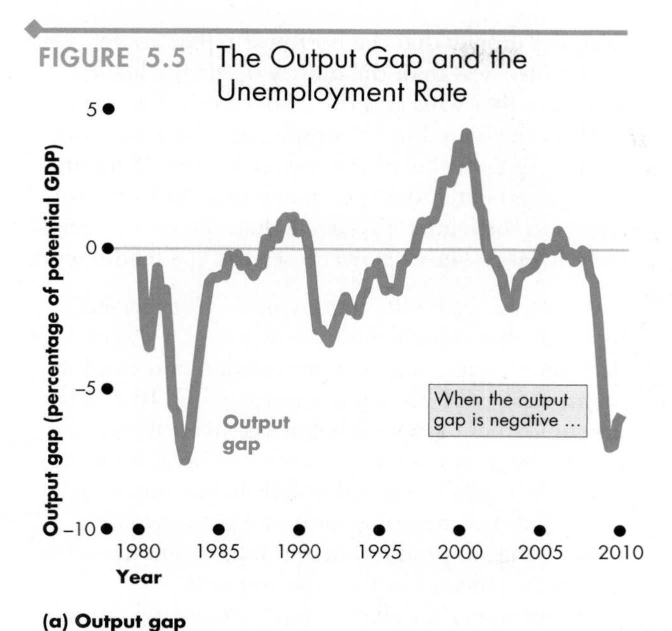

(a) Output gap

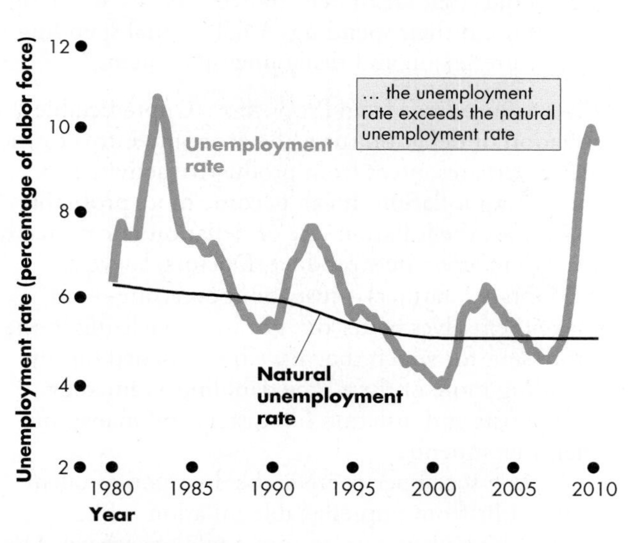

(b) Unemployment rate

As real GDP fluctuates around potential GDP in part (a), the unemployment rate fluctuates around the natural unemployment rate in part (b). In recessions, cyclical unemployment peaks and the output gap becomes negative. At business cycle peaks, the unemployment rate falls below the natural rate and the output gap becomes positive. The natural unemployment rate decreased during the 1980s and 1990s.

Sources of data: Bureau of Economic Analysis, Bureau of Labor Statistics, and Congressional Budget Office.

myeconlab animation

Figure 5.5 illustrates these fluctuations in the United States between 1980 and 2010—the output gap in part (a) and the unemployment rate and natural unemployment rate in part (b).

When the economy is at full employment, the unemployment rate equals the natural unemployment rate and real GDP equals potential GDP so the output gap is zero. When the unemployment rate is less than the natural unemployment rate, real GDP is greater than potential GDP and the output gap is positive. And when the unemployment rate is greater than the natural unemployment rate, real GDP is less than potential GDP and the output gap is negative.

Figure 5.5(b) shows the natural unemployment rate estimated by the Congressional Budget Office. This estimate puts the natural unemployment rate at 6.2 percent in 1980 and falling steadily through the 1980s and 1990s to 4.8 percent by 2000. This estimate of the natural unemployment rate in the United States is one that many, but not all, economists agree with.

REVIEW QUIZ

1. Why does unemployment arise and what makes some unemployment unavoidable?
2. Define frictional unemployment, structural unemployment, and cyclical unemployment. Give examples of each type of unemployment.
3. What is the natural unemployment rate?
4. How does the natural unemployment rate change and what factors might make it change?
5. Why is the unemployment rate never zero, even at full employment?
6. What is the output gap? How does it change when the economy goes into recession?
7. How does the unemployment rate fluctuate over the business cycle?

You can work these questions in Study Plan 5.2 and get instant feedback.

Your next task is to see how we monitor the price level and the inflation rate. You will learn about the Consumer Price Index (CPI), which is monitored every month. You will also learn about other measures of the price level and the inflation rate.

The Price Level, Inflation, and Deflation

What will it *really* cost you to pay off your student loan? What will your parent's life savings buy when they retire? The answers depend on what happens to the **price level**, the average level of prices, and the value of money. A persistently rising price level is called **inflation;** a persistently falling price level is called **deflation**.

We are interested in the price level, inflation, and deflation for two main reasons. First, we want to measure the annual percentage change of the price level—the inflation rate or deflation rate. Second, we want to distinguish between the money values and real values of economic variables such as your student loan and your parent's savings.

We begin by explaining why inflation and deflation are problems. Then we'll look at how we measure the price level and the inflation rate. Finally, we'll return to the task of distinguishing real values from money values.

Why Inflation and Deflation are Problems

Low, steady, and anticipated inflation or deflation isn't a problem, but an unexpected burst of inflation or period of deflation brings big problems and costs. An unexpected inflation or deflation:

- Redistributes income
- Redistributes wealth
- Lowers real GDP and employment
- Diverts resources from production

Redistribution of Income Workers and employers sign wage contracts that last for a year or more. An unexpected burst of inflation raises prices but doesn't immediately raise the wages. Workers are worse off because their wages buy less than they bargained for and employers are better off because their profits rise.

An unexpected period of deflation has the opposite effect. Wage rates don't fall but the prices fall. Workers are better off because their fixed wages buy more than they bargained for and employers are worse off with lower profits.

Redistribution of Wealth People enter into loan contracts that are fixed in money terms and that pay an interest rate agreed as a percentage of the money borrowed and lent. With an unexpected burst of inflation, the money that the borrower repays to the lender buys less than the money originally loaned. The borrower wins and the lender loses. The interest paid on the loan doesn't compensate the lender for the loss in the value of the money loaned. With an unexpected deflation, the money that the borrower repays to the lender buys *more* than the money originally loaned. The borrower loses and the lender wins.

Lowers Real GDP and Employment Unexpected inflation that raises firms' profits brings a rise in investment and a boom in production and employment. Real GDP rises above potential GDP and the unemployment rate falls below the natural rate. But this situation is *temporary*. Profitable investment dries up, spending falls, real GDP falls below potential GDP and the unemployment rate rises. Avoiding these swings in production and jobs means avoiding unexpected swings in the inflation rate.

An unexpected deflation has even greater consequences for real GDP and jobs. Businesses and households that are in debt (borrowers) are worse off and they cut their spending. A fall in total spending brings a recession and rising unemployment.

Diverts Resources from Production Unpredictable inflation or deflation turns the economy into a casino and diverts resources from productive activities to forecasting inflation. It can become more profitable to forecast the inflation rate or deflation rate correctly than to invent a new product. Doctors, lawyers, accountants, farmers—just about everyone—can make themselves better off, not by specializing in the profession for which they have been trained but by spending more of their time dabbling as amateur economists and inflation forecasters and managing their investments.

From a social perspective, the diversion of talent that results from unpredictable inflation is like throwing scarce resources onto a pile of garbage. This waste of resources is a cost of inflation.

At its worst, inflation becomes **hyperinflation**—an inflation rate of 50 percent a month or higher that grinds the economy to a halt and causes a society to collapse. Hyperinflation is rare, but Zimbabwe in recent years and several European and Latin American countries have experienced it.

We pay close attention to the inflation rate, even when its rate is low, to avoid its consequences. We monitor the price level every month and devote considerable resources to measuring it accurately. You're now going to see how we do this.

The Consumer Price Index

Every month, the Bureau of Labor Statistics (BLS) measures the price level by calculating the **Consumer Price Index (CPI)**, which is a measure of the average of the prices paid by urban consumers for a fixed basket of consumer goods and services. What you learn here will help you to make sense of the CPI and relate it to your own economic life. The CPI tells you about the *value* of the money in your pocket.

Reading the CPI Numbers

The CPI is defined to equal 100 for a period called the *reference base period*. Currently, the reference base period is 1982–1984. That is, for the average of the 36 months from January 1982 through December 1984, the CPI equals 100.

In June 2010, the CPI was 218. This number tells us that the average of the prices paid by urban consumers for a fixed market basket of consumer goods and services was 118 percent higher in 2010 than it was on the average during 1982–1984.

Constructing the CPI

Constructing the CPI involves three stages:

- Selecting the CPI basket
- Conducting the monthly price survey
- Calculating the CPI

The CPI Basket The first stage in constructing the CPI is to select what is called the *CPI basket*. This basket contains the goods and services represented in the index, each weighted by its relative importance. The idea is to make the relative importance of the items in the CPI basket the same as that in the budget of an average urban household. For example, because people spend more on housing than on bus rides, the CPI places more weight on the price of housing than on the price of a bus ride.

To determine the CPI basket, the BLS conducts a Consumer Expenditure Survey. Today's CPI basket is based on data gathered in the Consumer Expenditure Survey of 2008.

Figure 5.6 shows the CPI basket in June 2010. As you look at the relative importance of the items in the CPI basket, remember that it applies to the *average* household. *Individual* household's baskets are spread around the average. Think about what you buy and compare your basket with the CPI basket.

FIGURE 5.6 The CPI Basket

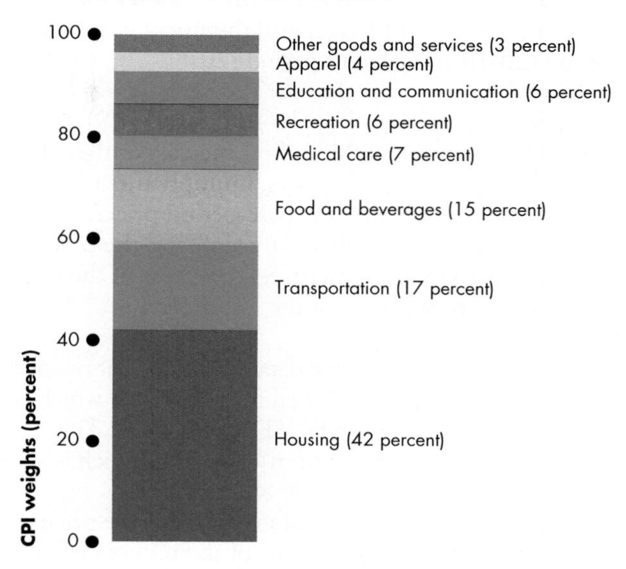

The CPI basket consists of the items that an average urban household buys. It consists mainly of housing (42 percent), transportation (17 percent), and food and beverages (15 percent). All other items add up to 26 percent of the total.

Sources of data: United States Census Bureau and Bureau of Labor Statistics.

myeconlab animation

The Monthly Price Survey Each month, BLS employees check the prices of the 80,000 goods and services in the CPI basket in 30 metropolitan areas. Because the CPI aims to measure price *changes*, it is important that the prices recorded each month refer to exactly the same item. For example, suppose the price of a box of jelly beans has increased but a box now contains more beans. Has the price of jelly beans increased? The BLS employee must record the details of changes in quality or packaging so that price changes can be isolated from other changes.

Once the raw price data are in hand, the next task is to calculate the CPI.

Calculating the CPI To calculate the CPI, we

1. Find the cost of the CPI basket at base-period prices.
2. Find the cost of the CPI basket at current-period prices.
3. Calculate the CPI for the base period and the current period.

We'll work through these three steps for the simple artificial economy in Table 5.1, which shows the quantities in the CPI basket and the prices in the base period (2010) and current period (2011).

Part (a) contains the data for the base period. In that period, consumers bought 10 oranges at $1 each and 5 haircuts at $8 each. To find the cost of the CPI basket in the base-period prices, multiply the quantities in the CPI basket by the base-period prices. The cost of oranges is $10 (10 at $1 each), and the cost of haircuts is $40 (5 at $8 each). So total cost of the CPI basket in the base period of the CPI basket is $50 ($10 + $40).

Part (b) contains the price data for the current period. The price of an orange increased from $1 to $2, which is a 100 percent increase—($1 ÷ $1) × 100 = 100. The price of a haircut increased from $8 to $10, which is a 25 percent increase—($2 ÷ $8) × 100 = 25.

The CPI provides a way of averaging these price increases by comparing the cost of the basket rather than the price of each item. To find the cost of the CPI basket in the current period, 2011, multiply the quantities in the basket by their 2011 prices. The cost of oranges is $20 (10 at $2 each), and the cost of haircuts is $50 (5 at $10 each). So total cost of the fixed CPI basket at current-period prices is $70 ($20 + $50).

TABLE 5.1 The CPI: A Simplified Calculation

(a) The cost of the CPI basket at base-period prices: 2010

Item (CPI basket)	Quantity (CPI basket)	Price	Cost of CPI Basket
Oranges	10	$1.00	$10
Haircuts	5	$8.00	$40
Cost of CPI basket at base-period prices			$50

(b) The cost of the CPI basket at current-period prices: 2011

Item (CPI basket)	Quantity (CPI basket)	Price	Cost of CPI Basket
Oranges	10	$2.00	$20
Haircuts	5	$10.00	$50
Cost of CPI basket at current-period prices			$70

You've now taken the first two steps toward calculating the CPI: calculating the cost of the CPI basket in the base period and the current period. The third step uses the numbers you've just calculated to find the CPI for 2010 and 2011.

The formula for the CPI is

$$\text{CPI} = \frac{\text{Cost of CPI basket at current prices}}{\text{Cost of CPI basket at base-period prices}} \times 100.$$

In Table 5.1, you established that in 2010 (the base period), the cost of the CPI basket was $50 and in 2011, it was $70. If we use these numbers in the CPI formula, we can find the CPI for 2010 and 2011. For 2010, the CPI is

$$\text{CPI in 2010} = \frac{\$50}{\$50} \times 100 = 100.$$

For 2011, the CPI is

$$\text{CPI in 2011} = \frac{\$70}{\$50} \times 100 = 140.$$

The principles that you've applied in this simplified CPI calculation apply to the more complex calculations performed every month by the BLS.

Measuring the Inflation Rate

A major purpose of the CPI is to measure changes in the cost of living and in the value of money. To measure these changes, we calculate the *inflation rate* as the annual percentage change in the CPI. To calculate the inflation rate, we use the formula:

$$\text{Inflation rate} = \frac{\text{CPI this year} - \text{CPI last year}}{\text{CPI last year}} \times 100.$$

We can use this formula to calculate the inflation rate in 2010. The CPI in June 2010 was 218.0, and the CPI in June 2009 was 215.7. So the inflation rate during the twelve months to June 2010 was

$$\text{Inflation rate} = \frac{(218.0 - 215.7)}{215.7} \times 100 = 1.1\%.$$

Distinguishing High Inflation from a High Price Level

Figure 5.7 shows the CPI and the inflation rate in the United States between 1970 and 2010. The two parts of the figure are related and emphasize the distinction between high inflation and high prices.

When the price level in part (a) *rises rapidly*, (1970 through 1982), the inflation rate in part (b) is *high*. When the price level in part (a) *rises slowly*, (after 1982), the inflation rate in part (b) is *low*.

A high inflation rate means that the price level is rising rapidly. A high price level means that there has been a sustained period of rising prices.

When the price level in part (a) *falls* (2009), the inflation rate in part (b) is negative—deflation.

The CPI is not a perfect measure of the price level and changes in the CPI probably overstate the inflation rate. Let's look at the sources of bias.

The Biased CPI

The main sources of bias in the CPI are

- New goods bias
- Quality change bias
- Commodity substitution bias
- Outlet substitution bias

New Goods Bias If you want to compare the price level in 2009 with that in 1969, you must somehow compare the price of a computer today with that of a typewriter in 1969. Because a PC is more expensive than a typewriter was, the arrival of the PC puts an upward bias into the CPI and its inflation rate.

Quality Change Bias Cars, CD players, and many other items get better every year. Part of the rise in the prices of these items is a payment for improved quality and is not inflation. But the CPI counts the entire price rise as inflation and so overstates inflation.

Commodity Substitution Bias Changes in relative prices lead consumers to change the items they buy. For example, if the price of beef rises and the price of chicken remains unchanged, people buy more chicken and less beef. This switch from beef to chicken might provide the same amount of protein and the same enjoyment as before and expenditure is the same as before. The price of protein has not changed. But because the CPI ignores the substitution of chicken for beef, it says the price of protein has increased.

FIGURE 5.7 The CPI and the Inflation Rate

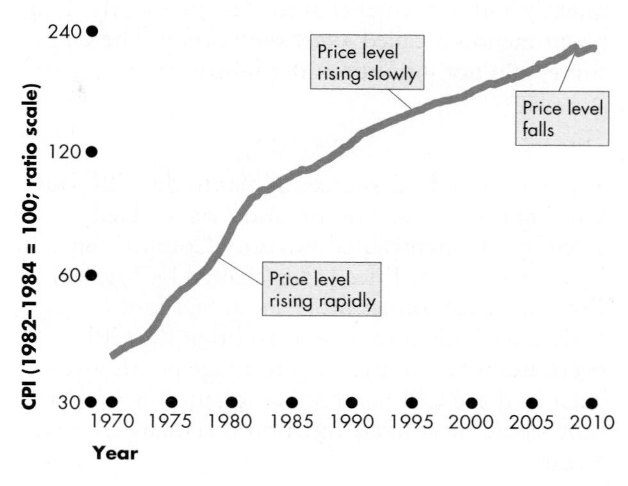

(a) CPI

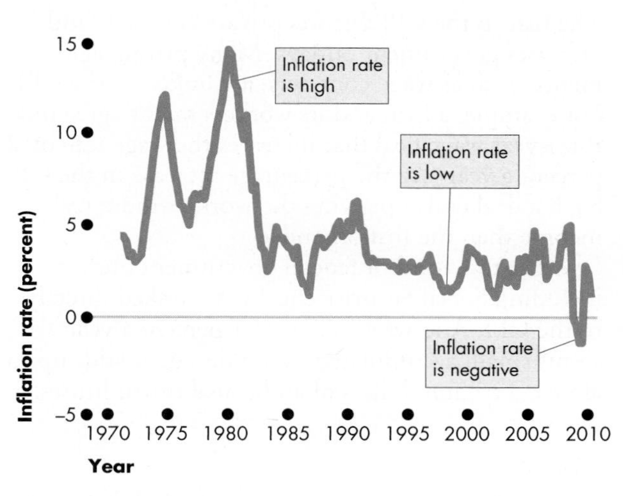

(b) Inflation rate

When the price level rises rapidly, the inflation rate is high, and when the price level rises slowly, the inflation rate is low. When the price level falls, the inflation rate is negative.

From 1970 through 1982, the price level increased rapidly in part (a) and the inflation rate was high in part (b). After 1982, the price level rose slowly in part (a) and the inflation rate was low in part (b). In 2009, the price level fell and the inflation rate was negative—there was deflation.

Source of data: Bureau of Labor Statistics.

myeconlab animation

Outlet Substitution Bias When confronted with higher prices, people use discount stores more frequently and convenience stores less frequently. This phenomenon is called *outlet substitution*. The CPI surveys do not monitor outlet substitutions.

The Magnitude of the Bias

You've reviewed the sources of bias in the CPI. But how big is the bias? This question was tackled in 1996 by a Congressional Advisory Commission on the Consumer Price Index chaired by Michael Boskin, an economics professor at Stanford University. This commission said that the CPI overstates inflation by 1.1 percentage points a year. That is, if the CPI reports that inflation is 3.1 percent a year, most likely inflation is actually 2 percent a year.

Some Consequences of the Bias

The bias in the CPI distorts private contracts and increases government outlays. Many private agreements, such as wage contracts, are linked to the CPI. For example, a firm and its workers might agree to a three-year wage deal that increases the wage rate by 2 percent a year *plus* the percentage increase in the CPI. Such a deal ends up giving the workers more real income than the firm intended.

Close to a third of federal government outlays, including Social Security checks, are linked directly to the CPI. And while a bias of 1 percent a year seems small, accumulated over a decade it adds up to almost a trillion dollars of additional expenditures.

Alternative Price Indexes

The CPI is just one of many alternative price level index numbers and because of the bias in the CPI, other measures are used for some purposes. We'll describe three alternatives to the CPI and explain when and why they might be preferred to the CPI. The alternatives are

- Chained CPI
- Personal consumption expenditure deflator
- GDP deflator

Chained CPI The *chained CPI* is a price index that is calculated using a similar method to that used to calculate *chained-dollar real GDP* described in Chapter 4 (see pp. 98–99).

The *chained* CPI overcomes the sources of bias in the CPI. It incorporates substitutions and new goods bias by using current and previous period quantities rather than fixed quantities from an earlier period.

The practical difference made by the chained CPI is small. This index has been calculated since 2000 and the average inflation rate since then as measured by the chained CPI is only 0.3 percentage points lower than the standard CPI—2.5 percent versus 2.8 percent per year.

Personal Consumption Expenditure Deflator The *personal consumption expenditure deflator* (or *PCE deflator*) is calculated from data in the national income accounts that you studied in Chapter 4. When the Bureau of Economic Analysis calculates *real GDP*, it also calculates the real values of its expenditure components: real consumption expenditure, real investment, real government expenditure, and real net exports. These calculations are done in the same way as that for real GDP described in simplified terms on p. 89 and more technically on pp. 98–99 in Chapter 4.

To calculate the PCE deflator, we use the formula:

$$\text{PCE deflator} = (\text{Nominal } C \div \text{Real } C) \times 100,$$

where C is personal consumption expenditure.

The basket of goods and services included in the PCE deflator is broader than that in the CPI because it includes all consumption expenditure, not only the items bought by a typical urban family.

The difference between the PCE deflator and the CPI is small. Since 2000, the inflation rate measured by the PCE deflator is 2.4 percent per year, 0.4 percentage points lower than the CPI inflation rate.

GDP Deflator The *GDP deflator* is a bit like the PCE deflator except that it includes all the goods and services that are counted as part of GDP. So it is an index of the prices of the items in consumption, investment, government expenditure, and net exports.

$$\text{GDP deflator} = (\text{Nominal GDP} \div \text{Real GDP}) \times 100.$$

This broader price index is appropriate for macroeconomics because it is a comprehensive measure of the cost of the real GDP basket of goods and services.

Since 2000, the GDP deflator has increased at an average rate of 2.6 percent per year, only 0.2 percentage points below the CPI inflation rate.

Core CPI Inflation

No matter whether we calculate the inflation rate using the CPI, the chained CPI, the personal consumption expenditure deflator, or the GDP deflator, the number bounces around a good deal from month to month or quarter to quarter. To determine the trend in the inflation rate, we need to strip the raw numbers of their volatility. The **core CPI inflation rate**, which is the CPI inflation rate excluding volatile elements, attempts to do just that and reveal the underlying inflation trend.

As a practical matter, the core CPI inflation rate is calculated as the percentage change in the CPI (or other price index) excluding food and fuel. The prices of these two items are among the most volatile.

While the core CPI inflation rate removes the volatile elements in inflation, it can give a misleading view of the true underlying inflation rate. If the relative prices of the excluded items are changing, the core CPI inflation rate will give a biased measure of the true underlying inflation rate.

Such a misleading account was given during the years between 2003 and 2008 when the relative prices of food and fuel were rising. The result was a core CPI inflation rate that was systematically below the CPI inflation rate. Figure 5.8 shows the two series since 2000. More refined measures of core inflation have been suggested that eliminate the bias.

The Real Variables in Macroeconomics

You saw in Chapter 4 how we measure real GDP. And you've seen in this chapter how we can use nominal GDP and real GDP to provide another measure of the price level—the GDP deflator. But viewing real GDP as nominal GDP deflated, opens up the idea of other real variables. By using the GDP deflator, we can deflate other nominal variables to find their real values. For example, the *real wage rate* is the nominal wage rate divided by the GDP deflator.

We can adjust any nominal quantity or price variable for inflation by deflating it—by dividing it by the price level.

There is one variable that is a bit different—an interest rate. A real interest rate is *not* a nominal interest rate divided by the price level. You'll learn how to adjust the nominal interest rate for inflation to find the real interest rate in Chapter 7. But all the other real variables of macroeconomics are calculated by dividing a nominal variable by the price level.

FIGURE 5.8 Core Inflation

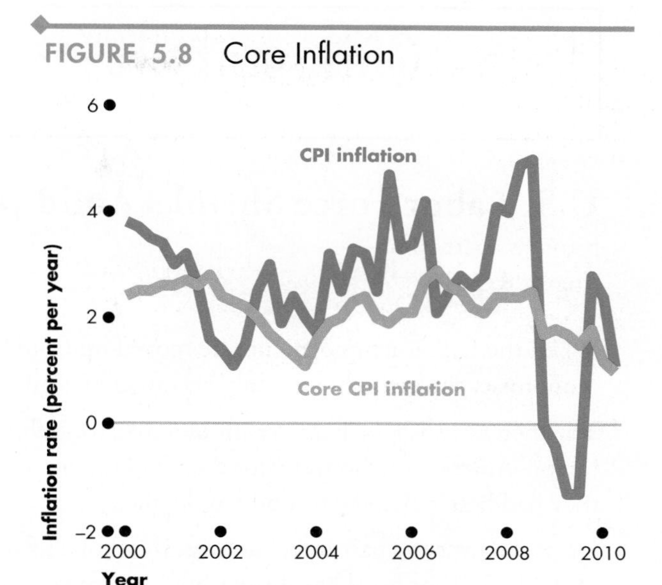

The core CPI inflation rate excludes volatile price changes of food and fuel. Since 2003, the core CPI inflation rate has mostly been below the CPI inflation rate because the relative prices of food and fuel have been rising.

Source of data: Bureau of Labor Statistics.

myeconlab animation

REVIEW QUIZ

1. What is the price level?
2. What is the CPI and how is it calculated?
3. How do we calculate the inflation rate and what is its relationship with the CPI?
4. What are the four main ways in which the CPI is an upward-biased measure of the price level?
5. What problems arise from the CPI bias?
6. What are the alternative measures of the price level and how do they address the problem of bias in the CPI?

You can work these questions in Study Plan 5.3 and get instant feedback.

You've now completed your study of the measurement of macroeconomic performance. Your next task is to learn what determines that performance and how policy actions might improve it. But first, take a close-up look at the labor market in 2009 and 2010 in *Reading Between the Lines* on pp. 122–123.

READING BETWEEN THE LINES

Jobs Growth Lags Recovery

U.S. Labor Force Shrinks Amid Jobs Market Woes

http://www.ft.com
August 8, 2010

When the U.S. unemployment rate moved up from 9.7 percent to 9.9 percent in April, economists cheered it as an oddly encouraging sign.

The increase was largely the result of a massive influx of 805,000 workers into the labor force—Americans who were not even looking for a job during the recession and finally felt they had better chances to find employment.

However, over the past three months, that hope seems to have vanished. Since May, the size of the U.S. labor force has shrunk by 1.15m people, with 188,000 of those dropping out last month, according to data released by the U.S. government on Friday.

Although labor force participation data are notoriously volatile, the underlying trend is unmistakable: the majority of the 1.65m people who jumped back into the labor force in the first four months of the year are back on the sidelines, cowed by the sudden slowdown in the U.S. economy and the tepid pace of private-sector job creation. …

Additionally, downward pressure on the size of the labor force could be exacerbated as Americans exhaust their unemployment benefits, which in some states last as long as 99 weeks. To receive jobless checks, workers have to prove that they are searching for a post, keeping them inside the labor force.

Indeed, in the latest government data, there were already signs of long-term unemployed Americans exiting the workforce in desperation after running out of benefits. In July, 179,000 people who had been unemployed for 27 weeks or longer left the labor force, accounting for most of the overall decline. …

ESSENCE OF THE STORY

- The U.S. unemployment rate increased from 9.7 percent to 9.9 percent in April 2010 mainly because 805,000 workers entered the labor force.
- In May, June, and July 2010, the U.S. labor force decreased by 1.15 million people.
- Monthly labor force participation data are volatile, but the underlying trend is downward and is being driven by slow economic growth and a slow pace of job creation in the private sector.
- To receive unemployment benefits, workers must search for work so that they are counted as unemployed and in the labor force.
- As benefits run out, a worker might stop looking for work and leave the labor force, which distorts the true change in unemployment.
- In July 2010, 179,000 people who had been unemployed for 27 weeks or longer left the labor force, accounting for most of the overall decline.

ECONOMIC ANALYSIS

- This news article reports and comments on some labor market data for April through July 2010.
- During 2010, the economy was expanding following a deep recession. Figure 1 shows real GDP bottomed in mid-2009.
- Despite the expanding economy, the labor force participation rate continued on a downward trend (as reported in the news article) and the unemployment rate continued to rise.
- Figure 2 shows that the unemployment rate continued to rise until October 2009 when it reached a peak.
- The tendency for the turning point in the unemployment rate to lag the turning point in real GDP by a few months is a normal feature of the business cycle.
- The unemployment path looks the same regardless of whether we use the official measure, U–3, or add in discouraged workers (U–4) or other marginally attached workers (U–5).
- Because all the unemployment rates move up and down together, we can conclude that the falling labor force participation rate is not being driven by a fall in the number of marginally attached workers.
- Rather, as the news article says, it is long-term unemployed who are withdrawing from the labor force.
- But as Fig. 3 shows, the percentage of the unemployed who are long-term unemployed (15 weeks or longer) continued to rise through mid-2010.
- The news article identifies one link between unemployment benefits and the unemployment rate—for those whose benefits run out, the incentive to remain unemployed weakens so these people are more likely to withdraw from the labor force.
- There is a second link between unemployment benefits and the unemployment rate: When benefits are extended (to 99 weeks in some states), for those who qualify, the incentive to remain unemployed and take longer to find a suitable job strengthens.
- The increase in the percentage of the unemployed who remain unemployed for 15 weeks or longer shown in Fig. 3 might be influenced by this effect.

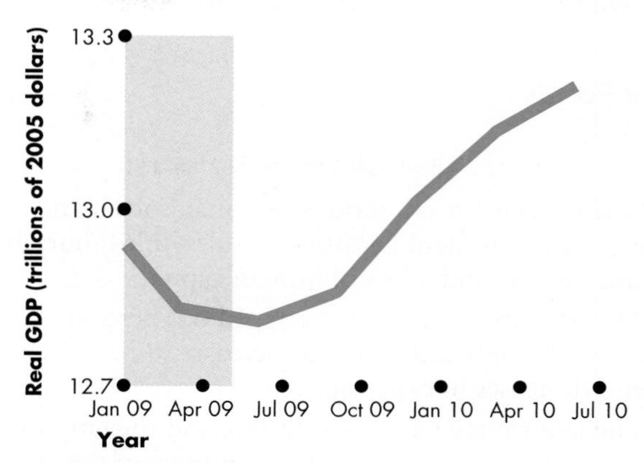

Figure 1 Real GDP

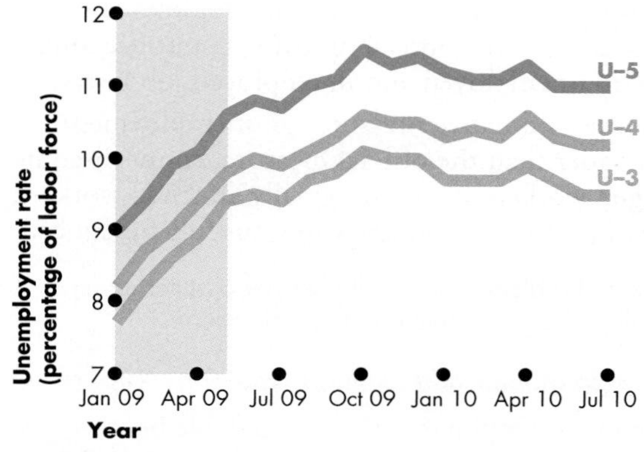

Figure 2 Unemployment

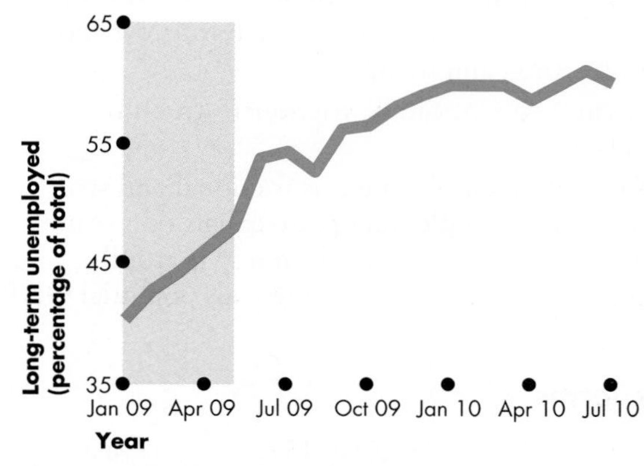

Figure 3 Long-term unemployment

SUMMARY

Key Points

Employment and Unemployment (pp. 108–112)

- Unemployment is a serious personal, social, and economic problem because it results in lost output and income and a loss of human capital.
- The unemployment rate averaged 6.2 percent between 1980 and 2010. It increases in recessions and decreases in expansions.
- The labor force participation rate and the employment-to-population ratio have an upward trend and fluctuate with the business cycle.
- Two alternative measures of unemployment, narrower than the official measure, count the long-term unemployed and unemployed job losers.
- Three alternative measures of unemployment, broader than the official measure, count discouraged workers, other marginally attached workers, and part-time workers who want full-time jobs.

Working Problems 1 to 5 will give you a better understanding of employment and unemployment.

Unemployment and Full Employment (pp. 113–115)

- Some unemployment is unavoidable because people are constantly entering and leaving the labor force and losing or quitting jobs; also firms that create jobs are constantly being borne, expanding, contracting, and dying.
- Unemployment can be frictional, structural, or cyclical.
- When all unemployment is frictional and structural, the unemployment rate equals the natural unemployment rate, the economy is at full employment, and real GDP equals potential GDP.
- Over the business cycle, real GDP fluctuates around potential GDP and the unemployment rate fluctuates around the natural unemployment rate.

Working Problems 6 to 11 will give you a better understanding of unemployment and full employment.

The Price Level, Inflation, and Deflation (pp. 116–121)

- Inflation and deflation that are unexpected redistribute income and wealth and divert resources from production.
- The Consumer Price Index (CPI) is a measure of the average of the prices paid by urban consumers for a fixed basket of consumer goods and services.
- The CPI is defined to equal 100 for a reference base period—currently 1982–1984.
- The inflation rate is the percentage change in the CPI from one period to the next.
- Changes in the CPI probably overstate the inflation rate because of the bias that arises from new goods, quality changes, commodity substitution, and outlet substitution.
- The bias in the CPI distorts private contracts and increases government outlays.
- Alternative price level measures such as the PCE deflator and GDP deflator avoid the bias of the CPI but do not make a large difference to the measured inflation rate.
- Real economic variables are calculated by dividing nominal variables by the price level.

Working Problems 12 to 20 will give you a better understanding of the price level, inflation, and deflation.

Key Terms

STUDY PLAN PROBLEMS AND APPLICATIONS

myeconlab You can work Problems 1 to 20 in MyEconLab Chapter 5 Study Plan and get instant feedback.

Employment and Unemployment (Study Plan 5.1)

1. The Bureau of Labor Statistics reported the following data for 2008:
   Labor force: 154,287,000
   Employment: 145,362,000
   Working-age population: 233,788,000
   Calculate the
   a. Unemployment rate.
   b. Labor force participation rate.
   c. Employment-to-population ratio.
2. In July 2009, in the economy of Sandy Island, 10,000 people were employed, 1,000 were unemployed, and 5,000 were not in the labor force. During August 2009, 80 people lost their jobs and didn't look for new ones, 20 people quit their jobs and retired, 150 unemployed people were hired, 50 people quit the labor force, and 40 people entered the labor force to look for work. Calculate for July 2009
   a. The unemployment rate.
   b. The employment-to-population ratio.

   And calculate for the end of August 2009
   c. The number of people unemployed.
   d. The number of people employed.
   e. The unemployment rate.

Use the following information to work Problems 3 and 4.

In March 2007, the U.S. unemployment rate was 4.4 percent. In August 2008, the unemployment rate was 6.1 percent. Predict what happened to

3. Unemployment between March 2007 and August 2008, assuming that the labor force was constant.
4. The labor force between March 2007 and August 2008, assuming that unemployment was constant.
5. **Shrinking U.S. Labor Force Keeps Unemployment Rate From Rising**

   An exodus of discouraged workers from the job market kept the unemployment rate from climbing above 10 percent. Had the labor force not decreased by 661,000, the unemployment rate would have been 10.4 percent. The number of discouraged workers rose to 929,000 last month.

   Source: Bloomberg, January 9, 2010

   What is a discouraged worker? Explain how an increase in discouraged workers influences the official unemployment rate and U–4.

Unemployment and Full Employment (Study Plan 5.2)

Use the following news clip to work Problems 6 to 8.

Nation's Economic Pain Deepens

A spike in the unemployment rate—the biggest in more than two decades—raised new concerns that the economy is heading into a recession. The U.S. unemployment rate soared to 5.5% in May from 5% in April—much higher than forecasted. The surge marked the biggest one-month jump in unemployment since February 1986, and the 5.5% rate is the highest seen since October 2004.

Source: CNN, June 6, 2008

6. How does the unemployment rate in May compare to the unemployment rate during the earlier recessions?
7. Why might the unemployment rate tend to actually underestimate the unemployment problem, especially during a recession?
8. How does the unemployment rate in May compare to the estimated natural unemployment rate? What does this imply about the relationship between real GDP and potential GDP at this time?

Use the following information to work Problems 9 and 10.

Some Firms Struggle to Hire Despite High Unemployment

Matching people with available jobs is always difficult after a recession as the economy remakes itself. But Labor Department data suggest the disconnect is particularly acute this time. Since the recovery began in mid-2009, the number of job openings has risen more than twice as fast as actual hires. If the job market were working normally, openings would be getting filled as they appear. Some five million more would be employed and the unemployment rate would be 6.8%, instead of 9.5%.

Source: *The Wall Street Journal*, August 9, 2010

9. If the labor market is working properly, why would there be any unemployment at all?
10. Are the 5 million workers who cannot find jobs because of mismatching in the labor market

counted as part of the economy's structural unemployment or part of its cyclical unemployment?

11. Which of the following people are unemployed because of labor market mismatching?
    - Michael has unemployment benefits of $450 a week and he turned down a full-time job paying $7.75 an hour.
    - Tory used to earn $60,000 a year and he turned down a low-paid job to search for one that pays at least $50,000 a year.
    - David turned down a temporary full-time job paying $15 an hour because it was an hour's drive away and the gas cost would be high.

The Price Level, Inflation, and Deflation

(Study Plan 5.3)

Use the following information to work Problems 12 and 13.

The people on Coral Island buy only juice and cloth. The CPI basket contains the quantities bought in 2009. The average household spent $60 on juice and $30 on cloth in 2009 when the price of juice was $2 a bottle and the price of cloth was $5 a yard. In the current year, 2010, juice is $4 a bottle and cloth is $6 a yard.

12. Calculate the CPI basket and the percentage of the household's budget spent on juice in 2009.
13. Calculate the CPI and the inflation rate in 2010.

Use the following data to work Problems 14 to 16. The BLS reported the following CPI data:

June 2006	201.9
June 2007	207.2
June 2008	217.4

14. Calculate the inflation rates for the years ended June 2007 and June 2008. How did the inflation rate change in 2008?
15. Why might these CPI numbers be biased?
16. How do alternative price indexes help to avoid the bias in the CPI numbers?
17. **Inflation Can Act as a Safety Valve**

    Workers will more readily accept a real wage cut that arises from an increase in the price level than a cut in their nominal wage rate.

    Source: FT.com, May 28, 2009

    Explain why inflation influences a worker's real wage rate. Why might this observation be true?

18. The IMF *World Economic Outlook* reported the following price level data (2000 = 100):

Region	2006	2007	2008
United States	117.1	120.4	124.0
Euro area	113.6	117.1	119.6
Japan	98.1	98.1	98.8

    a. In which region was the inflation rate highest in 2007 and in 2008?
    b. Describe the path of the price level in Japan.

19. **Inflation Getting "Uglier and Uglier"**

    The Labor Department reported that the CPI rose 4.2% through the 12 months ending in May and 0.6% in May. Energy costs rose 4.4% in May, and surged 17.4% over the 12 months ending in May; transportation costs increased 2% in May, and jumped 8.1% over the 12 months ending in May. The price of food increased 0.3% in May, and jumped 5.1% during the 12 months ending in May. The price of milk increased 10.2% over the 12 months. The price of clothing fell 0.2% in May, and decreased 0.4% over the 12 months. The core CPI rose 0.2% in May and 2.3% during the 12 months ending in May.

    Source: CNN, June 13, 2008

    a. Which components of the CPI basket experienced price increases (i) faster than the average and (ii) slower than the average?
    b. Distinguish between the CPI and the core CPI. Why might the core CPI be a useful measurement and why might it be misleading?

20. **Dress for Less**

    Since 1998, the price of the Louis Vuitton "Speedy" handbag has more than doubled, to $685, while the price of Joe Boxer's "licky face" underwear has dropped by nearly half, to $8.99. As luxury fashion has become more expensive, mainstream apparel has become markedly less so. Clothing is one of the few categories in the CPI in which overall prices have declined—about 10 percent—since 1998.

    Source: *The New York Times*, May 29, 2008

    a. What percentage of the CPI basket does apparel comprise?
    b. If luxury clothing prices have increased dramatically since the late 1990s, why has the clothing category of the CPI actually declined by about 10 percent?

ADDITIONAL PROBLEMS AND APPLICATIONS

myeconlab You can work these problems in MyEconLab if assigned by your instructor.

Employment and Unemployment

21. What is the unemployment rate supposed to measure and why is it an imperfect measure?
22. The Bureau of Labor Statistics reported the following data for 2005:

    Labor force participation rate: 66 percent
    Working-age population: 226 million
    Employment-to-population ratio: 62.7

    Calculate the
    a. Labor force.
    b. Employment.
    c. Unemployment rate.
23. In the New Orleans metropolitan area in August 2005, the labor force was 634,512 and 35,222 people were unemployed. In September 2005 following Hurricane Katrina, the labor force fell by 156,518 and the number employed fell by 206,024. Calculate the unemployment rate in August 2005 and in September 2005.
24. The BLS reported the following data: In July 2010, employment declined by 131,000 but the unemployment rate was unchanged at 9.5 percent. About 2.6 million persons were marginally attached to the labor force and among the marginally attached, 1.2 million workers were discouraged.
    a. Calculate the change in unemployment in July 2010.
    b. With 2.6 million marginally attached workers and 1.2 million of them discouraged workers, what are the characteristics of the other 1.4 million marginally attached workers?
25. A high unemployment rate tells us a large percentage of the labor force is unemployed, but it doesn't tell us why the unemployment rate is high. What measure of unemployment tells us if (i) people are taking longer than usual to find a job, (ii) more people are economic part-time workers, or (iii) more unemployed people are job losers?
26. **Some Firms Struggle to Hire Despite High Unemployment**

    With about 15 million Americans looking for work, some employers are swamped with job applicants, but many employers can't hire enough workers. What has changed in the jobs market? During the recession, millions of middle-skill, middle-wage jobs disappeared. Now with the recovery, these people can't find the skilled jobs that they seek and have a hard time adjusting to lower-skilled work with less pay.

    Source: *The Wall Street Journal*, August 9, 2010

    How will extending the period over which the government is willing to pay unemployment benefits to 99 weeks influence the cost of unemployment?
27. Why might the unemployment rate underestimate the underutilization of labor resources?

Unemployment and Full Employment

Use the following data to work Problems 28 and 29.

The IMF *World Economic Outlook* reports the following unemployment rates:

Region	2007	2008
United States	4.6	5.4
Euro area	7.4	7.3
Japan	3.9	3.9

28. What do these numbers tell you about the phase of the business cycle in the United States, Euro area, and Japan in 2008?
29 What do these numbers tell us about the relative size of the natural unemployment rates in the United States, the Euro area, and Japan?
30. Do these numbers tell us anything about the relative size of the labor force participation rates and employment-to-population ratios in the three regions?
31. **A Half-Year of Job Losses**

    Employers trimmed jobs in June for the sixth straight month, with the total for the first six months at 438,000 jobs lost by the U.S. economy. The job losses in June were concentrated in manufacturing and construction, two sectors that have been badly battered in the recession.

    Source: CNN, July 3, 2008

    a. Based on the news clip, what might be the main source of increased unemployment?
    b. Based on the news clip, what might be the main type of increased unemployment?

32. **Governor Plans to Boost Economy with Eco-friendly Jobs**

    Oregon's 5.6 percent unemployment rate hovers close to the national average of 5.5 percent. A few years ago, Oregon had one of the highest unemployment rates in the nation. To avoid rising unemployment, Oregon Governor Kulongoski introduced a plan that provides public schools and universities with enough state funds to meet growing demand for skilled workers. Also Kulongoski wants to use state and federal money for bridges, roads, and buildings to stimulate more construction jobs.

    Source: *The Oregonian*, July 8, 2008

    a. What is the main type of unemployment that Governor Kulongoski is using policies to avoid? Explain.
    b. How might these policies impact Oregon's natural unemployment rate? Explain.

The Price Level, Inflation, and Deflation

33. A typical family on Sandy Island consumes only juice and cloth. Last year, which was the base year, the family spent $40 on juice and $25 on cloth. In the base year, juice was $4 a bottle and cloth was $5 a length. This year, juice is $4 a bottle and cloth is $6 a length. Calculate
    a. The CPI basket.
    b. The CPI in the current year.
    c. The inflation rate in the current year.
34. Amazon.com agreed to pay its workers $20 an hour in 1999 and $22 an hour in 2001. The price level for these years was 166 in 1999 and 180 in 2001. Calculate the real wage rate in each year. Did these workers really get a pay raise between 1999 and 2001?
35. **News release**

    In June 2010, real personal consumption expenditure (PCE) was $9,283.4 billion and the PCE deflator was 110.8. In July 2010, real personal consumption expenditure was $9,301.3 billion and personal consumption expenditure was $10,325.5 billion.

    Source: Bureau of Economic Analysis, August 30, 2010

    Calculate personal consumption expenditure in June 2010 and the PCE deflator in July 2010. Was the percentage increase in real personal consumption expenditure greater or smaller than that in personal consumption expenditure?

Economics in the News

36. After you have studied *Reading Between the Lines* on pp. 122–123 answer the following questions.
    a. When did the unemployment rate peak after the 2008–2009 recession?
    b. What might we conclude from the three unemployment measures in Fig. 2 (p. 123)?
    c. Why might unemployment benefits influence the unemployment rate?
    d. Do unemployment benefits influence cyclical unemployment or natural unemployment? Explain.
    e. Is the rise in unemployment after mid-2009 most likely cyclical, structural, or frictional? Explain.
    f. Suggest some actions that the U.S. government might take to create more jobs.
37. **Out of a Job and Out of Luck at 54**

    Too young to retire, too old to get a new job. That's how many older workers feel after getting the pink slip and spending time on the unemployment line. Many lack the skills to craft resumes and search online, experts say. Older workers took an average of 21.1 weeks to land a new job in 2007, about 5 weeks longer than younger people. "Older workers will be more adversely affected because of the time it takes to transition into another job," said Deborah Russell, AARP's director of workforce issues.

    Source: CNN, May 21, 2008

    a. What type of unemployment might older workers be more prone to experience?
    b. Explain how the unemployment rate of older workers is influenced by the business cycle.
    c. Why might older unemployed workers become marginally attached or discouraged workers during a recession?

Data Graphing

Use the *Data Grapher* in MyEconLab to work Problems 38 to 40.

38. In which country in 2009 was the unemployment rate highest and in which was it lowest: Canada, Japan, France, or the United States?
39. In which country in 2009 was the inflation rate highest and in which was it lowest: Australia, United Kingdom, France, or the United States?
40. Make a scatter diagram of U.S. inflation and unemployment. Describe the relationship.

The Big Picture

PART TWO

MONITORING MACROECONOMIC PERFORMANCE

Macroeconomics is a large and controversial subject that is interlaced with political ideological disputes. And it is a field in which charlatans as well as serious thinkers have much to say.

You have just learned in Chapters 4 and 5 how we monitor and measure the main macroeconomic variables. We use real GDP to calculate the rate of economic growth and business cycle fluctuations. And we use the CPI and other measures of the price level to calculate the inflation rate and to "deflate" nominal values to find *real* values.

In the chapters that lie ahead, you will learn the theories that economists have developed to explain economic growth, fluctuations, and inflation.

First, in Chapters 6 through 9, you will study the long-term trends. This material is central to the oldest question in macroeconomics that Adam Smith tried to answer: What are the causes of the wealth of nations? You will also study three other old questions that Adam Smith's contemporary and friend David Hume first addressed: What causes inflation? What causes international deficits and surpluses? And why do exchange rates fluctuate?

In Chapters 10 through 12, you will study macroeconomic fluctuations.

Finally, in Chapters 13 and 14, you will study the policies that the federal government and Federal Reserve might adopt to make the economy perform well.

David Hume, *a Scot who lived from 1711 to 1776, did not call himself an economist. "Philosophy and general learning" is how he described the subject of his life's work. Hume was an extraordinary thinker and writer. Published in 1742, his* Essays, Moral and Political, *range across economics, political science, moral philosophy, history, literature, ethics, and religion and explore such topics as love, marriage, divorce, suicide, death, and the immortality of the soul!*

His economic essays provide astonishing insights into the forces that cause inflation, business cycle fluctuations, balance of payments deficits, and interest rate fluctuations; and they explain the effects of taxes and government deficits and debts.

Data were scarce in Hume's day, so he was not able to draw on detailed evidence to support his analysis. But he was empirical. He repeatedly appealed to experience and evidence as the ultimate judge of the validity of an argument. Hume's fundamentally empirical approach dominates macroeconomics today.

"... in every kingdom into which money begins to flow in greater abundance than formerly, everything takes a new face: labor and industry gain life; the merchant becomes more enterprising, the manufacturer more diligent and skillful, and even the farmer follows his plow with greater alacrity and attention."

DAVID HUME
Essays, Moral and Political

TALKING WITH **Richard Clarida**

Professor Clarida, why did you decide to become an economist and what drew you to macroeconomics?

I had the great fortune to have some excellent, inspiring economics professors in college (Fred Gotheil and Matt Canzoneri) and decided by my sophomore year to put myself on a path that would take me to Ph.D. work in economics. To me, there was (and still is!) enormous appeal and satisfaction from being able to distill the complexities of the economy, really the global economy, into the major fundamental forces that are driving the interactions that are of interest to people. I'm by nature a 'big picture' guy but require and respect rigor and robustness of analysis. In college and grad school, the rational expectations revolution was just emerging and so it was quite an exciting time to be jumping into macro.

To me, there was (and still is!) enormous appeal and satisfaction from being able to distill the complexities of the economy, really the global economy, into the major fundamental forces that are driving the interactions that are of interest to people.

When you consider the United States and global economies today, there are many topics that have made headlines, most notably, the state of our economy and the rise in power of developing countries. Let's start with the state of the U.S. economy. What brought the recession from which we're now slowly recovering?

The U.S. economy was hit in 2007 and 2008 by four significant, negative shocks: The bursting of the housing bubble, a major global dislocation in financial markets, a credit crunch as banks suffered losses and tightened lending standards, and record oil and gasoline prices.

The collapse of the housing market was a significant shock to aggregate demand. The dislocation in financial markets and the credit crunch were also negative shocks to aggregate demand. This is because tighter lending standards and higher credit spreads made it more expensive for firms and households to borrow for any given level of the interest rate set by the Fed. These three shocks shifted the aggregate demand curve to the left.

Higher oil and commodity prices were a negative supply shock,which shifted the aggregate supply curve to the left.

The combination of these shocks brought an unusually large decrease in real GDP and increase in unemployment. These shocks also severly disrupted international trade and financial markets and triggered the largest ever fiscal and monetary stimulus measures.

When did the recession begin and end and why is the recovery so painfully slow?

The National Bureau of Economic Research (with whom I am affiliated as a Research Associate) is the arbiter of when a recession begins and ends and the Bureau declared the recession began in December 2007 and ended in June 2009. So the U.S. economy is now in the second year of recovery from the worst recession in 75 years. But the recovery to date has been sluggish. Unemployment remains high and eco-

RICHARD H. CLARIDA is the C. Lowell Harriss Professor of Economics at Columbia University, where he has taught since 1988. He graduated with highest honors from the University of Illinois at Urbana in 1979 and received his masters and Ph.D. in Economics from Harvard University in 1983, writing his dissertation under the supervision of Benjamin Friedman.

Professor Clarida has taught at Yale University and held public service positions as Senior Staff Economist with the President's Council of Economic Advisers in President Ronald Reagan's Administration and most recently as Assistant Secretary of the Treasury for Economic Policy in the Administration of President George W. Bush. He has also been a visiting scholar at the International Monetary Fund and at many central banks around the world, including the Federal Reserve, the European Central Bank, the Bank of Canada, the Deutsche Bundesbank, the Bank of Italy, and the Bank of England.

Professor Clarida has published a large number of important articles in leading academic journals and books on monetary policy, exchange rates, interest rates, and international capital flows.

Michael Parkin talked with Richard Clarida about his research and some of the macroeconomic policy challenges facing the United States and the world today.

nomic growth, while positive, has been much slower than in a typical recovery. This is because the U.S. economy continues to suffer the consequences of the significant negative shocks that caused the recession. The bursting of the housing bubble, the financial crisis, and the credit crunch continue to hamper bank lending.

The collapse of the housing market and the financial crisis have forced U.S. households to reduce borrowing and increase savings, which has brought a further negative shock to aggregate demand that fiscal and monetary policy have been unable to fully offset.

Research by the International Monetary Fund has found that recoveries from recessions associated with financial crises are usually sluggish, with slower growth and higher unemployment than recoveries that are not associated with financial crises. In this case—I hope my forecast is wrong—it would seem that the United States runs the risk of going through a sustained period of slow growth.

As the recovery gains momentum, do you think we might have a period of stagflation like the 1970s?

Because of the recession, inflation in the United States was well below two percent, the level that the Fed and most central banks strive for. This is mostly due to the large output gap that opened up during the recession as well as surprisingly strong productivity growth. Despite these trends, measures of expected inflation remain well anchored at around 2 percent. Stagflation is not a near-term risk.

... measures of expected inflation remain well anchored at 2 percent.

The Fed has an implicit target for inflation over a horizon of three years. It realizes that monetary policy operates with long lags, so it seeks to set a path for policy that it expects will bring inflation to two percent over several years.

If inflation expectations start to drift up, I am confident that the Fed will eventually do what it takes to keep inflation around the two percent level.

Is the current account deficit sustainable? Do you see it correcting?

The U.S. current account deficit has been shrinking as a share of GDP for almost two years. In a growing global economy, with the dollar as reserve currency, the United States can run a sustainable current account deficit of two to three percent of GDP forever. Over time, as budget deficits fall and a more competitive dollar boosts exports, the current account deficit should stabilize at the high end of this range.

In the past, the dollar has been relatively strong when compared to the euro, the pound and the yen, but now we are experiencing a weaker dollar with drastically unfavorable exchange rates. Is the dollar going to continue to go down? Does it matter?

The dollar has been trending down for some time and I expect this to continue. The United States is

> **[The] United States is now lagging, not leading global growth, and the share of dollars in global portfolios will continue to trend down.**

now lagging, not leading global growth, and the share of dollars in global portfolios will continue to trend down. I don't see a free fall or crash landing in the dollar, if only because the euro, at this time, is not a viable alternative.

Why isn't the euro a viable alternative to the dollar?

At this time there isn't an integrated financial market in Europe. There is a collection of a dozen markets. Also, with the privileges of being a global reserve currency come obligations. Global growth drives growing global demand for currency of the reserve country and this implies that the reserve currency country on average, runs a balance of payments deficit as Britain did until World War I and as the United States has since the 1960s.

Many central banks around the world, including those at which you've been a visiting scholar, have an explicit inflation target. Should the Fed target inflation like these other central banks do?

The Fed has a dual mandate to keep prices stable and the economy at full employment. I do not foresee the Fed changing this mandate. But through its communication strategy, the Fed has moved pretty close to an inflation forecast target.

With the deep and sustained recession and the record low interest rates, has fiscal policy been reinstated as a stabilization tool?

Given the huge impact that falling house prices had on wealth and the balance sheets of financial institutions, fiscal policy is proving to be a necessary tool in the cycle to complement monetary policy. However, the 'bang per buck', or multiplier from fiscal policy, was less than many expected. This was because the impairment of credit markets and a desire to rebuild savings offset much of the impact of fiscal policy.

The world economy has been getting much attention in the press, as many Asian countries are growing in global market share in emerging and established industries. Are China and India going to keep nudging double digit growth rates for the foreseeable future?

I am bullish on global growth prospects for the next five years for China, India, and the many other "emerging" economies that are benefiting from a combination of favorable fundamentals and globalization.

Is China's exchange rate policy a problem for the United States?

China is allowing its currency to appreciate versus the dollar and will continue to do so. This is in China's interest as much as it is in the United States' interest.

China in recent years has seen a sharp rise in inflation and a surge in capital inflows in anticipation that its currency will strengthen. China has and will continue to allow its currency to strengthen in order to reduce inflation and short term capital inflows.

> **China ... has seen a sharp rise in inflation and a surge in capital inflows in anticipation that its currency will strengthen.**

What is your advice to a student who is just starting to study economics? Is it a good subject in which to major? What other subjects work well with it?

It won't surprise you to learn that I think economics is an excellent subject in which to major. In many colleges, including Columbia, it is among the most popular majors. My advice would be to take a broad range of electives and to avoid the temptation to specialize in one narrow area of economics. Also, do as much data, statistics, and presentation work as you can. You will learn the most when you have to explain yourself to others.

PART THREE Monitoring Macroeconomic Trends

After studying this chapter, you will be able to:

- Define and calculate the economic growth rate and explain the implications of sustained growth
- Describe the economic growth trends in the United States and other countries and regions
- Explain how population growth and labor productivity growth make potential GDP grow
- Explain the sources of labor productivity growth
- Explain the theories of economic growth, the empirical evidence on its causes, and policies to increase its rate

6 ECONOMIC GROWTH

Real GDP *per person* in the United States tripled between 1960 and 2010. If you live in a dorm that was built during the 1960s, it is likely to have just two power outlets: one for a desk lamp and one for a bedside lamp. Today, with the help of a power bar (or two), your room bulges with a personal computer, television and DVD player, microwave, refrigerator, coffeemaker, and toaster—and the list goes on. Economic growth has brought about this improvement in living standards.

We see even greater economic growth in modern Asia. At the mouth of the Yangtze River in one of the world's great cities, Shanghai, people are creating businesses, investing in new technologies, developing local and global markets, and transforming their lives. Incomes have tripled not in 50 years but in the 13 years since 1997. In the summer of 2010, China overtook Japan as the world's second largest economy. Why are incomes in China growing so rapidly?

In this chapter, we study the forces that make real GDP grow. In *Reading Between the Lines* at the end of the chapter, we return to the economic growth of China and see how it compares with that of Japan and the United States.

The Basics of Economic Growth

Economic growth is a sustained expansion of production possibilities measured as the increase in real GDP over a given period. Rapid economic growth maintained over a number of years can transform a poor nation into a rich one. Such have been the stories of Hong Kong, South Korea, and some other Asian economies. Slow economic growth or the absence of growth can condemn a nation to devastating poverty. Such has been the fate of Sierra Leone, Somalia, Zambia, and much of the rest of Africa.

The goal of this chapter is to help you to understand why some economies expand rapidly and others stagnate. We'll begin by learning how to calculate the economic growth rate and by discovering the magic of sustained growth.

Calculating Growth Rates

We express the **economic growth rate** as the annual percentage change of real GDP. To calculate this growth rate, we use the formula:

$$\text{Real GDP growth rate} = \frac{\text{Real GDP in current year} - \text{Real GDP in previous year}}{\text{Real GDP in previous year}} \times 100.$$

For example, if real GDP in the current year is $11 trillion and if real GDP in the previous year was $10 trillion, then the economic growth rate is 10 percent.

The growth rate of real GDP tells us how rapidly the *total* economy is expanding. This measure is useful for telling us about potential changes in the balance of economic power among nations. But it does not tell us about changes in the standard of living.

The standard of living depends on **real GDP per person** (also called *per capita* real GDP), which is real GDP divided by the population. So the contribution of real GDP growth to the change in the standard of living depends on the growth rate of real GDP per person. We use the above formula to calculate this growth rate, replacing real GDP with real GDP per person.

Suppose, for example, that in the current year, when real GDP is $11 trillion, the population is 202 million. Then real GDP per person is $11 trillion divided by 202 million, which equals $54,455. And suppose that in the previous year, when real GDP was $10 trillion, the population was 200 million. Then real GDP per person in that year was $10 trillion divided by 200 million, which equals $50,000.

Use these two values of real GDP per person with the growth formula above to calculate the growth rate of real GDP per person. That is,

$$\text{Real GDP per person growth rate} = \frac{\$54{,}455 - \$50{,}000}{\$50{,}000} \times 100 = 8.9 \text{ percent.}$$

The growth rate of real GDP per person can also be calculated (approximately) by subtracting the population growth rate from the real GDP growth rate. In the example you've just worked through, the growth rate of real GDP is 10 percent. The population changes from 200 million to 202 million, so the population growth rate is 1 percent. The growth rate of real GDP per person is approximately equal to 10 percent minus 1 percent, which equals 9 percent.

Real GDP per person grows only if real GDP grows faster than the population grows. If the growth rate of the population exceeds the growth of real GDP, then real GDP per person falls.

The Magic of Sustained Growth

Sustained growth of real GDP per person can transform a poor society into a wealthy one. The reason is that economic growth is like compound interest.

Compound Interest Suppose that you put $100 in the bank and earn 5 percent a year interest on it. After one year, you have $105. If you leave that $105 in the bank for another year, you earn 5 percent interest on the original $100 *and on the $5 interest that you earned last year*. You are now earning interest on interest! The next year, things get even better. Then you earn 5 percent on the original $100 and on the interest earned in the first year and the second year. You are even earning interest on the interest that you earned on the interest of the first year.

Your money in the bank is growing at a rate of 5 percent a year. Before too many years have passed, your initial deposit of $100 will have grown to $200. But after how many years?

The answer is provided by a formula called the **Rule of 70**, which states that the number of years it takes for the level of any variable to double is approx-

FIGURE 6.1 The Rule of 70

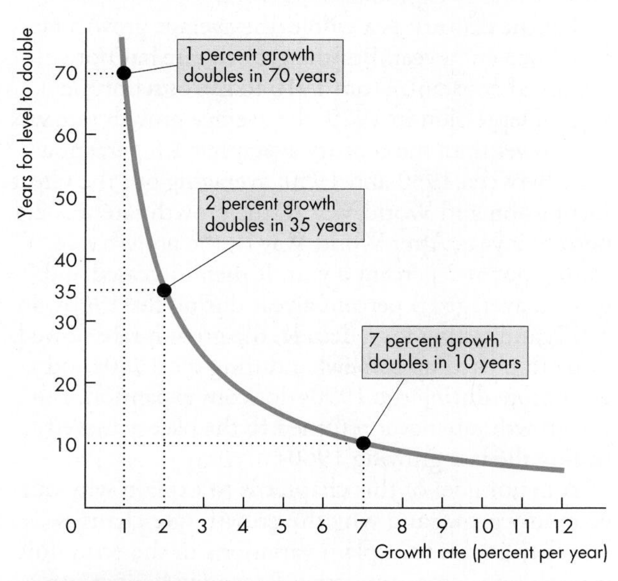

Growth rate (percent per year)	Years for level to double
1	70.0
2	35.0
3	23.3
4	17.5
5	14.0
6	11.7
7	10.0
8	8.8
9	7.8
10	7.0
11	6.4
12	5.8

The number of years it takes for the level of a variable to double is approximately 70 divided by the annual percentage growth rate of the variable.

myeconlab animation

imately 70 divided by the annual percentage growth rate of the variable. Using the Rule of 70, you can now calculate how many years it takes your $100 to become $200. It is 70 divided by 5, which is 14 years.

Applying the Rule of 70

The Rule of 70 applies to any variable, so it applies to real GDP per person. Figure 6.1 shows the doubling time for growth rates of 1 percent per year to 12 percent per year.

You can see that real GDP per person doubles in 70 years (70 divided by 1)—an average human life span—if the growth rate is 1 percent a year. It doubles in 35 years if the growth rate is 2 percent a year and in just 10 years if the growth rate is 7 percent a year.

We can use the Rule of 70 to answer other questions about economic growth. For example, in 2010, U.S. real GDP per person was approximately 4 times that of China. China's recent growth rate of real GDP per person was 10 percent a year. If this growth rate were maintained, how long would it take China's real GDP per person to reach that of the United States in 2010? The answer, provided by the Rule of 70, is 14 years. China's real GDP per person doubles in 7 years (70 divided by 10). It doubles again to 4 times its current level in another 7 years. So after 14 years of growth at 10 percent a year, China's real GDP per person is 4 times its current level and equals that of the United States in 2010. Of course, after 14 years, U.S. real GDP per person would have increased, so China would still not have caught up to the United States. But at the current growth rates, China's real GDP per person will equal that of the United States by 2026.

REVIEW QUIZ

1. What is economic growth and how do we calculate its rate?
2. What is the relationship between the growth rate of real GDP and the growth rate of real GDP per person?
3. Use the Rule of 70 to calculate the growth rate that leads to a doubling of real GDP per person in 20 years.

You can work these questions in Study Plan 6.1 and get instant feedback.

Economic Growth Trends

You have just seen the power of economic growth to increase incomes. At a 1 percent growth rate, it takes a human life span to double the standard of living. But at a 7 percent growth rate, the standard of living doubles every decade. How fast is our economy growing? How fast are other economies growing? Are poor countries catching up to rich ones, or do the gaps between the rich and poor persist or even widen? Let's answer these questions.

Growth in the U.S. Economy

Figure 6.2 shows real GDP per person in the United States for the hundred years from 1910 to 2010. The red line is actual real GDP and the black line (that starts in 1949) is potential GDP. The trend in potential GDP tells us about economic growth. Fluctuations around potential GDP tell us about the business cycle.

Two extraordinary events dominate the graph: the Great Depression of the 1930s, when growth stopped for a decade, and World War II of the 1940s, when growth briefly exploded.

For the century as a whole, the average growth rate was 2 percent a year. But the growth rate has not remained constant. From 1910 to the onset of the Great Depression in 1929, the average growth rate was a bit lower than the century average at 1.8 percent a year. Between 1930 and 1950, averaging out the Great Depression and World War II, the growth rate was 2.4 percent a year. After World War II, the growth rate started out at 2 percent a year. It then increased and growth averaged 3 percent a year during the 1960s. In 1973, and lasting for a decade, the growth rate slowed. Growth picked up somewhat during the 1980s and even more during the 1990s dot.com expansion. But the growth rate never returned to the pace achieved during the fast-growing 1960s.

A major goal of this chapter is to explain why our economy grows and why the growth rate changes. Another goal is to explain variations in the economic growth rate across countries. Let's now look at some of these growth rates.

FIGURE 6.2 A Hundred Years of Economic Growth in the United States

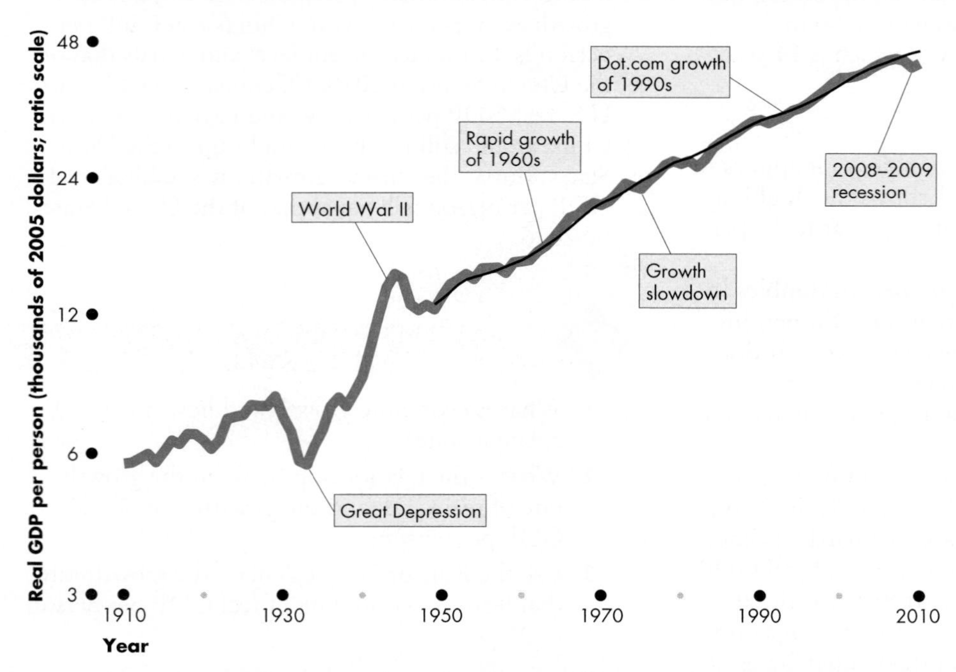

During the 100 years from 1910 to 2010, real GDP per person in the United States grew by 2 percent a year, on average. The growth rate was greater after World War II than it was before the Great Depression. Growth was most rapid during the 1960s. It slowed during the 1970s and speeded up again during the 1980s and 1990s, but it never returned to its 1960s' rate.

Sources of data: GDP (GNP)1908–1928, Christina D. Romer, "World War I and the Postwar Depression: A Reinterpretation Based on Alternative Estimates of GNP," *Journal of Monetary Economics*, 22, 1988; 1929–2008, Bureau of Economic Analysis. Population Census Bureau.

myeconlab animation

Real GDP Growth in the World Economy

Figure 6.3 shows real GDP per person in the United States and in other countries between 1960 and 2010. Part (a) looks at the seven richest countries—known as the G7 nations. Among these nations, the United States has the highest real GDP per person. In 2010, Canada had the second-highest real GDP per person, ahead of Japan and France, Germany, Italy, and the United Kingdom (collectively the Europe Big 4).

During the fifty years shown here, the gaps between the United States, Canada, and the Europe Big 4 have been almost constant. But starting from a long way below, Japan grew fastest. It caught up to Europe in 1970 and to Canada in 1990. But during the 1990s, Japan's economy stagnated.

Many other countries are growing more slowly than, and falling farther behind, the United States. Figure 6.3(b) looks at some of these countries.

Real GDP per person in Central and South America was 28 percent of the U.S. level in 1960. It grew more quickly than the United States and reached 30 percent of the U.S. level by 1980, but then growth slowed and by 2010, real GDP per person in these countries was 23 percent of the U.S. level.

In Eastern Europe, real GDP per person has grown more slowly than anywhere except Africa, and fell from 32 percent of the U.S. level in 1980 to 19 percent in 2003 and then increased again to 22 percent in 2010.

Real GDP per person in Africa, the world's poorest continent, fell from 10 percent of the U.S. level in 1960 to 5 percent in 2007 and then increased slightly to 6 percent in 2010.

FIGURE 6.3 Economic Growth Around the World: Catch-Up or Not?

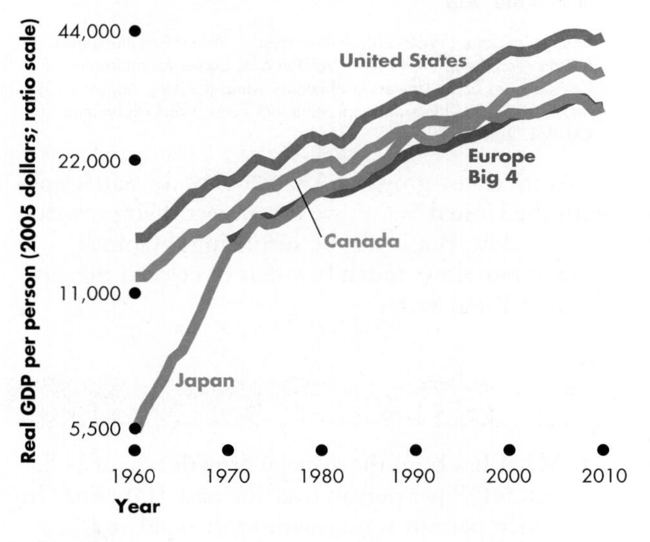

(a) Catch-up?

Real GDP per person has grown throughout the world. Among the rich industrial countries in part (a), real GDP per person has grown slightly faster in the United States than in Canada and the four big countries of Europe (France, Germany, Italy, and the United Kingdom). Japan had the fastest growth rate before 1973 but then growth slowed and Japan's economy stagnated during the 1990s.

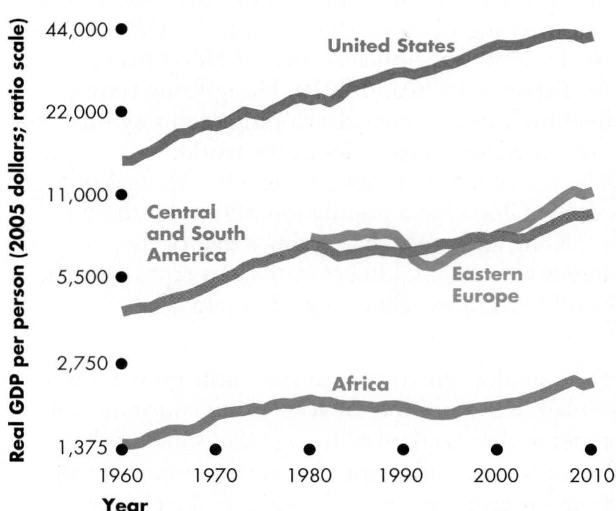

(b) No catch-up?

Among a wider range of countries shown in part (b), growth rates have been lower than that of the United States. The gaps between the real GDP per person in the United States and in these countries have widened. The gap between the real GDP per person in the United States and Africa has widened by a large amount.

Sources of data: (1960–2007) Alan Heston, Robert Summers, and Bettina Aten, Penn World Table Version 6.3, Center for International Comparisons of the University of Pennsylvania (CICUP), August 2009; and (2008–2010) International Monetary Fund, *World Economic Outlook*, April 2010.

Economics in Action

Fast Trains on the Same Track

Four Asian economies, Hong Kong, Korea, Singapore, and China, have experienced spectacular growth, which you can see in the figure. During the 1960s, real GDP per person in these economies ranged from 3 to 28 percent of that in the United States. But by 2010, real GDP per person in Singapore and Hong Kong had surpassed that of the United States.

The figure also shows that China is catching up rapidly but from a long way behind. China's real GDP per person increased from 3 percent of the U.S. level in 1960 to 26 percent in 2010.

The Asian economies shown here are like fast trains running on the same track at similar speeds and with a roughly constant gap between them. Singapore and Hong Kong are hooked together as the lead train, which runs about 20 years in front of Korea and about 40 years in front of China.

Real GDP per person in Korea in 2010 was similar to that in Hong Kong in 1988, and real GDP in China in 2010 was similar to that of Hong Kong in 1976. Between 1976 and 2010, Hong Kong transformed itself from a poor developing economy into one of the richest economies in the world.

The rest of China is now doing what Hong Kong has done. China has a population 200 times that of Hong Kong and more than 4 times that of the United States. So if China continues its rapid growth, the world economy will change dramatically.

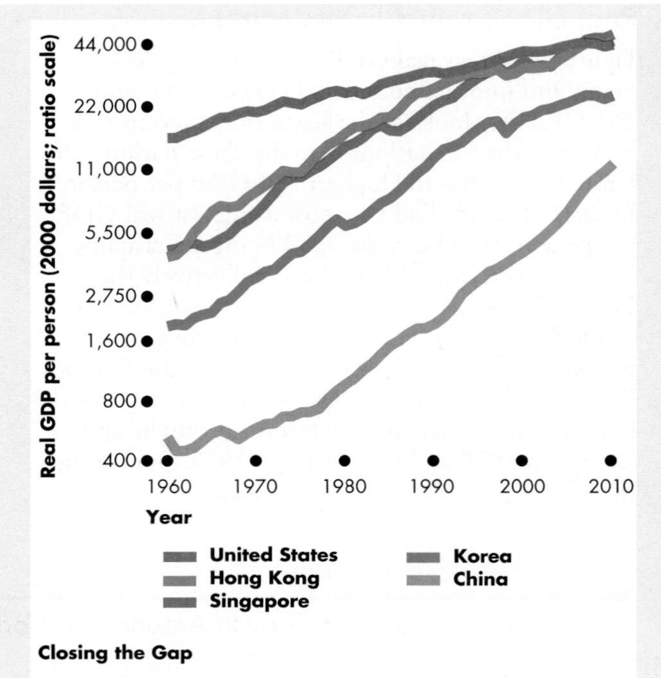

Closing the Gap

Sources of data: (1960–2007) Alan Heston, Robert Summers, and Bettina Aten, Penn World Table Version 6.3, Center for International Comparisons of the University of Pennsylvania (CICUP), August 2009; and (2008–2010) International Monetary Fund, *World Economic Outlook*, April 2010.

As these fast-growing Asian economies catch up with the United States, we can expect their growth rates to slow. But it will be surprising if China's growth rate slows much before it has closed the gap on the United States.

Even modest differences in economic growth rates sustained over a number of years bring enormous differences in the standard of living. And some of the differences that you've just seen are enormous. So the facts about economic growth in the United States and around the world raise some big questions.

What are the preconditions for economic growth? What sustains economic growth once it gets going? How can we identify the sources of economic growth and measure the contribution that each source makes? What can we do to increase the sustainable rate of economic growth?

We're now going to address these questions and discover the causes of economic growth. We start by seeing how potential GDP is determined and what makes it grow. You will see that labor productivity growth is the key to rising living standards and go on to explore the sources of this growth.

REVIEW QUIZ

1. What has been the average growth rate of U.S. real GDP per person over the past 100 years? In which periods was growth most rapid and in which periods was it slowest?
2. Describe the gaps between real GDP per person in the United States and in other countries. For which countries is the gap narrowing? For which is it widening? For which is it the same?
3. Compare real GDP per person and its growth rate in Hong Kong, Korea, Singapore, China, and the United States. In terms of real GDP per person, how far is China behind these others?

You can work these questions in Study Plan 6.2 and get instant feedback.

How Potential GDP Grows

Economic growth occurs when real GDP increases. But a one-shot rise in real GDP or a recovery from recession isn't economic growth. Economic growth is a sustained, year-after-year increase in *potential GDP*.

So what determines potential GDP and what are the forces that make it grow?

What Determines Potential GDP?

Labor, capital, land, and entrepreneurship produce real GDP, and the productivity of the factors of production determines the quantity of real GDP that can be produced.

The quantity of land is fixed and on any given day, the quantities of entrepreneurial ability and capital are also fixed and their productivities are given. The quantity of labor employed is the only *variable* factor of production. Potential GDP is the level of real GDP when the quantity of labor employed is the full-employment quantity.

To determine potential GDP, we use a model with two components:

- An aggregate production function
- An aggregate labor market

Aggregate Production Function When you studied the limits to production in Chapter 2 (see p. 30), you learned that the *production possibilities frontier* is the boundary between the combinations of goods and services that can be produced and those that cannot. We're now going to think about the production possibilities frontier for two special "goods": real GDP and the quantity of leisure time.

Think of real GDP as a number of big shopping carts. Each cart contains some of each kind of different goods and services produced, and one cartload of items costs $1 trillion. To say that real GDP is $13 trillion means that it is 13 very big shopping carts of goods and services.

The quantity of leisure time is the number of hours spent not working. Each leisure hour could be spent working. If we spent all our time taking leisure, we would do no work and produce nothing. Real GDP would be zero. The more leisure we forgo, the greater is the quantity of labor we supply and the greater is the quantity of real GDP produced.

But labor hours are not all equally productive. We use our most productive hours first and as more hours are worked less and less productive hours are used. So for each additional hour of leisure forgone (each additional hour of labor), real GDP increases but by successively smaller amounts.

The **aggregate production function** is the relationship that tells us how real GDP changes as the quantity of labor changes when all other influences on production remain the same. Figure 6.4 shows this relationship—the curve labeled *PF*. An increase in the quantity of labor (and a corresponding decrease in leisure hours) brings a movement along the production function and an increase in real GDP.

Aggregate Labor Market In macroeconomics, we pretend that there is one large labor market that determines the quantity of labor employed and the quantity of real GDP produced. To see how this aggregate labor market works, we study the demand for labor, the supply of labor, and labor market equilibrium.

The Demand for Labor The *demand for labor* is the relationship between the quantity of labor demanded and the real wage rate. The quantity of labor demanded is the number of labor hours hired by all the firms in the economy during a given period. This

FIGURE 6.4 The Aggregate Production Function

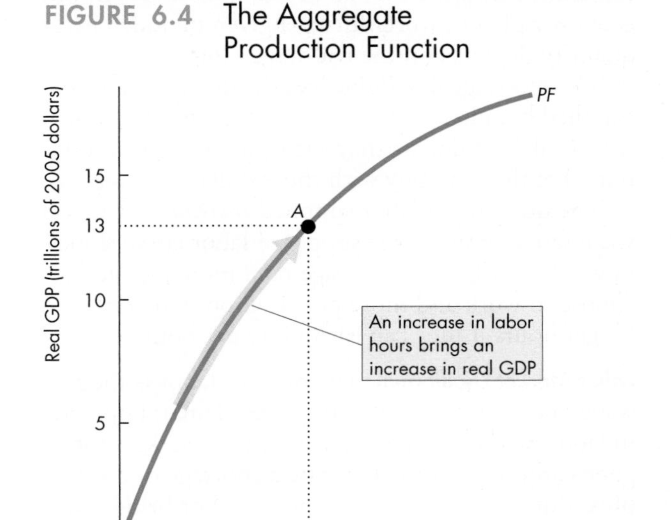

At point *A* on the aggregate production function *PF*, 200 billion hours of labor produce $13 trillion of real GDP.

quantity depends on the price of labor, which is the real wage rate.

The **real wage rate** is the money wage rate divided by the price level. The real wage rate is the quantity of goods and services that an hour of labor earns. It contrasts with the money wage rate, which is the number of dollars that an hour of labor earns.

The *real* wage rate influences the quantity of labor demanded because what matters to firms is not the number of dollars they pay (money wage rate) but how much output they must sell to earn those dollars.

The quantity of labor demanded *increases* as the real wage rate *decreases*—the demand for labor curve slopes downward. Why? The answer lies in the shape of the production function.

You've seen that along the production function, each additional hour of labor increases real GDP by successively smaller amounts. This tendency has a name: the *law of diminishing returns.* Because of diminishing returns, firms will hire more labor only if the real wage rate falls to match the fall in the extra output produced by that labor.

The Supply of Labor The *supply of labor* is the relationship between the quantity of labor supplied and the real wage rate. The quantity of labor supplied is the number of labor hours that all the households in the economy plan to work during a given period. This quantity depends on the real wage rate.

The *real* wage rate influences the quantity of labor supplied because what matters to households is not the number of dollars they earn (money wage rate) but what they can buy with those dollars.

The quantity of labor supplied *increases* as the real wage rate *increases*—the supply of labor curve slopes upward. At a higher real wage rate, more people choose to work and more people choose to work longer hours if they can earn more per hour.

Labor Market Equilibrium The price of labor is the real wage rate. The forces of supply and demand operate in labor markets just as they do in the markets for goods and services to eliminate a shortage or a surplus. But a shortage or a surplus of labor brings only a gradual change in the real wage rate. If there is a shortage of labor, the real wage rate rises to eliminate it; and if there is a surplus of labor, the real wage rate eventually falls to eliminate it. When there is neither a shortage nor a surplus, the labor market is in equilibrium—a full-employment equilibrium.

FIGURE 6.5 Labor Market Equilibrium

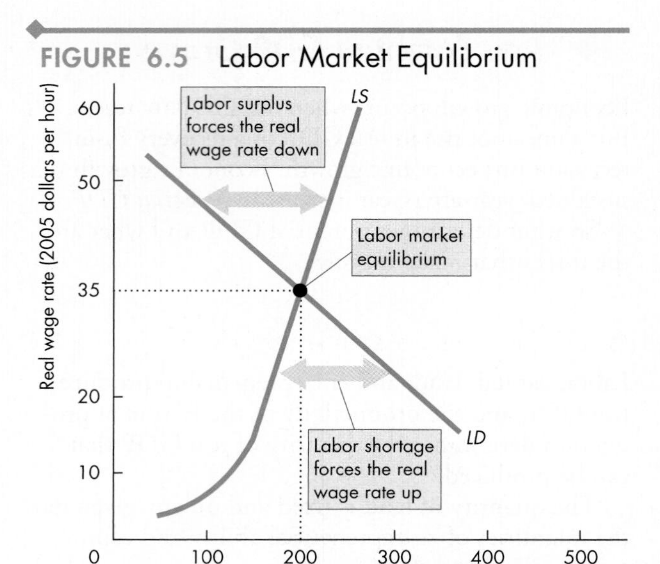

Labor market equilibrium occurs when the quantity of labor demanded equals the quantity of labor supplied. The equilibrium real wage rate is \$35 an hour, and equilibrium employment is 200 billion hours per year.

At a wage rate above \$35 an hour, there is a surplus of labor and the real wage rate falls to eliminate the surplus. At a wage rate below \$35 an hour, there is a shortage of labor and the real wage rate rises to eliminate the shortage.

myeconlab animation

Figure 6.5 illustrates labor market equilibrium. The demand for labor curve is *LD* and the supply of labor curve is *LS.* This labor market is in equilibrium at a real wage rate of \$35 an hour and 200 billion hours a year are employed.

If the real wage rate exceeds \$35 an hour, the quantity of labor supplied exceeds the quantity demanded and there is a surplus of labor. When there is a surplus of labor, the real wage rate falls toward the equilibrium real wage rate where the surplus is eliminated.

If the real wage rate is less than \$35 an hour, the quantity of labor demanded exceeds the quantity supplied and there is a shortage of labor. When there is a shortage of labor, the real wage rate rises toward the equilibrium real wage rate where the shortage is eliminated.

If the real wage rate is \$35 an hour, the quantity of labor demanded equals the quantity supplied and there is neither a shortage nor a surplus of labor. In this situation, there is no pressure in either direction on the real wage rate. So the real wage rate remains constant and the market is in equilibrium. At this equilibrium real wage rate and level of employment, the economy is at *full employment.*

Potential GDP You've seen that the production function tells us the quantity of real GDP that a given amount of labor can produce—see Fig. 6.4. The quantity of real GDP produced increases as the quantity of labor increases. At the equilibrium quantity of labor, the economy is at full employment, and the quantity of real GDP at full employment is potential GDP. So the full-employment quantity of labor produces potential GDP.

Figure 6.6 illustrates the determination of potential GDP. Part (a) shows labor market equilibrium. At the equilibrium real wage rate, equilibrium employment is 200 billion hours. Part (b) shows the production function. With 200 billion hours of labor, the economy can produce a real GDP of $13 trillion. This amount is potential GDP.

What Makes Potential GDP Grow?

We can divide all the forces that make potential GDP grow into two categories:

- Growth of the supply of labor
- Growth of labor productivity

Growth of the Supply of Labor When the supply of labor grows, the supply of labor curve shifts rightward. The quantity of labor at a given real wage rate increases.

The quantity of labor is the number of workers employed multiplied by average hours per worker; and the number employed equals the employment-to-population ratio multiplied by the working-age population (see Chapter 5, p. 110). So the quantity of labor changes as a result of changes in

1. Average hours per worker
2. The employment-to-population ratio
3. The working-age population

Average hours per worker have decreased as the workweek has become shorter, and the employment-to-population ratio has increased as more women have entered the labor force. The combined effect of

FIGURE 6.6 The Labor Market and Potential GDP

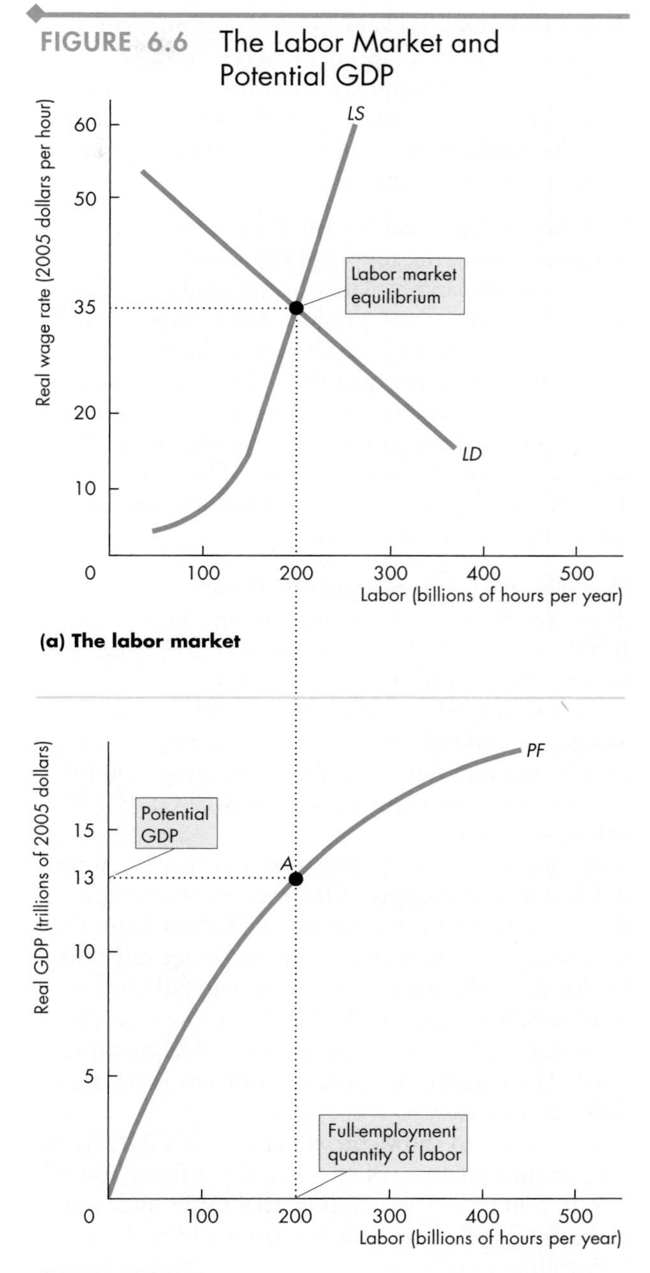

The economy is at full employment when the quantity of labor demanded equals the quantity of labor supplied, in part (a). The real wage rate is $35 an hour, and employment is 200 billion hours a year. Part (b) shows potential GDP. It is the quantity of real GDP determined by the production function at the full-employment quantity of labor.

these two factors has kept the average hours per working-age person (approximately) constant.

Growth in the supply of labor has come from growth in the working-age population. In the long run, the working-age population grows at the same rate as the total population.

The Effects of Population Growth Population growth brings growth in the supply of labor, but it does not change the demand for labor or the production function. The economy can produce more output by using more labor, but there is no change in the quantity of real GDP that a given quantity of labor can produce.

With an increase in the supply of labor and no change in the demand for labor, the real wage rate falls and the equilibrium quantity of labor increases. The increased quantity of labor produces more output and potential GDP increases.

Illustrating the Effects of Population Growth Figure 6.7 illustrates the effects of an increase in the population. In Fig. 6.7(a), the demand for labor curve is LD and initially the supply of labor curve is LS_0. The equilibrium real wage rate is \$35 an hour and the quantity of labor is 200 billion hours a year. In Fig. 6.7(b), the production function (PF) shows that with 200 billion hours of labor employed, potential GDP is \$13 trillion at point A.

An increase in the population increases the supply of labor and the supply of labor curve shifts rightward to LS_1. At a real wage rate of \$35 an hour, there is now a surplus of labor. So the real wage rate falls. In this example, the real wage rate will fall until it reaches \$25 an hour. At \$25 an hour, the quantity of labor demanded equals the quantity of labor supplied. The equilibrium quantity of labor increases to 300 billion a year.

Figure 6.7(b) shows the effect on real GDP. As the equilibrium quantity of labor increases from 200 billion to 300 billion hours, potential GDP increases along the production function from \$13 trillion to \$16 trillion at point B.

So an increase in the population increases the full-employment quantity of labor, increases potential GDP, and lowers the real wage rate. But the population increase *decreases* potential GDP per hour of labor. Initially, it was \$65 (\$13 trillion divided by 200 billion). With the population increase, potential GDP per hour of labor is \$53.33 (\$16 trillion divided by 300 billion). Diminishing returns are the source of the decrease in potential GDP per hour of labor.

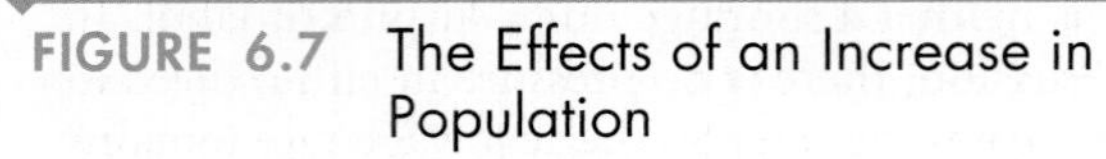
FIGURE 6.7 The Effects of an Increase in Population

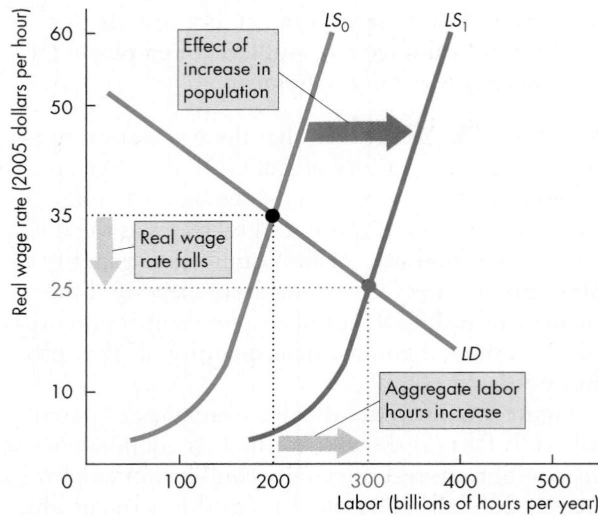

(a) The labor market

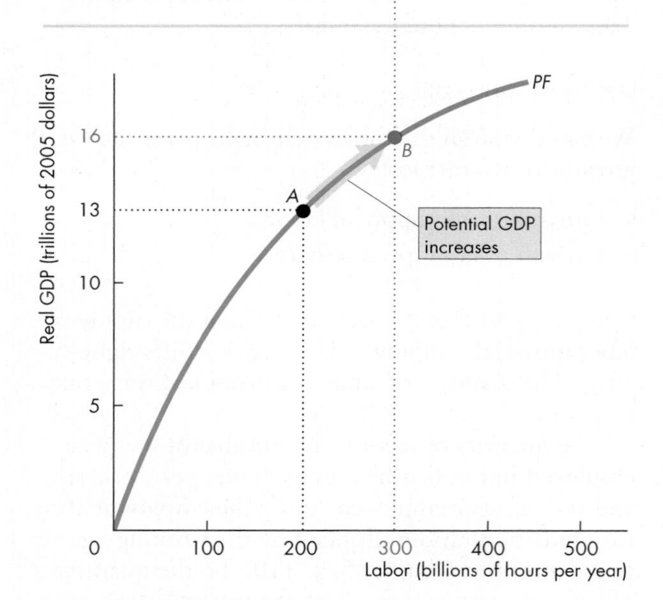

(b) Potential GDP

An increase in the population increases the supply of labor. In part (a), the supply of labor curve shifts rightward. The real wage rate falls and aggregate labor hours increase. In part (b), the increase in aggregate labor hours brings an increase in potential GDP. But diminishing returns bring a decrease in potential GDP per hour of labor.

Growth of Labor Productivity **Labor productivity** is the quantity of real GDP produced by an hour of labor. It is calculated by dividing real GDP by aggregate labor hours. For example, if real GDP is $13 trillion and aggregate hours are 200 billion, labor productivity is $65 per hour.

When labor productivity grows, real GDP per person grows and brings a rising standard of living. Let's see how an increase in labor productivity changes potential GDP.

Effects of an Increase in Labor Productivity If labor productivity increases, production possibilities expand. The quantity of real GDP that any given quantity of labor can produce increases. If labor is more productive, firms are willing to pay more for a given number of hours of labor so the demand for labor also increases.

With an increase in the demand for labor and *no change in the supply of labor*, the real wage rate rises and the quantity of labor supplied increases. The equilibrium quantity of labor also increases.

So an increase in labor productivity increases potential GDP for two reasons: Labor is more productive and more labor is employed.

Illustrating the Effects of an Increase in Labor Productivity Figure 6.8 illustrates the effects of an increase in labor productivity.

In part (a), the production function initially is PF_0. With 200 billion hours of labor employed, potential GDP is $13 trillion at point *A*.

In part (b), the demand for labor curve is LD_0 and the supply of labor curve is *LS*. The real wage rate is $35 an hour, and the equilibrium quantity of labor is 200 billion hours a year.

Now labor productivity increases. In Fig. 6.8(a), the increase in labor productivity shifts the production function upward to PF_1. At each quantity of labor, more real GDP can be produced. For example, at 200 billion hours, the economy can now produce $18 trillion of real GDP at point *B*.

In Fig. 6.8(b), the increase in labor productivity increases the demand for labor and the demand for labor curve shifts rightward to LD_1. At the initial real wage rate of $35 an hour, there is now a shortage of labor. The real wage rate rises. In this example, the real wage rate will rise until it reaches $45 an hour. At $45 an hour, the quantity of labor demanded equals the quantity of labor supplied and the equilibrium quantity of labor is 225 billion hours a year.

FIGURE 6.8 The Effects of an Increase in Labor Productivity

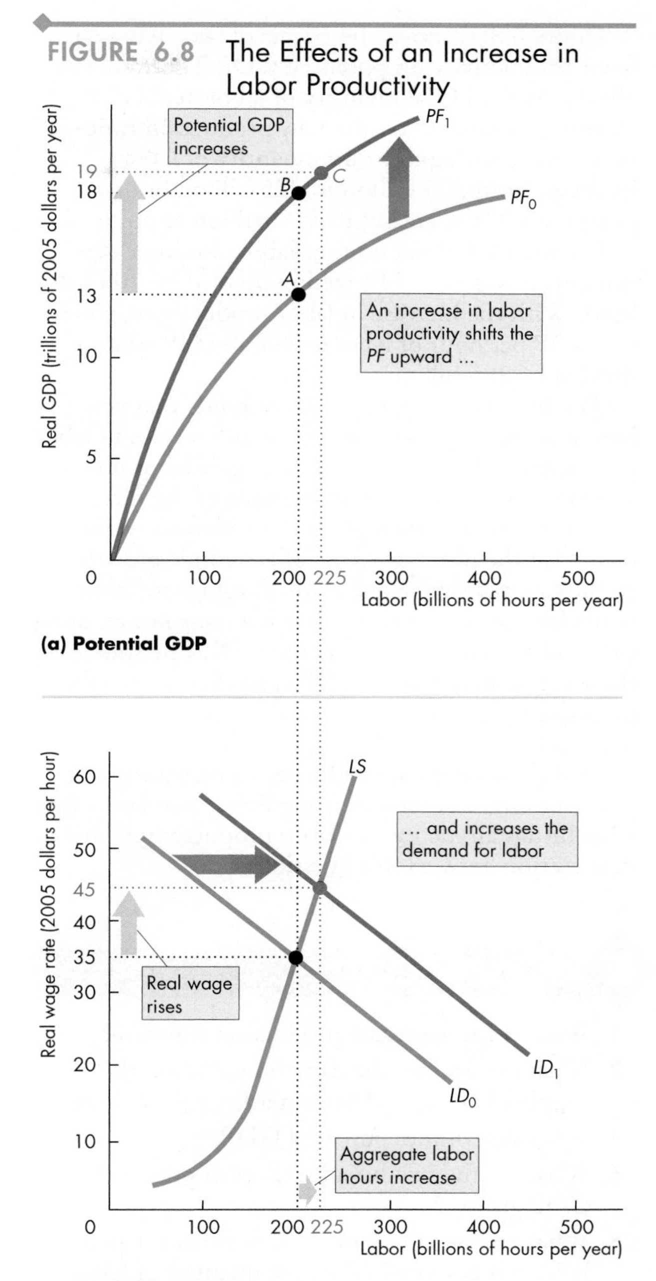

An increase in labor productivity shifts the production function upward from PF_0 to PF_1 in part (a) and shifts the demand for labor curve rightward from LD_0 to LD_1 in part (b). The real wage rate rises to $45 an hour, and aggregate labor hours increase from 200 billion to 225 billion. Potential GDP increases from $13 trillion to $19 trillion.

Figure 6.8(a) shows the effects of the increase in labor productivity on potential GDP. There are two effects. At the initial quantity of labor, real GDP increases to point B on the new production function. But as the equilibrium quantity of labor increases from 200 billion to 225 billion hours, potential GDP increases to \$19 trillion at point C.

Potential GDP per hour of labor also increases. Initially, it was \$65 (\$13 trillion divided by 200 billion). With the increase in labor productivity, potential GDP per hour of labor is \$84.44 (\$19 trillion divided by 225 billion).

The increase in aggregate labor hours that you have just seen is a consequence of an increase in labor productivity. This increase in aggregate labor hours and labor productivity is an example of the interaction effects that economists seek to identify in their search for the ultimate *causes* of economic growth. In the case that we've just studied, aggregate labor hours increase but that increase is a *consequence*, not a cause, of the growth of potential GDP. The source of the increase in potential GDP is an increase in labor productivity.

Labor productivity is the key to increasing output per hour of labor and rising living standards. But what brings an increase in labor productivity? The next section answers this question.

REVIEW QUIZ

1 What is the aggregate production function?
2 What determines the demand for labor, the supply of labor, and labor market equilibrium?
3 What determines potential GDP?
4 What are the two broad sources of potential GDP growth?
5 What are the effects of an increase in the population on potential GDP, the quantity of labor, the real wage rate, and potential GDP per hour of labor?
6 What are the effects of an increase in labor productivity on potential GDP, the quantity of labor, the real wage rate, and potential GDP per hour of labor?

You can work these questions in Study Plan 6.3 and get instant feedback.

Why Labor Productivity Grows

You've seen that labor productivity growth makes potential GDP grow; and you've seen that labor productivity growth is essential if real GDP per person and the standard of living are to grow. But *why* does labor productivity grow? What are the preconditions that make labor productivity growth possible and what are the forces that make it grow? Why does labor productivity grow faster at some times and in some places than others?

Preconditions for Labor Productivity Growth

The fundamental precondition for labor productivity growth is the *incentive* system created by firms, markets, property rights, and money. These four social institutions are the same as those described in Chapter 2 (see pp. 41–42) that enable people to gain by specializing and trading.

Economics in Action

Intellectual Property Rights Propel Growth

In 1760, when the states that 16 years later would become the United States of America were developing agricultural economies, England was on the cusp of an economic revolution, the *Industrial Revolution.*

For 70 dazzling years, technological advances in the use of steam power, the manufacture of cotton, wool, iron, and steel, and in transportation, accompanied by massive capital investment associated with these technologies, transformed the economy of England. Incomes rose and brought an explosion in an increasingly urbanized population.

By 1825, advances in steam technology had reached a level of sophistication that enabled Robert Stevenson to build the world's first steam-powered rail engine (the Rocket pictured here) and the birth of the world's first railroad.

Why did the Industrial Revolution happen? Why did it start in 1760? And why in England?

Economic historians say that intellectual property rights—England's patent system—provides the answer.

England's patent system began with the Statute of Monopolies of 1624, which gave inventors a monopoly to use their idea for a term of 14 years. For about 100 years, the system was used to reward friends of the

It was the presence of secure property rights in Britain in the middle 1700s that got the Industrial Revolution going (see Economics in Action below). And it is their absence in some parts of Africa today that is keeping labor productivity stagnant.

With the preconditions for labor productivity growth in place, three things influence its pace:

- Physical capital growth
- Human capital growth
- Technological advances

Physical Capital Growth

As the amount of capital per worker increases, labor productivity also increases. Production processes that use hand tools can create beautiful objects, but production methods that use large amounts of capital per worker are much more productive. The accumulation of capital on farms, in textile factories, in iron foundries and steel mills, in coal mines, on building sites, in chemical plants, in auto plants, in banks and insurance companies, and in shopping malls has added incredibly to the labor productivity of our economy. The next time you see a movie that is set in the Old West or colonial times, look carefully at the small amount of capital around. Try to imagine how productive you would be in such circumstances compared with your productivity today.

royal court rather than true inventors. But from around 1720 onward, the system started to work well. To be granted a 14-year monopoly, an inventor only had to pay the required £100 fee (about $22,000 in today's money) and register his or her invention. The inventor was not required to describe the invention in too much detail, so registering and getting a patent didn't mean sharing the invention with competitors.

This patent system, which is in all essentials the same as today's, aligned the self-interest of entrepreneurial inventors with the social interest and unleashed a flood of inventions, the most transformative of which was steam power and, by 1825, the steam locomotive.

Human Capital Growth

Human capital—the accumulated skill and knowledge of human beings—is the fundamental source of labor productivity growth. Human capital grows when a new discovery is made and it grows as more and more people learn how to use past discoveries.

The development of one of the most basic human skills—writing—was the source of some of the earliest major gains in productivity. The ability to keep written records made it possible to reap ever-larger gains from specialization and trade. Imagine how hard it would be to do any kind of business if all the accounts, invoices, and agreements existed only in people's memories.

Later, the development of mathematics laid the foundation for the eventual extension of knowledge about physical forces and chemical and biological processes. This base of scientific knowledge was the foundation for the technological advances of the Industrial Revolution and of today's information revolution.

But a lot of human capital that is extremely productive is much more humble. It takes the form of millions of individuals learning and becoming remarkably more productive by repetitively doing simple production tasks. One much-studied example of this type of human capital growth occurred in World War II. With no change in physical capital, thousands of workers and managers in U.S. shipyards learned from experience and accumulated human capital that more than doubled their productivity in less than two years.

Technological Advances

The accumulation of physical capital and human capital have made a large contribution to labor productivity growth. But technological change—the discovery and the application of new technologies—has made an even greater contribution.

FIGURE 6.9 The Sources of Economic Growth

Sources				
Change in average hours per worker Change in employment-to-population ratio Working-age population growth	Labor supply growth	Real GDP growth	Population growth	
Physical capital growth Human capital growth ▪ Education and training ▪ Job experience Technological advances	Labor productivity growth		Real GDP per person growth	

Labor supply growth and labor productivity growth combine to determine real GDP growth. Real GDP per person growth depends on real GDP growth and population growth.

myeconlab animation

Economics in Action

Women Are the Better Borrowers

Economic growth is driven by the decisions made by billions of individuals to save and invest, and borrow and lend. But most people are poor, have no credit history, and can't borrow from a bank.

These people—many of whom are women—can, however, start a business, employ a few people, and earn an income with the help of a *microloan*.

Microloans originated in Bangladesh but have spread throughout the developing world. Kiva.org and MicroPlace.com (owned by eBay) are Web sites that enable people to lend money that is used to make microloans in developing economies.

Throughout the developing world, microloans are helping women to feed and clothe their families and to grow their small businesses, often in agriculture. As the incomes of microloan borrowers rise, they pay off their loans and accumulate capital. A billion microloans pack a macro punch.

Labor is many times more productive today than it was a hundred years ago but not because we have more steam engines and more horse-drawn carriages per person. Rather, it is because we have transportation equipment that uses technologies that were unknown a hundred years ago and that are more productive than the old technologies were.

Technological advance arises from formal research and development programs and from informal trial and error, and it involves discovering new ways of getting more out of our resources.

To reap the benefits of technological change, capital must increase. Some of the most powerful and far-reaching fundamental technologies are embodied in human capital—for example, language, writing, and mathematics. But most technologies are embodied in physical capital. For example, to reap the benefits of the internal combustion engine, millions of horse-drawn carriages had to be replaced with automobiles; and to reap the benefits of digital music, millions of Discmans had to be replaced by iPods.

Figure 6.9 summarizes the sources of labor productivity growth and more broadly of real GDP growth. The figure also emphasizes that for real GDP per person to grow, real GDP must grow faster than the population.

REVIEW QUIZ

1. What are the preconditions for labor productivity growth?
2. Explain the influences on the pace of labor productivity growth.

You can work these questions in Study Plan 6.4 and get instant feedback.

Growth Theories, Evidence, and Policies

You've seen how population growth and labor productivity growth make potential GDP grow. You've also seen that the growth of physical capital and human capital and technological advances make labor productivity grow. How do all these factors interact? What is cause and what is effect? Growth theories address these questions.

Alternative theories of economic growth provide insights into the process of economic growth, but none provides a complete and definite answer to the basic questions: What causes economic growth and why do growth rates vary? Economics has some way to go before it can provide definite answers to these questions. We look at the current state of the empirical evidence. Finally, we'll look at the policies that might achieve faster growth.

Let's start by studying the three main theories of economic growth:

- Classical growth theory
- Neoclassical growth theory
- New growth theory

Classical Growth Theory

Classical growth theory is the view that the growth of real GDP per person is temporary and that when it rises above the subsistence level, a population explosion eventually brings it back to the subsistence level. Adam Smith, Thomas Robert Malthus, and David Ricardo—the leading economists of the late eighteenth century and early nineteenth century—proposed this theory, but the view is most closely associated with the name of Malthus and is sometimes called the *Malthusian theory*. Charles Darwin's ideas about evolution by natural selection were inspired by the insights of Malthus.

Modern-Day Malthusians Many people today are Malthusians. They say that if today's global population of 6.9 billion explodes to 11 billion by 2050 and perhaps 35 billion by 2300, we will run out of resources, real GDP per person will decline, and we will return to a primitive standard of living. We must, say Malthusians, contain population growth.

Modern-day Malthusians also point to global warming and climate change as reasons to believe that eventually, real GDP per person will decrease.

Neoclassical Growth Theory

Neoclassical growth theory is the proposition that real GDP per person grows because technological change induces saving and investment that make capital per hour of labor grow. Growth ends if technological change stops because of diminishing marginal returns to both labor and capital. Robert Solow of MIT suggested the most popular version of this growth theory in the 1950s.

Neoclassical growth theory's big break with its classical predecessor is its view about population growth.

The Neoclassical Theory of Population Growth The population explosion of eighteenth century Europe that created the classical theory of population eventually ended. The birth rate fell, and while the population continued to increase, its rate of increase moderated.

The key economic influence that slowed the population growth rate is the opportunity cost of a woman's time. As women's wage rates increase and their job opportunities expand, the opportunity cost of having children increases. Faced with a higher opportunity cost, families choose to have fewer children and the birth rate falls.

Technological advances that bring higher incomes also brings advances in health care that extends lives. So as incomes increase, both the birth rate and the death rate decrease. These opposing forces offset each other and result in a slowly rising population.

This modern view of population growth and the historical trends that support it contradict the views of the classical economists. They also call into question the modern doomsday view that the planet will be swamped with more people than it can support.

Technological Change and Diminishing Returns In neoclassical growth theory, the pace of technological change influences the economic growth rate but economic growth does not influence the pace of technological change. It is assumed that technological change results from chance. When we're lucky, we have rapid technological change, and when bad luck strikes, the pace of technological advance slows.

To understand neoclassical growth theory, imagine the world of the mid-1950s, when Robert Solow is explaining his idea. Income per person is around $12,000 a year in today's money. The population is growing at about 1 percent a year. Saving and investment are about 20 percent of GDP, enough to keep the quantity of capital per hour of labor constant. Income per person is growing but not very fast.

Then technology begins to advance at a more rapid pace across a range of activities. The transistor revolutionizes an emerging electronics industry. New plastics revolutionize the manufacture of household appliances. The interstate highway system revolutionizes road transportation. Jet airliners start to replace piston-engine airplanes and speed air transportation.

These technological advances bring new profit opportunities. Businesses expand, and new businesses are created to exploit the newly available profitable technologies. Investment and saving increase. The economy enjoys new levels of prosperity and growth. But will the prosperity last? And will the growth last? Neoclassical growth theory says that the *prosperity* will last but the *growth* will not last unless technology keeps advancing.

According to neoclassical growth theory, the prosperity will persist because there is no classical population growth to induce the wage rate to fall. So the gains in income per person are permanent.

But growth will eventually stop if technology stops advancing because of diminishing marginal returns to capital. The high profit rates that result from technological change bring increased saving and capital accumulation. But as more capital is accumulated, more and more projects are undertaken that have lower rates of return—diminishing marginal returns. As the return on capital falls, the incentive to keep investing weakens. With weaker incentives to save and invest, saving decreases and the rate of capital accumulation slows. Eventually, the pace of capital accumulation slows so that it is only keeping up with population growth. Capital per worker remains constant.

A Problem with Neoclassical Growth Theory

All economies have access to the same technologies, and capital is free to roam the globe, seeking the highest available real interest rate. Capital will flow until rates of return are equal, and rates of return will be equal when capital per hour of labor are equal. Real GDP growth rates and income levels per person around the world will converge. Figure 6.3 on p. 137 shows that while there is some sign of convergence among the rich countries in part (a), convergence is slow, and part (b) shows that it does not appear to be imminent for all countries. New growth theory overcomes this shortcoming of neoclassical growth theory. It also explains what determines the pace of technological change.

New Growth Theory

New growth theory holds that real GDP per person grows because of the choices people make in the pursuit of profit and that growth will persist indefinitely. Paul Romer of Stanford University developed this theory during the 1980s, based on ideas of Joseph Schumpeter during the 1930s and 1940s.

According to the new growth theory, the pace at which new discoveries are made—and at which technology advances—is not determined by chance. It depends on how many people are looking for a new technology and how intensively they are looking. The search for new technologies is driven by incentives.

Profit is the spur to technological change. The forces of competition squeeze profits, so to increase profit, people constantly seek either lower-cost methods of production or new and better products for which people are willing to pay a higher price. Inventors can maintain a profit for several years by taking out a patent or a copyright, but eventually, a new discovery is copied, and profits disappear. So more research and development is undertaken in the hope of creating a new burst of profitable investment and growth.

Two facts about discoveries and technological knowledge play a key role in the new growth theory: Discoveries are (at least eventually) a public capital good; and knowledge is capital that is not subject to diminishing marginal returns.

Economists call a good a *public good* when no one can be excluded from using it and when one person's use does not prevent others from using it. National defense is the classic example of a public good. The programming language used to write apps for the iPhone is another.

Because knowledge is a public good, as the benefits of a new discovery spread, free resources become available. Nothing is given up when they are used: They have a zero opportunity cost. When a student in Austin writes a new iPhone app, his use of the programming language doesn't prevent another student in Seattle from using it.

Knowledge is even more special because it is *not* subject to diminishing returns. But increasing the stock of knowledge makes both labor and machines more productive. Knowledge capital does not bring diminishing returns. Biotech knowledge illustrates this idea well. Biologists have spent a lot of time developing DNA sequencing technology. As more has been discovered, the productivity of this knowledge capital has relentlessly increased. In 1990, it cost about $50 to sequence one DNA base pair. That cost had fallen to $1 by 2000 and to 1/10,000th of a penny by 2010.

The implication of this simple and appealing observation is astonishing. Unlike the other two theories, new growth theory has no growth-stopping mechanism. As physical capital accumulates, the return to capital—the real interest rate—falls. But the incentive to innovate and earn a higher profit becomes stronger. So innovation occurs, capital becomes more productive, the demand for capital increases, and the real interest rate rises again.

Labor productivity grows indefinitely as people discover new technologies that yield a higher real interest rate. The growth rate depends only on people's incentives and ability to innovate.

A Perpetual Motion Economy New growth theory sees the economy as a perpetual motion machine, which Fig. 6.10 illustrates.

No matter how rich we become, our wants exceed our ability to satisfy them. We always want a higher standard of living. In the pursuit of a higher standard of living, human societies have developed incentive systems—markets, property rights, and money—that enable people to profit from innovation. Innovation leads to the development of new and better techniques of production and new and better products. To take advantage of new techniques and to produce new products, new firms start up and old firms go out of business—firms are born and die. As old firms die and new firms are born, some jobs are destroyed and others are created. The new jobs created are better than the old ones and they pay higher real wage rates. Also, with higher wage rates and more productive techniques, leisure increases. New and better jobs and new and better products lead to more consumption goods and services and, combined with increased leisure, bring a higher standard of living.

But our insatiable wants are still there, so the process continues: Wants and incentives create innovation, new and better products, and a yet higher standard of living.

FIGURE 6.10 A Perpetual Motion Machine

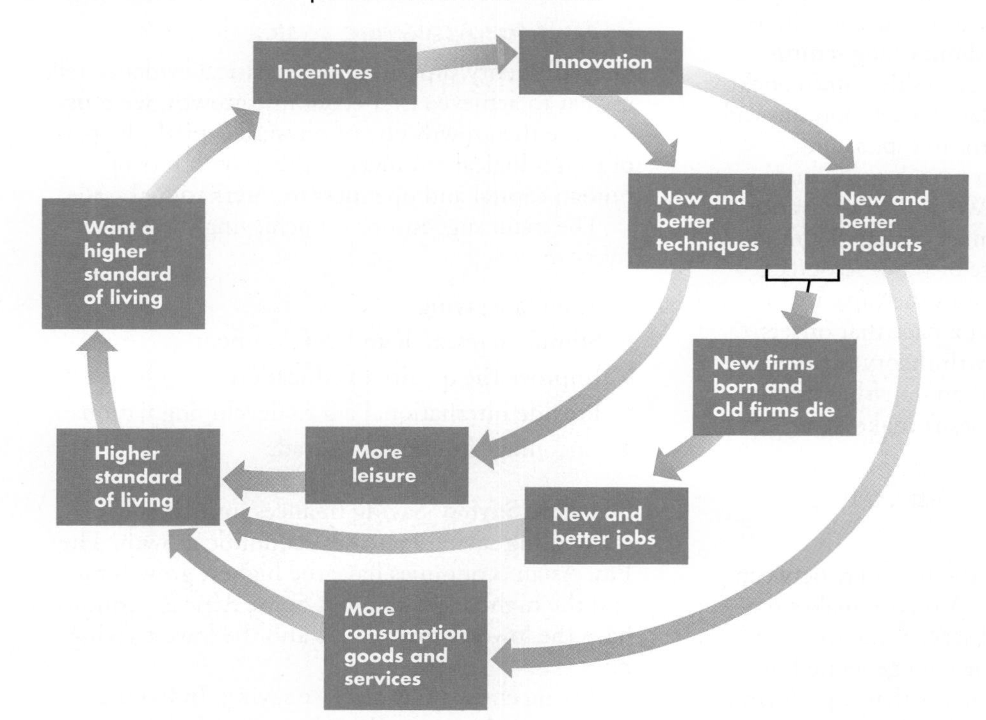

People want a higher standard of living and are spurred by profit incentives to make the innovations that lead to new and better techniques and new and better products.

These new and better techniques and products, in turn, lead to the birth of new firms and the death of some old firms, new and better jobs, and more leisure and more consumption goods and services.

The result is a higher standard of living, but people want a still higher standard of living, and the growth process continues.

Source: Based on a similar figure in *These Are the Good Old Days: A Report on U.S. Living Standards*, Federal Reserve Bank of Dallas 1993 Annual Report.

myeconlab animation

New Growth Theory Versus Malthusian Theory

The contrast between the Malthusian theory and new growth theory couldn't be more sharp. Malthusians see the end of prosperity as we know it today and new growth theorists see unending plenty. The contrast becomes clearest by thinking about the differing views about population growth.

To a Malthusian, population growth is part of the problem. To a new growth theorist, population growth is part of the solution. People are the ultimate economic resource. A larger population brings forth more wants, but it also brings a greater amount of scientific discovery and technological advance. So rather than being the source of falling real GDP per person, population growth generates faster labor productivity growth and rising real GDP per person. Resources are limited, but the human imagination and ability to increase productivity are unlimited.

Sorting Out the Theories

Which theory is correct? None of them tells us the whole story, but each teaches us something of value.

Classical growth theory reminds us that our physical resources are limited and that without advances in technology, we must eventually hit diminishing returns.

Neoclassical growth theory reaches the same conclusion but not because of a population explosion. Instead, it emphasizes diminishing returns to capital and reminds us that we cannot keep growth going just by accumulating physical capital. We must also advance technology and accumulate human capital. We must become more creative in our use of scarce resources.

New growth theory emphasizes the capacity of human resources to innovate at a pace that offsets diminishing returns. New growth theory fits the facts of today's world more closely than do either of the other two theories. But that doesn't make it correct.

The Empirical Evidence on the Causes of Economic Growth

Economics makes progress by the interplay between theory and empirical evidence. A theory makes predictions about what we will observe if the theory is correct. Empirical evidence, the data generated by history and the natural experiments that it performs, provide the data for testing the theory.

Economists have done an enormous amount of research confronting theories of growth with the empirical evidence. The way in which this research has been conducted has changed over the years.

In 1776, when Adam Smith wrote about "the nature and causes of the Wealth of Nations" in his celebrated book, empirical evidence took the form of carefully selected facts described in words and stories. Today, large databases, sophisticated statistical methods, and fast computers provide numerical measurements of the causes of economic growth.

Economists have looked at the growth rate data for more than 100 countries for the period since 1960 and explored the correlations between the growth rate and more than 60 possible influences on it. The conclusion of this data crunching is that most of these possible influences have variable and unpredictable effects, but a few of them have strong and clear effects. Table 6.1 summarizes these more robust influences. They are arranged in order of difficulty (or in the case of region, impossiblity) of changing. Political and economic systems are hard to change, but market distortions, investment, and openness to international trade are features of a nation's economy that can be influenced by policy.

Let's now look at growth policies.

Policies for Achieving Faster Growth

Growth theory supported by empirical evidence tells us that to achieve faster economic growth, we must increase the growth rate of physical capital, the pace of technological advance, or the growth rate of human capital and openness to international trade.

The main suggestions for achieving these objectives are

- Stimulate saving
- Stimulate research and development
- Improve the quality of education
- Provide international aid to developing nations
- Encourage international trade

Stimulate Saving Saving finances investment so stimulating saving increases economic growth. The East Asian economies have the highest growth rates and the highest saving rates. Some African economies have the lowest growth rates and the lowest saving rates.

Tax incentives can increase saving. Individual Retirement Accounts (IRAs) are a tax incentive to save. Economists claim that a tax on consumption rather than income provides the best saving incentive.

TABLE 6.1 The Influences on Economic Growth

Influence	Good for Economic Growth	Bad for Economic Growth
Region	■ Far from equator	■ Sub-Sahara Africa
Politics	■ Rule of law ■ Civil liberties	■ Revolutions ■ Military coups ■ Wars
Economic system	■ Capitalist	
Market distortions		■ Exchange rate distortions ■ Price controls and black markets
Investment	■ Human capital ■ Physical capital	
International trade	■ Open to trade	

Source of data: Xavier Sala-i-Martin, "I Just Ran Two Million Regressions," *The American Economic Review*, Vol. 87, No 2, (May 1997), pp. 178–183.

Stimulate Research and Development Everyone can use the fruits of *basic* research and development efforts. For example, all biotechnology firms can use advances in gene-splicing technology. Because basic inventions can be copied, the inventor's profit is limited and the market allocates too few resources to this activity. Governments can direct public funds toward financing basic research, but this solution is not foolproof. It requires a mechanism for allocating the public funds to their highest-valued use.

Improve the Quality of Education The free market produces too little education because it brings benefits beyond those valued by the people who receive the education. By funding basic education and by ensuring high standards in basic skills such as language, mathematics, and science, governments can contribute to a nation's growth potential. Education can also be stimulated and improved by using tax incentives to encourage improved private provision.

Provide International Aid to Developing Nations It seems obvious that if rich countries give financial aid to developing countries, investment and growth will increase in the recipient countries. Unfortunately, the obvious does not routinely happen. A large amount of data-driven research on the effects of aid on growth has turned up a zero and even negative effect. Aid often gets diverted and spent on consumption.

Encourage International Trade Trade, not aid, stimulates economic growth. It works by extracting the available gains from specialization and trade. The fastest-growing nations are those most open to trade. If the rich nations truly want to aid economic development, they will lower their trade barriers against developing nations, especially in farm products. The World Trade Organization's efforts to achieve more open trade are being resisted by the richer nations.

REVIEW QUIZ

1. What is the key idea of classical growth theory that leads to the dismal outcome?
2. What, according to neoclassical growth theory, is the fundamental cause of economic growth?
3. What is the key proposition of new growth theory that makes economic growth persist?

You can work these questions in Study Plan 6.5 and get instant feedback.

To complete your study of economic growth, take a look at *Reading Between the Lines* on pp. 152–153 and see how economic growth is changing the GDP rankings of nations.

Economic Growth in China

China Pips Japan but "Still a Developing Nation"

http://www.afp.com
August 17, 2010

China insisted Tuesday it was still a developing nation despite overtaking Japan as the world's second largest economy, in the face of pressure to take on a greater role in global affairs. ...

Thirty years after opening its doors to the outside world, China has enjoyed spectacular economic growth and already claimed the titles of world's top exporter, auto market, and steelmaker.

After outpacing its neighbor in the second quarter, China is on course this year to officially confirm its position as world number two—a title Japan held for 40 years—underscoring its emergence as a global economic and political force.

While some analysts are predicting that China could take on the top spot from the United States within a few decades, commentators insisted it remained a developing nation with tens of millions living in poverty.

Commerce ministry spokesman Yao Jian said China still lagged far behind its rivals in per capita terms and has a long way to go to becoming a world-class power.

"The quality of China's economic growth still needs to be improved, no matter whether it is in terms of people's quality of life or in terms of science, technology, and environmental protection," the spokesman said.

"We still have an enormous gap to make up."

He said China's per capita GDP was 3,800 dollars—putting it around 105th in the world—and that 150 million of its 1.3 billion people live below the poverty line, according to UN standards.

"China's economy will continue to develop because China has a large population and its economy lagged behind," he said. ...

ESSENCE OF THE STORY

- China is a large developing nation that ranks at 105 in the world on per capita income with 150 million of its 1.3 billion people living below the UN poverty line.
- After opening to global trade and investment 30 years ago, China has experienced rapid economic growth.
- In mid-2010, China displaced Japan as the world's number 2 economy. Japan held this spot for 40 years.
- Some analysts predict that China will take the top spot from the United States within a few decades.
- A commerce ministry spokesman says people's quality of life, and science, technology, and environmental protection need to be improved.

ECONOMIC ANALYSIS

- The news that China overtook Japan in mid-2010 to become the world's second largest economy is based on GDP data.
- When the GDP of China measured in yuan and the GDP of Japan measured in yen are converted to U.S. dollars at the current exchange rate, China's GDP became slightly larger than Japan's in the second quarter of 2010.
- Figure 1 shows the data on GDP in China, Japan, and the United States. You can see that Japan has stagnated since 1995 while China has streaked upward.
- You learned in Chapter 4 that PPP prices provide a more useful international comparison of GDP. You also learned that real GDP measures economic growth and nominal GDP (in Fig. 1) measures a combination of economic growth and inflation (or deflation).
- Comparing China and Japan using real GDP in PPP prices (in Fig. 2), China became the number 2 economy as long ago as 1995, and in 2010 it became not the number 2 economy but the number 1, overtaking the United States.
- In 2010, China had 4 times as many people as the United States and they earned, on average, 1/4 the income of Americans. So total income and GDP in China roughly equaled that in the United States.
- China remains a poor country in three respects: Income per person is low; income inequality is large so many people live in poverty; and most of the country's advanced technology is imported from the United States and Europe.
- How poor China appears depends on the numbers used. At the current exchange rate and in China's prices, income per person was $3,800 in 2010, but in PPP prices, it was $11,000. Figure 3 shows how far China is behind Japan and the United States when measured by income per person valued in PPP prices.
- The growth of physical capital and human capital and technological change are proceeding at a rapid pace in China and bringing rapid growth in real GDP per person.
- But China lags a long way behind the United States in science, technology, and environmental protection.
- As China's economy continues to expand, it will devote more resources to narrowing the gap in these areas as well as narrowing the income gap.

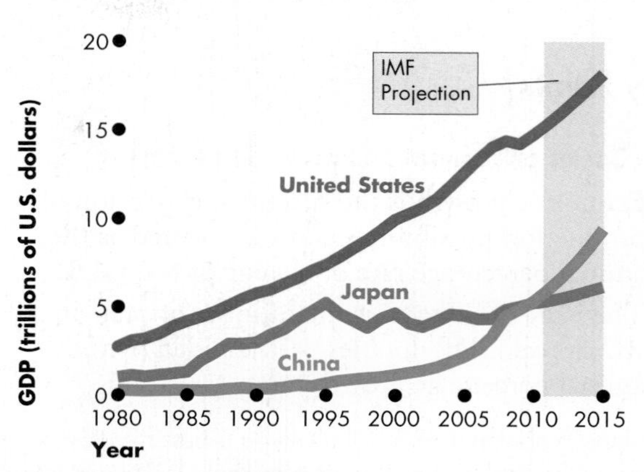

Figure 1 GDP in U.S. dollars

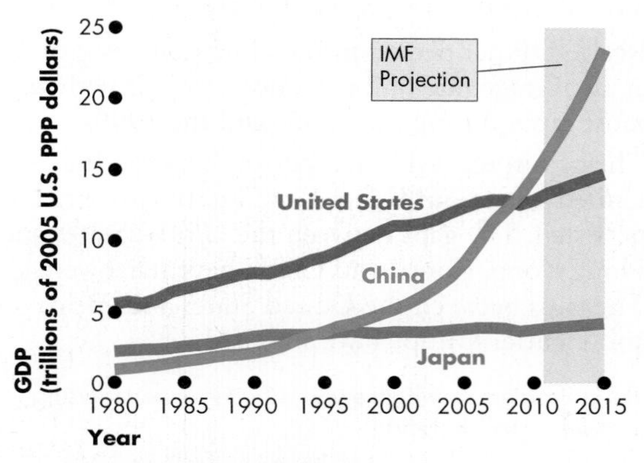

Figure 2 Real GDP in PPP prices

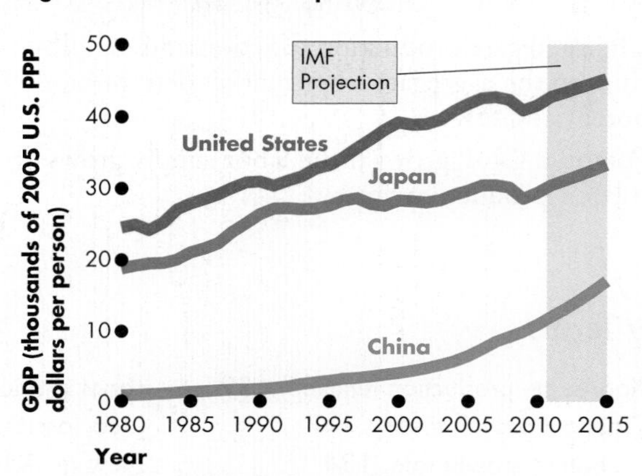

Figure 3 Real GDP per person in PPP prices

SUMMARY

Key Points

The Basics of Economic Growth (pp. 134–135)

- Economic growth is the sustained expansion of production possibilities and is measured as the annual percentage rate of change of real GDP.
- The Rule of 70 tells us the number of years in which real GDP doubles—70 divided by the annual percentage growth rate.

Working Problems 1 to 5 will give you a better understanding the basics of economic growth.

Economic Growth Trends (pp. 136–138)

- Real GDP per person in the United States grows at an average rate of 2 percent a year. Growth was most rapid during the 1960s and the 1990s.
- The gap in real GDP per person between the United States and Central and South America has persisted. The gaps between the United States and Hong Kong, Korea, and China have narrowed. The gaps between the United States and Africa and Central Europe have widened.

Working Problem 6 will give you a better understanding of economic growth trends.

How Potential GDP Grows (pp. 139–144)

- The aggregate production function and equilibrium in the aggregate labor market determine potential GDP.
- Potential GDP grows if the labor supply grows or if labor productivity grows.
- Only labor productivity growth makes real GDP per person and the standard of living grow.

Working Problems 7 to 14 will give you a better understanding of how potential GDP grows.

Why Labor Productivity Grows (pp. 144–146)

- Labor productivity growth requires an incentive system created by firms, markets, property rights, and money.
- The sources of labor productivity growth are growth of physical capital and human capital and advances in technology.

Working Problems 15 and 16 will give you a better understanding of why labor productivity grows.

Growth Theories, Evidence, and Policies (pp. 147–151)

- In classical theory, real GDP per person keeps returning to the subsistence level.
- In neoclassical growth theory, diminishing returns to capital limit economic growth.
- In new growth theory, economic growth persists indefinitely at a rate determined by decisions that lead to innovation and technological change.
- Policies for achieving faster growth include stimulating saving and research and development, encouraging international trade, and improving the quality of education.

Working Problems 17 and 18 will give you a better understanding of growth theories, evidence, and policies.

Key Terms

Aggregate production function, 139
Classical growth theory, 147
Economic growth rate, 134
Labor productivity, 143
Neoclassical growth theory, 147
New growth theory, 148
Real GDP per person, 134
Real wage rate, 140
Rule of 70, 134

STUDY PLAN PROBLEMS AND APPLICATIONS

myeconlab You can work Problems 1 to 18 in MyEconLab Chapter 6 Study Plan and get instant feedback.

The Basics of Economic Growth (Study Plan 6.1)

1. Brazil's real GDP was 1,360 trillion reais in 2009 and 1,434 trillion reais in 2010. Brazil's population was 191.5 million in 2009 and 193.3 million in 2010. Calculate
   a. The economic growth rate.
   b. The growth rate of real GDP per person.
   c. The approximate number of years it takes for real GDP per person in Brazil to double if the 2010 economic growth rate and population growth rate are maintained.
2. Japan's real GDP was 525 trillion yen in 2009 and 535 trillion yen in 2010. Japan's population was 127.6 million in 2009 and 127.5 million in 2010. Calculate
   a. The economic growth rate.
   b. The growth rate of real GDP per person.
   c. The approximate number of years it takes for real GDP per person in Japan to double if the real GDP economic growth rate returns to 3 percent a year and the population growth rate is maintained.

Use the following data to work Problems 3 and 4.

China's real GDP per person was 9,280 yuan in 2009 and 10,110 yuan in 2010. India's real GDP per person was 30,880 rupees in 2009 and 32,160 rupees in 2010.

3. By maintaining their current growth rates, which country will double its 2010 standard of living first?
4. The population of China is growing at 1 percent a year and the population of India is growing at 1.4 percent a year. Calculate the growth rate of real GDP in each country.
5. **China's Economy Picks Up Speed**

   China's trend growth rate of real GDP per person was 2.2 percent a year before 1980 and 8.7 percent a year after 1980. In the year to August 2009, China's output increased by 11.3 percent.

   Source: World Economic Outlook and FT.com, September 14, 2009

   Distinguish between a rise in China's economic growth rate and a temporary cyclical expansion. How long, at the current growth rate, will it take for China to double its real GDP per person?

Economic Growth Trends (Study Plan 6.2)

6. China was the largest economy for centuries because everyone had the same type of economy— subsistence—and so the country with the most people would be economically biggest. Then the Industrial Revolution sent the West on a more prosperous path. Now the world is returning to a common economy, this time technology- and information-based, so once again population triumphs.
   a. Why was China the world's largest economy until 1890?
   b. Why did the United States surpass China in 1890 to become the world's largest economy?

How Potential GDP Grows (Study Plan 6.3)

Use the following information to work Problems 7 and 8.

Suppose that the United States cracks down on illegal immigrants and returns millions of workers to their home countries.

7. Explain what will happen to U.S. potential GDP, employment, and the real wage rate.
8. Explain what will happen in the countries to which the immigrants return to potential GDP, employment, and the real wage rate.

Use the following news clip to work Problems 9 to 11.

U.S. Workers World's Most Productive

Americans work longer hours than those in other rich nations. Americans also produce more per person but only part of the U.S. productivity growth can be explained by the longer hours they work. Americans also create more wealth per hour of work. U.S. employees worked an average of 1,804 hours in 2006, compared to 1,564.4 for the French, but far less than the 2,200 hours that Asians worked. But in Asian countries the average labor productivity is lower.

Source: CBS News, September 3, 2007

9. What is the difference between productivity in this news clip and real GDP per person?
10. Identify and correct a confusion between levels and growth rates of productivity in the news clip.

11. If workers in developing Asian economies work more hours than Americans, why are they not the world's most productive?

Use the following tables to work Problems 12 to 14. The tables describe an economy's labor market and its production function in 2010.

Real wage rate (dollars per hour)	Labor hours supplied	Labor hours demanded
80	45	5
70	40	10
60	35	15
50	30	20
40	25	25
30	20	30
20	15	35

Labor (hours)	Real GDP (2005 dollars)
5	425
10	800
15	1,125
20	1,400
25	1,625
30	1,800
35	1,925
40	2,000

12. What are the equilibrium real wage rate, the quantity of labor employed in 2010, labor productivity, and potential GDP in 2010?
13. In 2011, the population increases and labor hours supplied increase by 10 at each real wage rate. What are the equilibrium real wage rate, labor productivity, and potential GDP in 2011?
14. In 2011, the population increases and labor hours supplied increase by 10 at each real wage rate. Does the standard of living in this economy increase in 2011? Explain why or why not.

Why Labor Productivity Grows (Study Plan 6.4)

15. **Labor Productivity on the Rise**

    The Bureau of Labor Statistics reported the following data for the year ended June 2009: In the nonfarm sector, output fell 5.5 percent as labor productivity increased 1.9 percent—the largest increase since 2003—but in the manufacturing sector, output fell 9.8 percent as labor productivity increased by 4.9 percent—the largest increase since the first quarter of 2005.

    Source: bls.gov/news.release, August 11, 2009

    In both sectors, output fell while labor productivity increased. Did the quantity of labor (aggregate hours) increase or decrease? In which sector was the change in the quantity of labor larger?
16. For three years, there was no technological change in Longland but capital per hour of labor increased from \$10 to \$20 to \$30 and real GDP per hour of labor increased from \$3.80 to \$5.70 to \$7.13. Then, in the fourth year, capital per hour of labor remained constant but real GDP per hour of labor increased to \$10. Does Longland experience diminishing returns? Explain why or why not.

Growth Theories, Evidence, and Policies

(Study Plan 6.5)

17. Explain the processes that will bring the growth of real GDP per person to a stop according to
    a. Classical growth theory.
    b. Neoclassical growth theory.
    c. New growth theory.
18. In the economy of Cape Despair, the subsistence real wage rate is \$15 an hour. Whenever real GDP per hour rises above \$15, the population grows, and whenever real GDP per hour of labor falls below this level, the population falls. The table shows Cape Despair's production function:

Labor (billions of hours per year)	Real GDP (billions of 2000 dollars)
0.5	8
1.0	15
1.5	21
2.0	26
2.5	30
3.0	33
3.5	35

Initially, the population of Cape Despair is constant and real GDP per hour of labor is at the subsistence level of \$15. Then a technological advance shifts the production function upward by 50 percent at each level of labor.

a. What are the initial levels of real GDP and labor productivity?
b. What happens to labor productivity immediately following the technological advance?
c. What happens to the population growth rate following the technological advance?
d. What are the eventual levels of real GDP and real GDP per hour of labor?

ADDITIONAL PROBLEMS AND APPLICATIONS

myeconlab You can work these problems in MyEconLab if assigned by your instructor.

The Basics of Economic Growth

19. If in 2010 China's real GDP is growing at 9 percent a year, its population is growing at 1 percent a year, and these growth rates continue, in what year will China's real GDP per person be twice what it is in 2010?
20. Mexico's real GDP was 8,600 trillion pesos in 2009 and 8,688 trillion pesos in 2010. Mexico's population was 107 million in 2009 and 108 million in 2010. Calculate
    a. The economic growth rate.
    b. The growth rate of real GDP per person.
    c. The approximate number of years it takes for real GDP per person in Mexico to double if the 2010 economic growth rate and population growth rate are maintained.
21. Venezuela's real GDP was 57,049 trillion bolivares in 2009 and 56,764 trillion bolivares in 2010. Venezuela's population was 28.6 million in 2009 and 29.2 million in 2010. Calculate
    a. The economic growth rate.
    b. The growth rate of real GDP per person.
    c. The approximate number of years it takes for real GDP per person in Venezuela to double if economic growth returns to its average since 2009 of 3.6 percent a year and is maintained.

Economic Growth Trends

22. **The New World Order**

    While gross domestic product growth is cooling a bit in emerging market economies, the results are still tremendous compared with the United States and much of Western Europe. The emerging market economies posted a 6.7% jump in real GDP in 2008, down from 7.5% in 2007. The advanced economies grew an estimated 1.6% in 2008. The difference in growth rates represents the largest spread between emerging market economies and advanced economies in the 37-year history of the survey.

    Source: *Fortune*, July 14, 2008

    Do growth rates over the past few decades indicate that gaps in real GDP per person around the world are shrinking, growing, or staying the same? Explain.

How Potential GDP Grows

23. If a large increase in investment increases labor productivity, explain what happens to
    a. Potential GDP.
    b. Employment.
    c. The real wage rate.
24. If a severe drought decreases labor productivity, explain what happens to
    a. Potential GDP.
    b. Employment.
    c. The real wage rate.

Use the following tables to work Problems 25 to 27. The first table describes an economy's labor market in 2010 and the second table describes its production function in 2010.

Real wage rate (dollars per hour)	Labor hours supplied	Labor hours demanded
80	55	15
70	50	20
60	45	25
50	40	30
40	35	35
30	30	40
20	25	45

Labor (hours)	Real GDP (2005 dollars)
15	1,425
20	1,800
25	2,125
30	2,400
35	2,625
40	2,800
45	2,925
50	3,000

25. What are the equilibrium real wage rate and the quantity of labor employed in 2010 ?
26. What are labor productivity and potential GDP in 2010?
27. Suppose that labor productivity increases in 2010. What effect does the increased labor productivity have on the demand for labor, the supply of labor, potential GDP, and real GDP per person?

Why Labor Productivity Grows

28. **India's Economy Hits the Wall**

    Just six months ago, India was looking good. Annual growth was 9%, consumer demand was huge, and foreign investment was growing. But now most economic forecasts expect growth to slow to 7%—a big drop for a country that needs to accelerate growth. India needs urgently to upgrade its infrastructure and education and health-care facilities. Agriculture is unproductive and needs better technology. The legal system needs to be strengthened with more judges and courtrooms.

    Source: *BusinessWeek*, July 1, 2008

    Explain five potential sources for faster economic growth in India suggested in this news clip.

Growth Theories, Evidence, and Policies

29. **The Productivity Watch**

    According to former Federal Reserve chairman Alan Greenspan, IT investments in the 1990s boosted productivity, which boosted corporate profits, which led to more IT investments, and so on, leading to a nirvana of high growth.

    Source: *Fortune*, September 4, 2006

    Which of the growth theories that you've studied in this chapter best corresponds to the explanation given by Mr. Greenspan?

30. Is faster economic growth always a good thing? Argue the case for faster growth and the case for slower growth. Then reach a conclusion on whether growth should be increased or slowed.

31. **Makani Power: A Mighty Wind**

    Makani Power aims to generate energy from what are known as high-altitude wind-extraction technologies. And that's about all its 34-year-old Aussie founder, Saul Griffith, wants to say about it. But Makani can't hide entirely, not when its marquee investor is Google.org, the tech company's philanthropic arm. Makani's plan is to capture that high-altitude wind with a very old tool: kites. Harnessing higher-altitude wind, at least in theory, has greater potential than the existing wind industry because at a thousand feet above the ground, the wind is stronger and more consistent.

    Source: *Fortune*, April 28, 2008

    Explain which growth theory best describes the news clip.

Economics in the News

32. After you have studied *Reading Between the Lines* on pp. 152–153 answer the following questions.
    a. On what criterion is China the second largest economy in the world?
    b. What is the distinction between the size of an economy and the standard of living of its people?
    c. Where does China rank on a standard of living comparison? How is that rank changing and why?
    d. What is the distinction between market prices and PPP prices?
    e. Using PPP prices, where does China's economy rank in size and standard of living?
    f. For what might the size of an economy matter?

33. **Make Way for India—The Next China**

    China grows at around 9 percent a year, but its one-child policy will start to reduce the size of China's working-age population within the next 10 years. India, by contrast, will have an increasing working-age population for another generation at least.

    Source: *The Independent*, March 1, 2006

    a. Given the expected population changes, do you think China or India will have the greater economic growth rate? Why?
    b. Would China's growth rate remain at 9 percent a year without the restriction on its population growth rate?
    c. India's population growth rate is 1.6 percent a year, and in 2005 its economic growth rate was 8 percent a year. China's population growth rate is 0.6 percent a year, and in 2005 its economic growth rate was 9 percent a year. In what year will real GDP per person double in each country?

Data Graphing

34. Use the *Data Grapher* to create a graph of the growth rate of real GDP per person in the United States, Canada, Germany, and the United Kingdom.
    a. Which country had the fastest growth of real GDP per person since 1980 and which had the slowest?
    b. In which country has real GDP per person fluctuated most?

After studying this chapter, you will be able to:

- Describe and define the flows of funds through financial markets and the financial institutions
- Explain how investment and saving along with borrowing and lending decisions are made and how these decisions interact in the loanable funds market
- Explain how a government deficit (or surplus) influences the real interest rate, saving, and investment in the loanable funds market
- Explain how international borrowing or lending influences the real interest rate, saving, and investment in the global loanable funds market

7

FINANCE, SAVING, AND INVESTMENT

During September 2008, Wall Street put on a spectacular show. To prevent the collapse of Fannie Mae and Freddie Mac, the two largest lenders to home buyers, the U.S. government took over their risky debts. When Lehman Brothers, a venerable Wall Street investment bank, was on the verge of bankruptcy, secure phone lines and limousines worked overtime as the Federal Reserve Bank of New York, the U.S. Treasury, and senior officials of Bank of America and Barclays Bank (a British bank) tried to find ways to save the bank. The effort failed. On the same weekend, Bank of America bought Merrill Lynch, another big Wall Street investment bank. And a few days later, the U.S. government bought insurance giant AIG and tried to get Congress to provide $700 billion to buy just about every risky debt that anyone wanted to unload.

Behind such drama, Wall Street plays a crucial unseen role funneling funds from savers and lenders to investors and borrowers. This chapter explains how financial markets work and their place in the economy.

In *Reading Between the Lines* at the end of the chapter, we'll look at the effects of government budget deficits and apply what you've learned to better understand what is happening in U.S. and global financial markets today.

Financial Institutions and Financial Markets

The financial institutions and markets that we study in this chapter play a crucial role in the economy. They provide the channels through which saving flows to finance the investment in new capital that makes the economy grow.

In studying the economics of financial institutions and markets, we distinguish between:

- Finance and money
- Physical capital and financial capital

Finance and Money

In economics, we use the term *finance* to describe the activity of providing the funds that finance expenditures on capital. The study of finance looks at how households and firms obtain and use financial resources and how they cope with the risks that arise in this activity.

Money is what we use to pay for goods and services and factors of production and to make financial transactions. The study of money looks at how households and firms use it, how much of it they hold, how banks create and manage it, and how its quantity influences the economy.

In the economic lives of individuals and businesses, finance and money are closely interrelated. And some of the main financial institutions, such as banks, provide both financial services and monetary services. Nevertheless, by distinguishing between *finance* and *money* and studying them separately, we will better understand our financial and monetary markets and institutions.

For the rest of this chapter, we study finance. Money is the topic of the next chapter.

Physical Capital and Financial Capital

Economists distinguish between physical capital and financial capital. *Physical capital* is the tools, instruments, machines, buildings, and other items that have been produced in the past and that are used today to produce goods and services. Inventories of raw materials, semifinished goods, and components are part of physical capital. When economists use the term capital, they mean *physical* capital. The funds that firms use to buy physical capital are called **financial capital**.

Along the *aggregate production function* in Chapter 6 (see p. 139), the quantity of capital is fixed. An increase in the quantity of capital increases production possibilities and shifts the aggregate production function upward. You're going to see, in this chapter, how investment, saving, borrowing, and lending decisions influence the quantity of capital and make it grow, and as a consequence, make real GDP grow.

We begin by describing the links between capital and investment and between wealth and saving.

Capital and Investment

The quantity of capital changes because of investment and depreciation. *Investment* increases the quantity of capital and *depreciation* decreases it (see Chapter 4, p. 86). The total amount spent on new capital is called **gross investment**. The change in the value of capital is called **net investment**. Net investment equals gross investment minus depreciation.

Figure 7.1 illustrates these terms. On January 1, 2010, Ace Bottling Inc. had machines worth \$30,000—Ace's initial capital. During 2010, the market value of Ace's machines fell by 67 percent—\$20,000. After this depreciation, Ace's machines were valued at \$10,000. During 2010, Ace spent \$30,000 on new machines. This amount is Ace's gross investment. By December 31, 2010, Ace Bottling had capital valued at \$40,000, so its capital had increased by \$10,000. This amount is Ace's net investment. Ace's net investment equals its gross investment of \$30,000 minus depreciation of its initial capital of \$20,000.

Wealth and Saving

Wealth is the value of all the things that people own. What people own is related to what they earn, but it is not the same thing. People earn an *income*, which is the amount they receive during a given time period from supplying the services of the resources they own. **Saving** is the amount of income that is not paid in taxes or spent on consumption goods and services. Saving increases wealth. Wealth also increases when the market value of assets rises—called *capital gains*—and decreases when the market value of assets falls—called *capital losses*.

For example, at the end of the school year you have \$250 in the bank and a coin collection worth \$300, so your wealth is \$550. During the summer,

FIGURE 7.1 Capital and Investment

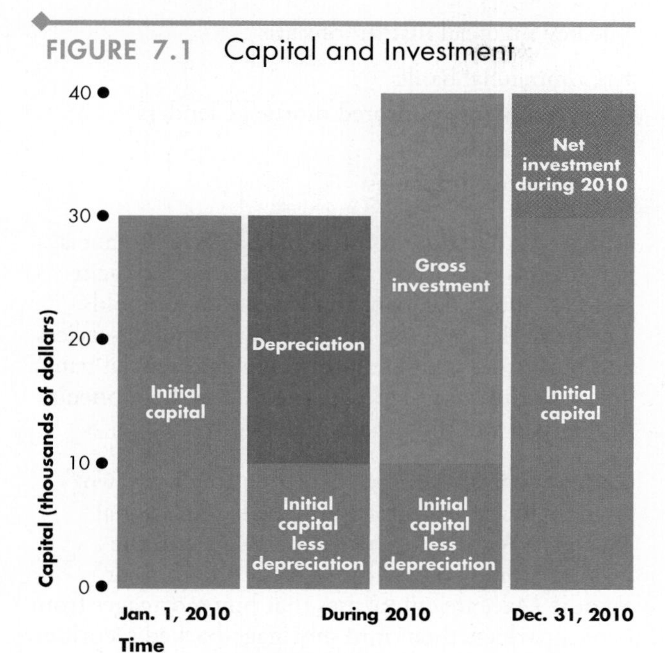

On January 1, 2010, Ace Bottling had capital worth $30,000. During the year, the value of Ace's capital fell by $20,000—depreciation—and it spent $30,000 on new capital—gross investment. Ace's net investment was $10,000 ($30,000 gross investment minus $20,000 depreciation) so that at the end of 2010, Ace had capital worth $40,000.

myeconlab animation

you earn $5,000 (net of taxes) and spend $1,000 on consumption goods and services so your saving is $4,000. Your bank account increases to $4,250 and your wealth becomes $4,550. The $4,000 increase in wealth equals saving. If coins rise in value and your coin collection is now worth $500, you have a capital gain of $200, which is also added to your wealth.

National wealth and national saving work like this personal example. The wealth of a nation at the end of a year equals its wealth at the start of the year plus its saving during the year, which equals income minus consumption expenditure.

To make real GDP grow, saving and wealth must be transformed into investment and capital. This transformation takes place in the markets for financial capital and through the activities of financial institutions. We're now going to describe these markets and institutions.

Financial Capital Markets

Saving is the source of the funds that are used to finance investment, and these funds are supplied and demanded in three types of financial markets:

- Loan markets
- Bond markets
- Stock markets

Loan Markets Businesses often want short-term finance to buy inventories or to extend credit to their customers. Sometimes they get this finance in the form of a loan from a bank. Households often want finance to purchase big ticket items, such as automobiles or household furnishings and appliances. They get this finance as bank loans, often in the form of outstanding credit card balances.

Households also get finance to buy new homes. (Expenditure on new homes is counted as part of investment.) These funds are usually obtained as a loan that is secured by a **mortgage**—a legal contract that gives ownership of a home to the lender in the event that the borrower fails to meet the agreed loan payments (repayments and interest). Mortgage loans were at the center of the U.S. credit crisis of 2007–2008.

All of these types of financing take place in loan markets.

Bond Markets When Wal-Mart expands its business and opens new stores, it gets the finance it needs by selling bonds. Governments—federal, state, and municipal—also raise finance by issuing bonds.

A **bond** is a promise to make specified payments on specified dates. For example, you can buy a Wal-Mart bond that promises to pay $5.00 every year until 2024 and then to make a final payment of $100 in 2025.

The buyer of a bond from Wal-Mart makes a loan to the company and is entitled to the payments promised by the bond. When a person buys a newly issued bond, he or she may hold the bond until the borrower has repaid the amount borrowed or sell it to someone else. Bonds issued by firms and governments are traded in the **bond market**.

The term of a bond might be long (decades) or short (just a month or two). Firms often issue very short-term bonds as a way of getting paid for their sales before the buyer is able to pay. For example, when GM sells $100 million of railway locomotives to Union Pacific, GM wants to be paid when the items are shipped. But Union Pacific doesn't want to pay until the locomotives are earning an income. In this situation, Union Pacific might promise to pay GM $101 million three months in the future. A bank would be willing to buy this promise for (say) $100 million. GM gets $100 million immediately and the bank gets $101 million in three months when Union Pacific honors its promise. The U.S. Treasury issues promises of this type, called Treasury bills.

Another type of bond is a **mortgage-backed security**, which entitles its holder to the income from a package of mortgages. Mortgage lenders create mortgage-backed securities. They make mortgage loans to homebuyers and then create securities that they sell to obtain more funds to make more mortgage loans. The holder of a mortgage-backed security is entitled to receive payments that derive from the payments received by the mortgage lender from the homebuyer–borrower.

Mortgage-backed securities were at the center of the storm in the financial markets in 2007–2008.

Stock Markets When Boeing wants finance to expand its airplane building business, it issues stock. A **stock** is a certificate of ownership and claim to the firm's profits. Boeing has issued about 900 million shares of its stock. So if you owned 900 Boeing shares, you would own one millionth of Boeing and be entitled to receive one millionth of its profits.

Unlike a stockholder, a bondholder does not own part of the firm that issued the bond.

A **stock market** is a financial market in which shares of stocks of corporations are traded. The New York Stock Exchange, the London Stock Exchange (in England), the Tokyo Stock Exchange (in Japan), and the Frankfurt Stock Exchange (in Germany) are all examples of stock markets.

Financial Institutions

Financial markets are highly competitive because of the role played by financial institutions in those markets. A **financial institution** is a firm that operates on both sides of the markets for financial capital. The financial institution is a borrower in one market and a lender in another.

Financial institutions also stand ready to trade so that households with funds to lend and firms or households seeking funds can always find someone on the other side of the market with whom to trade.

The key financial institutions are

- Commercial banks
- Government-sponsored mortgage lenders
- Pension funds
- Insurance companies

Commercial Banks Commercial banks are financial institutions that accept deposits, provide payment services, and make loans to firms and households. The bank that you use for your own banking services and that issues your credit card is a commercial bank. These institutions play a central role in the monetary system and we study them in detail in Chapter 8.

Government-Sponsored Mortgage Lenders Two large financial institutions, the Federal National Mortgage Association, or Fannie Mae, and the Federal Home Loan Mortgage Corporation, or Freddie Mac, are enterprises that buy mortgages from banks, package them into mortgage-backed securities, and sell them. In September 2008, Fannie and Freddie owned or guaranteed $6 trillion worth of mortgages (half of the U.S. $12 trillion of mortgages) and were taken over by the federal government.

Economics in Action

The Financial Crisis and the Fix

Bear Stearns: absorbed by JPMorgan Chase with help from the Federal Reserve. Lehman Brothers: gone. Fannie Mae and Freddie Mac: taken into government oversight. Merrill Lynch: absorbed by Bank of America. AIG: given an $85 billion lifeline by the Federal Reserve and sold off in parcels to financial institutions around the world. Wachovia: taken over by Wells Fargo. Washington Mutual: taken over by JPMorgan Chase. Morgan Stanley: 20 percent bought by Mitsubishi, a large Japanese bank. These are some of the events in the financial crisis of 2008. What was going on and how can a replay be avoided?

Between 2002 and 2005, mortgage lending exploded and home prices rocketed. Mortgage lenders bundled their loans into *mortgage-backed securities* and sold them to eager buyers around the world.

When interest rates began to rise in 2006 and asset prices fell, financial institutions took big losses. Some losses were too big to bear and big-name institutions failed.

Pension Funds Pension funds are financial institutions that use the pension contributions of firms and workers to buy bonds and stocks. The mortgage-backed securities of Fannie Mae and Freddie Mac are among the assets of pension funds. Some pension funds are very large and play an active role in the firms whose stock they hold.

Insurance Companies Insurance companies enable households and firms to cope with risks such as accident, theft, fire, ill-health, and a host of other misfortunes. They receive premiums from their customers and pay claims. Insurance companies use the funds they have received but not paid out as claims to buy bonds and stocks on which they earn interest income.

In normal times, insurance companies have a steady flow of funds coming in from premiums and interest on the financial assets they hold and a steady, but smaller, flow of funds paying claims. Their profit is the gap between the two flows. But in unusual times, when large and widespread losses are being incurred, insurance companies can run into difficulty in meeting their obligations. Such a situation arose in 2008 for one of the biggest insurers, AIG, and the firm was taken into public ownership.

Insolvency and Illiquidity

A financial institution's **net worth** is the market value of what it has lent minus the market value of what it has borrowed. If net worth is positive, the institution is *solvent*. But if net worth is negative, the institution is *insolvent* and must go out of business. The owners of an insolvent financial institution—usually its stockholders—bear the loss.

A financial institution both borrows and lends, so it is exposed to the risk that its net worth might become negative. To limit that risk, financial institutions are regulated and a minimum amount of their lending must be backed by their net worth.

Sometimes, a financial institution is solvent but illiquid. A firm is *illiquid* if it has made long-term loans with borrowed funds and is faced with a sudden demand to repay more of what it has borrowed than its available cash. In normal times, a financial institution that is illiquid can borrow from another institution. But if all the financial institutions are short of cash, the market for loans among financial institutions dries up.

Insolvency and illiquidity were at the core of the financial meltdown of 2007–2008.

In the hope of avoiding a replay, Congress has enacted the *Restoring American Financial Stability Act of 2010*. The main points of the Act are

- A Consumer Financial Protection Agency to enforce consumer-oriented regulation, ensure that the fine print on financial services contracts is clear and accurate, and maintain a toll-free hotline for consumers to report alleged deception.
- A Financial Services Oversight Council to anticipate financial market weakness.
- Authority for the Federal Deposit Insurance Corporation to seize, liquidate, and reconstruct troubled financial firms.
- Tight restrictions to stop banks gambling for their own profits and limit their risky investments.
- Mortgage reforms that require lenders to review the income and credit histories of applicants and ensure they can afford payments.
- Require firms that create mortgage-backed securities to keep at least 5 percent of them.

The 2010 Act does nothing to solve the problem that Fannie and Freddie remain under government oversight. Many people believe that the measures are too timid and leave the financial system fragile.

Interest Rates and Asset Prices

Stocks, bonds, short-term securities, and loans are collectively called *financial assets*. The interest rate on a financial asset is the interest received expressed as a percentage of the price of the asset.

Because the interest rate is a percentage of the price of an asset, if the asset price rises, other things remaining the same, the interest rate falls. Conversely, if the asset price falls, other things remaining the same, the interest rate rises.

To see this inverse relationship between an asset price and the interest rate, let's look at an example. We'll consider a bond that promises to pay its holder \$5 a year forever. What is the rate of return—the interest rate—on this bond? The answer depends on the price of the bond. If you could buy this bond for \$50, the interest rate would be 10 percent per year:

$$\text{Interest rate} = (\$5 \div \$50) \times 100 = 10 \text{ percent.}$$

But if the price of this bond increased to \$200, its rate of return or interest rate would be only 2.5 percent per year. That is,

$$\text{Interest rate} = (\$5 \div \$200) \times 100 = 2.5 \text{ percent.}$$

This relationship means that the price of an asset and the interest rate on that asset are determined simultaneously—one implies the other.

This relationship also means that if the interest rate on the asset rises, the price of the asset falls, debts become harder to pay, and the net worth of the financial institution falls. Insolvency can arise from a previously unexpected large rise in the interest rate.

In the next part of this chapter, we learn how interest rates and asset prices are determined in the financial markets.

REVIEW QUIZ

1. Distinguish between physical capital and financial capital and give two examples of each.
2. What is the distinction between gross investment and net investment?
3. What are the three main types of markets for financial capital?
4. Explain the connection between the price of a financial asset and its interest rate.

You can work these questions in Study Plan 7.1 and get instant feedback.

The Loanable Funds Market

In macroeconomics, we group all the financial markets that we described in the previous section into a single loanable funds market. The **loanable funds market** is the aggregate of all the individual financial markets.

The circular flow model of Chapter 4 (see p. 85) can be extended to include flows in the loanable funds market that finance investment.

Funds that Finance Investment

Figure 7.2 shows the flows of funds that finance investment. They come from three sources:

1. Household saving
2. Government budget surplus
3. Borrowing from the rest of the world

Households' income, Y, is spent on consumption goods and services, C, saved, S, or paid in net taxes, T. **Net taxes** are the taxes paid to governments minus the cash transfers received from governments (such as Social Security and unemployment benefits). So income is equal to the sum of consumption expenditure, saving, and net taxes:

$$Y = C + S + T.$$

You saw in Chapter 4 (p. 86) that Y also equals the sum of the items of aggregate expenditure: consumption expenditure, C, investment, I, government expenditure, G, and exports, X, minus imports, M. That is:

$$Y = C + I + G + X - M.$$

By using these two equations, you can see that

$$I + G + X = M + S + T.$$

Subtract G and X from both sides of the last equation to obtain

$$I = S + (T - G) + (M - X).$$

This equation tells us that investment, I, is financed by household saving, S, the government budget surplus, $(T - G)$, and borrowing from the rest of the world, $(M - X)$.

A government budget surplus $(T > G)$ contributes funds to finance investment, but a government budget deficit $(T < G)$ competes with investment for funds.

FIGURE 7.2 Financial Flows and the Circular Flow of Expenditure and Income

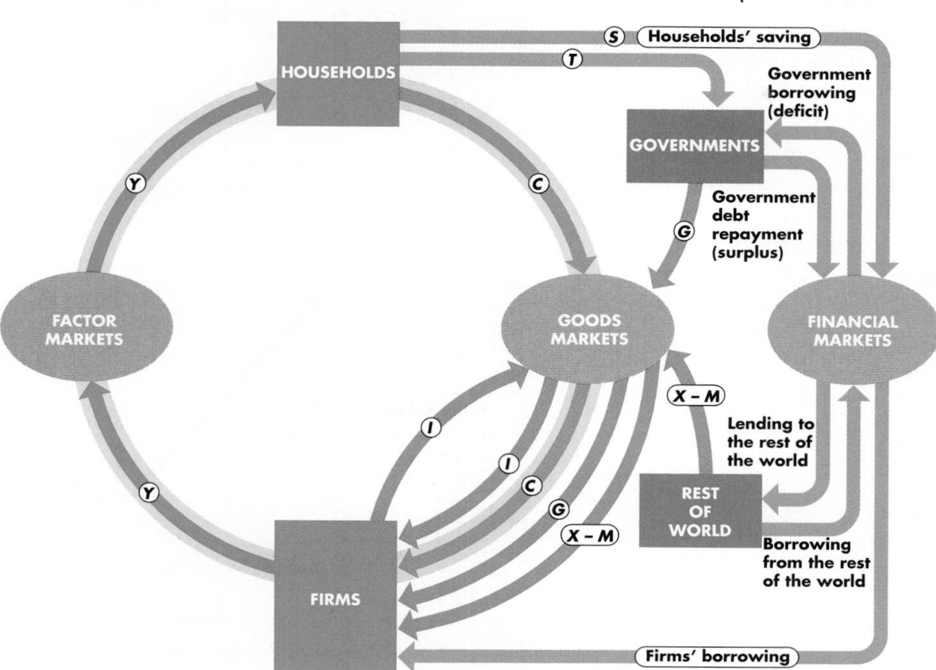

Households use their income for consumption expenditure (C), saving (S), and net taxes (T). Firms borrow to finance their investment expenditure. Governments borrow to finance a budget deficit or repay debt if they have a budget surplus. The rest of the world borrows to finance its deficit or lends its surplus.

myeconlab animation

If we export less than we import, we borrow $(M - X)$ from the rest of the world to finance some of our investment. If we export more than we import, we lend $(X - M)$ to the rest of the world and part of U.S. saving finances investment in other countries.

The sum of private saving, S, and government saving, $(T - G)$, is called **national saving**. National saving and foreign borrowing finance investment.

In 2010, U.S. investment was $1.8 trillion. Governments (federal, state, and local combined) had a deficit of $1.5 trillion. This total of $3.3 trillion was financed by private saving of $2.8 trillion and borrowing from the rest of the world (negative net exports) of $0.5 trillion.

You're going to see how investment and saving and the flows of loanable funds—all measured in constant 2005 dollars—are determined. The price in the loanable funds market that achieves equilibrium is an interest rate, which we also measure in real terms as the *real* interest rate. In the loanable funds market, there is just one interest rate, which is an average of the interest rates on all the different types of financial securities that we described earlier. Let's see what we mean by the real interest rate.

The Real Interest Rate

The **nominal interest rate** is the number of dollars that a borrower pays and a lender receives in interest in a year expressed as a percentage of the number of dollars borrowed and lent. For example, if the annual interest paid on a $500 loan is $25, the nominal interest rate is 5 percent per year: $25 ÷ $500 × 100 or 5 percent.

The **real interest rate** is the nominal interest rate adjusted to remove the effects of inflation on the buying power of money. The real interest rate is approximately equal to the nominal interest rate minus the inflation rate.

You can see why if you suppose that you have put $500 in a savings account that earns 5 percent a year. At the end of a year, you have $525 in your savings account. Suppose that the inflation rate is 2 percent per year—during the year, all prices increased by 2 percent. Now, at the end of the year, it costs $510 to buy what $500 would have bought one year ago. Your money in the bank has really only increased by $15, from $510 to $525. That $15 is equivalent to a real interest rate of 3 percent a year on your original

$500. So the real interest rate is the 5 percent nominal interest rate minus the 2 percent inflation rate[1].

The real interest rate is the opportunity cost of loanable funds. The real interest *paid* on borrowed funds is the opportunity cost of borrowing. And the real interest rate *forgone* when funds are used either to buy consumption goods and services or to invest in new capital goods is the opportunity cost of not saving or not lending those funds.

We're now going to see how the loanable funds market determines the real interest rate, the quantity of funds loaned, saving, and investment. In the rest of this section, we will ignore the government and the rest of the world and focus on households and firms in the loanable funds market. We will study

- The demand for loanable funds
- The supply of loanable funds
- Equilibrium in the loanable funds market

The Demand for Loanable Funds

The *quantity of loanable funds demanded* is the total quantity of funds demanded to finance investment, the government budget deficit, and international investment or lending during a given period. Our focus here is on investment. We'll bring the other two items into the picture in later sections of this chapter.

What determines investment and the demand for loanable funds to finance it? Many details influence this decision, but we can summarize them in two factors:

1. The real interest rate
2. Expected profit

Firms invest in capital only if they expect to earn a profit and fewer projects are profitable at a high real interest rate than at a low real interest rate, so

Other things remaining the same, the higher the real interest rate, the smaller is the quantity of loanable funds demanded; and the lower the real interest rate, the greater the quantity of loanable funds demanded.

[1]The *exact* real interest rate formula, which allows for the change in the purchasing power of both the interest and the loan is: Real interest rate = (Nominal interest rate – Inflation rate) ÷ (1 + Inflation rate/100). If the nominal interest rate is 5 percent a year and the inflation rate is 2 percent a year, the real interest rate is (5 – 2) ÷ (1 + 0.02) = 2.94 percent a year.

FIGURE 7.3 The Demand for Loanable Funds

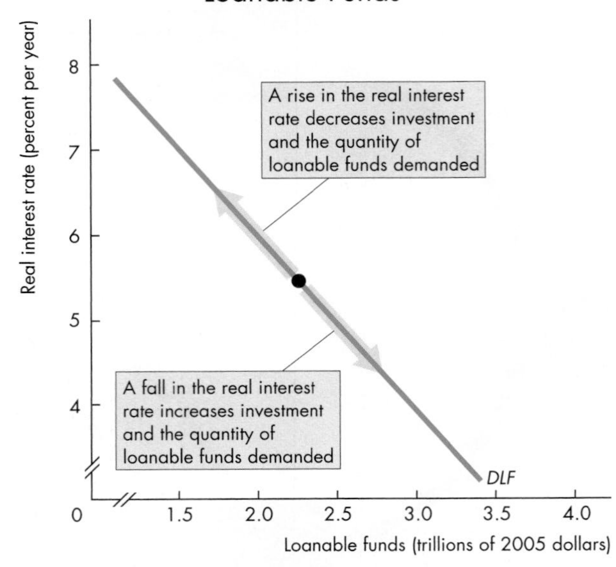

A change in the real interest rate changes the quantity of loanable funds demanded and brings a movement along the demand for loanable funds curve.

myeconlab animation

Demand for Loanable Funds Curve The **demand for loanable funds** is the relationship between the quantity of loanable funds demanded and the real interest rate, when all other influences on borrowing plans remain the same. The demand curve *DLF* in Fig. 7.3 is a demand for loanable funds curve.

To understand the demand for loanable funds, think about Amazon.com's decision to borrow $100 million to build some new warehouses. If Amazon expects to get a return of $5 million a year from this investment before paying interest costs and the interest rate is less than 5 percent a year, Amazon would make a profit, so it builds the warehouses. But if the interest rate is more than 5 percent a year, Amazon would incur a loss, so it doesn't build the warehouses. The quantity of loanable funds demanded is greater the lower is the real interest rate.

Changes in the Demand for Loanable Funds When the expected profit changes, the demand for loanable funds changes. Other things remaining the same, the greater the expected profit from new capital, the greater is the amount of investment and the greater the demand for loanable funds.

Expected profit rises during a business cycle expansion and falls during a recession; rises when technological change creates profitable new products; rises as a growing population brings increased demand for goods and services; and fluctuates with contagious swings of optimism and pessimism, called "animal spirits" by Keynes and "irrational exuberance" by Alan Greenspan.

When expected profit changes, the demand for loanable funds curve shifts.

The Supply of Loanable Funds

The *quantity of loanable funds supplied* is the total funds available from private saving, the government budget surplus, and international borrowing during a given period. Our focus here is on saving. We'll bring the other two items into the picture later.

How do you decide how much of your income to save and supply in the loanable funds market? Your decision is influenced by many factors, but chief among them are

1. The real interest rate
2. Disposable income
3. Expected future income
4. Wealth
5. Default risk

We begin by focusing on the real interest rate.

Other things remaining the same, the higher the real interest rate, the greater is the quantity of loanable funds supplied; and the lower the real interest rate, the smaller is the quantity of loanable funds supplied.

The Supply of Loanable Funds Curve The **supply of loanable funds** is the relationship between the quantity of loanable funds supplied and the real interest rate when all other influences on lending plans remain the same. The curve *SLF* in Fig. 7.4 is a supply of loanable funds curve.

Think about a student's decision to save some of what she earns from her summer job. With a real interest rate of 2 percent a year, she decides that it is not worth saving much—better to spend the income and take a student loan if funds run out during the semester. But if the real interest rate jumped to 10 percent a year, the payoff from saving would be high enough to encourage her to cut back on spending and increase the amount she saves.

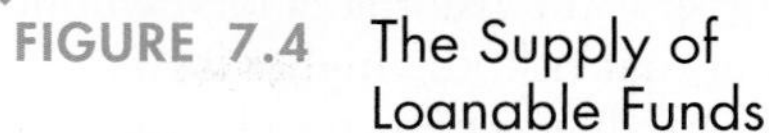

FIGURE 7.4 The Supply of Loanable Funds

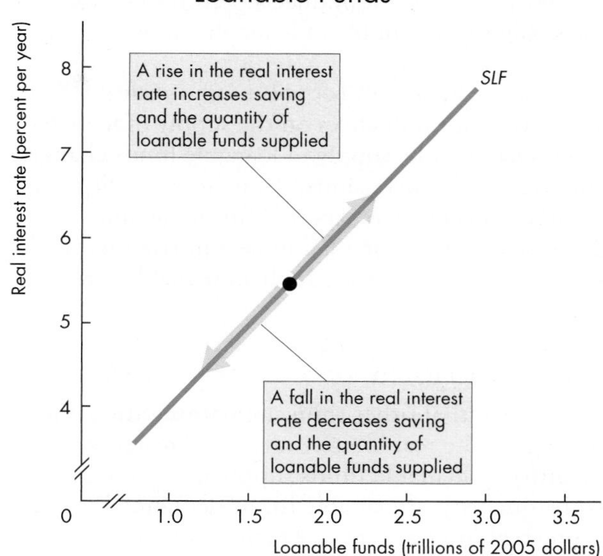

A change in the real interest rate changes the quantity of loanable funds supplied and brings a movement along the supply of loanable funds curve.

myeconlab animation

Changes in the Supply of Loanable Funds A change in disposable income, expected future income, wealth, or default risk changes the supply of loanable funds.

Disposable Income A household's *disposable income* is the income earned minus net taxes. When disposable income increases, other things remaining the same, consumption expenditure increases but by less than the increase in income. Some of the increase in income is saved. So the greater a household's disposable income, other things remaining the same, the greater is its saving.

Expected Future Income The higher a household's expected future income, other things remaining the same, the smaller is its saving today.

Wealth The higher a household's wealth, other things remaining the same, the smaller is its saving. If a person's wealth increases because of a capital gain, the person sees less need to save. For example, from 2002 through 2006, when house prices were rising rapidly, wealth increased despite the fact that personal saving dropped close to zero.

Default Risk Default risk is the risk that a loan will not be repaid. The greater that risk, the higher is the interest rate needed to induce a person to lend and the smaller is the supply of loanable funds.

Shifts of the Supply of Loanable Funds Curve When any of the four influences on the supply of loanable funds changes, the supply of loanable funds changes and the supply curve shifts. An increase in disposable income, a decrease in expected future income, a decrease in wealth, or a fall in default risk increases saving and increases the supply of loanable funds.

Equilibrium in the Loanable Funds Market

You've seen that other things remaining the same, the higher the real interest rate, the greater is the quantity of loanable funds supplied and the smaller is the quantity of loanable funds demanded. There is one real interest rate at which the quantities of loanable funds demanded and supplied are equal, and that interest rate is the equilibrium real interest rate.

Figure 7.5 shows how the demand for and supply of loanable funds determine the real interest rate. The *DLF* curve is the demand curve and the *SLF* curve is the supply curve. If the real interest rate exceeds 6 percent a year, the quantity of loanable funds supplied exceeds the quantity demanded—a surplus of funds. Borrowers find it easy to get funds, but lenders are unable to lend all the funds they have available. The real interest rate falls and continues to fall until the quantity of funds supplied equals the quantity of funds demanded.

If the real interest rate is less than 6 percent a year, the quantity of loanable funds supplied is less than the quantity demanded—a shortage of funds. Borrowers can't get the funds they want, but lenders are able to lend all the funds they have. So the real interest rate rises and continues to rise until the quantity of funds supplied equals the quantity demanded.

Regardless of whether there is a surplus or a shortage of loanable funds, the real interest rate changes and is pulled toward an equilibrium level. In Fig. 7.5, the equilibrium real interest rate is 6 percent a year. At this interest rate, there is neither a surplus nor a shortage of loanable funds. Borrowers can get the funds they want, and lenders can lend all the funds they have available. The investment plans of borrowers and the saving plans of lenders are consistent with each other.

FIGURE 7.5 Equilibrium in the Loanable Funds Market

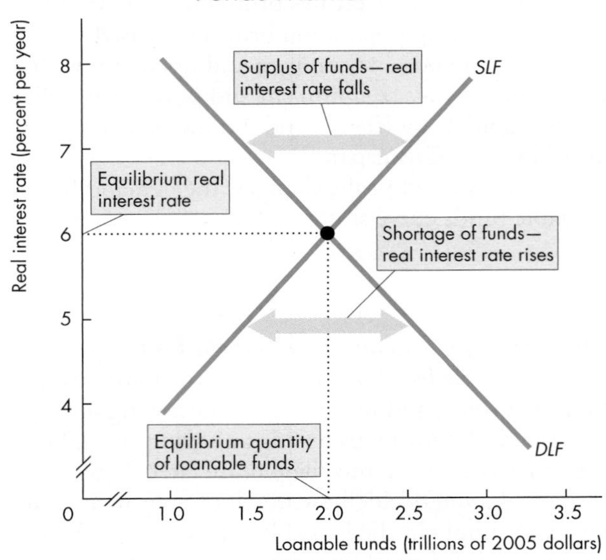

A surplus of funds lowers the real interest rate and a shortage of funds raises it. At an interest rate of 6 percent a year, the quantity of funds demanded equals the quantity supplied and the market is in equilibrium.

Changes in Demand and Supply

Financial markets are highly volatile in the short run but remarkably stable in the long run. Volatility in the market comes from fluctuations in either the demand for loanable funds or the supply of loanable funds. These fluctuations bring fluctuations in the real interest rate and in the equilibrium quantity of funds lent and borrowed. They also bring fluctuations in asset prices.

Here we'll illustrate the effects of *increases* in demand and supply in the loanable funds market.

An Increase in Demand If the profits that firms expect to earn increase, they increase their planned investment and increase their demand for loanable funds to finance that investment. With an increase in the demand for loanable funds, but no change in the supply of loanable funds, there is a shortage of funds. As borrowers compete for funds, the interest rate rises and lenders increase the quantity of funds supplied.

Figure 7.6(a) illustrates these changes. An increase in the demand for loanable funds shifts the demand curve rightward from DLF_0 to DLF_1. With no

FIGURE 7.6 Changes in Demand and Supply

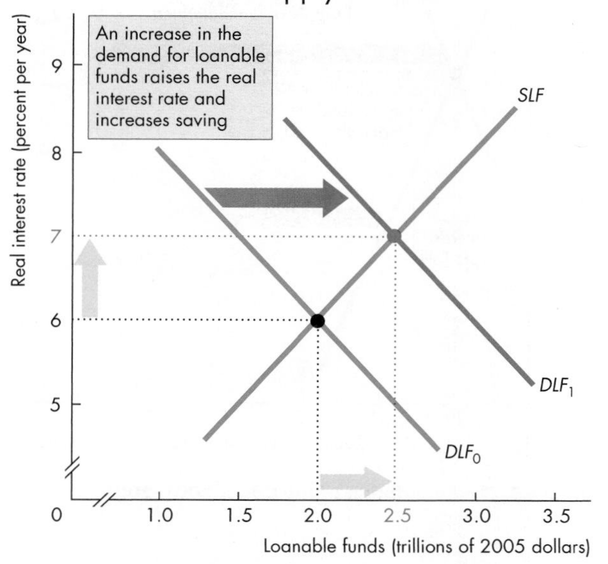

(a) An increase in demand

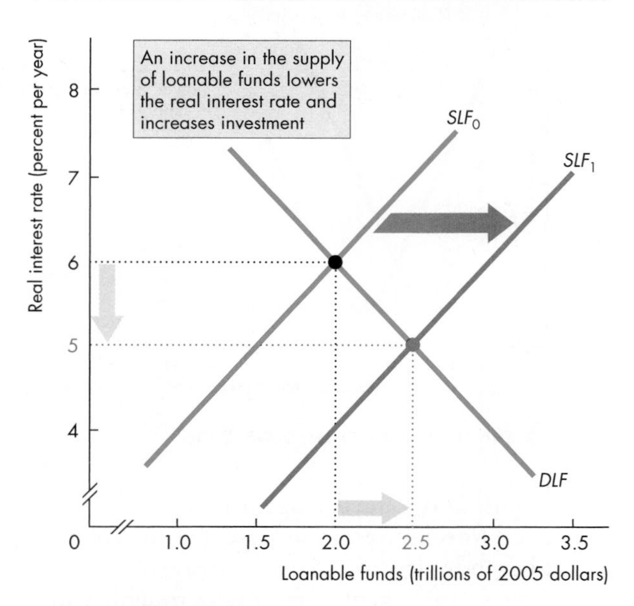

(b) An increase in supply

In part (a), the demand for loanable funds increases and supply doesn't change. The real interest rate rises (financial asset prices fall) and the quantity of funds increases.
In part (b), the supply of loanable funds increases and demand doesn't change. The real interest rate falls (financial asset prices rise) and the quantity of funds increases.

myeconlab animation

change in the supply of loanable funds, there is a shortage of funds at a real interest rate of 6 percent a year. The real interest rate rises until it is 7 percent a year. Equilibrium is restored and the equilibrium quantity of funds has increased.

An Increase in Supply If one of the influences on saving plans changes and increases saving, the supply of loanable funds increases. With no change in the demand for loanable funds, the market is flush with loanable funds. Borrowers find bargains and lenders find themselves accepting a lower interest rate. At the lower interest rate, borrowers find additional investment projects profitable and increase the quantity of loanable funds that they borrow.

Figure 7.6(b) illustrates these changes. An increase in supply shifts the supply curve rightward from SLF_0 to SLF_1. With no change in demand, there is a surplus of funds at a real interest rate of 6 percent a year. The real interest rate falls until it is 5 percent a year. Equilibrium is restored and the equilibrium quantity of funds has increased.

Long-Run Growth of Demand and Supply Over time, both demand and supply in the loanable funds market fluctuate and the real interest rate rises and falls. Both the supply of loanable funds and the demand for loanable funds tend to increase over time. On the average, they increase at a similar pace, so although demand and supply trend upward, the real interest rate has no trend. It fluctuates around a constant average level.

REVIEW QUIZ

1. What is the loanable funds market?
2. Why is the real interest rate the opportunity cost of loanable funds?
3. How do firms make investment decisions?
4. What determines the demand for loanable funds and what makes it change?
5. How do households make saving decisions?
6. What determines the supply of loanable funds and what makes it change?
7. How do changes in the demand for and supply of loanable funds change the real interest rate and quantity of loanable funds?

You can work these questions in Study Plan 7.2 and get instant feedback.

Economics in Actions

Loanable Funds Fuel Home Price Bubble

The financial crisis that gripped the U.S. and global economies in 2007 and cascaded through the financial markets in 2008 had its origins much earlier in events taking place in the loanable funds market.

Between 2001 and 2005, a massive injection of loanable funds occurred. Some funds came from the rest of the world, but that source of supply has been stable. The Federal Reserve provided funds to keep interest rates low and that was a major source of the increase in the supply of funds. (The next chapter explains how the Fed does this.)

Figure 1 illustrates the loanable funds market starting in 2001. In that year, the demand for loanable funds was DLF_{01} and the supply of loanable funds was SLF_{01}. The equilibrium real interest rate was 4 percent a year and the equilibrium quantity of loanable funds was $29 trillion (in 2005 dollars).

During the ensuing four years, a massive increase in the supply of loanable funds shifted the supply curve rightward to SLF_{05}. A smaller increase in demand shifted the demand for loanable funds curve to DLF_{05}. The real interest rate fell to 1 percent a year and the quantity of loanable funds increased to $36 trillion—a 24 percent increase in just four years.

With this large increase in available funds, much of it in the form of mortgage loans to home buyers, the demand for homes increased by more than the increase in the supply of homes. Home prices rose and the expectation of further increases fueled the demand for loanable funds.

By 2006, the expectation of continued rapidly rising home prices brought a very large increase in the demand for loanable funds. At the same time, the Federal Reserve began to tighten credit. (Again, you'll learn how this is done in the next chapter). The result of the Fed's tighter credit policy was a slowdown in the pace of increase in the supply of loanable funds.

Figure 2 illustrates these events. In 2006, the demand for loanable funds increased from DLF_{05} to DLF_{06} and the supply of loanable funds increased by a smaller amount from SLF_{05} to SLF_{06}. The real interest rate increased to 3 percent a year.

The rise in the real interest rate (and a much higher rise in the nominal interest rate) put many homeowners in financial difficulty. Mortgage payments increased and some borrowers stopped repaying their loans.

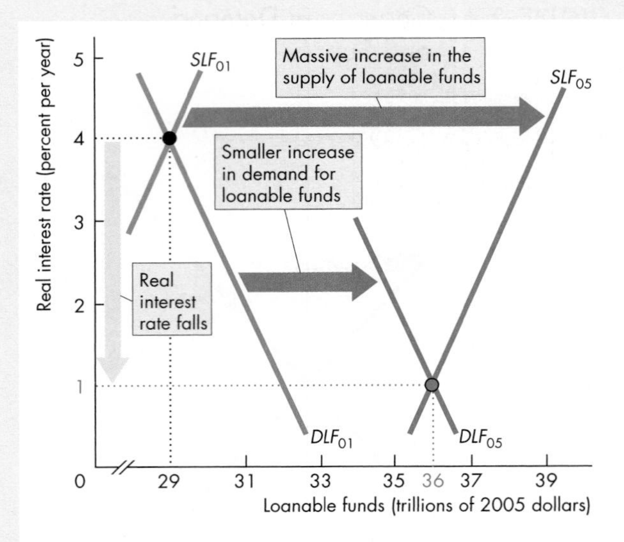

Figure 1 The Foundation of the Crisis: 2001–2005

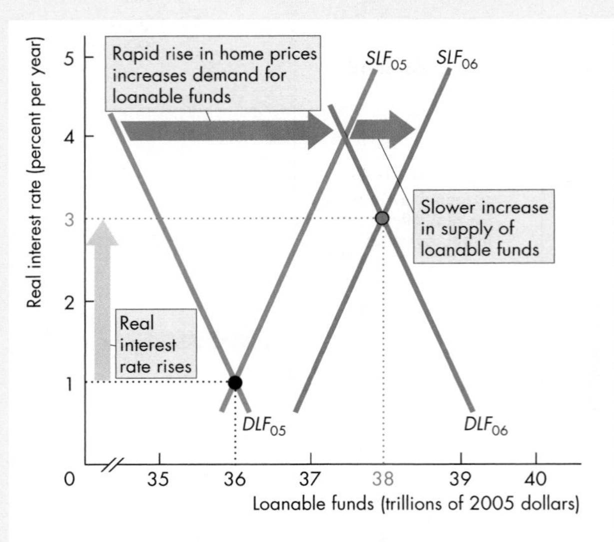

Figure 2 The Start of the Crisis: 2005–2006

By August 2007, the damage from mortgage default and foreclosure was so large that the credit market began to dry up. A large decrease in both demand and supply kept interest rates roughly constant but decreased the quantity of new business.

The total quantity of loanable funds didn't decrease, but the rate of increase slowed to a snail's pace and financial institutions most exposed to the bad mortgage debts and the securities that they backed (described on p. 162) began to fail.

These events illustrate the crucial role played by the loanable funds market in our economy.

Government in the Loanable Funds Market

Government enters the loanable funds market when it has a budget surplus or budget deficit. A government budget surplus increases the supply of loanable funds and contributes to financing investment; a government budget deficit increases the demand for loanable funds and competes with businesses for funds. Let's study the effects of government on the loanable funds market.

A Government Budget Surplus

A government budget surplus increases the supply of loanable funds. The real interest rate falls, which decreases household saving and decreases the quantity of private funds supplied. The lower real interest rate increases the quantity of loanable funds demanded, and increases investment.

FIGURE 7.7 A Government Budget Surplus

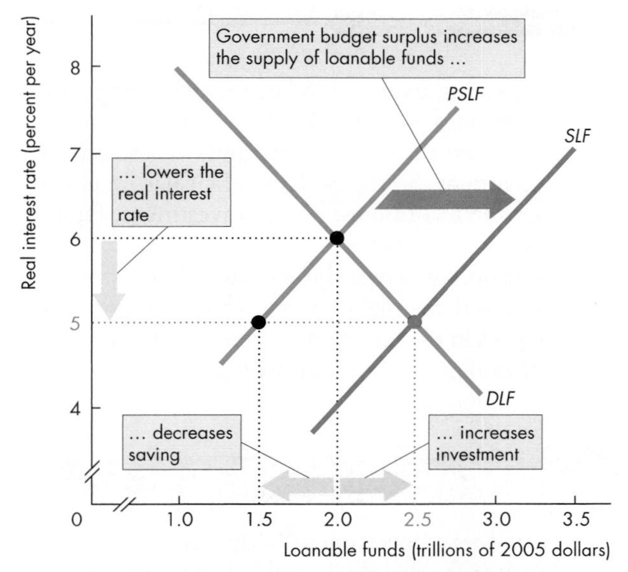

A government budget surplus of $1 trillion is added to private saving and the private supply of loanable funds (*PSLF*) to determine the supply of loanable funds, *SLF*. The real interest rate falls to 5 percent a year, private saving decreases, but investment increases to $2.5 trillion.

myeconlab animation

Figure 7.7 shows these effects of a government budget surplus. The private supply of loanable funds curve is *PSLF*. The supply of loanable funds curve, *SLF*, shows the sum of private supply and the government budget surplus. Here, the government budget surplus is $1 trillion, so at each real interest rate the *SLF* curve lies $1 trillion to the right of the *PSLF* curve. That is, the horizontal distance between the *PSLF* curve and the *SLF* curve equals the government budget surplus.

With no government surplus, the real interest rate is 6 percent a year, the quantity of loanable funds is $2 trillion a year, and investment is $2 trillion a year. But with the government surplus of $1 trillion a year, the equilibrium real interest rate falls to 5 percent a year and the equilibrium quantity of loanable funds increases to $2.5 trillion a year.

The fall in the interest rate decreases private saving to $1.5 trillion, but investment increases to $2.5 trillion, which is financed by private saving plus the government budget surplus (government saving).

A Government Budget Deficit

A government budget deficit increases the demand for loanable funds. The real interest rate rises, which increases household saving and increases the quantity of private funds supplied. But the higher real interest rate decreases investment and the quantity of loanable funds demanded by firms to finance investment.

Figure 7.8 shows these effects of a government budget deficit. The private demand for loanable funds curve is *PDLF*. The demand for loanable funds curve, *DLF*, shows the sum of private demand and the government budget deficit. Here, the government budget deficit is $1 trillion, so at each real interest rate the *DLF* curve lies $1 trillion to the right of the *PDLF* curve. That is, the horizontal distance between the *PDLF* curve and the *DLF* curve equals the government budget deficit.

With no government deficit, the real interest rate is 6 percent a year, the quantity of loanable funds is $2 trillion a year and investment is $2 trillion a year. But with the government budget deficit of $1 trillion a year, the equilibrium real interest rate rises to 7 percent a year and the equilibrium quantity of loanable funds increases to $2.5 trillion a year.

The rise in the real interest rate increases private saving to $2.5 trillion, but investment decreases to $1.5 trillion because $1 trillion of private saving must finance the government budget deficit.

FIGURE 7.8 A Government Budget Deficit

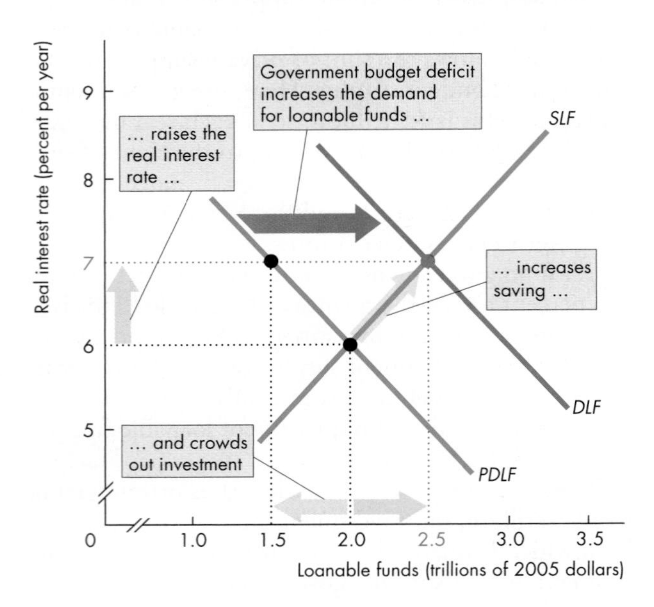

A government budget deficit adds to the private demand for loanable funds curve (*PDLF*) to determine the demand for loanable funds curve, *DLF*. The real interest rate rises, saving increases, but investment decreases—a crowding-out effect.

FIGURE 7.9 The Ricardo-Barro Effect

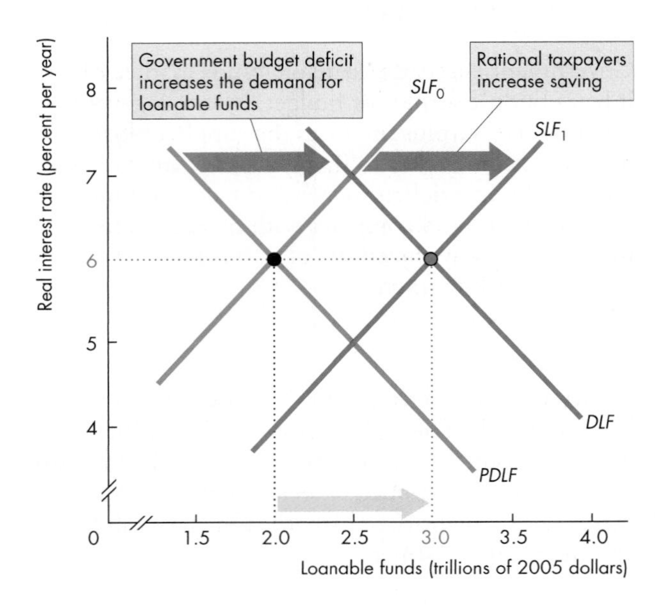

A budget deficit increases the demand for loanable funds. Rational taxpayers increase saving, which increases the supply of loanable funds curve from SLF_0 to SLF_1. Crowding out is avoided: Increased saving finances the budget deficit.

The Crowding-Out Effect The tendency for a government budget deficit to raise the real interest rate and decrease investment is called the **crowding-out effect.** The budget deficit crowds out investment by competing with businesses for scarce financial capital.

The crowding-out effect does not decrease investment by the full amount of the government budget deficit because the higher real interest rate induces an increase in private saving that partly contributes toward financing the deficit.

The Ricardo-Barro Effect First suggested by the English economist David Ricardo in the eighteenth century and refined by Robert J. Barro of Harvard University, the Ricardo-Barro effect holds that both of the effects we've just shown are wrong and the government budget, whether in surplus or deficit, has no effect on either the real interest rate or investment.

Barro says that taxpayers are rational. They can see that a budget deficit today means that future taxes will be higher and future disposable incomes will be smaller. With smaller expected future disposable incomes, saving increases today. Private saving and the private supply of loanable funds increase to match the quantity of loanable funds demanded by the government. So the budget deficit has no effect on either the real interest rate or investment. Figure 7.9 shows this outcome.

Most economists regard the Ricardo-Barro view as extreme. But there might be some change in private saving that goes in the direction suggested by the Ricardo-Barro effect that lessens the crowding-out effect.

REVIEW QUIZ

1. How does a government budget surplus or deficit influence the loanable funds market?
2. What is the crowding-out effect and how does it work?
3. What is the Ricardo-Barro effect and how does it modify the crowding-out effect?

You can work these questions in Study Plan 7.3 and get instant feedback.

The Global Loanable Funds Market

The loanable funds market is global, not national. Lenders on the supply side of the market want to earn the highest possible real interest rate and they will seek it by looking everywhere in the world. Borrowers on the demand side of the market want to pay the lowest possible real interest rate and they will seek it by looking everywhere in the world. Financial capital is mobile: It moves to the best advantage of lenders and borrowers.

International Capital Mobility

If a U.S. supplier of loanable funds can earn a higher interest rate in Tokyo than in New York, funds supplied in Japan will increase and funds supplied in the United States will decrease—funds will flow from the United States to Japan.

If a U.S. demander of loanable funds can pay a lower interest rate in Paris than in New York, the demand for funds in France will increase and the demand for funds in the United States will decrease—funds will flow from France to the United States.

Because lenders are free to seek the highest real interest rate and borrowers are free to seek the lowest real interest rate, the loanable funds market is a single, integrated, global market. Funds flow into the country in which the interest rate is highest and out of the country in which the interest rate is lowest.

When funds leave the country with the lowest interest rate, a shortage of funds raises the real interest rate. When funds move into the country with the highest interest rate, a surplus of funds lowers the real interest rate. The free international mobility of financial capital pulls real interest rates around the world toward equality.

Only when the real interest rates in New York, Tokyo, and Paris are equal does the incentive to move funds from one country to another stop.

Equality of real interest rates does not mean that if you calculate the average real interest rate in New York, Tokyo, and Paris, you'll get the same number. To compare real interest rates, we must compare financial assets of equal risk.

Lending is risky. A loan might not be repaid. Or the price of a stock or bond might fall. Interest rates include a risk premium—the riskier the loan, other things remaining the same, the higher is the interest rate. The interest rate on a risky loan minus that on a safe loan is called the *risk premium*.

International capital mobility brings *real* interest rates in all parts of the world to equality except for differences that reflect differences in risk—differences in the risk premium.

International Borrowing and Lending

A country's loanable funds market connects with the global market through net exports. If a country's net exports are negative ($X < M$), the rest of the world supplies funds to that country and the quantity of loanable funds in that country is greater than national saving. If a country's net exports are positive ($X > M$), the country is a net supplier of funds to the rest of the world and the quantity of loanable funds in that country is less than national saving.

Demand and Supply in the Global and National Markets

The demand for and supply of funds in the global loanable funds market determines the world equilibrium real interest rate. This interest rate makes the quantity of loanable funds demanded equal the quantity supplied in the world economy. But it does not make the quantity of funds demanded and supplied equal in each national economy. The demand for and supply of funds in a national economy determine whether the country is a lender to or a borrower from the rest of the world.

The Global Loanable Funds Market Figure 7.10(a) illustrates the global market. The demand for loanable funds, DLF_W is the sum of the demands in all countries. Similarly, the supply of loanable funds, SLF_W is the sum of the supplies in all countries. The world equilibrium real interest rate makes the quantity of funds supplied in the world as a whole equal to the quantity demanded. In this example, the equilibrium real interest rate is 5 percent a year and the quantity of funds is $10 trillion.

An International Borrower Figure 7.10(b) shows the loanable funds market in a country that borrows from the rest of the world. The country's demand for loanable funds, DLF, is part of the world demand in Fig. 7.10(a). The country's supply of loanable funds, SLF_D, is part of the world supply.

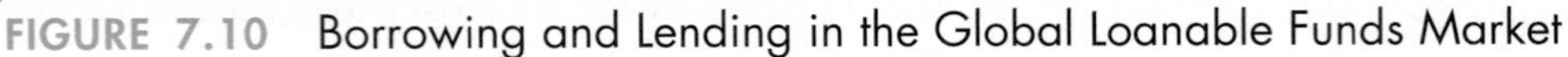

FIGURE 7.10 Borrowing and Lending in the Global Loanable Funds Market

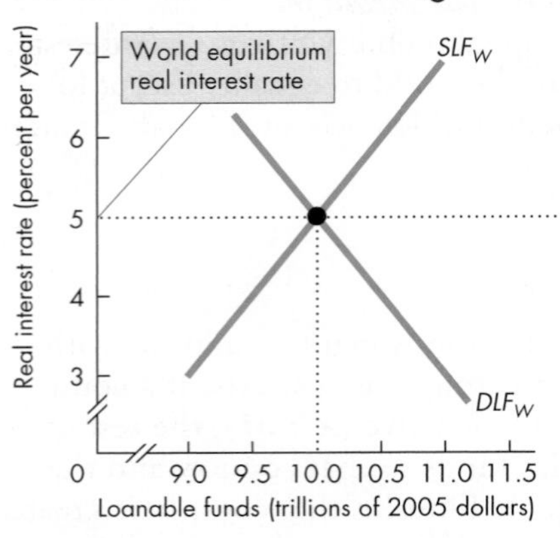

(a) The global market

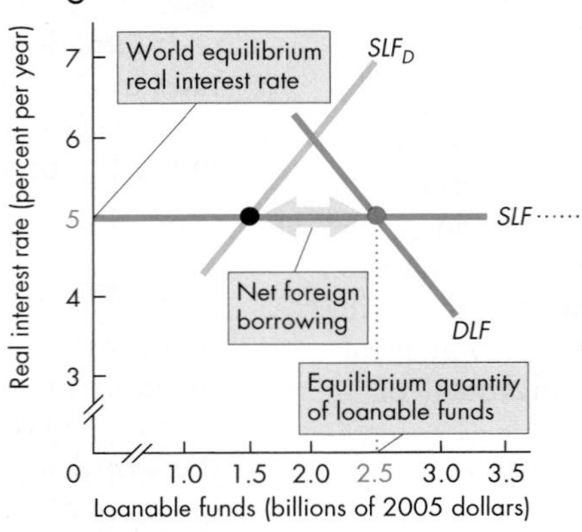

(b) An international borrower

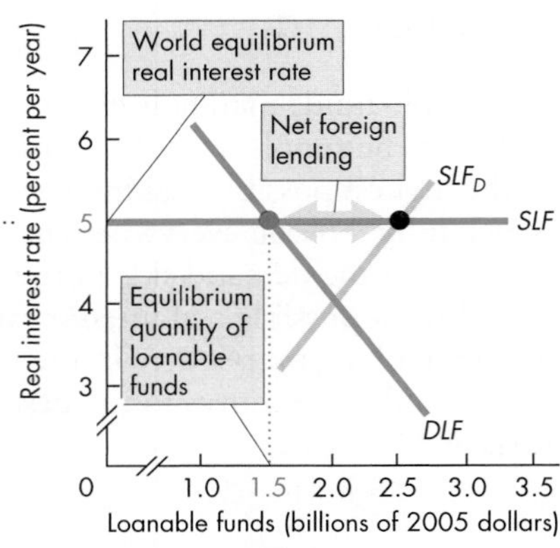

(c) An international lender

In the global loanable funds market in part (a), the demand for loanable funds, DLF_W, and the supply of funds, SLF_W, determine the world real interest rate. Each country can get funds at the world real interest rate and faces the (horizontal) supply curve *SLF* in parts (b) and (c).

At the world real interest rate, borrowers in part (b) want more funds than the quantity supplied by domestic lenders (SLF_D). The shortage is made up by international borrowing.

Domestic suppliers of funds in part (c) want to lend more than domestic borrowers demand. The excess quantity supplied goes to foreign borrowers.

myeconlab animation

If this country were isolated from the global market, the real interest rate would be 6 percent a year (where the *DLF* and SLF_D curves intersect). But if the country is integrated into the global economy, with an interest rate of 6 percent a year, funds would *flood into* it. With a real interest rate of 5 percent a year in the rest of the world, suppliers of loanable funds would seek the higher return in this country. In effect, the country faces the supply of loanable funds curve *SLF*, which is horizontal at the world equilibrium real interest rate.

The country's demand for loanable funds and the world interest rate determine the equilibrium quantity of loanable funds—\$2.5 billion in Fig. 7.10(b).

An International Lender Figure 7.10(c) shows the situation in a country that lends to the rest of the world. As before, the country's demand for loanable funds, *DLF*, is part of the world demand and the country's supply of loanable funds, SLF_D, is part of the world supply in Fig. 7.10(a).

If this country were isolated from the global economy, the real interest rate would be 4 percent a year (where the *DLF* and SLF_D curves intersect). But if this country is integrated into the global economy, with an interest rate of 4 percent a year, funds would quickly *flow out* of it. With a real interest rate of 5 percent a year in the rest of the world, domestic suppliers of loanable funds would seek the higher return in other countries. Again, the country faces the supply of loanable funds curve *SLF*, which is horizontal at the world equilibrium real interest rate.

The country's demand for loanable funds and the world interest rate determine the equilibrium quantity of loanable funds—\$1.5 billion in Fig. 7.10(c).

Changes in Demand and Supply A change in the demand or supply in the global loanable funds market changes the real interest rate in the way shown in Fig. 7.6 (see p. 169). The effect of a change in demand or supply in a national market depends on the size of the country. A change in demand or supply in a small country has no significant effect on global demand or supply, so it leaves the world real interest rate unchanged and changes only the country's net exports and international borrowing or lending. A change in demand or supply in a large country has a significant effect on global demand or supply, so it changes the world real interest rate as well as the country's net exports and international borrowing or lending. Every country feels some of the effect of a large country's change in demand or supply.

Economics in Action

Greenspan's Interest Rate Puzzle

The real interest rate paid by big corporations in the United States fell from 5.5 percent a year in 2001 to 2.5 percent a year in 2005. Alan Greenspan, then the Chairman of the Federal Reserve, said he was puzzled that the real interest rate was falling at a time when the U.S. government budget deficit was increasing.

Why did the real interest rate fall?

The answer lies in the global loanable funds market. Rapid economic growth in Asia and Europe brought a large increase in global saving, which in turn increased the global supply of loanable funds. The supply of loanable funds increased because Asian and European saving increased strongly.

The U.S. government budget deficit increased the U.S. and global demand for loanable funds. But this increase was very small compared to the increase in the global supply of loanable funds.

The result of a large increase in supply and a small increase in demand was a fall in the world equilibrium real interest rate and an increase in the equilibrium quantity of loanable funds.

The figure illustrates these events. The supply of loanable funds increased from SLF_{01} in 2001 to SLF_{05} in 2005. (In the figure, we ignore the change in the global demand for loanable funds because it was small relative to the increase in supply.)

With the increase in supply, the real interest rate fell from 5.5 percent to 2.5 percent a year and the quantity of loanable funds increased.

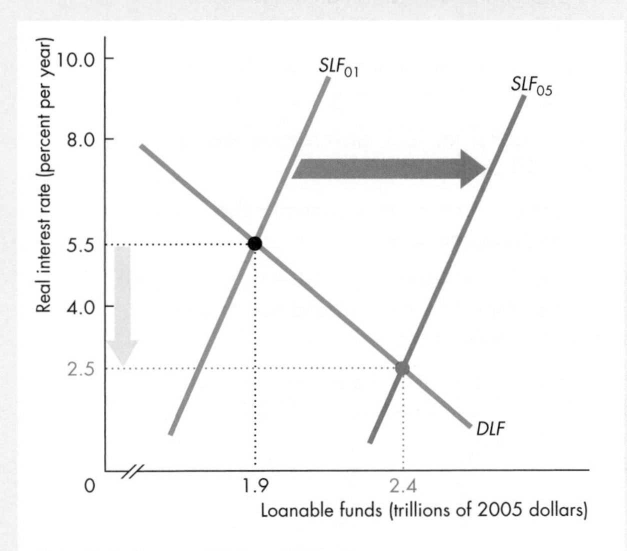

The Global Loanable Funds Market

In the United States, borrowing from the rest of the world increased to finance the increased government budget deficit.

The interest rate puzzle illustrates the important fact that the loanable funds market is a global market, not a national market.

REVIEW QUIZ

1. Why do loanable funds flow among countries?
2. What determines the demand for and supply of loanable funds in an individual economy?
3. What happens if a country has a shortage of loanable funds at the world real interest rate?
4. What happens if a country has a surplus of loanable funds at the world real interest rate?
5. How is a government budget deficit financed in an open economy?

You can work these questions in Study Plan 7.4 and get instant feedback.

To complete your study of financial markets, take a look at *Reading Between the Lines* on pp. 176–177 and see how you can use the model of the loanable funds market to understand the events in the financial market crisis of 2008.

Crowding Out in the Global Recession

"Borrowing to Live" Weighs on Families, Firms, Nation

http://www.dallasmorningnews.com
June 13, 2010

... In the last decade, American household, business, and government debts doubled to $39.2 trillion. We did not double the size of the economy. And that's the problem. ...

The average Dallas consumer owed $26,599 in March [2010] on credit cards and loans covering cars, tuition, and other personal needs. (The amount doesn't include mortgages.) Dallas County delinquency rates for student, auto, and credit card loans are above the national average.

Now the U.S. government is on a borrowing spree. For every dollar it spends, it is borrowing 40 cents. ...

Some politicians and policy wonks say we have 10 years. Gold bugs and debt Jeremiahs say the day [of reckoning] is at hand.

In April, Federal Reserve Chairman Ben Bernanke told a Dallas audience that we should plan now to cut spending, raise taxes, or both. That seems to be the middle ground—it's time we have a plan. ...

It would be easier if we owed the money to ourselves. More than $4 trillion of our federal debt of $8.572 trillion (not counting loans the government owes itself) was borrowed from foreigners.

China is our top creditor. It holds roughly $1.2 trillion in U.S. government debt. ...

ESSENCE OF THE STORY

- U.S. household, business, and government debts doubled to $39.2 trillion in the last decade.
- The average Dallas consumer owed $26,599 in March 2010, not counting mortgages.
- For every dollar the U.S. government spends, it borrows 40 cents.
- Some people think the government's deficit will bring financial collapse.
- Most people, including Fed chairman Ben Bernanke, think that taxes should rise and government spending be cut.
- More than $4 trillion of the federal debt of $8.6 trillion is owed to foreigners, $1.2 trillion to China alone.

ECONOMIC ANALYSIS

- This news article says that the growth of both U.S. government debt and U.S. international debt are unsustainable and must be stopped.
- The article speculates about impending doom at an unknown future date, perhaps in 10 years.
- Government debt grows when the government runs a budget deficit. The news article correctly points out that the U.S. government is running a whopping deficit.
- In 2009, of every dollar the government spent, it borrowed 40 cents.
- The U.S. government is not alone. Governments in Europe, Japan, China, and many other countries are running large budget deficits.
- These deficits might bring a "day of reckoning" as the article states, but they bring a more immediate problem: crowding out investment and slowing the pace of economic growth.
- In 2009, the increase in government borrowing in the loanable funds market sent the real interest rate on long-term corporate bonds to 6 percent per year, up from 2 percent per year in 2008.
- Figure 1, which is like Fig. 7.10(a) on p. 174, illustrates what happened in the global loanable funds market, and Fig. 2, which is like Fig. 7.10(b), illustrates the U.S. loanable funds market.
- In both figures, the supply of loanable funds curve is *SLF* and the private (non-government) demand for loanable funds curve is *PDLF*. These supply and demand curves are (assumed to be) the same in 2008 and 2009.
- In 2008, the demand for loanable funds curve was DLF_{08} in both figures. The real interest rate, determined in the global market, was 2 percent per year.
- Fiscal stimulus packages increased government budget deficits and increased the demand for loanable funds. The demand curves (both figures) shifted to DLF_{09}. The real interest rate increased in the global market to 6 percent per year.
- In the global market in Fig. 1, the higher real interest rate crowded out (lowered) investment by 25 percent.
- In the U.S. market in Fig. 2, the higher real interest rate crowded out (lowered) investment by almost 25 percent.
- The higher real interest rate had a second effect in the U.S. market: It increased saving and the quantity of loanable funds supplied.

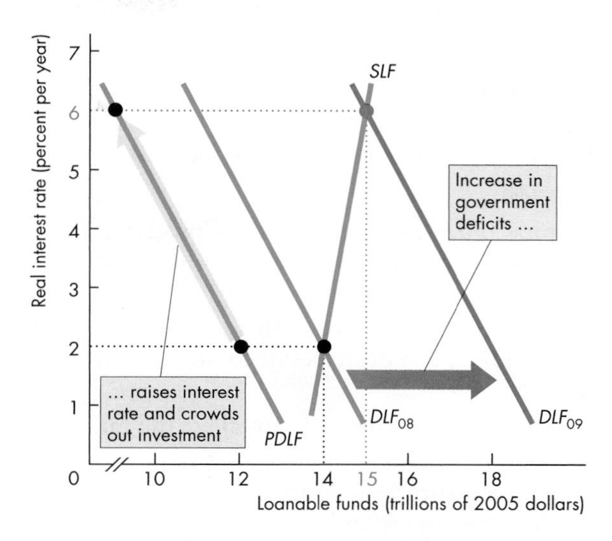

Figure 1 The global loanable funds market

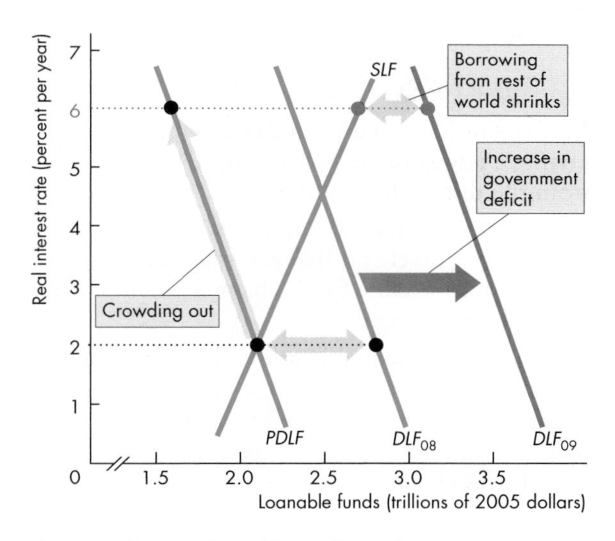

Figure 2 The U.S. loanable funds market

- The increase in the quantity of loanable funds supplied from U.S. sources decreased the amount borrowed from the rest of the world.
- So, although the long-term problems correctly identified in the news article are a concern, crowding out brings an immediate problem.
- But the drop in borrowing from the rest of the world is a move in the direction hoped for in the article.

SUMMARY

Key Points

Financial Institutions and Financial Markets

(pp. 160–164)

- Capital (*physical capital*) is a real productive resource; financial capital is the funds used to buy capital.
- Gross investment increases the quantity of capital and depreciation decreases it. Saving increases wealth.
- The markets for financial capital are the markets for loans, bonds, and stocks.
- Financial institutions ensure that borrowers and lenders can always find someone with whom to trade.

Working Study Plan Problems 1 to 5 will give you a better understanding of financial institutions and markets.

The Loanable Funds Market (pp. 164–170)

- Investment in capital is financed by household saving, a government budget surplus, and funds from the rest of the world.
- The quantity of loanable funds demanded depends negatively on the real interest rate and the demand for loanable funds changes when profit expectations change.
- The quantity of loanable funds supplied depends positively on the real interest rate and the supply of loanable funds changes when disposable income, expected future income, wealth, and default risk change.
- Equilibrium in the loanable funds market determines the real interest rate and quantity of funds.

Working Study Plan Problems 6 to 9 will give you a better understanding of the loanable funds market.

Government in the Loanable Funds Market

(pp. 171–172)

- A government budget surplus increases the supply of loanable funds, lowers the real interest rate, and increases investment and the equilibrium quantity of loanable funds.
- A government budget deficit increases the demand for loanable funds, raises the real interest rate, and increases the equilibrium quantity of loanable funds, but decreases investment in a crowding-out effect.
- The Ricardo-Barro effect is the response of rational taxpayers to a budget deficit: private saving increases to finance the budget deficit. The real interest rate remains constant and the crowding-out effect is avoided.

Working Study Plan Problems 10 to 15 will give you a better understanding of government in the loanable funds market.

The Global Loanable Funds Market (pp. 173–175)

- The loanable funds market is a global market.
- The equilibrium real interest rate is determined in the global loanable funds market and national demand and supply determine the quantity of international borrowing or lending.

Working Study Plan Problems 16 to 18 will give you a better understanding of the global loanable funds market.

Key Terms

Bond, 161
Bond market, 161
Crowding-out effect, 172
Demand for loanable funds, 166
Financial capital, 160
Financial institution, 162
Gross investment, 160
Loanable funds market, 164
Mortgage, 161
Mortgage-backed security, 162
National saving, 165
Net investment, 160
Net taxes, 164
Net worth, 163
Nominal interest rate, 165
Real interest rate, 165
Saving, 160
Stock, 162
Stock market, 162
Supply of loanable funds, 167
Wealth, 160

STUDY PLAN PROBLEMS AND APPLICATIONS

myeconlab You can work Problems 1 to 18 in MyEconLab Chapter 7 Study Plan and get instant feedback.

Financial Institutions and Financial Markets

(Study Plan 7.1)

Use the following information to work Problems 1 and 2.

Michael is an Internet service provider. On December 31, 2009, he bought an existing business with servers and a building worth $400,000. During his first year of operation, his business grew and he bought new servers for $500,000. The market value of some of his older servers fell by $100,000.

1. What was Michael's gross investment, depreciation, and net investment during 2010?
2. What is the value of Michael's capital at the end of 2010?
3. Lori is a student who teaches golf on the weekend and in a year earns $20,000 after paying her taxes. At the beginning of 2010, Lori owned $1,000 worth of books, CDs, and golf clubs and she had $5,000 in a savings account at the bank. During 2010, the interest on her savings account was $300 and she spent a total of $15,300 on consumption goods and services. There was no change in the market values of her books, CDs, and golf clubs.
   a. How much did Lori save in 2010?
   b. What was her wealth at the end of 2010?
4. In a speech at the CFA Society of Nebraska in February 2007, William Poole, former Chairman of the St. Louis Federal Reserve Bank said:

   Over most of the post–World War II period, the personal saving rate averaged about 6 percent, with some higher years from the mid-1970s to mid-1980s. The negative trend in the saving rate started in the mid-1990s, about the same time the stock market boom started. Thus it is hard to dismiss the hypothesis that the decline in the measured saving rate in the late 1990s reflected the response of consumption to large capital gains from corporate equity [stock]. Evidence from panel data of households also supports the conclusion that the decline in the personal saving rate since 1984 is largely a consequence of capital gains on corporate equities.

   a. Is the purchase of corporate equities part of household consumption or saving? Explain your answer.
   b. Equities reap a capital gain in the same way that houses reap a capital gain. Does this mean that the purchase of equities is investment? If not, explain why it is not.
5. **G-20 Leaders Look to Shake off Lingering Economic Troubles**

   The G-20 aims to take stock of the economic recovery. One achievement of the G-20 in Pittsburgh could be a deal to require that financial institutions hold more capital.

   Source: *USA Today*, September 24, 2009

   What are the financial institutions that the G-20 might require to hold more capital? What exactly is the "capital" referred to in the news clip? How might the requirement to hold more capital make financial institutions safer?

The Loanable Funds Market (Study Plan 7.2)

Use the following information to work Problems 6 and 7.

First Call, Inc., is a cellular phone company. It plans to build an assembly plant that costs $10 million if the real interest rate is 6 percent a year. If the real interest rate is 5 percent a year, First Call will build a larger plant that costs $12 million. And if the real interest rate is 7 percent a year, First Call will build a smaller plant that costs $8 million.

6. Draw a graph of First Call's demand for loanable funds curve.
7. First Call expects its profit from the sale of cellular phones to double next year. If other things remain the same, explain how this increase in expected profit influences First Call's demand for loanable funds.
8. Draw a graph to illustrate how an increase in the supply of loanable funds and a decrease in the demand for loanable funds can lower the real interest rate and leave the equilibrium quantity of loanable funds unchanged.
9. Use the information in Problem 4.

a. U.S. household income has grown considerably since 1984. Has U.S. saving been on a downward trend because Americans feel wealthier?

b. Explain why households preferred to buy corporate equities rather than bonds.

Government in the Loanable Funds Market

(Study Plan 7.3)

Use the following table to work Problems 10 to 12. The table shows an economy's demand for loanable funds and the supply of loanable funds schedules, when the government's budget is balanced.

Real interest rate (percent per year)	Loanable funds demanded (trillions of 2005 dollars)	Loanable funds supplied (trillions of 2005 dollars)
4	8.5	5.5
5	8.0	6.0
6	7.5	6.5
7	7.0	7.0
8	6.5	7.5
9	6.0	8.0
10	5.5	8.5

10. Suppose that the government has a budget surplus of $1 trillion. What are the real interest rate, the quantity of investment, and the quantity of private saving? Is there any crowding out in this situation?
11. Suppose that the government has a budget deficit of $1 trillion. What are the real interest rate, the quantity of investment, and the quantity of private saving? Is there any crowding out in this situation?
12. Suppose that the government has a budget deficit of $1 trillion and the Ricardo-Barro effect occurs. What are the real interest rate and the quantity of investment?

Use the table in Problem 10 to work Problems 13 to 15.

Suppose that the quantity of loanable funds demanded increases by $1 trillion at each real interest rate and the quantity of loanable funds supplied increases by $2 trillion at each interest rate.

13. If the government budget is balanced, what are the real interest rate, the quantity of loanable funds, investment, and private saving? Does any crowding out occur?
14. If the government budget becomes a deficit of $1 trillion, what are the real interest rate, the quantity of loanable funds, investment, and private saving? Does any crowding out occur?
15. If the government wants to stimulate investment and increase it to $9 trillion, what must it do?

The Global Loanable Funds Market (Study Plan 7.4)

Use the following information to work Problems 16 and 17.

Global Saving Glut and U.S. Current Account, remarks by Ben Bernanke (when a governor of the Federal Reserve) on March 10, 2005:

The U.S. economy appears to be performing well: Output growth has returned to healthy levels, the labor market is firming, and inflation appears to be under control. But, one aspect of U.S. economic performance still evokes concern: the nation's large and growing current account deficit (negative net exports). Most forecasters expect the nation's current account imbalance to decline slowly at best, implying a continued need for foreign credit and a concomitant decline in the U.S. net foreign asset position.

16. Why is the United States, with the world's largest economy, borrowing heavily on international capital markets—rather than lending, as would seem more natural?
17. a. What implications do the U.S. current account deficit (negative net exports) and our reliance on foreign credit have for economic performance in the United States?
    b. What policies, if any, should be used to address this situation?
18. **IMF Says It Battled Crisis Well**

    The International Monetary Fund (IMF) reported that it acted effectively in combating the global recession. Since September 2008, the IMF made $163 billion available to developing countries. While the IMF urged developed countries and China to run deficits to stimulate their economies, the IMF required developing countries with large deficits to cut spending and not increase spending.

    Source: *The Wall Street Journal,* September 29, 2009

    a. Explain how increased government budget deficits change the loanable funds market.

    b. Would the global recession have been less severe had the IMF made larger loans to developing countries?

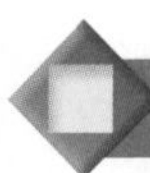

ADDITIONAL PROBLEMS AND APPLICATIONS

myeconlab You can work these problems in MyEconLab if assigned by your instructor.

Financial Institutions and Financial Markets

19. On January 1, 2009, Terry's Towing Service owned 4 tow trucks valued at $300,000. During 2009, Terry's bought 2 new trucks for a total of $180,000. At the end of 2009, the market value of all of the firm's trucks was $400,000. What was Terry's gross investment? Calculate Terry's depreciation and net investment.

Use the following information to work Problems 20 and 21.

The Bureau of Economic Analysis reported that the U.S. capital stock was $40.4 trillion at the end of 2007, $41.1 trillion at the end of 2008, and $41.4 trillion at the end of 2009. Depreciation in 2008 was $1.3 trillion, and gross investment during 2009 was $1.5 trillion (all in 2005 dollars).

20. Calculate U. S. net investment and gross investment during 2008.
21. Calculate U.S. depreciation and net investment during 2009.
22. Annie runs a fitness center. On December 31, 2009, she bought an existing business with exercise equipment and a building worth $300,000. During 2010, business improved and she bought some new equipment for $50,000. At the end of 2010, her equipment and buildings were worth $325,000. Calculate Annie's gross investment, depreciation, and net investment during 2010.
23. Karrie is a golf pro, and after she paid taxes, her income from golf and interest from financial assets was $1,500,000 in 2010. At the beginning of 2010, she owned $900,000 worth of financial assets. At the end of 2010, Karrie's financial assets were worth $1,900,000.
    a. How much did Karrie save during 2010?
    b. How much did she spend on consumption goods and services?

The Loanable Funds Market

Use the following information to work Problems 24 and 25.

In 2010, the Lee family had disposable income of $80,000, wealth of $140,000, and an expected future income of $80,000 a year. At a real interest rate of 4 percent a year, the Lee family saves $15,000 a year; at a real interest rate of 6 percent a year, they save $20,000 a year; and at a real interest rate of 8 percent, they save $25,000 a year.

24. Draw a graph of the Lee family's supply of loanable funds curve.
25. In 2011, suppose that the stock market crashes and the default risk increases. Explain how this increase in default risk influences the Lee family's supply of loanable funds curve.
26. Draw a graph to illustrate the effect of an increase in the demand for loanable funds and an even larger increase in the supply of loanable funds on the real interest rate and the equilibrium quantity of loanable funds.
27. **Greenspan's Conundrum Spells Confusion for Us All**

    In January 2005, the interest rate on bonds was 4% a year and it was expected to rise to 5% a year by the end of 2005. As the rate rose to 4.3% during February, most commentators focused, not on why the interest rate rose, but on why it was so low before. Explanations of this "conundrum" included that unusual buying and expectations for an economic slowdown were keeping the interest rate low.

    Source: *Financial Times*, February 26, 2005

    a. Explain how "unusual buying" might lead to a low real interest rate.
    b. Explain how investors' "expectations for an economic slowdown" might lead to a lower real interest rate.

Government in the Loanable Funds Market

Use the following information to work Problems 28 and 29.

India's Economy Hits the Wall

At the start of 2008, India had an annual growth of 9%, huge consumer demand, and increasing foreign investment. But by July 2008, India had 11.4% inflation, large government deficits, and rising interest rates. Economic growth is expected to fall to 7% by the end of 2008. A Goldman Sachs report suggests that India needs to lower the government's deficit, raise educational achievement, control inflation, and liberalize its financial markets.

Source: *Business Week*, July 1, 2008

28. If the Indian government reduces its deficit and returns to a balanced budget, how will the demand for or supply of loanable funds in India change?
29. With economic growth forecasted to slow, future incomes are expected to fall. If other things remain the same, how will the demand or supply of loanable funds in India change?
30. **Federal Deficit Surges to $1.38 trillion through August**

    House Republican Leader John Boehner of Ohio asks: When will the White House tackle these jaw-dropping deficits that pile more and more debt on future generations while it massively increases federal spending?

    Source: *USA Today*, September 11, 2009

    Explain the effect of the federal deficit and the mounting debt on U.S. economic growth.

The Global Loanable Funds Market

31. **The Global Savings Glut and Its Consequences**

    Several developing countries are running large current account surpluses (representing an excess of savings over investment) and rapid growth has led to high saving rates as people save a large fraction of additional income. In India, the saving rate has risen from 23% a decade ago to 33% today. China's saving rate is 55%. The glut of saving in Asia is being put into U.S. bonds. When a poor country buys U.S. bonds, it is in effect lending to the United States.

    Source: *The Cato Institute*, June 8, 2007

    a. Graphically illustrate and explain the impact of the "glut of savings" on the real interest rate and the quantity of loanable funds.
    b. How do the high saving rates in Asia impact investment in the United States?

Use the following information to work Problems 32 to 35.

Most economists agree that the problems we are witnessing today developed over a long period of time. For more than a decade, a massive amount of money flowed into the United States from investors abroad, because our country is an attractive and secure place to do business. This large influx of money to U.S. financial institutions—along with low interest rates—made it easier for Americans to get credit. These developments allowed more families to borrow money for cars and homes and college tuition—some for the first time. They allowed more entrepreneurs to get loans to start new businesses and create jobs.

President George W. Bush, *Address to the Nation*, September 24, 2008

32. Explain why, for more than a decade, a massive amount of money flowed into the United States. Compare and contrast your explanation with that of the President.
33. Provide a graphical analysis of the reasons why the interest rate was low.
34. Funds have been flowing into the United States since the early 1980s. Why might they have created problems in 2008 but not earlier?
35. Could the United States stop funds from flowing in from other countries? How?

Economics in the News

36. After you have studied *Reading Between the Lines* on pp. 176–177 answer the following questions.
    a. What are the long-term problems to which the news article draws attention?
    b. What was the major event in the global and U.S. loanable funds markets in 2009?
    c. How did the event identified in part (b) influence the world real interest rate and the global supply of and demand for loanable funds?
    d. How did the event identified in part (b) influence the U.S. supply of and demand for loanable funds and the amount that the United States borrowed from the rest of the world?
    e. If governments in other countries were to lower their budget deficits but the U.S. government did not lower its deficit, what would happen to the world real interest rate, the supply of and demand for loanable funds in the United States, and the amount that the United States borrows from the rest of the world?
    f. If the U.S. government lowered its budget deficit but the governments in other countries did not lower their deficits, what would happen to the world real interest rate, the supply of and demand for loanable funds in the United States, and the amount that the United States borrows from the rest of the world?

After studying this chapter, you will be able to:

- Define money and describe its functions
- Explain the economic functions of banks and other depository institutions
- Describe the structure and functions of the Federal Reserve System (the Fed)
- Explain how the banking system creates money
- Explain what determines the demand for money, the supply of money, and the nominal interest rate
- Explain how the quantity of money influences the price level and the inflation rate in the long run

8

MONEY, THE PRICE LEVEL, AND INFLATION

Money, like fire and the wheel, has been around for a long time, and it has taken many forms. Money was wampum (beads made from shells) for North American Indians, whale's teeth for Fijians, and tobacco for early American colonists. Cakes of salt served as money in Ethiopia and Tibet. Today, when we want to buy something, we use coins or dollar bills, write a check, or swipe a debit card or a credit card. Soon, we'll be using a "smart card" or even a cell phone to make payments. Are all these things money?

The quantity of money in our economy is regulated by the Federal Reserve—the Fed. How does the Fed influence the quantity of money? And what happens if the Fed creates too much money or too little money?

In this chapter, we study the functions of money, the banks that create it, the Federal Reserve and its influence on the quantity of money, and the long-run consequences of changes in the quantity of money. In *Reading Between the Lines* at the end of the chapter, we look at the extraordinary actions taken by the Fed during the recent financial crisis.

What Is Money?

What do wampum, tobacco, and nickels and dimes have in common? They are all examples of **money**, which is defined as any commodity or token that is generally acceptable as a means of payment. A **means of payment** is a method of settling a debt. When a payment has been made, there is no remaining obligation between the parties to a transaction. So what wampum, tobacco, and nickels and dimes have in common is that they have served (or still do serve) as the means of payment. Money serves three other functions:

- Medium of exchange
- Unit of account
- Store of value

Medium of Exchange

A *medium of exchange* is any object that is generally accepted in exchange for goods and services. Without a medium of exchange, goods and services must be exchanged directly for other goods and services—an exchange called *barter*. Barter requires a *double coincidence of wants*, a situation that rarely occurs. For example, if you want a hamburger, you might offer a CD in exchange for it. But you must find someone who is selling hamburgers and wants your CD.

A medium of exchange overcomes the need for a double coincidence of wants. Money acts as a medium of exchange because people with something to sell will always accept money in exchange for it. But money isn't the only medium of exchange. You can buy with a credit card, but a credit card isn't money. It doesn't make a final payment, and the debt it creates must eventually be settled by using money.

Unit of Account

A *unit of account* is an agreed measure for stating the prices of goods and services. To get the most out of your budget, you have to figure out whether seeing one more movie is worth its opportunity cost. But that cost is not dollars and cents. It is the number of ice-cream cones, sodas, or cups of coffee that you must give up. It's easy to do such calculations when all these goods have prices in terms of dollars and cents (see Table 8.1). If the price of a movie is $8 and the price of a cappuccino is $4, you know right away that seeing one movie costs you 2 cappuccinos.

TABLE 8.1 The Unit of Account Function of Money Simplifies Price Comparisons

Good	Price in money units	Price in units of another good
Movie	$8.00 each	2 cappuccinos
Cappuccino	$4.00 each	2 ice-cream cones
Ice cream	$2 per cone	2 packs of jelly beans
Jelly beans	$1 per pack	2 sticks of gum
Gum	$0.50 per stick	

Money as a unit of account: The price of a movie is $8 and the price of a stick of gum is 50¢, so the opportunity cost of a movie is 16 sticks of gum ($8.00 ÷ 50¢ = 16).

No unit of account: You go to a movie theater and learn that the cost of seeing a movie is 2 cappuccinos. You go to a grocery store and learn that a pack of jelly beans costs 2 sticks of gum. But how many sticks of gum does seeing a movie cost you? To answer that question, you go to the coffee shop and find that a cappuccino costs 2 ice-cream cones. Now you head for the ice-cream shop, where an ice-cream cone costs 2 packs of jelly beans. Now you get out your pocket calculator: 1 movie costs 2 cappuccinos, or 4 ice-cream cones, or 8 packs of jelly beans, or 16 sticks of gum!

If jelly beans are $1 a pack, one movie costs 8 packs of jelly beans. You need only one calculation to figure out the opportunity cost of any pair of goods and services.

Imagine how troublesome it would be if your local movie theater posted its price as 2 cappuccinos, the coffee shop posted the price of a cappuccino as 2 ice-cream cones, the ice-cream shop posted the price of an ice-cream cone as 2 packs of jelly beans, and the grocery store priced a pack of jelly beans as 2 sticks of gum! Now how much running around and calculating will you have to do to find out how much that movie is going to cost you in terms of the cappuccinos, ice cream cones, jelly beans, or gum that you must give up to see it? You get the answer for cappuccinos right away from the sign posted on the movie theater. But for all the other goods, you're going to have to visit many different stores to establish the price of each good in terms of another and then calculate the prices in units that are relevant for your own decision. The hassle of doing all this research might be enough to make a person swear off movies! You can see how much simpler it is if all the prices are expressed in dollars and cents.

Store of Value

Money is a *store of value* in the sense that it can be held and exchanged later for goods and services. If money were not a store of value, it could not serve as a means of payment.

Money is not alone in acting as a store of value. A house, a car, and a work of art are other examples.

The more stable the value of a commodity or token, the better it can act as a store of value and the more useful it is as money. No store of value has a completely stable value. The value of a house, a car, or a work of art fluctuates over time. The value of the commodities and tokens that are used as money also fluctuate over time.

Inflation lowers the value of money and the values of other commodities and tokens that are used as money. To make money as useful as possible as a store of value, a low inflation rate is needed.

Money in the United States Today

In the United States today, money consists of

- Currency
- Deposits at banks and other depository institutions

Currency The notes and coins held by individuals and businesses are known as **currency**. Notes are money because the government declares them so with the words "This note is legal tender for all debts, public and private." You can see these words on every dollar bill. Notes and coins *inside* banks are not counted as currency because they are not held by individuals and businesses.

Deposits Deposits of individuals and businesses at banks and other depository institutions, such as savings and loan associations, are also counted as money. Deposits are money because the owners of the deposits can use them to make payments.

Official Measures of Money Two official measures of money in the United States today are known as M1 and M2. **M1** consists of currency and traveler's checks plus checking deposits owned by individuals and businesses. M1 does *not* include currency held by banks, and it does not include currency and checking deposits owned by the U.S. government. **M2** consists of M1 plus time deposits, savings deposits, and money market mutual funds and other deposits.

Economics in Action

Official Measures of U.S. Money

The figure shows the relative magnitudes of the items that make up M1 and M2. Notice that M2 is almost five times as large as M1 and that currency is a small part of our money.

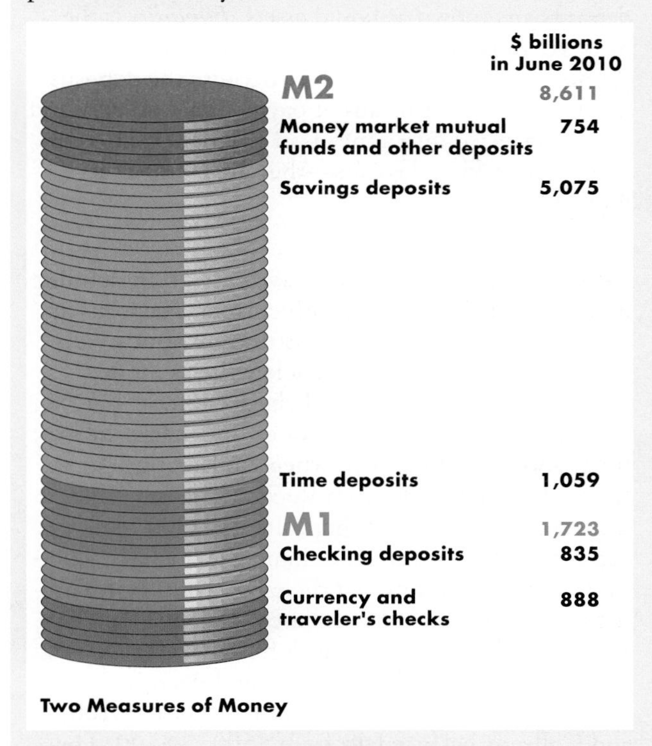

Two Measures of Money

M1
- Currency and traveler's checks
- Checking deposits at commercial banks, savings and loan associations, savings banks, and credit unions

M2
- M1
- Time deposits
- Savings deposits
- Money market mutual funds and other deposits

Source of data: The Federal Reserve Board. The data are for June 2010.

Are M1 and M2 Really Money? Money is the means of payment. So the test of whether an asset is money is whether it serves as a means of payment. Currency passes the test. But what about deposits? Checking deposits are money because they can be transferred from one person to another by writing a check or using a debit card. Such a transfer of ownership is equivalent to handing over currency. Because M1 consists of currency plus checking deposits and each of these is a means of payment, *M1 is money*.

But what about M2? Some of the savings deposits in M2 are just as much a means of payment as the checking deposits in M1. You can use an ATM to get funds from your savings account to pay for your purchase at the grocery store or the gas station. But some savings deposits are not means of payment. These deposits are known as liquid assets. *Liquidity* is the property of being easily convertible into a means of payment without loss in value. Because the deposits in M2 that are not means of payment are quickly and easily converted into a means of payment—into currency or checking deposits—they are counted as money.

Deposits Are Money but Checks Are Not In defining money, we include, along with currency, deposits at banks and other depository institutions. But we do not count the checks that people write as money. Why are deposits money and checks not?

To see why deposits are money but checks are not, think about what happens when Colleen buys some roller-blades for $100 from Rocky's Rollers. When Colleen goes to Rocky's shop, she has $500 in her deposit account at the Laser Bank. Rocky has $1,000 in his deposit account—at the same bank, as it happens. The total deposits of these two people are $1,500. Colleen writes a check for $100. Rocky takes the check to the bank right away and deposits it. Rocky's bank balance rises from $1,000 to $1,100, and Colleen's balance falls from $500 to $400. The total deposits of Colleen and Rocky are still the same as before: $1,500. Rocky now has $100 more than before, and Colleen has $100 less.

This transaction has transferred money from Colleen to Rocky, but the check itself was never money. There wasn't an extra $100 of money while the check was in circulation. The check instructs the bank to transfer money from Colleen to Rocky.

If Colleen and Rocky use different banks, there is an extra step. Rocky's bank credits $100 to Rocky's account and then takes the check to a check-clearing center. The check is then sent to Colleen's bank, which pays Rocky's bank $100 and then debits Colleen's account $100. This process can take a few days, but the principles are the same as when two people use the same bank.

Credit Cards Are Not Money You've just seen that checks are not money. What about credit cards? Isn't having a credit card in your wallet and presenting the card to pay for your roller-blades the same thing as using money? Why aren't credit cards somehow valued and counted as part of the quantity of money?

When you pay by check, you are frequently asked to prove your identity by showing your driver's license. It would never occur to you to think of your driver's license as money. It's just an ID card. A credit card is also an ID card, but one that lets you take out a loan at the instant you buy something. When you sign a credit card sales slip, you are saying, "I agree to pay for these goods when the credit card company bills me." Once you get your statement from the credit card company, you must make at least the minimum payment due. To make that payment, you need money—you need to have currency or a checking deposit to pay the credit card company. So although you use a credit card when you buy something, the credit card is not the *means of payment* and it is not money.

REVIEW QUIZ

1. What makes something money? What functions does money perform? Why do you think packs of chewing gum don't serve as money?
2. What are the problems that arise when a commodity is used as money?
3. What are the main components of money in the United States today?
4. What are the official measures of money? Are all the measures really money?
5. Why are checks and credit cards not money?

You can work these questions in Study Plan 8.1 and get instant feedback.

We've seen that the main component of money in the United States is deposits at banks and other depository institutions. Let's take a closer look at these institutions.

Depository Institutions

A **depository institution** is a financial firm that takes deposits from households and firms. These deposits are components of M1 and M2. You will learn what these institutions are, what they do, the economic benefits they bring, how they are regulated, and how they have innovated to create new financial products.

Types of Depository Institutions

The deposits of three types of financial firms make up the nation's money. They are

- Commercial banks
- Thrift institutions
- Money market mutual funds

Commercial Banks A *commercial bank* is a firm that is licensed to receive deposits and make loans. In 2010, about 7,000 commercial banks operated in the United States but mergers make this number fall each year as small banks disappear and big banks expand.

A few very large commercial banks offer a wide range of banking services and have extensive international operations. The largest of these banks are Bank of America, Wells Fargo, JPMorgan Chase, and Citigroup. Most commercial banks are small and serve their regional and local communities.

The deposits of commercial banks represent 40 percent of M1 and 65 percent of M2.

Thrift Institutions Savings and loan associations, savings banks, and credit unions are *thrift institutions.*

Savings and Loan Association A *savings and loan association* (S&L) is a depository institution that receives deposits and makes personal, commercial, and home-purchase loans.

Savings Bank A *savings bank* is a depository institution that accepts savings deposits and makes mostly home-purchase loans.

Credit Union A *credit union* is a depository institution owned by a social or economic group, such as a firm's employees, that accepts savings deposits and makes mostly personal loans.

The deposits of the thrift institutions represent 9 percent of M1 and 16 percent of M2.

Money Market Mutual Funds A *money market mutual fund* is a fund operated by a financial institution that sells shares in the fund and holds assets such as U.S. Treasury bills and short-term commercial bills.

Money market mutual fund shares act like bank deposits. Shareholders can write checks on their money market mutual fund accounts, but there are restrictions on most of these accounts. For example, the minimum deposit accepted might be $2,500, and the smallest check a depositor is permitted to write might be $500.

Money market mutual funds do not feature in M1 and represent 9 percent of M2.

What Depository Institutions Do

Depository institutions provide services such as check clearing, account management, credit cards, and Internet banking, all of which provide an income from service fees.

But depository institutions earn most of their income by using the funds they receive from depositors to make loans and to buy securities that earn a higher interest rate than that paid to depositors. In this activity, a depository institution must perform a balancing act weighing return against risk. To see this balancing act, we'll focus on the commercial banks.

A commercial bank puts the funds it receives from depositors and other funds that it borrows into four types of assets:

1. A bank's **reserves** are notes and coins in the bank's vault or in a deposit account at the Federal Reserve. (We'll study the Federal Reserve later in this chapter.) These funds are used to meet depositors' currency withdrawals and to make payments to other banks. In normal times, a bank keeps about a half of one percent of deposits as reserves. (You'll see in Table 8.2 on the next page that 2010 is not a normal time.)
2. *Liquid assets* are overnight loans to other banks, U.S. government Treasury bills, and commercial bills. These assets are the banks' first line of defense if they need reserves. Liquid assets can be sold and instantly converted into reserves with virtually no risk of loss. Because they have a low risk, they earn a low interest rate.

   The interest rate on overnight loans to other banks, called the **federal funds rate**, is targeted by the Fed. We explain how and why on pp. 350–351.

3. *Securities* are U.S. government bonds and other bonds such as mortgage-backed securities. These assets can be sold and converted into reserves but at prices that fluctuate, so they are riskier than liquid assets and have a higher interest rate.
4. *Loans* are funds committed for an agreed-upon period of time to corporations to finance investment and to households to finance the purchase of homes, cars, and other durable goods. The outstanding balances on credit card accounts are also bank loans. Loans are a bank's riskiest and highest-earning assets: They can't be converted into reserves until they are due to be repaid, and some borrowers default and never repay.

Table 8.2 provides a snapshot of the sources and uses of funds of all the commercial banks in June 2010 that serves as a summary of the above account.

Economic Benefits Provided by Depository Institutions

You've seen that a depository institution earns part of its profit because it pays a lower interest rate on deposits than what it earns on loans. What benefits do these institutions provide that make depositors willing to put up with a low interest rate and borrowers willing to pay a higher one?

TABLE 8.2 Commercial Banks: Sources and Uses of Funds

	Funds (billions of dollars)	Percentage of deposits
Total funds	11,096	144.3
Sources		
Deposits	7,694	100.0
Borrowing	1,997	26.0
Own capital and other sources	1,405	18.3
Uses		
Reserves	1,097	14.3
Liquid assets	98	1.3
Securities and other assets	3,040	39.5
Loans	6,861	89.2

Commercial banks get most of their funds from depositors and use most of them to make loans. In normal times banks hold about 0.5 percent of deposits as reserves. But in 2010, at a time of great financial uncertainty, they held an unusually large 14.3 percent as reserves.

Source of data: The Federal Reserve Board. The data are for June, 2010.

Depository institutions provide four benefits:

- Create liquidity
- Pool risk
- Lower the cost of borrowing
- Lower the cost of monitoring borrowers

Create Liquidity Depository institutions create liquidity by *borrowing short and lending long*—taking deposits and standing ready to repay them on short notice or on demand and making loan commitments that run for terms of many years.

Pool Risk A loan might not be repaid—a default. If you lend to one person who defaults, you lose the entire amount loaned. If you lend to 1,000 people (through a bank) and one person defaults, you lose almost nothing. Depository institutions pool risk.

Lower the Cost of Borrowing Imagine there are no depository institutions and a firm is looking for $1 million to buy a new factory. It hunts around for several dozen people from whom to borrow the funds. Depository institutions lower the cost of this search. The firm gets its $1 million from a single institution that gets deposits from a large number of people but spreads the cost of this activity over many borrowers.

Lower the Cost of Monitoring Borrowers By monitoring borrowers, a lender can encourage good decisions that prevent defaults. But this activity is costly. Imagine how costly it would be if each household that lent money to a firm incurred the costs of monitoring that firm directly. Depository institutions can perform this task at a much lower cost.

How Depository Institutions Are Regulated

Depository institutions are engaged in a risky business, and a failure, especially of a large bank, would have damaging effects on the entire financial system and economy. To make the risk of failure small, depository institutions are required to hold levels of reserves and owners' capital that equal or surpass ratios laid down by regulation. If a depository institution fails, its deposits are guaranteed up to $250,000 per depositor per bank by the *Federal Deposit Insurance Corporation* or FDIC. The FDIC can take over management of a bank that appears to be heading toward failure.

Economics in Action

Commercial Banks Flush with Reserves

When Lehman Brothers (a New York investment bank) failed in October 2008, panic spread through financial markets. Banks that are normally happy to lend to each other overnight for an interest rate barely above the rate they can earn on safe Treasury bills lost confidence and the interest rate in this market shot up to 3 percentage points above the Treasury bill rate. Banks wanted to be safe and to hold cash. The Fed created and the banks willingly held reserves at the unheard of level of $1 trillion or 14 percent of deposits.

Throughout 2009 and 2010, bank reserves remained at this extraordinary level. And despite having plenty of funds to lend, the level of bank loans barely changed over 2009 and 2010.

The figure compares the commercial banks' sources and uses of funds (sources are liabilities and uses are assets) in 2008 with those in 2010.

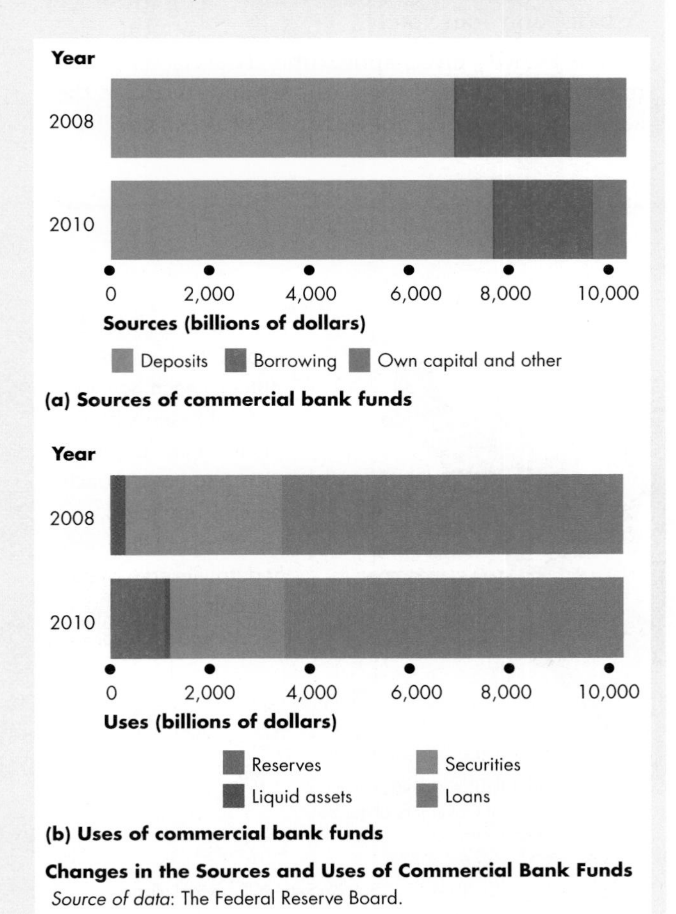

Changes in the Sources and Uses of Commercial Bank Funds

Source of data: The Federal Reserve Board.

Financial Innovation

In the pursuit of larger profit, depository institutions are constantly seeking ways to improve their products in a process called *financial innovation*.

During the late 1970s, a high inflation rate sent the interest rate on home-purchase loans to 15 percent a year. Traditional fixed interest rate mortgages became unprofitable and variable interest rate mortgages were introduced.

During the 2000s, when interest rates were low and depository institutions were flush with funds, sub-prime mortgages were developed. To avoid the risk of carrying these mortgages, mortgage-backed securities were developed. The original lending institution sold these securities, lowered their own exposure to risk, and obtained funds to make more loans.

The development of low-cost computing and communication brought financial innovations such as credit cards and daily interest deposit accounts.

Financial innovation has brought changes in the composition of money. Checking deposits at thrift institutions have become an increasing percentage of M1 while checking deposits at commercial banks have become a decreasing percentage. Savings deposits have decreased as a percentage of M2, while time deposits and money market mutual funds have expanded. Surprisingly, the use of currency has not fallen much.

REVIEW QUIZ

1. What are depository institutions?
2. What are the functions of depository institutions?
3. How do depository institutions balance risk and return?
4. How do depository institutions create liquidity, pool risks, and lower the cost of borrowing?
5. How have depository institutions made innovations that have influenced the composition of money?

You can work these questions in Study Plan 8.2 and get instant feedback.

You now know what money is. Your next task is to learn about the Federal Reserve System and the ways in which it can influence the quantity of money.

The Federal Reserve System

The **Federal Reserve System** (usually called the **Fed**) is the central bank of the United States. A **central bank** is a bank's bank and a public authority that regulates a nation's depository institutions and conducts *monetary policy,* which means that it adjusts the quantity of money in circulation and influences interest rates.

We begin by describing the structure of the Fed.

The Structure of the Fed

Three key elements of the Fed's structure are

- The Board of Governors
- The regional Federal Reserve banks
- The Federal Open Market Committee

The Board of Governors A seven-member board appointed by the President of the United States and confirmed by the Senate governs the Fed. Members have 14-year (staggered) terms and one seat on the board becomes vacant every two years. The President appoints one board member as chairman for a 4-year renewable term—currently Ben Bernanke, a former economics professor at Princeton University.

The Federal Reserve Banks The nation is divided into 12 Federal Reserve districts (shown in Fig. 8.1). Each district has a Federal Reserve Bank that provides check-clearing services to commercial banks and issues bank notes.

The Federal Reserve Bank of New York (known as the New York Fed), occupies a special place in the Federal Reserve System because it implements the Fed's policy decisions in the financial markets.

The Federal Open Market Committee The **Federal Open Market Committee** (FOMC) is the main policy-making organ of the Federal Reserve System. The FOMC consists of the following voting members:

- The chairman and the other six members of the Board of Governors
- The president of the Federal Reserve Bank of New York
- The presidents of the other regional Federal Reserve banks (of whom, on a yearly rotating basis, only four vote)

The FOMC meets approximately every six weeks to review the state of the economy and to decide the actions to be carried out by the New York Fed.

FIGURE 8.1 The Federal Reserve System

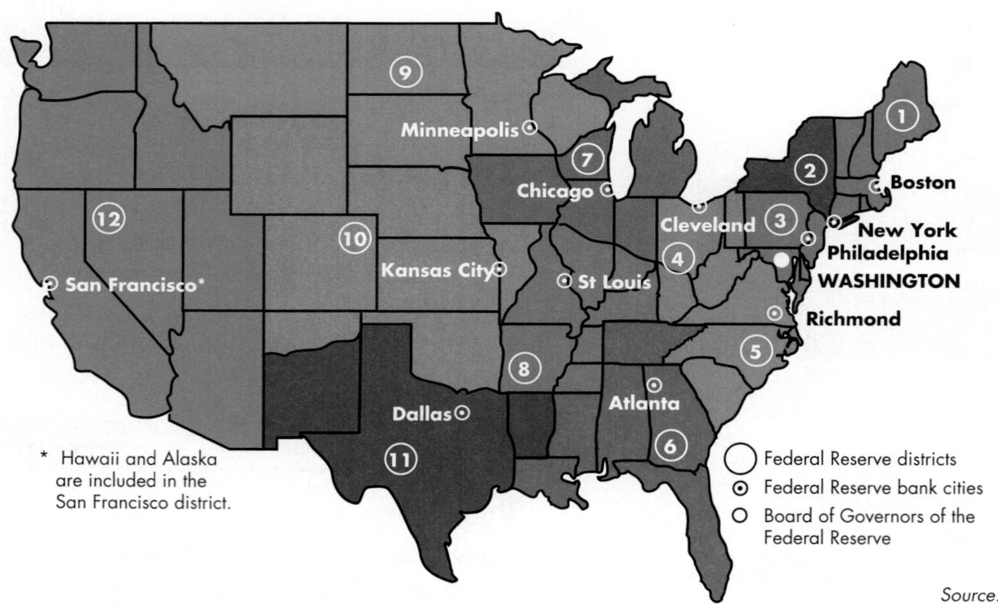

The nation is divided into 12 Federal Reserve districts, each having a Federal Reserve bank. (Some of the larger districts also have branch banks.) The Board of Governors of the Federal Reserve System is located in Washington, D.C.

Source: Federal Reserve Bulletin.

myeconlab animation

The Fed's Balance Sheet

The Fed influences the economy through the size and composition of its balance sheet—the assets that the Fed owns and the liabilities that it owes.

The Fed's Assets The Fed has two main assets:

1. U.S. government securities
2. Loans to depository institutions

The Fed holds U.S. securities—Treasury bills and Treasury bonds—that it buys in the bond market. When the Fed buys or sells bonds, it participates in the *loanable funds market* (see pp. 164–170).

The Fed makes loans to depository institutions. When these institutions in aggregate are short of reserves, they can borrow from the Fed. In normal times this item is small, but during 2007 and 2008, it grew as the Fed provided increasing amounts of relief from the financial crisis. By October 2008, loans to depository institutions exceeded government securities in the Fed's balance sheet.

The Fed's Liabilities The Fed has two liabilities:

1. Federal Reserve notes
2. Depository institution deposits

Federal Reserve notes are the dollar bills that we use in our daily transactions. Some of these notes are held by individuals and businesses; others are in the tills and vaults of banks and other depository institutions.

Depository institution deposits at the Fed are part of the reserves of these institutions (see p. 187).

The Monetary Base The Fed's liabilities together with coins issued by the Treasury (coins are not liabilities of the Fed) make up the monetary base. That is, the **monetary base** is the sum of currency (Federal Reserve notes and coins) and depository institution deposits at the Fed.

The Fed's assets are the sources of the monetary base. They are also called the backing for the monetary base. The Fed's liabilities are the uses of the monetary base as currency and bank reserves. Table 8.3 provides a snapshot of the sources and uses of the monetary base in June 2010.

When the Fed changes the monetary base, the quantity of money and interest rate change. You're going to see how these changes come about later in this chapter. First, we'll look at the Fed's tools that enable it to influence money and interest rates.

TABLE 8.3 The Sources and Uses of the Monetary Base

Sources (billions of dollars)		Uses (billions of dollars)	
U.S. government securities	777	Currency	900
Loans to depository institutions	70	Reserves of depository institutions	1,099
Other items (net)	1,152		
Monetary base	1,999	Monetary base	1,999

Source of data: Federal Reserve Board. The data are for June, 2010.

The Fed's Policy Tools

The Fed influences the quantity of money and interest rates by adjusting the quantity of reserves available to the banks and the reserves the banks must hold. To do this, the Fed manipulates three tools:

- Open market operations
- Last resort loans
- Required reserve ratio

Open Market Operations An **open market operation** is the purchase or sale of securities by the Fed in the *loanable funds market*. When the Fed buys securities, it pays for them with newly created bank reserves. When the Fed sells securities, the Fed is paid with reserves held by banks. So open market operations directly influence the reserves of banks. By changing the quantity of bank reserves, the Fed changes the quantity of monetary base, which influences the quantity of money.

An Open Market Purchase To see how an open market operation changes bank reserves, suppose the Fed buys $100 million of government securities from the Bank of America. When the Fed makes this transaction, two things happen:

1. The Bank of America has $100 million less securities, and the Fed has $100 million more securities.
2. The Fed pays for the securities by placing $100 million in the Bank of America's deposit account at the Fed.

Figure 8.2 shows the effects of these actions on the balance sheets of the Fed and the Bank of America. Ownership of the securities passes from the Bank of

FIGURE 8.2 The Fed Buys Securities in the Open Market

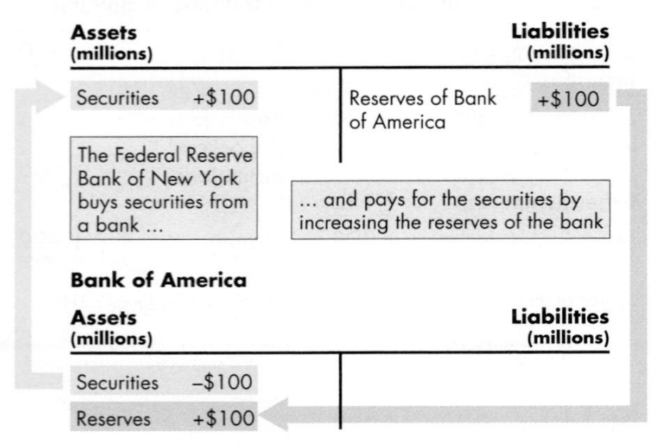

When the Fed buys securities in the open market, it creates bank reserves. The Fed's assets and liabilities increase, and the Bank of America exchanges securities for reserves.

America to the Fed, so the Bank of America's assets decrease by $100 million and the Fed's assets increase by $100 million, as shown by the blue arrow running from the Bank of America to the Fed.

The Fed pays for the securities by placing $100 million in the Bank of America's reserve account at the Fed, as shown by the green arrow running from the Fed to the Bank of America.

The Fed's assets and liabilities increase by $100 million. The Bank of America's total assets are unchanged: It sold securities to increase its reserves.

An Open Market Sale If the Fed sells $100 million of government securities to the Bank of America in the open market:

1. The Bank of America has $100 million more securities, and the Fed has $100 million less securities.
2. The Bank of America pays for the securities by using $100 million of its reserve deposit at the Fed.

You can follow the effects of these actions on the balance sheets of the Fed and the Bank of America by reversing the arrows and the plus and minus signs in Fig. 8.2. Ownership of the securities passes from the Fed to the Bank of America, so the Fed's assets decrease by $100 million and the Bank of America's assets increase by $100 million.

Economics in Action

The Fed's Balance Sheet Explodes

The Fed's balance sheet underwent some remarkable changes during the financial crisis of 2007–2008 and the recession that the crisis triggered. The figure shows the effects of these changes on the size and composition of the monetary base by comparing the situation in 2010 with that before the financial crisis began in late 2007.

In a normal year, 2007, the Fed's holding of U.S. government securities is almost as large as the monetary base and the monetary base is composed of almost all currency.

But between 2007 and 2010 the Fed made huge loans to banks and other financial institutions that more than doubled the monetary base. Almost all of this increase was composed of bank reserves.

When, and how quickly, to unwind the large increase in the monetary base and bank reserves was a source of disagreement at the Fed in 2010.

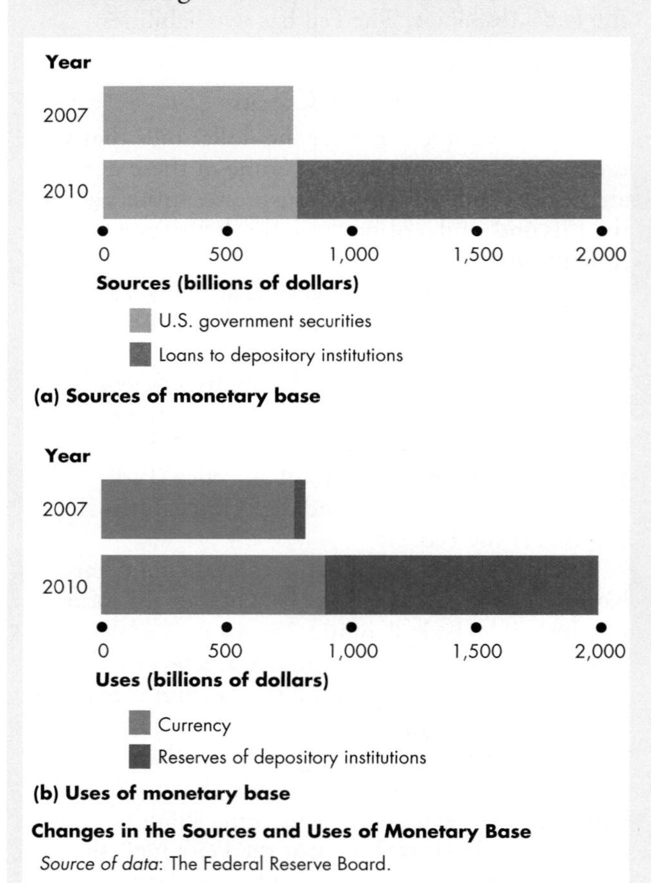

Changes in the Sources and Uses of Monetary Base

Source of data: The Federal Reserve Board.

The Bank of America uses $100 million of its reserves to pay for the securities.

Both the Fed's assets and liabilities decrease by $100 million. The Bank of America's total assets are unchanged: It has used reserves to buy securities.

The New York Fed conducts these open-market transactions on directions from the FOMC.

Last Resort Loans The Fed is the **lender of last resort**, which means that if a bank is short of reserves, it can borrow from the Fed. But the Fed sets the interest rate on last resort loans and this interest rate is called the *discount rate*.

During the period since August 2007 when the first effects of the financial crisis started to be felt, the Fed has been especially active as lender of last resort and, with the U.S. Treasury, has created a number of new lending facilities and initiatives to prevent banks from failing.

Required Reserve Ratio The **required reserve ratio** is the minimum percentage of deposits that depository institutions are required to hold as reserves. In 2010, required reserves were 3 percent of checking deposits between $10.7 million and $55.2 million and 10 percent of checking deposits in excess of $55.2 million. If the Fed requires the banks to hold more reserves, they must cut their lending.

REVIEW QUIZ

1. What is the central bank of the United States and what functions does it perform?
2. What is the monetary base and how does it relate to the Fed's balance sheet?
3. What are the Fed's three policy tools?
4. What is the Federal Open Market Committee and what are its main functions?
5. How does an open market operation change the monetary base?

You can work these questions in Study Plan 8.3 and get instant feedback.

Next, we're going to see how the banking system—the banks and the Fed—creates money and how the quantity of money changes when the Fed changes the monetary base.

How Banks Create Money

Banks create money. But this doesn't mean that they have smoke-filled back rooms in which counterfeiters are busily working. Remember, money is both currency and bank deposits. What banks create is deposits, and they do so by making loans.

Creating Deposits by Making Loans

The easiest way to see that banks create deposits is to think about what happens when Andy, who has a Visa card issued by Citibank, uses his card to buy a tank of gas from Chevron. When Andy signs the card sales slip, he takes a loan from Citibank and obligates himself to repay the loan at a later date. At the end of the business day, a Chevron clerk takes a pile of signed credit card sales slips, including Andy's, to Chevron's bank. For now, let's assume that Chevron also banks at Citibank. The bank immediately credits Chevron's account with the value of the slips (minus the bank's commission).

You can see that these transactions have created a bank deposit and a loan. Andy has increased the size of his loan (his credit card balance), and Chevron has increased the size of its bank deposit. Because bank deposits are money, Citibank has created money.

If, as we've just assumed, Andy and Chevron use the same bank, no further transactions take place. But the outcome is essentially the same when two banks are involved. If Chevron's bank is Bank of America, then Citibank uses its reserves to pay Bank of America. Citibank has an increase in loans and a decrease in reserves; Bank of America has an increase in reserves and an increase in deposits. The banking system as a whole has an increase in loans and deposits but no change in reserves.

If Andy had swiped his card at an automatic payment pump, all these transactions would have occurred at the time he filled his tank, and the quantity of money would have increased by the amount of his purchase (minus the bank's commission for conducting the transactions).

Three factors limit the quantity of loans and deposits that the banking system can create through transactions like Andy's. They are:

- The monetary base
- Desired reserves
- Desired currency holding

The Monetary Base You've seen that the *monetary base* is the sum of Federal Reserve notes, coins, and banks' deposits at the Fed. The size of the monetary base limits the total quantity of money that the banking system can create. The reason is that banks have a desired level of reserves, households and firms have a desired holding of currency, and both of these desired holdings of the monetary base depend on the quantity of deposits.

Desired Reserves A bank's *desired reserves* are the reserves that it *plans* to hold. They contrast with a bank's *required reserves*, which is the minimum quantity of reserves that a bank *must* hold.

The quantity of desired reserves depends on the level of deposits and is determined by the **desired reserve ratio**—the ratio of reserves to deposits that the banks *plan* to hold. The *desired* reserve ratio exceeds the *required* reserve ratio by an amount that the banks determine to be prudent on the basis of their daily business requirements and in the light of the current outlook in financial markets.

Desired Currency Holding The proportions of money held as currency and bank deposits—the ratio of currency to deposits— depend on how households and firms choose to make payments: Whether they plan to use currency or debit cards and checks.

Choices about how to make payments change slowly so the ratio of desired currency to deposits also changes slowly, and at any given time this ratio is fixed. If bank deposits increase, desired currency holding also increases. For this reason, when banks make loans that increase deposits, some currency leaves the banks—the banking system leaks reserves. We call the leakage of bank reserves into currency the *currency drain*, and we call the ratio of currency to deposits the **currency drain ratio**.

We've sketched the way that a loan creates a deposit and described the three factors that limit the amount of loans and deposits that can be created. We're now going to examine the money creation process more closely and discover a money multiplier.

The Money Creation Process

The money creation process begins with an increase in the monetary base, which occurs if the Fed conducts an open market operation in which it buys securities from banks and other institutions. The Fed pays for the securities it buys with newly created bank reserves.

When the Fed buys securities from a bank, the bank's reserves increase but its deposits don't change. So the bank has excess reserves. A bank's **excess reserves** are its actual reserves minus its desired reserves.

When a bank has excess reserves, it makes loans and creates deposits. When the entire banking system has excess reserves, total loans and deposits increase and the quantity of money increases.

One bank can make a loan and get rid of excess reserves. But the banking system as a whole can't get rid of excess reserves so easily. When the banks make loans and create deposits, the extra deposits lower excess reserves for two reasons. First, the increase in deposits increases desired reserves. Second, a currency drain decreases total reserves. But excess reserves don't completely disappear. So the banks lend some more and the process repeats.

As the process of making loans and increasing deposits repeats, desired reserves increase, total reserves decrease through the currency drain, and eventually enough new deposits have been created to use all the new monetary base.

Figure 8.3 summarizes one round in the process we've just described. The sequence has the following eight steps:

1. Banks have excess reserves.
2. Banks lend excess reserves.
3. The quantity of money increases.
4. New money is used to make payments.
5. Some of the new money remains on deposit.
6. Some of the new money is a *currency drain*.
7. Desired reserves increase because deposits have increased.
8. Excess reserves decrease.

If the Fed *sells* securities in an open market operation, then banks have negative excess reserves—they are short of reserves. When the banks are short of reserves, loans and deposits decrease and the process we've described above works in a downward direction until desired reserves plus desired currency holding has decreased by an amount equal to the decrease in monetary base.

A money multiplier determines the change in the quantity of money that results from a change in the monetary base.

FIGURE 8.3 How the Banking System Creates Money by Making Loans

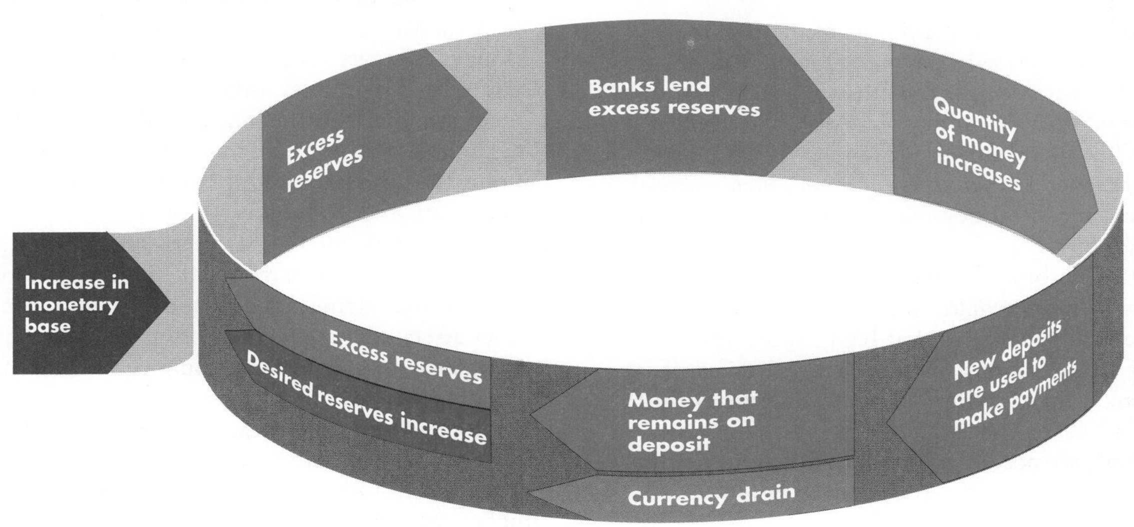

The Federal Reserve increases the monetary base, which increases bank reserves and creates excess reserves. Banks lend the excess reserves, which creates new deposits. The quantity of money increases. New deposits are used to make payments. Some of the new money remains on deposit at banks and some leaves the banks in a currency drain. The increase in bank deposits increases banks' desired reserves. But the banks still have excess reserves, though less than before. The process repeats until excess reserves have been eliminated.

The Money Multiplier

The **money multiplier** is the ratio of the change in the quantity of money to the change in monetary base. For example, if a $1 million increase in the monetary base increases the quantity of money by $2.5 million, then the money multiplier is 2.5.

The smaller the banks' desired reserve ratio and the smaller the currency drain ratio, the larger is the money multiplier. (See the Mathematical Note on pp. 204–205 for details on the money multiplier).

REVIEW QUIZ

1 How do banks create money?
2 What limits the quantity of money that the banking system can create?
3 A bank manager tells you that she doesn't create money. She just lends the money that people deposit. Explain why she's wrong.

You can work these questions in Study Plan 8.4 and get instant feedback.

Economics in Action

The Variable Money Multipliers

We can measure the money multiplier, other things remaining the same, as the ratio of the quantity of money (M1 or M2) to the monetary base. In normal times, these ratios (and the money multipliers) change slowly.

In the early 1990s, the M1 multiplier—the ratio of M1 to the monetary base—was about 3 and the M2 multiplier—the ratio of M2 to the monetary base—was about 12. Through the 1990s and 2000s, the currency drain ratio gradually increased and the money multipliers decreased. By 2007 the M1 multiplier was 2 and the M2 multiplier was 9.

Then, in 2008 and 2009 when the Fed increased the monetary base by an unprecedented $1 trillion, almost all of the newly created reserves were willingly held by the banks. In an environment of enormous uncertainty, desired reserves increased by an amount similar to the increase in actual reserves. The quantity of money barely changed.

The Money Market

There is no limit to the amount of money we would like to *receive* in payment for our labor or as interest on our savings. But there *is* a limit to how big an inventory of money we would like to *hold* and neither spend nor use to buy assets that generate an income. The *quantity of money demanded* is the inventory of money that people plan to hold on any given day. It is the quantity of money in our wallets and in our deposit accounts at banks. The quantity of money held must equal the quantity supplied, and the forces that bring about this equality in the money market have powerful effects on the economy, as you will see in the rest of this chapter.

But first, we need to explain what determines the amount of money that people plan to hold.

The Influences on Money Holding

The quantity of money that people plan to hold depends on four main factors:

- The price level
- The *nominal* interest rate
- Real GDP
- Financial innovation

The Price Level The quantity of money measured in dollars is *nominal money*. The quantity of nominal money demanded is proportional to the price level, other things remaining the same. If the price level rises by 10 percent, people hold 10 percent more nominal money than before, other things remaining the same. If you hold $20 to buy your weekly movies and soda, you will increase your money holding to $22 if the prices of movies and soda—and your wage rate—increase by 10 percent.

The quantity of money measured in constant dollars (for example, in 2005 dollars) is real money. *Real money* is equal to nominal money divided by the price level and is the quantity of money measured in terms of what it will buy. In the above example, when the price level rises by 10 percent and you increase your money holding by 10 percent, your *real* money holding is constant. Your $22 at the new price level buys the same quantity of goods and is the same quantity of *real money* as your $20 at the original price level. The quantity of real money demanded is independent of the price level.

The *Nominal* Interest Rate A fundamental principle of economics is that as the opportunity cost of something increases, people try to find substitutes for it. Money is no exception. The higher the opportunity cost of holding money, other things remaining the same, the smaller is the quantity of real money demanded. The nominal interest rate on other assets minus the nominal interest rate on money is the opportunity cost of holding money.

The interest rate that you earn on currency and checking deposits is zero. So the opportunity cost of holding these items is the nominal interest rate on other assets such as a savings bond or Treasury bill. By holding money instead, you forgo the interest that you otherwise would have received.

Money loses value because of inflation, so why isn't the inflation rate part of the cost of holding money? It is. Other things remaining the same, the higher the expected inflation rate, the higher is the nominal interest rate.

Real GDP The quantity of money that households and firms plan to hold depends on the amount they are spending. The quantity of money demanded in the economy as a whole depends on aggregate expenditure—real GDP.

Again, suppose that you hold an average of $20 to finance your weekly purchases of movies and soda. Now imagine that the prices of these goods and of all other goods remain constant but that your income increases. As a consequence, you now buy more goods and services and you also keep a larger amount of money on hand to finance your higher volume of expenditure.

Financial Innovation Technological change and the arrival of new financial products influence the quantity of money held. Financial innovations include

1. Daily interest checking deposits
2. Automatic transfers between checking and saving deposits
3. Automatic teller machines
4. Credit cards and debit cards
5. Internet banking and bill paying

These innovations have occurred because of the development of computing power that has lowered the cost of calculations and record keeping.

We summarize the effects of the influences on money holding by using a demand for money curve.

The Demand for Money

The **demand for money** is the relationship between the quantity of real money demanded and the nominal interest rate when all other influences on the amount of money that people wish to hold remain the same.

Figure 8.4 shows a demand for money curve, *MD*. When the interest rate rises, other things remaining the same, the opportunity cost of holding money rises and the quantity of real money demanded decreases—there is a movement up along the demand for money curve. Similarly, when the interest rate falls, the opportunity cost of holding money falls, and the quantity of real money demanded increases—there is a movement down along the demand for money curve.

When any influence on money holding other than the interest rate changes, there is a change in the demand for money and the demand for money curve shifts. Let's study these shifts.

Shifts in the Demand for Money Curve

A change in real GDP or financial innovation changes the demand for money and shifts the demand for money curve.

Figure 8.5 illustrates the change in the demand for money. A decrease in real GDP decreases the demand for money and shifts the demand for money curve leftward from MD_0 to MD_1. An increase in real GDP has the opposite effect: It increases the demand for money and shifts the demand for money curve rightward from MD_0 to MD_2.

The influence of financial innovation on the demand for money curve is more complicated. It decreases the demand for currency and might increase the demand for some types of deposits and decrease the demand for others. But generally, financial innovation decreases the demand for money.

Changes in real GDP and financial innovation have brought large shifts in the demand for money in the United States.

FIGURE 8.4 The Demand for Money

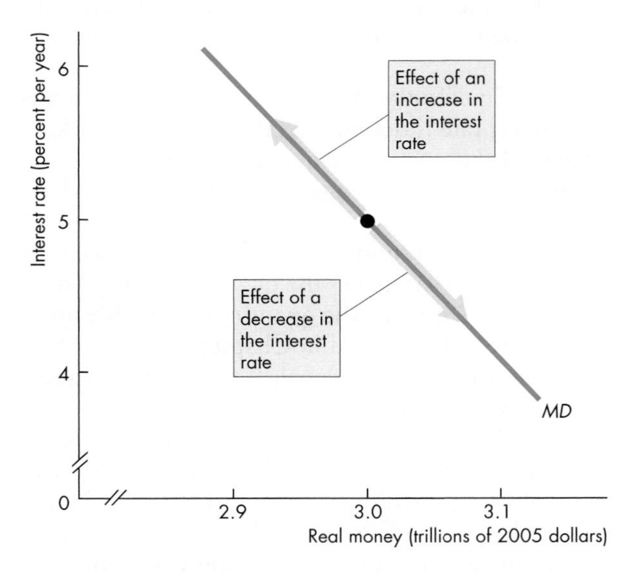

The demand for money curve, *MD*, shows the relationship between the quantity of real money that people plan to hold and the nominal interest rate, other things remaining the same. The interest rate is the opportunity cost of holding money. A change in the interest rate brings a movement along the demand for money curve.

myeconlab animation

FIGURE 8.5 Changes in the Demand for Money

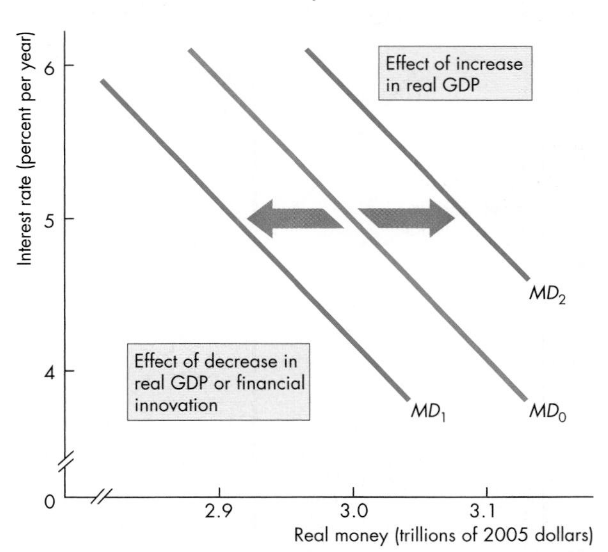

A decrease in real GDP decreases the demand for money. The demand for money curve shifts leftward from MD_0 to MD_1. An increase in real GDP increases the demand for money. The demand for money curve shifts rightward from MD_0 to MD_2. Financial innovation generally decreases the demand for money.

myeconlab animation

Money Market Equilibrium

You now know what determines the demand for money, and you've seen how the banking system creates money. Let's now see how the money market reaches an equilibrium.

Money market equilibrium occurs when the quantity of money demanded equals the quantity of money supplied. The adjustments that occur to bring money market equilibrium are fundamentally different in the short run and the long run.

Short-Run Equilibrium The quantity of money supplied is determined by the actions of the banks and the Fed. As the Fed adjusts the quantity of money, the interest rate changes.

In Fig. 8.6, the Fed uses open market operations to make the quantity of real money supplied $3.0 trillion and the supply of money curve *MS*. With demand for money curve *MD*, the equilibrium interest rate is 5 percent a year.

If the interest rate were 4 percent a year, people would want to hold more money than is available. They would sell bonds, bid down their price, and the interest rate would rise. If the interest rate were 6 percent a year, people would want to hold less money than is available. They would buy bonds, bid up their price, and the interest rate would fall.

FIGURE 8.6 Money Market Equilibrium

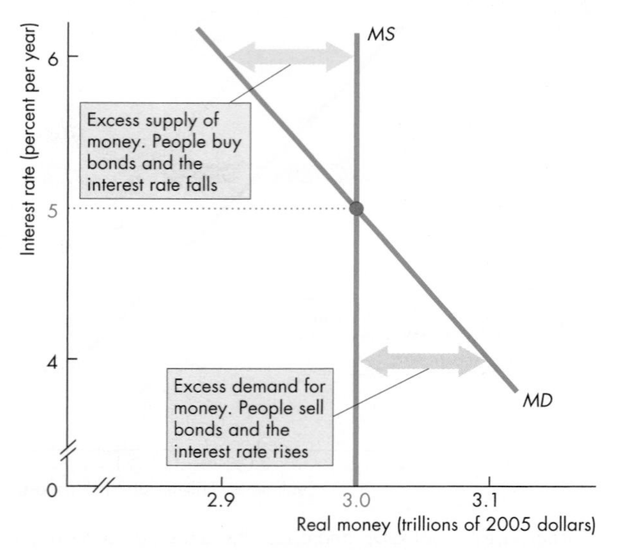

Money market equilibrium occurs when the quantity of money demanded equals the quantity supplied. In the short run, real GDP determines the demand for money curve, *MD*, and the Fed determines the quantity of real money supplied and the supply of money curve, *MS*. The interest rate adjusts to achieve equilibrium, here 5 percent a year.

myeconlab animation

The Short-Run Effect of a Change in the Supply of Money Starting from a short-run equilibrium, if the Fed increases the quantity of money, people find themselves holding more money than the quantity demanded. With a surplus of money holding, people enter the loanable funds market and buy bonds. The increase in demand for bonds raises the price of a bond and lowers the interest rate (refresh your memory by looking at Chapter 7, p. 164).

If the Fed decreases the quantity of money, people find themselves holding less money than the quantity demanded. They now enter the loanable funds market to sell bonds. The decrease in the demand for bonds lowers their price and raises the interest rate.

Figure 8.7 illustrates the effects of the changes in the quantity of money that we've just described. When the supply of money curve shifts rightward from MS_0 to MS_1, the interest rate falls to 4 percent a year; when the supply of money curve shifts leftward to MS_2, the interest rate rises to 6 percent a year.

Long-Run Equilibrium You've just seen how the nominal interest rate is determined in the money market at the level that makes the quantity of money demanded equal the quantity supplied by the Fed. You learned in Chapter 7 (on p. 168) that the real interest rate is determined in the loanable funds market at the level that makes the quantity of loanable funds demanded equal the quantity of loanable funds supplied. You also learned in Chapter 7 (on p. 165) that the real interest rate equals the nominal interest rate minus the inflation rate.

When the inflation rate equals the expected (or forecasted) inflation rate and when real GDP equals potential GDP, the money market, the loanable funds market, the goods market, and the labor market are in long-run equilibrium—the economy is in long-run equilibrium.

If in long-run equilibrium, the Fed increases the quantity of money, eventually a new long-run equilibrium is reached in which nothing real has changed. Real GDP, employment, the real quantity of money, and the real interest rate all return to their original levels. But something does change: the price level. The price level rises by the same percentage as the rise

FIGURE 8.7 A Change in the Supply of Money

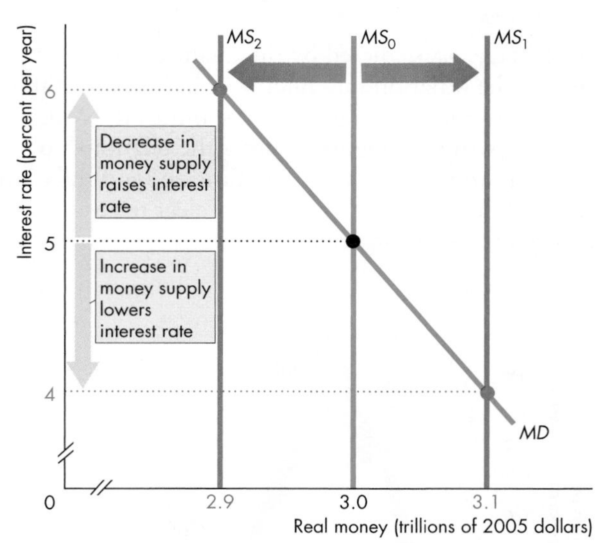

An increase in the supply of money shifts the supply of money curve from MS_0 to MS_1 and the interest rate falls. A decrease in the supply of money shifts the supply of money curve from MS_0 to MS_2 and the interest rate rises.

myeconlab animation

in the quantity of money. Why does this outcome occur in the long run?

The reason is that real GDP and employment are determined by the demand for labor, the supply of labor, and the production function—the real forces described in Chapter 6 (pp. 139–141); and the real interest rate is determined by the demand for and supply of (real) loanable funds—the real forces described in Chapter 7 (pp. 166–168). The only variable that is free to respond to a change in the supply of money in the long run is the price level. The price level adjusts to make the quantity of real money supplied equal to the quantity demanded.

So when the Fed changes the nominal quantity of money, in the long run the price level changes by a percentage equal to the percentage change in the quantity of nominal money. In the long run, the change in the price level is proportional to the change in the quantity of money.

The Transition from the Short Run to the Long Run
How does the economy move from the first short-run response to an increase in the quantity of money to the long-run response?

The adjustment process is lengthy and complex. Here, we'll only provide a sketch of the process. A more thorough account must wait until you've studied Chapter 9.

We start out in long-run equilibrium and the Fed increases the quantity of money by 10 percent. Here are the steps in what happens next.

First, the nominal interest rate falls (just like you saw on p. 198 and in Fig. 8.6). The real interest rate falls too, as people try to get rid of their excess money holdings and buy bonds.

With a lower real interest rate, people want to borrow and spend more. Firms want to borrow to invest and households want to borrow to invest in bigger homes or to buy more consumer goods.

The increase in the demand for goods cannot be met by an increase in supply because the economy is already at full employment. So there is a general shortage of all kinds of goods and services.

The shortage of goods and services forces the price level to rise.

As the price level rises, the real quantity of money decreases. The decrease in the quantity of real money raises the nominal interest rate and the real interest rate. As the interest rate rises, spending plans are cut back, and eventually the original full-employment equilibrium is restored. At the new long-run equilibrium, the price level has risen by 10 percent and nothing real has changed.

REVIEW QUIZ

1. What are the main influences on the quantity of real money that people and businesses plan to hold?
2. Show the effects of a change in the nominal interest rate and a change in real GDP using the demand for money curve.
3. How is money market equilibrium determined in the short run?
4. How does a change in the supply of money change the interest rate in the short run?
5. How does a change in the supply of money change the interest rate in the long run?

You can work these questions in Study Plan 8.5 and get instant feedback.

Let's explore the long-run link between money and the price level a bit further.

The Quantity Theory of Money

In the long run, the price level adjusts to make the quantity of real money demanded equal the quantity supplied. A special theory of the price level and inflation—the quantity theory of money—explains this long-run adjustment of the price level.

The **quantity theory of money** is the proposition that in the long run, an increase in the quantity of money brings an equal percentage increase in the price level. To explain the quantity theory of money, we first need to define *the velocity of circulation.*

The **velocity of circulation** is the average number of times a dollar of money is used annually to buy the goods and services that make up GDP. But GDP equals the price level (P) multiplied by *real* GDP (Y). That is,

$$GDP = PY.$$

Call the quantity of money M. The velocity of circulation, V, is determined by the equation

$$V = PY/M.$$

For example, if GDP is $1,000 billion ($PY$ = $1,000 billion) and the quantity of money is $250 billion, then the velocity of circulation is 4.

From the definition of the velocity of circulation, the *equation of exchange* tells us how M, V, P, and Y are connected. This equation is

$$MV = PY.$$

Given the definition of the velocity of circulation, the equation of exchange is always true—it is true by definition. It becomes the quantity theory of money if the quantity of money does not influence the velocity of circulation or real GDP. In this case, the equation of exchange tells us that in the long run, the price level is determined by the quantity of money. That is,

$$P = M(V/Y),$$

where (V/Y) is independent of M. So a change in M brings a proportional change in P.

We can also express the equation of exchange in growth rates,[1] in which form it states that

$$\text{Money growth rate} + \text{Rate of velocity change} = \text{Inflation rate} + \text{Real GDP growth rate}$$

Economics in Action

Does the Quantity Theory Work?

On average, as predicted by the quantity theory of money, the inflation rate fluctuates in line with fluctuations in the money growth rate minus the real GDP growth rate. Figure 1 shows the relationship between money growth (M2 definition) and inflation in the United States. You can see a clear relationship between the two variables.

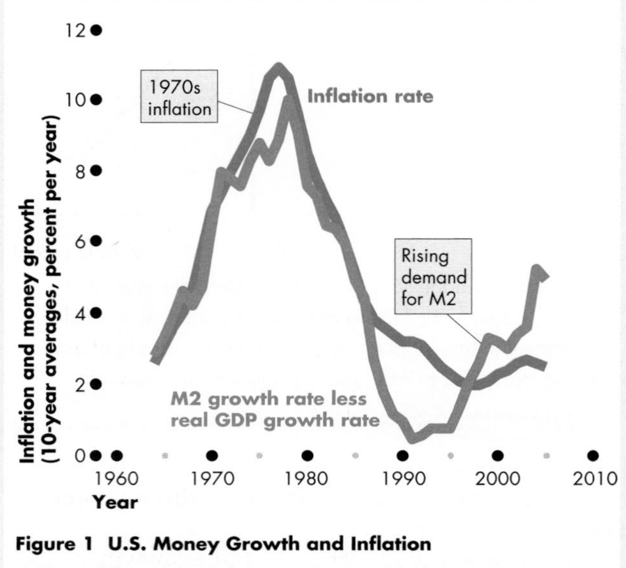

Figure 1 U.S. Money Growth and Inflation

Sources of data: Federal Reserve and Bureau of Labor Statistics.

Solving this equation for the inflation rate gives

$$\text{Inflation rate} = \text{Money growth rate} + \text{Rate of velocity change} - \text{Real GDP growth rate}$$

In the long run, the rate of velocity change is not influenced by the money growth rate. More strongly, in the long run, the rate of velocity change is approxi-

[1] To obtain this equation, begin with

$$MV = PY.$$

Then changes in these variables are related by the equation

$$\Delta MV + M\Delta V = \Delta PY + P\Delta Y.$$

Divide this equation by the equation of exchange to obtain

$$\Delta M/M + \Delta V/V = \Delta P/P + \Delta Y/Y.$$

The term $\Delta M/M$ is the money growth rate, $\Delta V/V$ is the rate of velocity change, $\Delta P/P$ is the inflation rate, and $\Delta Y/Y$ is the real GDP growth rate.

International data also support the quantity theory. Figure 2 shows a scatter diagram of the inflation rate and the money growth rate in 134 countries and Fig. 3 shows the inflation rate and money growth rate in countries with inflation rates below 20 percent a year. You can see a general tendency for money growth and inflation to be correlated, but the quantity theory (the red line) does not predict inflation precisely.

The correlation between money growth and inflation isn't perfect, and the correlation does not tell us that money growth *causes* inflation. Money growth might cause inflation; inflation might cause money growth; or some third variable might cause both inflation and money growth. Other evidence does confirm, though, that causation runs from money growth to inflation.

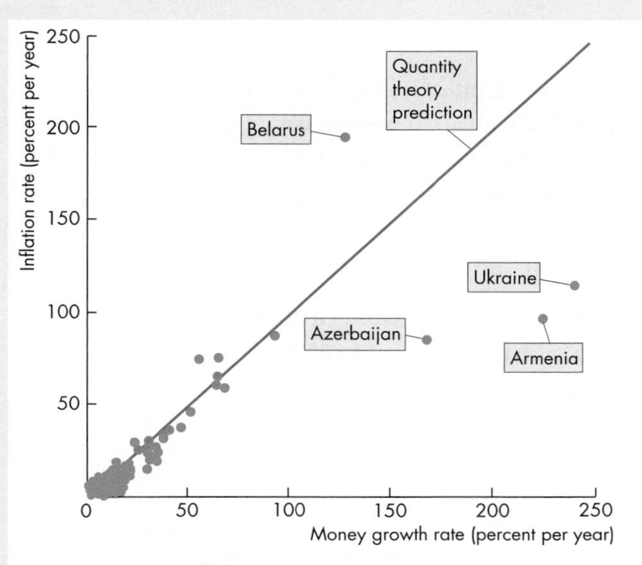

Figure 2 134 Countries: 1990–2005

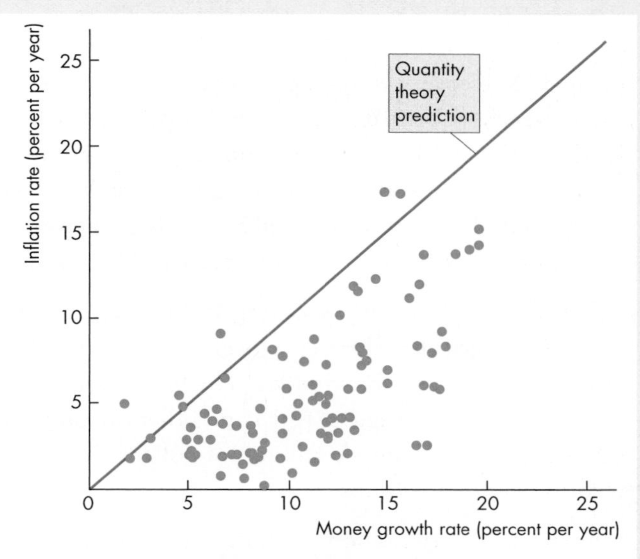

Figure 3 Lower-Inflation Countries: 1990–2005

Sources of data: International Financial Statistics Yearbook, 2008 and International Monetary Fund, *World Economic Outlook*, October, 2008.

mately zero. With this assumption, the inflation rate in the long run is determined as

$$\text{Inflation rate} = \text{Money growth rate} - \text{Real GDP growth rate}.$$

In the long run, fluctuations in the money growth rate minus the real GDP growth rate bring equal fluctuations in the inflation rate.

Also, in the long run, with the economy at full employment, real GDP equals potential GDP, so the real GDP growth rate equals the potential GDP growth rate. This growth rate might be influenced by inflation, but the influence is most likely small and the quantity theory assumes that it is zero. So the real GDP growth rate is given and doesn't change when the money growth rate changes—inflation is correlated with money growth.

REVIEW QUIZ

1. What is the quantity theory of money?
2. How is the velocity of circulation calculated?
3. What is the equation of exchange?
4. Does the quantity theory correctly predict the effects of money growth on inflation?

You can work these questions in Study Plan 8.6 and get instant feedback.

You now know what money is, how the banks create it, and how the quantity of money influences the nominal interest rate in the short run and the price level in the long run. *Reading Between the Lines* on pp. 202–203 looks at the Fed's incredible actions in the recent financial crisis.

Can More Money Keep the Recovery Going?

It Falls to the Fed to Fuel Recovery

The Financial Times
August 30, 2010

The U.S. recovery is stalling. ... The recovery is in danger of petering out altogether. Recent numbers have been dismal. Second-quarter growth was marked down to 1.6 percent on Friday. Earlier, signs of a new crunch in the housing market gave the stock market another pummelling. Already low expectations were disappointed nonetheless: Sales of existing single-family homes in July fell by nearly 30 percent, to their lowest for 15 years. Sales of new homes were at their lowest since the series began to be reported in 1963. ...

At the end of last week, speaking at the Jackson Hole conference, Ben Bernanke, Fed chief, acknowledged the faltering recovery, and reminded his audience that the central bank has untapped capacity for stimulus. The benchmark interest rate is effectively zero, but that leaves quantitative easing (QE) and other unconventional measures. So far as QE goes, the Fed has already pumped trillions of dollars into the economy by buying debt. If it chose, it could pump in trillions more. ...

As the monetary economist Scott Sumner has pointed out, Milton Friedman—name me a less reconstructed monetarist—talked of "the fallacy of identifying tight money with high interest rates and easy money with low interest rates." When long-term nominal interest rates are very low, and inflation expectations are therefore also very low, money is tight in the sense that matters. When money is loose, inflation expectations rise, and so do long-term interest rates. ... Under current circumstances, better to print money and be damned. ...

ESSENCE OF THE STORY

- The 2010 second-quarter real GDP growth rate was a low1.6 percent a year and home sales were at their lowest since measurement started in 1963.
- Fed Chairman Ben Bernanke agrees the recovery is weak but says the Fed has weapons to fight recession.
- Interest rates are close to zero but the Fed has pumped trillions of dollars into the economy by buying debt (quantitative easing) and the Fed can pump in trillions more.
- Economist Scott Sumner, citing Milton Friedman, says the interest rate that influences spending decisions is the real interest rate and that isn't low when inflation is expected to be low.
- With the U.S. recovery stalling and possibly ending, the Fed should pump in more money.

ECONOMIC ANALYSIS

- Between October 2007 and October 2008, to counter a global financial crisis, the Fed cut the federal funds interest rate to almost zero.
- Between October 2008 and October 2009, the Fed increased the monetary base by an unprecedented $900 billion.
- Between October 2009 and March 2010, the Fed added a further $300 billion to the monetary base—a total increase of $1.2 trillion over 18 months.
- Figure 1 shows these extraordinary increases in the monetary base.
- As you've seen in this chapter, most of the increase in monetary base was willingly held by the banks. They increased their desired reserves.
- These monetary actions by the Fed lowered the interest rates that firms and households pay on very short-term loans, as you can see in Fig. 2.
- But the interest rate on long-term loans that finance business investment barely changed.
- You can see in Fig. 2 that the long-term corporate bond rate (the rate paid by the safest big firms) hovered around 5.5 percent.
- For the Fed's injection of monetary base to lower the long-term corporate bond rate, the banks would have to get into the loanable funds market and start to lend their large volume of reserves.
- As the news article notes, it is the real interest rate, not the nominal interest rate, that influences expenditure. And because for a few months, deflation was expected (a falling price level), the real interest rate spiked upward.
- Figure 3 shows the real interest rate on long-term corporate borrowing.
- Despite massive injections of monetary base (quantitative easing) and powerful effects on the short-term interest rate, it is hard to see the effects of the Fed's actions on the long-term real interest rate.
- Increasing the monetary base further, as advocated in the news article, might lower the long-term real interest rate, but it might alternatively merely add to bank reserves and leave the long-term interest rate unchanged.

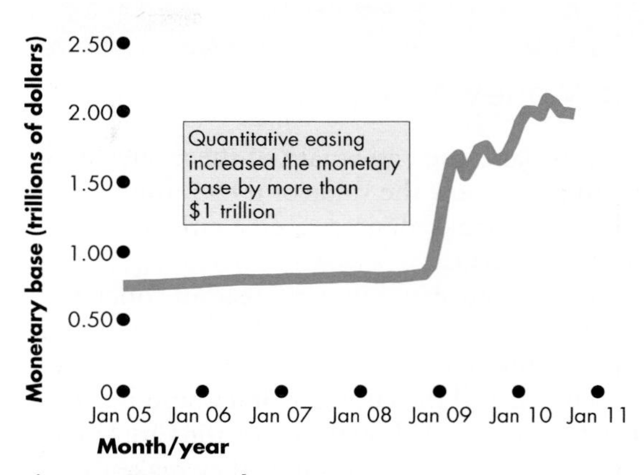

Figure 1 Monetary base

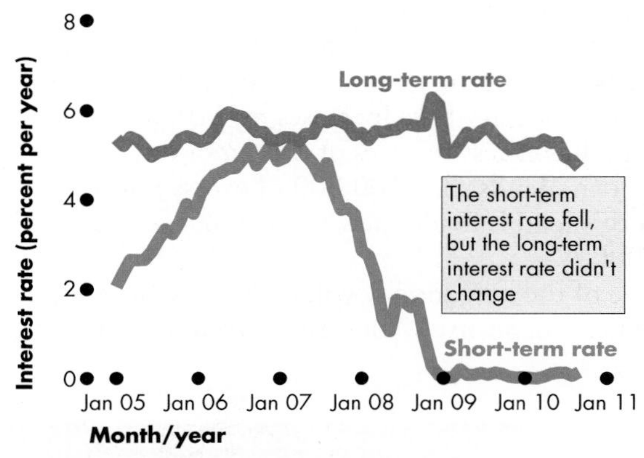

Figure 2 Nominal interest rates

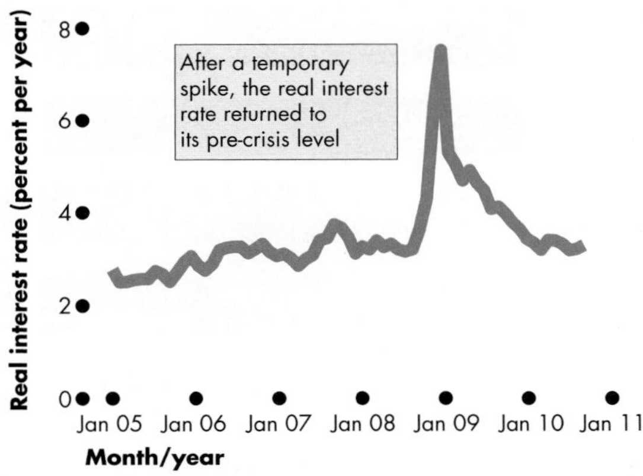

Figure 3 The long-term real interest rate

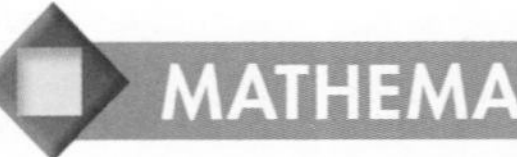

MATHEMATICAL NOTE

The Money Multiplier

This note explains the basic math of the money multiplier and shows how the value of the multiplier depends on the banks' desired reserve ratio and the currency drain ratio.

To make the process of money creation concrete, we work through an example for a banking system in which each bank has a desired reserve ratio of 10 percent of deposits and the currency drain ratio is 50 percent of deposits. (Although these ratios are larger than the ones in the U.S. economy, they make the process end more quickly and enable you to see more clearly the principles at work.)

The figure keeps track of the numbers. Before the process begins, all the banks have no excess reserves. Then the monetary base increases by $100,000 and one bank has excess reserves of this amount.

The bank lends the $100,000 of excess reserves. When this loan is made, new money increases by $100,000.

Some of the new money will be held as currency and some as deposits. With a currency drain ratio of 50 percent of deposits, one third of the new money will be held as currency and two thirds will be held as deposits. That is, $33,333 drains out of the banks as currency and $66,667 remains in the banks as deposits. The increase in the quantity of money of $100,000 equals the increase in deposits plus the increase in currency holdings.

The increased bank deposits of $66,667 generate an increase in desired reserves of 10 percent of that amount, which is $6,667. Actual reserves have increased by the same amount as the increase in deposits: $66,667. So the banks now have excess reserves of $60,000.

The process we've just described repeats but begins with excess reserves of $60,000. The figure shows the next two rounds. At the end of the process, the quantity of money has increased by a multiple of the increase in the monetary base. In this case, the increase is $250,000, which is 2.5 times the increase in the monetary base.

The sequence in the figure shows the first stages of the process that finally reaches the total shown in the final row of the "money" column.

To calculate what happens at the later stages in the process and the final increase in the quantity of

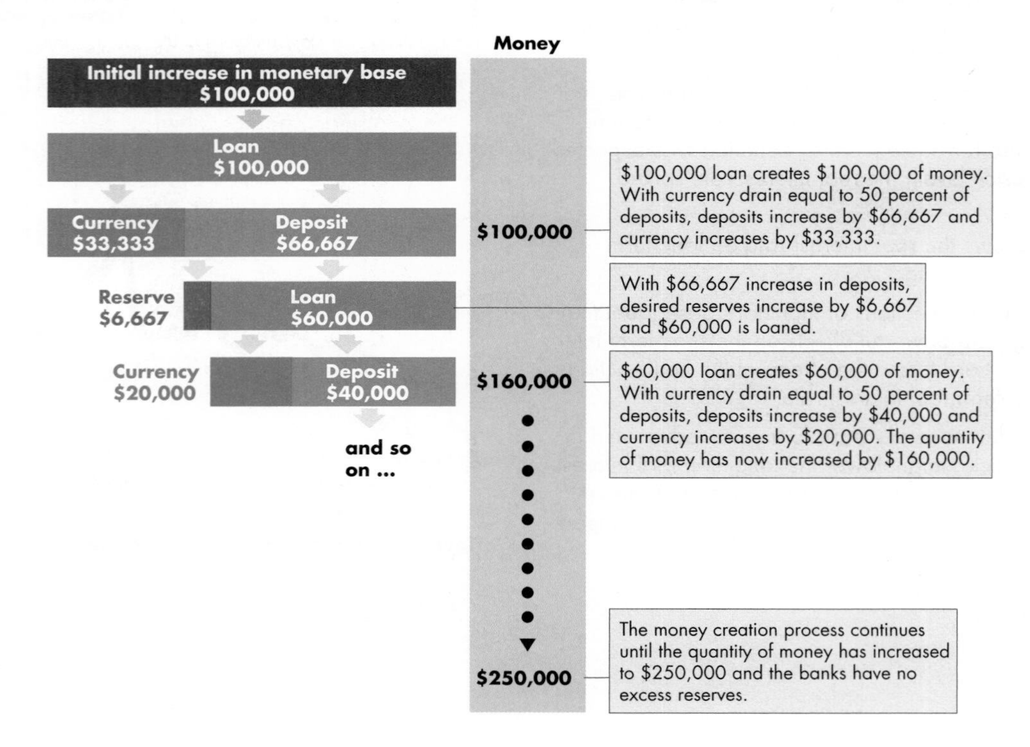

Figure 1 The money creation process

money, look closely at the numbers in the figure. The initial increase in reserves is \$100,000 (call it A). At each stage, the loan is 60 percent (0.6) of the previous loan and the quantity of money increases by 0.6 of the previous increase. Call that proportion L ($L = 0.6$). We can write down the complete sequence for the increase in the quantity of money as

$$A + AL + AL^2 + AL^3 + AL^4 + AL^5 + \ldots .$$

Remember, L is a fraction, so at each stage in this sequence, the amount of new loans and new money gets smaller. The total value of loans made and money created at the end of the process is the sum of the sequence, which is[1]

$$A/(1 - L).$$

If we use the numbers from the example, the total increase in the quantity of money is

$$\$100{,}000 + 60{,}000 + 36{,}000 + \ldots$$

$$= \$100{,}000\ (1 + 0.6 + 0.36 + \ldots)$$

$$= \$100{,}000\ (1 + 0.6 + 0.6^2 + \ldots)$$

$$= \$100{,}000 \times 1/(1 - 0.6)$$

$$= \$100{,}000 \times 1/(0.4)$$

$$= \$100{,}000 \times 2.5$$

$$= \$250{,}000.$$

The magnitude of the money multiplier depends on the desired reserve ratio and the currency drain ratio. Let's explore this relationship

The money multiplier is the ratio of money to the monetary base. Call the money multiplier mm, the quantity of money M, and the monetary base MB. Then

$$mm = M/MB.$$

Next recall that money, M, is the sum of deposits and currency. Call deposits D and currency C. Then

$$M = D + C.$$

Finally, recall that the monetary base, MB, is the sum of banks' reserves and currency. Call banks' reserves R. Then

$$MB = R + C.$$

Use the equations for M and MB in the mm equation to give:

$$mm = M/MB = (D + C)/(R + C).$$

Now divide all the variables on the right side of the equation by D to give:

$$mm = M/MB = (1 + C/D)/(R/D + C/D).$$

In this equation, C/D is the currency drain ratio and R/D is the banks' reserve ratio. If we use the values in the example on the previous page, C/D is 0.5 and R/D is 0.1, and

$$mm = (1 + 0.5)/(0.1 + 0.5).$$

$$= 1.5/0.6 = 2.5.$$

The U.S. Money Multiplier

The money multiplier in the United States can be found by using the formula above along with the values of C/D and R/D in the U.S. economy.

Because we have two definitions of money, M1 and M2, we have two money multipliers. Call the M1 deposits $D1$ and call the M2 deposits $D2$.

The numbers for M1 in 2010 are $C/D1 = 1.06$ and $R/D1 = 1.32$. So

$$\text{M1 multiplier} = (1 + 1.06)/(1.32 + 1.06) = 0.87.$$

For M2 in 2010, $C/D2 = 0.11$ and $R/D2 = 0.14$, so

$$\text{M2 multiplier} = (1 + 0.11)/(0.14 + 0.11) = 4.44.$$

[1] The sequence of values is called a convergent geometric series. To find the sum of a series such as this, begin by calling the sum S. Then write the sum as

$$S = A + AL + AL^2 + AL^3 + AL^4 + AL^5 + \ldots .$$

Multiply by L to get

$$LS = AL + AL^2 + AL^3 + AL^4 + AL^5 + \ldots$$

and then subtract the second equation from the first to get

$$S(1 - L) = A$$

or

$$S = A/(1 - L).$$

SUMMARY

Key Points

What Is Money? (pp. 184–186)

- Money is the means of payment. It functions as a medium of exchange, a unit of account, and a store of value.
- Today, money consists of currency and deposits.

Working Problems 1 to 4 will give you a better understanding of what money is.

Depository Institutions (pp. 187–189)

- Commercial banks, S&Ls, savings banks, credit unions, and money market mutual funds are depository institutions whose deposits are money.
- Depository institutions provide four main economic services: They create liquidity, minimize the cost of obtaining funds, minimize the cost of monitoring borrowers, and pool risks.

Working Problems 5 and 6 will give you a better understanding of depository institutions.

The Federal Reserve System (pp. 190–193)

- The Federal Reserve System is the central bank of the United States.
- The Fed influences the quantity of money by setting the required reserve ratio, making last resort loans, and by conducting open market operations.
- When the Fed buys securities in an open market operation, the monetary base increases; when the Fed sells securities, the monetary base decreases.

Working Problems 7 to 9 will give you a better understanding of the Federal Reserve System

How Banks Create Money (pp. 193–195)

- Banks create money by making loans.
- The total quantity of money that can be created depends on the monetary base, the desired reserve ratio, and the currency drain ratio.

Working Problems 10 to 14 will give you a better understanding of how banks create money.

The Money Market (pp. 196–199)

- The quantity of money demanded is the amount of money that people plan to hold.
- The quantity of real money equals the quantity of nominal money divided by the price level.
- The quantity of real money demanded depends on the nominal interest rate, real GDP, and financial innovation.
- The nominal interest rate makes the quantity of money demanded equal the quantity supplied.
- When the Fed increases the supply of money, the nominal interest rate falls (the short-run effect).
- In the long run, when the Fed increases the supply of money, the price level rises and the nominal interest rate returns to its initial level.

Working Problems 15 and 16 will give you a better understanding of the money market.

The Quantity Theory of Money (pp. 200–201)

- The quantity theory of money is the proposition that money growth and inflation move up and down together in the long run.

Working Problem 17 will give you a better understanding of the quantity theory of money.

Key Terms

STUDY PLAN PROBLEMS AND APPLICATIONS

myeconlab You can work Problems 1 to 19 in MyEconLab Chapter 8 Study Plan and get instant feedback.

What Is Money? (Study Plan 8.1)

1. In the United States today, money includes which of the following items?
   a. Federal Reserve bank notes in Citibank's cash machines
   b. Your Visa card
   c. Coins inside a vending machine
   d. U.S. dollar bills in your wallet
   e. The check you have just written to pay for your rent
   f. The loan you took out last August to pay for your school fees
2. In June 2009, currency held by individuals and businesses was $853 billion; traveler's checks were $5 billion; checkable deposits owned by individuals and businesses were $792 billion; savings deposits were $4,472 billion; time deposits were $1281 billion; and money market funds and other deposits were $968 billion. Calculate M1 and M2 in June 2009.
3. In June 2008, M1 was $1,394 billion; M2 was $7,681 billion; checkable deposits owned by individuals and businesses were $619 billion; time deposits were $1,209 billion; and money market funds and other deposits were $1,057 billion. Calculate currency and traveler's checks held by individuals and businesses and calculate savings deposits.
4. **One More Thing Cell Phones Could Do: Replace Wallets**

   Soon you'll be able to pull out your cell phone and wave it over a scanner to make a payment. The convenience of whipping out your phone as a payment mechanism is driving the transition.

   Source: *USA Today*, November 21, 2007

   If people can use their cell phones to make payments, will currency disappear? How will the components of M1 change?

Depository Institutions (Study Plan 8.2)

Use the following news clip to work Problems 5 and 6.

Regulators Give Bleak Forecast for Banks

Regulators said that they were bracing for an uptick in the number of bank failures. The Fed declined to comment on the health of specific companies but said that Wall Street firms have learned a great deal from Bear Stearns and have reduced leverage and built up their liquidity. Today, investment banks are stronger than they were a month-and-a-half ago.

Source: CNN, June 5, 2008

5. Explain a bank's "balancing act" and how the over-pursuit of profit or underestimation of risk can lead to a bank failure.
6. During a time of uncertainty, why might it be necessary for a bank to build up its liquidity?

The Federal Reserve System (Study Plan 8.3)

7. Suppose that at the end of December 2009, the monetary base in the United States was $700 billion, Federal Reserve notes were $650 billion, and banks' reserves at the Fed were $20 billion. Calculate the quantity of coins.
8. **Risky Assets: Counting to a Trillion**

   Prior to the financial crisis, the Fed held less than $1 trillion in assets and most were in safe U.S. government securities. By mid-December 2008, the Fed's balance sheet had increased to over $2.3 trillion. The massive expansion began when the Fed rolled out its lending program: sending banks cash in exchange for risky assets.

   Source: CNNMoney, September 29, 2009

   What are the Fed's policy tools and which policy tool did the Fed use to increase its assets to $2.3 trillion in 2008?
9. The FOMC sells $20 million of securities to Wells Fargo. Enter the transactions that take place to show the changes in the following balance sheets.

Federal Reserve Bank of New York

Assets (millions)	Liabilities (millions)

Wells Fargo

Assets (millions)	Liabilities (millions)

How Banks Create Money (Study Plan 8.4)

10. The commercial banks in Zap have

Reserves	\$250 million
Loans	\$1,000 million
Deposits	\$2,000 million
Total assets	\$2,500 million

If the banks hold no excess reserves, calculate their desired reserve ratio.

Use the following information to work Problems 11 and 12.

In the economy of Nocoin, banks have deposits of \$300 billion. Their reserves are \$15 billion, two thirds of which is in deposits with the central bank. Households and firms hold \$30 billion in bank notes. There are no coins!

11. Calculate the monetary base and the quantity of money.
12. Calculate the banks' desired reserve ratio and the currency drain ratio (as percentages).

Use the following news clip to work Problems 13 and 14.

Banks Drop on Higher Reserve Requirement

China's central bank will raise its reserve ratio requirement by a percentage point to a record 17.5 percent, stepping up a battle to contain lending growth. Banks' ratio of excess reserves to deposits was 2 percent. Every half-point increase in the required reserve ratio cuts banks' profits by 1.5 percent.

Source: *People's Daily Online*, June 11, 2008

13. Explain how increasing the required reserve ratio impacts banks' money creation process.
14. Why might a higher required reserve ratio decrease bank profits?

The Money Market (Study Plan 8.5)

15. The spreadsheet provides information about the demand for money in Minland. Column A is the nominal interest rate, r. Columns B and C show the quantity of money demanded at two values of real GDP: Y_0 is \$10 billion and Y_1 is \$20 billion. The quantity of money supplied is \$3 billion. Initially, real GDP is \$20 billion. What happens in Minland if the interest rate (i) exceeds 4 percent a year and (ii) is less than 4 percent a year?

	A	B	C
1	r	Y_0	Y_1
2	7	1.0	1.5
3	6	1.5	2.0
4	5	2.0	2.5
5	4	2.5	3.0
6	3	3.0	3.5
7	2	3.5	4.0
8	1	4.0	4.5

16. The figure shows the demand for money curve.

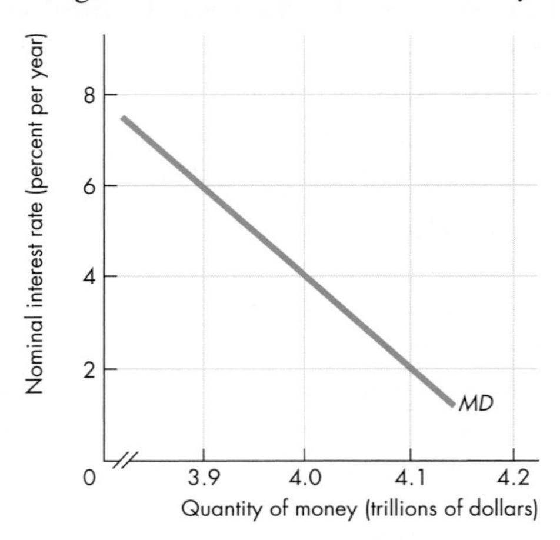

If the Fed decreases the quantity of real money supplied from \$4 trillion to \$3.9 trillion, explain how the price of a bond will change.

The Quantity Theory of Money (Study Plan 8.6)

17. Quantecon is a country in which the quantity theory of money operates. In year 1, the economy is at full employment and real GDP is \$400 million, the price level is 200, and the velocity of circulation is 20. In year 2, the quantity of money increases by 20 percent. Calculate the quantity of money, the price level, real GDP, and the velocity of circulation in year 2.

Mathematical Note (Study Plan 8.MN)

18. In Problem 11, the banks have no excess reserves. Suppose that the Bank of Nocoin, the central bank, increases bank reserves by \$0.5 billion.
    a. What happens to the quantity of money?
    b. Explain why the change in the quantity of money is not equal to the change in the monetary base.
    c. Calculate the money multiplier.
19. In Problem 11, the banks have no excess reserves. Suppose that the Bank of Nocoin, the central bank, decreases bank reserves by \$0.5 billion.
    a. Calculate the money multiplier.
    b. What happens to the quantity of money, deposits, and currency?

ADDITIONAL PROBLEMS AND APPLICATIONS

myeconlab You can work these problems in MyEconLab if assigned by your instructor.

What Is Money?

20. Sara withdraws $1,000 from her savings account at the Lucky S&L, keeps $50 in cash, and deposits the balance in her checking account at the Bank of Illinois. What is the immediate change in M1 and M2?
21. Rapid inflation in Brazil in the early 1990s caused the cruzeiro to lose its ability to function as money. Which of the following commodities would most likely have taken the place of the cruzeiro in the Brazilian economy? Explain why.
    a. Tractor parts
    b. Packs of cigarettes
    c. Loaves of bread
    d. Impressionist paintings
    e. Baseball trading cards
22. **From Paper-Clip to House, in 14 Trades**

    A 26-year-old Montreal man appears to have succeeded in his quest to barter a single, red paper-clip all the way up to a house. It took almost a year and 14 trades. …

    Source: *CBC News*, 7 July 2006

    Is barter a means of payment? Is it just as efficient as money when trading on e-Bay? Explain.

Depository Institutions

Use the following news clip to work Problems 23 and 24.

What Bad Banking Means to You

Bad news about the banking industry makes you wonder about the safety of your cash in the bank. Regulators expect 100–200 bank failures over the next 12–24 months. Expected loan losses, the deteriorating housing market, and the credit squeeze are blamed for the drop in bank profits. The number of institutions classed as "problem" institutions was at 76 at the end of 2007, but, to put that number in perspective, at the end of the banking crisis in 1992 1,063 banks were on that "trouble" list. One thing that will save your money if your bank goes under is FDIC insurance. The FDIC insures deposits in banks and thrift institutions and it maintains that not one depositor has lost a single cent of insured funds as a result of a bank failure since it was created in 1934.

Source: CNN, February 28, 2008

23. Explain how attempts by banks to maximize profits can sometimes lead to bank failures.
24. How does FDIC insurance help minimize bank failures and bring more stability to the banking system?

The Federal Reserve System

25. Explain the distinction between a central bank and a commercial bank.
26. If the Fed makes an open market sale of $1 million of securities to a bank, what initial changes occur in the economy?
27. Set out the transactions that the Fed undertakes to increase the quantity of money.
28. Describe the Fed's assets and liabilities. What is the monetary base and how does it relate to the Fed's balance sheet?
29. **Banks Using Fewer Emergency Loans**

    In a sign of some improvement in the financial crisis, during the week ending July 9 investment banks didn't borrow from the Federal Reserve's emergency lending program and commercial banks also scaled back. In March the Fed scrambled to avert the crisis by giving investment banks a place to go for emergency overnight loans. In exchange for short-term loans of Treasury securities, companies can put up as collateral more risky investments.

    Source: *Time*, July 11, 2008

    What is the rationale behind allowing the Federal Reserve to make loans to banks?

How Banks Create Money

30. Banks in New Transylvania have a desired reserve ratio of 10 percent and no excess reserves. The currency drain ratio is 50 percent. Then the central bank increases the monetary base by $1,200 billion.
    a. How much do the banks lend in the first round of the money creation process?
    b. How much of the initial amount lent flows back to the banking system as new deposits?
    c. How much of the initial amount lent does not return to the banks but is held as currency?
    d. Why does a second round of lending occur?

The Money Market

31. Explain the change in the nominal interest rate in the short run if
   a. Real GDP increases.
   b. The money supply increases.
   c. The price level rises.
32. In Minland in Problem 15, the interest rate is 4 percent a year. Suppose that real GDP decreases to $10 billion and the quantity of money supplied remains unchanged. Do people buy bonds or sell bonds? Explain how the interest rate changes.

The Quantity Theory of Money

33. The table provides some data for the United States in the first decade following the Civil War.

	1869	1879
Quantity of money	$1.3 billion	$1.7 billion
Real GDP (1929 dollars)	$7.4 billion	Z
Price level (1929 = 100)	X	54
Velocity of circulation	4.50	4.61

Source of data: Milton Friedman and Anna J. Schwartz, *A Monetary History of the United States 1867–1960*

   a. Calculate the value of X in 1869.
   b. Calculate the value of Z in 1879.
   c. Are the data consistent with the quantity theory of money? Explain your answer.

Mathematical Note

34. In the United Kingdom, the currency drain ratio is 0.38 of deposits and the reserve ratio is 0.002. In Australia, the quantity of money is $150 billion, the currency drain ratio is 33 percent of deposits, and the reserve ratio is 8 percent.
   a. Calculate the U.K. money multiplier.
   b. Calculate the monetary base in Australia.

Economics in the News

35. After you have studied *Reading Between the Lines* on pp. 202–203 answer the following questions.
   a. What changes in the monetary base have occurred since October 2008?
   b. How does the Fed bring about an increase in the monetary base?
   c. How did the increase in the monetary base change the quantities of M1 and M2? Why?
   d. How did the change in monetary base influence short-term nominal interest rates? Why?
   e. How did the change in monetary base influence long-term nominal interest rates? Why?
   f. How did the change in monetary base influence long-term real interest rates? Why?
36. **Fed at Odds with ECB over Value of Policy Tool**

   Financial innovation and the spread of U.S. currency throughout the world has broken down relationships between money, inflation, and growth, making monetary gauges a less useful tool for policy makers, the U.S. Federal Reserve chairman, Ben Bernanke, said. Many other central banks use monetary aggregates as a guide to policy decision, but Bernanke believes reliance on monetary aggregates would be unwise because empirical relationship between U.S. money growth, inflation, and output growth is unstable. Bernanke said that the Fed had "philosophical" and economic differences with the European Central Bank and the Bank of England regarding the role of money and that debate between institutions was healthy. "Unfortunately, forecast errors for money growth are often significant," reducing their effectiveness as a tool for policy, Bernanke said. "There are differences between the U.S. and Europe in terms of the stability of money demand," Bernanke said. Ultimately, the risk of bad policy arising from a devoted following of money growth led the Fed to downgrade the importance of money measures.

   Source: *International Herald Tribune*, November 10, 2006

   a. Explain how the debate surrounding the quantity theory of money could make "monetary gauges a less useful tool for policy makers."
   b. What do Bernanke's statements reveal about his stance on the accuracy of the quantity theory of money?

After studying this chapter, you will be able to:

- Describe the foreign exchange market and explain how the exchange rate is determined day by day
- Explain the trends and fluctuations in the exchange rate and explain interest rate parity and purchasing power parity
- Describe the alternative exchange rate policies and explain their effects
- Describe the balance of payments accounts and explain what causes an international deficit

9 THE EXCHANGE RATE AND THE BALANCE OF PAYMENTS

The dollar ($), the euro (€), and the yen (¥) are three of the world's monies and most international payments are made using one of them. But the world has more than 100 different monies.

In October 2000, one U.S. dollar bought 1.17 euros, but from 2000 through 2008, the dollar sank against the euro and by July 2008 one U.S. dollar bought only 63 euro cents. Why did the dollar fall against the euro? Can or should the United States do anything to stabilize the value of the dollar?

Every year since 1988, foreign entrepreneurs have roamed the United States with giant virtual shopping carts and loaded them up with Gerber, Firestone, Columbia Pictures, Ben & Jerry's, and Anheuser-Busch, all of which are now controlled by Japanese or European companies. Why have foreigners been buying U.S. businesses?

In this chapter, you're going to discover the answers to these questions. In *Reading Between the Lines* at the end of the chapter, we'll look at a risky investment strategy that exploits interest rate differences and the foreign exchange market.

The Foreign Exchange Market

When Wal-Mart imports DVD players from Japan, it pays for them using Japanese yen. And when Japan Airlines buys an airplane from Boeing, it pays using U.S. dollars. Whenever people buy things from another country, they use the currency of that country to make the transaction. It doesn't make any difference what the item is that is being traded internationally. It might be a DVD player, an airplane, insurance or banking services, real estate, the stocks and bonds of a government or corporation, or even an entire business.

Foreign money is just like U.S. money. It consists of notes and coins issued by a central bank and mint and deposits in banks and other depository institutions. When we described U.S. money in Chapter 8, we distinguished between currency (notes and coins) and deposits. But when we talk about foreign money, we refer to it as foreign currency. **Foreign currency** is the money of other countries regardless of whether that money is in the form of notes, coins, or bank deposits.

We buy these foreign currencies and foreigners buy U.S. dollars in the foreign exchange market.

Trading Currencies

The currency of one country is exchanged for the currency of another in the **foreign exchange market.** The foreign exchange market is not a place like a downtown flea market or a fruit and vegetable market. The foreign exchange market is made up of thousands of people—importers and exporters, banks, international investors and speculators, international travelers, and specialist traders called *foreign exchange brokers.*

The foreign exchange market opens on Monday morning in Sydney, Australia, and Hong Kong, which is still Sunday evening in New York. As the day advances, markets open in Singapore, Tokyo, Bahrain, Frankfurt, London, New York, Chicago, and San Francisco. As the West Coast markets close, Sydney is only an hour away from opening for the next day of business. The sun barely sets in the foreign exchange market. Dealers around the world are in continual contact by telephone and computer, and on a typical day in 2010, around $3 trillion (of all currencies) were traded in the foreign exchange market—or more than $600 trillion in a year.

Exchange Rates

An **exchange rate** is the price at which one currency exchanges for another currency in the foreign exchange market. For example, on September 1, 2010, $1 would buy 84 Japanese yen or 79 euro cents. So the exchange rate was 84 yen per dollar or, equivalently, 79 euro cents per dollar.

The exchange rate fluctuates. Sometimes it rises and sometimes it falls. A rise in the exchange rate is called an *appreciation* of the dollar, and a fall in the exchange rate is called a *depreciation* of the dollar. For example, when the exchange rate rises from 84 yen to 100 yen per dollar, the dollar appreciates, and when the exchange rate falls from 100 yen to 84 yen per dollar, the dollar depreciates.

Economics in Action on the next page shows the fluctuations in the U.S. dollar against three currencies since 2000.

Questions About the U.S. Dollar Exchange Rate

The performance of the U.S. dollar in the foreign exchange market raises a number of questions that we address in this chapter.

First, how is the exchange rate determined? Why did the U.S. dollar appreciate from 2000 to 2002 and then begin to depreciate?

Second, how do the Fed and other central banks operate in the foreign exchange market? In particular, how was the exchange rate between the U.S. dollar and the Chinese yuan fixed and why did it remain constant for many years?

Third, how do exchange rate fluctuations influence our international trade and international payments? In particular, could we eliminate, or at least decrease, our international deficit by changing the exchange rate? Would an appreciation of the yuan change the balance of trade and payments between the United States and China?

We begin by learning how trading in the foreign exchange market determines the exchange rate.

An Exchange Rate Is a Price

An exchange rate is a price—the price of one currency in terms of another. And like all prices, an exchange rate is determined in a market—the *foreign exchange market.*

The U.S. dollar trades in the foreign exchange market and is supplied and demanded by tens of

Economics in Action

The U.S. Dollar: More Down than Up

The figure shows the U.S. dollar exchange rate against the three currencies that feature prominently in U.S. imports—the Chinese yuan, the European euro, and the Japanese yen—between 2000 and 2010.

Against the Chinese yuan, the dollar was constant before 2005 and then started to depreciate. Against the European euro and the Japanese yen, the dollar appreciated before 2002 and then mainly depreciated but staged a brief appreciation against the yen in 2005–2007.

Notice the high-frequency fluctuations (rapid brief up and down movements) of the dollar against the euro and the yen compared to the smooth changes against the yuan. Think about why that might be, and we'll check your answer later in this chapter.

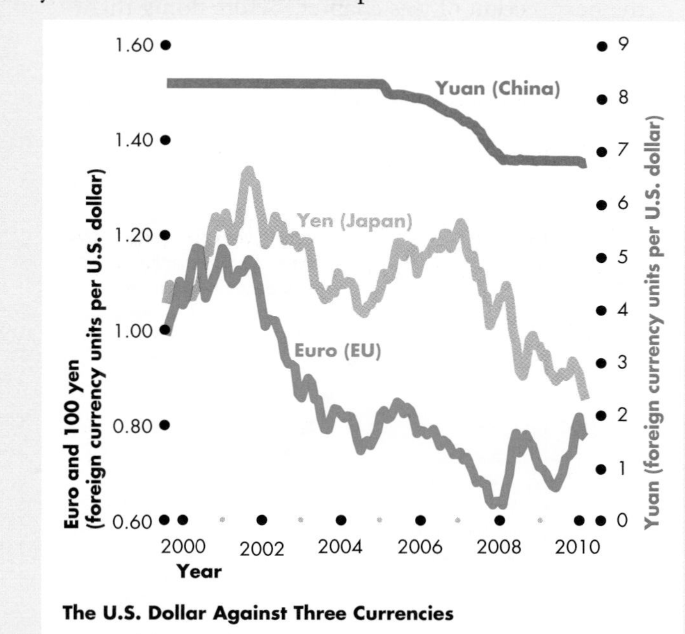

The U.S. Dollar Against Three Currencies

Source of data: Pacific Exchange Rate Service

thousands of traders every hour of every business day. Because it has many traders and no restrictions on who may trade, the foreign exchange market is a *competitive market.*

In a competitive market, demand and supply determine the price. So to understand the forces that determine the exchange rate, we need to study the factors that influence demand and supply in the foreign exchange market. But there is a feature of the foreign exchange market that makes it special.

The Demand for One Money Is the Supply of Another Money

When people who are holding the money of some other country want to exchange it for U.S. dollars, they demand U.S. dollars and supply that other country's money. And when people who are holding U.S. dollars want to exchange them for the money of some other country, they supply U.S. dollars and demand that other country's money.

So the factors that influence the demand for U.S. dollars also influence the supply of European Union euros, or Japanese yen, or Chinese yuan. And the factors that influence the demand for that other country's money also influence the supply of U.S. dollars.

We'll first look at the influences on the demand for U.S. dollars in the foreign exchange market.

Demand in the Foreign Exchange Market

People buy U.S. dollars in the foreign exchange market so that they can buy U.S.-produced goods and services—U.S. exports. They also buy U.S. dollars so that they can buy U.S. assets such as bonds, stocks, businesses, and real estate or so that they can keep part of their money holding in a U.S. dollar bank account.

The quantity of U.S. dollars demanded in the foreign exchange market is the amount that traders plan to buy during a given time period at a given exchange rate. This quantity depends on many factors, but the main ones are

1. The exchange rate
2. World demand for U.S. exports
3. Interest rates in the United States and other countries
4. The expected future exchange rate

We look first at the relationship between the quantity of U.S. dollars demanded in the foreign exchange market and the exchange rate when the other three influences remain the same.

The Law of Demand for Foreign Exchange The law of demand applies to U.S. dollars just as it does to anything else that people value. Other things remaining the same, the higher the exchange rate, the smaller is the quantity of U.S. dollars demanded in the foreign exchange market. For example, if the price of the U.S. dollar rises from 100 yen to 120 yen but nothing else changes, the quantity of U.S. dollars that people plan to buy in the foreign exchange market decreases. The exchange rate influences the quantity of U.S. dollars demanded for two reasons:

- Exports effect
- Expected profit effect

Exports Effect The larger the value of U.S. exports, the larger is the quantity of U.S. dollars demanded in the foreign exchange market. But the value of U.S. exports depends on the prices of U.S.-produced goods and services *expressed in the currency of the foreign buyer*. And these prices depend on the exchange rate. The lower the exchange rate, other things remaining the same, the lower are the prices of U.S.-produced goods and services to foreigners and the greater is the volume of U.S. exports. So if the exchange rate falls (and other influences remain the same), the quantity of U.S. dollars demanded in the foreign exchange market increases.

To see the exports effect at work, think about orders for Boeing's new 787 airplane. If the price of a 787 is $100 million and the exchange rate is 90 euro cents per U.S. dollar, the price of this airplane to KLM, a European airline, is €90 million. KLM decides that this price is too high, so it doesn't buy a new 787. If the exchange rate falls to 80 euro cents per U.S. dollar and other things remain the same, the price of a 787 falls to €80 million. KLM now decides to buy a 787 and buys U.S. dollars in the foreign exchange market.

Expected Profit Effect The larger the expected profit from holding U.S. dollars, the greater is the quantity of U.S. dollars demanded in the foreign exchange market. But expected profit depends on the exchange rate. For a given expected future exchange rate, the lower the exchange rate today, the larger is the expected profit from buying U.S. dollars today and holding them, so the greater is the quantity of U.S. dollars demanded in the foreign exchange market today. Let's look at an example.

Suppose that Mizuho Bank, a Japanese bank, expects the exchange rate to be 120 yen per U.S. dollar at the end of the year. If today's exchange rate is also 120 yen per U.S. dollar, Mizuho Bank expects no profit from buying U.S. dollars and holding them until the end of the year. But if today's exchange rate is 100 yen per U.S. dollar and Mizuho Bank buys U.S. dollars, it expects to sell those dollars at the end of the year for 120 yen per dollar and make a profit of 20 yen per U.S. dollar.

The lower the exchange rate today, other things remaining the same, the greater is the expected profit from holding U.S. dollars and the greater is the quantity of U.S. dollars demanded in the foreign exchange market today.

Demand Curve for U.S. Dollars

Figure 9.1 shows the demand curve for U.S. dollars in the foreign exchange market. A change in the exchange rate, other things remaining the same, brings a change in the quantity of U.S. dollars demanded and a movement along the demand curve. The arrows show such movements.

We will look at the factors that *change* demand in the next section of this chapter. Before doing that, let's see what determines the supply of U.S. dollars.

FIGURE 9.1 The Demand for U.S. Dollars

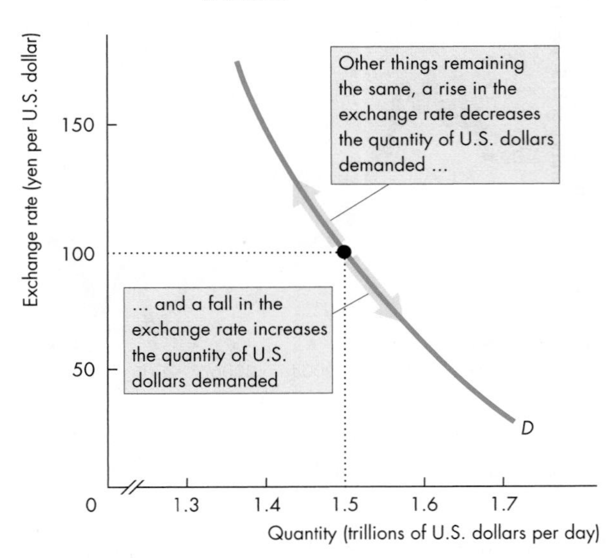

The quantity of U.S. dollars demanded depends on the exchange rate. Other things remaining the same, if the exchange rate rises, the quantity of U.S. dollars demanded decreases and there is a movement up along the demand curve for U.S. dollars. If the exchange rate falls, the quantity of U.S. dollars demanded increases and there is a movement down along the demand curve for U.S. dollars.

Supply in the Foreign Exchange Market

People sell U.S. dollars and buy other currencies so that they can buy foreign-produced goods and services—U.S. imports. People also sell U.S. dollars and buy foreign currencies so that they can buy foreign assets such as bonds, stocks, businesses, and real estate or so that they can hold part of their money in bank deposits denominated in a foreign currency.

The quantity of U.S. dollars supplied in the foreign exchange market is the amount that traders plan to sell during a given time period at a given exchange rate. This quantity depends on many factors, but the main ones are

1. The exchange rate
2. U.S. demand for imports
3. Interest rates in the United States and other countries
4. The expected future exchange rate

Let's look at the law of supply in the foreign exchange market—the relationship between the quantity of U.S. dollars supplied in the foreign exchange market and the exchange rate when the other three influences remain the same.

The Law of Supply of Foreign Exchange Other things remaining the same, the higher the exchange rate, the greater is the quantity of U.S. dollars supplied in the foreign exchange market. For example, if the exchange rate rises from 100 yen to 120 yen per U.S. dollar and other things remain the same, the quantity of U.S. dollars that people plan to sell in the foreign exchange market increases.

The exchange rate influences the quantity of dollars supplied for two reasons:

- Imports effect
- Expected profit effect

Imports Effect The larger the value of U.S. imports, the larger is the quantity of U.S. dollars supplied in the foreign exchange market. But the value of U.S. imports depends on the prices of foreign-produced goods and services *expressed in U.S. dollars*. These prices depend on the exchange rate. The higher the exchange rate, other things remaining the same, the lower are the prices of foreign-produced goods and services to Americans and the greater is the volume of U.S. imports. So if the exchange rate rises (and other influences remain the same), the quantity of U.S. dollars supplied in the foreign exchange market increases.

Expected Profit Effect This effect works just like that on the demand for the U.S. dollar but in the opposite direction. The higher the exchange rate today, other things remaining the same, the larger is the expected profit from selling U.S. dollars today and holding foreign currencies, so the greater is the quantity of U.S. dollars supplied.

Supply Curve for U.S. Dollars

Figure 9.2 shows the supply curve of U.S. dollars in the foreign exchange market. A change in the exchange rate, other things remaining the same, brings a change in the quantity of U.S. dollars supplied and a movement along the supply curve. The arrows show such movements.

FIGURE 9.2 The Supply of U.S. Dollars

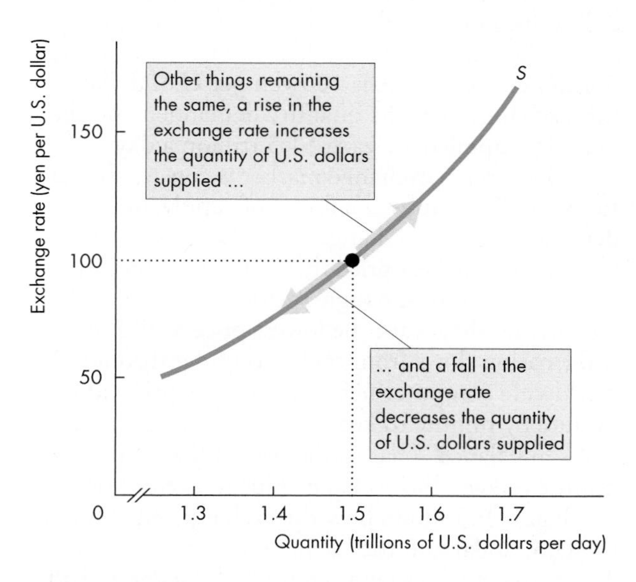

The quantity of U.S. dollars supplied depends on the exchange rate. Other things remaining the same, if the exchange rate rises, the quantity of U.S. dollars supplied increases and there is a movement up along the supply curve of U.S. dollars. If the exchange rate falls, the quantity of U.S. dollars supplied decreases and there is a movement down along the supply curve of U.S. dollars.

myeconlab animation

Market Equilibrium

Equilibrium in the foreign exchange market depends on how the Federal Reserve and other central banks operate. Here, we will study equilibrium when central banks keep out of this market. In a later section (on pp. 222–224), we examine the effects of alternative actions that the Fed or another central bank might take in the foreign exchange market.

Figure 9.3 shows the demand curve for U.S. dollars, *D*, from Fig. 9.1 and the supply curve of U.S. dollars, *S*, from Fig. 9.2, and the equilibrium exchange rate.

The exchange rate acts as a regulator of the quantities demanded and supplied. If the exchange rate is too high, there is a surplus—the quantity supplied exceeds the quantity demanded. For example, in Fig. 9.3, if the exchange rate is 150 yen per U.S. dollar, there is a surplus of U.S. dollars. If the exchange rate is too low, there is a shortage—the quantity supplied is less than the quantity demanded. For example, if the exchange rate is 50 yen per U.S. dollar, there is a shortage of U.S. dollars.

At the equilibrium exchange rate, there is neither a shortage nor a surplus—the quantity supplied equals the quantity demanded. In Fig. 9.3, the equilibrium exchange rate is 100 yen per U.S. dollar. At this exchange rate, the quantity demanded and the quantity supplied are each $1.5 trillion a day.

The foreign exchange market is constantly pulled to its equilibrium by the forces of supply and demand. Foreign exchange traders are constantly looking for the best price they can get. If they are selling, they want the highest price available. If they are buying, they want the lowest price available. Information flows from trader to trader through the worldwide computer network, and the price adjusts minute by minute to keep buying plans and selling plans in balance. That is, the price adjusts minute by minute to keep the exchange rate at its equilibrium.

Figure 9.3 shows how the exchange rate between the U.S. dollar and the Japanese yen is determined. The exchange rates between the U.S. dollar and all other currencies are determined in a similar way. So are the exchange rates among the other currencies. But the exchange rates are tied together so that no profit can be made by buying one currency, selling it for a second one, and then buying back the first one. If such a profit were available, traders would spot it, demand and supply would change, and the exchange rates would snap into alignment.

FIGURE 9.3 Equilibrium Exchange Rate

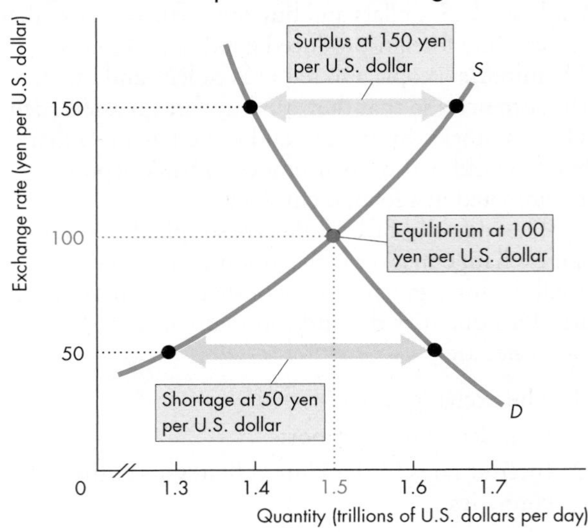

The demand curve for U.S. dollars is *D*, and the supply curve of U.S. dollars is *S*. If the exchange rate is 150 yen per U.S. dollar, there is a surplus of U.S. dollars and the exchange rate falls. If the exchange rate is 50 yen per U.S. dollar, there is a shortage of U.S. dollars and the exchange rate rises. If the exchange rate is 100 yen per U.S. dollar, there is neither a shortage nor a surplus of U.S. dollars and the exchange rate remains constant. The foreign exchange market is in equilibrium.

REVIEW QUIZ

1. What are the influences on the demand for U.S. dollars in the foreign exchange market?
2. Provide an example of the exports effect on the demand for U.S. dollars.
3. What are the influences on the supply of U.S. dollars in the foreign exchange market?
4. Provide an example of the imports effect on the supply of U.S. dollars.
5. How is the equilibrium exchange rate determined?
6. What happens if there is a shortage or a surplus of U.S. dollars in the foreign exchange market?

You can work these questions in Study Plan 9.1 and get instant feedback.

Exchange Rate Fluctuations

You've seen (in *Economics in Action* on p. 213) that the U.S. dollar fluctuates a lot against the yen and the euro. Changes in the demand for U.S. dollars or the supply of U.S. dollars bring these exchange rate fluctuations. We'll now look at the factors that make demand and supply change, starting with the demand side of the market.

Changes in the Demand for U.S. Dollars

The demand for U.S. dollars in the foreign exchange market changes when there is a change in

- World demand for U.S. exports
- U.S. interest rate relative to the foreign interest rate
- The expected future exchange rate

World Demand for U.S. Exports An increase in world demand for U.S. exports increases the demand for U.S. dollars. To see this effect, think about Boeing's airplane sales. An increase in demand for air travel in Australia sends that country's airlines on a global shopping spree. They decide that the 787 is the ideal product, so they order 50 airplanes from Boeing. The demand for U.S. dollars now increases.

U.S. Interest Rate Relative to the Foreign Interest Rate People and businesses buy financial assets to make a return. The higher the interest rate that people can make on U.S. assets compared with foreign assets, the more U.S. assets they buy.

What matters is not the *level* of the U.S. interest rate, but the U.S. interest rate minus the foreign interest rate—a gap that is called the **U.S. interest rate differential.** If the U.S. interest rate rises and the foreign interest rate remains constant, the U.S. interest rate differential increases. The larger the U.S. interest rate differential, the greater is the demand for U.S. assets and the greater is the demand for U.S. dollars in the foreign exchange market.

The Expected Future Exchange Rate For a given current exchange rate, other things remaining the same, a rise in the expected future exchange rate increases the profit that people expect to make by holding U.S. dollars and the demand for U.S. dollars increases today.

Figure 9.4 summarizes the influences on the demand for U.S. dollars. An increase in the demand for U.S. exports, a rise in the U.S. interest rate differential, or a rise in the expected future exchange rate increases the demand for U.S. dollars today and shifts the demand curve rightward from D_0 to D_1. A decrease in the demand for U.S. exports, a fall in the U.S. interest rate differential, or a fall in the expected future exchange rate decreases the demand for U.S. dollars today and shifts the demand curve leftward from D_0 to D_2.

FIGURE 9.4 Changes in the Demand for U.S. Dollars

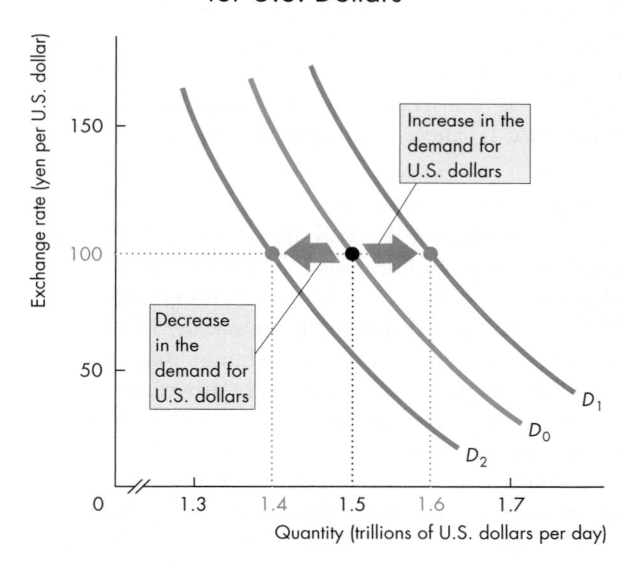

A change in any influence on the quantity of U.S. dollars that people plan to buy, other than the exchange rate, brings a change in the demand for U.S. dollars.

The demand for U.S. dollars

Increases if:	*Decreases if:*
World demand for U.S. exports increases	World demand for U.S. exports decreases
The U.S. interest rate differential rises	The U.S. interest rate differential falls
The expected future exchange rate rises	The expected future exchange rate falls

myeconlab animation

Changes in the Supply of U.S. Dollars

The supply of U.S. dollars in the foreign exchange market changes when there is a change in

- U.S. demand for imports
- U.S. interest rate relative to the foreign interest rate
- The expected future exchange rate

U.S. Demand for Imports An increase in the U.S. demand for imports increases the supply of U.S. dollars in the foreign exchange market. To see why, think about Wal-Mart's purchase of DVD players. An increase in the demand for DVD players sends Wal-Mart out on a global shopping spree. Wal-Mart decides that Panasonic DVD players produced in Japan are the best buy, so Wal-Mart increases its purchases of these players. The supply of U.S. dollars now increases as Wal-Mart goes to the foreign exchange market for Japanese yen to pay Panasonic.

U.S. Interest Rate Relative to the Foreign Interest Rate The effect of the U.S. interest rate differential on the supply of U.S. dollars is the opposite of its effect on the demand for U.S. dollars. The larger the U.S. interest rate differential, the *smaller* is the supply of U.S. dollars in the foreign exchange market.

With a higher U.S. interest rate differential, people decide to keep more of their funds in U.S. dollar assets and less in foreign currency assets. They buy a smaller quantity of foreign currency and sell a smaller quantity of dollars in the foreign exchange market.

So, a rise in the U.S. interest rate, other things remaining the same, decreases the supply of U.S. dollars in the foreign exchange market.

The Expected Future Exchange Rate For a given current exchange rate, other things remaining the same, a fall in the expected future exchange rate decreases the profit that can be made by holding U.S. dollars and decreases the quantity of U.S. dollars that people want to hold. To reduce their holdings of U.S. dollar assets, people must sell U.S. dollars. When they do so, the supply of U.S. dollars in the foreign exchange market increases.

Figure 9.5 summarizes the influences on the supply of U.S. dollars. If the supply of U.S. dollars decreases, the supply curve shifts leftward from S_0 to S_1. And if the supply of U.S. dollars increases, the supply curve shifts rightward from S_0 to S_2.

FIGURE 9.5 Changes in the Supply of U.S. Dollars

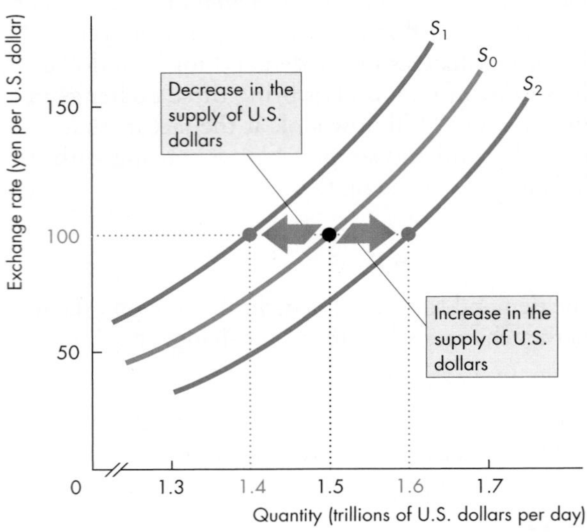

A change in any influence on the quantity of U.S. dollars that people plan to sell, other than the exchange rate, brings a change in the supply of dollars.

The supply of U.S. dollars

Increases if:	*Decreases if:*
■ U.S. import demand increases	■ U.S. import demand decreases
■ The U.S. interest rate differential falls	■ The U.S. interest rate differential rises
■ The expected future exchange rate falls	■ The expected future exchange rate rises

Changes in the Exchange Rate

If the demand for U.S. dollars increases and the supply does not change, the exchange rate rises. If the demand for U.S. dollars decreases and the supply does not change, the exchange rate falls. Similarly, if the supply of U.S. dollars decreases and the demand does not change, the exchange rate rises. If the supply of U.S. dollars increases and the demand does not change, the exchange rate falls.

These predictions are exactly the same as those for any other market. Two episodes in the life of the U.S. dollar (next page) illustrate these predictions.

Economics in Action

The Dollar on a Roller Coaster

The foreign exchange market is a striking example of a competitive market. The expectations of thousands of traders around the world influence this market minute-by-minute throughout the 24-hour global trading day.

Demand and supply rarely stand still and their fluctuations bring a fluctuating exchange rate. Two episodes in the life of the dollar illustrate these fluctuations: 2005–2007, when the dollar appreciated and 2007–2008, when the dollar depreciated.

An Appreciating U.S. Dollar: 2005–2007 Between January 2005 and July 2007, the U.S. dollar appreciated against the yen. It rose from 103 yen to 123 yen per U.S. dollar. Part (a) of the figure provides an explanation for this appreciation.

In 2005, the demand and supply curves were those labeled D_{05} and S_{05}. The exchange rate was 103 yen per U.S. dollar.

During 2005 and 2006, the Federal Reserve raised the interest rate, but the interest rate in Japan barely changed. With an increase in the U.S. interest rate differential, funds flowed into the United States. Also, currency traders, anticipating this increased flow of funds into the United States, expected the dollar to appreciate against the yen. The demand for U.S. dollars increased, and the supply of U.S. dollars decreased.

In the figure, the demand curve shifted rightward from D_{05} to D_{07} and the supply curve shifted leftward from S_{05} to S_{07}. The exchange rate rose to 123 yen per U.S. dollar. In the figure, the equilibrium quantity remained unchanged—an assumption.

A Depreciating U.S. Dollar: 2007–2008 Between July 2007 and September 2008, the U.S. dollar depreciated against the yen. It fell from 123 yen to 107 yen per U.S. dollar. Part (b) of the figure provides a possible explanation for this depreciation. The demand and supply curves labeled D_{07} and S_{07} are the same as in part (a).

During the last quarter of 2007 and the first three quarters of 2008, the U.S. economy entered a severe credit crisis and the Federal Reserve cut the interest rate in the United States. But the Bank of Japan kept the interest rate unchanged in Japan. With a narrowing of the U.S. interest rate differential, funds flowed out of the United States. Also, currency traders expected the U.S. dollar to depreciate against the yen. The demand for U.S. dollars decreased and the supply of U.S. dollars increased.

In part (b) of the figure, the demand curve shifted leftward from D_{07} to D_{08}, the supply curve shifted rightward from S_{07} to S_{08}, and the exchange rate fell to 107 yen per U.S. dollar.

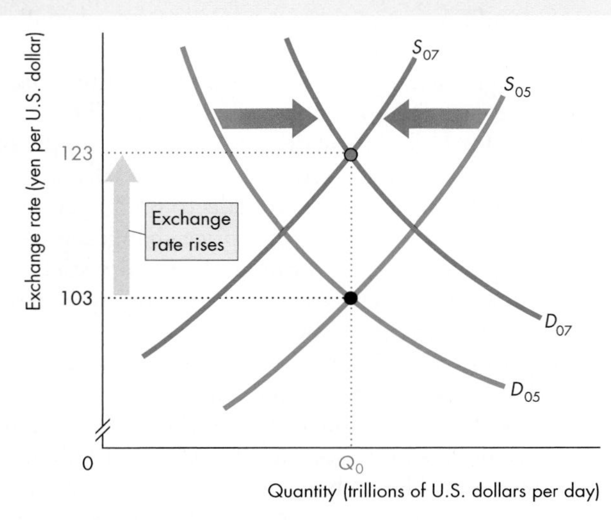

(a) 2005–2007

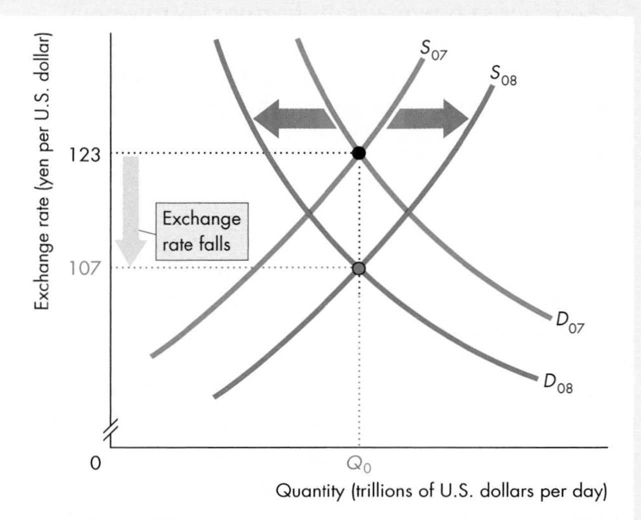

(b) 2007–2008

The Rising and Falling U.S. Dollar

Fundamentals, Expectations, and Arbitrage

Changes in the *expected* exchange rate change the *actual* exchange rate. But what makes the expected exchange rate change? The answer is new information about the *fundamental influences* on the exchange rate—the world demand for U.S. exports, U.S. demand for imports, and the U.S. interest rate relative to the foreign interest rate. Expectations about these variables change the exchange rate through their influence on the expected exchange rate, and the effect is instant.

To see why, suppose news breaks that the Fed will raise the interest rate next week. Traders now expect the demand for dollars to increase and the dollar to appreciate: They expect to profit by buying dollars today and selling them next week for a higher price than they paid. The rise in the expected future value of the dollar increases the demand for dollars today, decreases the supply of dollars today, and raises the exchange rate. The exchange rate changes as soon as the news about a fundamental influence is received.

Profiting by trading in the foreign exchange market often involves *arbitrage*: The practice of buying in one market and selling for a higher price in another related market. Arbitrage ensures that the exchange rate is the same in New York, London, and all other trading centers. It isn't possible to buy at a low price in London and sell for a higher price in New York. If it were possible, demand would increase in London and decrease in New York to make the prices equal.

Arbitrage also removes profit from borrowing in one currency and lending in another and buying goods in one currency and selling them in another. These arbitrage activities bring about

- Interest rate parity
- Purchasing power parity

Interest Rate Parity Suppose a bank deposit earns 1 percent a year in Tokyo and 3 percent a year in New York. Why wouldn't people move their funds to New York, and even borrow in Japan to do so? The answer is that some would, in an activity called the "carry trade" (see *Reading Between the Lines* on pp. 230–231). The New York deposit is in dollars and the Tokyo deposit is in yen. So a change in the exchange rate brings risk to borrowing in one currency and lending in another. If investors *expect* the yen to appreciate by 2 percent a year and they buy and hold yen for a year they will earn 1 percent interest and *expect* a 2 percent return from the higher yen. The total *expected* return is 3 percent, the same as on U.S. dollars in New York.

This situation is called **interest rate parity**, which means equal rates of return. Adjusted for risk, interest rate parity always prevails. Funds move to get the highest *expected* return available. If for a few seconds a higher return is available in New York than in Tokyo, the demand for U.S. dollars increases and the exchange rate rises until the expected rates of return are equal.

Purchasing Power Parity Suppose a memory stick costs 5,000 yen in Tokyo and $50 in New York. If the exchange rate is 100 yen per dollar, the two monies have the same value. You can buy a memory stick in either Tokyo or New York for the same price. You can express that price as either 5,000 yen or $50, but the price is the same in the two currencies.

The situation we've just described is called **purchasing power parity**, which means *equal value of money*. If purchasing power parity does not prevail, powerful arbitrage forces go to work. To see these forces, suppose that the price of a memory stick in New York rises to $60, but in Tokyo it remains at 5,000 yen. Further, suppose the exchange rate remains at 100 yen per dollar. In this case, a memory stick in Tokyo still costs 5,000 yen or $50, but in New York, it costs $60 or 6,000 yen. Money buys more in Japan than in the United States. Money is not of equal value in the two countries.

If all (or most) prices have increased in the United States and not increased in Japan, then people will generally expect that the value of the U.S. dollar in the foreign exchange market must fall. In this situation, the exchange rate is expected to fall. The demand for U.S. dollars decreases, and the supply of U.S. dollars increases. The exchange rate falls, as expected. If the exchange rate falls to 83.33 yen per dollar and there are no further price changes, purchasing power parity is restored. A memory stick that costs $60 in New York also costs the equivalent of $60 ($60 \times 83.33 = 5{,}000$) in Tokyo.

If prices rise in Japan and other countries but remain constant in the United States, then people will expect the U.S. dollar to appreciate. The demand for U.S. dollars increases, and the supply of U.S. dollars decreases. The exchange rate rises, as expected.

So far we've been looking at the forces that determine the *nominal* exchange rate—the amount of one money that another money buys. We're now going to study the *real* exchange rate.

The Real Exchange Rate

The **real exchange rate** is the relative price of U.S.-produced goods and services to foreign-produced goods and services. It is a measure of the quantity of the real GDP of other countries that a unit of U.S. real GDP buys.

The real Japanese yen exchange rate, *RER*, is

$$RER = (E \times P)/P^*,$$

where E is the exchange rate (yen per U.S. dollar), P is the U.S. price level, and P^* is the Japanese price level.

To understand the real exchange rate, suppose that each country produces only one good and that the exchange rate E is 100 yen per dollar. The United States produces only computer chips priced at $150 each, so P equals $150 and $E \times P$ equals 15,000 yen. Japan produces only iPods priced at 5,000 yen each, so P^* equals 5,000 yen. Then the real Japanese yen exchange rate is

$$RER = (100 \times 150)/5{,}000 = 3 \text{ iPods per chip.}$$

The Short Run In the short run, if the nominal exchange rate changes, the real exchange rate also changes. The reason is that prices and the price levels in the United States and Japan don't change every time the exchange rate changes. Sticking with the chips and iPods example, if the dollar appreciates to 200 yen per dollar and prices don't change, the real exchange rate rises to 6 iPods per chip. The price of an iPod in the United States falls to $25 (5,000 yen ÷ 200 yen per dollar = $25).

Changes in the real exchange rate bring short-run changes in the quantity of imports demanded and the quantity of exports supplied.

The Long Run But in the long run, the situation is radically different: In the long run, the nominal exchange rate and the price level are determined together and the real exchange rate does *not* change when the nominal exchange rate changes.

In the long run, demand and supply in the markets for goods and services determine prices. In the chips and iPod example, the world markets for chips and iPods determine their *relative* price. In our example the relative price is 3 iPods per chip. The same forces determine all relative prices and so determine nations' relative price levels.

In the long run, if the dollar appreciates prices *do* change. To see why, recall the quantity theory of money that you met in Chapter 8 (pp. 200–201).

In the long run, the quantity of money determines the price level. But the quantity theory of money applies to all countries, so the quantity of money in Japan determines the price level in Japan, and the quantity of money in the United States determines the price level in the United States.

For a given real exchange rate, a change in the quantity of money brings a change in the price level *and* a change in the exchange rate.

Suppose that the quantity of money doubles in Japan. The dollar appreciates (the yen depreciatates) from 100 yen per dollar to 200 yen per dollar and all prices double, so the price of an iPod rises from 5,000 yen to 10,000 yen.

At the new price in Japan and the new exchange rate, an iPod still costs $50 (10,000 yen ÷ 200 yen per dollar = $50). The real exchange rate remains at 3 iPods per chip.

If Japan and the United States produced identical goods (if GDP in both countries consisted only of computer chips), the real exchange rate in the long run would equal 1.

In reality, although there is overlap in what each country produces, U.S. real GDP is a different bundle of goods and services from Japanese real GDP. So the relative price of Japanese and U.S. real GDP—the real exchange rate—is not 1, and it changes over time. The forces of demand and supply in the markets for the millions of goods and services that make up real GDP determine the relative price of Japanese and U.S. real GDP, and changes in these forces change the real exchange rate.

REVIEW QUIZ

1. Why does the demand for U.S. dollars change?
2. Why does the supply of U.S. dollars change?
3. What makes the U.S. dollar exchange rate fluctuate?
4. What is interest rate parity and what happens when this condition doesn't hold?
5. What is purchasing power parity and what happens when this condition doesn't hold?
6. What determines the real exchange rate and the nominal exchange rate in the short run?
7. What determines the real exchange rate and the nominal exchange rate in the long run?

You can work these questions in Study Plan 9.2 and get instant feedback.

Exchange Rate Policy

Because the exchange rate is the price of a country's money in terms of another country's money, governments and central banks must have a policy toward the exchange rate. Three possible exchange rate policies are

- Flexible exchange rate
- Fixed exchange rate
- Crawling peg

Flexible Exchange Rate

A **flexible exchange rate** is an exchange rate that is determined by demand and supply in the foreign exchange market with no direct intervention by the central bank.

Most countries, including the United States, operate a flexible exchange rate, and the foreign exchange market that we have studied so far in this chapter is an example of a flexible exchange rate regime.

But even a flexible exchange rate is influenced by central bank actions. If the Fed raises the U.S. interest rate and other countries keep their interest rates unchanged, the demand for U.S. dollars increases, the supply of U.S. dollars decreases, and the exchange rate rises. (Similarly, if the Fed lowers the U.S. interest rate, the demand for U.S. dollars decreases, the supply increases, and the exchange rate falls.)

In a flexible exchange rate regime, when the central bank changes the interest rate, its purpose is not usually to influence the exchange rate, but to achieve some other monetary policy objective. (We return to this topic at length in Chapter 14.)

Fixed Exchange Rate

A **fixed exchange rate** is an exchange rate that is determined by a decision of the government or the central bank and is achieved by central bank intervention in the foreign exchange market to block the unregulated forces of demand and supply.

The world economy operated a fixed exchange rate regime from the end of World War II to the early 1970s. China had a fixed exchange rate until recently. Hong Kong has had a fixed exchange rate for many years and continues with that policy today.

Active intervention in the foreign exchange market is required to achieve a fixed exchange rate.

If the Fed wanted to fix the U.S. dollar exchange rate against the Japanese yen, the Fed would have to sell U.S. dollars to prevent the exchange rate from rising above the target value and buy U.S. dollars to prevent the exchange rate from falling below the target value.

There is no limit to the quantity of U.S. dollars that the Fed can *sell*. The Fed creates U.S. dollars and can create any quantity it chooses. But there is a limit to the quantity of U.S. dollars the Fed can *buy*. That limit is set by U.S. official foreign currency reserves because to buy U.S. dollars the Fed must sell foreign currency. Intervention to buy U.S. dollars stops when U.S. official foreign currency reserves run out.

Let's look at the foreign exchange interventions that the Fed can make.

Suppose the Fed wants the exchange rate to be steady at 100 yen per U.S. dollar. If the exchange rate rises above 100 yen, the Fed sells dollars. If the exchange rate falls below 100 yen, the Fed buys dollars. By these actions, the Fed keeps the exchange rate close to its target rate of 100 yen per U.S. dollar.

Figure 9.6 shows the Fed's intervention in the foreign exchange market. The supply of dollars is S and initially the demand for dollars is D_0. The equilibrium exchange rate is 100 yen per dollar. This exchange rate is also the Fed's target exchange rate, shown by the horizontal red line.

When the demand for U.S. dollars increases and the demand curve shifts rightward to D_1, the Fed sells \$100 billion. This action prevents the exchange rate from rising. When the demand for U.S. dollars decreases and the demand curve shifts leftward to D_2, the Fed buys \$100 billion. This action prevents the exchange rate from falling.

If the demand for U.S. dollars fluctuates between D_1 and D_2 and on average is D_0, the Fed can repeatedly intervene in the way we've just seen. Sometimes the Fed buys and sometimes it sells but, on average, it neither buys nor sells.

But suppose the demand for U.S. dollars *increases permanently* from D_0 to D_1. To maintain the exchange rate at 100 yen per U.S. dollar, the Fed must sell dollars and buy foreign currency, so U.S. official foreign currency reserves would be increasing. At some point, the Fed would abandon the exchange rate of 100 yen per U.S. dollar and stop piling up foreign currency reserves.

Now suppose the demand for U.S. dollars *decreases permanently* from D_0 to D_2. In this situation, the Fed

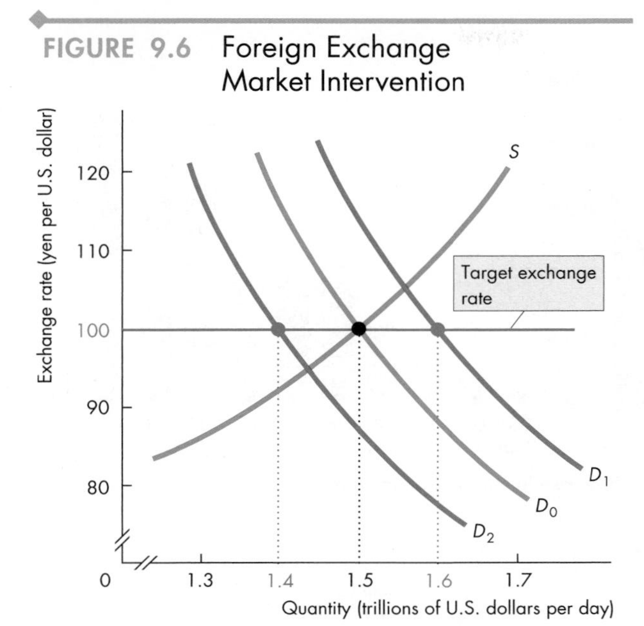

FIGURE 9.6 Foreign Exchange Market Intervention

Initially, the demand for U.S. dollars is D_0, the supply of U.S. dollars is S, and the exchange rate is 100 yen per U.S. dollar. The Fed can intervene in the foreign exchange market to keep the exchange rate close to its target rate (100 yen in this example). If the demand for U.S. dollars increases and the demand curve shifts from D_0 to D_1, the Fed sells dollars. If the demand for U.S. dollars decreases and the demand curve shifts from D_0 to D_2, the Fed buys dollars. Persistent intervention on one side of the market cannot be sustained.

myeconlab animation

cannot maintain the exchange rate at 100 yen per U.S. dollar indefinitely. To hold the exchange rate at 100 yen, the Fed must *buy* U.S. dollars. When the Fed buys U.S. dollars in the foreign exchange market, it uses U.S. official foreign currency reserves. So the Fed's action decreases its foreign currency reserves. Eventually, the Fed would run out of foreign currency and would then have to abandon the target exchange rate of 100 yen per U.S. dollar.

Crawling Peg

A **crawling peg** is an exchange rate that follows a path determined by a decision of the government or the central bank and is achieved in a similar way to a fixed exchange rate by central bank intervention in the foreign exchange market. A crawling peg works like a fixed exchange rate except that the target value changes. The target might change at fixed intervals (daily, weekly, monthly) or at random intervals.

The Fed has never operated a crawling peg, but some prominent countries do use this system. When China abandoned its fixed exchange rate, it replaced it with a crawling peg. Developing countries might use a crawling peg as a method of trying to control inflation—of keeping the inflation rate close to target.

The ideal crawling peg sets a target for the exchange rate equal to the equilibrium exchange rate

Economics in Action

The People's Bank of China in the Foreign Exchange Market

You saw in the figure on p. 213 that the exchange rate between the U.S. dollar and the Chinese yuan was constant for several years. The reason for this near constant exchange rate is that China's central bank, the People's Bank of China, intervened to operate a *fixed exchange rate policy*. From 1997 until 2005, the yuan was pegged at 8.28 yuan per U.S. dollar. Since 2005, the yuan has appreciated slightly but it has not been permitted to fluctuate freely. Since 2005, the yuan has been on a crawling peg.

Why Does China Manage Its Exchange Rate? The popular story is that China manages its exchange rate to keep its export prices low and to make it easier to compete in world markets. You've seen that this story is correct *only in the short run*. With prices in China unchanged, a lower yuan–U.S. dollar exchange rate brings lower U.S. dollar prices for China's exports. But the yuan–U.S. dollar exchange rate was fixed for almost 10 years and has been managed for five more years. This long period of a fixed exchange rate has long-run, not short-run, effects. In the long run, the exchange rate has no effect on competitiveness. The reason is that prices adjust to reflect the exchange rate and the real exchange rate is unaffected by the nominal exchange rate.

So why does China fix its exchange rate? The most convincing answer is that China sees a fixed exchange rate as a way of controlling its inflation rate. By making the yuan crawl against the U.S. dollar, China's inflation rate is anchored to the U.S. inflation rate and will depart from U.S. inflation by an amount determined by the speed of the crawl.

The bottom line is that in the long run, exchange rate policy is monetary policy, not foreign trade policy. To change its exports and imports, a country must change its comparative advantage (Chapter 2).

How Does China Manage Its Exchange Rate? The People's Bank pegs the yuan at 7 yuan per U.S. dollar by intervening in the foreign exchange market and buying U.S. dollars. But to do so, it must pile up U.S. dollars.

Part (a) of the figure shows the scale of China's increase in official foreign currency reserves, some of which are euros and yen but most of which are U.S. dollars. You can see that China's reserves increased by more than $400 billion in 2007, 2008, and 2009.

The demand and supply curves in part (b) of the figure illustrate what is happening in the market for U.S. dollars priced in terms of the yuan and explains why China's reserves have increased. The demand curve D and supply curve S intersect at 5 yuan per U.S. dollar. If the People's Bank of China takes no actions in the market, this exchange rate is the equilibrium rate (an assumed value).

The consequence of the fixed (and crawling peg) yuan exchange rate is that China has piled up U.S. dollar reserves on a huge scale. By mid-2006, China's official foreign currency reserves approached $1 trillion and by the end of 2009, they exceeded $2 trillion!

If the People's Bank stopped buying U.S. dollars, the U.S. dollar would depreciate and the yuan would appreciate—the yuan–U.S. dollar exchange rate would fall—and China would stop piling up U.S. dollar reserves.

In the example in the figure, the dollar would depreciate to 5 yuan per dollar.

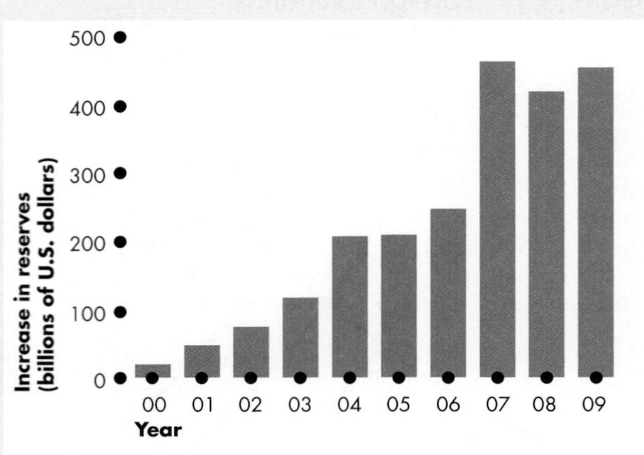

(a) Increase in U.S. dollar reserves

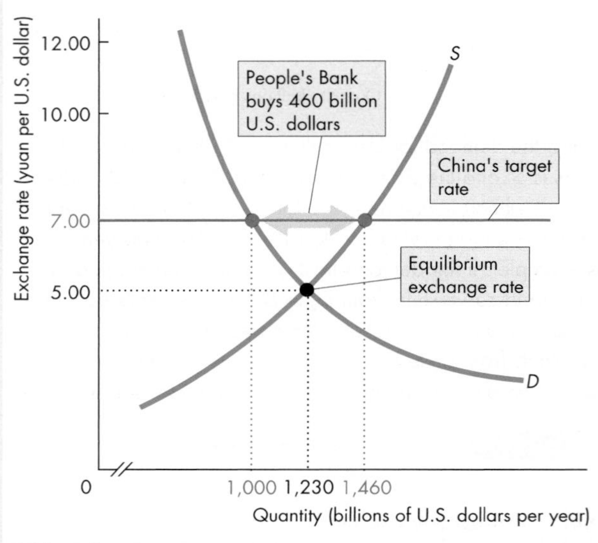

(b) Pegging the yuan

China's Foreign Exchange Market Intervention

on average. The peg seeks only to prevent large swings in the expected future exchange rate that change demand and supply and make the exchange rate fluctuate too wildly.

A crawling peg departs from the ideal if, as often happens with a fixed exchange rate, the target rate departs from the equilibrium exchange rate for too long. When this happens, the country either runs out of reserves or piles up reserves.

In the final part of this chapter, we explain how the balance of international payments is determined.

REVIEW QUIZ

1. What is a flexible exchange rate and how does it work?
2. What is a fixed exchange rate and how is its value fixed?
3. What is a crawling peg and how does it work?
4. How has China operated in the foreign exchange market, why, and with what effect?

You can work these questions in Study Plan 9.3 and get instant feedback.

Financing International Trade

You now know how the exchange rate is determined, but what is the effect of the exchange rate? How does currency depreciation or currency appreciation influence our international trade and payments? We're going to lay the foundation for addressing these questions by looking at the scale of international trading, borrowing, and lending and at the way in which we keep our records of international transactions. These records are called the *balance of payments accounts*.

Balance of Payments Accounts

A country's **balance of payments accounts** records its international trading, borrowing, and lending in three accounts:

1. Current account
2. Capital and financial account
3. Official settlements account

The **current account** records receipts from exports of goods and services sold abroad, payments for imports of goods and services from abroad, net interest income paid abroad, and net transfers abroad (such as foreign aid payments). The *current account balance* equals the sum of exports minus imports, net interest income, and net transfers.

The **capital and financial account** records foreign investment in the United States minus U.S. investment abroad. (This account also has a statistical discrepancy that arises from errors and omissions in measuring international capital transactions.)

The **official settlements account** records the change in **U.S. official reserves**, which are the government's holdings of foreign currency. If U.S. official reserves *increase*, the official settlements account balance is *negative*. The reason is that holding foreign money is like investing abroad. U.S. investment abroad is a minus item in the capital and financial account and in the official settlements account.

The sum of the balances on the three accounts *always* equals zero. That is, to pay for our current account deficit, we must either borrow more from abroad than we lend abroad or use our official reserves to cover the shortfall.

Table 9.1 shows the U.S. balance of payments accounts in 2010. Items in the current account and the capital and financial account that provide foreign currency to the United States have a plus sign; items that cost the United States foreign currency have a minus sign. The table shows that in 2010, U.S. imports exceeded U.S. exports and the current account had a deficit of $436 billion. How do we pay for imports that exceed the value of our exports? That is, how do we pay for our current account deficit?

We pay by borrowing from the rest of the world. The capital account tells us by how much. We borrowed $1,408 billion (foreign investment in the United States) but made loans of $1,200 billion (U.S. investment abroad). Our *net* foreign borrowing was $1,408 billion minus $1,200 billion, which equals $208 billion. There is almost always a statistical discrepancy between our capital account and current account transactions, and in 2010, the discrepancy was $231 billion. Combining the discrepancy with the measured net foreign borrowing gives a capital and financial account balance of $439 billion.

TABLE 9.1 U.S. Balance of Payments Accounts in 2010

Current account	**Billions of dollars**
Exports of goods and services	+1,754
Imports of goods and services	–2,215
Net interest income	+167
Net transfers	–142
Current account balance	–436
Capital and financial account	
Foreign investment in the United States	+1,408
U.S. investment abroad	–1,200
Statistical discrepancy	231
Capital and financial account balance	+439
Official settlements account	
Official settlements account balance	–3

Source of data: Bureau of Economic Analysis (based on first quarter).

The capital and financial account balance plus the current account balance equals the change in U.S. official reserves. In 2010, the capital and financial account balance of $439 billion plus the current account balance of –$436 billion equaled $3 billion. Official reserves *increased* in 2010 by $3 billion. Holding more foreign reserves is like lending to the rest of the world, so this amount appears in the official settlements account in Table 9.1 as –$3 billion. The sum of the balances on the three balance of payments accounts equals zero.

To see more clearly what the nation's balance of payments accounts mean, think about your own balance of payments accounts. They are similar to the nation's accounts.

An Individual's Balance of Payments Accounts An individual's current account records the income from supplying the services of factors of production and the expenditure on goods and services. Consider Jackie, for example. She worked in 2010 and earned an income of $25,000. Jackie has $10,000 worth of investments that earned her an interest income of $1,000. Jackie's current account shows an income of $26,000. Jackie spent $18,000 buying consumption goods and services. She also bought a new house, which cost her $60,000. So Jackie's total expenditure was $78,000. Jackie's expenditure minus her income is $52,000 ($78,000 minus $26,000). This amount is Jackie's current account deficit.

Economics in Action

Three Decades of Deficits

The numbers that you reviewed in Table 9.1 give a snapshot of the balance of payments accounts in 2010. The figure below puts that snapshot into perspective by showing the balance of payments between 1980 and 2010.

Because the economy grows and the price level rises, changes in the dollar value of the balance of payments do not convey much information. To remove the influences of economic growth and inflation, the figure shows the balance of payments expressed as a percentage of nominal GDP.

As you can see, a large current account deficit emerged during the 1980s but declined from 1987 to 1991. The current account deficit then increased through 2000, decreased slightly in 2001, and then increased through 2006 after which it decreased again but increased slightly in 2010. The capital and financial account balance is almost a mirror image of the current account balance. The official settlements balance is very small in comparison with the balances on the other two accounts.

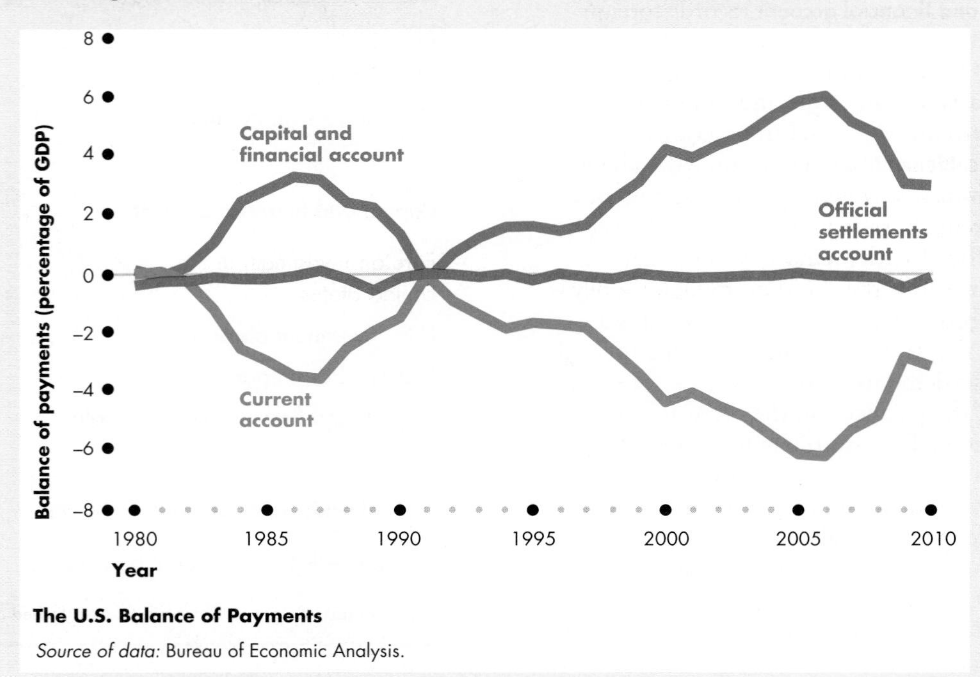

The U.S. Balance of Payments

Source of data: Bureau of Economic Analysis.

To pay for expenditure of $52,000 in excess of her income, Jackie must either use the money that she has in the bank or take out a loan. Suppose that Jackie took out a loan of $50,000 to help buy her house and that this loan was the only borrowing that she did. Borrowing is an *inflow* in the capital account, so Jackie's capital account *surplus* was $50,000. With a current account deficit of $52,000 and a capital account surplus of $50,000, Jackie was still $2,000 short. She got that $2,000 from her own bank account. Her cash holdings decreased by $2,000.

Jackie's income from her work is like a country's income from its exports. Her income from her investments is like a country's interest income from foreigners. Her purchases of goods and services, including her purchase of a house, are like a country's imports. Jackie's loan—borrowing from someone else—is like a country's borrowing from the rest of the world. The change in Jackie's bank account is like the change in the country's official reserves.

Borrowers and Lenders

A country that is borrowing more from the rest of the world than it is lending to the rest of the world is called a **net borrower**. Similarly, a **net lender** is a country that is lending more to the rest of the world than it is borrowing from the rest of the world.

The United States is a net borrower, but it has not always been in this situation. Throughout the 1960s and most of the 1970s, the United States was a net lender to the rest of the world—the United States had a current account surplus and a capital account deficit. But from the early 1980s, with the exception of only a single year, 1991, the United States has been a net borrower from the rest of the world. And during the years since 1992, the scale of U.S. borrowing has mushroomed.

Most countries are net borrowers like the United States. But a few countries, including China, Japan, and oil-rich Saudi Arabia, are net lenders. In 2010, when the United States borrowed more than $400 billion from the rest of the world, most of it came from China.

Debtors and Creditors

A net borrower might be decreasing its net assets held in the rest of the world, or it might be going deeper into debt. A nation's total stock of foreign investment determines whether it is a debtor or a creditor. A **debtor nation** is a country that during its entire history has borrowed more from the rest of the world than it has lent to it. It has a stock of outstanding debt to the rest of the world that exceeds the stock of its own claims on the rest of the world. A **creditor nation** is a country that during its entire history has invested more in the rest of the world than other countries have invested in it.

The United States was a debtor nation through the nineteenth century as we borrowed from Europe to finance our westward expansion, railroads, and industrialization. We paid off our debt and became a creditor nation for most of the twentieth century. But following a string of current account deficits, we became a debtor nation again in 1986.

Since 1986, the total stock of U.S. borrowing from the rest of the world has exceeded U.S. lending to the rest of the world. The largest debtor nations are the capital-hungry developing countries (such as the United States was during the nineteenth century). The international debt of these countries grew from less than a third to more than a half of their gross domestic product during the 1980s and created what was called the "Third World debt crisis."

Should we be concerned that the United States is a net borrower and a debtor? The answer to this question depends mainly on what the net borrower is doing with the borrowed money. If borrowing is financing investment that in turn is generating economic growth and higher income, borrowing is not a problem. It earns a return that more than pays the interest. But if borrowed money is used to finance consumption, to pay the interest and repay the loan, consumption will eventually have to be reduced. In this case, the greater the borrowing and the longer it goes on, the greater is the reduction in consumption that will eventually be necessary.

Is U.S. Borrowing for Consumption?

In 2010, we borrowed $439 billion from abroad. In that year, private investment in buildings, plant, and equipment was $1,840 billion and government investment in defense equipment and social projects was $500 billion. All this investment added to the nation's capital, and increased productivity. Government also spends on education and health care services, which increase *human capital.* Our international borrowing is financing private and public investment, not consumption.

Current Account Balance

What determines a country's current account balance and net foreign borrowing? You've seen that net exports (NX) is the main item in the current account. We can define the current account balance (CAB) as

$$CAB = NX + \text{Net interest income} + \text{Net transfers.}$$

We can study the current account balance by looking at what determines net exports because the other two items are small and do not fluctuate much.

Net Exports

Net exports are determined by the government budget and private saving and investment. To see how net exports are determined, we need to recall some of the things that we learned in Chapter 7 about the flows of funds that finance investment. Table 9.2 refreshes your memory and summarizes some calculations.

Part (a) lists the national income variables that are needed, with their symbols. Part (b) defines three balances: net exports, the government sector balance, and the private sector balance.

Net exports is exports of goods and services minus imports of goods and services.

The **government sector balance** is equal to net taxes minus government expenditures on goods and services. If that number is positive, a government sector surplus is lent to other sectors; if that number is negative, a government deficit must be financed by borrowing from other sectors. The government sector deficit is the sum of the deficits of the federal, state, and local governments.

The **private sector balance** is saving minus investment. If saving exceeds investment, a private sector surplus is lent to other sectors. If investment exceeds saving, a private sector deficit is financed by borrowing from other sectors.

Part (b) also shows the values of these balances for the United States in 2010. As you can see, net exports were –\$536 billion, a deficit of \$536 billion. The government sector's revenue from *net* taxes was \$1,698 billion and its expenditure was \$2,993 billion, so the government sector balance was –\$1,295 billion—a deficit of \$1,295 billion. The private sector saved \$2,598 billion and invested \$1,839 billion, so its balance was \$759 billion—a surplus of \$759 billion.

Part (c) shows the relationship among the three balances. From the *National Income and Product Accounts*, we know that real GDP, Y, is the sum of consumption expenditure (C), investment, government expenditure, and net exports. Real GDP also equals the sum of consumption expenditure, saving, and net taxes. Rearranging these equations tells us that net exports is the sum of the government sector balance and the private sector balance. In the United States in 2010, the government sector balance was

TABLE 9.2 Net Exports, the Government Budget, Saving, and Investment

	Symbols and equations	United States in 2010 (billions of dollars)
(a) Variables		
Exports*	X	1,818
Imports*	M	2,354
Government expenditures	G	2,993
Net taxes	T	1,698
Investment	I	1,839
Saving	S	2,598
(b) Balances		
Net exports	$X - M$	1,818 – 2,354 = –536
Government sector	$T - G$	1,698 – 2,993 = –1,295
Private sector	$S - I$	2,598 – 1,839 = 759
(c) Relationship among balances		
National accounts	$Y = C + I + G + X - M$	
	$= C + S + T$	
Rearranging:	$X - M = S - I + T - G$	
Net exports	$X - M$	–536
equals:		
Government sector	$T - G$	–1,295
plus		
Private sector	$S - I$	759

Source of data: Bureau of Economic Analysis. The data are for 2010, average of first two quarters, seasonally adjusted at annual rate.

* The *National Income and Product Accounts* measures of exports and imports are slightly different from the balance of payments accounts measures in Table 9.1 on p. 225.

Economics in Action

The Three Sector Balances

You've seen that net exports equal the sum of the government sector balance and the private sector balance. How do these three sector balances fluctuate over time?

The figure answers this question. It shows the government sector balance (the red line), net exports (the blue line), and the private sector balance (the green line).

The private sector balance and the government sector balance move in opposite directions. When the government sector deficit increased during the late 1980s and early 1990s, the private sector surplus increased. And when the government sector deficit decreased and became a surplus during the 1990s and early 2000s, the private sector's surplus decreased and became a deficit. And when the government deficit increased yet again from 2007 to 2009, the private sector deficit shrank and became a surplus.

Sometimes, when the government sector deficit increases, as it did during the first half of the 1980s, net exports become more negative. But after the early 1990s, net exports did not follow the government sector balance closely. Rather, net exports respond to the *sum* of the government sector and private sector balances. When both the private sector and the government sector have a deficit, net exports are negative and the combined private and government deficit is financed by borrowing from the rest of the world. But the dominant trend in net exports is negative.

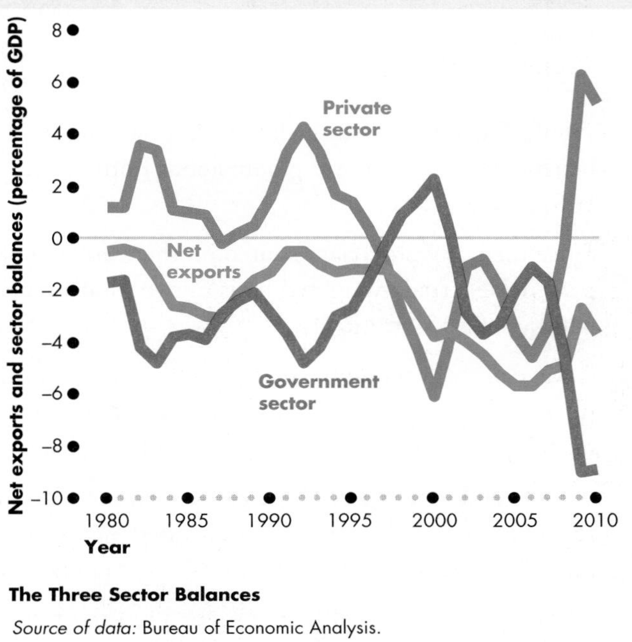

The Three Sector Balances

Source of data: Bureau of Economic Analysis.

–$1,295 billion and the private sector balance was $759 billion. The government sector balance plus the private sector balance equaled net exports of –$536 billion.

Where Is the Exchange Rate?

We haven't mentioned the exchange rate while discussing the balance of payments. Doesn't it play a role? The answer is that in the short run it does but in the long run it doesn't.

In the short run, a fall in the dollar lowers the real exchange rate, which makes U.S. imports more costly and U.S. exports more competitive. A higher price of imported consumption goods and services might induce a decrease in consumption expenditure and an increase in saving. A higher price of imported capital goods might induce a decrease in investment. Other things remaining the same, an increase in saving or a decrease in investment decreases the private sector deficit and decreases the current account deficit.

But in the long run, a change in the nominal exchange rate leaves the real exchange rate unchanged and plays no role in influencing the current account balance.

REVIEW QUIZ

1. What are the transactions that the balance of payments accounts record?
2. Is the United States a net borrower or a net lender? Is it a debtor or a creditor nation?
3. How are net exports and the government sector balance linked?

You can work these questions in Study Plan 9.4 and get instant feedback.

Reading Between the Lines on pp. 230–231 looks at risky trading that exploits the U.S. interest rate differential in the foreign exchange market.

The Dollar and "Carry Trade"

Dollar Faces Increasingly Strong Set of Headwinds

http://www.financialtimes.com
August 5, 2010

Only a few weeks ago, the dollar was powering toward its highest levels in four years, the beneficiary of widespread gloom about Europe's debt crisis and rising optimism about the U.S. recovery.

Since then, investors have soured on the world's largest economy. The dollar has tumbled 9 percent on a trade-weighted basis in two months, and yesterday fell to ¥85.29, within a whisker of a 15-year low. ...

A wave of weak economic data, including disappointing jobs figures, and expectations of further monetary easing by the U.S. Federal Reserve to head off the risk of a double-dip recession have been the main drivers of the dollar's fall. ...

As they pull money out of the greenback, investors are betting the recovery in other parts of the world will outpace that of the United States. Asian countries, expected to enjoy stronger growth than the debt-burdened west, have enjoyed strong inflows of funds. ...

The conditions are building, too, for a return of the dollar "carry trade", in which investors take advantage of low U.S. borrowing costs to invest in higher-yielding assets elsewhere. ...

One dollar "carry trade" has involved buying Indonesian bonds. Foreign ownership of Indonesian bonds has risen to a record, while bond yields—which move inversely to prices—have fallen to record lows. Tim Lee at Pi Economics, a consultancy, says the dollar carry trade may now be worth more than $750 billion. ...

In the longer term, the success of the dollar "carry trade" will depend on the U.S. economy remaining weak—but not too weak. ...

ESSENCE OF THE STORY

- Concern about Europe's debt crisis and optimism about U.S. real GDP growth brought an appreciation of the U.S. dollar.
- Disappointing jobs figures and expectations of further monetary easing by the Fed changed the outlook, ended the rise in the dollar, and lowered its value by 9 percent on average and close to a 15-year low against the Japanese yen (¥).
- Investors are pulling funds out of the U.S. dollar and moving them to the Asian currencies.
- The dollar "carry trade" is expanding and one estimate puts it at more than $750 billion.
- The longer term success of the dollar "carry trade" will depend on the U.S. economy remaining weak so that interest rates remain low.

ECONOMIC ANALYSIS

- The news article says the dollar will keep depreciating and U.S. interest rates will remain low, so the "carry trade" will be profitable.
- The *carry trade* is borrowing at a low interest rate in one currency, converting the funds to another currency to earn a higher interest rate, then converting the funds back to the original currency.
- Carry trade is profitable provided the interest rate difference doesn't get wiped out by a fall in the value of the currency with the higher interest rate.
- If the carry trade was persistently profitable, it would mean that *interest rate parity* did not hold.
- *Interest rate parity* (explained on p. 220) is a situation in which, adjusted for risk, expected rates of return are equal in all currencies.
- The "carry trade" was profitable in 2009 and 2010.
- Figure 1 shows that the Indonesian rupiah has *appreciated* against the U.S. dollar (the dollar has depreciated).
- Figure 2 shows the interest rates in Indonesia and the United States. Large investors can borrow at the U.S. commercial bill rate (almost zero) and small investors can borrow at an interest rate of about 2 percentage points above the prime lending rate.
- Large investors can buy and sell rupiah for a small percentage transaction fee. Small investors pay a large percentage transaction fee.
- Figure 3 shows the profit (and loss) from borrowing $100 and using the carry trade to earn the Indonesian interest rate.
- Because the Indonesian interest rate exceeds the U.S. interest rate *and the rupiah has appreciated,* the carry trade has been profitable.
- But the percentage rate of return has fallen, and it turned negative for small investors.
- Does the profitable carry trade mean that interest rate parity doesn't hold?
- It does not. Investing in Indonesian rupiah is risky. The rupiah might depreciate and wipe out the interest rate difference.
- The economic rear-view mirror is much clearer than the windshield.
- Expected returns are equal, but actual past returns are unequal. As people have increased investments in Indonesia, the "carry trade" profit has shrunk.

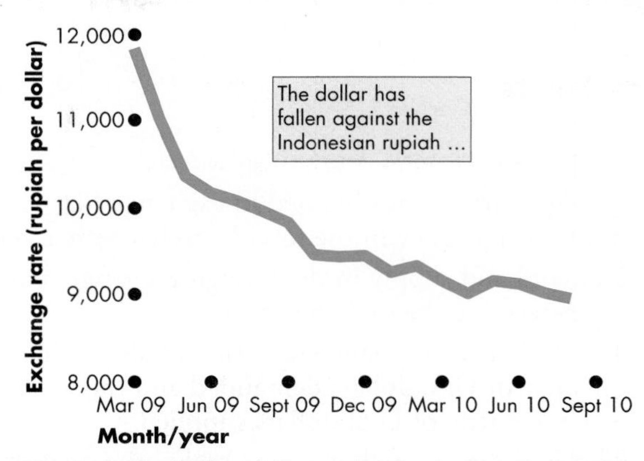

Figure 1 The falling dollar and rising Indonesian rupiah

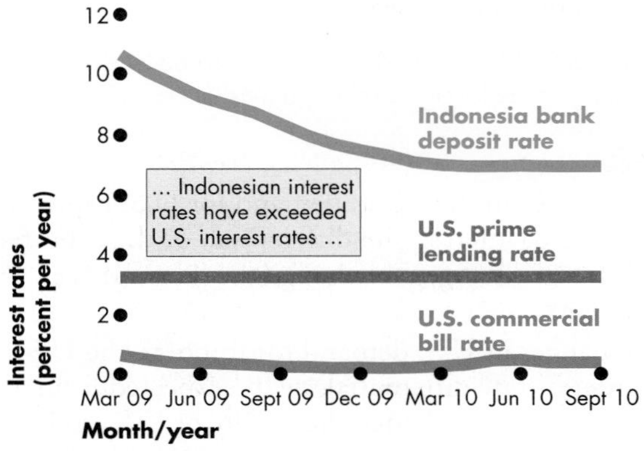

Figure 2 U.S. and Indonesian interest rates

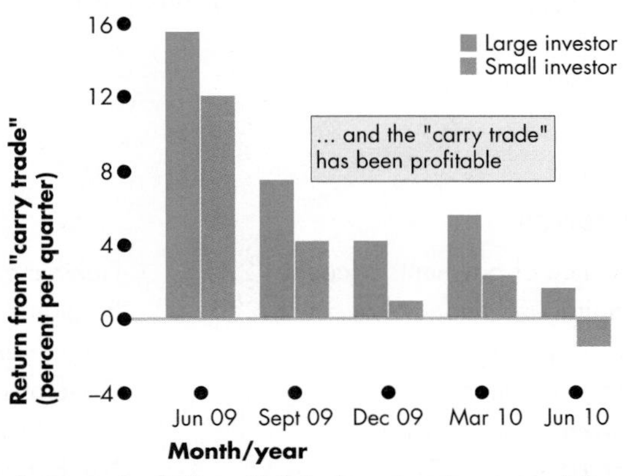

Figure 3 Profit from U.S.–Indonesian "carry trade"

SUMMARY

Key Points

The Foreign Exchange Market (pp. 212–216)

- Foreign currency is obtained in exchange for domestic currency in the foreign exchange market.
- Demand and supply in the foreign exchange market determine the exchange rate.
- The higher the exchange rate, the smaller is the quantity of U.S. dollars demanded and the greater is the quantity of U.S. dollars supplied.
- The equilibrium exchange rate makes the quantity of U.S. dollars demanded equal the quantity of U.S. dollars supplied.

Working Problems 1 to 6 will give you a better understanding of the foreign exchange market.

Exchange Rate Fluctuations (pp. 217–221)

- Changes in the world demand for U.S. exports, the U.S. interest rate differential, or the expected future exchange rate change the demand for U.S. dollars.
- Changes in U.S. demand for imports, the U.S. interest rate differential, or the expected future exchange rate change the supply of U.S. dollars.
- Exchange rate expectations are influenced by purchasing power parity and interest rate parity.
- In the long run, the nominal exchange rate is a monetary phenomenon and the real exchange rate is independent of the nominal exchange rate.

Working Problems 7 to 15 will give you a better understanding of exchange rate fluctuations.

Exchange Rate Policy (pp. 222–224)

- An exchange rate can be flexible, fixed, or a crawling peg.
- To achieve a fixed or a crawling exchange rate, a central bank must intervene in the foreign exchange market and either buy or sell foreign currency.

Working Problems 16 and 17 will give you a better understanding of exchange rate policy.

Financing International Trade (pp. 225–229)

- International trade, borrowing, and lending are financed by using foreign currency.
- A country's international transactions are recorded in its current account, capital account, and official settlements account.
- The current account balance is similar to net exports and is determined by the government sector balance plus the private sector balance.

Working Problems 18 and 19 will give you a better understanding of financing international trade.

Key Terms

Balance of payments accounts, 225
Capital and financial account, 225
Crawling peg, 223
Creditor nation, 227
Current account, 225
Debtor nation, 227
Exchange rate, 212
Fixed exchange rate, 222
Flexible exchange rate, 222
Foreign currency, 212
Foreign exchange market, 212
Government sector balance, 228
Interest rate parity, 220
Net borrower, 227
Net exports, 228
Net lender, 227
Official settlements account, 225
Private sector balance, 228
Purchasing power parity, 220
Real exchange rate, 221
U.S. interest rate differential, 217
U.S. official reserves, 225

STUDY PLAN PROBLEMS AND APPLICATIONS

myeconlab You can work Problems 1 to 19 in MyEconLab Chapter 9 Study Plan and get instant feedback.

The Foreign Exchange Market (Study Plan 9.1)

Use the following data to work Problems 1 to 3.
The U.S. dollar exchange rate increased from $0.89 Canadian in June 2009 to $0.96 Canadian in June 2010, and it decreased from 83.8 euro cents in January 2009 to 76.9 euro cents in January 2010.

1. Did the U.S. dollar appreciate or depreciate against the Canadian dollar? Did the U.S. dollar appreciate or depreciate against the euro?
2. What was the value of the Canadian dollar in terms of U.S. dollars in June 2009 and June 2010? Did the Canadian dollar appreciate or depreciate against the U.S. dollar over the year June 2009 to June 2010?
3. What was the value of one euro (100 euro cents) in terms of U.S. dollars in January 2009 and January 2010? Did the euro appreciate or depreciate against the U.S. dollar in 2009?

Use the following data to work Problems 4 to 6.

In January 2010, the exchange rate was 91 yen per U.S. dollar. By September 2010, the exchange rate had fallen to 84 yen per U.S. dollar.

4. Explain the exports effect of this change in the exchange rate.
5. Explain the imports effect of this change in the exchange rate.
6. Explain the expected profit effect of this change in the exchange rate.

Exchange Rate Fluctuations (Study Plan 9.2)

7. On August 3, 2010, the U.S. dollar was trading at 86 yen per U.S. dollar on the foreign exchange market. On September 13, 2010, the U.S. dollar was trading at 83 yen per U.S. dollar.
   a. What events in the foreign exchange market might have brought this fall in the value of the U.S. dollar?
   b. Did the events change the demand for U.S. dollars, the supply of U.S. dollars, or both demand and supply in the foreign exchange market?
8. Colombia is the world's biggest producer of roses. The global demand for roses increases and at the same time, the central bank in Colombia increases the interest rate. In the foreign exchange market for Colombian pesos, what happens to
   a. The demand for pesos?
   b. The supply of pesos?
   c. The quantity of pesos demanded?
   d. The quantity of pesos supplied?
   e. The exchange rate of the peso against the U.S. dollar?
9. If a euro deposit in a bank in Paris, France, earns interest of 4 percent a year and a yen deposit in Tokyo, Japan, earns 0.5 percent a year, everything else remaining the same and adjusted for risk, what is the exchange rate expectation of the Japanese yen?
10. The U.K. pound is trading at 1.54 U.S. dollars per U.K. pound. There is purchasing power parity at this exchange rate. The interest rate in the United States is 2 percent a year and the interest rate in the United Kingdom is 4 percent a year.
    a. Calculate the U.S. interest rate differential.
    b. What is the U.K. pound expected to be worth in terms of U.S. dollars one year from now?
    c. Which country more likely has the lower inflation rate? How can you tell?
11. You can purchase a laptop in Mexico City for 12,960 Mexican pesos. If the exchange rate is 10.8 Mexican pesos per U.S. dollar and if purchasing power parity prevails, at what price can you buy an identical computer in Dallas, Texas?
12. **When the Chips Are Down**

    The *Economist* magazine uses the price of a Big Mac to determine whether a currency is undervalued or overvalued. In July 2010, the price of a Big Mac was $3.73 in New York, 13.2 yuan in Beijing, and 6.50 Swiss francs in Geneva. The exchanges rates were 6.78 yuan per U.S. dollar and 1.05 Swiss francs per U.S. dollar.

    Source: *The Economist*, July 22, 2010

    a. Was the yuan undervalued or overvalued relative to purchasing power parity?
    b. Was the Swiss franc undervalued or overvalued relative to purchasing power parity?
    c. Do you think the price of a Big Mac in different countries provides a valid test of purchasing power parity?

13. The price level in the Eurozone is 112.4, the price level in the United States is 109.1, and the nominal exchange rate was 80 euro cents per U.S. dollar. What is the real exchange rate expressed as Eurozone real GDP per unit of U.S. real GDP?
14. The U.S. price level is 106.3, the Japanese price level is 95.4, and the real exchange rate is 103.6 Japanese real GDP per unit of U.S. real GDP. What is the nominal exchange rate?
15. **Dollar Hits 15-Year Low vs Yen**

    Today in Tokyo a dollar bought only 84.71 yen, the lowest since 1995. The dollar's weakness against the yen is making Japanese exports more expensive. Investors stepped up selling of U.S. dollars after the Federal Reserve announced yesterday only small steps aimed at shoring up the flagging U.S. economy. "Investors were unnerved by the Fed's statement. It just confirmed that the U.S. economic recovery is slowing," said a dealer at a Japanese bank in Tokyo.

    Source: *USA Today*, August 11, 2010

    On a graph of the foreign exchange market show the effects of
    a. Japanese exports becoming more expensive.
    b. Investors stepping up the sale of dollars.

Exchange Rate Policy (Study Plan 9.3)

16. With the strengthening of the yen against the U.S. dollar in 2010, Japan's central bank did not take any action. A leading Japanese politician has called on the central bank to take actions to weaken the yen, saying it will help exporters in the short run and have no long-run effects.
    a. What is Japan's current exchange rate policy?
    b. What does the politician want the exchange rate policy to be in the short run? Why would such a policy have no effect on the exchange rate in the long run?
17. **Double-Talking the Dollar**

    In the 1970s and 1980s, the United States was constantly buying and selling foreign currencies to change the value of the dollar, but since 1995 it has made only a few transactions and since 2000 none at all. The foreign exchange market is so huge, trying to manipulate the dollar is largely futile. A currency's value reflects an economy's fundamentals: How well a country allocates resources, how productive its workers are, how it contains inflation, etc., but for years on end, currencies can move in directions that seem to have little to do with fundamentals. They overshoot their correct values, in part because nobody is ever sure exactly what those correct values are.

    Source: *Time*, May 5, 2008

    a. How has U.S. exchange rate policy evolved since the early 1970s?
    b. Explain why "trying to manipulate the dollar is largely futile," especially in the long run.
    c. Explain why a currency can experience short-run fluctuations "that seem to have little to do with fundamentals." Illustrate with a graph.

Financing International Trade (Study Plan 9.4)

18. The table gives some information about the U.S. international transactions in 2008.

Item	Billions of U.S. dollars
Imports of goods and services	2,561
Foreign investment in the United States	955
Exports of goods and services	1,853
U.S. investment abroad	300
Net interest income	121
Net transfers	–123
Statistical discrepancy	66

    a. Calculate the current account balance.
    b. Calculate the capital and financial account balance.
    c. Did U.S. official reserves increase or decrease?
    d. Was the United States a net borrower or a net lender in 2008? Explain your answer.
19. **The United States, Debtor Nation**

    The United States is a debtor nation, and for most of the past 30 years it has been piling up large trade deficits. The current account has now reached a deficit of 6 percent of GDP, and must be financed by capital inflows. Foreigners must purchase large amounts of U.S. assets, or the current account deficit cannot be financed.

    Source: *Asia Times*, September 28, 2006

    a. Explain why a current account deficit "must be financed by capital inflows."
    b. Under what circumstances should the debtor nation status of the United States be a concern?

ADDITIONAL PROBLEMS AND APPLICATIONS

myeconlab You can work these problems in MyEconLab if assigned by your instructor.

The Foreign Exchange Market

20. Suppose that yesterday, the U.S. dollar was trading on the foreign exchange market at 0.75 euros per U.S. dollar and today the U.S. dollar is trading at 0.78 euros per U.S. dollar. Which of the two currencies (the U.S. dollar or the euro) has appreciated and which has depreciated today?
21. Suppose that the exchange rate fell from 84 yen per U.S. dollar to 71 yen per U.S. dollar. What is the effect of this change on the quantity of U.S. dollars that people plan to buy in the foreign exchange market?
22. Suppose that the exchange rate rose from 71 yen per U.S. dollar to 100 yen per U.S. dollar. What is the effect of this change on the quantity of U.S. dollars that people plan to sell in the foreign exchange market?
23. Today's exchange rate between the yuan and the U.S. dollar is 6.78 yuan per dollar and the central bank of China is buying U.S. dollars in the foreign exchange market. If the central bank of China did not purchase U.S. dollars would there be excess demand or excess supply of U.S. dollars in the foreign exchange market? Would the exchange rate remain at 6.78 yuan per U.S. dollar? If not, which currency would appreciate?

Exchange Rate Fluctuations

24. Yesterday, the current exchange rate was $1.05 Canadian per U.S. dollar and traders expected the exchange rate to remain unchanged for the next month. Today, with new information, traders now expect the exchange rate next month to fall to $1 Canadian per U.S. dollar. Explain how the revised expected future exchange rate influences the demand for U.S. dollars, or the supply of U.S. dollars, or both in the foreign exchange market.
25. On January 1, 2010, the exchange rate was 91 yen per U.S. dollar. Over the year, the supply of U.S. dollars increased and by January, 2011, the exchange rate fell to 84 yen per U.S. dollar. What happened to the quantity of U.S. dollars that people planned to buy in the foreign exchange market?
26. On August 1, 2010, the exchange rate was 84 yen per U.S. dollar. Over the year, the demand for U.S. dollars increased and by August 1, 2011, the exchange rate was 100 yen per U.S. dollar. What happened to the quantity of U.S. dollars that people planned to sell in the foreign exchange market?

Use the following news clip to work Problems 27 and 28.

Top U.S. Real Estate Markets for Investment

Rahul Reddy has been investing in Australian real estate for the last two years. Now, with the Australian dollar growing in strength and the American housing market strained, he's got his eye on real estate in Florida and California. Encouraged by a weak dollar and a belief in the resiliency of the U.S. economy, investors are seeking investment properties and development opportunities in the United States. "The United States is good for speculative higher-risk investments from our perspective because the strong Australian dollar will enable us to gain hold of real estate at prices we will probably not see for a long time," says Reddy. "The United States is an economic powerhouse that I think will recover, and if the exchange rate goes back to what it was a few years ago, we will benefit."

Source: *Forbes*, July 10, 2008

27. Explain why foreigners are "seeking investment properties and development opportunities in the United States."
28. Explain what would happen if the speculation made by Reddy became widespread. Would expectations become self-fulfilling?

Use the following information to work Problems 29 and 30.

Brazil's Overvalued Real

The Brazilian real has appreciated 33 percent against the U.S. dollar and has pushed up the price of a Big Mac in Sao Paulo to $4.60, higher than the New York price of $3.99. Despite Brazil's interest rate being at 8.75 percent a year compared to the U.S. interest rate at near zero, foreign funds flowing into Brazil surged in October.

Source: Bloomberg News, October 27, 2009

29. Does purchasing power parity hold? If not, does PPP predict that the Brazilian real will appreciate or depreciate against the U.S. dollar? Explain.
30. Does interest rate parity hold? If not, why not? Will the Brazilian real appreciate further or depreciate against the U.S. dollar if the Fed raises the interest rate while the Brazilian interest rate remains at 8.75 percent a year?

Exchange Rate Policy

Use the following news clip to work Problems 31 to 34.

U.S. Declines to Cite China as Currency Manipulator

The Bush administration has declined to cite China for manipulating its currency to gain unfair trade advantages against the United States. America's growing trade deficit with China, which last year hit an all-time high of $256.3 billion, is the largest deficit ever recorded with a single country. Chinese currency, the yuan, has risen in value by 18.4 percent against the U.S. dollar since the Chinese government loosened its currency system in July 2005. However, American manufacturers contend the yuan is still undervalued by as much as 40 percent, making Chinese products more competitive in this country and U.S. goods more expensive in China. China buys U.S. dollar-denominated securities to maintain the value of the yuan in terms of the U.S. dollar.

Source: MSN, May 15, 2008

31. What was the exchange rate policy adopted by China until July 2005? Explain how it worked. Draw a graph to illustrate your answer.
32. What was the exchange rate policy adopted by China after July 2005? Explain how it works.
33. Explain how fixed and crawling peg exchange rates can be used to manipulate trade balances in the short run, but not the long run.
34. Explain the long-run effect of China's current exchange rate policy.
35. **Aussie Dollar Hit by Interest Rate Talk**

    The Australian dollar fell against the U.S. dollar to its lowest value in the past two weeks. The CPI inflation rate was reported to be generally as expected but not high enough to justify previous expectations for an aggressive interest rate rise by Australia's central bank next week.

    Source: Reuters, October 28, 2009

    a. What is Australia's exchange rate policy? Explain why expectations about the Australian interest rate lowered the value of the Australian dollar against the U.S. dollar.
    b. To avoid the fall in the value of the Australian dollar against the U.S. dollar, what action could the central bank of Australia have taken? Would such an action signal a change in Australia's exchange rate policy?

Financing International Trade

Use the following table to work Problems 36 to 38. The table gives some data about the U.K. economy:

Item	Billions of U.K. pounds
Consumption expenditure	721
Exports of goods and services	277
Government expenditures	230
Net taxes	217
Investment	181
Saving	162

36. Calculate the private sector balance.
37. Calculate the government sector balance.
38. Calculate net exports and show the relationship between the government sector balance and net exports.

Economics in the News

39. After you have studied *Reading Between the Lines* on pp. 230–231 answer the following questions.
    a. What is the "carry trade" and between what types of countries and currencies is it likely to take place?
    b. What are the risks in the "carry trade"?
    c. Is it possible to earn a profit in the "carry trade" in the long run? Explain why or why not.
    d. Explain how participating in the "carry trade" reduces the profit available to other traders.
    e. Define interest rate parity and explain its connection with the "carry trade."
    f. Define purchasing power parity and explain how this concept might be used in the "carry trade."

Expanding the Frontier

PART THREE

UNDERSTANDING MACROECONOMIC TRENDS

Economics is about how we cope with scarcity. We cope as individuals by making choices that balance marginal benefits and marginal costs so that we use our scarce resources efficiently. We cope as societies by creating incentive systems and social institutions that encourage specialization and exchange.

These choices and the incentive systems that guide them determine what we specialize in; how much work we do; how hard we work at school to learn the mental skills that form our human capital and that determine the kinds of jobs we get and the incomes we earn; how much we save for future big-ticket expenditures; how much businesses and governments spend on new capital—on auto assembly lines, computers and fiber cables for improved Internet services, shopping malls, highways, bridges, and tunnels; how intensively existing capital and natural resources are used and how quickly they wear out or are used up; and the problems that scientists, engineers, and other inventors work on to develop new technologies.

All the choices we've just described combine to determine the standard of living and the rate at which it improves—the economic growth rate.

Money that makes specialization and exchange in markets possible is a huge contributor to economic growth. But too much money brings a rising cost of living with no improvement in the standard of living.

Joseph Schumpeter, *the son of a textile factory owner, was born in Austria in 1883. He moved from Austria to Germany during the tumultuous 1920s when those two countries experienced hyperinflation. In 1932, in the depths of the Great Depression, he came to the United States and became a professor of economics at Harvard University.*

This creative economic thinker wrote about economic growth and development, business cycles, political systems, and economic biography. He was a person of strong opinions who expressed them forcefully and delighted in verbal battles.

Schumpeter saw the development and diffusion of new technologies by profit-seeking entrepreneurs as the source of economic progress. But he saw economic progress as a process of creative destruction—the creation of new profit opportunities and the destruction of currently profitable businesses. For Schumpeter, economic growth and the business cycle were a single phenomenon.

"Economic progress, in capitalist society, means turmoil."

JOSEPH SCHUMPETER
Capitalism, Socialism, and Democracy

TALKING WITH **Xavier Sala-i-Martin**

What attracted you to economics?

It was a random event. I wanted to be rich, so I asked my mom, "In my family, who is the richest guy?" She said, "Your uncle John." And I asked, "What did he study?" And she said, "Economics." So I went into economics!

In Spain, there are no liberal arts colleges where you can study lots of things. At age 18, you must decide what career you will follow. If you choose economics, you go to economics school and take economics five years in a row. So you have to make a decision in a crazy way, like I did.

How did economic growth become your major field of research?

I studied economics. I liked it. I studied mathematical economics. I liked it too, and I went to graduate school. In my second year at Harvard, Jeffrey Sachs hired me to go to Bolivia. I saw poor people for the first time in my life. I was shocked. I decided I should try to answer the question "Why are these people so poor and why are we so rich, and what can we do to turn their state into our state?" We live in a bubble world in the United States and Europe, and we don't realize how poor people really are. When you see poverty at first hand, it is very hard to think about something else. So I decided to study economic growth. Coincidentally, when I returned from Bolivia, I was assigned to be Robert Barro's teaching assistant. He was teaching economic growth, so I studied with him and eventually wrote books and articles with him.

In your first research on economic growth, you tested the neoclassical growth model using data for a number of countries and for the states of the United States. What did you discover?

Neoclassical theory was criticized on two grounds. First, its source of growth, technological change, is exogenous—not explained. Second, its assumption of diminishing marginal returns to capital seems to imply that income per person should converge to the same level in every country. If you are poor, your marginal product should be high. Every cookie that you save should generate huge growth. If you are rich, your marginal product should be low. Every cookie you save should generate very little growth. Therefore poor countries should grow faster than rich countries, and convergence of income levels should occur. Convergence doesn't occur, so, said its critics, neoclassical theory must be wrong.

It turned out that it was this criticism that was wrong. Growth depends on the productivity of your cookies and on how many cookies you save. If you don't save any cookies, you don't grow, even if your marginal product is large.

Conditional convergence is the idea that income per person will converge only if countries have similar savings rates, similar technologies, and similar everything. That's what I tested. To hold every relevant factor equal, I tested the hypothesis using regions: states within the United States or countries that are similar. And once you're careful to hold other things equal, you see a perfect negative relationship between growth rates and income levels.

> **Growth through capital accumulation is very, very hard. Growth has to come from other things, such as technological change.**

XAVIER SALA-I-MARTIN is Professor of Economics at Columbia University. He is also a Research Associate at the National Bureau of Economic Research, Senior Economic Advisor to the World Economic Forum, Associate Editor of the *Journal of Economic Growth,* founder and CEO of Umbele Foundation: A Future for Africa, and President of the Economic Commission of the Barcelona Football Club.

Professor Sala-i-Martin was an undergraduate at Universitat Autonoma de Barcelona and a graduate student at Harvard University, where he obtained his Ph.D. in 1990.

In 2004, he was awarded the Premio Juan Carlos I de Economía, a biannual prize given by the Bank of Spain to the best economist in Spain and Latin America. With Robert Barro, he is the author of *Economic Growth* Second Edition (MIT Press, 2003), the definitive graduate level text on this topic.

Michael Parkin talked with Xavier Sala-i-Martin about his work and the progress that economists have made in understanding economic growth.

As predicted by neoclassical theory, poor countries grow faster than rich countries if they are similar. So my research shows that it is not so easy to reject neoclassical theory. The law of diminishing returns that comes from Adam Smith and Malthus and Ricardo is very powerful. Growth through capital accumulation is very, very hard. Growth has to come from other things, such as technological change.

What do we know today about the nature and causes of the wealth of nations that Adam Smith didn't know?

Actually, even though over the last two hundred years some of the best minds have looked at the question, we know surprisingly little. We have some general principles that are not very easy to apply in practice. We know, for example, that markets are good. We know that for the economy to work, we need property rights to be guaranteed. If there are thieves—government or private thieves—that can steal the proceeds of the investment, there's no investment and there's no growth. We know that the incentives are very important.

These are general principles. Because we know these principles we should ask: How come Africa is still poor? The answer is, it is very hard to translate "Markets are good" and "Property rights work" into practical actions. We know that Zimbabwe has to guarantee property rights. With the government it has, that's not going to work. The U.S. constitution works in the United States. If you try to copy the constitution and impose the system in Zimbabwe, it's not going to work.

You've done a lot of work on distribution of income, and you say we've made a lot of progress. What is the evidence to support this conclusion?

There are two issues: poverty and inequality. When in 2001 I said poverty is going down, everyone said I was crazy. The United Nations Development Report, which uses World Bank data, was saying the exact opposite. I said the World Bank methodology was flawed. After a big public argument that you can see in *The Economist*, the World Bank revised their poverty numbers and they now agree with me that poverty rates are falling.

Now why is poverty falling? In 1970, 80 percent of the world's poor were in Asia—in China, India, Bangladesh, and Indonesia. China's "Great Leap Forward" was a great leap backward. People were starving to death. Now, the growth of these countries has been spectacular and the global poverty rate has fallen. Yes, if you look at Africa, Africa is going backwards. But Africa has 700 million people. China has 1.3 billion. India has 1.1 billion. Indonesia has 300 million. Asia has 4 billion of the world's 6 billion people. These big guys are growing. It's impossible that global poverty is not going down.

But what we care about is poverty in different regions of the world. Asia has been doing very well, but Africa has not. Unfortunately, Africa is still going in the wrong direction.

You've made a big personal commitment to Africa. What is the Africa problem? Why does this continent lag behind Asia? Why, as you've just put it, is Africa going in the wrong direction?

Number one, Africa is a very violent continent. There are twenty-two wars in Africa as we speak. Two, nobody will invest in Africa. Three, we in the rich world—the United States, Europe, and Japan—won't let them trade. Because we have agricultural subsidies, trade barriers, and tariffs for their products, they can't sell to us.

Africans should globalize themselves. They should open, and we should let them open. They should introduce markets. But to get markets, you need legal systems, police, transparency, less red tape. You need a lot of the things we have now. They have corrupt economies, very bureaucratic, with no property rights, the judiciary is corrupt. All of that has to change.

They need female education. One of the biggest rates of return that we have is educating girls. To educate girls, they'll need to build schools, they need to pay teachers, they need to buy uniforms, they need to provide the incentives for girls to go to school, which usually is like a string. You pull it, you don't push it. Pushing education doesn't work. What you need is: Let the girls know that the rate of return on education is very high by providing jobs after they leave school. So you need to change the incentives of the girls to go to school and educate themselves. That's going to increase the national product, but it will also increase health, and it will also reduce fertility.

Returning to the problems of poverty and inequality, how can inequality be increasing within countries but decreasing globally—across countries?

Because most inequality comes from the fact that some people live in rich countries and some people live in poor countries. The big difference across people is not that there are rich Americans and poor Americans. Americans are very close to each other relative to the difference between Americans and people from Senegal. What is closing today is the gap *across* countries—and for the first time in history. Before the Industrial Revolution, everybody was equal. Equal and poor. Equally poor. People were living at subsistence levels, which means you eat, you're clothed, you have a house, you die. No movies, no travel, no music, no toothbrush. Just subsist. And if the weather is not good, one third of the population dies. That was the history of the world between 10,000 B.C. and today.

Yes, there was a king, there was Caesar, but the majority of the population were peasants.

All of a sudden, the Industrial Revolution means that one small country, England, takes off and there is 2 percent growth every year. The living standard of the workers of England goes up and up and up. Then the United States, then France, then the rest of Europe, then Canada all begin to grow.

In terms of today's population, one billion people become rich and five billion remain poor. Now for the first time in history, the majority of these five billion people are growing more rapidly than the rich guys. They're catching up quickly. The incomes of the majority of poor citizens of the world are growing faster than those of Americans.

What advice do you have for someone who is just beginning to study economics?

Question! Question everything! Take some courses in history and math. And read my latest favorite book, Bill Easterly's *White Man's Burden.** It shows why we have not been doing the right thing in the aid business. I'm a little bit less dramatic than he is. He says that nothing has worked. I think some things have worked, and we have to take advantage of what has worked to build on it. But I agree with the general principle that being nice, being good, doesn't necessarily mean doing good. Lots of people with good intentions do harm. Economic science teaches us that incentives are the key.

Question! Question everything!

*William Easterly, *The White Man's Burden: Why the West's Efforts to Aid the Rest Have Done So Much Ill and So Little Good.* New York, Penguin Books, 2006.

PART FOUR Macroeconomic Fluctuations

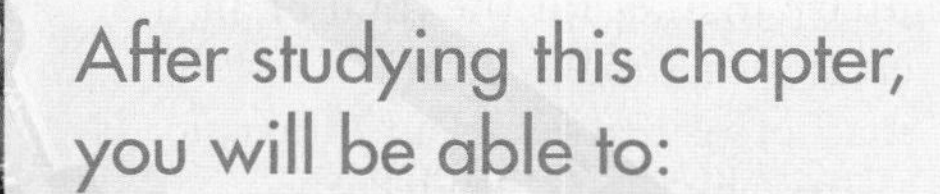

After studying this chapter, you will be able to:

- Explain what determines aggregate supply in the long run and in the short run
- Explain what determines aggregate demand
- Explain how real GDP and the price level are determined and how changes in aggregate supply and aggregate demand bring economic growth, inflation, and the business cycle
- Describe the main schools of thought in macroeconomics today

10 AGGREGATE SUPPLY AND AGGREGATE DEMAND

The pace at which production grows and prices rise is uneven. In 2004, real GDP grew by 3.6 percent, but 2008 had zero growth and 2009 saw real GDP shrink by more than 2 percent.

Similarly, during recent years, prices have increased at rates ranging from more than 3 percent in 2005 to a barely perceptible less than 1 percent in 2009.

The uneven pace of economic growth and inflation—the business cycle—is the subject of this chapter and the two that follow it.

This chapter explains a model of real GDP and the price level—the *aggregate supply–aggregate demand model* or *AS-AD model*. This model represents the consensus view of macroeconomists on how real GDP and the price level are determined. The model provides a framework for understanding the forces that make our economy expand, that bring inflation, and that cause business cycle fluctuations. The *AS-AD* model also provides a framework within which we can see the range of views of macroeconomists in different schools of thought.

In *Reading Between the Lines* at the end of the chapter, we use the *AS-AD* model to interpret the course of U.S. real GDP and the price level in 2010.

Aggregate Supply

The purpose of the aggregate supply–aggregate demand model that you study in this chapter is to explain how real GDP and the price level are determined and how they interact. The model uses similar ideas to those that you encountered in Chapter 3 when you learned how the quantity and price in a competitive market are determined. But the *aggregate* supply–*aggregate* demand model (*AS-AD* model) isn't just an application of the competitive market model. Some differences arise because the *AS-AD* model is a model of an imaginary market for the total of all the final goods and services that make up real GDP. The quantity in this "market" is real GDP and the price is the price level measured by the GDP deflator.

One thing that the *AS-AD* model shares with the competitive market model is that both distinguish between *supply* and the *quantity supplied.* We begin by explaining what we mean by the quantity of real GDP supplied.

Quantity Supplied and Supply

The *quantity of real GDP supplied* is the total quantity of goods and services, valued in constant base-year (2005) dollars, that firms plan to produce during a given period. This quantity depends on the quantity of labor employed, the quantity of physical and human capital, and the state of technology.

At any given time, the quantity of capital and the state of technology are fixed. They depend on decisions that were made in the past. The population is also fixed. But the quantity of labor is not fixed. It depends on decisions made by households and firms about the supply of and demand for labor.

The labor market can be in any one of three states: at full employment, above full employment, or below full employment. At full employment, the quantity of real GDP supplied is *potential GDP*, which depends on the full-employment quantity of labor (see Chapter 6, pp. 139–141). Over the business cycle, employment fluctuates around full employment and the quantity of real GDP supplied fluctuates around potential GDP.

Aggregate supply is the relationship between the quantity of real GDP supplied and the price level. This relationship is different in the long run than in the short run and to study aggregate supply, we distinguish between two time frames:

- Long-run aggregate supply
- Short-run aggregate supply

Long-Run Aggregate Supply

Long-run aggregate supply is the relationship between the quantity of real GDP supplied and the price level when the money wage rate changes in step with the price level to maintain full employment. The quantity of real GDP supplied at full employment equals potential GDP and this quantity is the same regardless of the price level.

The long-run aggregate supply curve in Fig. 10.1 illustrates long-run aggregate supply as the vertical line at potential GDP labeled *LAS*. Along the long-run aggregate supply curve, as the price level changes, the money wage rate also changes so the real wage rate remains at the full-employment equilibrium level and real GDP remains at potential GDP. The long-run aggregate supply curve is always vertical and is always located at potential GDP.

The long-run aggregate supply curve is vertical because potential GDP is independent of the price level. The reason for this independence is that a movement along the *LAS* curve is accompanied by a change in *two* sets of prices: the prices of goods and services—the price level—and the prices of the factors of production, most notably, the money wage rate. A 10 percent increase in the prices of goods and services is matched by a 10 percent increase in the money wage rate. Because the price level and the money wage rate change by the same percentage, the *real wage rate* remains unchanged at its full-employment equilibrium level. So when the price level changes and the real wage rate remains constant, employment remains constant and real GDP remains constant at potential GDP.

Production at a Pepsi Plant You can see more clearly why real GDP is unchanged when all prices change by the same percentage by thinking about production decisions at a Pepsi bottling plant. How does the quantity of Pepsi supplied change if the price of Pepsi changes and the wage rate of the workers and prices of all the other resources used vary by the same percentage? The answer is that the quantity supplied doesn't change. The firm produces the quantity that maximizes profit. That quantity depends on the price of Pepsi relative to the cost of producing it. With no change in price *relative to cost*, production doesn't change.

Short-Run Aggregate Supply

Short-run aggregate supply is the relationship between the quantity of real GDP supplied and the price level *when the money wage rate, the prices of other resources, and potential GDP remain constant.* Figure 10.1 illustrates this relationship as the short-run aggregate supply curve *SAS* and the short-run aggregate supply schedule. Each point on the *SAS* curve corresponds to a row of the short-run aggregate supply schedule. For example, point *A* on the *SAS* curve and row *A* of the schedule tell us that if the price level is 100, the quantity of real GDP supplied is $12 trillion. In the short run, a rise in the price level brings an increase in the quantity of real GDP supplied. The short-run aggregate supply curve slopes upward.

With a given money wage rate, there is one price level at which the real wage rate is at its full-employment equilibrium level. At this price level, the quantity of real GDP supplied equals potential GDP and the *SAS* curve intersects the *LAS* curve. In this example, that price level is 110. If the price level rises above 110, the quantity of real GDP supplied increases along the *SAS* curve and exceeds potential GDP; if the price level falls below 110, the quantity of real GDP supplied decreases along the *SAS* curve and is less than potential GDP.

Back at the Pepsi Plant You can see why the short-run aggregate supply curve slopes upward by returning to the Pepsi bottling plant. If production increases, marginal cost rises and if production decreases, marginal cost falls (see Chapter 2, p. 33).

If the price of Pepsi rises with no change in the money wage rate and other costs, Pepsi can increase profit by increasing production. Pepsi is in business to maximize its profit, so it increases production.

Similarly, if the price of Pepsi falls while the money wage rate and other costs remain constant, Pepsi can avoid a loss by decreasing production. The lower price weakens the incentive to produce, so Pepsi decreases production.

What's true for Pepsi bottlers is true for the producers of all goods and services. When all prices rise, the *price level rises.* If the price level rises and the money wage rate and other factor prices remain constant, all firms increase production and the quantity of real GDP supplied increases. A fall in the price level has the opposite effect and decreases the quantity of real GDP supplied.

FIGURE 10.1 Long-Run and Short-Run Aggregate Supply

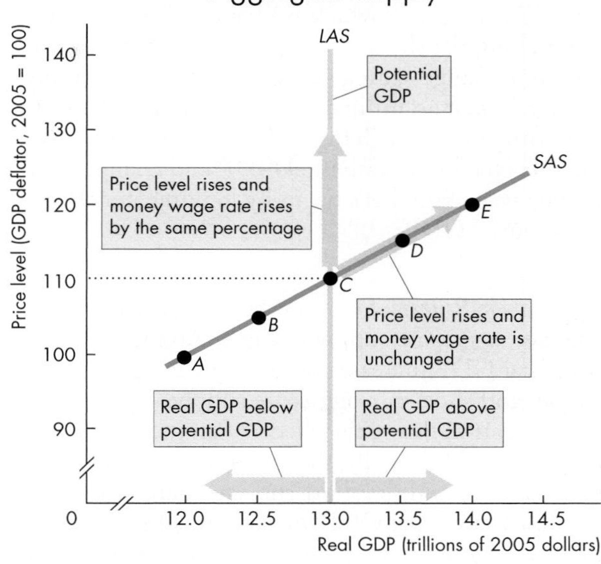

	Price level (GDP deflator)	Real GDP supplied (trillions of 2005 dollars)
A	100	12.0
B	105	12.5
C	**110**	**13.0**
D	115	13.5
E	120	14.0

In the long run, the quantity of real GDP supplied is potential GDP and the *LAS* curve is vertical at potential GDP. In the short-run, the quantity of real GDP supplied increases if the price level rises, while all other influences on supply plans remain the same.

The short-run aggregate supply curve, *SAS*, slopes upward. The short-run aggregate supply curve is based on the aggregate supply schedule in the table. Each point *A* through *E* on the curve corresponds to the row in the table identified by the same letter.

When the price level is 110, the quantity of real GDP supplied is $13 trillion, which is potential GDP. If the price level rises above 110, the quantity of real GDP supplied increases and exceeds potential GDP; if the price level falls below 110, the quantity of real GDP supplied decreases below potential GDP.

myeconlab animation

Changes in Aggregate Supply

A change in the price level changes the quantity of real GDP supplied, which is illustrated by a movement along the short-run aggregate supply curve. It does not change aggregate supply. Aggregate supply changes when an influence on production plans other than the price level changes. These other influences include changes in potential GDP and changes in the money wage rate. Let's begin by looking at a change in potential GDP.

Changes in Potential GDP When potential GDP changes, aggregate supply changes. An increase in potential GDP increases both long-run aggregate supply and short-run aggregate supply.

Figure 10.2 shows the effects of an increase in potential GDP. Initially, the long-run aggregate supply curve is LAS_0 and the short-run aggregate supply curve is SAS_0. If potential GDP increases to $14 trillion, long-run aggregate supply increases and the long-run aggregate supply curve shifts rightward to LAS_1. Short-run aggregate supply also increases, and the short-run aggregate supply curve shifts rightward to SAS_1. The two supply curves shift by the same amount only if the full-employment price level remains constant, which we will assume to be the case.

Potential GDP can increase for any of three reasons:

- An increase in the full-employment quantity of labor
- An increase in the quantity of capital
- An advance in technology

Let's look at these influences on potential GDP and the aggregate supply curves.

An Increase in the Full-Employment Quantity of Labor A Pepsi bottling plant that employs 100 workers bottles more Pepsi than does an otherwise identical plant that employs 10 workers. The same is true for the economy as a whole. The larger the quantity of labor employed, the greater is real GDP.

Over time, potential GDP increases because the labor force increases. But (with constant capital and technology) *potential* GDP increases only if the full-employment quantity of labor increases. Fluctuations in employment over the business cycle bring fluctuations in real GDP. But these changes in real GDP are fluctuations around potential GDP. They are not changes in potential GDP and long-run aggregate supply.

FIGURE 10.2 A Change in Potential GDP

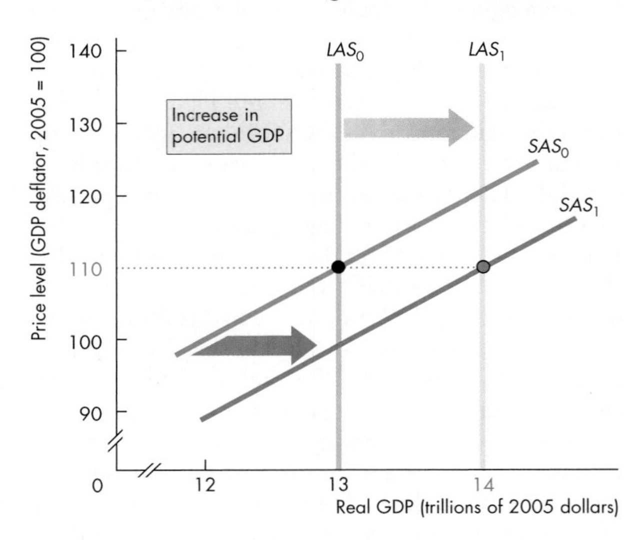

An increase in potential GDP increases both long-run aggregate supply and short-run aggregate supply. The long-run aggregate supply curve shifts rightward from LAS_0 to LAS_1 and the short-run aggregate supply curve shifts from SAS_0 to SAS_1.

myeconlab animation

An Increase in the Quantity of Capital A Pepsi bottling plant with two production lines bottles more Pepsi than does an otherwise identical plant that has only one production line. For the economy, the larger the quantity of capital, the more productive is the labor force and the greater is its potential GDP. Potential GDP per person in the capital-rich United States is vastly greater than that in capital-poor China or Russia.

Capital includes *human capital.* One Pepsi plant is managed by an economics major with an MBA and has a labor force with an average of 10 years of experience. This plant produces a larger output than does an otherwise identical plant that is managed by someone with no business training or experience and that has a young labor force that is new to bottling. The first plant has a greater amount of human capital than the second. For the economy as a whole, the larger the quantity of *human capital*—the skills that people have acquired in school and through on-the-job training—the greater is potential GDP.

An Advance in Technology A Pepsi plant that has pre-computer age machines produces less than one that uses the latest robot technology. Technological change enables firms to produce more from any given amount of factors of production. So even with fixed quantities of labor and capital, improvements in technology increase potential GDP.

Technological advances are by far the most important source of increased production over the past two centuries. As a result of technological advances, one farmer in the United States today can feed 100 people and in a year one autoworker can produce almost 14 cars and trucks.

Let's now look at the effects of changes in the money wage rate.

Changes in the Money Wage Rate When the money wage rate (or the money price of any other factor of production such as oil) changes, short-run aggregate supply changes but long-run aggregate supply does not change.

Figure 10.3 shows the effect of an increase in the money wage rate. Initially, the short-run aggregate supply curve is SAS_0. A rise in the money wage rate *decreases* short-run aggregate supply and shifts the short-run aggregate supply curve leftward to SAS_2.

A rise in the money wage rate decreases short-run aggregate supply because it increases firms' costs. With increased costs, the quantity that firms are willing to supply at each price level decreases, which is shown by a leftward shift of the *SAS* curve.

A change in the money wage rate does not change long-run aggregate supply because on the *LAS* curve, the change in the money wage rate is accompanied by an equal percentage change in the price level. With no change in *relative* prices, firms have no incentive to change production and real GDP remains constant at potential GDP. With no change in potential GDP, the long-run aggregate supply curve *LAS* does not shift.

What Makes the Money Wage Rate Change? The money wage rate can change for two reasons: departures from full employment and expectations about inflation. Unemployment above the natural rate puts downward pressure on the money wage rate, and unemployment below the natural rate puts upward pressure on it. An expected rise in the inflation rate makes the money wage rate rise faster, and an expected fall in the inflation rate slows the rate at which the money wage rate rises.

FIGURE 10.3 A Change in the Money Wage Rate

A rise in the money wage rate decreases short-run aggregate supply and shifts the short-run aggregate supply curve leftward from SAS_0 to SAS_2. A rise in the money wage rate does not change potential GDP, so the long-run aggregate supply curve does not shift.

myeconlab animation

REVIEW QUIZ

1. If the price level and the money wage rate rise by the same percentage, what happens to the quantity of real GDP supplied? Along which aggregate supply curve does the economy move?
2. If the price level rises and the money wage rate remains constant, what happens to the quantity of real GDP supplied? Along which aggregate supply curve does the economy move?
3. If potential GDP increases, what happens to aggregate supply? Does the *LAS* curve shift or is there a movement along the *LAS* curve? Does the *SAS* curve shift or is there a movement along the *SAS* curve?
4. If the money wage rate rises and potential GDP remains the same, does the *LAS* curve or the *SAS* curve shift or is there a movement along the *LAS* curve or the *SAS* curve?

You can work these questions in Study Plan 10.1 and get instant feedback.

Aggregate Demand

The quantity of real GDP demanded (Y) is the sum of real consumption expenditure (C), investment (I), government expenditure (G), and exports (X) minus imports (M). That is,

$$Y = C + I + G + X - M.$$

The *quantity of real GDP demanded* is the total amount of final goods and services produced in the United States that people, businesses, governments, and foreigners plan to buy.

These buying plans depend on many factors. Some of the main ones are

1. The price level
2. Expectations
3. Fiscal policy and monetary policy
4. The world economy

We first focus on the relationship between the quantity of real GDP demanded and the price level. To study this relationship, we keep all other influences on buying plans the same and ask: How does the quantity of real GDP demanded vary as the price level varies?

The Aggregate Demand Curve

Other things remaining the same, the higher the price level, the smaller is the quantity of real GDP demanded. This relationship between the quantity of real GDP demanded and the price level is called **aggregate demand.** Aggregate demand is described by an *aggregate demand schedule* and an *aggregate demand curve.*

Figure 10.4 shows an aggregate demand curve (AD) and an aggregate demand schedule. Each point on the AD curve corresponds to a row of the schedule. For example, point C' on the AD curve and row C' of the schedule tell us that if the price level is 110, the quantity of real GDP demanded is $13 trillion.

The aggregate demand curve slopes downward for two reasons:

- Wealth effect
- Substitution effects

Wealth Effect When the price level rises but other things remain the same, *real* wealth decreases. Real wealth is the amount of money in the bank, bonds, stocks, and other assets that people own, measured not in dollars but in terms of the goods and services that the money, bonds, and stocks will buy.

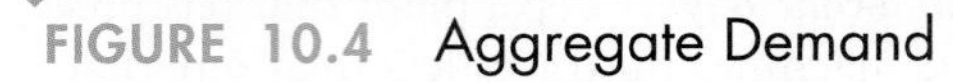

FIGURE 10.4 Aggregate Demand

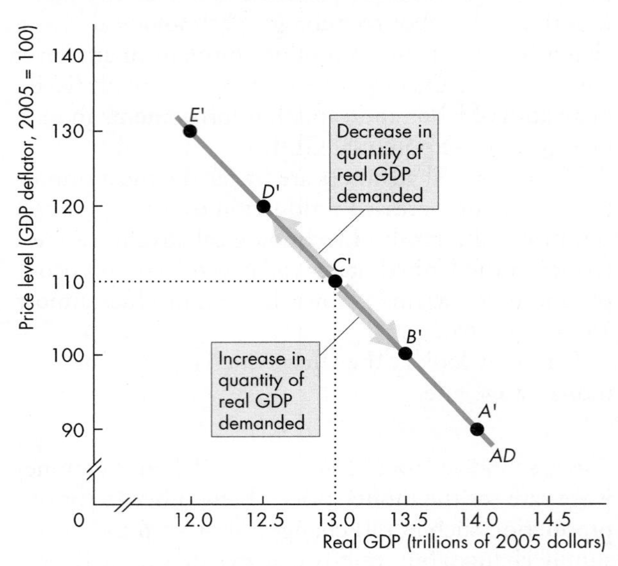

	Price level (GDP deflator)	Real GDP demanded (trillions of 2005 dollars)
A'	90	14.0
B'	100	13.5
C'	**110**	**13.0**
D'	120	12.5
E'	130	12.0

The aggregate demand curve (AD) shows the relationship between the quantity of real GDP demanded and the price level. The aggregate demand curve is based on the aggregate demand schedule in the table. Each point A' through E' on the curve corresponds to the row in the table identified by the same letter. When the price level is 110, the quantity of real GDP demanded is $13 trillion, as shown by point C' in the figure. A change in the price level, when all other influences on aggregate buying plans remain the same, brings a change in the quantity of real GDP demanded and a movement along the AD curve.

People save and hold money, bonds, and stocks for many reasons. One reason is to build up funds for education expenses. Another reason is to build up enough funds to meet possible medical expenses or other big bills. But the biggest reason is to build up enough funds to provide a retirement income.

If the price level rises, real wealth decreases. People then try to restore their wealth. To do so, they must increase saving and, equivalently, decrease current consumption. Such a decrease in consumption is a decrease in aggregate demand.

Maria's Wealth Effect You can see how the wealth effect works by thinking about Maria's buying plans. Maria lives in Moscow, Russia. She has worked hard all summer and saved 20,000 rubles (the ruble is the currency of Russia), which she plans to spend attending graduate school when she has finished her economics degree. So Maria's wealth is 20,000 rubles. Maria has a part-time job, and her income from this job pays her current expenses. The price level in Russia rises by 100 percent, and now Maria needs 40,000 rubles to buy what 20,000 once bought. To try to make up some of the fall in value of her savings, Maria saves even more and cuts her current spending to the bare minimum.

Substitution Effects When the price level rises and other things remain the same, interest rates rise. The reason is related to the wealth effect that you've just studied. A rise in the price level decreases the real value of the money in people's pockets and bank accounts. With a smaller amount of real money around, banks and other lenders can get a higher interest rate on loans. But faced with a higher interest rate, people and businesses delay plans to buy new capital and consumer durable goods and cut back on spending.

This substitution effect involves changing the timing of purchases of capital and consumer durable goods and is called an *intertemporal* substitution effect—a substitution across time. Saving increases to increase future consumption.

To see this intertemporal substitution effect more clearly, think about your own plan to buy a new computer. At an interest rate of 5 percent a year, you might borrow $1,000 and buy the new computer. But at an interest rate of 10 percent a year, you might decide that the payments would be too high. You don't abandon your plan to buy the computer, but you decide to delay your purchase.

A second substitution effect works through international prices. When the U.S. price level rises and other things remain the same, U.S.-made goods and services become more expensive relative to foreign-made goods and services. This change in *relative prices* encourages people to spend less on U.S.-made items and more on foreign-made items. For example, if the U.S. price level rises relative to the Japanese price level, Japanese buy fewer U.S.-made cars (U.S. exports decrease) and Americans buy more Japanese-made cars (U.S. imports increase). U.S. GDP decreases.

Maria's Substitution Effects In Moscow, Russia, Maria makes some substitutions. She was planning to trade in her old motor scooter and get a new one. But with a higher price level and a higher interest rate, she decides to make her old scooter last one more year. Also, with the prices of Russian goods sharply increasing, Maria substitutes a low-cost dress made in Malaysia for the Russian-made dress she had originally planned to buy.

Changes in the Quantity of Real GDP Demanded When the price level rises and other things remain the same, the quantity of real GDP demanded decreases—a movement up along the *AD* curve as shown by the arrow in Fig. 10.4. When the price level falls and other things remain the same, the quantity of real GDP demanded increases—a movement down along the *AD* curve.

We've now seen how the quantity of real GDP demanded changes when the price level changes. How do other influences on buying plans affect aggregate demand?

Changes in Aggregate Demand

A change in any factor that influences buying plans other than the price level brings a change in aggregate demand. The main factors are

- Expectations
- Fiscal policy and monetary policy
- The world economy

Expectations An increase in expected future income increases the amount of consumption goods (especially big-ticket items such as cars) that people plan to buy today and increases aggregate demand.

An increase in the expected future inflation rate increases aggregate demand today because people decide to buy more goods and services at today's relatively lower prices.

An increase in expected future profits increases the investment that firms plan to undertake today and increases aggregate demand.

Fiscal Policy and Monetary Policy The government's attempt to influence the economy by setting and changing taxes, making transfer payments, and purchasing goods and services is called **fiscal policy**. A tax cut or an increase in transfer payments—for example, unemployment benefits or welfare payments—increases aggregate demand. Both of these influences operate by increasing households' *disposable* income. **Disposable income** is aggregate income minus taxes plus transfer payments. The greater the disposable income, the greater is the quantity of consumption goods and services that households plan to buy and the greater is aggregate demand.

Government expenditure on goods and services is one component of aggregate demand. So if the government spends more on spy satellites, schools, and highways, aggregate demand increases.

The Federal Reserve's (Fed's) attempt to influence the economy by changing interest rates and the quantity of money is called **monetary policy**. The Fed influences the quantity of money and interest rates by using the tools and methods described in Chapter 8.

An increase in the quantity of money increases aggregate demand through two main channels: It lowers interest rates and makes it easier to get a loan.

With lower interest rates, businesses plan a greater level of investment in new capital and households plan greater expenditure on new homes, on home improvements, on automobiles, and a host of other consumer durable goods. Banks and others eager to lend lower their standards for making loans and more people are able to get home loans and other consumer loans.

A decrease in the quantity of money has the opposite effects and lowers aggregate demand.

The World Economy Two main influences that the world economy has on aggregate demand are the exchange rate and foreign income. The *exchange rate* is the amount of a foreign currency that you can buy with a U.S. dollar. Other things remaining the same, a rise in the exchange rate decreases aggregate

Economics in Action

Fiscal Policy to Fight Recession

In February 2008, Congress passed legislation that gave $168 billion to businesses and low- and middle-income Americans—$600 to a single person and $1,200 to a couple with an additional $300 for each child. The benefit was scaled back for individuals with incomes above $75,000 a year and for families with incomes greater than $150,000 a year.

The idea of the package was to stimulate business investment and consumption expenditure and increase aggregate demand.

Deal makers Senators Harry Reid and Mitch McConnell

Monetary Policy to Fight Recession

In October 2008 and the months that followed, the Federal Reserve, in concert with the European Central Bank, the Bank of Canada, and the Bank of England, cut the interest rate and took other measures to ease credit and encourage banks and other financial institutions to increase their lending. The U.S. interest rate was the lowest (see below).

Like the earlier fiscal stimulus package, the idea of these interest rate cuts and easier credit was to stimulate business investment and consumption expenditure and increase aggregate demand.

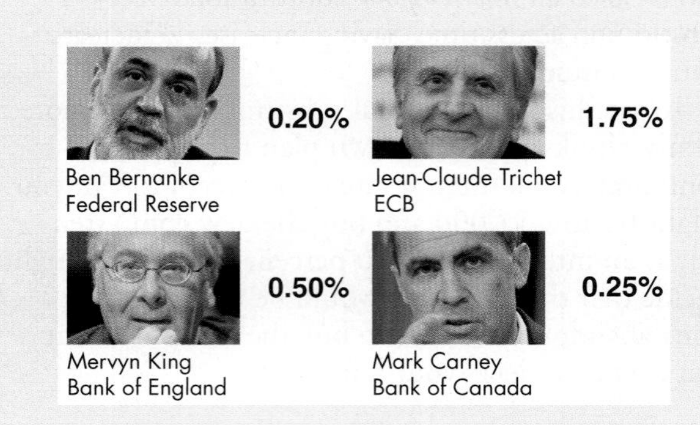

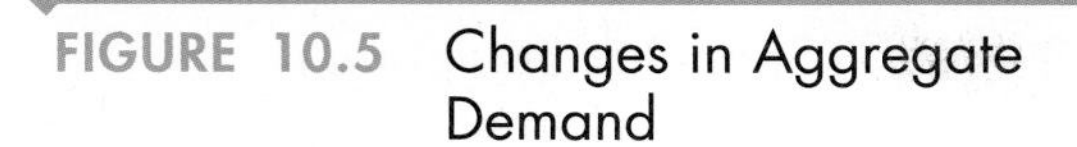

FIGURE 10.5 Changes in Aggregate Demand

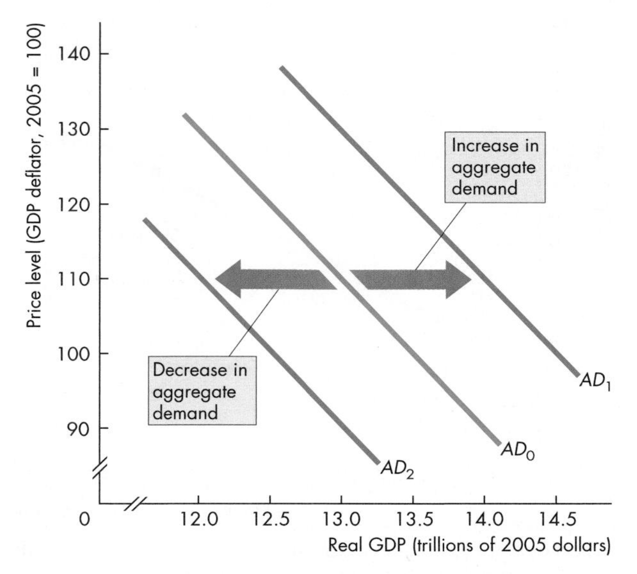

Aggregate demand

Decreases if:

- Expected future income, inflation, or profit decreases
- Fiscal policy decreases government expenditure, increases taxes, or decreases transfer payments
- Monetary policy decreases the quantity of money and increases interest rates
- The exchange rate increases or foreign income decreases

Increases if:

- Expected future income, inflation, or profit increases
- Fiscal policy increases government expenditure, decreases taxes, or increases transfer payments
- Monetary policy increases the quantity of money and decreases interest rates
- The exchange rate decreases or foreign income increases

myeconlab animation

demand. To see how the exchange rate influences aggregate demand, suppose that the exchange rate is 1.20 euros per U.S. dollar. A Nokia cell phone made in Finland costs 120 euros, and an equivalent Motorola phone made in the United States costs \$110. In U.S. dollars, the Nokia phone costs \$100, so people around the world buy the cheaper phone from Finland. Now suppose the exchange rate falls to 1 euro per U.S. dollar. The Nokia phone now costs \$120 and is more expensive than the Motorola phone. People will switch from the Nokia phone to the Motorola phone. U.S. exports will increase and U.S. imports will decrease, so U.S. aggregate demand will increase.

An increase in foreign income increases U.S. exports and increases U.S. aggregate demand. For example, an increase in income in Japan and Germany increases Japanese and German consumers' and producers' planned expenditures on U.S.-produced goods and services.

Shifts of the Aggregate Demand Curve When aggregate demand changes, the aggregate demand curve shifts. Figure 10.5 shows two changes in aggregate demand and summarizes the factors that bring about such changes.

Aggregate demand increases and the *AD* curve shifts rightward from AD_0 to AD_1 when expected future income, inflation, or profit increases; government expenditure on goods and services increases; taxes are cut; transfer payments increase; the quantity of money increases and the interest rate falls; the exchange rate falls; or foreign income increases.

Aggregate demand decreases and the *AD* curve shifts leftward from AD_0 to AD_2 when expected future income, inflation, or profit decreases; government expenditure on goods and services decreases; taxes increase; transfer payments decrease; the quantity of money decreases and the interest rate rises; the exchange rate rises; or foreign income decreases.

REVIEW QUIZ

1. What does the aggregate demand curve show? What factors change and what factors remain the same when there is a movement along the aggregate demand curve?
2. Why does the aggregate demand curve slope downward?
3. How do changes in expectations, fiscal policy and monetary policy, and the world economy change aggregate demand and the aggregate demand curve?

You can work these questions in Study Plan 10.2 and get instant feedback.

Explaining Macroeconomic Trends and Fluctuations

The purpose of the *AS-AD* model is to explain changes in real GDP and the price level. The model's main purpose is to explain business cycle fluctuations in these variables. But the model also aids our understanding of economic growth and inflation trends. We begin by combining aggregate supply and aggregate demand to determine real GDP and the price level in equilibrium. Just as there are two time frames for aggregate supply, there are two time frames for macroeconomic equilibrium: a long-run equilibrium and a short-run equilibrium. We'll first look at short-run equilibrium.

Short-Run Macroeconomic Equilibrium

The aggregate demand curve tells us the quantity of real GDP demanded at each price level, and the short-run aggregate supply curve tells us the quantity of real GDP supplied at each price level. **Short-run macroeconomic equilibrium** occurs when the quantity of real GDP demanded equals the quantity of real GDP supplied. That is, short-run macroeconomic equilibrium occurs at the point of intersection of the *AD* curve and the *SAS* curve.

Figure 10.6 shows such an equilibrium at a price level of 110 and real GDP of $13 trillion (points *C* and *C*').

To see why this position is the equilibrium, think about what happens if the price level is something other than 110. Suppose, for example, that the price level is 120 and that real GDP is $14 trillion (at point *E* on the *SAS* curve). The quantity of real GDP demanded is less than $14 trillion, so firms are unable to sell all their output. Unwanted inventories pile up, and firms cut both production and prices. Production and prices are cut until firms can sell all their output. This situation occurs only when real GDP is $13 trillion and the price level is 110.

Now suppose the price level is 100 and real GDP is $12 trillion (at point *A* on the *SAS* curve). The quantity of real GDP demanded exceeds $12 trillion, so firms are unable to meet the demand for their output. Inventories decrease, and customers clamor for goods and services, so firms increase production and raise prices. Production and prices increase until firms can meet the demand for their output. This situation occurs only when real GDP is $13 trillion and the price level is 110.

FIGURE 10.6 Short-Run Equilibrium

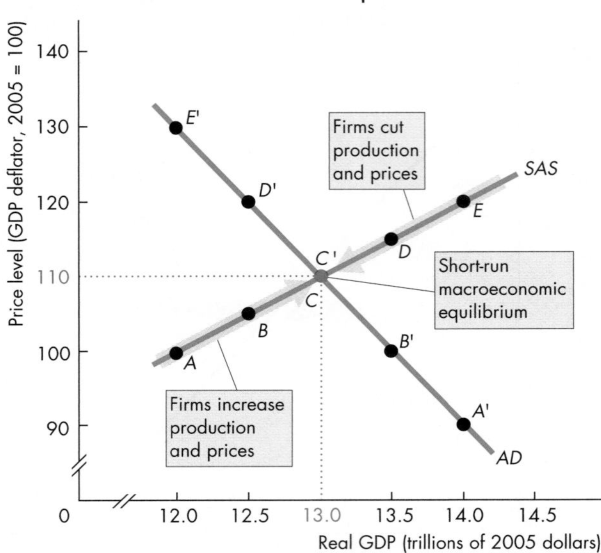

Short-run macroeconomic equilibrium occurs when real GDP demanded equals real GDP supplied—at the intersection of the aggregate demand curve (*AD*) and the short-run aggregate supply curve (*SAS*).

myeconlab animation

In the short run, the money wage rate is fixed. It does not adjust to move the economy to full employment. So in the short run, real GDP can be greater than or less than potential GDP. But in the long run, the money wage rate does adjust and real GDP moves toward potential GDP. Let's look at long-run equilibrium and see how we get there.

Long-Run Macroeconomic Equilibrium

Long-run macroeconomic equilibrium occurs when real GDP equals potential GDP—equivalently, when the economy is on its *LAS* curve.

When the economy is a away from long-run equilibrium, the money wage rate adjusts. If the money wage rate is too high, short-run equilibrium is below potential GDP and the unemployment rate is above the natural rate. With an excess supply of labor, the money wage rate falls. If the money wage rate is too low, short-run equilibrium is above potential GDP and the unemployment rate is below the natural rate.

With an excess demand for labor, the money wage rate rises.

Figure 10.7 shows the long-run equilibrium and how it comes about. If short-run aggregate supply curve is SAS_1, the money wage rate is too high to achieve full employment. A fall in the money wage rate shifts the *SAS* curve to *SAS** and brings full employment. If short-run aggregate supply curve is SAS_2, the money wage rate is too low to achieve full employment. Now, a rise in the money wage rate shifts the *SAS* curve to *SAS** and brings full employment.

In long-run equilibrium, potential GDP determines real GDP and potential GDP and aggregate demand together determine the price level. The money wage rate adjusts until the *SAS* curve passes through the long-run equilibrium point.

Let's now see how the *AS-AD* model helps us to understand economic growth and inflation.

FIGURE 10.7 Long-Run Equilibrium

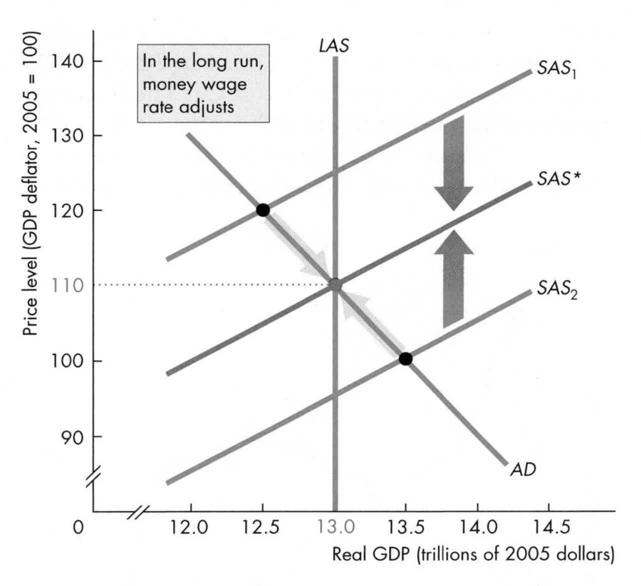

In long-run macroeconomic equilibrium, real GDP equals potential GDP. So long-run equilibrium occurs where the aggregate demand curve, *AD*, intersects the long-run aggregate supply curve, *LAS*. In the long run, aggregate demand determines the price level and has no effect on real GDP. The money wage rate adjusts in the long run, so that the *SAS* curve intersects the *LAS* curve at the long-run equilibrium price level.

myeconlab animation

Economic Growth and Inflation in the *AS-AD* Model

Economic growth results from a growing labor force and increasing labor productivity, which together make potential GDP grow (Chapter 6, pp. 141–144). Inflation results from a growing quantity of money that outpaces the growth of potential GDP (Chapter 8, pp. 200–201).

The *AS-AD* model explains and illustrates economic growth and inflation. It explains economic growth as increasing long-run aggregate supply and it explains inflation as a persistent increase in aggregate demand at a faster pace than that of the increase in potential GDP.

Economics in Action

U.S. Economic Growth and Inflation

The figure is a *scatter diagram* of U.S. real GDP and the price level. The graph has the same axes as those of the *AS-AD* model. Each dot represents a year between 1960 and 2010. The red dots are recession years. The pattern formed by the dots shows the combination of economic growth and inflation. Economic growth was fastest during the 1960s; inflation was fastest during the 1970s.

The *AS-AD* model interprets each dot as being at the intersection of the *SAS* and *AD* curves.

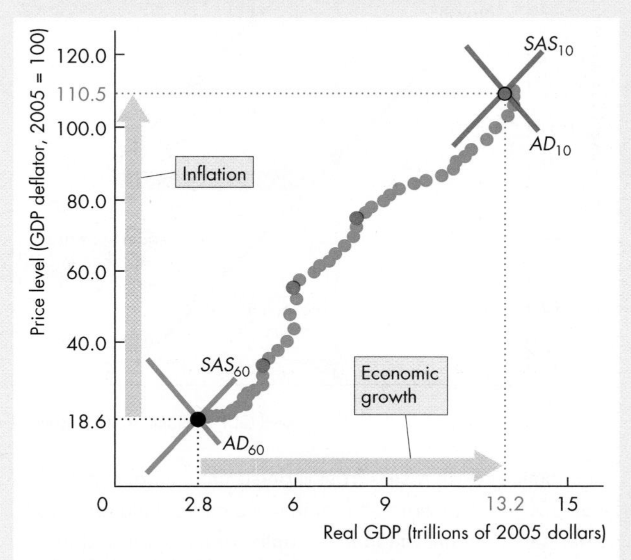

The Path of Real GDP and the Price Level

Source of data: Bureau of Economic Analysis.

Figure 10.8 illustrates this explanation in terms of the shifting *LAS* and *AD* curves.

When the *LAS* curve shifts rightward from LAS_0 to LAS_1, potential GDP grows from $13 trillion to $14 trillion and in long-run equilibrium, real GDP also grows to $14 trillion.

Whan the *AD* curve shifts rightward from AD_0 to AD_1, which is a growth of aggregate demand that outpaces the growth of potential GDP, the price level rises from 110 to 120.

If aggregate demand were to increase at the same pace as long-run aggregate supply, real GDP would grow with no inflation.

Our economy experiences periods of growth and inflation, like those shown in Fig. 10.8, but it does not experience *steady* growth and *steady* inflation. Real GDP fluctuates around potential GDP in a business cycle. When we study the business cycle, we ignore economic growth and focus on the fluctuations around the trend. By doing so, we see the business cycle more clearly. Let's now see how the *AS-AD* model explains the business cycle.

FIGURE 10.8 Economic Growth and Inflation

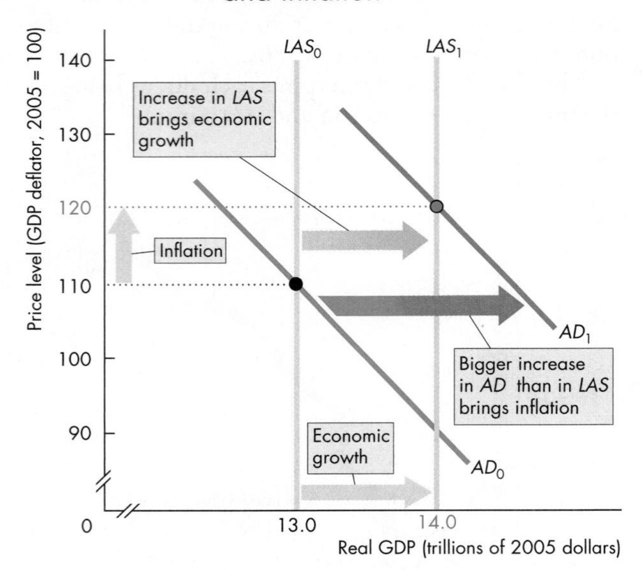

Economic growth results from a persistent increase in potential GDP—a rightward shift of the *LAS* curve. Inflation results from persistent growth in the quantity of money that shifts the *AD* curve rightward at a faster pace than the real GDP growth rate.

myeconlab animation

The Business Cycle in the *AS-AD* Model

The business cycle occurs because aggregate demand and short-run aggregate supply fluctuate but the money wage rate does not adjust quickly enough to keep real GDP at potential GDP. Figure 10.9 shows three types of short-run equilibrium.

Figure 10.9(a) shows an above full-employment equilibrium. An **above full-employment equilibrium** is an equilibrium in which real GDP exceeds potential GDP. The gap between real GDP and potential GDP is the **output gap.** When real GDP exceeds potential GDP, the output gap is called an **inflationary gap.**

The above full-employment equilibrium shown in Fig. 10.9(a) occurs where the aggregate demand curve AD_0 intersects the short-run aggregate supply curve SAS_0 at a real GDP of $13.2 trillion. There is an inflationary gap of $0.2 trillion.

Economics in Action

The U.S. Business Cycle

The U.S. economy had an inflationary gap in 2006 (at *A* in the figure), full employment in 2006 (at *B*), and a recessionary gap in 2009 (at *C*). The fluctuating output gap in the figure is the real-world version of Fig. 10.9(d) and is generated by fluctuations in aggregate demand and short-run aggregate supply.

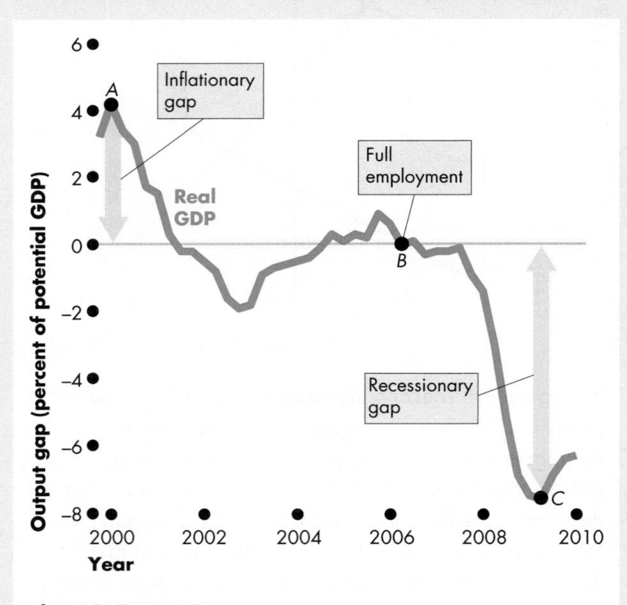

The U.S. Output Gap

Sources of data: Bureau of Economic Analysis and Congressional Budget Office.

Figure 10.9(b) is an example of **full-employment equilibrium,** in which real GDP equals potential GDP. In this example, the equilibrium occurs where the aggregate demand curve AD_1 intersects the short-run aggregate supply curve SAS_1 at an actual and potential GDP of $13 trillion.

In part (c), there is a below full-employment equilibrium. A **below full-employment equilibrium** is an equilibrium in which potential GDP exceeds real GDP. When potential GDP exceeds real GDP, the output gap is called a **recessionary gap.**

The below full-employment equilibrium shown in Fig. 10.9(c) occurs where the aggregate demand curve AD_2 intersects the short-run aggregate supply curve SAS_2 at a real GDP of $12.8 trillion. Potential GDP is $13 trillion, so the recessionary gap is $0.2 trillion.

The economy moves from one type of macroeconomic equilibrium to another as a result of fluctuations in aggregate demand and in short-run aggregate supply. These fluctuations produce fluctuations in real GDP. Figure 10.9(d) shows how real GDP fluctuates around potential GDP.

Let's now look at some of the sources of these fluctuations around potential GDP.

FIGURE 10.9 The Business Cycle

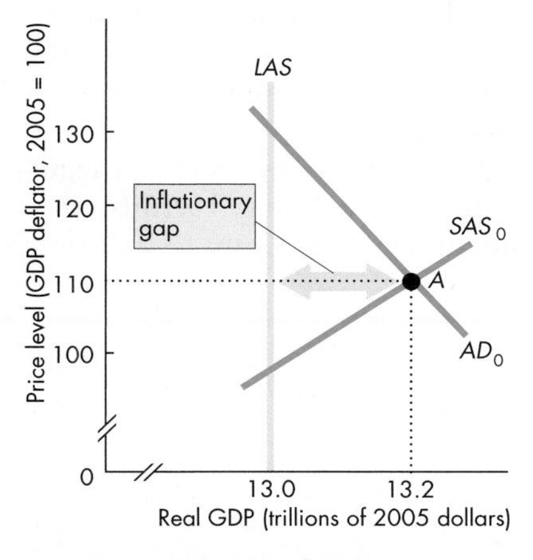

(a) Above full-employment equilibrium

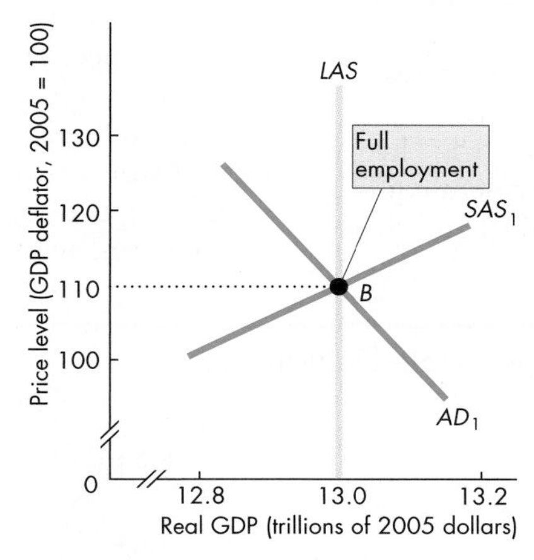

(b) Full-employment equilibrium

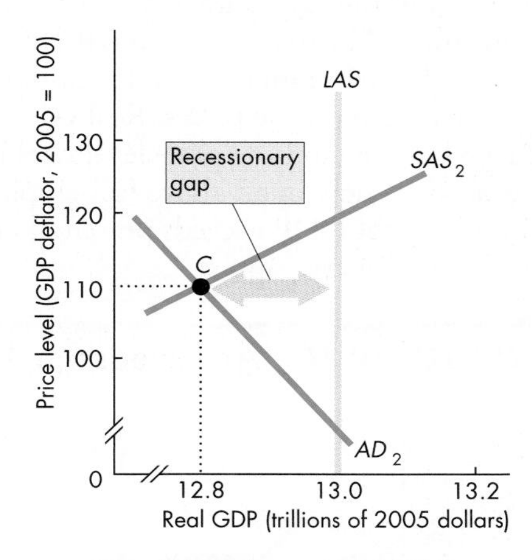

(c) Below full-employment equilibrium

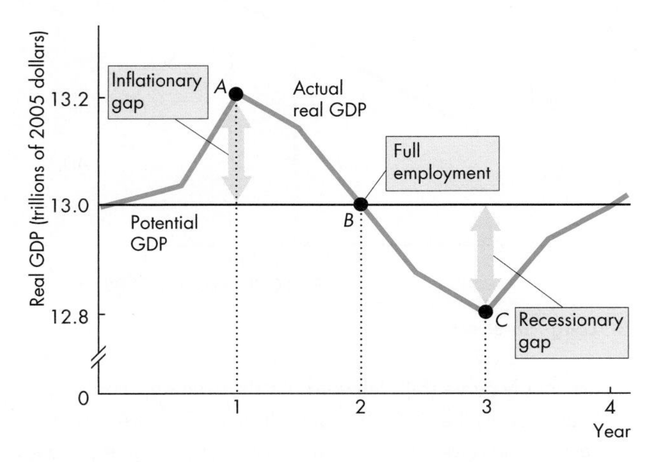

(d) Fluctuations in real GDP

Part (a) shows an above full-employment equilibrium in year 1; part (b) shows a full-employment equilibrium in year 2; and part (c) shows a below full-employment equilibrium in year 3. Part (d) shows how real GDP fluctuates around potential GDP in a business cycle.

In year 1, an inflationary gap exists and the economy is at point *A* in parts (a) and (d). In year 2, the economy is at full employment and the economy is at point *B* in parts (b) and (d). In year 3, a recessionary gap exists and the economy is at point *C* in parts (c) and (d).

Fluctuations in Aggregate Demand

One reason real GDP fluctuates around potential GDP is that aggregate demand fluctuates. Let's see what happens when aggregate demand increases.

Figure 10.10(a) shows an economy at full employment. The aggregate demand curve is AD_0, the short-run aggregate supply curve is SAS_0, and the long-run aggregate supply curve is *LAS*. Real GDP equals potential GDP at $13 trillion, and the price level is 110.

Now suppose that the world economy expands and that the demand for U.S.-produced goods increases in Asia and Europe. The increase in U.S. exports increases aggregate demand in the United States, and the aggregate demand curve shifts rightward from AD_0 to AD_1 in Fig. 10.10(a).

Faced with an increase in demand, firms increase production and raise prices. Real GDP increases to $13.5 trillion, and the price level rises to 115. The economy is now in an above full-employment equilibrium. Real GDP exceeds potential GDP, and there is an inflationary gap.

The increase in aggregate demand has increased the prices of all goods and services. Faced with higher prices, firms increased their output rates. At this stage, prices of goods and services have increased but the money wage rate has not changed. (Recall that as we move along the *SAS* curve, the money wage rate is constant.)

The economy cannot produce in excess of potential GDP forever. Why not? What are the forces at work that bring real GDP back to potential GDP?

Because the price level has increased and the money wage rate is unchanged, workers have experienced a fall in the buying power of their wages and firms' profits have increased. Under these circumstances, workers demand higher wages and firms, anxious to maintain their employment and output levels, meet those demands. If firms do not raise the money wage rate, they will either lose workers or have to hire less productive ones.

As the money wage rate rises, the short-run aggregate supply begins to decrease. In Fig. 10.10(b), the short-run aggregate supply curve begins to shift from

FIGURE 10.10 An Increase in Aggregate Demand

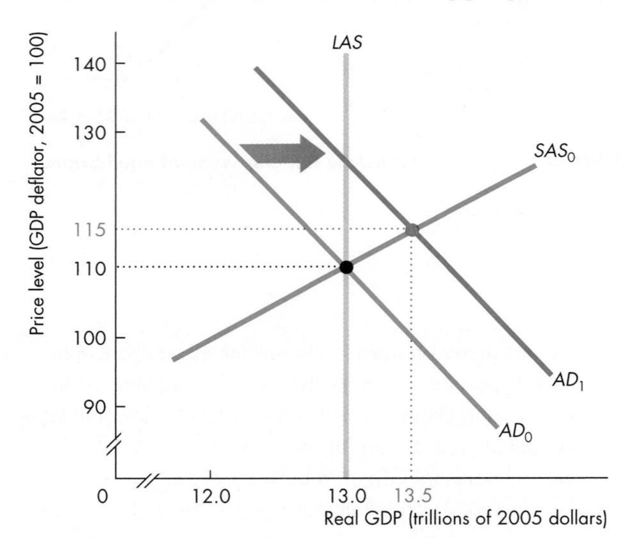

(a) Short-run effect

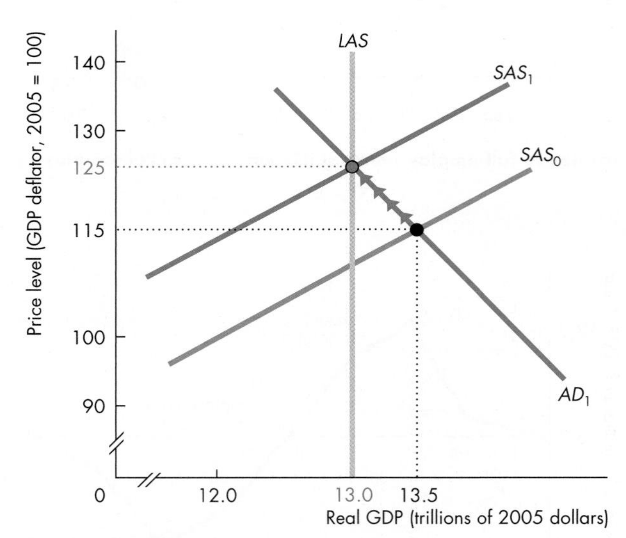

(b) Long-run effect

An increase in aggregate demand shifts the aggregate demand curve from AD_0 to AD_1. In short-run equilibrium, real GDP increases to $13.5 trillion and the price level rises to 115. In this situation, an inflationary gap exists. In the long run in part (b), the money wage rate rises and the short-run aggregate supply curve shifts leftward. As short-run aggregate supply decreases, the *SAS* curve shifts from SAS_0 to SAS_1 and intersects the aggregate demand curve AD_1 at higher price levels and real GDP decreases. Eventually, the price level rises to 125 and real GDP decreases to $13 trillion—potential GDP.

myeconlab animation

SAS_0 toward SAS_1. The rise in the money wage rate and the shift in the *SAS* curve produce a sequence of new equilibrium positions. Along the adjustment path, real GDP decreases and the price level rises. The economy moves up along its aggregate demand curve as shown by the arrows in the figure.

Eventually, the money wage rate rises by the same percentage as the price level. At this time, the aggregate demand curve AD_1 intersects SAS_1 at a new full-employment equilibrium. The price level has risen to 125, and real GDP is back where it started, at potential GDP.

A decrease in aggregate demand has effects similar but opposite to those of an increase in aggregate demand. That is, a decrease in aggregate demand shifts the aggregate demand curve leftward. Real GDP decreases to less than potential GDP, and a recessionary gap emerges. Firms cut prices. The lower price level increases the purchasing power of wages and increases firms' costs relative to their output prices because the money wage rate is unchanged. Eventually, the money wage rate falls and the short-run aggregate supply increases.

Let's now work out how real GDP and the price level change when aggregate supply changes.

Fluctuations in Aggregate Supply

Fluctuations in short-run aggregate supply can bring fluctuations in real GDP around potential GDP. Suppose that initially real GDP equals potential GDP. Then there is a large but temporary rise in the price of oil. What happens to real GDP and the price level?

Figure 10.11 answers this question. The aggregate demand curve is AD_0, the short-run aggregate supply curve is SAS_0, and the long-run aggregate supply curve is *LAS*. Real GDP is $13 trillion, which equals potential GDP, and the price level is 110. Then the price of oil rises. Faced with higher energy and transportation costs, firms decrease production. Short-run aggregate supply decreases, and the short-run aggregate supply curve shifts leftward to SAS_1. The price level rises to 120, and real GDP decreases to $12.5 trillion. Because real GDP decreases, the economy experiences recession. Because the price level increases, the economy experiences inflation. A combination of recession and inflation, called **stagflation**, actually occurred in the United States in the mid-1970s and early 1980s, but events like this are not common.

When the price of oil returns to its original level, the economy returns to full employment.

FIGURE 10.11 A Decrease in Aggregate Supply

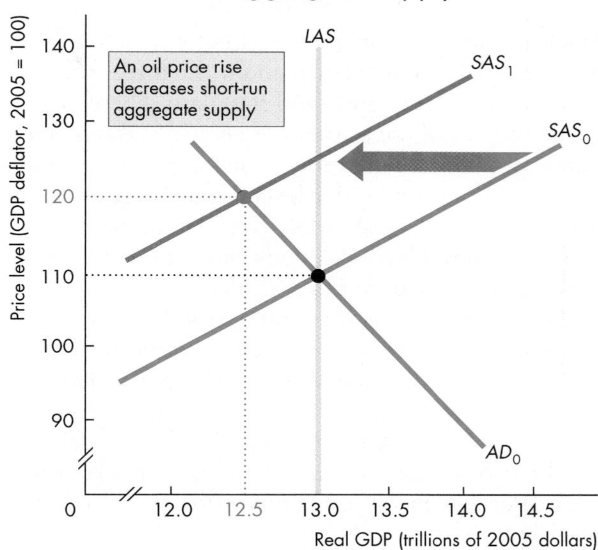

An increase in the price of oil decreases short-run aggregate supply and shifts the short-run aggregate supply curve from SAS_0 to SAS_1. Real GDP falls from $13 trillion to $12.5 trillion, and the price level rises from 110 to 120. The economy experiences stagflation.

REVIEW QUIZ

1. Does economic growth result from increases in aggregate demand, short-run aggregate supply, or long-run aggregate supply?
2. Does inflation result from increases in aggregate demand, short-run aggregate supply, or long-run aggregate supply?
3. Describe three types of short-run macroeconomic equilibrium.
4. How do fluctuations in aggregate demand and short-run aggregate supply bring fluctuations in real GDP around potential GDP?

You can work these questions in Study Plan 10.3 and get instant feedback.

We can use the *AS-AD* model to explain and illustrate the views of the alternative schools of thought in macroeconomics. That is your next task.

Macroeconomic Schools of Thought

Macroeconomics is an active field of research, and much remains to be learned about the forces that make our economy grow and fluctuate. There is a greater degree of consensus and certainty about economic growth and inflation—the longer-term trends in real GDP and the price level—than there is about the business cycle—the short-term fluctuations in these variables. Here, we'll look only at differences of view about short-term fluctuations.

The *AS-AD* model that you've studied in this chapter provides a good foundation for understanding the range of views that macroeconomists hold about this topic. But what you will learn here is just a first glimpse at the scientific controversy and debate. We'll return to these issues at various points later in the text and deepen your appreciation of the alternative views.

Classification usually requires simplification, and classifying macroeconomists is no exception to this general rule. The classification that we'll use here is simple, but it is not misleading. We're going to divide macroeconomists into three broad schools of thought and examine the views of each group in turn. The groups are

- Classical
- Keynesian
- Monetarist

The Classical View

A **classical** macroeconomist believes that the economy is self-regulating and always at full employment. The term "classical" derives from the name of the founding school of economics that includes Adam Smith, David Ricardo, and John Stuart Mill.

A **new classical** view is that business cycle fluctuations are the efficient responses of a well-functioning market economy that is bombarded by shocks that arise from the uneven pace of technological change.

The classical view can be understood in terms of beliefs about aggregate demand and aggregate supply.

Aggregate Demand Fluctuations In the classical view, technological change is the most significant influence on both aggregate demand and aggregate supply. For this reason, classical macroeconomists don't use the *AS-AD* framework. But their views can be interpreted in this framework. A technological change that increases the productivity of capital brings an increase in aggregate demand because firms increase their expenditure on new plant and equipment. A technological change that lengthens the useful life of existing capital decreases the demand for new capital, which decreases aggregate demand.

Aggregate Supply Response In the classical view, the money wage rate that lies behind the short-run aggregate supply curve is instantly and completely flexible. The money wage rate adjusts so quickly to maintain equilibrium in the labor market that real GDP always adjusts to equal potential GDP.

Potential GDP itself fluctuates for the same reasons that aggregate demand fluctuates: technological change. When the pace of technological change is rapid, potential GDP increases quickly and so does real GDP. And when the pace of technological change slows, so does the growth rate of potential GDP.

Classical Policy The classical view of policy emphasizes the potential for taxes to stunt incentives and create inefficiency. By minimizing the disincentive effects of taxes, employment, investment, and technological advance are at their efficient levels and the economy expands at an appropriate and rapid pace.

The Keynesian View

A **Keynesian** macroeconomist believes that left alone, the economy would rarely operate at full employment and that to achieve and maintain full employment, active help from fiscal policy and monetary policy is required.

The term "Keynesian" derives from the name of one of the twentieth century's most famous economists, John Maynard Keynes (see p. 317).

The Keynesian view is based on beliefs about the forces that determine aggregate demand and short-run aggregate supply.

Aggregate Demand Fluctuations In the Keynesian view, *expectations* are the most significant influence on aggregate demand. Those expectations are based on herd instinct, or what Keynes himself called "animal spirits." A wave of pessimism about future profit prospects can lead to a fall in aggregate demand and plunge the economy into recession.

Aggregate Supply Response In the Keynesian view, the money wage rate that lies behind the short-run aggregate supply curve is extremely sticky in the downward direction. Basically, the money wage rate doesn't fall. So if there is a recessionary gap, there is no automatic mechanism for getting rid of it. If it were to happen, a fall in the money wage rate would increase short-run aggregate supply and restore full employment. But the money wage rate doesn't fall, so the economy remains stuck in recession.

A modern version of the Keynesian view, known as the **new Keynesian** view, holds not only that the money wage rate is sticky but also that prices of goods and services are sticky. With a sticky price level, the short-run aggregate supply curve is horizontal at a fixed price level.

Policy Response Needed The Keynesian view calls for fiscal policy and monetary policy to actively offset changes in aggregate demand that bring recession.

By stimulating aggregate demand in a recession, full employment can be restored.

The Monetarist View

A **monetarist** is a macroeconomist who believes that the economy is self-regulating and that it will normally operate at full employment, provided that monetary policy is not erratic and that the pace of money growth is kept steady.

The term "monetarist" was coined by an outstanding twentieth-century economist, Karl Brunner, to describe his own views and those of Milton Friedman (see p. 375).

The monetarist view can be interpreted in terms of beliefs about the forces that determine aggregate demand and short-run aggregate supply.

Aggregate Demand Fluctuations In the monetarist view, *the quantity of money* is the most significant influence on aggregate demand. The quantity of money is determined by the Federal Reserve (the Fed). If the Fed keeps money growing at a steady pace, aggregate demand fluctuations will be minimized and the economy will operate close to full employment. But if the Fed decreases the quantity of money or even just slows its growth rate too abruptly, the economy will go into recession. In the monetarist view, all recessions result from inappropriate monetary policy.

Aggregate Supply Response The monetarist view of short-run aggregate supply is the same as the Keynesian view: the money wage rate is sticky. If the economy is in recession, it will take an unnecessarily long time for it to return unaided to full employment.

Monetarist Policy The monetarist view of policy is the same as the classical view on fiscal policy. Taxes should be kept low to avoid disincentive effects that decrease potential GDP. Provided that the quantity of money is kept on a steady growth path, no active stabilization is needed to offset changes in aggregate demand.

The Way Ahead

In the chapters that follow, you're going to encounter Keynesian, classical, and monetarist views again. In the next chapter, we study the original Keynesian model of aggregate demand. This model remains useful today because it explains how expenditure fluctuations are magnified and bring changes in aggregate demand that are larger than the changes in expenditure. We then go on to apply the *AS-AD* model to a deeper look at U.S. inflation and business cycles.

Our attention then turns to short-run macroeconomic policy—the fiscal policy of the Administration and Congress and the monetary policy of the Fed.

REVIEW QUIZ

1. What are the defining features of classical macroeconomics and what policies do classical macroeconomists recommend?
2. What are the defining features of Keynesian macroeconomics and what policies do Keynesian macroeconomists recommend?
3. What are the defining features of monetarist macroeconomics and what policies do monetarist macroeconomists recommend?

You can work these questions in Study Plan 10.4 and get instant feedback.

To complete your study of the *AS-AD* model, *Reading Between the Lines* on pp. 258–259 looks at the U.S. economy in 2010 through the eyes of this model.

Aggregate Supply and Aggregate Demand in Action

GDP Figures Revised Downward

Associated Press
August 27, 2010

The economy grew at a much slower pace this spring than previously estimated, mostly because of the largest surge in imports in 26 years and a slower buildup in inventories.

The nation's gross domestic product—the broadest measure of the economy's output—grew at a 1.6 percent annual rate in the April-to-June period, the Commerce Department said Friday. That's down from an initial estimate of 2.4 percent last month and much slower than the first quarter's 3.7 percent pace. Many economists had expected a sharper drop.

Shortly after the revision was announced, Federal Reserve Chairman Ben Bernanke ... described the economic outlook as "inherently uncertain" and said the economy "remains vulnerable to unexpected developments." The lower estimate for economic growth and Bernanke's comments follow a week of disappointing economic reports. The housing sector is slumping badly after the expiration of a government home buyer tax credit. And business spending on big-ticket manufactured items such as machinery and software, an important source of growth earlier this year, is also tapering off.

Most analysts expect the economy will grow at a similarly weak pace for the rest of this year.

"We seem to be in the early stages of what might be called a 'growth recession'," said Ethan Harris, an economist at Bank of America-Merrill Lynch. The economy is likely to keep expanding, but at a snail's pace and without creating many more jobs. Harris expects the nation's output will grow at about a 2 percent pace in the second half of this year. As a result, the jobless rate could rise from its current level of 9.5 percent.

ESSENCE OF THE STORY

- Real GDP grew at a 1.6 percent annual rate in the second quarter of 2010, down from a previously estimated 2.4 percent and down from 3.7 percent in the first quarter.
- Imports increased at their fastest pace in 26 years and inventories increased at a slow pace.
- Fed Chairman Ben Bernanke says the economic outlook is uncertain.
- Other bad news included a slump in home construction and lower investment expenditure.
- Most forecasters expect slow 2 percent growth for the rest of 2010 and a rise in the unemployment rate.

ECONOMIC ANALYSIS

- U.S. real GDP grew at a 1.6 percent annual rate during the second quarter of 2010—a slower than average growth rate and slower than the original estimate a month earlier.
- In the second quarter of 2010, real GDP was estimated to be $13.2 trillion, up from $12.8 trillion in the second quarter of 2009. The price level was 110 (up 10 percent since 2005).
- Figure 1 illustrates the situation in the second quarter of 2009. The aggregate demand curve was AD_{09} and the short-run aggregate supply curve was SAS_{09}. Real GDP ($12.8 trillion) and the price level (110) are at the intersection of these curves.
- The Congressional Budget Office (CBO) estimated that potential GDP in the second quarter of 2009 was $13.9 trillion, so the long-run aggregate supply curve in 2009 was LAS_{09} in Fig. 1.
- Figure 1 shows the output gap in 2009, which was a recessionary gap of $1.1 trillion or 8 percent of potential GDP.
- During the year from June 2009 to June 2010, the labor force increased, the capital stock increased, and labor productivity increased. Potential GDP increased to an estimated $14.1 trillion.
- In Fig. 2, the *LAS* curve shifted rightward to LAS_{10}.
- Also during the year from June 2009 to June 2010, a combination of fiscal and monetary policy stimulus and an increase in demand from an expanding world economy increased aggregate demand.
- The increase in aggregate demand exceeded the increase in long-run aggregate supply and the *AD* curve shifted rightward to AD_{10}. Short-run aggregate supply increased by a similar amount to the increase in *AD* and the *SAS* shifted rightward to SAS_{10}.
- Real GDP increased to $13.2 trillion and the price level remained constant at 110.
- The output gap narrowed slightly to $0.9 trillion or 6.4 percent of potential GDP.
- With real GDP forecast to grow at only 2 percent a year for the rest of 2010, the output gap would remain very large.
- Real GDP would need to grow faster than potential GDP for some time for the output gap to close.

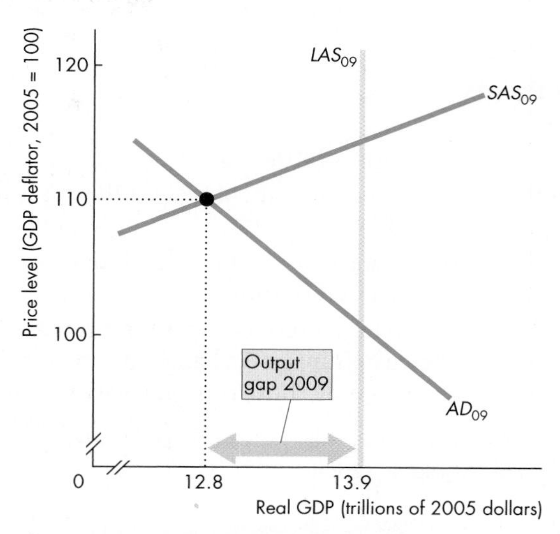

Figure 1 *AS-AD* in second quarter of 2009

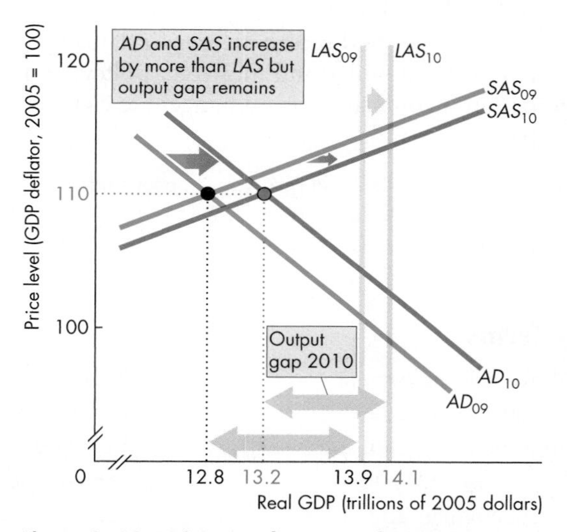

Figure 2 *AS-AD* in second quarter of 2010

SUMMARY

Key Points

Aggregate Supply (pp. 242–245)

- In the long run, the quantity of real GDP supplied is potential GDP.
- In the short run, a rise in the price level increases the quantity of real GDP supplied.
- A change in potential GDP changes long-run and short-run aggregate supply. A change in the money wage rate changes only short-run aggregate supply.

Working Problems 1 to 3 will give you a better understanding of aggregate supply.

Aggregate Demand (pp. 246–249)

- A rise in the price level decreases the quantity of real GDP demanded.
- Changes in expected future income, inflation, and profits; in fiscal policy and monetary policy; and in foreign income and the exchange rate change aggregate demand.

Working Problems 4 to 7 will give you a better understanding of aggregate demand.

Explaining Macroeconomic Trends and Fluctuations (pp. 250–255)

- Aggregate demand and short-run aggregate supply determine real GDP and the price level.
- In the long run, real GDP equals potential GDP and aggregate demand determines the price level.
- The business cycle occurs because aggregate demand and aggregate supply fluctuate.

Working Problems 8 to 16 will give you a better understanding of macroeconomic trends and fluctuations.

Macroeconomic Schools of Thought (pp. 256–257)

- Classical economists believe that the economy is self-regulating and always at full employment.
- Keynesian economists believe that full employment can be achieved only with active policy.
- Monetarist economists believe that recessions result from inappropriate monetary policy.

Working Problems 17 to 19 will give you a better understanding of the macroeconomic schools of thought.

Key Terms

Above full-employment equilibrium, 252
Aggregate demand, 246
Below full-employment equilibrium, 253
Classical, 256
Disposable income, 248
Fiscal policy, 248
Full-employment equilibrium, 253
Inflationary gap, 252
Keynesian, 256
Long-run aggregate supply, 242
Long-run macroeconomic equilibrium, 250
Monetarist, 257
Monetary policy, 248
New classical, 256
New Keynesian, 257
Output gap, 252
Recessionary gap, 253
Short-run aggregate supply, 243
Short-run macroeconomic equilibrium, 250
Stagflation, 255

STUDY PLAN PROBLEMS AND APPLICATIONS

myeconlab You can work Problems 1 to 19 in MyEconLab Chapter 10 Study Plan and get instant feedback.

Aggregate Supply (Study Plan 10.1)

1. Explain the influence of each of the following events on the quantity of real GDP supplied and aggregate supply in India and use a graph to illustrate.
   - U.S. firms move their call handling, IT, and data functions to India.
   - Fuel prices rise.
   - Wal-Mart and Starbucks open in India.
   - Universities in India increased the number of engineering graduates.
   - The money wage rate rises.
   - The price level in India increases.
2. **Wages Could Hit Steepest Plunge in 18 Years**

   A bad economy is starting to drag down wages for millions of workers. The average weekly wage has fallen 1.4% this year through September. Colorado will become the first state to lower its minimum wage since the federal minimum wage law was passed in 1938, when the state cuts its rate by 4 cents an hour.

   Source: *USA Today*, October 16, 2009

   Explain how the fall in the average weekly wage and the minimum wage will influence aggregate supply.
3. Chinese Premier Wen Jiabao has warned Japan that its companies operating in China should raise pay for their workers. Explain how a rise in wages in China will influence the quantity of real GDP supplied and aggregate supply in China.

Aggregate Demand (Study Plan 10.2)

4. Canada trades with the United States. Explain the effect of each of the following events on Canada's aggregate demand.
   - The government of Canada cuts income taxes.
   - The United States experiences strong economic growth.
   - Canada sets new environmental standards that require power utilities to upgrade their production facilities.
5. The Fed cuts the quantity of money and all other things remain the same. Explain the effect of the cut in the quantity of money on aggregate demand in the short run.
6. Mexico trades with the United States. Explain the effect of each of the following events on the quantity of real GDP demanded and aggregate demand in Mexico.
   - The United States goes into a recession.
   - The price level in Mexico rises.
   - Mexico increases the quantity of money.
7. **Durable Goods Orders Surge in May, New-Homes Sales Dip**

   The Commerce Department announced that demand for durable goods rose 1.8 percent, while new-home sales dropped 0.6 percent in May. U.S. companies suffered a sharp drop in exports as other countries struggle with recession.

   Source: *USA Today*, June 24, 2009

   Explain how the items in the news clip influence U.S. aggregate demand.

Explaining Macroeconomic Trends and Fluctuations (Study Plan 10.3)

Use the following graph to work Problems 8 to 10. Initially, the short-run aggregate supply curve is SAS_0 and the aggregate demand curve is AD_0.

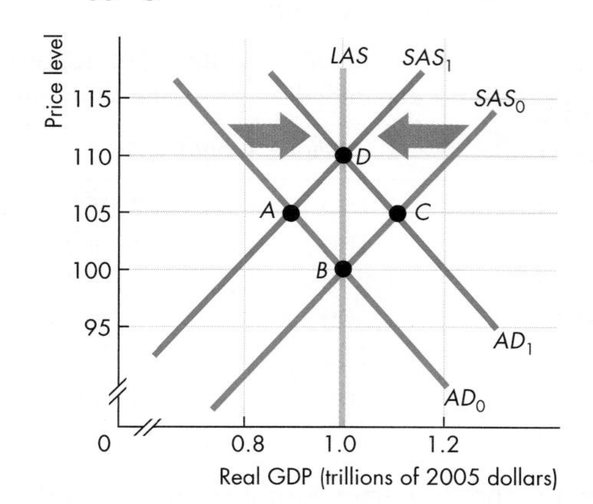

8. Some events change aggregate demand from AD_0 to AD_1. Describe two events that could have created this change in aggregate demand. What is the equilibrium after aggregate demand changed? If potential GDP is $1 trillion, the economy is at what type of macroeconomic equilibrium?
9. Some events change aggregate supply from SAS_0 to SAS_1. Describe two events that could have created this change in aggregate supply. What is the

equilibrium after aggregate supply changed? If potential GDP is $1 trillion, does the economy have an inflationary gap, a recessionary gap, or no output gap?

10. Some events change aggregate demand from AD_0 to AD_1 and aggregate supply from SAS_0 to SAS_1. What is the new macroeconomic equilibrium?

Use the following data to work Problems 11 to 13.

The following events have occurred in the history of the United States:

- A deep recession hits the world economy.
- The world oil price rises sharply.
- U.S. businesses expect future profits to fall.

11. Explain for each event whether it changes short-run aggregate supply, long-run aggregate supply, aggregate demand, or some combination of them.
12. Explain the separate effects of each event on U.S. real GDP and the price level, starting from a position of long-run equilibrium.
13. Explain the combined effects of these events on U.S. real GDP and the price level, starting from a position of long-run equilibrium.

Use the following data to work Problems 14 and 15.

The table shows the aggregate demand and short-run aggregate supply schedules of a country in which potential GDP is $1,050 billion.

Price level	Real GDP demanded	Real GDP supplied in the short run
	(billions of 2005 dollars)	
100	1,150	1,050
110	1,100	1,100
120	1,050	1,150
130	1,000	1,200
140	950	1,250
150	900	1,300
160	850	1,350

14. What is the short-run equilibrium real GDP and price level?
15. Does the country have an inflationary gap or a recessionary gap and what is its magnitude?
16. **Geithner Urges Action on Economy**
    Treasury Secretary Timothy Geithner is reported as having said that the United States can no longer rely on consumer spending to be the growth engine of recovery from recession. Washington needs to plant the seeds for business investment and exports. "We can't go back to a situation where we're depending on a near short-term boost in consumption to carry us forward," he said.

    Source: *The Wall Street Journal*, September 12, 2010

    a. Explain the effects of an increase in consumer spending on the short-run macroeconomic equilibrium.
    b. Explain the effects of an increase in business investment on the short-run macroeconomic equilibrium.
    c. Explain the effects of an increase in exports on the short-run macroeconomic equilibrium.

Macroeconomic Schools of Thought (Study Plan 10.4)

17. Describe what a classical macroeconomist, a Keynesian, and a monetarist would want to do in response to each of the events listed in Problem 11.
18. **Adding Up the Cost of Obama's Agenda**
    When campaigning, Barack Obama has made a long list of promises for new federal programs costing tens of billions of dollars. Obama has said he would strengthen the nation's bridges and dams ($6 billion a year), extend health insurance to more people (part of a $65-billion-a-year health plan), develop cleaner energy sources ($15 billion a year), curb home foreclosures ($10 billion in one-time spending) and add $18 billion a year to education spending. In total a $50-billion plan to stimulate the economy through increased government spending. A different blueprint offered by McCain proposes relatively little new spending and tax cuts as a more effective means of solving problems.

    Source: *Los Angeles Times*, July 8, 2008

    a. Based upon this news clip, explain what macroeconomic school of thought Barack Obama most likely follows.
    b. Based upon this news clip, explain what macroeconomic school of thought John McCain most likely follows.
19. Based upon the news clip in Problem 16, explain what macroeconomics school of thought Treasury Secretary Timothy Geithner most likely follows?

ADDITIONAL PROBLEMS AND APPLICATIONS

myeconlab You can work these problems in MyEconLab if assigned by your instructor.

Aggregate Supply

20. Explain for each event whether it changes the quantity of real GDP supplied, short-run aggregate supply, long-run aggregate supply, or a combination of them.
    - Automotive firms in the United States switch to a new technology that raises productivity.
    - Toyota and Honda build additional plants in the United States.
    - The prices of auto parts imported from China rise.
    - Autoworkers agree to a cut in the nominal wage rate.
    - The U.S. price level rises.

Aggregate Demand

21. Explain for each event whether it changes the quantity of real GDP demanded or aggregate demand.
    - Automotive firms in the United States switch to a new technology that raises productivity.
    - Toyota and Honda build new plants in the United States.
    - Autoworkers agree to a lower money wage rate.
    - The U.S. price level rises.
22. **Inventories Surge**

    The Commerce Department reported that wholesale inventories rose 1.3 percent in July, the best performance since July 2008. A major driver of the economy since late last year has been the restocking of depleted store shelves.

    Source: *Associated Press*, September 13, 2010

    Explain how a surge in inventories influences current aggregate demand.
23. **Low Spending Is Taking Toll on Economy**

    The Commerce Department reported that the economy continued to stagnate during the first three months of the year, with a sharp pullback in consumer spending the primary factor at play. Consumer spending fell for a broad range of goods and services, including cars, auto parts, furniture, food and recreation, reflecting a growing inclination toward thrift.

    Source: *The New York Times*, May 1, 2008

    Explain how a fall in consumer expenditure influences the quantity of real GDP demanded and aggregate demand.

Explaining Macroeconomic Trends and Fluctuations

Use the following information to work Problems 24 to 26.

The following events have occurred at times in the history of the United States:

- The world economy goes into an expansion.
- U.S. businesses expect future profits to rise.
- The government increases its expenditure on goods and services in a time of war or increased international tension.

24. Explain for each event whether it changes short-run aggregate supply, long-run aggregate supply, aggregate demand, or some combination of them.
25. Explain the separate effects of each event on U.S. real GDP and the price level, starting from a position of long-run equilibrium.
26. Explain the combined effects of these events on U.S. real GDP and the price level, starting from a position of long-run equilibrium.

Use the following information to work Problems 27 and 28.

In Japan, potential GDP is 600 trillion yen and the table shows the aggregate demand and short-run aggregate supply schedules.

Price level	Real GDP demanded (trillions of 2005 yen)	Real GDP supplied in the short run (trillions of 2005 yen)
75	600	400
85	550	450
95	500	500
105	450	550
115	400	600
125	350	650
135	300	700

27. a. Draw a graph of the aggregate demand curve and the short-run aggregate supply curve.
    b. What is the short-run equilibrium real GDP and price level?
28. Does Japan have an inflationary gap or a recessionary gap and what is its magnitude?

Use the following information to work Problems 29 and 30.

Spending by Women Jumps

The magazine *Women of China* reported that Chinese women in big cities spent 63% of their income on consumer goods last year, up from a meager 26% in 2007. Clothing accounted for the biggest chunk of that spending, at nearly 30%, followed by digital products such as cellphones and cameras (11%) and travel (10%). Chinese consumption as a whole grew faster than the overall economy in the first half of the year and is expected to reach 42% of GDP by 2020, up from the current 36%.

Source: *The Wall Street Journal*, August 27, 2010

29. Explain the effect of a rise in consumption expenditure on real GDP and the price level in the short run.
30. If the economy had been operating at a full-employment equilibrium,
    a. Describe the macroeconomic equilibrium after the rise in consumer spending.
    b. Explain and draw a graph to illustrate how the economy can adjust in the long run to restore a full-employment equilibrium.
31. Why do changes in consumer spending play a large role in the business cycle?
32. **It's Pinching Everyone**

    The current inflationary process is a global phenomenon, but emerging and developing countries have been growing significantly faster than the rest of the world. Because there is no reason to believe that world production will rise miraculously at least in the immediate future, many people expect that prices will keep on rising. These expectations in turn exacerbate the inflationary process. Households buy more of non-perishable goods than they need for their immediate consumption because they expect prices to go up even further. What is worse is that traders withhold stocks from the market in the hope of being able to sell these at higher prices later on. In other words, expectations of higher prices become self-fulfilling.

    Source: *The Times of India*, June 24, 2008

    Explain and draw a graph to illustrate how inflation and inflation expectations "become self-fulfilling."

Macroeconomic Schools of Thought

33. **Should Congress Pass a New Stimulus Bill? No, Cut Taxes and Curb Spending Instead**

    The first stimulus was not too meager, but it was the wrong policy prescription. Anybody who studies economic history would know that government spending doesn't produce long-term, sustainable growth, and jobs. The only sure way to perk up the job market is to cut taxes permanently and rein in public spending and excessive regulation.

    Source: sgvtribune.com, September 11, 2010

    Economists from which macroeconomic school of thought would recommend a second spending stimulus and which a permanent tax cut?

Economics in the News

34. After you have studied *Reading Between the Lines* on pp. 258–259 answer the following questions.
    a. What are the main features of the U.S. economy in the second quarter of 2010?
    b. Did the United States have a recessionary gap or an inflationary gap in 2010? How do you know?
    c. Use the *AS-AD* model to show the changes in aggregate demand and aggregate supply that occurred in 2009 and 2010 that brought the economy to its situation in mid-2010.
    d. Use the *AS-AD* model to show the changes in aggregate demand and aggregate supply that would occur if monetary policy cut the interest rate and increased the quantity of money by enough to restore full employment.
    e. Use the *AS-AD* model to show the changes in aggregate demand and aggregate supply that would occur if the federal government increased its expenditure on goods and services or cut taxes further by enough to restore full employment.
    f. Use the *AS-AD* model to show the changes in aggregate demand and aggregate supply that would occur if monetary and fiscal policy stimulus turned out to be too much and took the economy into an inflationary gap. Show the short-run and the long-run effects.

After studying this chapter, you will be able to:

- Explain how expenditure plans are determined when the price level is fixed
- Explain how real GDP is determined when the price level is fixed
- Explain the expenditure multiplier when the price level is fixed
- Explain the relationship between aggregate expenditure and aggregate demand and explain the multiplier when the price level changes

11

EXPENDITURE MULTIPLIERS: THE KEYNESIAN MODEL

Alicia Keys sings into a microphone in a barely audible whisper and through the magic of electronic amplification, her voice fills Central Park.

Michael Bloomberg, the mayor of New York, and an assistant are being driven to a business meeting along one of the cobblestone streets of downtown Manhattan. The car's wheels bounce and vibrate over the uneven surface, but the assistant's notes are tapped into a BlackBerry without missing a keystroke, thanks to the car's efficient shock absorbers.

Investment and exports fluctuate like the volume of Alicia Keys' voice and the uneven surface of a New York City street. How does the economy react to those fluctuations? Does it behave like an amplifier, blowing up the fluctuations and spreading them out to affect the many millions of participants in an economic rock concert? Or does it react like a limousine, absorbing the shocks and providing a smooth ride for the economy's passengers?

You will explore these questions in this chapter and in *Reading Between the Lines* at the end of the chapter you will see the role played by inventory investment during 2010 as the economy expanded.

Fixed Prices and Expenditure Plans

In the Keynesian model that we study in this chapter, all the firms are like your grocery store: They set their prices and sell the quantities their customers are willing to buy. If they persistently sell a greater quantity than they plan to and are constantly running out of inventory, they eventually raise their prices. And if they persistently sell a smaller quantity than they plan to and have inventories piling up, they eventually cut their prices. But on any given day, their prices are fixed and the quantities they sell depend on demand, not supply.

Because each firm's prices are fixed, for the economy as a whole:

1. The *price level* is fixed, and
2. *Aggregate demand* determines real GDP.

The Keynesian model explains fluctuations in aggregate demand at a fixed price level by identifying the forces that determine expenditure plans.

Expenditure Plans

Aggregate expenditure has four components: consumption expenditure, investment, government expenditure on goods and services, and net exports (exports *minus* imports). These four components of aggregate expenditure sum to real GDP (see Chapter 4, pp. 85–86).

Aggregate planned expenditure is equal to the sum of the *planned* levels of consumption expenditure, investment, government expenditure on goods and services, and exports minus imports. Two of these components of planned expenditure, consumption expenditure and imports, change when income changes and so they depend on real GDP.

A Two-Way Link Between Aggregate Expenditure and Real GDP There is a two-way link between aggregate expenditure and real GDP. Other things remaining the same,

- An increase in real GDP increases aggregate expenditure, and
- An increase in aggregate expenditure increases real GDP.

You are now going to study this two-way link.

Consumption and Saving Plans

Several factors influence consumption expenditure and saving plans. The more important ones are

1. Disposable income
2. Real interest rate
3. Wealth
4. Expected future income

Disposable income is aggregate income minus taxes plus transfer payments. Aggregate income equals real GDP, so disposable income depends on real GDP. To explore the two-way link between real GDP and planned consumption expenditure, we focus on the relationship between consumption expenditure and disposable income when the other three factors listed above are constant.

Consumption Expenditure and Saving The table in Fig. 11.1 lists the consumption expenditure and the saving that people plan at each level of disposable income. Households can only spend their disposable income on consumption or save it, so planned consumption expenditure plus planned saving *always* equals disposable income.

The relationship between consumption expenditure and disposable income, other things remaining the same, is called the **consumption function.** The relationship between saving and disposable income, other things remaining the same, is called the **saving function**.

Consumption Function Figure 11.1(a) shows a consumption function. The *y*-axis measures consumption expenditure, and the *x*-axis measures disposable income. Along the consumption function, the points labeled *A* through *F* correspond to the rows of the table. For example, point *E* shows that when disposable income is $8 trillion, consumption expenditure is $7.5 trillion. As disposable income increases, consumption expenditure also increases.

At point *A* on the consumption function, consumption expenditure is $1.5 trillion even though disposable income is zero. This consumption expenditure is called *autonomous consumption*, and it is the amount of consumption expenditure that would take place in the short run even if people had no current income. Consumption expenditure in excess of this amount is called *induced consumption*, which is the consumption expenditure that is induced by an increase in disposable income.

45° Line Figure 11.1(a) also contains a 45° line, the height of which measures disposable income. At each point on this line, consumption expenditure equals disposable income. Between *A* and *D,* consumption expenditure exceeds disposable income, between *D* and *F* consumption expenditure is less than disposable income, and at point *D*, consumption expenditure equals disposable income.

Saving Function Figure 11.1(b) shows a saving function. Again, the points *A* through *F* correspond to the rows of the table. For example, point *E* shows that when disposable income is $8 trillion, saving is $0.5 trillion. As disposable income increases, saving increases. Notice that when consumption expenditure exceeds disposable income in part (a), saving is negative, called *dissaving,* in part (b).

FIGURE 11.1 Consumption Function and Saving Function

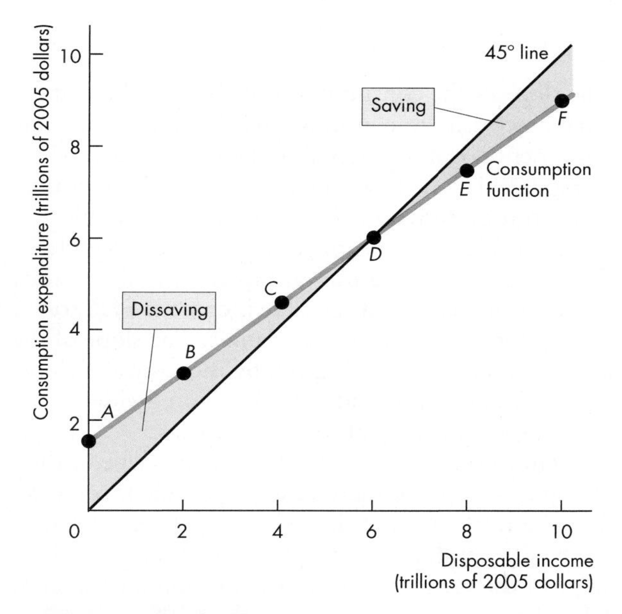

(a) Consumption function

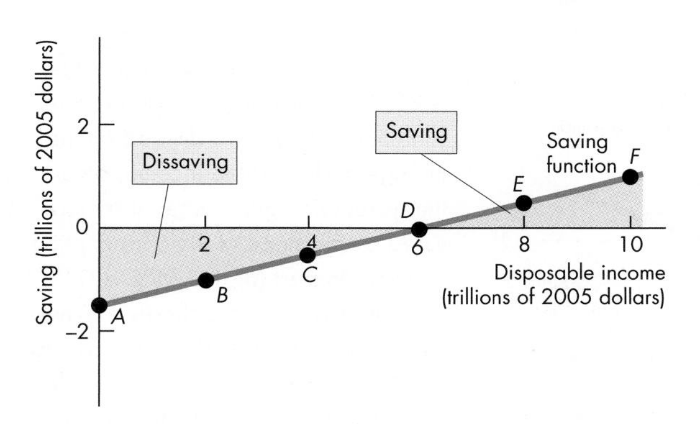

(b) Saving function

	Disposable income	Planned consumption expenditure	Planned saving
	(trillions of 2005 dollars)		
A	0	1.5	–1.5
B	2	3.0	–1.0
C	4	4.5	–0.5
D	6	6.0	0
E	8	7.5	0.5
F	10	9.0	1.0

The table shows consumption expenditure and saving plans at various levels of disposable income. Part (a) of the figure shows the relationship between consumption expenditure and disposable income (the consumption function). The height of the consumption function measures consumption expenditure at each level of disposable income. Part (b) shows the relationship between saving and disposable income (the saving function). The height of the saving function measures saving at each level of disposable income. Points *A* through *F* on the consumption and saving functions correspond to the rows in the table.

The height of the 45° line in part (a) measures disposable income. So along the 45° line, consumption expenditure equals disposable income. Consumption expenditure plus saving equals disposable income. When the consumption function is above the 45° line, saving is negative (dissaving occurs). When the consumption function is below the 45° line, saving is positive. At the point where the consumption function intersects the 45° line, all disposable income is spent on consumption and saving is zero.

myeconlab animation

Marginal Propensities to Consume and Save

The **marginal propensity to consume** (MPC) is the fraction of a *change* in disposable income that is spent on consumption. It is calculated as the *change* in consumption expenditure (ΔC) divided by the *change* in disposable income (ΔYD). The formula is

$$MPC = \frac{\Delta C}{\Delta YD}.$$

In the table in Fig. 11.1, when disposable income increases by $2 trillion, consumption expenditure increases by $1.5 trillion. The MPC is $1.5 trillion divided by $2 trillion, which equals 0.75.

The **marginal propensity to save** (MPS) is the fraction of a *change* in disposable income that is saved. It is calculated as the *change* in saving (ΔS) divided by the *change* in disposable income (ΔYD). The formula is

$$MPS = \frac{\Delta S}{\Delta YD}.$$

In the table in Fig. 11.1, when disposable income increases by $2 trillion, saving increases by $0.5 trillion. The MPS is $0.5 trillion divided by $2 trillion, which equals 0.25.

Because an increase in disposable income is either spent on consumption or saved, the marginal propensity to consume plus the marginal propensity to save equals 1. You can see why by using the equation:

$$\Delta C + \Delta S = \Delta YD.$$

Divide both sides of the equation by the change in disposable income to obtain

$$\frac{\Delta C}{\Delta YD} + \frac{\Delta S}{\Delta YD} = 1.$$

$\Delta C/\Delta YD$ is the marginal propensity to consume (MPC), and $\Delta S/\Delta YD$ is the marginal propensity to save (MPS), so

$$MPC + MPS = 1.$$

Slopes and Marginal Propensities

The slope of the consumption function is the marginal propensity to consume, and the slope of the saving function is the marginal propensity to save.

Figure 11.2(a) shows the MPC as the slope of the consumption function. An increase in disposable income of $2 trillion is the base of the red triangle. The increase in consumption expenditure that results from this increase in disposable income is $1.5 trillion and is the height of the triangle. The slope of the consumption function is given by the formula "slope equals rise over run" and is $1.5 trillion divided by $2 trillion, which equals 0.75—the MPC.

Figure 11.2(b) shows the MPS as the slope of the saving function. An increase in disposable income of $2 trillion (the base of the red triangle) increases saving by $0.5 trillion (the height of the triangle). The slope of the saving function is $0.5 trillion divided by $2 trillion, which equals 0.25—the MPS.

FIGURE 11.2 The Marginal Propensities to Consume and Save

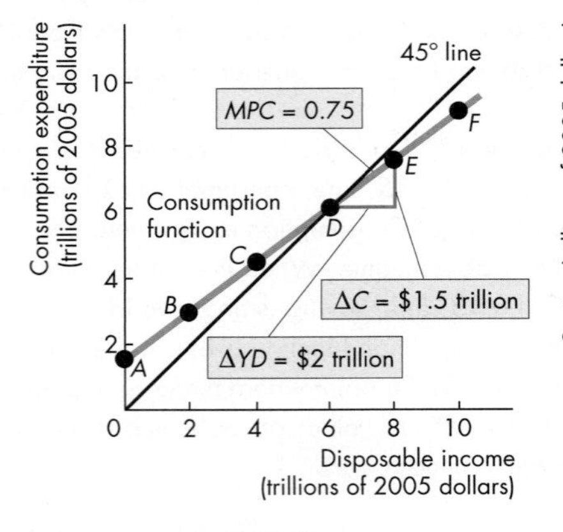

(a) Consumption function

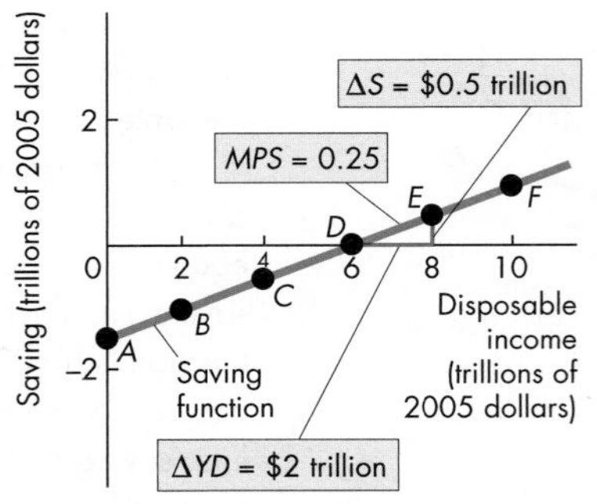

(b) Saving function

The marginal propensity to consume, MPC, is equal to the change in consumption expenditure divided by the change in disposable income, other things remaining the same. It is measured by the slope of the consumption function. In part (a), the MPC is 0.75.

The marginal propensity to save, MPS, is equal to the change in saving divided by the change in disposable income, other things remaining the same. It is measured by the slope of the saving function. In part (b), the MPS is 0.25.

myeconlab animation

Economics in Action

The U.S. Consumption Function

The figure shows the U.S. consumption function. Each point identified by a blue dot represents consumption expenditure and disposable income for a particular year. (The dots are for the years 1970 to 2010, and the dots for five of those years are identified in the figure.)

The U.S. consumption function is CF_0 in 1970 and CF_1 in 2010.

The slope of the consumption function in the figure is 0.9, which means that a $1 increase in disposable income increases consumption expenditure by 90 cents. This slope, which is an estimate of the marginal propensity to consume, is an assumption that is at the upper end of the range of values that economists have estimated for the marginal propensity to consume.

The consumption function shifts upward over time as other influences on consumption expenditure change. Of these other influences, the real interest rate and wealth fluctuate and so bring upward and downward shifts in the consumption function.

But rising wealth and rising expected future income bring a steady upward shift in the consumption function. As the consumption function shifts upward, autonomous consumption increases.

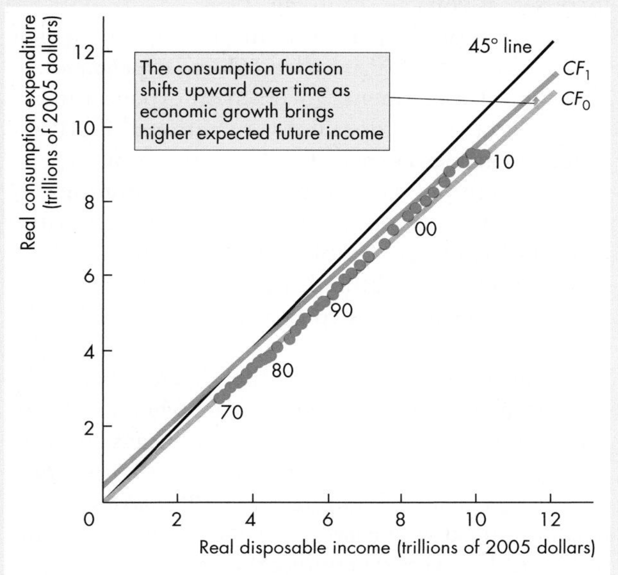

The U.S. Consumption Function

Source of data: Bureau of Economic Analysis.

Consumption as a Function of Real GDP

Consumption expenditure changes when disposable income changes and disposable income changes when real GDP changes. So consumption expenditure depends not only on disposable income but also on real GDP. We use this link between consumption expenditure and real GDP to determine equilibrium expenditure. But before we do so, we need to look at one further component of aggregate expenditure: imports. Like consumption expenditure, imports are influenced by real GDP.

Import Function

Of the many influences on U.S. imports in the short run, U.S. real GDP is the main influence. Other things remaining the same, an increase in U.S. real GDP increases the quantity of U.S. imports.

The relationship between imports and real GDP is determined by the **marginal propensity to import**, which is the fraction of an increase in real GDP that is spent on imports. It is calculated as the change in imports divided by the change in real GDP, other things remaining the same. For example, if an increase in real GDP of $1 trillion increases imports by $0.25 trillion, the marginal propensity to import is 0.25.

REVIEW QUIZ

1. Which components of aggregate expenditure are influenced by real GDP?
2. Define and explain how we calculate the marginal propensity to consume and the marginal propensity to save.
3. How do we calculate the effects of real GDP on consumption expenditure and imports by using the marginal propensity to consume and the marginal propensity to import?

You can work these questions in Study Plan 11.1 and get instant feedback.

Real GDP influences consumption expenditure and imports, which in turn influence real GDP. Your next task is to study this second piece of the two-way link between aggregate expenditure and real GDP and see how all the components of aggregate planned expenditure interact to determine real GDP.

Real GDP with a Fixed Price Level

You are now going to see how, at a given price level, aggregate expenditure plans determine real GDP. We start by looking at the relationship between aggregate planned expenditure and real GDP. This relationship can be described by an aggregate expenditure schedule or an aggregate expenditure curve. The *aggregate expenditure schedule* lists aggregate planned expenditure generated at each level of real GDP. The *aggregate expenditure curve* is a graph of the aggregate expenditure schedule.

Aggregate Planned Expenditure

The table in Fig. 11.3 sets out an aggregate expenditure schedule. To calculate aggregate planned expenditure at a given real GDP, we add the expenditure components together. The first column of the table shows real GDP, and the second column shows the planned consumption at each level of real GDP. A $1 trillion increase in real GDP increases consumption expenditure by $0.7 trillion—the *MPC* is 0.7.

The next two columns show investment and government expenditure on goods and services, both of which are independent of the level of real GDP. Investment depends on the real interest rate and the expected profit (see Chapter 7, p. 166). At a given point in time, these factors generate a given level of investment. Suppose this level of investment is $2.0 trillion. Also, suppose that government expenditure is $2.5 trillion.

The next two columns show exports and imports. Exports are influenced by events in the rest of the world, prices of foreign-produced goods and services relative to the prices of similar U.S.-produced goods and services, and exchange rates. But they are not directly affected by U.S. real GDP. Exports are a constant $2.0 trillion. Imports increase as U.S. real GDP increases. A $1 trillion increase in U.S. real GDP generates a $0.2 trillion increase in imports—the marginal propensity to import is 0.2.

The final column shows aggregate planned expenditure—the sum of planned consumption expenditure, investment, government expenditure on goods and services, and exports minus imports.

Figure 11.3 plots an aggregate expenditure curve. Real GDP is shown on the *x*-axis, and aggregate planned expenditure is shown on the *y*-axis. The aggregate expenditure curve is the red line *AE*. Points *A* through *F* on that curve correspond to the rows of the table. The *AE* curve is a graph of aggregate planned expenditure (the last column) plotted against real GDP (the first column).

Figure 11.3 also shows the components of aggregate expenditure. The constant components—investment (I), government expenditure on goods and services (G), and exports (X)—are shown by the horizontal lines in the figure. Consumption expenditure (C) is the vertical gap between the lines labeled $I + G + X$ and $I + G + X + C$.

To construct the *AE* curve, subtract imports (M) from the $I + G + X + C$ line. Aggregate expenditure is expenditure on U.S.-produced goods and services. But the components of aggregate expenditure—C, I, and G—include expenditure on imported goods and services. For example, if you buy a new cell phone, your expenditure is part of consumption expenditure. But if the cell phone is a Nokia made in Finland, your expenditure on it must be subtracted from consumption expenditure to find out how much is spent on goods and services produced in the United States—on U.S. real GDP. Money paid to Nokia for cell phone imports from Finland does not add to aggregate expenditure in the United States.

Because imports are only a part of aggregate expenditure, when we subtract imports from the other components of aggregate expenditure, aggregate planned expenditure still increases as real GDP increases, as you can see in Fig. 11.3.

Consumption expenditure minus imports, which varies with real GDP, is called **induced expenditure**. The sum of investment, government expenditure, and exports, which does not vary with real GDP, is called **autonomous expenditure**. Consumption expenditure and imports can also have an autonomous component—a component that does not vary with real GDP. Another way of thinking about autonomous expenditure is that it would be the level of aggregate planned expenditure if real GDP were zero.

In Fig. 11.3, autonomous expenditure is $6.5 trillion—aggregate planned expenditure when real GDP is zero (point *A*). For each $1 trillion increase in real GDP, induced expenditure increases by $0.5 trillion.

The aggregate expenditure curve summarizes the relationship between aggregate *planned* expenditure and real GDP. But what determines the point on the aggregate expenditure curve at which the economy operates? What determines *actual* aggregate expenditure?

FIGURE 11.3 Aggregate Planned Expenditure: The *AE* Curve

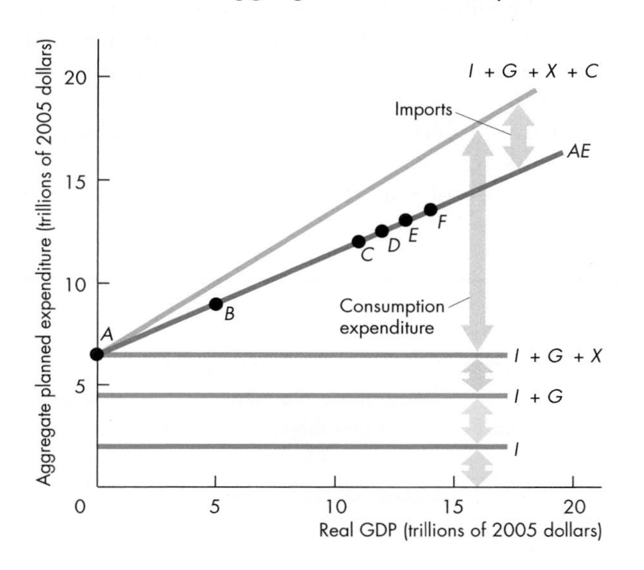

Aggregate planned expenditure is the sum of planned consumption expenditure, investment, government expenditure on goods and services, and exports minus imports. For example, in row *C* of the table, when real GDP is $11 trillion, planned consumption expenditure is $7.7 trillion, planned investment is $2.0 trillion, planned government expenditure is $2.5 trillion, planned exports are $2.0 trillion, and planned imports are $2.2 trillion. So when real GDP is $11 trillion, aggregate planned expenditure is $12 trillion ($7.7 + $2.0 + $2.5 + $2.0 – $2.2). The schedule shows that aggregate planned expenditure increases as real GDP increases. This relationship is graphed as the aggregate expenditure curve *AE*. The components of aggregate expenditure that increase with real GDP are consumption expenditure and imports. The other components—investment, government expenditure, and exports—do not vary with real GDP.

	Real GDP (*Y*)	Consumption expenditure (*C*)	Investment (*I*)	Government expenditure (*G*)	Exports (*X*)	Imports (*M*)	Aggregate planned expenditure ($AE = C + I + G + X - M$)
		Planned expenditure (trillions of 2005 dollars)					
A	0	0	2.0	2.5	2.0	0.0	6.5
B	5	3.5	2.0	2.5	2.0	1.0	9.0
C	11	7.7	2.0	2.5	2.0	2.2	12.0
D	12	8.4	2.0	2.5	2.0	2.4	12.5
E	13	9.1	2.0	2.5	2.0	2.6	13.0
F	14	9.8	2.0	2.5	2.0	2.8	13.5

Actual Expenditure, Planned Expenditure, and Real GDP

Actual aggregate expenditure is always equal to real GDP, as we saw in Chapter 4 (p. 86). But aggregate *planned* expenditure is not always equal to actual aggregate expenditure and therefore is not always equal to real GDP. How can actual expenditure and planned expenditure differ? The answer is that firms can end up with inventories that are greater or smaller than planned. People carry out their consumption expenditure plans, the government implements its planned expenditure on goods and services, and net exports are as planned. Firms carry out their plans to purchase new buildings, plant, and equipment. But one component of investment is the change in firms' inventories. If aggregate planned expenditure is less than real GDP, firms sell less than they planned to sell and end up with unplanned inventories. If aggregate planned expenditure exceeds real GDP, firms sell more than they planned to sell and end up with inventories being too low.

Equilibrium Expenditure

Equilibrium expenditure is the level of aggregate expenditure that occurs when aggregate *planned* expenditure equals real GDP. Equilibrium expenditure is a level of aggregate expenditure and real GDP at which spending plans are fulfilled. At a given price level, equilibrium expenditure determines real GDP. When aggregate planned expenditure and actual aggregate expenditure are unequal, a process of convergence toward equilibrium expenditure occurs. Throughout this process, real GDP adjusts. Let's examine equilibrium expenditure and the process that brings it about.

Figure 11.4(a) illustrates equilibrium expenditure. The table sets out aggregate planned expenditure at various levels of real GDP. These values are plotted as

FIGURE 11.4 Equilibrium Expenditure

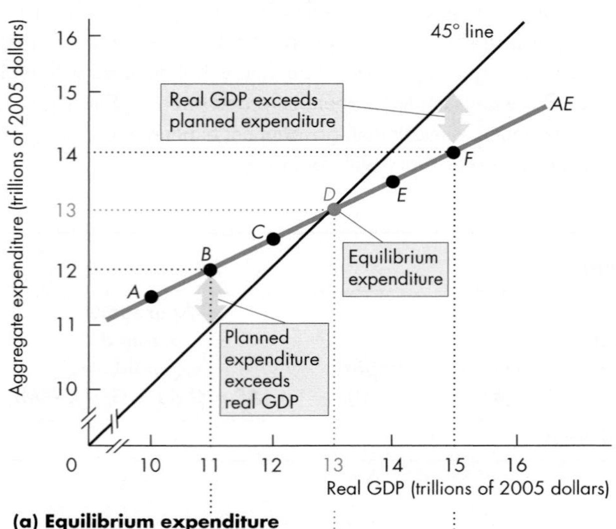

(a) Equilibrium expenditure

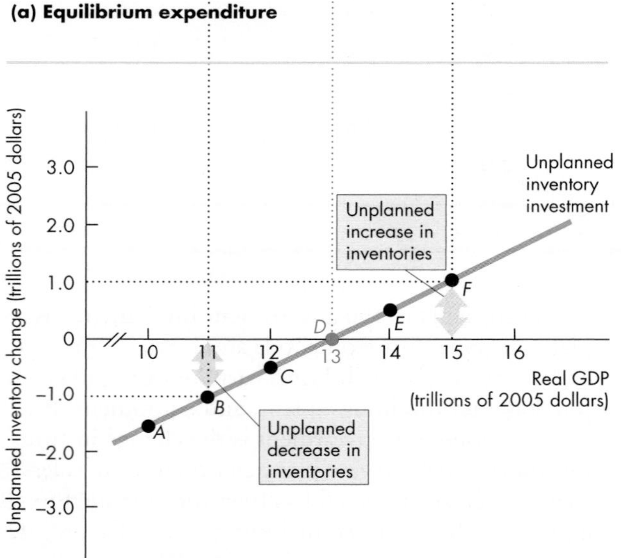

(b) Unplanned inventory changes

	Real GDP (*Y*)	Aggregate planned expenditure (*AE*)	Unplanned inventory change (*Y* – *AE*)
	(trillions of 2005 dollars)		
A	10	11.5	–1.5
B	11	12.0	–1.0
C	12	12.5	–0.5
D	13	13.0	0
E	14	13.5	0.5
F	15	14.0	1.0

The table shows expenditure plans at different levels of real GDP. When real GDP is $13 trillion, aggregate planned expenditure equals real GDP.

Part (a) of the figure illustrates equilibrium expenditure, which occurs when aggregate planned expenditure equals real GDP at the intersection of the 45° line and the *AE* curve. Part (b) of the figure shows the forces that bring about equilibrium expenditure. When aggregate planned expenditure exceeds real GDP, inventories decrease—for example, at point *B* in both parts of the figure. Firms increase production, and real GDP increases.

When aggregate planned expenditure is less than real GDP, inventories increase—for example, at point *F* in both parts of the figure. Firms decrease production, and real GDP decreases. When aggregate planned expenditure equals real GDP, there are no unplanned inventory changes and real GDP remains constant at equilibrium expenditure.

myeconlab animation

points *A* through *F* along the *AE* curve. The 45° line shows all the points at which aggregate planned expenditure equals real GDP. So where the *AE* curve lies above the 45° line, aggregate planned expenditure exceeds real GDP; where the *AE* curve lies below the 45° line, aggregate planned expenditure is less than real GDP; and where the *AE* curve intersects the 45° line, aggregate planned expenditure equals real GDP. Point *D* illustrates equilibrium expenditure. At this point, real GDP is $13 trillion.

Convergence to Equilibrium

What are the forces that move aggregate expenditure toward its equilibrium level? To answer this question, we must look at a situation in which aggregate expenditure is away from its equilibrium level.

From Below Equilibrium Suppose that in Fig. 11.4, real GDP is $11 trillion. With real GDP at $11 trillion, actual aggregate expenditure is also $11 trillion. But aggregate *planned* expenditure is $12 trillion, point *B* in Fig. 11.4(a). Aggregate planned expenditure exceeds *actual* expenditure. When people spend $12 trillion and firms produce goods and services worth $11 trillion, firms' inventories fall by $1 trillion, point *B* in Fig. 11.4(b). Because the change in inventories is part of investment, *actual* investment is $1 trillion less than *planned* investment.

Real GDP doesn't remain at $11 trillion for very long. Firms have inventory targets based on their sales. When inventories fall below target, firms increase production to restore inventories to the target level. To increase inventories, firms hire additional labor and increase production. Suppose that they increase production in the next period by $1 trillion. Real GDP increases by $1.0 trillion to $12.0 trillion. But again, aggregate planned expenditure exceeds real GDP. When real GDP is $12.0 trillion, aggregate planned expenditure is $12.5 trillion, point *C* in Fig. 11.4(a). Again, inventories decrease, but this time by less than before. With real GDP of $12.0 trillion and aggregate planned expenditure of $12.5 trillion, inventories decrease by $0.5 trillion, point *C* in Fig. 11.4(b). Again, firms hire additional labor and production increases; real GDP increases yet further.

The process that we've just described—planned expenditure exceeds real GDP, inventories decrease, and production increases to restore inventories—ends when real GDP has reached $13 trillion. At this real GDP, there is equilibrium. Unplanned inventory changes are zero. Firms do not change their production.

From Above Equilibrium If in Fig. 11.4, real GDP is $15 trillion, the process that we've just described works in reverse. With real GDP at $15 trillion, actual aggregate expenditure is also $15 trillion. But aggregate planned expenditure is $14 trillion, point *F* in Fig. 11.4(a). Actual expenditure exceeds planned expenditure. When people spend $14 trillion and firms produce goods and services worth $15 trillion, firms' inventories rise by $1 trillion, point *F* in Fig. 11.4(b). Now, real GDP begins to fall. As long as actual expenditure exceeds planned expenditure, inventories rise, and production decreases. Again, the process ends when real GDP has reached $13 trillion, the equilibrium at which unplanned inventory changes are zero and firms do not change their production.

REVIEW QUIZ

1 What is the relationship between aggregate planned expenditure and real GDP at equilibrium expenditure?
2 How does equilibrium expenditure come about? What adjusts to achieve equilibrium?
3 If real GDP and aggregate expenditure are less than equilibrium expenditure, what happens to firms' inventories? How do firms change their production? And what happens to real GDP?
4 If real GDP and aggregate expenditure are greater than equilibrium expenditure, what happens to firms' inventories? How do firms change their production? And what happens to real GDP?

You can work these questions in Study Plan 11.2 and get instant feedback.

We've learned that when the price level is fixed, real GDP is determined by equilibrium expenditure. And we have seen how unplanned changes in inventories and the production response they generate bring a convergence toward equilibrium expenditure. We're now going to study *changes* in equilibrium expenditure and discover an economic amplifier called the *multiplier*.

The Multiplier

Investment and exports can change for many reasons. A fall in the real interest rate might induce firms to increase their planned investment. A wave of innovation, such as occurred with the spread of multimedia computers in the 1990s, might increase expected future profits and lead firms to increase their planned investment. An economic boom in Western Europe and Japan might lead to a large increase in their expenditure on U.S.-produced goods and services—on U.S. exports. These are all examples of increases in autonomous expenditure.

When autonomous expenditure increases, aggregate expenditure increases and so does equilibrium expenditure and real GDP. But the increase in real GDP is *larger* than the change in autonomous expenditure. The **multiplier** is the amount by which a change in autonomous expenditure is magnified or multiplied to determine the change in equilibrium expenditure and real GDP.

To get the basic idea of the multiplier, we'll work with an example economy in which there are no income taxes and no imports. So we'll first assume that these factors are absent. Then, when you understand the basic idea, we'll bring these factors back into play and see what difference they make to the multiplier.

The Basic Idea of the Multiplier

Suppose that investment increases. The additional expenditure by businesses means that aggregate expenditure and real GDP increase. The increase in real GDP increases disposable income, and with no income taxes, real GDP and disposable income increase by the same amount. The increase in disposable income brings an increase in consumption expenditure. And the increased consumption expenditure adds even more to aggregate expenditure. Real GDP and disposable income increase further, and so does consumption expenditure. The initial increase in investment brings an even bigger increase in aggregate expenditure because it induces an increase in consumption expenditure. The magnitude of the increase in aggregate expenditure that results from an increase in autonomous expenditure is determined by the *multiplier*.

The table in Fig. 11.5 sets out an aggregate planned expenditure schedule. Initially, when real GDP is $12 trillion, aggregate planned expenditure is $12.25 trillion. For each $1 trillion increase in real GDP, aggregate planned expenditure increases by $0.75 trillion. This aggregate expenditure schedule is shown in the figure as the aggregate expenditure curve AE_0. Initially, equilibrium expenditure is $13 trillion. You can see this equilibrium in row *B* of the table and in the figure where the curve AE_0 intersects the 45° line at the point marked *B*.

Now suppose that autonomous expenditure increases by $0.5 trillion. What happens to equilibrium expenditure? You can see the answer in Fig. 11.5. When this increase in autonomous expenditure is added to the original aggregate planned expenditure, aggregate planned expenditure increases by $0.5 trillion at each level of real GDP. The new aggregate expenditure curve is AE_1. The new equilibrium expenditure, highlighted in the table (row *D*'), occurs where AE_1 intersects the 45° line and is $15 trillion (point *D*'). At this real GDP, aggregate planned expenditure equals real GDP.

The Multiplier Effect

In Fig. 11.5, the increase in autonomous expenditure of $0.5 trillion increases equilibrium expenditure by $2 trillion. That is, the change in autonomous expenditure leads, like Alicia Keys' electronic equipment, to an amplified change in equilibrium expenditure. This amplified change is the *multiplier effect*—equilibrium expenditure increases by *more than* the increase in autonomous expenditure. The multiplier is greater than 1.

Initially, when autonomous expenditure increases, aggregate planned expenditure exceeds real GDP. As a result, inventories decrease. Firms respond by increasing production so as to restore their inventories to the target level. As production increases, so does real GDP. With a higher level of real GDP, *induced expenditure* increases. Equilibrium expenditure increases by the sum of the initial increase in autonomous expenditure and the increase in induced expenditure. In this example, equilibrium expenditure increases by $2 trillion following the increase in autonomous expenditure of $0.5 trillion, so induced expenditure increases by $1.5 trillion.

Although we have just analyzed the effects of an *increase* in autonomous expenditure, this analysis also applies to a decrease in autonomous expenditure. If initially the aggregate expenditure curve is AE_1, equilibrium expenditure and real GDP are $15 trillion. A decrease in autonomous expenditure of $0.5 trillion shifts the aggregate expenditure curve downward by

FIGURE 11.5 The Multiplier

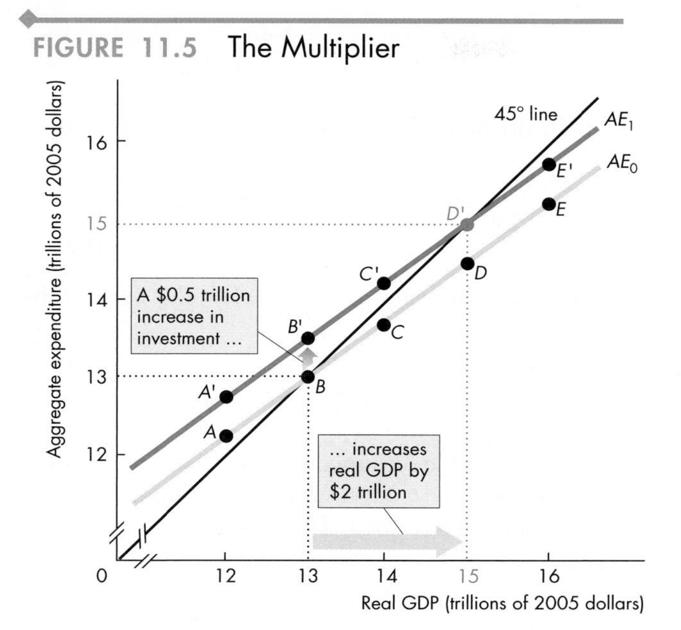

Real GDP (Y)	Aggregate planned expenditure: Original (AE_0)		New (AE_1)	
	(trillions of 2005 dollars)			
12	*A*	12.25	*A'*	12.75
13	***B***	**13.00**	*B'*	13.50
14	*C*	13.75	*C'*	14.25
15	*D*	14.50	*D'*	15.00
16	*E*	15.25	*E'*	15.75

A $0.5 trillion increase in autonomous expenditure shifts the *AE* curve upward by $0.5 trillion from AE_0 to AE_1. Equilibrium expenditure increases by $2 trillion from $13 trillion to $15 trillion. The increase in equilibrium expenditure is 4 times the increase in autonomous expenditure, so the multiplier is 4.

$0.5 trillion to AE_0. Equilibrium expenditure decreases from $15 trillion to $13 trillion. The decrease in equilibrium expenditure ($2 trillion) is larger than the decrease in autonomous expenditure that brought it about ($0.5 trillion).

Why Is the Multiplier Greater Than 1?

We've seen that equilibrium expenditure increases by more than the increase in autonomous expenditure. This makes the multiplier greater than 1. How come? Why does equilibrium expenditure increase by more than the increase in autonomous expenditure?

The multiplier is greater than 1 because induced expenditure increases—an increase in autonomous expenditure *induces* further increases in expenditure. The NASA space shuttle program costs about $5 billion a year. This expenditure adds $5 billion a year directly to real GDP. But that is not the end of the story. Astronauts and engineers now have more income, and they spend part of the extra income on goods and services. Real GDP now rises by the initial $5 billion plus the extra consumption expenditure induced by the $5 billion increase in income. The producers of cars, flat-screen TVs, vacations, and other goods and services now have increased incomes, and they, in turn, spend part of the increase in their incomes on consumption goods and services. Additional income induces additional expenditure, which creates additional income.

How big is the multiplier effect?

The Size of the Multiplier

Suppose that the economy is in a recession. Profit prospects start to look better, and firms are planning a large increase in investment. The world economy is also heading toward expansion. The question on everyone's lips is: How strong will the expansion be? This is a hard question to answer, but an important ingredient in the answer is the size of the multiplier.

The *multiplier* is the amount by which a change in autonomous expenditure is multiplied to determine the change in equilibrium expenditure that it generates. To calculate the multiplier, we divide the change in equilibrium expenditure by the change in autonomous expenditure.

Let's calculate the multiplier for the example in Fig. 11.5. Initially, equilibrium expenditure is $13 trillion. Then autonomous expenditure increases by $0.5 trillion, and equilibrium expenditure increases by $2 trillion, to $15 trillion. Then

$$\text{Multiplier} = \frac{\text{Change in equilibrium expenditure}}{\text{Change in autonomous expenditure}}$$

$$\text{Multiplier} = \frac{\$2 \text{ trillion}}{\$0.5 \text{ trillion}} = 4.$$

The Multiplier and the Slope of the *AE* Curve

The magnitude of the multiplier depends on the slope of the *AE* curve. In Fig. 11.6, the *AE* curve in part (a) is steeper than the *AE* curve in part (b), and the multiplier is larger in part (a) than in part (b). To see why, let's do a calculation.

Aggregate expenditure and real GDP change because induced expenditure and autonomous expenditure change. The change in real GDP (ΔY) equals the change in induced expenditure (ΔN) plus the change in autonomous expenditure (ΔA). That is,

$$\Delta Y = \Delta N + \Delta A.$$

But the change in induced expenditure is determined by the change in real GDP and the slope of the *AE* curve. To see why, begin with the fact that the slope of the *AE* curve equals the "rise," ΔN, divided by the "run," ΔY. That is,

$$\text{Slope of } AE \text{ curve} = \Delta N \div \Delta Y.$$

So

$$\Delta N = \text{Slope of } AE \text{ curve} \times \Delta Y.$$

Now, use this equation to replace ΔN in the first equation above to give

$$\Delta Y = \text{Slope of } AE \text{ curve} \times \Delta Y + \Delta A.$$

Now, solve for ΔY as

$$(1 - \text{Slope of } AE \text{ curve}) \times \Delta Y = \Delta A$$

and rearrange to give

$$\Delta Y = \frac{\Delta A}{1 - \text{Slope of } AE \text{ curve}}.$$

Finally, divide both sides of this equation by ΔA to give

$$\text{Multiplier} = \frac{\Delta Y}{\Delta A} = \frac{1}{1 - \text{Slope of } AE \text{ curve}}.$$

If we use the example in Fig. 11.5, the slope of the *AE* curve is 0.75, so

$$\text{Multiplier} = \frac{1}{1 - 0.75} = \frac{1}{0.25} = 4.$$

Where there are no income taxes and no imports, the slope of the *AE* curve equals the marginal propensity to consume (*MPC*). So

$$\text{Multiplier} = \frac{1}{1 - MPC}.$$

But (1 – *MPC*) equals *MPS*. So another formula is

$$\text{Multiplier} = \frac{1}{MPS}.$$

Again using the numbers in Fig. 11.5, we have

$$\text{Multiplier} = \frac{1}{0.25} = 4.$$

Because the marginal propensity to save (*MPS*) is a fraction—a number between 0 and 1—the multiplier is greater than 1.

FIGURE 11.6 The Multiplier and the Slope of the *AE* Curve

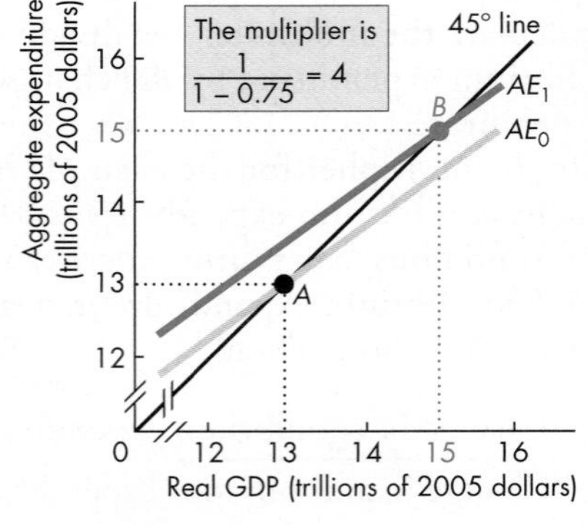

(a) Multiplier is 4

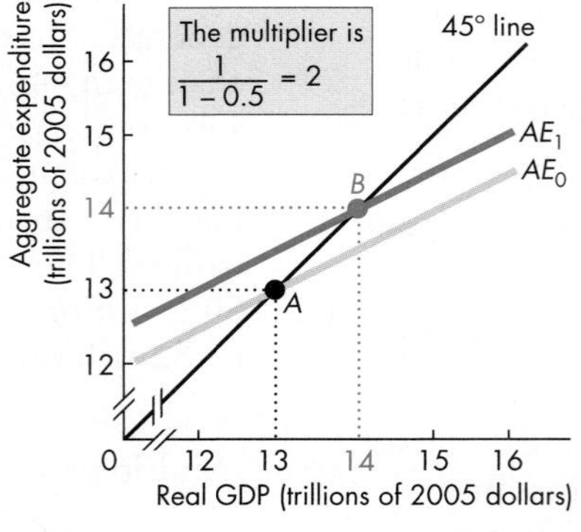

(b) Multiplier is 2

Imports and income taxes make the *AE* curve less steep and reduce the value of the multiplier. In part (a), with no imports and no income taxes, the slope of the *AE* curve is 0.75 (the marginal propensity to consume) and the multiplier is 4. But with imports and income taxes, the slope of the *AE* curve is less than the marginal propensity to consume. In part (b), the slope of the *AE* curve is 0.5. In this case, the multiplier is 2.

myeconlab animation

Imports and Income Taxes

Imports and income taxes influence the size of the multiplier and make it smaller than it otherwise would be.

To see why imports make the multiplier smaller, think about what happens following an increase in investment. The increase in investment increases real GDP, which in turn increases consumption expenditure. But part of the increase in expenditure is on imported goods and services. Only expenditure on U.S.-produced goods and services increases U.S. real GDP. The larger the marginal propensity to import, the smaller is the change in U.S. real GDP. The Mathematical Note on pp. 286–289 shows the effects of imports and income taxes on the multiplier.

Income taxes also make the multiplier smaller than it otherwise would be. Again, think about what happens following an increase in investment. The increase in investment increases real GDP. Income tax payments increase so disposable income increases by less than the increase in real GDP and consumption expenditure increases by less than it would if taxes had not changed. The larger the income tax rate, the smaller is the change in real GDP.

The marginal propensity to import and the income tax rate together with the marginal propensity to consume determine the multiplier. And their combined influence determines the slope of the *AE* curve.

Over time, the value of the multiplier changes as tax rates change and as the marginal propensity to consume and the marginal propensity to import change. These ongoing changes make the multiplier hard to predict. But they do not change the fundamental fact that an initial change in autonomous expenditure leads to a magnified change in aggregate expenditure and real GDP.

The Multiplier Process

The multiplier effect isn't a one-shot event. It is a process that plays out over a few months. Figure 11.7 illustrates the multiplier process. Autonomous expenditure increases by $0.5 trillion and real GDP increases by $0.5 trillion (the green bar in round 1). This increase in real GDP increases induced expenditure in round 2. With the slope of the *AE* curve equal to 0.75, induced expenditure increases by 0.75 times the increase in real GDP, so the increase in real GDP of $0.5 trillion induces a further increase in expenditure of $0.375 trillion. This change in induced expenditure (the green bar in round 2) when added to the previous increase in expenditure (the blue bar in round 2) increases real GDP by $0.875 trillion. The round 2 increase in real GDP induces a round 3 increase in induced expenditure. The process repeats through successive rounds. Each increase in real GDP is 0.75 times the previous increase and eventually real GDP increases by $2 trillion.

FIGURE 11.7 The Multiplier Process

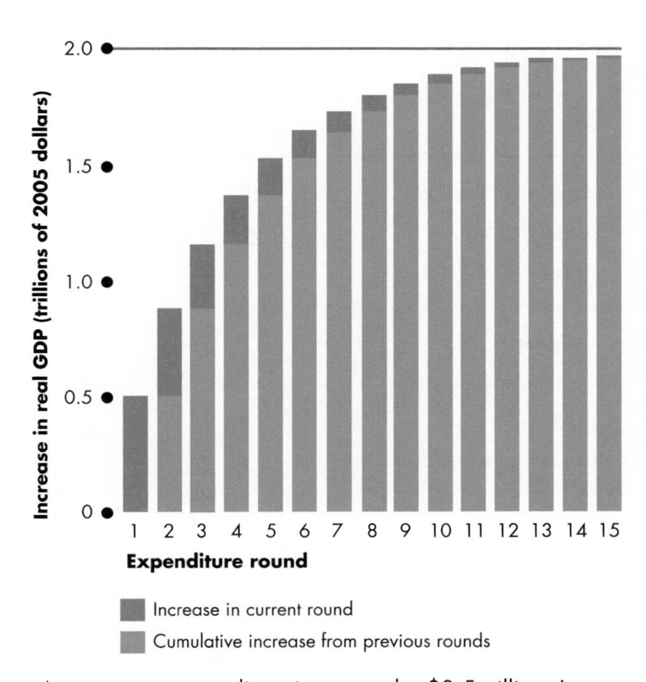

Autonomous expenditure increases by $0.5 trillion. In round 1, real GDP increases by the same amount. With the slope of the *AE* curve equal to 0.75, each additional dollar of real GDP induces an additional 0.75 of a dollar of induced expenditure. The round 1 increase in real GDP brings an increase in induced expenditure of $0.375 trillion in round 2. At the end of round 2, real GDP has increased by $0.875 trillion. The extra $0.375 trillion of real GDP in round 2 brings a further increase in induced expenditure of $0.281 trillion in round 3. At the end of round 3, real GDP has increased by $1.156 trillion. This process continues with real GDP increasing by ever-smaller amounts. When the process comes to an end, real GDP has increased by a total of $2 trillion.

myeconlab animation

Economics in Action

The Multiplier in the Great Depression

The aggregate expenditure model and its multiplier were developed during the 1930s by John Maynard Keynes to understand the most traumatic event in economic history, the *Great Depression.*

In 1929, the U.S. and global economies were booming. U.S. real GDP and real GDP per person had never been higher. By 1933, real GDP had fallen to 73 percent of its 1929 level and more than a quarter of the labor force was unemployed.

The table shows the GDP numbers and components of aggregate expenditure in 1929 and 1933.

	1929		1933	
	(billions of 1929 dollars)			
Induced consumption	47		34	
Induced imports	–6		–4	
Induced expenditure		41		30
Autonomous consumption	30		30	
Investment	17		3	
Government expenditure	10		10	
Exports	6		3	
Autonomous expenditure		63		46
GDP		**104**		**76**

Source of data: Bureau of Economic Analysis.

Autonomous expenditure collapsed as investment fell from \$17 billion to \$3 billion and exports fell by a large amount. Government expenditure held steady.

The figure uses the *AE* model to illustrate the Great Depression. In 1929, with autonomous expenditure of \$63 billion, the *AE* curve was AE_{29}. Equilibrium expenditure and real GDP were \$104 billion.

By 1933, autonomous expenditure had fallen by \$17 billion to \$46 billion and the *AE* curve had shifted downward to AE_{33}. Equilibrium expenditure and real GDP had fallen to \$76 billion.

The decrease in autonomous expenditure of \$17 billion brought a decrease in real GDP of \$28 billion. The multiplier was \$28/\$17 = 1.6. The slope of the *AE* curve is 0.39—the fall in induced expenditure, \$11 billion, divided by the fall in real GDP, \$28 billion. The multiplier formula, 1/(1 – Slope of *AE* curve), delivers a multiplier equal to 1.6.

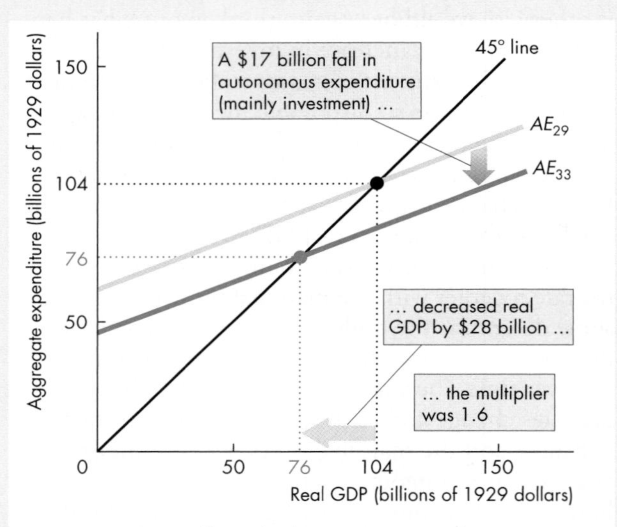

Aggregate Expenditure in the Great Depression

Business Cycle Turning Points

At business cycle turning points, the economy moves from expansion to recession or from recession to expansion. Economists understand these turning points as seismologists understand earthquakes. They know quite a lot about the forces and mechanisms that produce them, but they can't predict them. The forces that bring business cycle turning points are the swings in autonomous expenditure, such as investment and exports. The multiplier that you've just studied is the mechanism that gives momentum to the economy's new direction.

REVIEW QUIZ

1. What is the multiplier? What does it determine? Why does it matter?
2. How do the marginal propensity to consume, the marginal propensity to import, and the income tax rate influence the multiplier?
3. How do fluctuations in autonomous expenditure influence real GDP?

You can work these questions in Study Plan 11.3 and get instant feedback.

The Multiplier and the Price Level

We have just considered adjustments in spending that occur in the very short run when the price level is fixed. In this time frame, the economy's cobblestones, which are changes in investment and exports, are not smoothed by shock absorbers like those on Michael Bloomberg's car. Instead, they are amplified like Alicia Keys' voice. But these outcomes occur only when the price level is fixed. We now investigate what happens after a long enough time lapse for the price level to change.

Adjusting Quantities and Prices

When firms can't keep up with sales and their inventories fall below target, they increase production, but at some point, they raise their prices. Similarly, when firms find unwanted inventories piling up, they decrease production, but eventually they cut their prices. So far, we've studied the macroeconomic consequences of firms changing their production levels when their sales change, but we haven't looked at the effects of price changes. When individual firms change their prices, the economy's price level changes.

To study the simultaneous determination of real GDP and the price level, we use the *AS-AD model*, which is explained in Chapter 10. But to understand how aggregate demand adjusts, we need to work out the connection between the *AS-AD* model and the aggregate expenditure model that we've used in this chapter. The key to understanding the relationship between these two models is the distinction between the aggregate *expenditure* and aggregate *demand* and the related distinction between the aggregate *expenditure curve* and the aggregate *demand curve.*

Aggregate Expenditure and Aggregate Demand

The aggregate expenditure curve is the relationship between the aggregate planned expenditure and real GDP, all other influences on aggregate planned expenditure remaining the same. The aggregate demand curve is the relationship between the aggregate quantity of goods and services demanded and the price level, all other influences on aggregate demand remaining the same. Let's explore the links between these two relationships.

Deriving the Aggregate Demand Curve

When the price level changes, aggregate planned expenditure changes and the quantity of real GDP demanded changes. The aggregate demand curve slopes downward. Why? There are two main reasons:

- Wealth effect
- Substitution effects

Wealth Effect Other things remaining the same, the higher the price level, the smaller is the purchasing power of wealth. For example, suppose you have $100 in the bank and the price level is 105. If the price level rises to 125, your $100 buys fewer goods and services. You are less wealthy. With less wealth, you will probably want to try to spend a bit less and save a bit more. The higher the price level, other things remaining the same, the lower is aggregate planned expenditure.

Substitution Effects For a given expected future price level, a rise in the price level today makes current goods and services more expensive relative to future goods and services and results in a delay in purchases—an *intertemporal substitution.* A rise in the U.S. price level, other things remaining the same, makes U.S.-produced goods and services more expensive relative to foreign-produced goods and services. As a result, U.S. imports increase and U.S. exports decrease—an *international substitution.*

When the price level rises, each of these effects reduces aggregate planned expenditure at each level of real GDP. As a result, when the price level *rises,* the aggregate expenditure curve shifts *downward.* A fall in the price level has the opposite effect. When the price level *falls,* the aggregate expenditure curve shifts *upward.*

Figure 11.8(a) shows the shifts of the *AE* curve. When the price level is 110, the aggregate expenditure curve is AE_0, which intersects the 45° line at point *B*. Equilibrium expenditure is $13 trillion. If the price level increases to 130, the aggregate expenditure curve shifts downward to AE_1, which intersects the 45° line at point *A*. Equilibrium expenditure decreases to \$12 trillion. If the price level decreases to 90, the aggregate expenditure curve shifts upward to AE_2, which intersects the 45° line at point *C*. Equilibrium expenditure increases to \$14 trillion.

We've just seen that when the price level changes, other things remaining the same, the aggregate expenditure curve shifts and the equilibrium expenditure changes. But when the price level changes, other things remaining the same, there is a movement along the aggregate demand curve.

Figure 11.8(b) shows the movements along the aggregate demand curve. At a price level of 110, the aggregate quantity of goods and services demanded is \$13 trillion—point *B* on the *AD* curve. If the price level rises to 130, the aggregate quantity of goods and services demanded decreases to \$12 trillion. There is a movement up along the aggregate demand curve to point *A*. If the price level falls to 90, the aggregate quantity of goods and services demanded increases to \$14 trillion. There is a movement down along the aggregate demand curve to point *C*.

Each point on the aggregate demand curve corresponds to a point of equilibrium expenditure. The equilibrium expenditure points *A, B,* and *C* in Fig. 11.8(a) correspond to the points *A, B,* and *C* on the aggregate demand curve in Fig. 11.8(b).

Changes in Aggregate Expenditure and Aggregate Demand

When any influence on aggregate planned expenditure other than the price level changes, both the aggregate expenditure curve and the aggregate demand curve shift. For example, an increase in investment or exports increases both aggregate planned expenditure and aggregate demand and shifts both the *AE* curve and the *AD* curve. Figure 11.9 illustrates the effect of such an increase.

Initially, the aggregate expenditure curve is AE_0 in part (a) and the aggregate demand curve is AD_0 in part (b). The price level is 110, real GDP is \$13 trillion, and the economy is at point *A* in both parts of Fig. 11.9. Now suppose that investment increases by \$1 trillion. At a constant price level of 110, the aggregate expenditure curve shifts upward to AE_1. This curve intersects the 45° line at an equilibrium expenditure of \$15 trillion (point *B*). This equilibrium expenditure of \$15 trillion is the aggregate quantity of goods and services demanded at a price level of 110, as shown by point *B* in part (b). Point *B* lies on

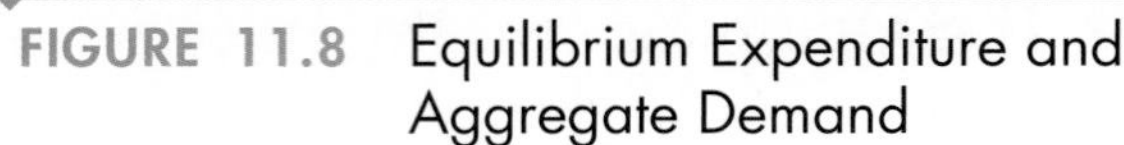

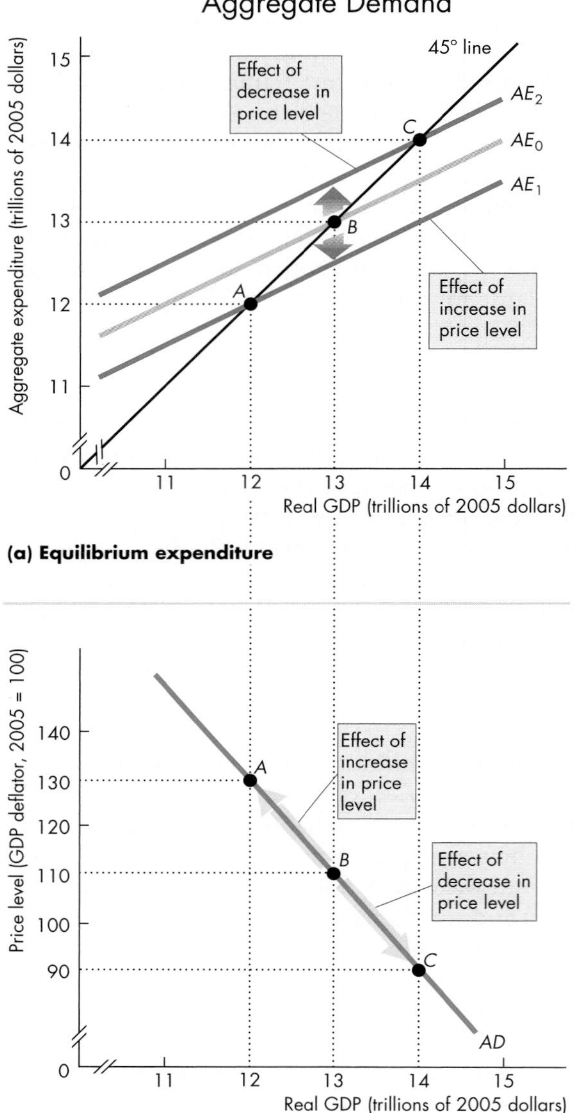

(b) Aggregate demand

A change in the price level *shifts* the *AE* curve and results in a *movement along* the *AD* curve. When the price level is 110, the *AE* curve is AE_0 and equilibrium expenditure is \$13 trillion at point *B*. When the price level rises to 130, the *AE* curve is AE_1 and equilibrium expenditure is \$12 trillion at point *A*. When the price level falls to 90, the *AE* curve is AE_2 and equilibrium expenditure is \$14 trillion at point *C*. Points *A, B,* and *C* on the *AD* curve in part (b) correspond to the equilibrium expenditure points *A, B,* and *C* in part (a).

myeconlab animation

FIGURE 11.9 A Change in Aggregate Demand

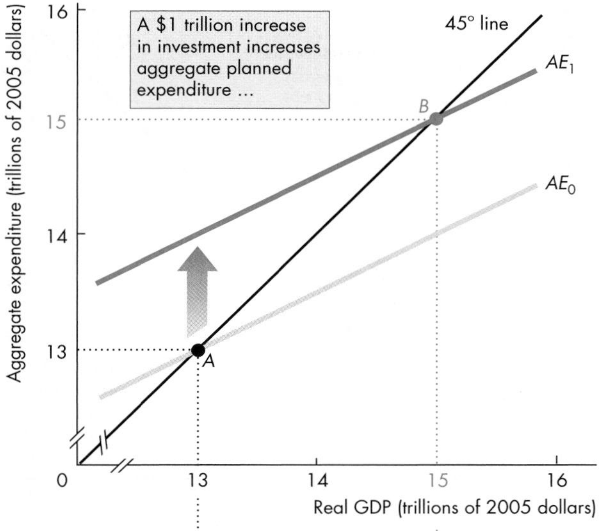

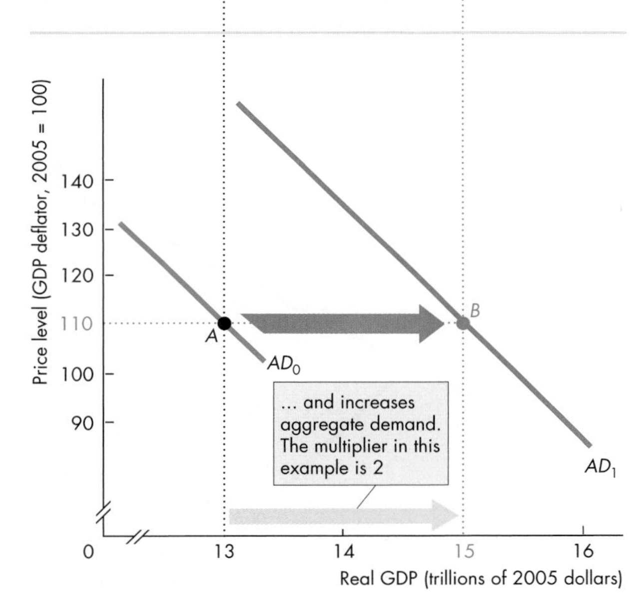

(b) Aggregate demand

The price level is 110. When the aggregate expenditure curve is AE_0 in part (a), the aggregate demand curve is AD_0 in part (b). An increase in autonomous expenditure shifts the *AE* curve upward to AE_1. In the new equilibrium, real GDP is $15 trillion (at point *B*). Because the quantity of real GDP demanded at a price level of 110 increases to $15 trillion, the *AD* curve shifts rightward to AD_1.

myeconlab animation

a new aggregate demand curve. The aggregate demand curve has shifted rightward to AD_1.

But how do we know by how much the *AD* curve shifts? The multiplier determines the answer. The larger the multiplier, the larger is the shift in the aggregate demand curve that results from a given change in autonomous expenditure. In this example, the multiplier is 2. A $1 trillion increase in investment produces a $2 trillion increase in the aggregate quantity of goods and services demanded at each price level. That is, a $1 trillion increase in autonomous expenditure shifts the aggregate demand curve rightward by $2 trillion.

A decrease in autonomous expenditure shifts the aggregate expenditure curve downward and shifts the aggregate demand curve leftward. You can see these effects by reversing the change that we've just described. If the economy is initially at point *B* on the aggregate expenditure curve AE_1 and on the aggregate demand curve AD_1, a decrease in autonomous expenditure shifts the aggregate expenditure curve downward to AE_0. The aggregate quantity of goods and services demanded decreases from $15 trillion to $13 trillion, and the aggregate demand curve shifts leftward to AD_0.

Let's summarize what we have just discovered:

If some factor other than a change in the price level increases autonomous expenditure, the *AE* curve shifts upward and the *AD* curve shifts rightward. The size of the *AD* curve shift equals the change in autonomous expenditure multiplied by the multiplier.

Equilibrium Real GDP and the Price Level

In Chapter 10, we learned that aggregate demand and short-run aggregate supply determine equilibrium real GDP and the price level. We've now put aggregate demand under a more powerful microscope and have discovered that a change in investment (or in any component of autonomous expenditure) changes aggregate demand and shifts the aggregate demand curve. The magnitude of the shift depends on the multiplier. But whether a change in autonomous expenditure results ultimately in a change in real GDP, a change in the price level, or a combination of the two depends on aggregate supply. There are two time frames to consider: the short run and the long run. First we'll see what happens in the short run.

An Increase in Aggregate Demand in the Short Run

Figure 11.10 describes the economy. Initially, in part (a), the aggregate expenditure curve is AE_0 and equilibrium expenditure is $13 trillion—point *A*. In part (b), aggregate demand is AD_0 and the short-run aggregate supply curve is *SAS*. (Chapter 10, pp. 243–245, explains the *SAS* curve.) Equilibrium is at point *A* in part (b), where the aggregate demand and short-run aggregate supply curves intersect. The price level is 110, and real GDP is $13 trillion.

Now suppose that investment increases by $1 trillion. With the price level fixed at 110, the aggregate expenditure curve shifts upward to AE_1. Equilibrium expenditure increases to $15 trillion—point *B* in part (a). In part (b), the aggregate demand curve shifts rightward by $2 trillion, from AD_0 to AD_1. How far the aggregate demand curve shifts is determined by the multiplier when the price level is fixed.

But with this new aggregate demand curve, the price level does not remain fixed. The price level rises, and as it does, the aggregate expenditure curve shifts downward. The short-run equilibrium occurs when the aggregate expenditure curve has shifted downward to AE_2 and the new aggregate demand curve, AD_1, intersects the short-run aggregate supply curve at point *C* in both part (a) and part (b). Real GDP is $14.3 trillion, and the price level is 123.

When price level effects are taken into account, the increase in investment still has a multiplier effect on real GDP, but the multiplier is smaller than it would be if the price level were fixed. The steeper the slope of the short-run aggregate supply curve, the larger is the increase in the price level and the smaller is the multiplier effect on real GDP.

An Increase in Aggregate Demand in the Long Run

Figure 11.11 illustrates the long-run effect of an increase in aggregate demand. In the long run, real GDP equals potential GDP and there is full employment. Potential GDP is $13 trillion, and the long-run aggregate supply curve is *LAS*. Initially, the economy is at point *A* in parts (a) and (b).

Investment increases by $1 trillion. In Fig. 11.11, the aggregate expenditure curve shifts to AE_1 and the aggregate demand curve shifts to AD_1. With no change in the price level, the economy would move to point *B* and real GDP would increase to $15 trillion. But in the short run, the price level rises to 123 and real GDP increases to only $14.3 trillion. With the higher price level, the *AE* curve shifts from AE_1 to

FIGURE 11.10 The Multiplier in the Short Run

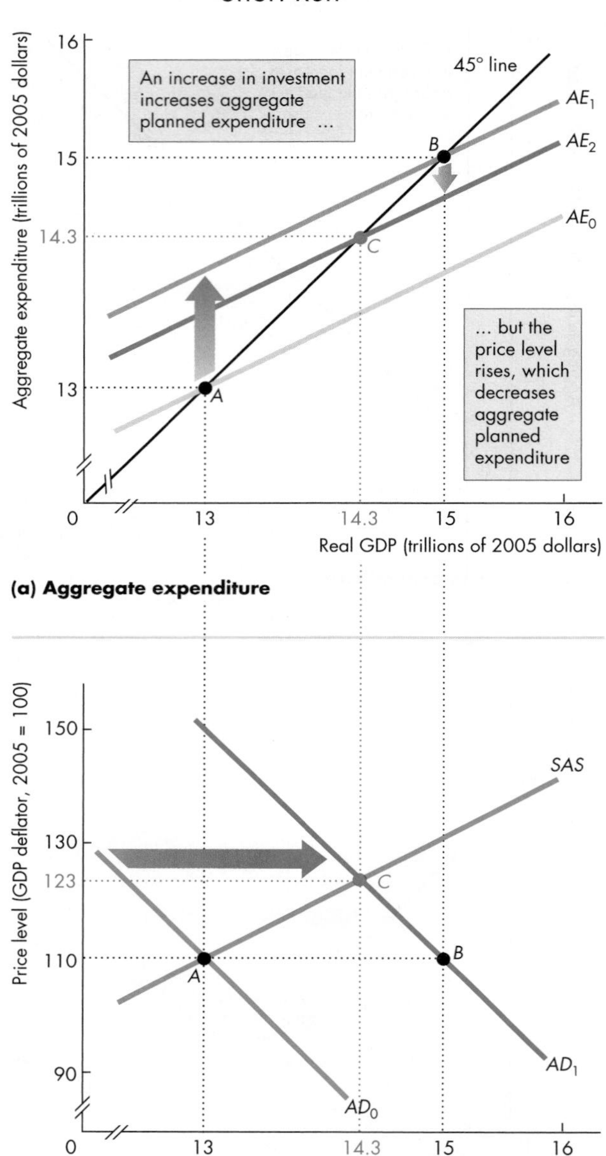

An increase in investment shifts the *AE* curve from AE_0 to AE_1 and the *AD* curve from AD_0 to AD_1. The price level rises, and the higher price level shifts the *AE* curve downward from AE_1 to AE_2. The economy moves to point *C* in both parts. In the short run, when prices are flexible, the multiplier effect is smaller than when the price level is fixed.

myeconlab animation

FIGURE 11.11 The Multiplier in the Long Run

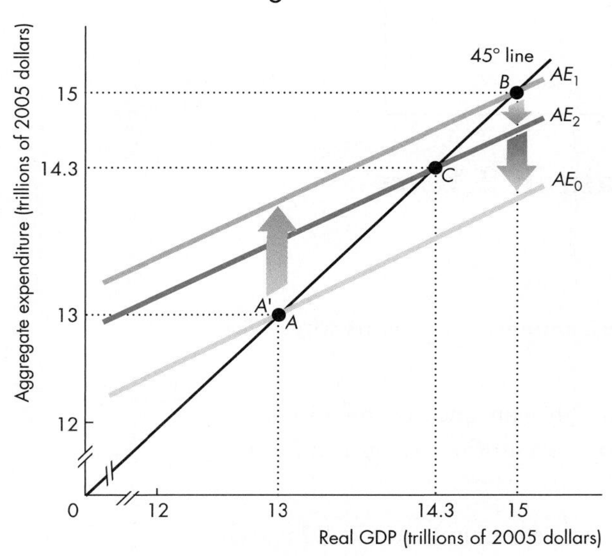

(a) Aggregate expenditure

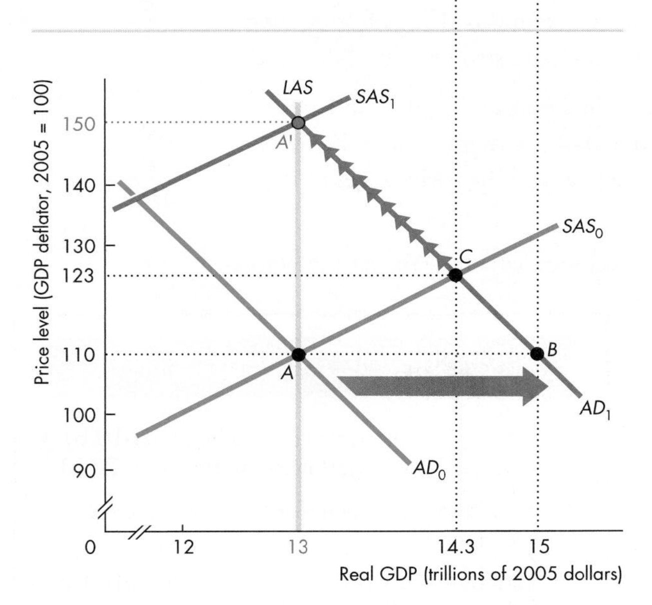

(b) Aggregate demand

Starting from point *A*, an increase in investment shifts the *AE* curve to AE_1 and the *AD* curve to AD_1. In the short run, the economy moves to point *C*. In the long run, the money wage rate rises and the *SAS* curve shifts to SAS_1. As the price level rises, the *AE* curve shifts back to AE_0 and the economy moves to point *A*'. In the long run, the multiplier is zero.

myeconlab animation

AE_2. The economy is now in a short-run equilibrium at point *C* in both part (a) and part (b).

Real GDP now exceeds potential GDP. The labor force is more than fully employed, and in the long run, shortages of labor increase the money wage rate. The higher money wage rate increases firms' costs, which decreases short-run aggregate supply and shifts the *SAS* curve leftward to SAS_1. The price level rises further, and real GDP decreases. There is a movement along AD_1, and the *AE* curve shifts downward from AE_2 toward AE_0. When the money wage rate and the price level have increased by the same percentage, real GDP is again equal to potential GDP and the economy is at point *A*'. In the long run, the multiplier is zero.

REVIEW QUIZ

1. How does a change in the price level influence the *AE* curve and the *AD* curve?
2. If autonomous expenditure increases with no change in the price level, what happens to the *AE* curve and the *AD* curve? Which curve shifts by an amount that is determined by the multiplier and why?
3. How does an increase in autonomous expenditure change real GDP in the short run? Does real GDP change by the same amount as the change in aggregate demand? Why or why not?
4. How does real GDP change in the long run when autonomous expenditure increases? Does real GDP change by the same amount as the change in aggregate demand? Why or why not?

You can work these questions in Study Plan 11.4 and get instant feedback.

You are now ready to build on what you've learned about aggregate expenditure fluctuations. We'll study the business cycle and the roles of fiscal policy and monetary policy in smoothing the cycle while achieving price stability and sustained economic growth. In Chapter 12 we study the U.S. business cycle and inflation, and in Chapters 13 and 14 we study fiscal policy and monetary policy, respectively. But before you leave the current topic, look at *Reading Between the Lines* on pp. 284–285 and see the aggregate expenditure model in action in the U.S. economy during 2009 and 2010.

Inventory Investment in the 2010 Expansion

Business Inventories Post Biggest Gain in 2 Years

http://www.seattletimes.com
September 14, 2010

Inventories held by businesses jumped in July by the largest amount in two years while sales rebounded after two months of declines.

Business inventories rose 1 percent in July, the biggest monthly gain since a similar increase in July 2008, the Commerce Department reported Tuesday. Inventories have grown for seven consecutive months.

Total business sales were up 0.7 percent in July after falling 0.5 percent in June and 1.2 percent in May.

The rebound in sales was an encouraging sign that consumer demand is rising after the two weak months. Businesses build up their stocks when they anticipate stronger retail demand.

Inventory growth helped drive economic expansion in the final quarter of 2009 and early this year. Many businesses replenished their stockpiles after slashing them during the recession. That led to rising orders at American factories and helped lead the early stages of the modest economic recovery.

For July, sales were up 1.1 percent at the manufacturing level with smaller gains at the wholesale and retail levels. A separate report Tuesday showed that retail sales increased in August by the largest amount since March, another encouraging sign that consumers are beginning to spend again.

The big jump in inventories in July might not have been voluntary. Businesses may have been caught with some unwanted stockpiles with the unexpected slowdown in sales in the previous two months. However, the hope is that sales will keep growing in coming months and this will spur businesses to continue stocking their shelves in anticipation of further gains in demand. …

ESSENCE OF THE STORY

- Business inventories increased in July 2010 by 1 percent, the largest increase since July 2008.
- Inventories have increased for seven consecutive months.
- Total business sales increased in July 2010 by 0.7 percent after falling in May and June.
- The increase in business inventories contributed to the increase in real GDP in the final quarter of 2009 and early 2010.
- Businesses replenished inventories after cutting them during the recession.
- The large increase in inventories in July might not have been voluntary.

ECONOMIC ANALYSIS

- The news article reports that inventories decreased during the recession of 2009 and were increasing in 2010 but not all of the increase was voluntary.
- Table 1 shows the real GDP and aggregate expenditure numbers for the second quarters of 2009 and 2010 along with the change over the year.
- The increase in investment and exports increased aggregate planned expenditure, which induced the increases in consumption expenditure and imports.
- Figure 1 shows how the change in inventories lags the change in real GDP. When real GDP starts to expand, inventories are still falling.
- Figure 2 uses the aggregate expenditure model to explain the behavior of inventories.
- In 2009 Q2, the *AE* curve was AE_0 and real GDP was $12.8 trillion, which we're assuming to be an expenditure equilibrium.
- The increase in investment and exports increased aggregate planned expenditure and shifted the *AE* curve upward to AE_1. Part of the increase in investment was a planned increase in inventories.
- When investment and exports increased, aggregate planned expenditure temporarily exceeded real GDP and an unplanned decrease in inventories occurred.
- In contrast to what the news article says, the planned increase in inventories in 2010 most likely *exceeded* the actual increase as the economy expanded.

Table 1 The Components of Aggregate Expenditure

Item	2009 Q2	2010 Q2	Change
	(billions of 2005 dollars)		
Consumption expenditure	9,117	9,270	153
Investment	1,453	1,787	334
Government expenditure	2,549	2,567	18
Exports	1,448	1,652	204
Imports	1,790	2,097	307
Residual*	33	13	–20
Real GDP	**12,810**	**13,192**	**382**
Change in inventories	–162	–39	123

*The residual arises because chain-dollar real variables are calculated for each expenditure component independently of chain-dollar real GDP and the components don't exactly sum to real GDP.

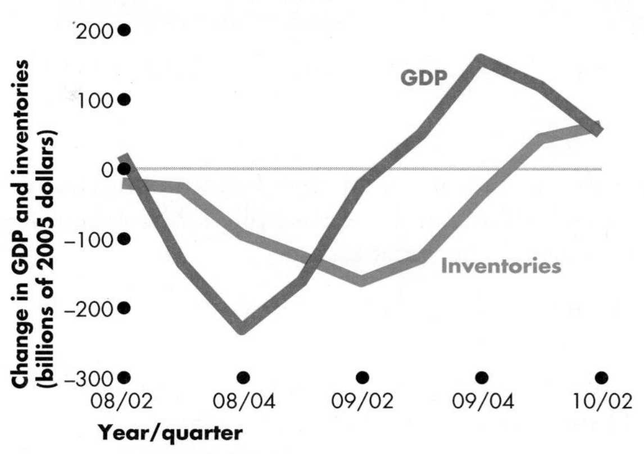

Figure 1 Real GDP and inventories

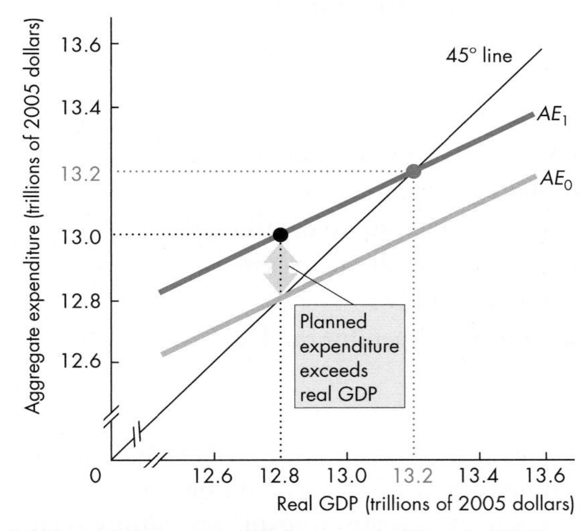

(a) Convergence to equilibrium expenditure in 2010

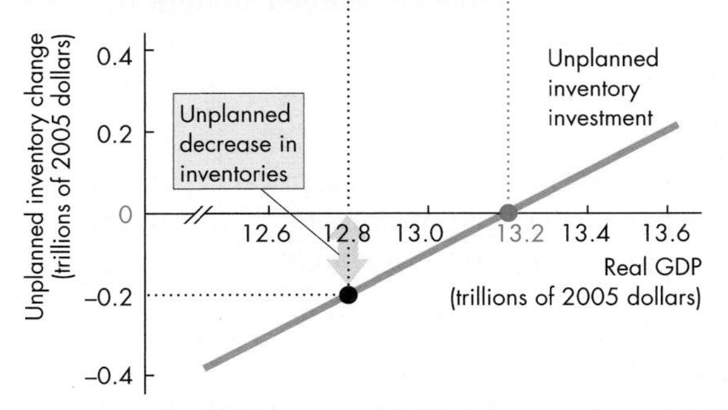

(b) Unplanned inventory change in 2010

Figure 2 Equilibrium expenditure in 2010

MATHEMATICAL NOTE

The Algebra of the Keynesian Model

This mathematical note derives formulas for equilibrium expenditure and the multipliers when the price level is fixed. The variables are

- Aggregate planned expenditure, *AE*
- Real GDP, *Y*
- Consumption expenditure, *C*
- Disposable income, *YD*
- Investment, *I*
- Government expenditure, *G*
- Exports, *X*
- Imports, *M*
- Net taxes, *T*
- Autonomous consumption expenditure, *a*
- Autonomous taxes, T_a
- Marginal propensity to consume, *b*
- Marginal propensity to import, *m*
- Marginal tax rate, *t*
- Autonomous expenditure, *A*

Aggregate Expenditure

Aggregate planned expenditure (*AE*) is the sum of the planned amounts of consumption expenditure (*C*), investment (*I*), government expenditure (*G*), and exports (*X*) minus the planned amount of imports (*M*).

$$AE = C + I + G + X - M.$$

Consumption Function Consumption expenditure (*C*) depends on disposable income (*YD*), and we write the consumption function as

$$C = a + bYD.$$

Disposable income (*YD*) equals real GDP minus net taxes (*Y* − *T*). So if we replace *YD* with (*Y* − *T*), the consumption function becomes

$$C = a + b(Y - T).$$

Net taxes, *T*, equal autonomous taxes (that are independent of income), T_a, plus induced taxes (that vary with income), *tY*.

So we can write net taxes as

$$T = T_a + tY.$$

Use this last equation to replace *T* in the consumption function. The consumption function becomes

$$C = a - bT_a + b(1 - t)Y.$$

This equation describes consumption expenditure as a function of real GDP.

Import Function Imports depend on real GDP, and the import function is

$$M = mY.$$

Aggregate Expenditure Curve Use the consumption function and the import function to replace *C* and *M* in the *AE* equation. That is,

$$AE = a - bT_a + b(1 - t)Y + I + G + X - mY.$$

Collect the terms that involve *Y* on the right side of the equation to obtain

$$AE = (a - bT_a + I + G + X) + [b(1 - t) - m]Y.$$

Autonomous expenditure (*A*) is $(a - bT_a + I + G + X)$, and the slope of the *AE* curve is $[b(1 - t) - m]$. So the equation for the *AE* curve, which is shown in Fig. 1, is

$$AE = A + [b(1 - t) - m]Y.$$

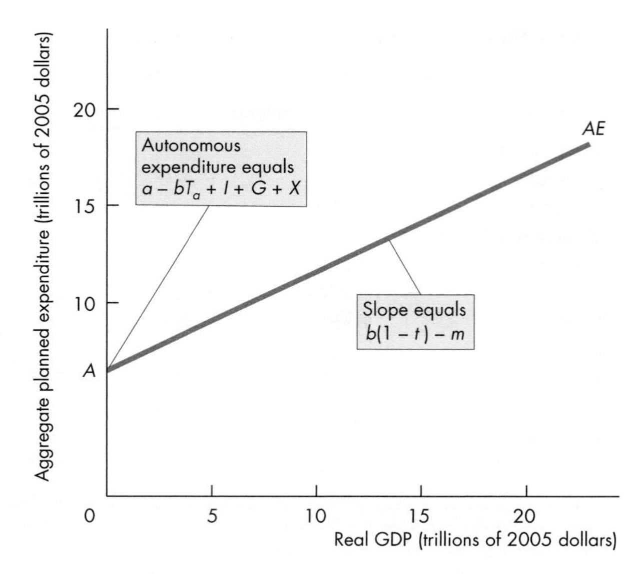

Figure 1 The *AE* curve

Equilibrium Expenditure

Equilibrium expenditure occurs when aggregate planned expenditure (AE) equals real GDP (Y). That is,

$$AE = Y.$$

In Fig. 2, the scales of the x-axis (real GDP) and the y-axis (aggregate planned expenditure) are identical, so the 45° line shows the points at which aggregate planned expenditure equals real GDP.

Figure 2 shows the point of equilibrium expenditure at the intersection of the AE curve and the 45° line.

To calculate equilibrium expenditure, solve the equations for the AE curve and the 45° line for the two unknown quantities AE and Y. So starting with

$$AE = A + [b(1 - t) - m]Y$$

$$AE = Y,$$

replace AE with Y in the AE equation to obtain

$$Y = A + [b(1 - t) - m]Y.$$

The solution for Y is

$$Y = \frac{1}{1 - [b(1 - t) - m]}A.$$

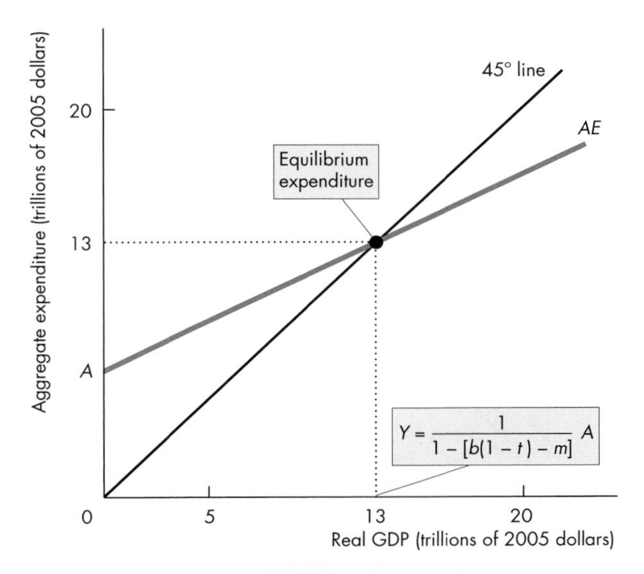

Figure 2 Equilibrium expenditure

The Multiplier

The *multiplier* equals the change in equilibrium expenditure and real GDP (Y) that results from a change in autonomous expenditure (A) divided by the change in autonomous expenditure.

A change in autonomous expenditure (ΔA) changes equilibrium expenditure and real GDP by

$$\Delta Y = \frac{1}{1 - [b(1 - t) - m]}\Delta A.$$

$$\text{Multiplier} = \frac{1}{1 - [b(1 - t) - m]}.$$

The size of the multiplier depends on the slope of the AE curve, $b(1 - t) - m$. The larger the slope, the larger is the multiplier. So the multiplier is larger,

- The greater the marginal propensity to consume (b)
- The smaller the marginal tax rate (t)
- The smaller the marginal propensity to import (m)

An economy with no imports and no income taxes has $m = 0$ and $t = 0$. In this special case, the multiplier equals $1/(1 - b)$. If b is 0.75, then the multiplier is 4, as shown in Fig. 3.

In an economy with imports and income taxes, if $b = 0.75$, $t = 0.2$, and $m = 0.1$, the multiplier equals 1 divided by $[1 - 0.75(1 - 0.2) - 0.1]$, which equals 2. Make up some more examples to show the effects of b, t, and m on the multiplier.

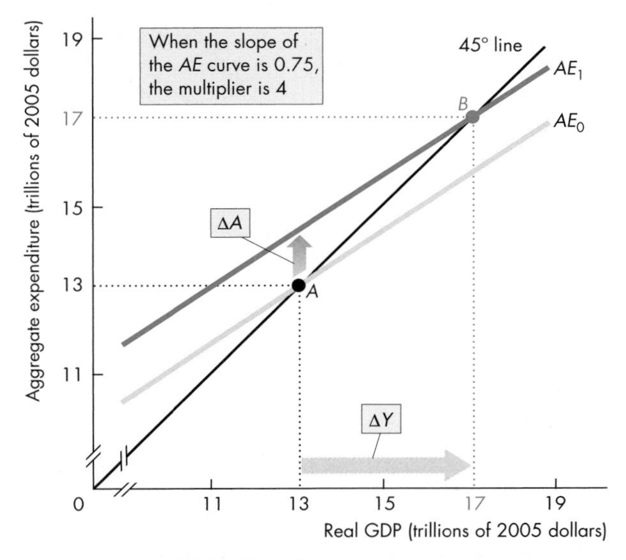

Figure 3 The multiplier

Government Expenditure Multiplier

The **government expenditure multiplier** equals the change in equilibrium expenditure and real GDP (Y) that results from a change in government expenditure (G) divided by the change in government expenditure. Because autonomous expenditure is equal to

$$A = a - bT_a + I + G + X,$$

the change in autonomous expenditure equals the change in government expenditure. That is,

$$\Delta A = \Delta G.$$

You can see from the solution for equilibrium expenditure Y that

$$\Delta Y = \frac{1}{1 - [b(1 - t) - m]} \Delta G.$$

The government expenditure multiplier equals

$$\frac{1}{1 - [b(1 - t) - m]}.$$

In an economy in which $t = 0$ and $m = 0$, the government expenditure multiplier is $1/(1 - b)$. With $b = 0.75$, the government expenditure multiplier is 4, as Fig. 4 shows. Make up some examples and use the above formula to show how b, m, and t influence the government expenditure multiplier.

Autonomous Tax Multiplier

The **autonomous tax multiplier** equals the change in equilibrium expenditure and real GDP (Y) that results from a change in autonomous taxes (T_a) divided by the change in autonomous taxes. Because autonomous expenditure is equal to

$$A = a - bT_a + I + G + X,$$

the change in autonomous expenditure equals *minus* b multiplied by the change in autonomous taxes. That is,

$$\Delta A = -b\Delta T_a.$$

You can see from the solution for equilibrium expenditure Y that

$$\Delta Y = \frac{-b}{1 - [b(1 - t) - m]} \Delta T_a.$$

The autonomous tax multiplier equals

$$\frac{-b}{1 - [b(1 - t) - m]}.$$

In an economy in which $t = 0$ and $m = 0$, the autonomous tax multiplier is $-b/(1 - b)$. In this special case, with $b = 0.75$, the autonomous tax multiplier equals -3, as Fig. 5 shows. Make up some examples and use the above formula to show how b, m, and t influence the autonomous tax multiplier.

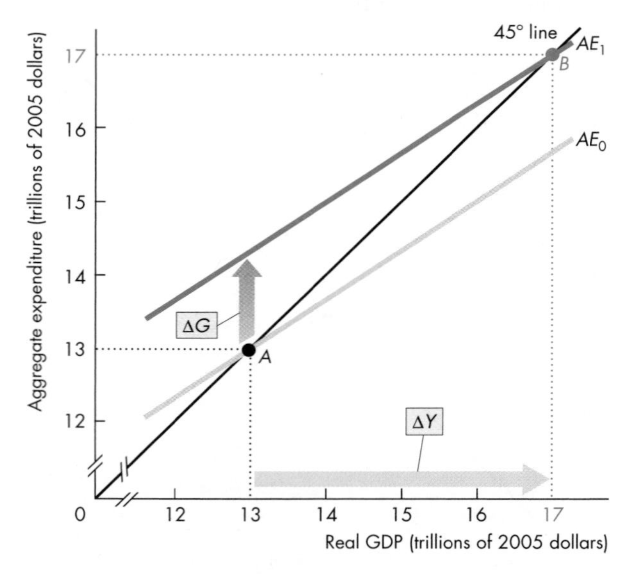

Figure 4 Government expenditure multiplier

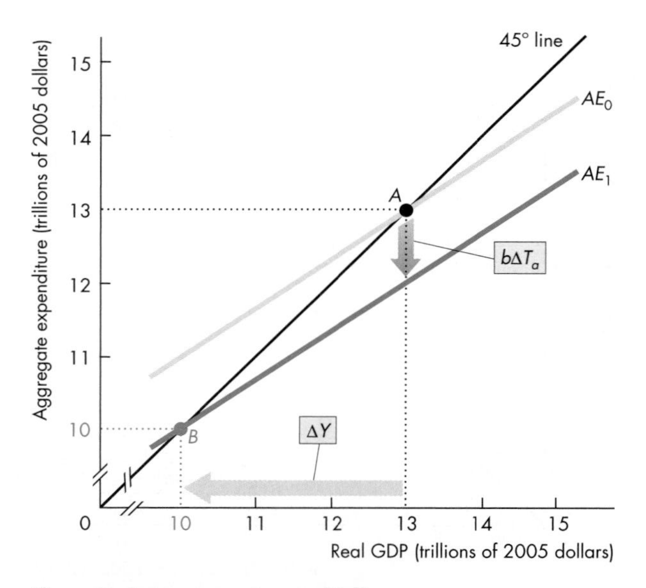

Figure 5 Autonomous tax multiplier

Balanced Budget Multiplier

The **balanced budget multiplier** equals the change in equilibrium expenditure and real GDP (Y) that results from equal changes in government expenditure and lump-sum taxes divided by the change in government expenditure. Because government expenditure and autono-mous taxes change by the same amount, the budget balance does not change.

The change in equilibrium expenditure that results from the change in government expenditure is

$$\Delta Y = \frac{1}{1 - [b(1 - t) - m]}\Delta G.$$

And the change in equilibrium expenditure that results from the change in autonomous taxes is

$$\Delta Y = \frac{-b}{1 - [b(1 - t) - m]}\Delta T_a.$$

So the change in equilibrium expenditure resulting from the changes in government expenditure and autonomous taxes is

$$\Delta Y = \frac{1}{1 - [b(1 - t) - m]}\Delta G + \frac{-b}{1-[b(1 - t)-m]}\Delta T_a.$$

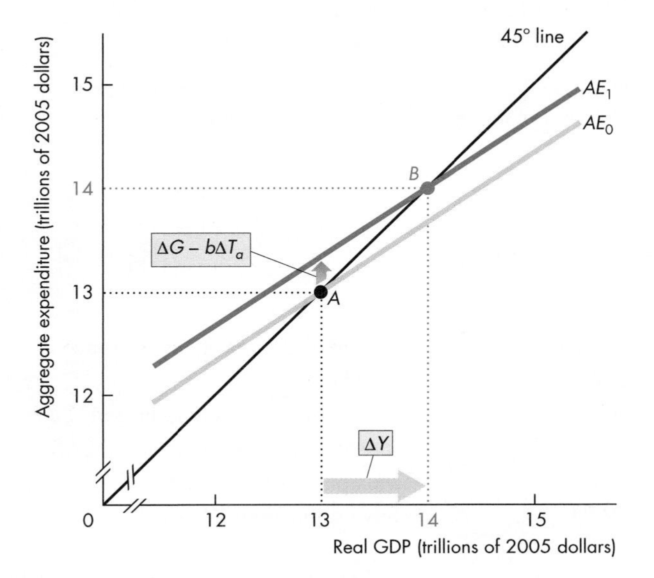

Figure 6 Balanced budget multiplier

Notice that

$$\frac{1}{1-[b(1 - t)-m]}$$

is common to both terms on the right side. So we can rewrite the equation as

$$\Delta Y = \frac{1}{1 - [b(1 - t) - m]}(\Delta G - b\Delta T_a)$$

The AE curve shifts upward by $\Delta G - b\Delta T_a$ as shown in Fig. 6.

But the change in government expenditure equals the change in autonomous taxes. That is,

$$\Delta G = \Delta T_a.$$

So we can write the equation as

$$\Delta Y = \frac{1 - b}{1 - [b(1 - t) - m]}\Delta G.$$

The balanced budget multiplier equals

$$\frac{1 - b}{1 - [b(1 - t) - m]}.$$

In an economy in which $t = 0$ and $m = 0$, the balanced budget multiplier is $(1 - b)/(1 - b)$, which equals 1, as Fig. 6 shows. Make up some examples and use the above formula to show how b, m, and t influence the balanced budget multiplier.

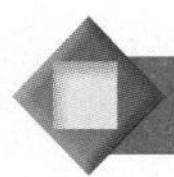

SUMMARY

Key Points

Fixed Prices and Expenditure Plans (pp. 266–269)

- When the price level is fixed, expenditure plans determine real GDP.
- Consumption expenditure is determined by disposable income, and the marginal propensity to consume (*MPC*) determines the change in consumption expenditure brought about by a change in disposable income. Real GDP determines disposable income.
- Imports are determined by real GDP, and the marginal propensity to import determines the change in imports brought about by a change in real GDP.

Working Problems 1 to 3 will give you a better understanding of fixed prices and expenditure plans.

Real GDP with a Fixed Price Level (pp. 270–273)

- Aggregate *planned* expenditure depends on real GDP.
- Equilibrium expenditure occurs when aggregate planned expenditure equals actual expenditure and real GDP.

Working Problems 4 to 7 will give you a better understanding of real GDP with a fixed price level.

The Multiplier (pp. 274–278)

- The multiplier is the magnified effect of a change in autonomous expenditure on equilibrium expenditure and real GDP.
- The multiplier is determined by the slope of the *AE* curve.
- The slope of the *AE* curve is influenced by the marginal propensity to consume, the marginal propensity to import, and the income tax rate.

Working Problems 8 to 11 will give you a better understanding of the multiplier.

The Multiplier and the Price Level (pp. 279–283)

- The *AD* curve is the relationship between the quantity of real GDP demanded and the price level, other things remaining the same.
- The *AE* curve is the relationship between aggregate planned expenditure and real GDP, other things remaining the same.
- At a given price level, there is a given *AE* curve. A change in the price level changes aggregate planned expenditure and shifts the *AE* curve. A change in the price level also creates a movement along the *AD* curve.
- A change in autonomous expenditure that is not caused by a change in the price level shifts the *AE* curve and shifts the *AD* curve. The magnitude of the shift of the *AD* curve depends on the multiplier and on the change in autonomous expenditure.
- The multiplier decreases as the price level changes, and the long-run multiplier is zero.

Working Problems 12 to 21 will give you a better understanding of the multiplier and the price level.

Key Terms

Aggregate planned expenditure, 266
Autonomous expenditure, 270
Autonomous tax multiplier, 288
Balanced budget multiplier, 289
Consumption function, 266
Disposable income, 266
Equilibrium expenditure, 272
Government expenditure multiplier, 288
Induced expenditure, 270
Marginal propensity to consume, 268
Marginal propensity to import, 269
Marginal propensity to save, 268
Multiplier, 274
Saving function, 266

STUDY PLAN PROBLEMS AND APPLICATIONS

myeconlab You can work Problems 1 to 22 in MyEconLab Chapter 11 Study Plan and get instant feedback.

Fixed Prices and Expenditure Plans (Study Plan 11.1)

Use the following data to work Problems 1 and 2.

You are given the following information about the economy of the United Kingdom.

Disposable income	Consumption expenditure
(billions of pounds per year)	
300	340
400	420
500	500
600	580
700	660

1. Calculate the marginal propensity to consume.
2. Calculate saving at each level of disposable income and calculate the marginal propensity to save.
3. **The U.S. and China's Savings Problems**

   Last year China saved about half of its gross domestic product while the United States saved only 13 percent of its national income. The contrast is even starker at the household level—a personal saving rate in China of about 30 percent of household income, compared with a U.S. rate that dipped into negative territory last year (–0.4% of after-tax household income). Similar extremes show up in the consumption shares of the two economies.

   Source: *Fortune*, March 8, 2006

   Compare the *MPC* and *MPS* in the United States and China. Why might they differ?

Real GDP with a Fixed Price Level (Study Plan 11.2)

Use the following figure to work Problems 4 and 5.

The figure illustrates the components of aggregate planned expenditure on Turtle Island. Turtle Island has no imports or exports, no incomes taxes, and the price level is fixed.

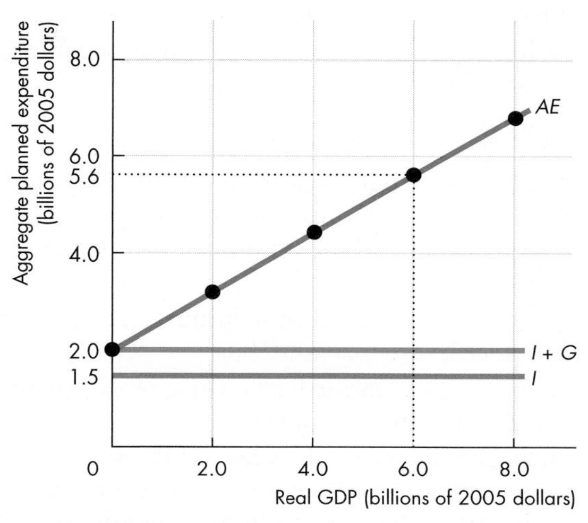

4. Calculate autonomous expenditure and the marginal propensity to consume.
5. a. What is aggregate planned expenditure when real GDP is $6 billion?

   b. If real GDP is $4 billion, what is happening to inventories?

   c. If real GDP is $6 billion, what is happening to inventories?
6. Explain the difference between induced consumption expenditure and autonomous consumption expenditure. Why isn't all consumption expenditure induced expenditure?
7. **Recovery?**

   In the second quarter, businesses increased spending on equipment and software by 21.9%, while a category that includes home building grew amid a rush by consumers to take advantage of tax credits for homes.

   Source: *The Wall Street Journal*, July 31, 2010

   Explain how an increase in business investment at a constant price level changes equilibrium expenditure.

The Multiplier (Study Plan 11.3)

Use the following data to work Problems 8 and 9.

An economy has a fixed price level, no imports, and no income taxes. *MPC* is 0.80, and real GDP is $150 billion. Businesses increase investment by $5 billion.

8. Calculate the multiplier and the change in real GDP.
9. Calculate the new real GDP and explain why real GDP increases by more than $5 billion.

Use the following data to work Problems 10 and 11.

An economy has a fixed price level, no imports, and no income taxes. An increase in autonomous expenditure of $2 trillion increases equilibrium expenditure by $8 trillion.

10. Calculate the multiplier and the marginal propensity to consume.
11. What happens to the multiplier if an income tax is introduced?

The Multiplier and the Price Level (Study Plan 11.4)

Use the following data to work Problems 12 to 16. Suppose that the economy is at full employment, the price level is 100, and the multiplier is 2. Investment increases by $100 billion.

12. What is the change in equilibrium expenditure if the price level remains at 100?
13. a. What is the immediate change in the quantity of real GDP demanded?
    b. In the short run, does real GDP increase by more than, less than, or the same amount as the immediate change in the quantity of real GDP demanded?
14. In the short run, does the price level remain at 100? Explain why or why not.
15. a. In the long run, does real GDP increase by more than, less than, or the same amount as the immediate increase in the quantity of real GDP demanded?
    b. Explain how the price level changes in the long run.
16. Are the values of the multipliers in the short run and the long run larger or smaller than 2?

Use the following news clip to work Problems 17 and 18.

Understimulated

A stimulus package would send more than $100 billion to American taxpayers before the end of 2008. The theory behind the rebates is that American taxpayers will take the cash and spend it—thus providing a jolt of stimulus to the economy. But will they? In 2001, Washington sought to jolt the economy back into life with tax rebates. In all, 90 million households received some $38 billion in cash. Months later, economists discovered that households spent 20 to 40 percent of their rebates during the first three months and about another third during the following three months. People with low incomes spent more.

Source: *Newsweek*, February 7, 2008

17. Will $100 billion of tax rebates to American consumers increase aggregate expenditure by more than, less than, or exactly $100 billion? Explain.
18. Explain and draw a graph to illustrate how this fiscal stimulus will influence aggregate expenditure and aggregate demand in both the short run and the long run.

Use the following news clip to work Problems 19 to 21.

Working Poor More Pinched as Rich Cut Back

Cutbacks by the wealthy have a ripple effect across all consumer spending, said Michael P. Niemira, chief economist at the International Council of Shopping Centers. The top 20 percent of households spend about $94,000 annually, almost five times what the bottom 20 percent spend and more than what the bottom sixty percent combined spend. Then there's also the multiplier effect: When shoppers splurge on $1,000 dinners and $300 limousine rides, that means fatter tips for the waiter and the driver. Sales clerks at upscale stores, who typically earn sales commissions, also depend on spending sprees of mink coats and jewelry. But the trickling down is starting to dry up, threatening to hurt a broad base of low-paid workers.

Source: MSNBC, January 28, 2008

19. Explain and draw a graph to illustrate the process by which "cutbacks by the wealthy have a ripple effect."
20. Explain and draw a graph to illustrate how real GDP will be driven back to potential GDP in the long run.
21. Why is the multiplier only a short-run influence on real GDP?

Mathematical Note (Study Plan 11.MN)

22. In the Canadian economy, autonomous consumption expenditure is $50 billion, investment is $200 billion, and government expenditure is $250 billion. The marginal propensity to consume is 0.7 and net taxes are $250 billion. Exports are $500 billion and imports are $450 billion. Assume that net taxes and imports are autonomous and the price level is fixed.
    a. What is the consumption function?
    b. What is the equation of the *AE* curve?
    c. Calculate equilibrium expenditure.
    d. Calculate the multiplier.
    e. If investment decreases to $150 billion, what is the change in equilibrium expenditure?
    f. Describe the process in part (e) that moves the economy to its new equilibrium expenditure.

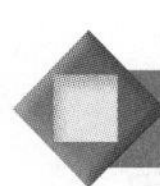

ADDITIONAL PROBLEMS AND APPLICATIONS

myeconlab You can work these problems in MyEconLab if assigned by your instructor.

Fixed Prices and Expenditure Plans

Use the following data to work Problems 23 and 24.

You are given the following information about the economy of Australia.

Disposable income	Saving
(billions of dollars per year)	
0	–5
100	20
200	45
300	70
400	95

23. Calculate the marginal propensity to save.
24. Calculate consumption at each level of disposable income. Calculate the marginal propensity to consume.

Use the following news clip to work Problems 25 to 27.

Americans $1.7 trillion Poorer

Americans saw their net worth decline by $1.7 trillion in the first quarter of 2008. Until then, net worth had been rising steadily since 2003. "The recent declines, however, may not affect consumer spending," said Michael Englund, senior economist with Action Economics. Americans have actually spent more in recent months—spending everything in their wallet and borrowing more. Household debt grew by 3.5 percent with consumer credit rising at an annual rate of 5.75 percent.

Source: CNN, June 5, 2008

25. Explain and draw a graph to illustrate how a decrease in household wealth theoretically impacts the consumption function and saving function.
26. According to the news clip, how did consumption expenditure respond in the first quarter of 2008? What factors might explain why consumers' actual response differs from what the consumption function model predicts?
27. Draw a graph of a consumption function and show at what point consumers were actually operating in the first quarter. Explain your answer.

Real GDP with a Fixed Price Level

Use the following spreadsheet, which lists real GDP (Y) and the components of aggregate planned expenditure in billions of dollars, to work Problems 28 and 29.

	A	B	C	D	E	F	G
1		Y	C	I	G	X	M
2	A	100	110	50	60	60	15
3	B	200	170	50	60	60	30
4	C	300	230	50	60	60	45
5	D	400	290	50	60	60	60
6	E	500	350	50	60	60	75
7	F	600	410	50	60	60	90

28. Calculate autonomous expenditure. Calculate the marginal propensity to consume.
29. a. What is aggregate planned expenditure when real GDP is $200 billion?
    b. If real GDP is $200 billion, explain the process that moves the economy toward equilibrium expenditure.
    c. If real GDP is $500 billion, explain the process that moves the economy toward equilibrium expenditure.
30. **Wholesale Inventories Decline, Sales Rise**

    The Commerce Department reported that wholesale inventories fell 1.3 percent in August for a record 12th consecutive month, evidence that companies are trimming orders to factories, which helped depress economic output during the recession. Economists hope that the rising sales will encourage businesses to begin restocking their inventories, which would boost factory production and help bolster broad economic growth in coming months.

    Source: *The New York Times*, October 8, 2009

    Explain why a fall in inventories is associated with recession and a restocking of inventories might bolster economic growth.

The Multiplier

31. **Obama's New Stimulus**

    The Obama recovery plan announced on Monday includes proposed spending of $50 billion to rebuild 150,000 miles of roads, construct and maintain 4,000 miles of rail, and fix or rebuild 150 miles of runways.

    Source: *USA Today*, September 10, 2010

    If the slope of the *AE* curve is 0.7, calculate the immediate change in aggregate planned expenditure and the change in real GDP in the short run if the price level remains unchanged.

32. **Obama's Economic Recovery Plan**

    President Obama's proposal to jolt a listless recovery with $180 billion worth of tax breaks and transportation projects left economists largely unimpressed Tuesday.

    Source: *USA Today*, September 10, 2010

    If taxes fall by $90 billion and the spending on transport projects increase by $90 billion, which component of Obama's recovery plan would have the larger effect on equilibrium expenditure, other things remaining the same?

The Multiplier and the Price Level

33. **Price Jump Worst Since '91**

    The biggest annual jump in the CPI since 1991 has fanned fears about growing pressures on consumers. The Labor Department report confirms what every consumer in America has known for months: Inflation is soaring and it's having an adverse impact on the economy.

    Source: CNN, July 16, 2008

    Explain and draw a graph to illustrate the effect of a rise in the price level on equilibrium expenditure.

Use the following news clip to work Problems 34 to 36.

Where Americans Will (and Won't) Cut Back

Consumer confidence has tumbled but even as consumers cut back on spending, there are some things they refuse to give up. Market research reports that Americans are demonstrating a strong reluctance to give up everyday pleasures, but many are forced to prioritize and scale back some of their spending. Spending on dining out, out-of-the-home entertainment, clothes, vacations, and buying lunch tend to be the first to be cut and many Americans are driving less and staying at home more. A whopping 50 percent of Americans plan to buy an HD or flat-panel TV in the next year. Cable and satellite TV subscriptions are also way down the list on cutbacks. Despite the expense, another thing consumers refuse to go without completely is travel. Even in these tough times, 59 percent of Americans plan to take a trip in the next six months.

Source: CNN, July 16, 2008

34. Which of the expenditures listed in the news clip are part of induced consumption expenditure and which is part of autonomous consumption expenditure? Explain why all consumption expenditure is not induced expenditure.
35. Explain and draw a graph to illustrate how declining consumer confidence influences aggregate expenditure and aggregate demand in the short run.
36. Explain and draw a graph to illustrate the long-run effect on aggregate expenditure and aggregate demand of the decline in consumer confidence.

Economics in the News

37. After you have studied *Reading Between the Lines* on pp. 284–285 answer the following questions.
    a. If the 2010 changes in inventories were mainly *planned* changes, what role did they play in shifting the *AE* curve and changing equilibrium expenditure? Use a two-part figure (similar to that on p. 272) to answer this question.
    b. Could the news article report that some of the rise in inventories in 2010 was unplanned be consistent with the *AE* model? Draw an appropriate graph to illustrate your answer.
    c. What do you think will happen to unplanned inventory changes when real GDP returns to potential GDP?

Mathematical Note

38. In an economy autonomous spending is $20 trillion and the slope of the *AE* curve is 0.6.
    a. What is the equation of the *AE* curve?
    b. Calculate equilibrium expenditure.
    c. Calculate the multiplier if the price level is unchanged.

After studying this chapter, you will be able to:

- Explain how demand-pull and cost-push forces bring cycles in inflation and output
- Explain the short-run and long-run tradeoff between inflation and unemployment
- Explain how the mainstream business cycle theory and real business cycle theory account for fluctuations in output and employment

12 U.S. INFLATION, UNEMPLOYMENT, AND BUSINESS CYCLE

Back in the 1970s, when inflation was raging at a double-digit rate, economist Arthur M. Okun proposed what he called the "misery index." Misery, he suggested, could be measured as the sum of the inflation rate and the unemployment rate. At its peak, in 1980, the misery index hit 22. At its lowest, in 1953, the misery index was 3.

Inflation and unemployment make us miserable for good reasons. We care about inflation because it raises our cost of living. And we care about unemployment because either it hits us directly and takes our jobs or it scares us into thinking that we might lose our jobs.

We want rapid income growth, low unemployment, and low inflation. But can we have all these things at the same time? Or do we face a tradeoff among them? As this chapter explains, we face a tradeoff in the short run but not in the long run.

At the end of the chapter, in *Reading Between the Lines*, we examine the state of unemployment and inflation and the "misery index" in 2010 compared with some earlier episodes.

Inflation Cycles

In the long run, inflation is a monetary phenomenon. It occurs if the quantity of money grows faster than potential GDP. But in the short run, many factors can start an inflation, and real GDP and the price level interact. To study these interactions, we distinguish between two sources of inflation:

- Demand-pull inflation
- Cost-push inflation

Demand-Pull Inflation

An inflation that starts because aggregate demand increases is called **demand-pull inflation**. Demand-pull inflation can be kicked off by *any* of the factors that change aggregate demand. Examples are a cut in the interest rate, an increase in the quantity of money, an increase in government expenditure, a tax cut, an increase in exports, or an increase in investment stimulated by an increase in expected future profits.

Initial Effect of an Increase in Aggregate Demand Suppose that last year the price level was 110 and real GDP was $13 trillion. Potential GDP was also $13 trillion. Figure 12.1(a) illustrates this situation. The aggregate demand curve is AD_0, the short-run aggregate supply curve is SAS_0, and the long-run aggregate supply curve is *LAS*.

Now suppose that the Fed cuts the interest rate. The quantity of money increases and the aggregate demand curve shifts from AD_0 to AD_1. With no change in potential GDP and no change in the money wage rate, the long-run aggregate supply curve and the short-run aggregate supply curve remain at *LAS* and SAS_0, respectively.

The price level and real GDP are determined at the point where the aggregate demand curve AD_1 intersects the short-run aggregate supply curve. The price level rises to 113, and real GDP increases above potential GDP to $13.5 trillion. Unemployment falls below its natural rate. The economy is at an above full-employment equilibrium and there is an inflationary gap. The next step in the unfolding story is a rise in the money wage rate.

FIGURE 12.1 A Demand-Pull Rise in the Price Level

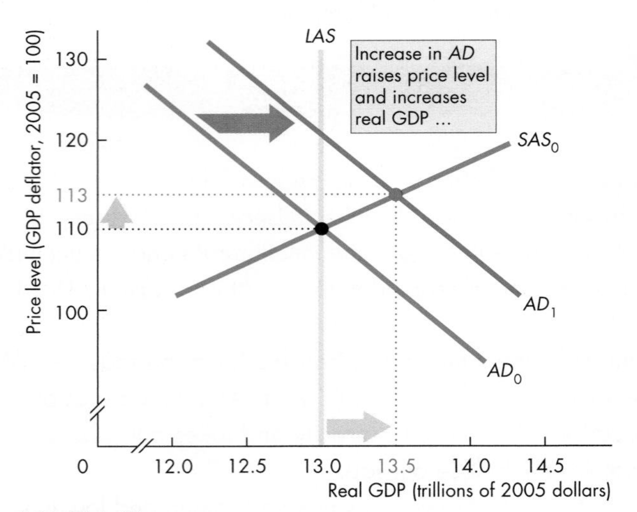

(a) Initial effect

In part (a), the aggregate demand curve is AD_0, the short-run aggregate supply curve is SAS_0, and the long-run aggregate supply curve is *LAS*. The price level is 110, and real GDP is $13 trillion, which equals potential GDP. Aggregate demand increases to AD_1. The price level rises to 113, and real GDP increases to $13.5 trillion.

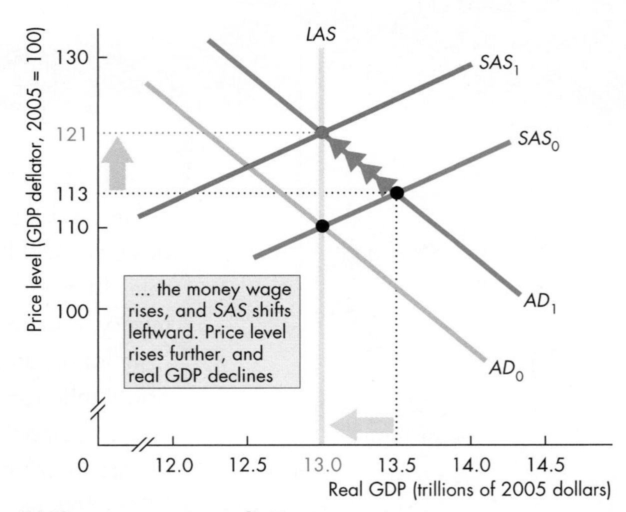

(b) The money wage adjusts

In part (b), starting from the above full-employment equilibrium, the money wage rate begins to rise and the short-run aggregate supply curve shifts leftward toward SAS_1. The price level rises further, and real GDP returns to potential GDP.

myeconlab animation

Money Wage Rate Response Real GDP cannot remain above potential GDP forever. With unemployment below its natural rate, there is a shortage of labor. In this situation, the money wage rate begins to rise. As it does so, short-run aggregate supply decreases and the *SAS* curve starts to shift leftward. The price level rises further, and real GDP begins to decrease.

With no further change in aggregate demand—that is, the aggregate demand curve remains at AD_1—this process ends when the short-run aggregate supply curve has shifted to SAS_1 in Fig. 12.1(b). At this time, the price level has increased to 121 and real GDP has returned to potential GDP of $13 trillion, the level at which it started.

A Demand-Pull Inflation Process The events that we've just described bring a *one-time rise in the price level*, not an inflation. For inflation to proceed, aggregate demand must *persistently* increase.

The only way in which aggregate demand can persistently increase is if the quantity of money persistently increases. Suppose the government has a budget deficit that it finances by selling bonds. Also suppose that the Fed buys some of these bonds. When the Fed buys bonds, it creates more money. In this situation, aggregate demand increases year after year. The aggregate demand curve keeps shifting rightward. This persistent increase in aggregate demand puts continual upward pressure on the price level. The economy now experiences demand-pull inflation.

Figure 12.2 illustrates the process of demand-pull inflation. The starting point is the same as that shown in Fig. 12.1. The aggregate demand curve is AD_0, the short-run aggregate supply curve is SAS_0, and the long-run aggregate supply curve is *LAS*. Real GDP is $13 trillion, and the price level is 110. Aggregate demand increases, shifting the aggregate demand curve to AD_1. Real GDP increases to $13.5 trillion, and the price level rises to 113. The economy is at an above full-employment equilibrium. There is a shortage of labor, and the money wage rate rises. The short-run aggregate supply curve shifts to SAS_1. The price level rises to 121, and real GDP returns to potential GDP.

But the Fed increases the quantity of money again, and aggregate demand continues to increase. The aggregate demand curve shifts rightward to AD_2. The price level rises further to 125, and real GDP again exceeds potential GDP at $13.5 trillion. Yet again,

FIGURE 12.2 A Demand-Pull Inflation Spiral

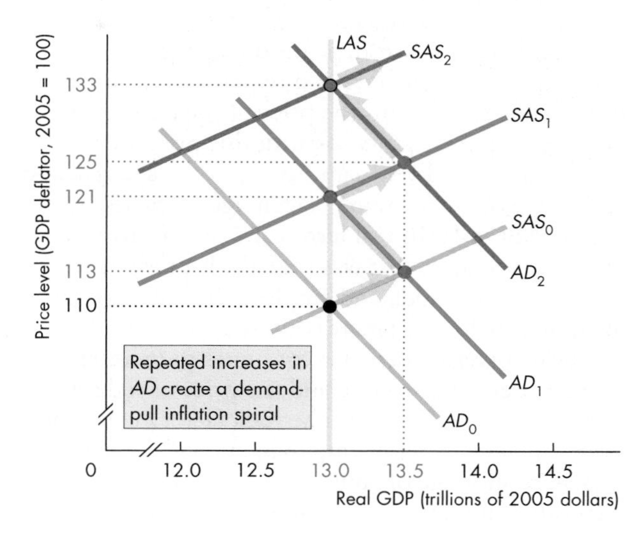

Each time the quantity of money increases, aggregate demand increases and the aggregate demand curve shifts rightward from AD_0 to AD_1 to AD_2, and so on. Each time real GDP increases above potential GDP, the money wage rate rises and the short-run aggregate supply curve shifts leftward from SAS_0 to SAS_1 to SAS_2, and so on. The price level rises from 110 to 113, 121, 125, 133, and so on. There is a demand-pull inflation spiral. Real GDP fluctuates between $13 trillion and $13.5 trillion.

myeconlab animation

the money wage rate rises and decreases short-run aggregate supply. The *SAS* curve shifts to SAS_2, and the price level rises further, to 133. As the quantity of money continues to grow, aggregate demand increases and the price level rises in an ongoing demand-pull inflation process.

The process you have just studied generates inflation—an ongoing process of a rising price level.

Demand-Pull Inflation in Kalamazoo You may better understand the inflation process that we've just described by considering what is going on in an individual part of the economy, such as a Kalamazoo soda-bottling plant. Initially, when aggregate demand increases, the demand for soda increases and the price of soda rises. Faced with a higher price, the soda plant works overtime and increases production. Conditions are good for workers in Kalamazoo, and the soda factory finds it hard to hang on to its best people. To do so, it offers a higher money wage rate. As the wage rate rises, so do the soda factory's costs.

What happens next depends on aggregate demand. If aggregate demand remains constant, the firm's costs increase but the price of soda does not increase as quickly as its costs. In this case, the firm cuts production. Eventually, the money wage rate and costs increase by the same percentage as the rise in the price of soda. In real terms, the soda factory is in the same situation as it was initially. It produces the same amount of soda and employs the same amount of labor as before the increase in demand.

But if aggregate demand continues to increase, so does the demand for soda and the price of soda rises at the same rate as wages. The soda factory continues to operate at above full employment and there is a persistent shortage of labor. Prices and wages chase each other upward in a demand-pull inflation spiral.

Demand-Pull Inflation in the United States A demand-pull inflation like the one you've just studied occurred in the United States during the late 1960s. In 1960, inflation was a moderate 2 percent a year, but its rate increased slowly to 3 percent by 1966. Then, in 1967, a large increase in government expenditure on the Vietnam War and an increase in spending on social programs, together with an increase in the growth rate of the quantity of money, increased aggregate demand more quickly. Consequently, the rightward shift of the aggregate demand curve accelerated and the price level increased more quickly. Real GDP moved above potential GDP, and the unemployment rate fell below its natural rate.

With unemployment below its natural rate, the money wage rate started to rise more quickly and the short-run aggregate supply curve shifted leftward. The Fed responded with a further increase in the money growth rate, and a demand-pull inflation spiral unfolded. By 1970, the inflation rate had reached 5 percent a year.

For the next few years, aggregate demand grew even more quickly and the inflation rate kept rising. By 1974, the inflation rate had reached 11 percent a year.

Next, let's see how shocks to aggregate supply can create cost-push inflation.

Cost-Push Inflation

An inflation that is kicked off by an increase in costs is called **cost-push inflation**. The two main sources of cost increases are

1. An increase in the money wage rate
2. An increase in the money prices of raw materials

At a given price level, the higher the cost of production, the smaller is the amount that firms are willing to produce. So if the money wage rate rises or if the prices of raw materials (for example, oil) rise, firms decrease their supply of goods and services. Aggregate supply decreases, and the short-run aggregate supply curve shifts leftward.[1] Let's trace the effects of such a decrease in short-run aggregate supply on the price level and real GDP.

Initial Effect of a Decrease in Aggregate Supply
Suppose that last year the price level was 110 and real GDP was \$13 trillion. Potential real GDP was also \$13 trillion. Figure 12.3(a) illustrates this situation. The aggregate demand curve was AD_0, the short-run aggregate supply curve was SAS_0, and the long-run aggregate supply curve was *LAS*. In the current year, the world's oil producers form a price-fixing organization that strengthens their market power and increases the relative price of oil. They raise the price of oil, and this action decreases short-run aggregate supply. The short-run aggregate supply curve shifts leftward to SAS_1. The price level rises to 117, and real GDP decreases to \$12.5 trillion. The economy is at a below full-employment equilibrium and there is a recessionary gap.

This event is a *one-time rise in the price level.* It is not inflation. In fact, a supply shock on its own cannot cause inflation. Something more must happen to enable a one-time supply shock, which causes a one-time rise in the price level, to be converted into a process of ongoing inflation. The quantity of money must persistently increase. Sometimes it does increase, as you will now see.

[1] Some cost-push forces, such as an increase in the price of oil accompanied by a decrease in the availability of oil, can also decrease long-run aggregate supply. We'll ignore such effects here and examine cost-push factors that change only short-run aggregate supply. Later in the chapter, we study the effects of shocks to long-run aggregate supply.

FIGURE 12.3 A Cost-Push Rise in the Price Level

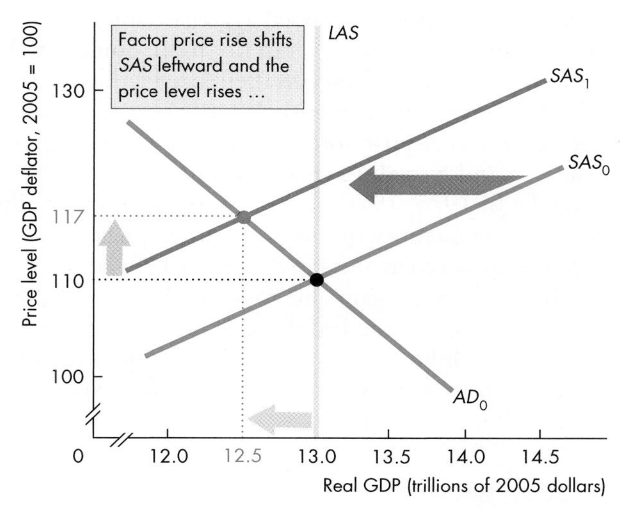

(a) Initial cost push

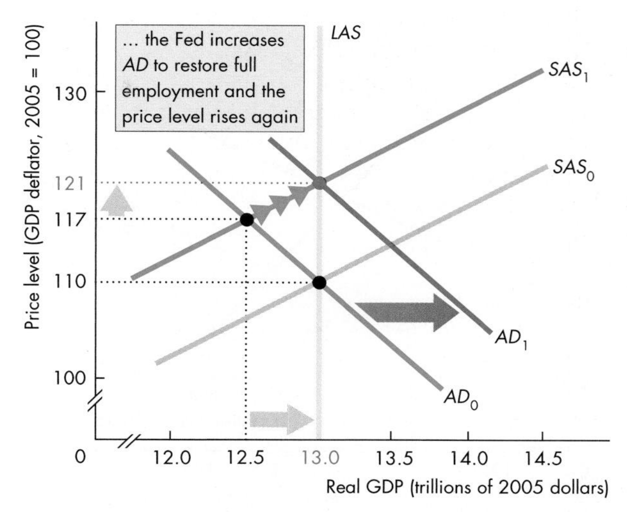

(b) The Fed responds

Initially, the aggregate demand curve is AD_0, the short-run aggregate supply curve is SAS_0, and the long-run aggregate supply curve is *LAS*. A decrease in aggregate supply (for example, resulting from a rise in the world price of oil) shifts the short-run aggregate supply curve to SAS_1. The economy moves to the point where the short-run aggregate supply curve SAS_1 intersects the aggregate demand curve AD_0. The price level rises to 117, and real GDP decreases to $12.5 trillion.

In part (b), if the Fed responds by increasing aggregate demand to restore full employment, the aggregate demand curve shifts rightward to AD_1. The economy returns to full employment, but the price level rises further to 121.

Aggregate Demand Response When real GDP decreases, unemployment rises above its natural rate. In such a situation, there is often an outcry of concern and a call for action to restore full employment. Suppose that the Fed cuts the interest rate and increases the quantity of money. Aggregate demand increases. In Fig. 12.3(b), the aggregate demand curve shifts rightward to AD_1 and full employment is restored. But the price level rises further to 121.

A Cost-Push Inflation Process The oil producers now see the prices of everything they buy increasing, so oil producers increase the price of oil again to restore its new high relative price. Figure 12.4 continues the story. The short-run aggregate supply curve now shifts to SAS_2. The price level rises and real GDP decreases.

The price level rises further, to 129, and real GDP decreases to $12.5 trillion. Unemployment increases above its natural rate. If the Fed responds yet again with an increase in the quantity of money, aggregate demand increases and the aggregate demand curve shifts to AD_2. The price level rises even higher—to 133—and full employment is again restored. A cost-push inflation spiral results. The combination of a rising price level and decreasing real GDP is called **stagflation.**

You can see that the Fed has a dilemma. If it does not respond when producers raise the oil price, the economy remains below full employment. If the Fed increases the quantity of money to restore full employment, it invites another oil price hike that will call forth yet a further increase in the quantity of money.

If the Fed responds to each oil price hike by increasing the quantity of money, inflation will rage along at a rate decided by oil producers. But if the Fed keeps the lid on money growth, the economy remains below full employment.

FIGURE 12.4 A Cost-Push Inflation Spiral

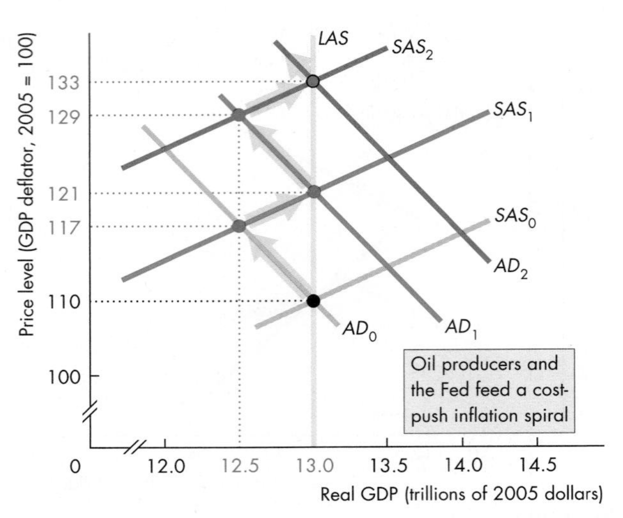

Each time a cost increase occurs, the short-run aggregate supply curve shifts leftward from SAS_0 to SAS_1 to SAS_2, and so on. Each time real GDP decreases below potential GDP, the Fed increases the quantity of money and the aggregate demand curve shifts rightward from AD_0 to AD_1 to AD_2, and so on. The price level rises from 110 to 117, 121, 129, 133, and so on. There is a cost-push inflation spiral. Real GDP fluctuates between $13 trillion and $12.5 trillion.

myeconlab animation

Cost-Push Inflation in Kalamazoo What is going on in the Kalamazoo soda-bottling plant when the economy is experiencing cost-push inflation?

When the oil price increases, so do the costs of bottling soda. These higher costs decrease the supply of soda, increasing its price and decreasing the quantity produced. The soda plant lays off some workers.

This situation persists until either the Fed increases aggregate demand or the price of oil falls. If the Fed increases aggregate demand, the demand for soda increases and so does its price. The higher price of soda brings higher profits, and the bottling plant increases its production. The soda factory rehires the laid-off workers.

Cost-Push Inflation in the United States A cost-push inflation like the one you've just studied occurred in the United States during the 1970s. It began in 1974 when the Organization of the Petroleum Exporting Countries (OPEC) raised the price of oil fourfold. The higher oil price decreased aggregate supply, which caused the price level to rise more quickly and real GDP to shrink. The Fed then faced a dilemma: Would it increase the quantity of money and accommodate the cost-push forces, or would it keep aggregate demand growth in check by limiting money growth? In 1975, 1976, and 1977, the Fed repeatedly allowed the quantity of money to grow quickly and inflation proceeded at a rapid rate. In 1979 and 1980, OPEC was again able to push oil prices higher. On that occasion, the Fed decided not to respond to the oil price hike with an increase in the quantity of money. The result was a recession but also, eventually, a fall in inflation.

Expected Inflation

If inflation is expected, the fluctuations in real GDP that accompany demand-pull and cost-push inflation that you've just studied don't occur. Instead, inflation proceeds as it does in the long run, with real GDP equal to potential GDP and unemployment at its natural rate. Figure 12.5 explains why.

Suppose that last year the aggregate demand curve was AD_0, the aggregate supply curve was SAS_0, and the long-run aggregate supply curve was *LAS*. The price level was 110, and real GDP was $13 trillion, which is also potential GDP.

To keep things as simple as possible, suppose that potential GDP does not change, so the *LAS* curve doesn't shift. Also suppose that aggregate demand is *expected to increase* to AD_1.

In anticipation of this increase in aggregate demand, the money wage rate rises and the short-run aggregate supply curve shifts leftward. If the money wage rate rises by the same percentage as the price level is expected to rise, the short-run aggregate supply curve for next year is SAS_1.

If aggregate demand turns out to be the same as expected, the aggregate demand curve is AD_1. The short-run aggregate supply curve, SAS_1, and AD_1 determine the actual price level at 121. Between last year and this year, the price level increased from 110 to 121 and the economy experienced an inflation rate equal to that expected. If this inflation is ongoing, aggregate demand increases (as expected) in the following year and the aggregate demand curve shifts to AD_2. The money wage rate rises to reflect the expected inflation, and the short-run aggregate sup-

FIGURE 12.5 Expected Inflation

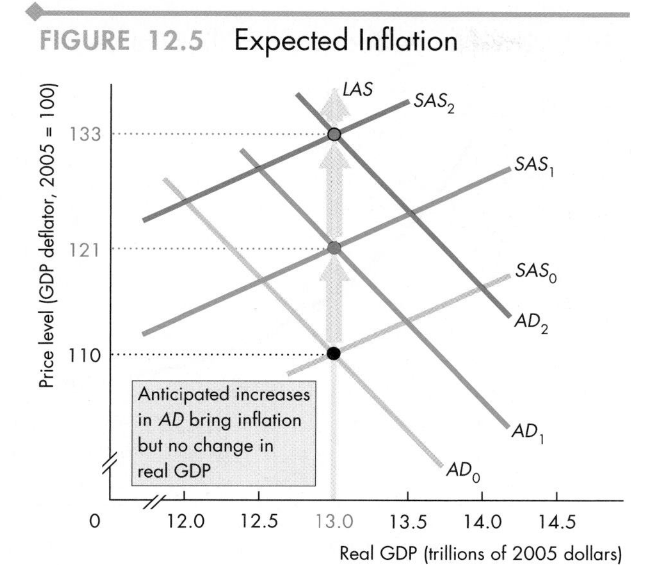

Potential real GDP is $13 trillion. Last year, aggregate demand was AD_0 and the short-run aggregate supply curve was SAS_0. The actual price level was the same as the expected price level: 110. This year, aggregate demand is expected to increase to AD_1 and the price level is expected to rise from 110 to 121. As a result, the money wage rate rises and the short-run aggregate supply curve shifts to SAS_1. If aggregate demand actually increases as expected, the actual aggregate demand curve AD_1 is the same as the expected aggregate demand curve. Real GDP is $13 trillion, and the actual price level rises to 121. The inflation is expected. Next year, the process continues with aggregate demand increasing as expected to AD_2 and the money wage rate rising to shift the short-run aggregate supply curve to SAS_2. Again, real GDP remains at $13 trillion, and the price level rises, as expected, to 133.

myeconlab animation

ply curve shifts to SAS_2. The price level rises, as expected, to 133.

What caused this inflation? The immediate answer is that because people expected inflation, the money wage rate increased and the price level increased. But the expectation was correct. Aggregate demand was expected to increase, and it did increase. It is the actual and expected increase in aggregate demand that caused the inflation.

An expected inflation at full employment is exactly the process that the quantity theory of money predicts. To review the quantity theory of money, see Chapter 8, pp. 200–201.

This broader account of the inflation process and its short-run effects show why the quantity theory of money doesn't explain the *fluctuations* in inflation. The economy follows the course described in Fig. 12.5, but as predicted by the quantity theory, only if aggregate demand growth is forecasted correctly.

Forecasting Inflation

To anticipate inflation, people must forecast it. Some economists who work for macroeconomic forecasting agencies, banks, insurance companies, labor unions, and large corporations specialize in inflation forecasting. The best forecast available is one that is based on all the relevant information and is called a **rational expectation**. A rational expectation is not necessarily a correct forecast. It is simply the best forecast with the information available. It will often turn out to be wrong, but no other forecast that could have been made with the information available could do better.

Inflation and the Business Cycle

When the inflation forecast is correct, the economy operates at full employment. If aggregate demand grows faster than expected, real GDP rises above potential GDP, the inflation rate exceeds its expected rate, and the economy behaves like it does in a demand-pull inflation. If aggregate demand grows more slowly than expected, real GDP falls below potential GDP and the inflation rate slows.

REVIEW QUIZ

1. How does demand-pull inflation begin?
2. What must happen to create a demand-pull inflation spiral?
3. How does cost-push inflation begin?
4. What must happen to create a cost-push inflation spiral?
5. What is stagflation and why does cost-push inflation cause stagflation?
6. How does expected inflation occur?
7. How do real GDP and the price level change if the forecast of inflation is incorrect?

You can work these questions in Study Plan 12.1 and get instant feedback.

Inflation and Unemployment: The Phillips Curve

Another way of studying inflation cycles focuses on the relationship and the short-run tradeoff between inflation and unemployment, a relationship called the **Phillips curve**—so named because it was first suggested by New Zealand economist A.W. Phillips.

Why do we need another way of studying inflation? What is wrong with the *AS-AD* explanation of the fluctuations in inflation and real GDP? The first answer to both questions is that we often want to study changes in both the expected and actual inflation rates and for this purpose, the Phillips curve provides a simpler tool and clearer insights than the *AS-AD* model provides. The second answer to both questions is that we often want to study changes in the short-run tradeoff between inflation and real economic activity (real GDP and unemployment) and again, the Phillips curve serves this purpose well.

To begin our explanation of the Phillips curve, we distinguish between two time frames (similar to the two aggregate supply time frames). We study

- The short-run Phillips curve
- The long-run Phillips curve

The Short-Run Phillips Curve

The **short-run Phillips curve** shows the relationship between inflation and unemployment, holding constant:

1. The expected inflation rate
2. The natural unemployment rate

You've just seen what determines the expected inflation rate. The natural unemployment rate and the factors that influence it are explained in Chapter 5, pp. 113–114.

Figure 12.6 shows a short-run Phillips curve, *SRPC*. Suppose that the expected inflation rate is 10 percent a year and the natural unemployment rate is 6 percent, point *A* in the figure. A short-run Phillips curve passes through this point. If inflation rises above its expected rate, unemployment falls below its natural rate. This joint movement in the inflation rate and the unemployment rate is illustrated as a movement up along the short-run Phillips curve from point *A* to point *B*. Similarly, if inflation falls below its expected rate, unemployment rises above its natural rate. In this case, there is movement down along the short-run Phillips curve from point *A* to point *C*.

FIGURE 12.6 A Short-Run Phillips Curve

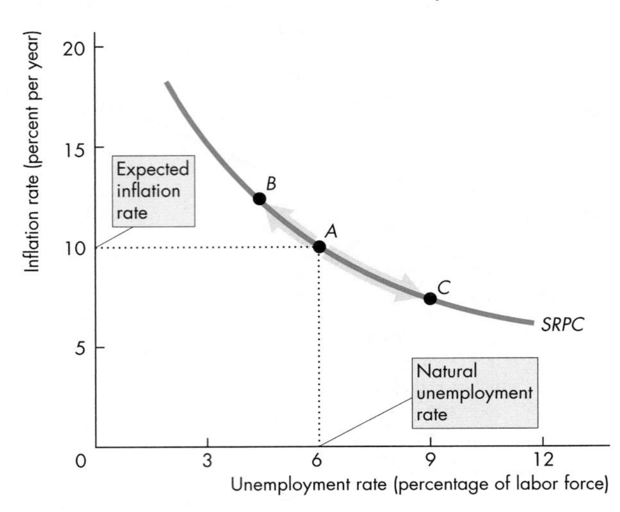

The short-run Phillips curve (*SRPC*) shows the relationship between inflation and unemployment at a given expected inflation rate and a given natural unemployment rate. With an expected inflation rate of 10 percent a year and a natural unemployment rate of 6 percent, the short-run Phillips curve passes through point *A*.

An unexpected increase in aggregate demand lowers unemployment and increases the inflation rate—a movement up along the short-run Phillips curve to point *B*. An unexpected decrease in aggregate demand increases unemployment and lowers the inflation rate—a movement down along the short-run Phillips curve to point *C*.

The short-run Phillips curve is like the short-run aggregate supply curve. A movement along the *SAS* curve that brings a higher price level and an increase in real GDP is equivalent to a movement along the short-run Phillips curve from *A* to *B* that brings an increase in the inflation rate and a decrease in the unemployment rate.

Similarly, a movement along the *SAS* curve that brings a lower price level and a decrease in real GDP is equivalent to a movement along the short-run Phillips curve from *A* to *C* that brings a decrease in the inflation rate and an increase in the unemployment rate.

The Long-Run Phillips Curve

The **long-run Phillips curve** shows the relationship between inflation and unemployment when the actual inflation rate equals the expected inflation rate. The long-run Phillips curve is vertical at the natural unemployment rate. In Fig. 12.7, it is the vertical line *LRPC*.

The long-run Phillips curve tells us that any expected inflation rate is possible at the natural unemployment rate. This proposition is consistent with the *AS-AD* model, which predicts (and which Fig. 12.5 illustrates) that when inflation is expected, real GDP equals potential GDP and unemployment is at its natural rate.

The short-run Phillips curve intersects the long-run Phillips curve at the expected inflation rate. A change in the expected inflation rate shifts the short-run Phillips curve but it does not shift the long-run Phillips curve.

In Fig. 12.7, if the expected inflation rate is 10 percent a year, the short-run Phillips curve is $SRPC_0$. If the expected inflation rate falls to 6 percent a year, the short-run Phillips curve shifts downward to $SRPC_1$. The vertical distance by which the short-run Phillips curve shifts from point *A* to point *D* is equal to the change in the expected inflation rate. If the actual inflation rate also falls from 10 percent to 6 percent, there is a movement down the long-run Phillips curve from *A* to *D*. An increase in the expected inflation rate has the opposite effect to that shown in Fig. 12.7.

The other source of a shift in the Phillips curve is a change in the natural unemployment rate.

Changes in the Natural Unemployment Rate

The natural unemployment rate changes for many reasons (see Chapter 5, pp. 113–114). A change in the natural unemployment rate shifts both the short-run and long-run Phillips curves. Figure 12.8 illustrates such shifts.

FIGURE 12.7 Short-Run and Long-Run Phillips Curves

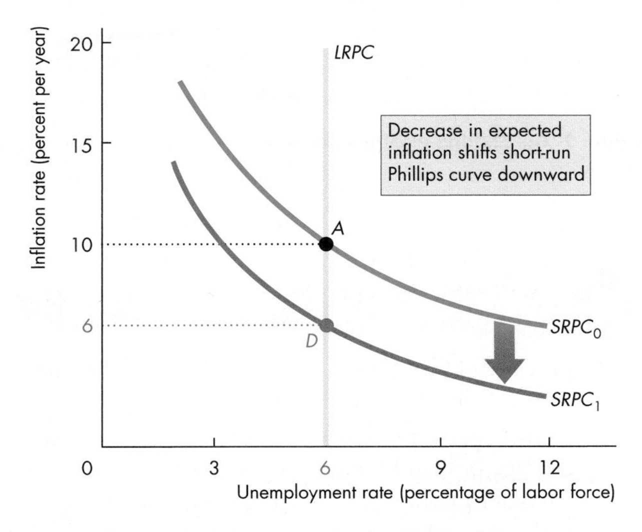

The long-run Phillips curve is *LRPC*. A fall in expected inflation from 10 percent a year to 6 percent a year shifts the short-run Phillips curve downward from $SRPC_0$ to $SRPC_1$. The long-run Phillips curve does not shift. The new short-run Phillips curve intersects the long-run Phillips curve at the new expected inflation rate—point *D*.

myeconlab animation

FIGURE 12.8 A Change in the Natural Unemployment Rate

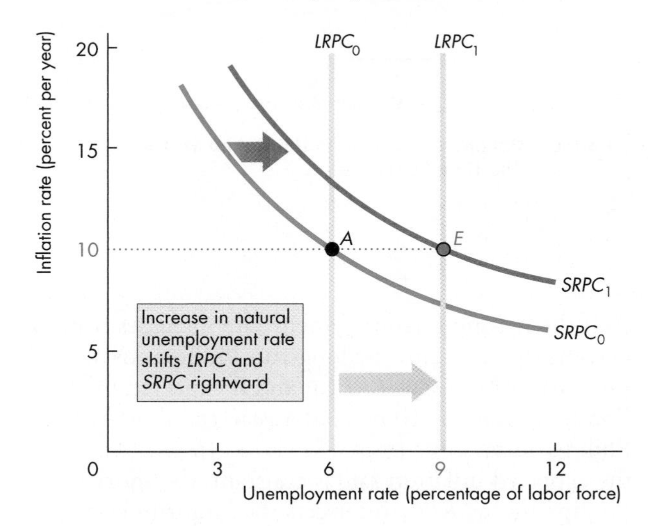

A change in the natural unemployment rate shifts both the short-run and long-run Phillips curves. An increase in the natural unemployment rate from 6 percent to 9 percent shifts the Phillips curves rightward to $SRPC_1$ and $LRPC_1$. The new long-run Phillips curve intersects the new short-run Phillips curve at the expected inflation rate—point *E*.

myeconlab animation

Economics in Action

The Shifting Short-Run Tradeoff

Figure 1 is a scatter diagram of the U.S. inflation rate (measured by the GDP deflator) and the unemployment rate since 1961. We can interpret the data in terms of the shifting short-run Phillips curve in Fig. 2.

During the 1960s, the short-run Phillips curve was $SRPC_0$, with a natural unemployment rate of 4.5 percent and an expected inflation rate of 2 percent a year (point *A*).

During the early 1970s, the short-run Phillips curve was $SRPC_1$, with a natural unemployment rate of 5 percent and an expected inflation rate of 6 percent a year (point *B*).

During the late 1970s, the natural unemployment rate increased to 8 percent (point *C*) and the short-run Phillips curve shifted to $SRPC_2$. Briefly in 1975 and again in 1981, the expected inflation rate surged to 9 percent a year (point *D*) and the short-run Phillips curve shifted to $SRPC_3$.

During the 1980s and 1990s, the expected inflation rate and the natural unemployment rate decreased and the short-run Phillips curve shifted leftward back to $SRPC_1$ and, by the mid-1990s, back to $SRPC_0$, where it remained into the 2000s.

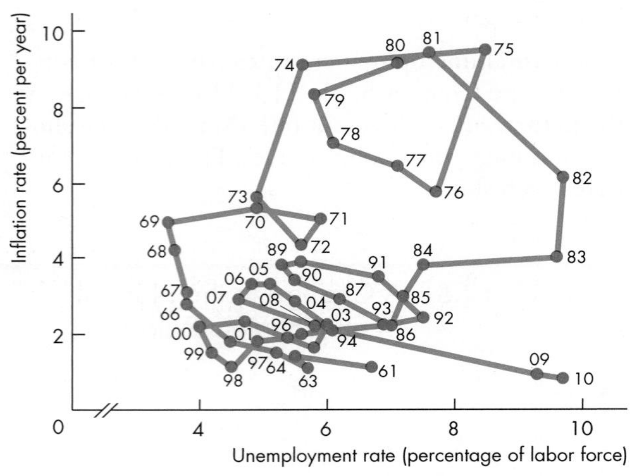

Figure 1 Phillips Curve Data in the United States: The Time Sequence

Source of data: Bureau of Labor Statistics.

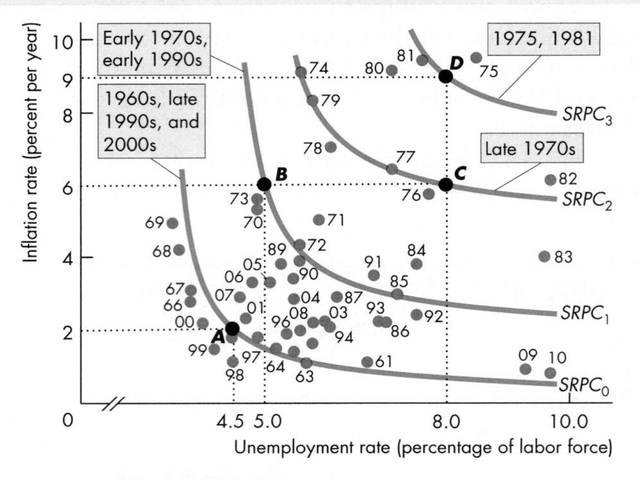

Figure 2 The Shifting Phillips Curves

If the natural unemployment rate increases from 6 percent to 9 percent, the long-run Phillips curve shifts from $LRPC_0$ to $LRPC_1$, and if expected inflation is constant at 10 percent a year, the short-run Phillips curve shifts from $SRPC_0$ to $SRPC_1$. Because the expected inflation rate is constant, the short-run Phillips curve $SRPC_1$ intersects the long-run curve $LRPC_1$ (point *E*) at the same inflation rate at which the short-run Phillips curve $SRPC_0$ intersects the long-run curve $LRPC_0$ (point *A*).

Changes in both the expected inflation rate and the natural unemployment rate have shifted the U.S. Phillips curve but the expected inflation rate has had the greater effect.

REVIEW QUIZ

1. How would you use the Phillips curve to illustrate an unexpected change in inflation?
2. If the expected inflation rate increases by 10 percentage points, how do the short-run Phillips curve and the long-run Phillips curve change?
3. If the natural unemployment rate increases, what happens to the short-run Phillips curve and the long-run Phillips curve?
4. Does the United States have a stable short-run Phillips curve? Explain why or why not.

You can work these questions in Study Plan 12.2 and get instant feedback.

The Business Cycle

The business cycle is easy to describe but hard to explain and business cycle theory remains unsettled and a source of controversy. We'll look at two approaches to understanding the business cycle:

- Mainstream business cycle theory
- Real business cycle theory

Mainstream Business Cycle Theory

The mainstream business cycle theory is that potential GDP grows at a steady rate while aggregate demand grows at a fluctuating rate. Because the money wage rate is sticky, if aggregate demand grows faster than potential GDP, real GDP moves above potential GDP and an inflationary gap emerges. And if aggregate demand grows slower than potential GDP, real GDP moves below potential GDP and a recessionary gap emerges. If aggregate demand decreases, real GDP also decreases in a recession.

Figure 12.9 illustrates this business cycle theory. Initially, actual and potential GDP are $10 trillion. The long-run aggregate supply curve is LAS_0, the aggregate demand curve is AD_0, and the price level is 100. The economy is at full employment at point *A*.

An expansion occurs when potential GDP increases and the *LAS* curve shifts rightward to LAS_1. During an expansion, aggregate demand also increases, and usually by more than potential GDP, so the price level rises. Assume that in the current expansion, the price level is expected to rise to 110 and the money wage rate has been set based on that expectation. The short-run aggregate supply curve is SAS_1.

If aggregate demand increases to AD_1, real GDP increases to $13 trillion, the new level of potential GDP, and the price level rises, as expected, to 110. The economy remains at full employment but now at point *B*.

If aggregate demand increases more slowly to AD_2, real GDP grows by less than potential GDP and the economy moves to point *C*, with real GDP at $12.5 trillion and the price level at 107. Real GDP growth is slower and inflation is lower than expected.

If aggregate demand increases more quickly to AD_3, real GDP grows by more than potential GDP and the economy moves to point *D*, with real GDP at $13.5 trillion and the price level at 113. Real GDP growth is faster and inflation is higher than expected.

Growth, inflation, and the business cycle arise from the relentless increases in potential GDP, faster (on average) increases in aggregate demand, and fluctuations in the pace of aggregate demand growth.

FIGURE 12.9 The Mainstream Business Cycle Theory

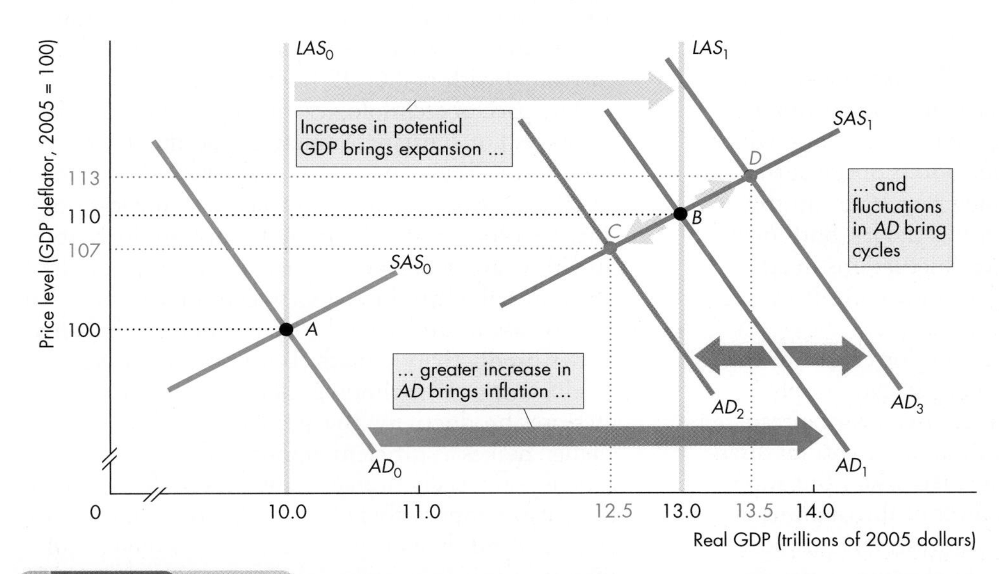

In a business cycle expansion, potential GDP increases and the *LAS* curve shifts rightward from LAS_0 to LAS_1. A greater than expected increase in aggregate demand brings inflation.

If the aggregate demand curve shifts to AD_1, the economy remains at full employment. If the aggregate demand curve shifts to AD_2, a recessionary gap arises. If the aggregate demand curve shifts to AD_3, an inflationary gap arises.

myeconlab animation

This mainstream theory comes in a number of special forms that differ regarding the source of fluctuations in aggregate demand growth and the source of money wage stickiness.

Keynesian Cycle Theory In **Keynesian cycle theory**, fluctuations in investment driven by fluctuations in business confidence—summarized by the phrase "animal spirits"—are the main source of fluctuations in aggregate demand.

Monetarist Cycle Theory In **monetarist cycle theory**, fluctuations in both investment and consumption expenditure, driven by fluctuations in the growth rate of the quantity of money, are the main source of fluctuations in aggregate demand.

Both the Keynesian and monetarist cycle theories simply assume that the money wage rate is rigid and don't explain that rigidity.

Two newer theories seek to explain money wage rate rigidity and to be more careful about working out its consequences.

New Classical Cycle Theory In **new classical cycle theory**, the rational expectation of the price level, which is determined by potential GDP and *expected* aggregate demand, determines the money wage rate and the position of the *SAS* curve. In this theory, only *unexpected* fluctuations in aggregate demand bring fluctuations in real GDP around potential GDP.

New Keynesian Cycle Theory The **new Keynesian cycle theory** emphasizes the fact that today's money wage rates were negotiated at many past dates, which means that *past* rational expectations of the current price level influence the money wage rate and the position of the *SAS* curve. In this theory, both unexpected and currently expected fluctuations in aggregate demand bring fluctuations in real GDP around potential GDP.

The mainstream cycle theories don't rule out the possibility that occasionally an aggregate supply shock might occur. An oil price rise, a widespread drought, a major hurricane, or another natural disaster, could, for example, bring a recession. But supply shocks are not the normal source of fluctuations in the mainstream theories. In contrast, real business cycle theory puts supply shocks at center stage.

Real Business Cycle Theory

The newest theory of the business cycle, known as **real business cycle theory** (or RBC theory), regards random fluctuations in productivity as the main source of economic fluctuations. These productivity fluctuations are assumed to result mainly from fluctuations in the pace of technological change, but they might also have other sources, such as international disturbances, climate fluctuations, or natural disasters. The origins of RBC theory can be traced to the rational expectations revolution set off by Robert E. Lucas, Jr., but the first demonstrations of the power of this theory were given by Edward Prescott and Finn Kydland and by John Long and Charles Plosser. Today, RBC theory is part of a broad research agenda called dynamic general equilibrium analysis, and hundreds of young macroeconomists do research on this topic.

We'll explore RBC theory by looking first at its impulse and then at the mechanism that converts that impulse into a cycle in real GDP.

The RBC Impulse The impulse in RBC theory is the growth rate of productivity that results from technological change. RBC theorists believe this impulse to be generated mainly by the process of research and development that leads to the creation and use of new technologies.

To isolate the RBC theory impulse, economists measure the change in the combined productivity of capital and labor. Figure 12.10 shows the RBC impulse for the United States from 1964 through 2009. You can see that fluctuations in productivity growth are correlated with real GDP fluctuations.

The pace of technological change and productivity growth is not constant. Sometimes productivity growth speeds up, sometimes it slows, and occasionally it even *falls*—labor and capital become less productive, on average. A period of rapid productivity growth brings a business cycle expansion, and a slowdown or fall in productivity triggers a recession.

It is easy to understand why technological change brings productivity growth. But how does it *decrease* productivity? All technological change eventually increases productivity. But if initially, technological change makes a sufficient amount of existing capital—especially human capital—obsolete, productivity can temporarily fall. At such a time, more jobs are destroyed than created and more businesses fail than start up.

FIGURE 12.10 The Real Business Cycle Impulse

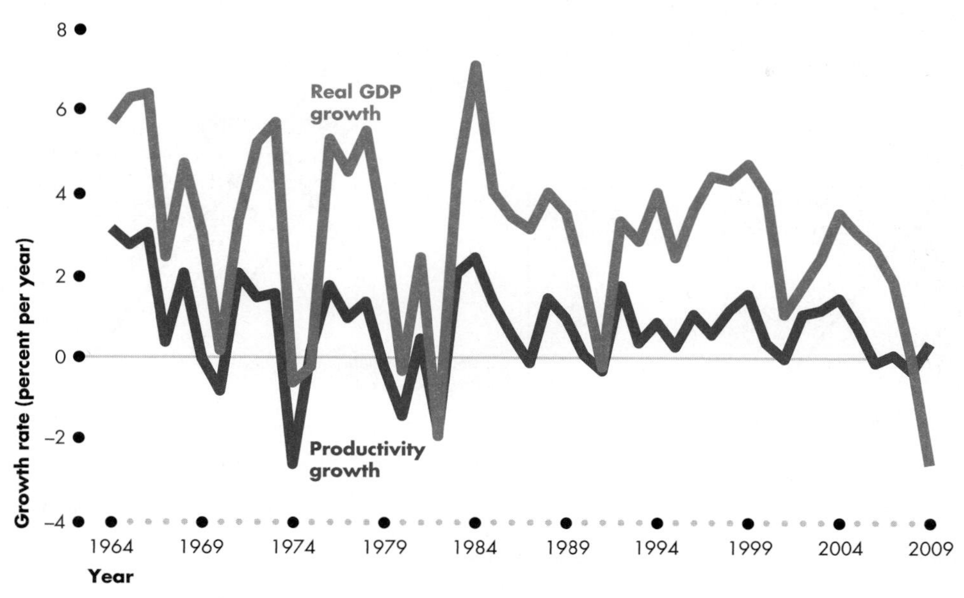

Source of data: Bureau of Economic Analysis.

The real business cycle is caused by changes in technology that bring fluctuations in the growth rate of productivity*. Productivity fluctuations are correlated with real GDP fluctuations and most recessions are associated with a slowdown in productivity growth. The 2008-2009 recession is an exception and occurred at a time when productivity growth increased.

*Productivity growth calculations are based on assumptions about the aggregate production function.

myeconlab animation

The RBC Mechanism Two effects follow from a change in productivity that sparks an expansion or a contraction:

1. Investment demand changes.
2. The demand for labor changes.

We'll study these effects and their consequences during a recession. In an expansion, they work in the direction opposite to what is described here.

Technological change makes some existing capital obsolete and temporarily decreases productivity. Firms expect the future profits to fall and see their labor productivity falling. With lower profit expectations, they cut back their purchases of new capital, and with lower labor productivity, they plan to lay off some workers. So the initial effect of a temporary fall in productivity is a decrease in investment demand and a decrease in the demand for labor.

Figure 12.11 illustrates these two initial effects of a decrease in productivity. Part (a) shows the effects of a decrease in investment demand in the loanable funds market. The demand for loanable funds curve is *DLF* and the supply of loanable funds curve is *SLF* (both of which are explained in Chapter 7, pp. 166–168). Initially, the demand for loanable funds curve is DLF_0 and the equilibrium quantity of funds is $2 trillion at a real interest rate of 6 percent a year. A decrease in productivity decreases investment demand, and the demand for loanable funds curve shifts leftward from *DLF* to DLF_1. The real interest rate falls to 4 percent a year, and the equilibrium quantity of loanable funds decreases to $1.7 trillion.

Figure 12.11(b) shows the demand for labor and supply of labor (which are explained in Chapter 6, pp. 139–140). Initially, the demand for labor curve is LD_0, the supply of labor curve LS_0, and equilibrium employment is 200 billion hours a year at a real wage rate of $35 an hour. The decrease in productivity decreases the demand for labor, and the demand for labor curve shifts leftward from LD_0 to LD_1.

Before we can determine the new level of employment and real wage rate, we need to take a ripple effect into account—the key effect in RBC theory.

The Key Decision: When to Work? According to RBC theory, people decide *when* to work by doing a cost-benefit calculation. They compare the return

FIGURE 12.11 Loanable Funds and Labor Markets in a Real Business Cycle

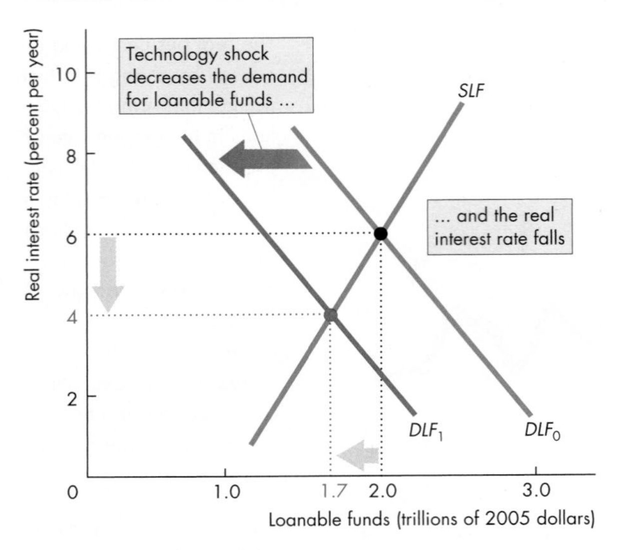

(a) Loanable funds and interest rate

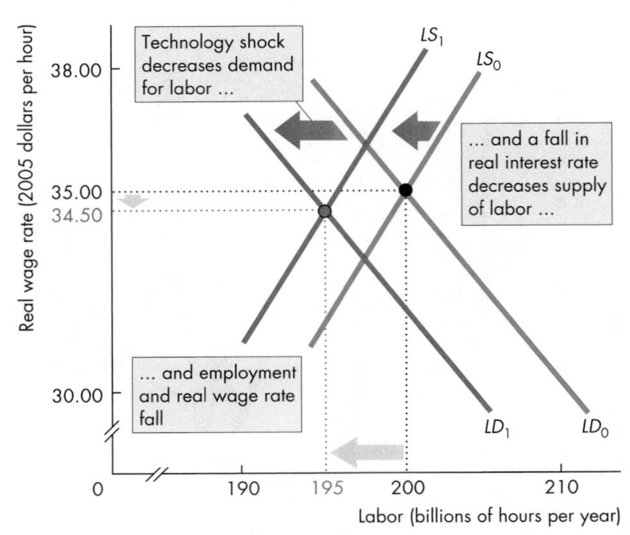

(b) Labor and wage rate

In part (a), the supply of loanable funds *SLF* and initial demand for loanable funds DLF_0 determine the real interest rate at 6 percent a year. In part (b), the initial demand for labor LD_0 and supply of labor, LS_0, determine the real wage rate at $35 an hour and employment at 200 billion hours. A technological change temporarily decreases productivity, and both the demand for loanable funds and the demand for labor decrease. The two demand curves shift leftward to DLF_1 and LD_1. In part (a), the real interest rate falls to 4 percent a year. In part (b), the fall in the real interest rate decreases the supply of labor (the when-to-work decision) and the supply of labor curve shifts leftward to LS_1. Employment decreases to 195 billion hours, and the real wage rate falls to $34.50 an hour. A recession is under way.

from working in the current period with the *expected* return from working in a later period. You make such a comparison every day in school. Suppose your goal in this course is to get an A. To achieve this goal, you work hard most of the time. But during the few days before the midterm and final exams, you work especially hard. Why? Because you believe that the return from studying close to the exam is greater than the return from studying when the exam is a long time away. So during the term, you take time off for the movies and other leisure pursuits, but at exam time, you study every evening and weekend.

RBC theory says that workers behave like you. They work fewer hours, sometimes zero hours, when the real wage rate is temporarily low, and they work more hours when the real wage rate is temporarily high. But to properly compare the current wage rate with the expected future wage rate, workers must use the real interest rate. If the real interest rate is 6 percent a year, a real wage of $1 an hour earned this week will become $1.06 a year from now. If the real wage rate is expected to be $1.05 an hour next year, today's real wage of $1 looks good. By working longer hours now and shorter hours a year from now, a person can get a 1 percent higher real wage. But suppose the real interest rate is 4 percent a year. In this case, $1 earned now is worth $1.04 next year. Working fewer hours now and more next year is the way to get a 1 percent higher real wage.

So the when-to-work decision depends on the real interest rate. The lower the real interest rate, other things remaining the same, the smaller is the supply of labor today. Many economists believe this *intertemporal substitution* effect to be of negligible size. RBC theorists believe that the effect is large, and it is the key feature of the RBC mechanism.

You saw in Fig. 12.11(a) that the decrease in the demand for loanable funds lowers the real interest rate. This fall in the real interest rate lowers the return to current work and decreases the supply of labor.

In Fig. 12.11(b), the labor supply curve shifts leftward to LS_1. The effect of the decrease in productivity on the demand for labor is larger than the effect of the fall in the real interest rate on the supply of labor. That is, the demand curve shifts farther leftward than does the supply curve. As a result, the real wage rate falls to $34.50 an hour and employment decreases to 195 billion hours. A recession has begun and is intensifying.

What Happened to Money? The name *real* business cycle theory is no accident. It reflects the central prediction of the theory. Real things, not nominal or monetary things, cause the business cycle. If the quantity of money changes, aggregate demand changes. But if there is no real change—with no change in the use of resources and no change in potential GDP—the change in the quantity of money changes only the price level. In RBC theory, this outcome occurs because the aggregate supply curve is the *LAS* curve, which pins real GDP down at potential GDP, so when aggregate demand changes, only the price level changes.

Cycles and Growth The shock that drives the business cycle of RBC theory is the same as the force that generates economic growth: technological change. On average, as technology advances, productivity grows; but as you saw in Fig. 12.10, it grows at an uneven pace. Economic growth arises from the upward trend in productivity growth and, according to RBC theory, the mostly positive but occasionally negative higher frequency shocks to productivity bring the business cycle.

Criticisms and Defenses of RBC Theory The three main criticisms of RBC theory are that (1) the money wage rate *is* sticky, and to assume otherwise is at odds with a clear fact; (2) intertemporal substitution is too weak a force to account for large fluctuations in labor supply and employment with small real wage rate changes; and (3) productivity shocks are as likely to be caused by *changes in aggregate demand* as by technological change.

If aggregate demand fluctuations cause the fluctuations in productivity, then the traditional aggregate demand theories are needed to explain them. Fluctuations in productivity do not cause the business cycle but are caused by it!

Building on this theme, the critics point out that the so-called productivity fluctuations that growth accounting measures are correlated with changes in the growth rate of money and other indicators of changes in aggregate demand.

The defenders of RBC theory claim that the theory explains the macroeconomic facts about the business cycle and is consistent with the facts about economic growth. In effect, a single theory explains *both growth and the business cycle.* The growth accounting exercise that explains slowly changing trends also explains the more frequent business cycle swings. Its defenders also claim that RBC theory is consistent with a wide range of *micro*economic evidence about labor supply decisions, labor demand and investment demand decisions, and information on the distribution of income between labor and capital.

REVIEW QUIZ

1. Explain the mainstream theory of the business cycle.
2. What are the four special forms of the mainstream theory of the business cycle and how do they differ?
3. According to RBC theory, what is the source of the business cycle? What is the role of fluctuations in the rate of technological change?
4. According to RBC theory, how does a fall in productivity growth influence investment demand, the market for loanable funds, the real interest rate, the demand for labor, the supply of labor, employment, and the real wage rate?
5. What are the main criticisms of RBC theory and how do its supporters defend it?

You can work these questions in Study Plan 12.3 and get instant feedback.

You can complete your study of economic fluctuations in *Reading Between the Lines* on pp. 310–311, which looks at the shifting inflation–unemployment tradeoff and misery index in the United States.

The Shifting Inflation–Unemployment Tradeoff

Evidence and Denial; Obama Advisers Refuse to Believe They're Failing

The Washington Times
August 4, 2010

... President Obama likes to say that he inherited the "worst" economy since the Great Depression, but the fact is that the economic "Misery Index" (inflation plus unemployment) ... was twice as high when President Reagan took office [in 1981]. (By the time President Reagan left the presidency, the Misery Index had dropped to less than half of what it had been when he assumed office.) ...

Reagan's policy was to sharply cut individual and corporate tax rates, and to restrain the growth in government spending and regulation. The Democrats, who were in control of the House of Representatives, resisted and delayed the Reagan tax cuts, so they were not fully implemented until 1983. Mr. Obama had the luxury of having his party in control of both houses of Congress, so he was able to get his proposed, massive government spending increases enacted almost immediately. ...

Keynesian economics, practiced during the late 1960s and 1970s, became thoroughly discredited with the stagflation of the 1970s ... and the subsequent Reagan supply-side boom. The Clinton administration ... partially reverted to Reaganomics in its second term; with a capital-gains rate cut and reductions in spending as a percentage of GDP. The result was very strong economic growth and budget surpluses.

Given the above facts ... would you follow the Reagan/Clinton II economic policies or the Obama ones? Where is the evidence ... that Obamanomics will work, particularly since it is not now working as advertised? Will the Misery Index be cut by more than half during the Obama administration, as it was during Reagan's terms, or will it rise?...

ESSENCE OF THE STORY

- The misery index, which is the inflation rate plus the unemployment rate, was twice as high in 1981 when President Reagan took office as it was in 2009 when President Obama's term began.
- President Reagan lowered the misery index to less than half its 1981 level by cutting taxes and restraining the growth in government spending and regulation.
- President Obama is trying to lower the misery index by increasing government spending.
- This approach is the Keynesian policy of the late 1960s and 1970s that brought stagflation and a rising misery index.

ECONOMIC ANALYSIS

- When President Obama assumed office in January 2009, the CPI inflation rate was zero and the unemployment rate was 7.7 percent, so the misery index was 7.7.
- When President Reagan assumed office in January 1981, the CPI inflation rate was 11.8 percent and the unemployment rate was 7.5 percent, so the misery index was 19.3.
- When President Reagan left office in January 1989, the CPI inflation rate was 4.7 percent and the unemployment rate was 5.4 percent, so the misery index was 10.1 (approximately half its 1981 level, as stated in the news article).
- In the year to August 2010, the CPI inflation rate was 1.1 percent and the unemployment rate was 9.6 percent. Combining these numbers generates a misery index of 10.7.
- Figure 1 puts these snapshots of the misery index in a longer perspective.
- The index was trending upward before 1980 and downward after its peak in June1980 when it reached 22 (the sum of an unemployment rate of 7.6 percent and an inflation rate of 14.4 percent a year).
- The misery index increases when the expected inflation rate rises, which shifts the short-run Phillips curve upward, and the natural unemployment rate rises, which shifts the short-run Phillips curve rightward.
- Figure 2 shows the paths followed by inflation and unemployment.
- In 1976, on the eve of Jimmy Carter's term as president, the economy was at point *A*. The unemployment rate was 7.5 percent and the inflation rate was 5.2 percent a year.
- By 1980, when Jimmy Carter left office and Ronald Reagan came into office, the economy was at point *B*.
- When Ronald Reagan left office, the economy had moved to point *C*.
- In January 2009, when President Obama entered office, the economy was at point *D* and by August 2010, the economy had moved to point *E*.
- Figure 2 contrasts the current and previous rises in the misery index. The rise of the index during the 1970s was the result of rising inflation and the rise of the index during 2009 and 2010 was the result of rising unemployment.

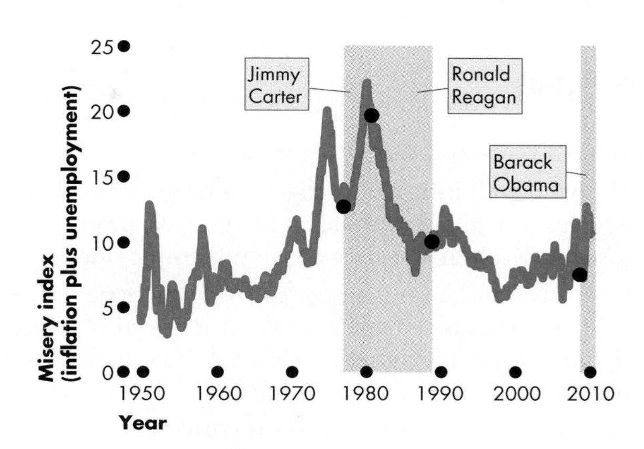

Figure 1 The U.S. misery index

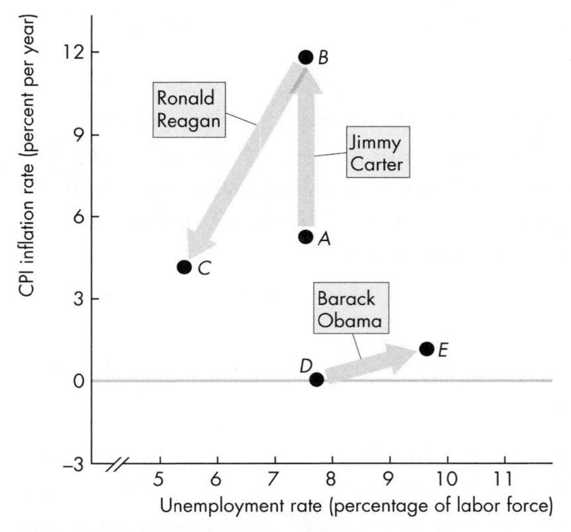

Figure 2 The inflation–unemployment paths

- Ronald Reagan's term in office saw a lower unemployment rate *and* a lower inflation rate.
- To lower the 2010 misery index, the Obama Administration must lower the unemployment rate while avoiding inflation.
- Economists were divided on the policies most likely to succeed. The author of the article (Richard W. Rahn) says that Reagan "supply-side" policies are needed. The Administration economists say more fiscal and monetary stimulus is needed.
- You can enter this debate in Chapters 13 and 14.

SUMMARY

Key Points

Inflation Cycles (pp. 296–301)

- Demand-pull inflation is triggered by an increase in aggregate demand and fueled by ongoing money growth. Real GDP cycles above full employment.
- Cost-push inflation is triggered by an increase in the money wage rate or raw material prices and is fueled by ongoing money growth. Real GDP cycles below full employment in a stagflation.
- When the forecast of inflation is correct, real GDP remains at potential GDP.

Working Problems 1 to 11 will give you a better understanding of inflation cycles.

Inflation and Unemployment: The Phillips Curve (pp. 302–304)

- The short-run Phillips curve shows the tradeoff between inflation and unemployment when the expected inflation rate and the natural unemployment rate are constant.
- The long-run Phillips curve, which is vertical, shows that when the actual inflation rate equals the expected inflation rate, the unemployment rate equals the natural unemployment rate.

Working Problems 12 to 14 will give you a better understanding of inflation and unemployment: the Phillips curve.

The Business Cycle (pp. 305–309)

- The mainstream business cycle theory explains the business cycle as fluctuations of real GDP around potential GDP and as arising from a steady expansion of potential GDP combined with an expansion of aggregate demand at a fluctuating rate.
- Real business cycle theory explains the business cycle as fluctuations of potential GDP, which arise from fluctuations in the influence of technological change on productivity growth.

Working Problem 15 will give you a better understanding of the business cycle.

Key Terms

Cost-push inflation, 298
Demand-pull inflation, 296
Keynesian cycle theory, 306
Long-run Phillips curve, 303
Monetarist cycle theory, 306
New classical cycle theory, 306
New Keynesian cycle theory, 306
Phillips curve, 302
Rational expectation, 301
Real business cycle theory, 306
Short-run Phillips curve, 302
Stagflation, 299

STUDY PLAN PROBLEMS AND APPLICATIONS

myeconlab You can work Problems 1 to 15 in MyEconLab Chapter 12 Study Plan and get instant feedback.

Inflation Cycles (Study Plan 12.1)

1. **Pakistan: Is It Cost-Push Inflation?**

   With CPI already spiking 11.8 percent for the first ten months of the fiscal year, the average CPI inflation for the same period last year stood at 22.35 percent. Some economists insist the current bout of inflationary pressures is spawned by increasing prices of fuel, food, raw materials, transportation, construction materials, elimination of energy subsidies, etc. as indicated by the spike in the wholesale price index (WPI), which rose 21.99 percent in April from a year earlier.

   Source: *Daily the Pak Banker,* May 22, 2010

   Explain what type of inflation Pakistan is experiencing.

Use the following figure to answer Problems 2, 3, 4, and 5. In each question, the economy starts out on the curves labeled AD_0 and SAS_0.

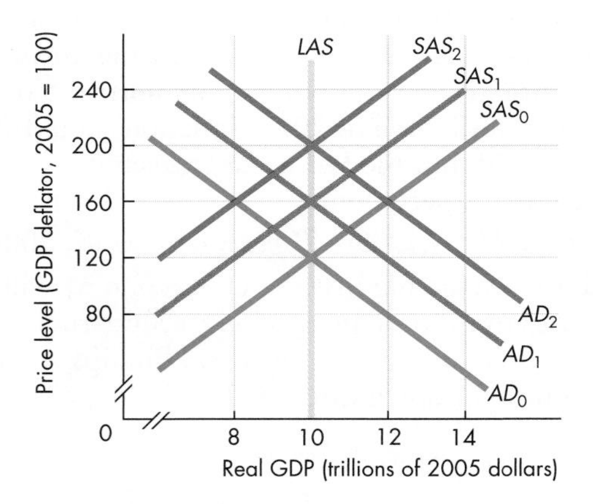

2. Some events occur and the economy experiences a demand-pull inflation.
   a. List the events that might cause a demand-pull inflation.
   b. Describe the initial effects of a demand-pull inflation.
   c. Describe what happens as a demand-pull inflation spiral proceeds.
3. Some events occur and the economy experiences a cost-push inflation.
   a. List the events that might cause a cost-push inflation.
   b. Describe the initial effects of a cost-push inflation.
   c. Describe what happens as a cost-push inflation spiral proceeds.
4. Some events occur and the economy is expected to experience inflation.
   a. List the events that might cause an expected inflation.
   b. Describe the initial effects of an expected inflation.
   c. Describe what happens as an expected inflation proceeds.
5. Suppose that people expect deflation (a falling price level), but aggregate demand remains at AD_0.
   a. What happens to the short-run and long-run aggregate supply curves? (Draw some new curves if you need to.)
   b. Describe the initial effects of an expected deflation.
   c. Describe what happens as it becomes obvious to everyone that the expected deflation is not going to occur.

Use the following news clip to work Problems 6 to 8.

The Right Way to Beat Chinese Inflation

High inflation is threatening social stability in China, soaring from 3.3 percent in March 2007 to 8.3 percent in March 2008. China's accelerating inflation reflects a similar climb in its GDP growth rate, from 11 percent in 2006 to 11.5 percent in 2007. The proximate cause of price growth since mid-2007 is the appearance of production bottlenecks as domestic demand exceeds supply in an increasing number of sectors, such as power generation, transportation, and intermediate-goods industries. The prolonged rapid increase in Chinese aggregate demand has been fueled by an investment boom, as well as a growing trade surplus.

Source: Brookings Institution, July 2, 2008

6. Is China experiencing demand-pull or cost-push inflation? Explain.
7. Draw a graph to illustrate the initial rise in the price level and the money wage rate response to a one-time rise in the price level.
8. Draw a graph to illustrate and explain how China might experience an inflation spiral.

Use the following news clip to work Problems 9 to 11.

Tight Money Won't Slay Food, Energy Inflation

It's important to differentiate between a general increase in prices—a situation in which aggregate demand exceeds their aggregate supply—and a relative price shock. For example, a specific shock to energy prices can become generalized if producers are able to pass on the higher costs. So far, global competition has made that difficult for companies, while higher input costs have largely been neutralized by rising labor productivity. Since 2003, core inflation has averaged less than 2 percent a year in the 30 major economies. History also suggests the Fed's gamble that slowing growth will shackle core inflation is a winning wager. The risk is that if U.S. consumers don't believe price increases will slow, growing inflation expectations may become self-fulfilling.

Source: *Bloomberg*, May 9, 2008

9. a. Explain the two types of inflation described in this news clip.
   b. Explain why "rising labor productivity" can neutralize the effect on inflation of "higher input costs."
10. Explain how "slowing growth" can reduce inflationary pressure.
11. Draw a graph to illustrate and explain how "growing inflation expectations may become self-fulfilling."

Inflation and Unemployment: The Phillips Curve

(Study Plan 12.2)

12. **Iran Postpones Cutting Gasoline Subsidies**

    Inflation is about 10 percent and the unemployment rate is about 14 percent. Earlier this month Iran's main audit body slammed the government's plan to scrap gasoline subsidies, warning that implementing such a reform might result in unrest. The government also intends to scrap subsidies on natural gas, which most Iranians use for cooking and heating, as well as electricity, but the new prices are still not known. However, in recent weeks some households have received electricity bills with nearly sevenfold price increases.

    Source: AFP, September 15, 2010

    a. If Iran removes the subsidies and consumers don't know what the higher prices will be, draw a graph to show the most likely path of inflation and unemployment.
    b. If Iran removes the subsidies and announces the new prices so that consumers know what they are, draw a graph to show the most likely path of inflation and unemployment.

13. **Recession? Maybe. Depression? Get Real.**

    The unemployment rate during the Great Depression peaked at nearly 25 percent in 1933, after an initial spike from 3 percent in 1929 to nearly 8.7 percent in 1930. The unemployment rate is just 5 percent, only up from 4.5 percent a year ago. Also during the Great Depression there was deflation, which is not happening today.

    Source: CNN, May 28, 2008

    a. Can the inflation and unemployment trends during the Great Depression be explained by a movement along a short-run Phillips curve?
    b. Can the inflation and unemployment trends during 2008 be explained by a movement along a short-run Phillips curve?

14. **From the Fed's Minutes**

    The Fed expects the unemployment rate will drop from 9.8 percent today to 9.25 percent by the end of 2010 and to 8 percent by the end of 2011. Private economists predict that the unemployment rate won't drop to a more normal 5 or 6 percent until 2013 or 2014. Inflation should stay subdued, but the Fed needs to keep its eye on inflation expectations.

    Source: *The New York Times*, October 14, 2009

    Is the Fed predicting that the U.S. economy will move rightward or leftward along a short-run Phillips curve or that the short-run Phillips curve will shift up or down through 2011?

The Business Cycle (Study Plan 12.3)

15. **Debate on Causes of Joblessness Grows**

    What is the cause of the high unemployment rate? One side says more government spending can reduce it. The other says its a structural problem—people who can't move to take new jobs because they are tied down to burdensome mortgages or firms that can't find workers with the requisite skills to fill job openings.

    Source: *The Wall Street Journal*, September 4, 2010

    Which business cycle theory would say that the rise in unemployment is cyclical? Which would say it is an increase in the natural rate? Why?

ADDITIONAL PROBLEMS AND APPLICATIONS

myeconlab You can work these problems in MyEconLab if assigned by your instructor.

Inflation Cycles

Use the following news clip to work Problems 16 and 17.

Bernanke Sees No Repeat of '70s-Style Inflation

There is little indication today of the beginnings of a 1970s-style wage-price spiral. Then, as now, a serious oil price shock occurred, but today's economy is more flexible in responding to difficulties and the country is more energy efficient than a generation ago, Bernanke said. Also, today the Fed monitors "inflation expectations." If people believe inflation will keep going up, they will change their behavior in ways that aggravate inflation—thus, a self-fulfilling prophecy. In the 1970s, people were demanding—and getting —higher wages in anticipation of rapidly rising prices; hence, the "wage-price" spiral Bernanke cited. The inflation rate has averaged about 3.5 percent over the past four quarters. That is "significantly higher" than the Fed would like but much less than the double-digit inflation rates of the mid-1970s and 1980, Bernanke said.

Source: *USA Today*, June 4, 2008

16. Draw a graph to illustrate and explain the inflation spiral that the U.S. experienced in the 1970s.
17. a. Explain the role that inflation expectations play in creating a self-fulfilling prophecy.
    b. Explain Bernanke's predictions about the impact of the 2008 oil price shock as compared to the 1970s shock.

Inflation and Unemployment: The Phillips Curve

Use the following information to work Problems 18 and 19.

The Reserve Bank of New Zealand signed an agreement with the New Zealand government in which the Bank agreed to maintain inflation inside a low target range. Failure to achieve the target would result in the governor of the Bank (the equivalent of the chairman of the Fed) losing his job.

18. Explain how this arrangement might have influenced New Zealand's short-run Phillips curve.
19. Explain how this arrangement might have influenced New Zealand's long-run Phillips curve.

Use the following information to work Problems 20 and 21.

An economy has an unemployment rate of 4 percent and an inflation rate of 5 percent a year at point *A* in the figure.

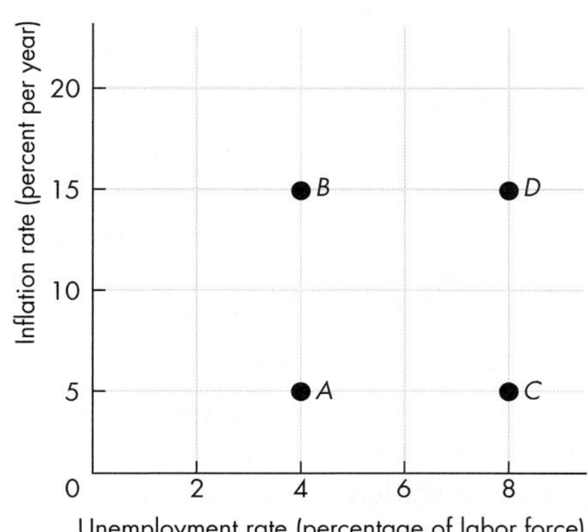

Some events occur that move the economy in a clockwise loop from *A* to *B* to *D* to *C* and back to *A*.

20. Describe the events that could create this sequence. Has the economy experienced demand-pull inflation, cost-push inflation, expected inflation, or none of these?
21. Draw in the figure the sequence of the economy's short-run and long-run Phillips curves.

Use the following news clip to work Problems 22 and 23.

Fed Pause Promises Financial Disaster

The indication is that inflationary expectations have become entrenched and strongly rooted in world markets. As a result, the risk of global stagflation has become significant. A drawn-out inflationary process always precedes stagflation, anathema to the so-called Phillips Curve. Following the attritional effect of inflation, the economy starts to grow below its potential. It experiences a persistent output gap, rising unemployment, and increasingly entrenched inflationary expectations.

Source: *Asia Times Online*, May 20, 2008

22. Evaluate the claim that stagflation is anathema to the Phillips curve.
23. Evaluate the claim made in this article that if "inflationary expectations" become strongly

"entrenched" an economy will experience "a persistent output gap."

Use the following information to work Problems 24 and 25.

Because the Fed doubled the monetary base in 2008 and the government spent billions of dollars bailing out troubled banks, insurance companies, and auto producers, some people are concerned that a serious upturn in the inflation rate will occur, not immediately but in a few years' time. At the same time, massive changes in the global economy might bring the need for structural change in the United States.

24. Explain how the Fed's doubling of the monetary base and government bailouts might influence the short-run and long-run unemployment–inflation tradeoffs. Will the influence come from changes in the expected inflation rate, the natural unemployment rate, or both?
25. Explain how large-scale structural change might influence the short-run and long-run unemployment–inflation tradeoffs. Will the influence come from changes in the expected inflation rate, the natural unemployment rate, or both?

The Business Cycle

Use the following information to work Problems 26 to 28.

Suppose that the business cycle in the United States is best described by RBC theory and that a new technology increases productivity.

26. Draw a graph to show the effect of the new technology in the market for loanable funds.
27. Draw a graph to show the effect of the new technology in the labor market.
28. Explain the when-to-work decision when technology advances.
29. **Real Wages Fail to Match a Rise in Productivity**

    For most of the last century, wages and productivity—the key measure of the economy's efficiency—have risen together, increasing rapidly through the 1950s and '60s and far more slowly in the 1970s and '80s. But in recent years, the productivity gains have continued while the pay increases have not kept up.

    Source: *The New York Times*, August 28, 2006

    Explain the relationship between wages and productivity in this news clip in terms of real business cycle theory.

Economics in the News

30. After you have studied *Reading Between the Lines* on pp. 310–311 answer the following questions.
    a. What are the main features of U.S. inflation and unemployment since 1950 that brought fluctuations in the misery index?
    b. When the misery index was at its peak in 1980, did inflation or unemployment contribute most to the high index?
    c. Do you think the U.S. economy had a recessionary gap or an inflationary gap or no gap in 1980? How might you be able to tell?
    d. Use the *AS-AD* model to show the changes in aggregate demand and aggregate supply that are consistent with the rise of the misery index to its peak in June 1980.
    e. Use the *AS-AD* model to show the changes in aggregate demand and aggregate supply that are consistent with the rise of the misery index since President Obama assumed office.
31. **Germany Leads Slowdown in Eurozone**

    The pace of German economic growth has weakened "markedly," but the reason is the weaker global prospects. Although German policymakers worry about the country's exposure to a fall in demand for its export goods, evidence is growing that the recovery is broadening with real wage rates rising and unemployment falling, which will lead into stronger consumer spending.

    Source: *The Financial Times*, September 23, 2010

    a. How does "exposure to a fall in demand for its export goods" influence Germany's aggregate demand, aggregate supply, unemployment, and inflation?
    b. Use the *AS-AD* model to illustrate your answer to part (a).
    c. Use the Phillips curve model to illustrate your answer to part (a).
    d. What do you think the news clip means by "the recovery is broadening with real wage rates rising and unemployment falling, which will lead into stronger consumer spending"?
    e. Use the *AS-AD* model to illustrate your answer to part (d).
    f. Use the Phillips curve model to illustrate your answer to part (d).

Boom and Bust

PART FOUR

UNDERSTANDING MACROECONOMIC FLUCTUATIONS

To cure a disease, doctors must first understand how the disease responds to different treatments. It helps to understand the mechanisms that operate to cause the disease, but sometimes a workable cure can be found even before the full story of the causes has been told.

Curing economic ills is similar to curing our medical ills. We need to understand how the economy responds to the treatments we might prescribe for it. And sometimes, we want to try a cure even though we don't fully understand the reasons for the problem we're trying to control.

You've seen how the pace of capital accumulation and technological change determine the long-term growth trend. You've learned how fluctuations around the long-term trend can be generated by changes in aggregate demand and aggregate supply. And you've learned about the key sources of fluctuations in aggregate demand and aggregate supply.

The *AS-AD* model explains the forces that determine real GDP and the price level in the short run. The model also enables us to see the big picture or grand vision of the different schools of macroeconomic thought concerning the sources of aggregate fluctuations. The Keynesian aggregate expenditure model provides an account of the factors that determine aggregate demand and make it fluctuate.

An alternative real business cycle theory puts all the emphasis on fluctuations in long-run aggregate supply. According to this theory, money changes aggregate demand and the price level but leaves the real economy untouched. The events of 2008 and 2009 will provide a powerful test of this theory.

John Maynard Keynes, *born in England in 1883, was one of the outstanding minds of the twentieth century. He represented Britain at the Versailles peace conference at the end of World War I, was a master speculator on international financial markets (an activity he conducted from bed every morning and which made and lost him several fortunes), and played a prominent role in creating the International Monetary Fund.*

He was a member of the Bloomsbury Group, a circle of outstanding artists and writers that included E. M. Forster, Bertrand Russell, and Virginia Woolf.

Keynes was a controversial and quick-witted figure. A critic once complained that Keynes had changed his opinion on some matter, to which Keynes retorted: "When I discover I am wrong, I change my mind. What do you do?"

Keynes' book, The General Theory of Employment, Interest and Money, *written during the Great Depression and published in 1936, revolutionanized macroeconomics.*

"The ideas of economists and political philosophers, both when they are right and when they are wrong, are more powerful than is commonly understood. Indeed the world is ruled by little else."

JOHN MAYNARD KEYNES
The General Theory of Employment, Interest and Money

TALKING WITH Ricardo J. Caballero

Professor Caballero, why did you decide to become an economist?

Did I decide? I'm convinced that one is either born an economist or not. I began studying business, but as soon as I took the first course in economics, I was captivated by the simple but elegant logic of (good) economic reasoning. Given the complexity of the real world, economic analysis is necessarily abstract. But at the same time, economics is mostly about concrete and important issues that affect the lives of millions of people. Abstraction and relevance—this is a wonderful but strange combination. Not everybody feels comfortable with it, but if you do, economics is for you.

Most of your work has been on business cycles and other high-frequency phenomena. Can we begin by reviewing the costs of recessions? Robert Lucas says that postwar U.S. recessions have cost very little. Do you agree?

No . . . but I'm not sure Robert Lucas was really trying to say that. My sense is that he was trying to push the profession to focus a bit more on long-run growth issues. Putting down the costs of recessions was a useful debating device to make his important point.

I believe that the statement that recessions are not costly is incorrect. First, I think his calculation of this magnitude reflects some fundamental flaw in the way the workhorse models we use in economics fail to account for the costs of risk and volatility. This flaw shows up in many different puzzles in economics, including the well-known equity premium puzzle. Economic models underestimate, by an order of magnitude, how unhappy agents are about facing uncertainty. Second, it is highly unlikely that recessions and medium-term growth are completely separable. In particular, the ongoing process of restructuring, which is central to productivity growth, is severely hampered by deep recessions.

Recessions are costly because they waste enormous resources, affect physical and human investment decisions, have large negative distributional consequences, influence political outcomes, and so on.

What about the costs of recessions in other parts of the world, especially Latin America?

The cost of recessions grows exponentially with their size and the country's inability to soften the impact on the most affected. Less developed economies suffer much larger shocks because their economies are not well diversified, and they experience capital outflows that exacerbate the impact of recessionary shocks. Their domestic financial sectors are small and often become strained during recessions, making it difficult to reallocate scarce resources toward those who need them the most. To make matters worse, the government's ability to use fiscal policy becomes impaired by the capital outflows, and monetary policy is also out of the question when the currency is in free fall and liabilities are dollarized. There are many things that we take for granted in the United States that simply are not feasible for emerging markets in distress. One has to be careful with extrapolating too directly the countercyclical recipes used for developed economies to these countries.

Recessions are costly because they waste enormous resources [and] affect physical and human investment decisions.

Your first work, in your M.A. dissertation, was to build a macroeconomic model of the economy of Chile. What do we learn by comparing economies? Does the Chilean economy behave essentially like the U.S. economy or are there fundamental differences?

RICARDO J. CABALLERO is Ford Professor of International Economics at MIT. He has received many honors, the most notable of which are the Frisch Medal of the Econometric Society (2002) and being named Chile's Economist of the Year (2001). A highly regarded teacher, he is much sought as a special lecturer and in 2005 gave the prestigious Yrjo Johnsson Lecture at the University of Helsinki.

Professor Caballero earned his B.S. degree in 1982 and M.A. in 1983 at Pontificia Universidad Católica de Chile. He then moved to the United States and obtained his Ph.D. at MIT in 1988.

Michael Parkin talked with Ricardo Caballero about his work and the progress that economists have made in understanding economic fluctuations.

Chile is a special economy among emerging markets. It began pro-market reforms many years before the rest and has had very prudent macroeconomic management for several decades by now. For that reason, it is a bit more "like the U.S. economy" than most other emerging market economies. However, there are still important differences, of the sort described in my answer to the previous question.

Beyond the specifics of Chile, at some deep level, macroeconomic principles, and economic principles more generally, are the same everywhere. It is all about incentives, tradeoffs, effort, commitment, discipline, transparency, insurance, and so on. But different economies hurt in different places, and hence the practice of economics has plenty of diversity.

You've studied situations in which capital suddenly stops flowing into an economy from abroad. What are the lessons you've learned from this research?

First things first. I think we need to get used to the presence of speculative bubbles. The reason is that the world today has a massive shortage of financial assets that savers can use to store value. Because of this shortage, "artificial" assets are ready to emerge at all times. Specific bubbles come and go—from the NASDAQ, to real estate, to commodities—but the total is much more stable.

I do not think the distinction between bubbles and fundamentals is as clear-cut as people describe. Probably outside periods of liquidity crises, all assets have some bubble component in them. The question is how much.

You've studied situations in which capital suddenly stops flowing into an economy from abroad. What are the lessons you've learned from this research?

The most basic lesson for emerging markets is that capital flows are volatile. Sometimes they simply magnify domestic problems, but in many other cases, they are the direct source of volatility. However, the conclusion from this observation is not that capital flows should be limited, just as we do not close the banks in the United States to eliminate the possibility of bank runs. On the contrary, much of the volatility comes from insufficient integration with international capital markets, which makes emerging markets illiquid and the target of specialists and speculators. For the short and medium run, the main policy lesson is that sudden stops to the inflow of capital must be put at the center of macroeconomic policy design in emerging markets. This has deep implications for the design of monetary and fiscal policy, as well as for international reserves management practices and domestic financial markets regulation.

The most basic lesson for emerging markets is that capital flows are volatile.

The U.S. current account deficit has been large and increasing for many years, and dollar debt levels around the world have increased. Do you see any danger in this process for either the United States or the rest of the world?

I believe the persistent current account deficits in the United States are not the result of an anomaly that, as such, must go away in a sudden crash, as theattractive to international private and public investors.

Absent major shocks, this process may still last for quite some time. But of course shocks do happen, and in that sense, leverage is dangerous. However, there isn't much we can or should do, short of implementing structural reforms around the world aimed at improving growth potential in some cases and domestic financial development in others.

You've suggested that an insatiable appetite for safe securities is the root cause of the global financial crisis and that governments must accept a larger responsibility for bearing risk arising from the financial system. Would you explain this idea?

Foreign central banks and investors and U.S. financial institutions have an insatiable demand for safe securities, which puts enormous pressure on the U.S. financial system. The global financial crisis was the result of an interaction between the initial tremors caused by the rise in subprime mortgage defaults and securities created from these mortgages to feed the demand for safe-assets.

By 2001, the demand for safe assets began to exceed their supply, and financial institutions searched for ways to create safe assets from previously untapped and riskier ones. Subprime mortgage borrowers were a source of raw material. To convert risky mortgages (and other risky assets, ranging from auto loans to student loans) into safe assets, "banks" created complex securities made from large numbers of risky mortgages broken into tiers of increasing risk.

By 2001, the demand for safe assets began to exceed their supply . . .

How did these new complex securities get out of control and lead to the real estate bubble and financial crisis?

A positive feedback loop was created: Supplied with safe assets, funds flowed into banks to finance real estate purchases financed by mortgages. Real estate prices rose rapidly, which reinforced the belief that the securities created from mortgages were indeed safe. But for the banking system and economy, the new-found source of "safe" assets was not safe at all. Combining a large number of risky mortgages to create a safe security works if the risk of default by the initial borrower is uncorrelated with that of others. But in the environment of 2007, the risks were highly correlated. There was one source of default—generally falling home prices.

The triggering event was the crash in the real estate "bubble" and the rise in subprime mortgage defaults that followed it. But this cannot be all of it. The global financial system went into cardiac arrest in response to a relatively small shock which was well within the range of possible scenarios. The real damage came from the unexpected and sudden freezing of the entire securitization industry. Almost instantaneously, confidence vanished and the complexity which made possible the "multiplication of bread" during the boom, turned into a source of counterparty risk, both real and imaginary. Fear fed into more fear, causing reluctance to engage in financial transactions, even among the prime financial institutions. Safe interest rates plummeted to record low levels.

Addressing these issues requires governments to explicitly bear a greater share of systemic risk. There are two prongs within this approach. The first prong is for the countries that demand safe financial assets to rebalance their portfolios toward riskier assets. The second prong is for governments in countries that produce safe assets to provide a greater share of risk-bearing. There are many detailed ways in which this might be done.

What advice do you have for someone who is just beginning to study economics but who wants to become an economist? If they are not in the United States, should they come here for graduate work as you did?

There is no other place in the world like the United States to pursue a Ph.D. and do research in economics. However, this is only the last stage in the process of becoming an economist. There are many superb economists, especially applied ones, all around the world.

Almost everything in life has an economic angle to it—look for it . . .

I believe the most important step is to learn to think like an economist. I heard Milton Friedman say that he knows many economists who have never gone through a Ph.D. program, and equally many who have completed their Ph.D. but are not really economists. I agree with him on this one. A good undergraduate program and talking about economics is a great first step. Almost everything in life has an economic angle to it—look for it and discuss it with your friends. It will not improve your social life, but it will make you a better economist.

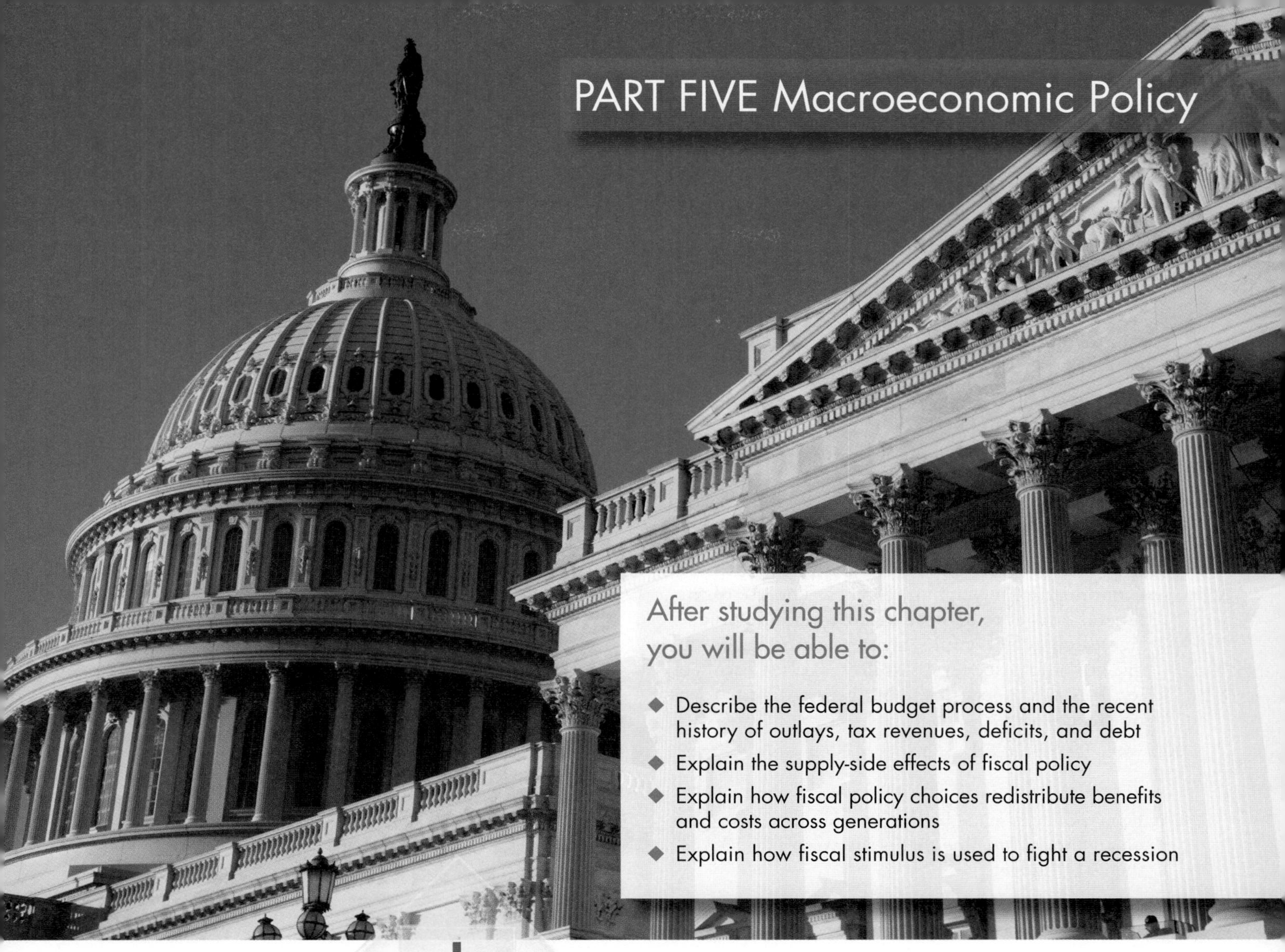

PART FIVE Macroeconomic Policy

After studying this chapter, you will be able to:

- Describe the federal budget process and the recent history of outlays, tax revenues, deficits, and debt
- Explain the supply-side effects of fiscal policy
- Explain how fiscal policy choices redistribute benefits and costs across generations
- Explain how fiscal stimulus is used to fight a recession

13 FISCAL POLICY

In 2010, the federal government spent 28 cents of every dollar that Americans earned. It raised 16 of those cents in taxes and borrowed the other 12. The government had a deficit of 12 cents on every dollar earned and a total deficit of $1.5 trillion. The 2010 deficit was exceptionally large, but federal government deficits are not new. Aside from the four years 1998–2001, the government's budget has been in deficit every year since 1970. Deficits bring debts, and your share of the federal government's debt is around $40,000.

Does it matter if the government doesn't balance its books? What are the effects of an ongoing government deficit and accumulating debt? Do they slow economic growth? Do they impose a burden on future generations—on you and your children?

What are the effects of taxes and government spending on the economy? Does a dollar spent by the government on goods and services have the same effect as a dollar spent by someone else? Does it create jobs, or does it destroy them?

These are the fiscal policy issues that you will study in this chapter. In *Reading Between the Lines* at the end of the chapter, we look at fiscal policy ideas to create jobs and boost real GDP in 2010.

The Federal Budget

The **federal budget** is an annual statement of the outlays and receipts of the government of the United States together with the laws and regulations that approve and support them. The federal budget has two purposes:

1. To finance federal government programs and activities, and
2. To achieve macroeconomic objectives

The first purpose of the federal budget was its only purpose before the Great Depression of the 1930s. The second purpose arose as a reaction to the Great Depression and the rise of the ideas of economist John Maynard Keynes. The use of the federal budget to achieve macroeconomic objectives such as full employment, sustained economic growth, and price level stability is called **fiscal policy**. It is this aspect of the budget that is the focus of this chapter.

The Institutions and Laws

Fiscal policy is made by the president and Congress on an annual timeline that is shown in Fig. 13.1 for the 2011 budget.

The Roles of the President and Congress The president *proposes* a budget to Congress each February. Congress debates the proposed budget and passes the budget acts in September. The president either signs those acts into law or vetoes the *entire* budget bill. The president does not have the veto power to eliminate specific items in a budget bill and approve others—known as a *line-item veto*. Many state governors have long had line-item veto authority. Congress attempted to grant these powers to the president of the United States in 1996, but in a 1998 Supreme Court ruling, the line-item veto for the president was declared unconstitutional. Although the president proposes and ultimately approves the budget, the task of making the tough decisions on spending and taxes rests with Congress.

Congress begins its work on the budget with the president's proposal. The House of Representatives and the Senate develop their own budget ideas in their respective House and Senate Budget Committees. Formal conferences between the two houses eventually resolve differences of view, and a series of spending acts and an overall budget act are usually passed by both houses before the start of the fiscal year. A *fiscal year* is a year that runs from October 1 to September 30 in the next calendar year. *Fiscal* 2011 is the fiscal year that *begins* on October 1, 2010.

FIGURE 13.1 The Federal Budget Timeline in Fiscal 2011

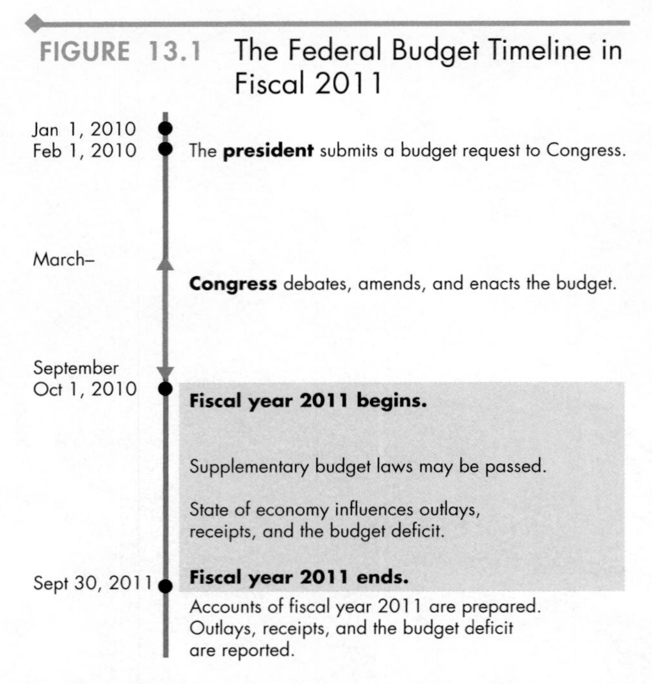

The federal budget process begins with the president's request in February. Congress debates and amends the request and enacts a budget before the start of the fiscal year on October 1. The president signs the budget acts into law or vetoes the entire budget bill. Throughout the fiscal year, Congress might pass supplementary budget laws. The budget outcome is calculated after the end of the fiscal year.

During a fiscal year, Congress often passes supplementary budget laws, and the budget outcome is influenced by the evolving state of the economy. For example, if a recession begins, tax revenues fall and welfare payments increase.

The Employment Act of 1946 Fiscal policy operates within the framework of the landmark **Employment Act of 1946** in which Congress declared that

> . . . it is the continuing policy and responsibility of the Federal Government to use all practicable means . . . to coordinate and utilize all its plans, functions, and resources . . . to promote maximum employment, production, and purchasing power.

This act recognized a role for government actions to keep unemployment low, the economy expanding, and inflation in check. The *Full Employment and Balanced Growth Act of 1978*, more commonly known as the *Humphrey-Hawkins Act*, went farther than the Employment Act of 1946 and set a specific target of 4 percent for the unemployment rate. But this target has never been treated as an unwavering policy goal. Under the 1946 act, the president must describe the current economic situation and the policies he believes are needed in the annual *Economic Report of the President*, which the Council of Economic Advisers writes.

The Council of Economic Advisers The president's Council of Economic Advisers was established in the Employment Act of 1946. The Council consists of a chairperson and two other members, all of whom are economists on a one- or two-year leave from their regular university or public service jobs. In 2010, the chair of President Obama's Council of Economic Advisers was Austan Goolsbee of the University of Chicago. The **Council of Economic Advisers** monitors the economy and keeps the President and the public well informed about the current state of the economy and the best available forecasts of where it is heading. This economic intelligence activity is one source of data that informs the budget-making process.

Let's look at the most recent federal budget.

Highlights of the 2011 Budget

Table 13.1 shows the main items in the federal budget proposed by President Obama for 2011. The numbers are projected amounts for the fiscal year beginning on October 1, 2010—fiscal 2011. Notice the three main parts of the table: *Receipts* are the government's tax revenues, *outlays* are the government's payments, and the *deficit* is the amount by which the government's outlays exceed its receipts.

Receipts Receipts were projected to be $2,807 billion in fiscal 2011. These receipts come from four sources:

1. Personal income taxes
2. Social Security taxes
3. Corporate income taxes
4. Indirect taxes and other receipts

The largest source of receipts is *personal income taxes*, which in 2011 are expected to be $1,076 billion. These taxes are paid by individuals on their incomes. The second largest source is *Social Security taxes*. These taxes are paid by workers and their employers to finance the government's Social Security programs. Third in size are *corporate income taxes*. These taxes are paid by companies on their profits. Finally, the smallest source of federal receipts is what are called *indirect taxes*. These taxes are on the sale of gasoline, alcoholic beverages, and a few other items.

Outlays Outlays are classified into three categories:

1. Transfer payments
2. Expenditure on goods and services
3. Debt interest

The largest item of outlays, *transfer payments*, is the payment to individuals, businesses, other levels of government, and the rest of the world. In 2011, this item is expected to be $2,588 billion. It includes Social Security benefits, Medicare and Medicaid, unemployment checks, welfare payments, farm subsidies, grants to state and local governments, and payments to international agencies. It also includes capital transfers to bail out failing financial institutions. Transfer payments, especially those for Medicare and Medicaid, are sources of persistent growth in

TABLE 13.1 Federal Budget in Fiscal 2011

Item	Projections (billions of dollars)	
Receipts	**2,807**	
Personal income taxes		1,076
Social Security taxes		1,054
Corporate income taxes		432
Indirect taxes and other receipts		245
Outlays	**4,129**	
Transfer payments		2,588
Expenditure on goods and services		1,181
Debt interest		360
Deficit	**1,322**	

Source of data: Budget of the United States Government, Fiscal Year 2011, Table 14.1.

government expenditures and are a major source of concern and political debate.

Expenditure on goods and services is the expenditure on final goods and services, and in 2011, it is expected to total $1,181 billion. This expenditure, which includes that on national defense, homeland security, research on cures for AIDS, computers for the Internal Revenue Service, government cars and trucks, and federal highways, has decreased in recent years. This component of the federal budget is the *government expenditure on goods and services* that appears in the circular flow of expenditure and income and in the National Income and Product Accounts (see Chapter 4, pp. 85–86).

Debt interest is the interest on the government debt. In 2011, this item is expected to be $360 billion—about 9 percent of total expenditure. This interest payment is large because the government has a debt of more than $6 trillion, which has arisen from many years of budget deficits during the 1970s, 1980s, 1990s, and 2000s.

Surplus or Deficit The government's budget balance is equal to receipts minus outlays.

$$\text{Budget balance} = \text{Receipts} - \text{Outlays}.$$

If receipts exceed outlays, the government has a **budget surplus**. If outlays exceed receipts, the government has a **budget deficit**. If receipts equal outlays, the government has a **balanced budget**. For fiscal 2011, with projected outlays of $4,129 billion and receipts of $2,807 billion, the government projected a budget deficit of $1,322 billion.

Big numbers like these are hard to visualize and hard to compare over time. To get a better sense of the magnitude of receipts, outlays, and the deficit, we often express them as percentages of GDP. Expressing them in this way lets us see how large government is relative to the size of the economy and also helps us to study *changes* in the scale of government over time.

How typical is the federal budget of 2011? Let's look at the recent history of the budget.

The Budget in Historical Perspective

Figure 13.2 shows the government's receipts, outlays, and budget surplus or deficit since 1980. You can see that except for the four years around 2000, the budget has been in persistent deficit.

You can also see that after 2008, the deficit was extraordinarily large, peaking in 2010 at almost 12 percent of GDP. The next highest deficit had been in 1983 at 6 percent of GDP.

The large deficit of the 1980s gradually shrank through 1990s expansion and in 1998 the first budget

FIGURE 13.2 The Budget Surplus and Deficit

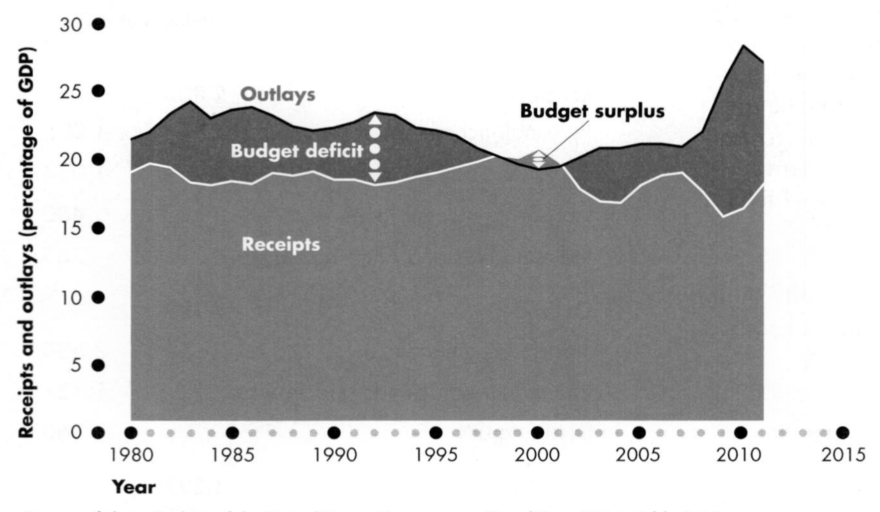

The figure records the federal government's outlays, receipts, and budget balance from 1980 to 2011. Except for the four years 1998 through 2001, the budget has been in deficit. The deficit after 2008 reached a new all-time high and occurred because outlays increased. Receipts have fluctuated but have displayed no trend (as a percentage of GDP).

Source of data: Budget of the United States Government, Fiscal Year 2011, Table 14.2.

myeconlab animation

surplus since 1969 emerged. But by 2002, the budget was again in deficit and during the 2008–2009 recession, the deficit reached a new all-time high.

Why did the budget deficit grow during the 1980s, vanish in the late 1990s, and re-emerge in the 2000s? Did outlays increase, or did receipts shrink, and which components of outlays and receipts changed most to swell and then shrink the deficit? Let's look at receipts and outlays in a bit more detail.

Receipts Figure 13.3(a) shows the components of government receipts as percentages of GDP from 1980 to 2011. Total receipts fluctuate because personal income taxes and corporate income taxes fluctuate. Other receipts (Social Security taxes and indirect taxes) are a near constant percentage of GDP.

Income tax receipts trended downward during the early 1980s and 2000s, upward during the 1990s, and slightly downward over the 30 years to 2010.

FIGURE 13.3 Federal Government Receipts and Outlays

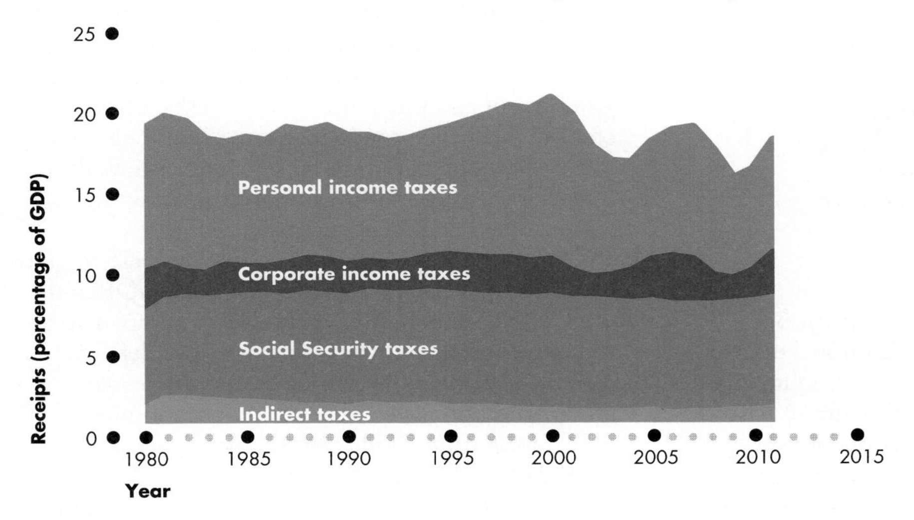

(a) Receipts

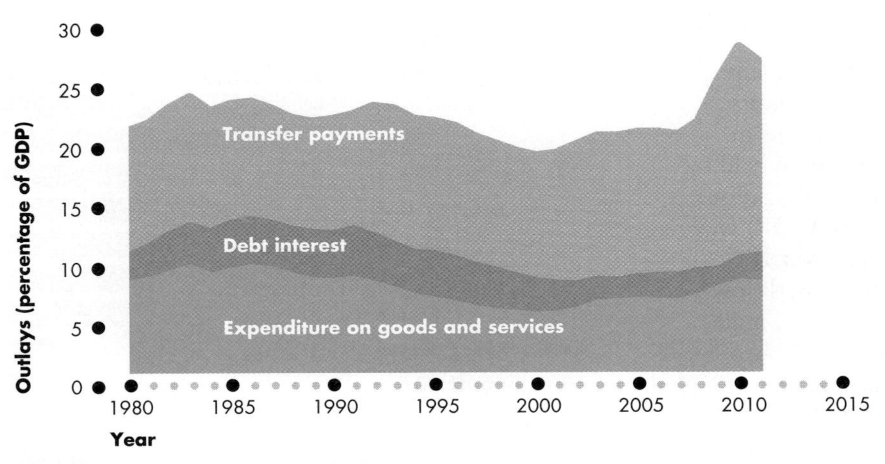

(b) Outlays

Source of data: Budget of the United States Government, Fiscal Year 2011, Table 14.2.

In part (a), receipts from personal and corporate income taxes (as a percentage of GDP) fell during the early1980s, increased during the 1990s, and fluctuated wildly during the 2000s. The other components of receipts remained steady. Over the entire period, receipts fell slightly.

In part (b), expenditure on goods and services as a percentage of GDP decreased through 2001 but then increased because expenditure on security-related goods and services increased sharply after 2001. Transfer payments increased over the entire period and exploded to a new all-time high percentage of GDP after 2008. Debt interest held steady during the 1980s and decreased during the 1990s and 2000s, helped by a shrinking budget deficit during the 1990s and low interest rates after 2008.

myeconlab animation

Outlays Figure 13.3(b) shows the components of government outlays as percentages of GDP from 1980 to 2011. Two features of government outlays stand out. First, expenditure on goods and services decreased from 1983 through 2000 and then increased. The increase after 2000 was mainly on security-related goods and services in the wake of the attacks that occurred on September 11, 2001, and defense expenditure. Second, transfer payments increased over the entire period and exploded after 2008 when the government tried to stimulate economic activity.

You've seen that the U.S. government budget deficit is large. But how does it compare to the deficits of other countries? The answer is that it is one of the largest, as *Economics in Action* shows. Of the major economies, only the United Kingdom has a larger deficit as a percentage of GDP.

Deficits bring debts, as you will now see.

Budget Balance and Debt

When the government has a budget deficit it borrows, and when it has a budget surplus it makes loan repayments. **Government debt** is the total amount that the government has borrowed. It is the sum of past budget deficits minus the sum of past budget surpluses. A government budget deficit increases government debt. A persistent budget deficit feeds itself: It leads to increased borrowing, which leads to larger interest payments, which in turn lead to a larger deficit. That is the story of the increasing budget deficit during the 1970s and 1980s.

Figure 13.4 shows two measures of government debt since 1940. Gross debt includes the amounts that the government owes to future generations in Social Security payments. Net debt is the debt held by the public, and it excludes Social Security obligations.

Government debt (as a percentage of GDP) was at an all-time high at the end of World War II. Budget surpluses and rapid economic growth lowered the debt-to-GDP ratio through 1974. Small budget deficits increased the debt-to-GDP ratio slightly through the 1970s, and large budget deficits increased it dramatically during the 1980s and the 1990–1991 recession. The growth rate of the debt-to-GDP ratio slowed as the economy expanded during the mid-1990s, fell when the budget went into surplus in the late 1990s and early 2000s, and began to rise again as the budget returned to deficit.

Economics in Action

The U.S. Government Budget in Global Perspective

The U.S. government budget deficit in Fiscal 2010 was projected to be 11.8 percent of GDP. You've seen that this deficit is historically high but how does it compare with the deficits of other countries?

To compare the deficits of governments across countries, we must take into account the differences in local and regional government arrangements. Some countries, and the United States is one of them, have large state and local governments. Other countries, and the United Kingdom is one, have larger central government and small local governments. These differences make the international comparison more valid at the level of total government. The figure shows the budget balances of all levels of government in the United States and other countries.

Of the countries shown here, the United Kingdom has the largest deficit, as a percentage of GDP, and the United States has the second largest. Japan and some European countries also have large deficits.

Italy, Canada, other advanced economies as a group, and the newly industrialized economies of Asia (Hong Kong, South Korea, Singapore, and Taiwan) had the smallest deficits in 2010. It is notable that none of the world's major economies had a budget surplus in 2010. Fiscal stimulus to fight recession resulted in deficits everywhere.

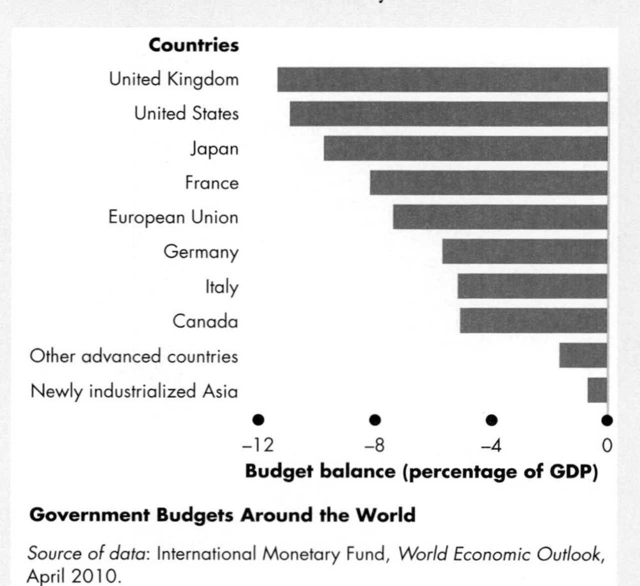

Government Budgets Around the World

Source of data: International Monetary Fund, *World Economic Outlook*, April 2010.

FIGURE 13.4 The Federal Government Debt

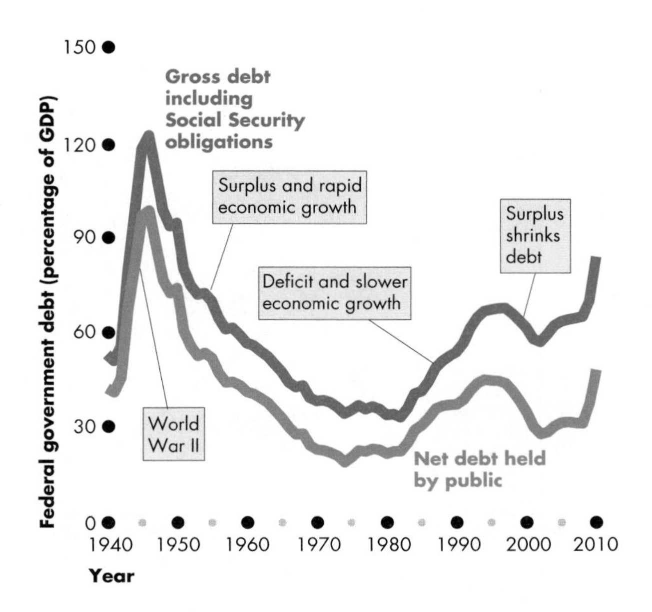

Gross and net government debt (the accumulation of past budget deficits less past budget surpluses) was at its highest at the end of World War II. Debt as a percentage of GDP fell through 1974 but then started to increase. After a further brief decline during the late 1970s, it exploded during the 1980s and continued to increase through 1995, after which it fell. After 2002, it began to rise again.

Source of data: Budget of the United States Government, Fiscal Year 2011, Table 7.1.

myeconlab animation

Debt and Capital Businesses and individuals incur debts to buy capital—assets that yield a return. In fact, the main point of debt is to enable people to buy assets that will earn a return that exceeds the interest paid on the debt. The government is similar to individuals and businesses in this regard. Much government expenditure is on public assets that yield a return. Highways, public schools and universities, and the stock of national defense capital all yield a social rate of return that probably far exceeds the interest rate the government pays on its debt.

But total government debt, which exceeds $4 trillion, is four times the value of the government's capital stock. So some government debt has been incurred to finance public consumption expenditure and transfer payments, which do not have a social return. Future generations bear the cost of this debt.

State and Local Budgets

The *total government* sector of the United States includes state and local governments as well as the federal government. In 2010, when federal government outlays were $4,129 billion, state and local outlays were a further $2,000 billion. Most of these expenditures were on public schools, colleges, and universities ($550 billion); local police and fire services; and roads.

It is the combination of federal, state, and local government receipts, outlays, and budget deficits that influences the economy. But state and local budgets are not designed to stabilize the aggregate economy. So sometimes, when the federal government cuts taxes or outlays, state and local governments do the reverse and, to a degree, cancel out the effects of the federal actions. For example, since 2000, federal taxes decreased as a percentage of GDP, but state and local taxes and total government taxes increased.

REVIEW QUIZ

1. What is fiscal policy, who makes it, and what is it designed to influence?
2. What special role does the president play in creating fiscal policy?
3. What special roles do the Budget Committees of the House of Representatives and the Senate play in creating fiscal policy?
4. What is the timeline for the U.S. federal budget each year? When does a fiscal year begin and end?
5. Is the federal government budget today in surplus or deficit?

You can work these questions in Study Plan 13.1 and get instant feedback.

Now that you know what the federal budget is and what the main components of receipts and outlays are, it is time to study the *effects* of fiscal policy. We'll begin by learning about the effects of taxes on employment, aggregate supply, and potential GDP. Then we'll study the effects of budget deficits and see how fiscal policy brings redistribution across generations. Finally, we'll look at fiscal stimulus and see how it might be used to speed recovery from recession and stabilize the business cycle.

Supply-Side Effects of Fiscal Policy

How do taxes on personal and corporate income affect real GDP and employment? The answer to these questions is controversial. Some economists, known as *supply-siders*, believe these effects to be large and an accumulating body of evidence suggests that they are correct. To see why these effects might be large, we'll begin with a refresher on how full employment and potential GDP are determined in the absence of taxes. Then we'll introduce an income tax and see how it changes the economic outcome.

Full Employment and Potential GDP

You learned in Chapter 6 (pp. 139–141) how the full-employment quantity of labor and potential GDP are determined. At full employment, the real wage rate adjusts to make the quantity of labor demanded equal the quantity of labor supplied. Potential GDP is the real GDP that the full-employment quantity of labor produces.

Figure 13.5 illustrates a full-employment situation. In part (a), the demand for labor curve is *LD*, and the supply of labor curve is *LS*. At a real wage rate of \$30 an hour and 250 billion hours of labor a year employed, the economy is at full employment.

In Fig. 13.5(b), the production function is *PF*. When 250 billion hours of labor are employed, real GDP—which is also potential GDP—is \$13 trillion.

Let's now see how an income tax changes potential GDP.

The Effects of the Income Tax

The tax on labor income influences potential GDP and aggregate supply by changing the full-employment quantity of labor. The income tax weakens the incentive to work and drives a wedge between the take-home wage of workers and the cost of labor to firms. The result is a smaller quantity of labor and a lower potential GDP.

Figure 13.5 shows this outcome. In the labor market, the income tax has no effect on the demand for labor, which remains at *LD*. The reason is that the quantity of labor that firms plan to hire depends only on how productive labor is and what it costs—its real wage rate.

FIGURE 13.5 The Effects of the Income Tax on Aggregate Supply

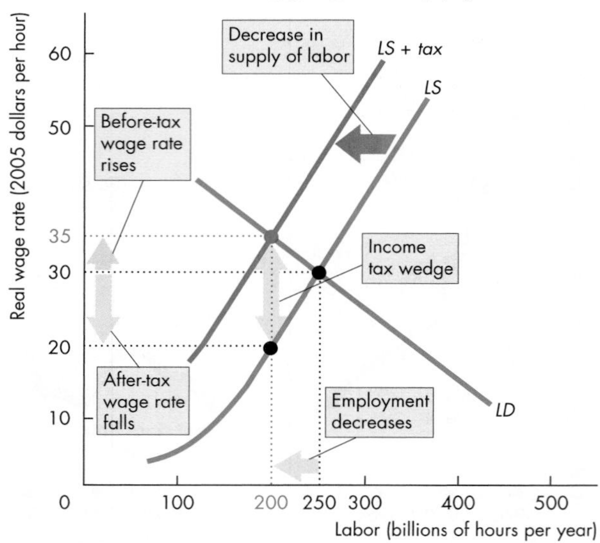

(a) Income tax and the labor market

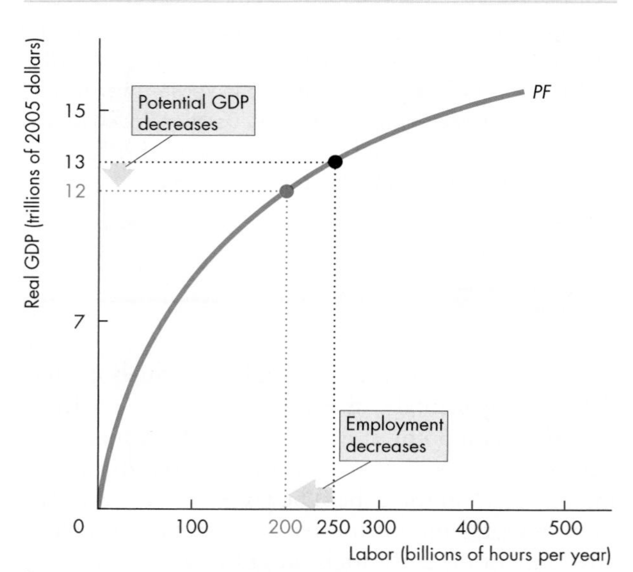

(b) Income tax and potential GDP

In part (a), with no income tax, the real wage rate is \$30 an hour and employment is 250 billion hours. In part (b), potential GDP is \$13 trillion. An income tax shifts the supply of labor curve leftward to *LS + tax*. The before-tax wage rate rises to \$35 an hour, the after-tax wage rate falls to \$20 an hour, and the quantity of labor employed decreases to 200 billion hours. With less labor, potential GDP decreases.

myeconlab animation

But the supply of labor *does* change. With no income tax, the real wage rate is $30 an hour and 250 billion hours of labor a year are employed. An income tax weakens the incentive to work and decreases the supply of labor. The reason is that for each dollar of before-tax earnings, workers must pay the government an amount determined by the income tax code. So workers look at the after-tax wage rate when they decide how much labor to supply. An income tax shifts the supply curve leftward to *LS + tax*. The vertical distance between the *LS* curve and the *LS + tax* curve measures the amount of income tax. With the smaller supply of labor, the *before-tax* wage rate rises to $35 an hour but the *after-tax* wage rate falls to $20 an hour. The gap created between the before-tax and after-tax wage rates is called the **tax wedge**.

The new equilibrium quantity of labor employed is 200 billion hours a year—less than in the no-tax case. Because the full-employment quantity of labor decreases, so does potential GDP. And a decrease in potential GDP decreases aggregate supply.

In this example, the tax rate is high—$15 tax on a $35 wage rate is a tax rate of about 43 percent. A lower tax rate would have a smaller effect on employment and potential GDP.

An increase in the tax rate to above 43 percent would decrease the supply of labor by more than the decrease shown in Fig. 13.5. Equilibrium employment and potential GDP would also decrease still further. A tax cut would increase the supply of labor, increase equilibrium employment, and increase potential GDP.

Taxes on Expenditure and the Tax Wedge

The tax wedge that we've just considered is only a part of the wedge that affects labor-supply decisions. Taxes on consumption expenditure add to the wedge. The reason is that a tax on consumption raises the prices paid for consumption goods and services and is equivalent to a cut in the real wage rate.

The incentive to supply labor depends on the goods and services that an hour of labor can buy. The higher the taxes on goods and services and the lower the after-tax wage rate, the less is the incentive to supply labor. If the income tax rate is 25 percent and the tax rate on consumption expenditure is 10 percent, a dollar earned buys only 65 cents worth of goods and services. The tax wedge is 35 percent.

Economics in Action

Some Real World Tax Wedges

Edward C. Prescott of Arizona State University, who shared the 2004 Nobel Prize for Economic Science, has estimated the tax wedges for a number of countries, among them the United States, the United Kingdom, and France.

The U.S. tax wedge is a combination of 13 percent tax on consumption and 32 percent tax on incomes. The income tax component of the U.S. tax wedge includes Social Security taxes and is the *marginal* tax rate—the tax rate paid on the marginal dollar earned.

Prescott estimates that in France, taxes on consumption are 33 percent and taxes on incomes are 49 percent.

The estimates for the United Kingdom fall between those for the United States and France. The figure shows these components of the tax wedges in the three countries.

Does the Tax Wedge Matter?

According to Prescott's estimates, the tax wedge has a powerful effect on employment and potential GDP. Potential GDP in France is 14 percent below that of the United States (per person), and the entire difference can be attributed to the difference in the tax wedge in the two countries.

Potential GDP in the United Kingdom is 41 percent below that of the United States (per person), and about a third of the difference arises from the different tax wedges. (The rest is due to different productivities.)

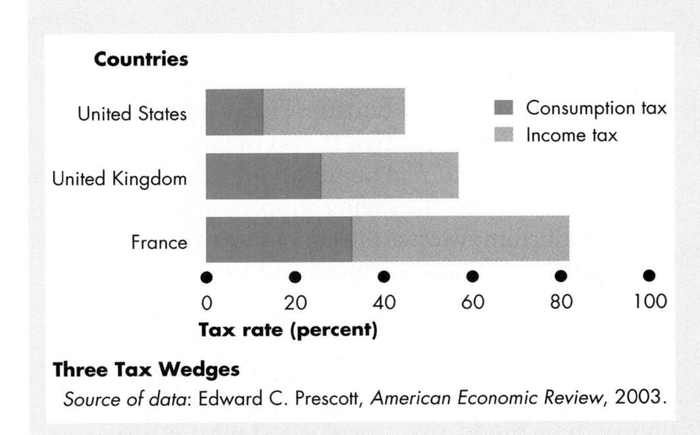

Three Tax Wedges

Source of data: Edward C. Prescott, *American Economic Review*, 2003.

Taxes and the Incentive to Save and Invest

A tax on interest income weakens the incentive to save and drives a wedge between the after-tax interest rate earned by savers and the interest rate paid by firms. These effects are analogous to those of a tax on labor income. But they are more serious for two reasons.

First, a tax on labor income lowers the quantity of labor employed and lowers potential GDP, while a tax on capital income lowers the quantity of saving and investment and *slows the growth rate of real GDP*.

Second, the true tax rate on interest income is much higher than that on labor income because of the way in which inflation and taxes on interest income interact. Let's examine this interaction.

Effect of Tax Rate on Real Interest Rate The interest rate that influences investment and saving plans is the *real after-tax interest rate*. The real *after-tax* interest rate subtracts the income tax rate paid on interest income from the real interest rate. But the taxes depend on the nominal interest rate, not the real interest rate. So the higher the inflation rate, the higher is the true tax rate on interest income. Here is an example. Suppose the real interest rate is 4 percent a year and the tax rate is 40 percent.

If there is no inflation, the nominal interest rate equals the real interest rate. The tax on 4 percent interest is 1.6 percent (40 percent of 4 percent), so the real after-tax interest rate is 4 percent minus 1.6 percent, which equals 2.4 percent.

If the inflation rate is 6 percent a year, the nominal interest rate is 10 percent. The tax on 10 percent interest is 4 percent (40 percent of 10 percent), so the real after-tax interest rate is 4 percent minus 4 percent, which equals zero. The true tax rate in this case is not 40 percent but 100 percent!

Effect of Income Tax on Saving and Investment In Fig. 13.6, initially there are no taxes. Also, the government has a balanced budget. The demand for loanable funds curve, which is also the investment demand curve, is *DLF*. The supply of loanable funds curve, which is also the saving supply curve, is *SLF*. The equilibrium interest rate is 3 percent a year, and the quantity of funds borrowed and lent is $2 trillion a year.

A tax on interest income has no effect on the demand for loanable funds. The quantity of investment and borrowing that firms plan to undertake depends only on how productive capital is and what it costs—its real interest rate. But a tax on interest income weakens the incentive to save and lend and decreases the supply of loanable funds. For each dollar of before-tax interest, savers must pay the government an amount determined by the tax code. So savers look at the after-tax real interest rate when they decide how much to save.

When a tax is imposed, saving decreases and the supply of loanable funds curve shifts leftward to *SLF + tax*. The amount of tax payable is measured by the vertical distance between the *SLF* curve and the *SLF + tax* curve. With this smaller supply of loanable funds, the interest rate rises to 4 percent a year but the *after-tax* interest rate falls to 1 percent a year. A tax wedge is driven between the interest rate and the after-tax interest rate, and the equilibrium quantity of loanable funds decreases. Saving and investment also decrease.

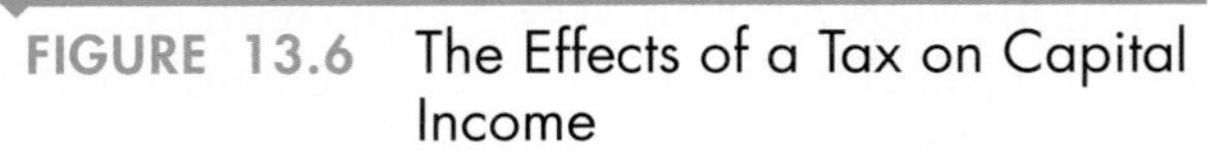

FIGURE 13.6 The Effects of a Tax on Capital Income

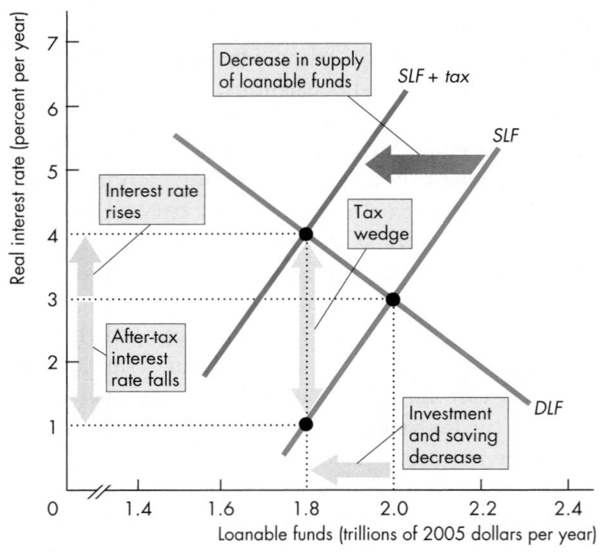

The demand for loanable funds and investment demand curve is *DLF*, and the supply of loanable funds and saving supply curve is *SLF*. With no income tax, the real interest rate is 3 percent a year and investment is $2 trillion. An income tax shifts the supply curve leftward to *SLF + tax*. The interest rate rises to 4 percent a year, the after-tax interest rate falls to 1 percent a year, and investment decreases to $1.8 trillion. With less investment, the real GDP growth rate decreases.

myeconlab animation

Tax Revenues and the Laffer Curve

An interesting consequence of the effect of taxes on employment and saving is that a higher tax *rate* does not always bring greater tax *revenue*. A higher tax rate brings in more revenue per dollar earned. But because a higher tax rate decreases the number of dollars earned, two forces operate in opposite directions on the tax revenue collected.

The relationship between the tax rate and the amount of tax revenue collected is called the **Laffer curve**. The curve is so named because Arthur B. Laffer, a member of President Reagan's Economic Policy Advisory Board, drew such a curve on a table napkin and launched the idea that tax *cuts* could *increase* tax revenue.

Figure 13.7 shows a Laffer curve. The tax *rate* is on the *x*-axis, and total tax *revenue* is on the *y*-axis. For tax rates below T^*, an increase in the tax rate increases tax revenue; at T^*, tax revenue is maximized; and a tax rate increase above T^* decreases tax revenue.

Most people think that the United States is on the upward-sloping part of the Laffer curve; so is the United Kingdom. But France might be close to the maximum point or perhaps even beyond it.

FIGURE 13.7 A Laffer Curve

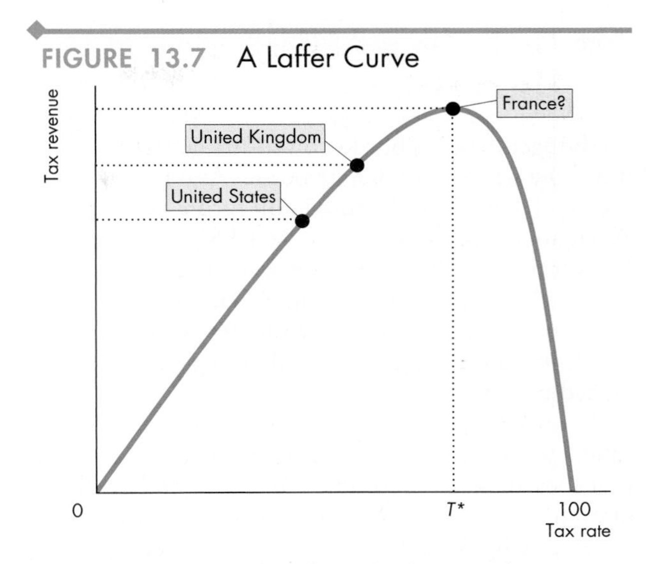

A Laffer curve shows the relationship between the tax rate and tax revenues. For tax rates below T^*, an increase in the tax rate increases tax revenue. At the tax rate T^*, tax revenue is maximized. For tax rates above T^*, an increase in the tax rate decreases tax revenue.

The Supply-Side Debate

Before 1980, few economists paid attention to the supply-side effects of taxes on employment and potential GDP. Then, when Ronald Reagan took office as president, a group of supply-siders began to argue the virtues of cutting taxes. Arthur Laffer was one of them. Laffer and his supporters were not held in high esteem among mainstream economists, but they were influential for a period. They correctly argued that tax cuts would increase employment and increase output. But they incorrectly argued that tax cuts would increase tax revenues and decrease the budget deficit. For this prediction to be correct, the United States would have had to be on the "wrong" side of the Laffer curve. Given that U.S. tax rates are among the lowest in the industrial world, it is unlikely that this condition was met. And when the Reagan administration did cut taxes, the budget deficit increased, a fact that reinforces this view.

Supply-side economics became tarnished because of its association with Laffer and came to be called "voodoo economics." But mainstream economists, including Martin Feldstein, a Harvard professor who was Reagan's chief economic adviser, recognized the power of tax cuts as incentives but took the standard view that tax cuts without spending cuts would swell the budget deficit and bring serious further problems. This view is now widely accepted by economists of all political persuasions.

REVIEW QUIZ

1. How does a tax on labor income influence the equilibrium quantity of employment?
2. How does the tax wedge influence potential GDP?
3. Why are consumption taxes relevant for measuring the tax wedge?
4. Why are income taxes on capital income more powerful than those on labor income?
5. What is the Laffer curve and why is it unlikely that the United States is on the "wrong" side of it?

You can work these questions in Study Plan 13.2 and get instant feedback.

You now know how taxes influence potential GDP and saving and investment. Next we look at the intergenerational effects of fiscal policy.

Generational Effects of Fiscal Policy

Is a budget deficit a burden on future generations? If it is, how will the burden be borne? And is the budget deficit the only burden on future generations? What about the deficit in the Social Security fund? Does it matter who owns the bonds that the government sells to finance its deficit? What about the bonds owned by foreigners? Won't repaying those bonds impose a bigger burden than repaying bonds owned by Americans?

To answer questions like these, we use a tool called **generational accounting**—an accounting system that measures the lifetime tax burden and benefits of each generation. This accounting system was developed by Alan Auerbach of the University of Pennsylvania and Laurence Kotlikoff of Boston University. Generational accounts for the United States have been prepared by Jagadeesh Gokhale of the Cato Institute and Kent Smetters of the Wharton School at the University of Pennsylvania.

Generational Accounting and Present Value

Income taxes and Social Security taxes are paid by people who have jobs. Social Security benefits are paid to people after they retire. So to compare taxes and benefits, we must compare the value of taxes paid by people during their working years with the benefits received in their retirement years. To compare the value of an amount of money at one date with that at a later date, we use the concept of present value. A **present value** is an amount of money that, if invested today, will grow to equal a given future amount when the interest that it earns is taken into account. We can compare dollars today with dollars in 2030 or any other future year by using present values.

For example, if the interest rate is 5 percent a year, $1,000 invested today will grow, with interest, to $11,467 after 50 years. So the present value (in 2010) of $11,467 in 2060 is $1,000.

By using present values, we can assess the magnitude of the government's debts to older Americans in the form of pensions and medical benefits.

But the assumed interest rate and growth rate of taxes and benefits critically influence the answers we get. For example, at an interest rate of 3 percent a year, the present value (in 2010) of $11,467 in 2060 is $2,616. The lower the interest rate, the greater is the present value of a given future amount.

Because there is uncertainty about the proper interest rate to use to calculate present values, plausible alternative numbers are used to estimate a range of present values.

Using generational accounting and present values, economists have studied the situation facing the federal government arising from its Social Security obligations, and they have found a time bomb!

The Social Security Time Bomb

When Social Security was introduced in the New Deal of the 1930s, today's demographic situation was not foreseen. The age distribution of the U.S. population today is dominated by the surge in the birth rate after World War II that created what is called the "baby boom generation." There are 77 million "baby boomers."

The first of the baby boomers start collecting Social Security pensions in 2008 and in 2011 they became eligible for Medicare benefits. By 2030, all the baby boomers will have reached retirement age and the population supported by Social Security and Medicare benefits will have doubled.

Under the existing laws, the federal government has an obligation to this increasing number of citizens to pay pensions and Medicare benefits on an already declared scale. These obligations are a debt owed by the government and are just as real as the bonds that the government issues to finance its current budget deficit.

To assess the full extent of the government's obligations, economists use the concept of fiscal imbalance. **Fiscal imbalance** is the present value of the government's commitments to pay benefits minus the present value of its tax revenues. Fiscal imbalance is an attempt to measure the scale of the government's true liabilities.

Gokhale and Smetters estimated that the fiscal imbalance was $79 trillion in 2010. To put the $79 trillion in perspective, note that U.S. GDP in 2010 was $13.6 trillion. So the fiscal imbalance was 5.8 times the value of one year's production. And the fiscal imbalance grows every year by an amount that in 2010 was approaching $2 trillion.

These are enormous numbers and point to a catastrophic future. How can the federal government meet its Social Security obligations? Gokhale and Smetters consider four alternatives:

- Raise income taxes
- Raise Social Security taxes
- Cut Social Security benefits
- Cut federal government discretionary spending

They estimated that if we had started in 2003 and made only one of these changes, income taxes would need to be raised by 69 percent, or Social Security taxes raised by 95 percent, or Social Security benefits cut by 56 percent. Even if the government stopped all its discretionary spending, including that on national defense, it would not be able to pay its bills. By combining the four measures, the pain from each could be lessened, but the pain would still be severe.

A further way of meeting these obligations is to pay by printing money. As you learned in Chapter 8 (see pp. 200–201), the consequence of this solution would be a seriously high inflation rate.

Generational Imbalance

A fiscal imbalance must eventually be corrected and when it is, people either pay higher taxes or receive lower benefits. The concept of generational imbalance tells us who will pay. **Generational imbalance** is the division of the fiscal imbalance between the current and future generations, assuming that the current generation will enjoy the existing levels of taxes and benefits.

Figure 13.8 shows an estimate of how the fiscal imbalance is distributed across the current (born before 1988) and future (born in or after 1988) generations. It also shows that the major source of the imbalances is Medicare. Social Security pension benefits create a fiscal imbalance, but these benefits will be more than fully paid for by the current generation. But the current generation will pay less than 50 percent of its Medicare costs, and the balance will fall on future generations. If we sum all the items, the current generation will pay 43 percent and future generations will pay 57 percent of the fiscal imbalance.

Because the estimated fiscal imbalance is so large, it is not possible to predict how it will be resolved. But we can predict that the outcome will involve both lower benefits and higher taxes or paying bills with new money and creating inflation.

The Fed would have to cooperate if inflation were to be used to deal with the imbalance, and this cooperation might be hard to obtain.

FIGURE 13.8 Fiscal and Generational Imbalances

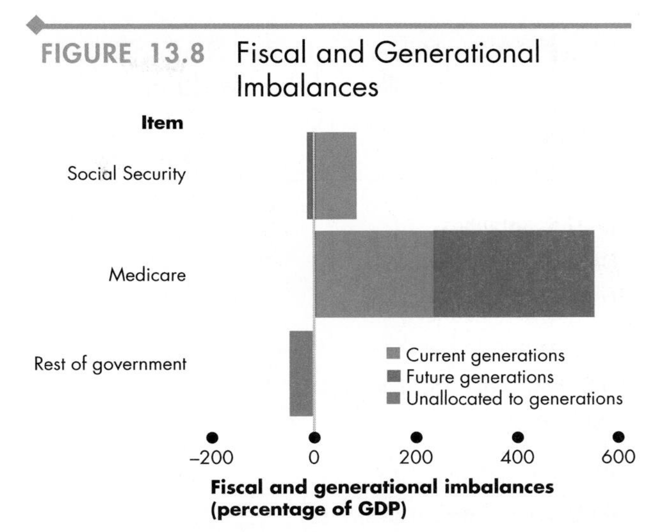

The bars show the scale of the fiscal imbalance. The largest component at almost 600 percent of GDP is Medicare benefits. These benefits are also the main component of the generational imbalance. Social Security pensions are paid for entirely by the current generation.

Source of data: Jagadeesh Gokhale and Kent Smetters, "Fiscal and Generational Imbalances: An Update" *Tax Policy and the Economy*, Vol. 20, pp. 193-223, University of Chicago Press, 2006.

International Debt

So far in our discussion of government deficits and debts, we've ignored the role played by the rest of the world. We'll conclude this discussion by considering the role and magnitude of international debt.

You've seen that borrowing from the rest of the world is one source of loanable funds. And you've also seen that this source of funds became larger during the late 1990s and 2000s.

How large is the contribution of the rest of the world? How much business investment have we paid for by borrowing from the rest of the world? And how much U.S. government debt is held abroad?

Table 13.2 answers these questions. In June 2010, the United States had a net debt to the rest of the world of $9.5 trillion. Of that debt, $4.0 trillion was U.S. government debt. U.S. corporations had used $4.7 trillion of foreign funds ($2.4 trillion in bonds and $2.3 trillion in equities). About two thirds of U.S. government debt is held by foreigners.

The international debt of the United States is important because, when that debt is repaid, the United States will transfer real resources to the rest of

TABLE 13.2 What the United States Owed the Rest of the World in June 2010

	$ trillions
(a) U.S. liabilities	
Deposits in U.S. banks	0.6
U.S. government securities	4.0
U.S. corporate bonds	2.4
U.S. corporate equities	2.3
Other (net)	0.2
Total	**9.5**
(b) U.S. government securities	
Held by rest of world	4.0
Held in the United States	2.0
Total	**6.0**

Source of data: Federal Reserve Board.

the world. Instead of running a large net exports deficit, the United States will need a surplus of exports over imports. To make a surplus possible, U.S. saving must increase and consumption must decrease. Some tough choices lie ahead.

REVIEW QUIZ

1. What is a present value?
2. Distinguish between fiscal imbalance and generational imbalance.
3. How large was the estimated U.S. fiscal imbalance in 2010 and how did it divide between current and future generations?
4. What is the source of the U.S. fiscal imbalance and what are the painful choices that we face?
5. How much of U.S. government debt is held by the rest of the world?

You can work these questions in Study Plan 13.3 and get instant feedback.

You now know how the supply-side effects of fiscal policy work and you've seen the shocking scale of fiscal imbalance. We conclude this chapter by looking at fiscal policy as a tool for fighting a recession.

Fiscal Stimulus

The 2008–2009 recession brought Keynesian macroeconomic ideas (see p. 256) back into fashion and put a spotlight on **fiscal stimulus**—the use of fiscal policy to increase production and employment. But whether fiscal policy is truly stimulating, and if so, how stimulating, are questions that generate much discussion and disagreement. You're now going to explore these questions.

Fiscal stimulus can be either *automatic* or *discretionary*. A fiscal policy action that is triggered by the state of the economy with no action by government is called **automatic fiscal policy**. The increase in total unemployment benefits triggered by the massive rise in the unemployment rate through 2009 is an example of automatic fiscal policy.

A fiscal policy action initiated by an act of Congress is called **discretionary fiscal policy**. It requires a change in a spending program or in a tax law. A fiscal stimulus act passed by Congress in 2009 (see *Economics in Action* on p. 336) is an example of discretionary fiscal policy.

Whether automatic or discretionary, an increase in government outlays or a decrease in government receipts can stimulate production and jobs. An increase in expenditure on goods and services directly increases aggregate expenditure. And an increase in transfer payments (such as unemployment benefits) or a decrease in tax revenues increases disposable income, which enables people to increase consumption expenditure. Lower taxes also strengthen the incentives to work and invest.

We'll begin by looking at automatic fiscal policy and the interaction between the business cycle and the budget balance.

Automatic Fiscal Policy and Cyclical and Structural Budget Balances

Two items in the government budget change automatically in response to the state of the economy. They are *tax revenues* and *needs-tested spending.*

Automatic Changes in Tax Revenues The tax laws that Congress enacts don't legislate the number of tax *dollars* the government will raise. Rather they define the tax *rates* that people must pay. Tax dollars paid depend on tax rates and incomes. But incomes vary with real GDP, so tax revenues depend on real GDP. When real GDP increases in a business cycle expansion, wages and profits rise, so tax revenues from these incomes rise. When real GDP decreases in a recession, wages and profits fall, so tax revenues fall.

Needs-Tested Spending The government creates programs that pay benefits to qualified people and businesses. The spending on these programs results in transfer payments that depend on the economic state of individual citizens and businesses. When the economy expands, unemployment falls, the number of people experiencing economic hardship decreases, so needs-tested spending decreases. When the economy is in a recession, unemployment is high and the number of people experiencing economic hardship increases, so needs-tested spending on unemployment benefits and food stamps increases.

Automatic Stimulus Because government receipts fall and outlays increase in a recession, the budget provides automatic stimulus that helps to shrink the recessionary gap. Similarly, because receipts rise and outlays decrease in a boom, the budget provides automatic restraint to shrink an inflationary gap.

Cyclical and Structural Budget Balances To identify the government budget deficit that arises from the business cycle, we distinguish between the **structural surplus or deficit**, which is the budget balance that would occur if the economy were at full employment, and the **cyclical surplus or deficit**, which is the actual surplus or deficit *minus* the structural surplus or deficit.

Figure 13.9 illustrates these concepts. Outlays *decrease* as real GDP *increases*, so the outlays curve slopes downward; and receipts *increase* as real GDP *increases*, so the receipts curve slopes upward.

In Fig. 13.9(a), potential GDP is $14 trillion and if real GDP equals potential GDP, the government has a *balanced budget*. There is no structural surplus or deficit. But there might be a cyclical surplus or deficit. If real GDP is less than potential GDP at $13 trillion, outlays exceed receipts and there is a *cyclical deficit*. If real GDP is greater than potential GDP at $15 trillion, outlays are less than receipts and there is a *cyclical surplus*.

In Fig. 13.9(b), if potential GDP equals $14 trillion (line *B*), the *structural balance is zero*. But if potential GDP is $13 trillion (line *A*), the government budget has a *structural deficit*. And if potential GDP is $15 trillion (line *C*), the government budget has a *structural surplus*.

FIGURE 13.9 Cyclical and Structural Surpluses and Deficits

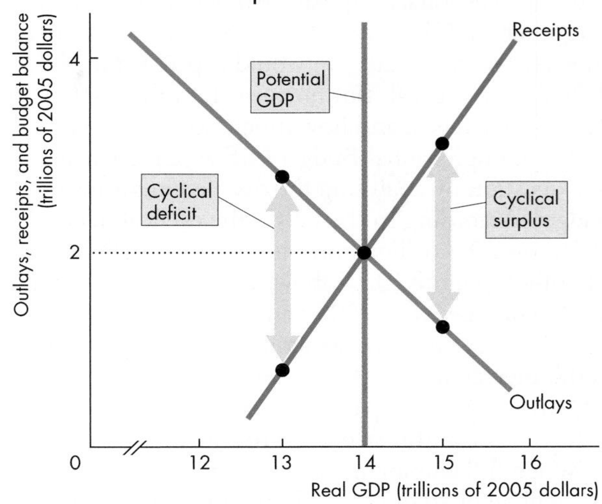

(a) Cyclical deficit and cyclical surplus

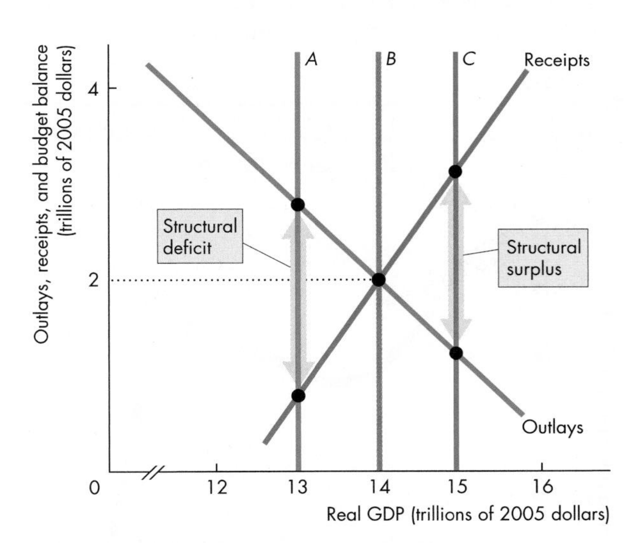

(b) Structural deficit and structural surplus

In part (a), potential GDP is $14 trillion. When real GDP is less than potential GDP, the budget is in a *cyclical deficit*. When real GDP exceeds potential GDP, the budget is in a *cyclical surplus*. The government has a *balanced budget* when real GDP equals potential GDP.

In part (b), if potential GDP is $13 trillion, there is a *structural deficit* and if potential GDP is $15 trillion, there is a *structural surplus*. If potential GDP is $14 trillion, the budget is in structural balance.

myeconlab animation

U.S. Structural Budget Balance in 2010 The U.S. federal budget in 2010 was in deficit at $1.4 trillion and the recessionary gap (the gap between real GDP and potential GDP) was close to $1 trillion. With a large recessionary gap, you would expect some of the deficit to be cyclical. But how much of the 2010 deficit was cyclical and how much was structural?

The Congressional Budget Office (CBO) answers this question by analyzing the detailed items in the budget. According to the CBO, the cyclical deficit in 2010 was $0.4 trillion and the structural deficit was $1 trillion. Figure 13.10 shows the cyclical and structural deficit between 2000 and 2010.

You can see that the structural deficit was small in 2007, increased in 2008, and exploded in 2009. The 2009 fiscal stimulus package (see *Economics in Action*) created most of this structural deficit.

When full employment returns, which the CBO says will be in 2014, the cyclical deficit will vanish. But the structural deficit must be addressed by further acts of Congress. No one knows the discretionary measures that will be taken to reduce the structural deficit and this awkward fact creates enormous uncertainty.

FIGURE 13.10 U.S. Cyclical and Structural Budget Balance

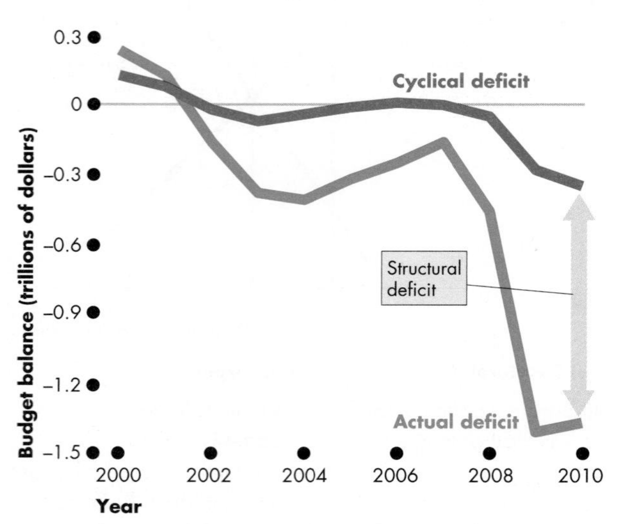

As real GDP shrank in the 2008–2009 recession, receipts fell, outlays increased, and the budget deficit increased. The cyclical deficit was small compared to the actual deficit; most of the 2010 deficit was structural.

Source of data: Congressional Budget Office.

myeconlab animation

Economics in Action

The 2009 Fiscal Stimulus Package

Congress passed the *American Recovery and Reinvestment Act of 2009* (the 2009 Fiscal Stimulus Act) in February 2009, and President Obama signed it into law at an economic forum he hosted in Denver. This act was the third and most ambitious in a series of stimulus packages and its purpose was to increase investment and consumer expenditure and lead to the creation of jobs.

The total package added $862 billion to the federal government's budget deficit: $288 billion from tax cuts and the rest from increased spending. The spending increases included payments to state and local governments ($144 billion), spending on infrastructure and science projects ($111 billion), programs in health care ($59 billion), education and training ($53 billion), and energy ($43 billion).

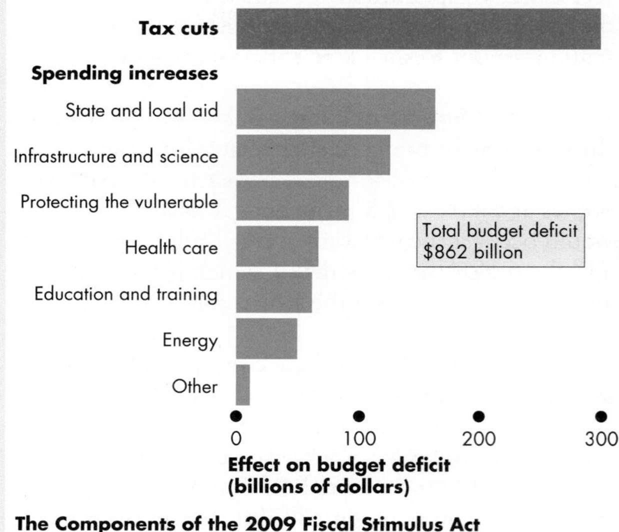

The Components of the 2009 Fiscal Stimulus Act

The president signs the 2009 fiscal stimulus act.

Discretionary Fiscal Stimulus

Most discussion of *discretionary* fiscal stimulus focuses on its effects on aggregate demand. But you've seen (on pp. 328–331) that taxes influence aggregate supply and that the balance of taxes and spending—the government budget deficit—can crowd out investment and slow the pace of economic growth. So discretionary fiscal stimulus has both supply-side and demand-side effects that end up determining its overall effectiveness.

We're going to begin our examination of discretionary fiscal stimulus by looking at its effects on aggregate demand.

Fiscal Stimulus and Aggregate Demand Changes in government expenditure and changes in taxes change aggregate demand by their influence on spending plans, and they also have multiplier effects.

Let's look at the two main fiscal policy multipliers: the government expenditure and tax multipliers.

The **government expenditure multiplier** is the quantitative effect of a change in government expenditure on real GDP. Because government expenditure is a component of aggregate expenditure, an increase in government spending increases aggregate expenditure and real GDP. But does a $1 billion increase in government expenditure increase real GDP by $1 billion, or more than $1 billion, or less than $1 billion?

When an increase in government expenditure increases real GDP, incomes rise and the higher incomes bring an increase in consumption expenditure. If this were the only consequence of increased government expenditure, the government expenditure multiplier would be greater than 1.

But an increase in government expenditure increases government borrowing (or decreases government lending if there is a budget surplus) and raises the real interest rate. With a higher cost of borrowing, investment decreases, which partly offsets the increase in government spending. If this were the only consequence of increased government expenditure, the multiplier would be less than 1.

The actual multiplier depends on which of the above effects is stronger and the consensus is that the crowding-out effect is strong enough to make the government expenditure multiplier less than 1.

The **tax multiplier** is the quantitative effect of a change in taxes on real GDP. The demand-side effects of a tax cut are likely to be smaller than an equivalent increase in government expenditure. The reason is that a tax cut influences aggregate demand by increasing disposable income, only part of which gets spent. So the initial injection of expenditure from a $1 billion tax cut is less than $1 billion.

A tax cut has similar crowding-out consequences to a spending increase. It increases government borrowing (or decreases government lending), raises the real interest rate, and cuts investment.

The tax multiplier effect on aggregate demand depends on these two opposing effects and is probably quite small.

Graphical Illustration of Fiscal Stimulus Figure 13.11 shows how fiscal stimulus is supposed to work if it is perfectly executed and has its desired effects.

Potential GDP is $14 trillion and real GDP is below potential at $13 trillion so the economy has a recessionary gap of $1 trillion.

To restore full employment, the government passes a fiscal stimulus package. An increase in

FIGURE 13.11 Expansionary Fiscal Policy

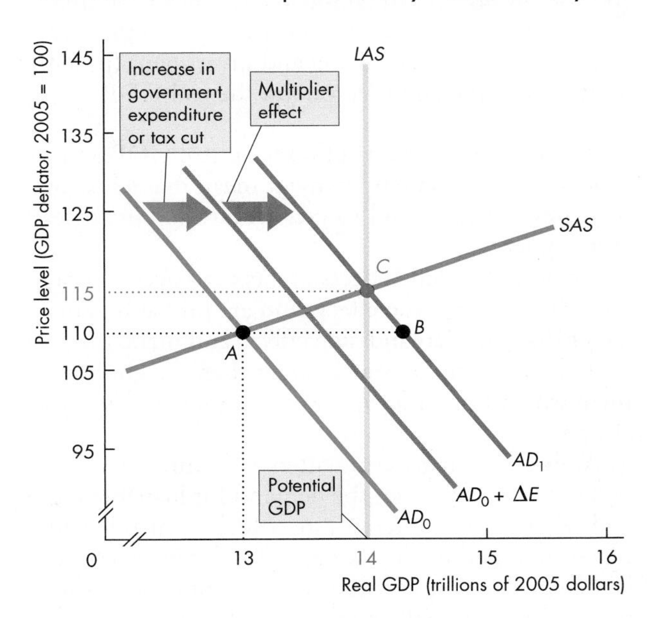

Potential GDP is $14 trillion, real GDP is $13 trillion, and there is a $1 trillion recessionary gap. An increase in government expenditure and a tax cut increase aggregate expenditure by ΔE. The multiplier increases consumption expenditure. The *AD* curve shifts rightward to AD_1, the price level rises to 115, real GDP increases to $14 trillion, and the recessionary gap is eliminated.

myeconlab animation

government expenditure and a tax cut increase aggregate expenditure by ΔE. If this were the only change in spending plans, the *AD* curve would shift rightward to become the curve labeled $AD_0 + \Delta E$ in Fig. 13.11. But if fiscal stimulus sets off a multiplier process that increases consumption expenditure, and does not crowd out much investment expenditure, aggregate demand increases further and the *AD* curve shifts to AD_1.

With no change in the price level, the economy would move from point *A* to point *B* on AD_1. But the increase in aggregate demand brings a rise in the price level along the upward-sloping *SAS* curve and the economy moves to point *C*.

At point *C*, the economy returns to full employment and the recessionary gap is eliminated.

Fiscal Stimulus and Aggregate Supply You've seen earlier in this chapter that taxes influence aggregate supply. A tax on labor income (on wages) drives a wedge between the cost of labor and the take-home pay of workers and lowers employment and output (p. 328). A tax on capital income (on interest) drives a wedge between the cost of borrowing and the return to lending and lowers saving and investment (p. 330). With less saving and investment, the real GDP growth rate slows.

These negative effects of taxes on real GDP and its growth rate and on employment mean that a tax *cut* increases real GDP and its growth rate and increases employment.

These supply-side effects of a tax cut occur along with the demand-side effects and are probably much larger than the demand-side effects and make the overall tax multiplier much larger than the government expenditure multiplier—see *Economics in Action.*

An increase in government expenditure financed by borrowing increases the demand for loanable funds and raises the real interest rate, which in turn lowers investment and private saving. This cut in investment is the main reason why the government expenditure multiplier is so small and why a deficit-financed increase in government spending ends up making only a small contribution to job creation. And because government expenditure crowds out investment, it lowers future real GDP.

So a fiscal stimulus package that is heavy on tax cuts and light on government spending works. But an increase in government expenditure alone is not an effective way to stimulate production and create jobs.

The description of the effects of discretionary fiscal stimulus and its graphical illustration in Fig. 13.11 make it look easy: Calculate the recessionary gap and the multipliers, change government expenditure and taxes, and eliminate the gap. In reality, things are not that easy.

Getting the magnitude and the timing right is difficult, and we'll now examine this challenge.

Magnitude of Stimulus Economists have diverging views about the size of the government spending and tax multipliers because there is insufficient empirical evidence on which to pin their size with accuracy. This fact makes it impossible for Congress to determine the amount of stimulus needed to close a given

Economics in Action

How Big Are the Fiscal Stimulus Multipliers?

When the 2009 fiscal stimulus package cut taxes by \$300 billion and increased government spending by almost \$500 billion, by how much did aggregate expenditure and real GDP change? How big were the fiscal policy multipliers? Was the government expenditure multiplier larger than the tax multiplier? These questions are about the multiplier effects on *equilibrium real GDP*, not just on aggregate demand.

President Obama's chief economic adviser in 2009, Christina Romer, a University of California, Berkeley, professor, expected the government expenditure multiplier to be about 1.5. So she was expecting the spending increase of \$500 billion to go a long way toward closing the \$1 trillion output gap by some time in 2010.

Robert Barro, a professor at Harvard University, says this multiplier number is not in line with previous experience. Based on his calculations, an additional \$500 billion of government spending would increase aggregate expenditure by only \$250 billion because it would lower private spending in a crowding-out effect by \$250 billion—the multiplier is 0.5.

Harald Uhlig, a professor at the University of Chicago, says that the government expenditure multiplier on real GDP is even smaller and lies between 0.3 and 0.4, so that a \$500 billion increase in government spending increases aggregate expenditure by between \$150 billion and \$200 billion.

output gap. Further, the actual output gap is not known and can only be estimated with error. For these two reasons, discretionary fiscal policy is risky.

Time Lags Discretionary fiscal stimulus actions are also seriously hampered by three time lags:

- Recognition lag
- Law-making lag
- Impact lag

Recognition Lag The recognition lag is the time it takes to figure out that fiscal policy actions are needed. This process involves assessing the current state of the economy and forecasting its future state.

Law-Making Lag The *law-making lag* is the time it takes Congress to pass the laws needed to change taxes or spending. This process takes time because each member of Congress has a different idea about what is the best tax or spending program to change, so long debates and committee meetings are needed to reconcile conflicting views. The economy might benefit from fiscal stimulation today, but by the time Congress acts, a different fiscal medicine might be needed.

Impact Lag The *impact lag* is the time it takes from passing a tax or spending change to its effects on real GDP being felt. This lag depends partly on the speed with which government agencies can act and partly on the timing of changes in spending plans by households and businesses. These changes are spread out over a number of quarters and possibly a number of years.

Economic forecasting is steadily improving, but it remains inexact and subject to error. The range of uncertainty about the magnitudes of the spending and tax mulitpliers make discretionary fiscal stimulus an imprecise tool for boosting production and jobs and the crowding out consequences raise serious questions about its effects on long-term economic growth.

There is greater agreement about tax multipliers. Because tax cuts strengthen the incentive to work and to invest, they increase aggregate supply as well as aggregate demand.

These multipliers get bigger as more time elapses. Harald Uhlig says that after one year, the tax multiplier is 0.5 so that the $300 billion tax cut would increase real GDP by about $150 billion by early 2010. But with two years of time to respond, real GDP would be $600 billion higher—a multiplier of 2. And after three years, the tax multiplier builds up to more than 6.

The implications of the work of Barro and Uhlig are that tax cuts are a powerful way to stimulate real GDP and employment but spending increases are not effective.

Christina Romer agrees that the economy hasn't performed in line with a multiplier of 1.5 but says other factors deteriorated and without the fiscal stimulus, the outcome would have been even worse.

Christina Romer: 1.5

Robert Barro: 0.5

Harald Uhlig: 0.4

REVIEW QUIZ

1. What is the distinction between automatic and discretionary fiscal policy?
2. How do taxes and needs-tested spending programs work as automatic fiscal policy to dampen the business cycle?
3. How do we tell whether a budget deficit needs discretionary action to remove it?
4. How can the federal government use discretionary fiscal policy to stimulate the economy?
5. Why might fiscal stimulus crowd out investment?

You can work these questions in Study Plan 13.4 and get instant feedback.

◆ You've now seen the effects of fiscal policy, and *Reading Between the Lines* on pp. 340–341 applies what you've learned to U.S. fiscal policy.

Obama Fiscal Policy

Republicans' Two-Point Plan to Create Jobs: Can It Work?

http://www.csmonitor.com
September 21, 2010

Republicans in Congress are urging two simple steps they say will help put Americans back to work: Freeze all tax rates at current levels and reduce federal spending. ... Cut government spending when the private sector is in slow gear? That's not what the textbooks typically offer as a way to rev up growth. ... So how viable is that "two-point plan," espoused recently by House Republican leader John Boehner? Would it work?

Economists are divided on these questions, but fairly broad agreement exists on a few points. One is that it would be beneficial to provide clarity on tax rates—which the first part of the Republican plan seeks to achieve and critics say President Obama has failed to do. Another is that spending cuts hold less promise than tax-rate policy as a lever for job creation.

Supporters and critics of these GOP proposals concur on one more thing: Voters shouldn't expect a quick fix. Good policies can help the job market heal faster, but the process will still take several years, forecasters predict. ...

Spending cuts could help signal that Washington policymakers are starting to get serious about tackling America's long-term fiscal challenge—a persistent gap between federal spending and revenues. ...

The case for spending cuts is partly an expression of doubt about the effectiveness of traditional stimulus via deficit spending. Researchers, including Harvard University's Robert Barro, have published studies suggesting that increased spending serves mainly to shift money around within the economy, while doing relatively little to expand the gross domestic product. ...

Foes of spending cuts say the move would harm a still-fragile economy that remains at risk of falling back into recession. When the economy is weak, economists in this camp argue, government spending acts to fuel demand for goods and services, rather than "crowding out" private-sector activity. ...

By Mark Trumball. Reproduced with permission from the September 21, 2010 issue of the Christian Science Monitor (www.CSMonitor.com).

ESSENCE OF THE STORY

- Republicans in Congress say freezing all tax rates at current levels and cutting government spending will help put Americans back to work.
- Economists are divided on whether the plan would work.
- Economists agree that clarity on tax rates would be beneficial, that tax policy holds more promise than spending, and that there is no quick fix.
- Republicans say spending cuts signal that policymakers are serious about tackling the long-term fiscal deficit.
- Research by Robert Barro and others suggests that increased spending does little to expand GDP.
- Others say government spending does not crowd out private spending and cuts in government spending would create a risk of a fall back into recession.

ECONOMIC ANALYSIS

- The policies proposed in the news article are designed to tackle a daunting problem.
- In mid-2010, after more than $800 billion of fiscal stimulus, the U.S. economy remained in a deep and stubborn recessionary gap.
- Cyclical unemployment—the excess of unemployment above the natural unemployment rate—was running at about 8 million workers.
- The output gap—the shortfall of real GDP below potential GDP—was $1 trillion.
- Figure 1 illustrates the situation in the labor market. The demand for labor is *LD* and the supply of labor is *LS*. The real wage rate is $25 per hour (an assumed level) and at the market real wage rate, 139 million workers are demanded but 147 million are supplied, so 8 million are unemployed.
- A very large increase in the demand for labor is needed to shift the demand for labor curve to *LD** and restore full employment.
- Figure 2 illustrates the situation in the market for real GDP. The aggregate demand curve is *AD* and the short-run aggregate supply curve is *SAS*. Equilibrium real GDP is $13 trillion and the price level is 115. Potential GDP, and long-run aggregate supply (*LAS*), is $14 trillion so the recessionary gap is $1 trillion.
- A very large fiscal stimulus is needed to shift the aggregate demand curve to *AD** to close the recessionary gap.
- Which components of aggregate demand are the source of the problem? What type of expenditure needs to be stimulated?
- The answer is investment. Consumption, government expenditure, and net exports were all greater both in dollars and as a percentage of real GDP than they had been at full employment in 2006.
- But investment was lower by $400 billion and had slipped from 17.2 percent of GDP to 13.6 percent.
- The proposed fiscal stimulus policy must be judged by its likely effect on investment.
- Two influences on investment need to be considered: the real interest rate, which is the opportunity cost of the funds used to finance investment, and the expected future return from investment including the degree of uncertainty about that future return.
- More government spending has an adverse effect on both of these influences on investment.

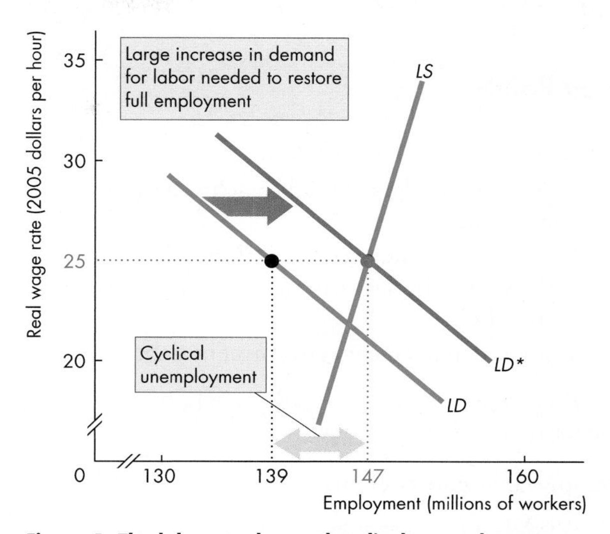

Figure 1 The labor market and cyclical unemployment

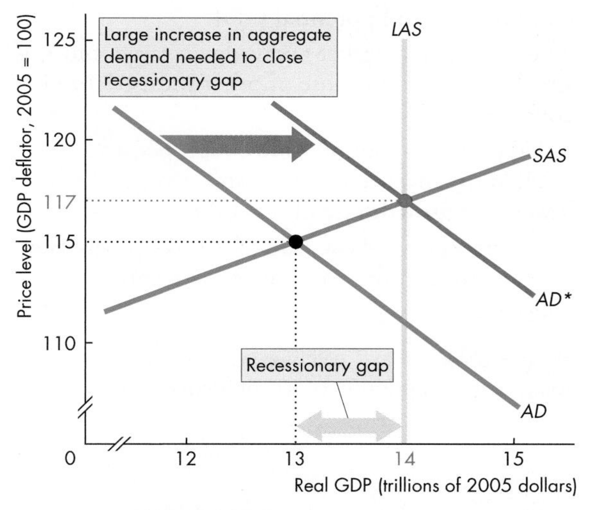

Figure 2 Aggregate supply and aggregate demand in 2010

- A larger budget deficit puts upward pressure on the real interest rate and crowds out some investment.
- A larger budget deficit also brings uncertainty about what future tax and expenditure changes will be made to eventually bring the deficit under control.

SUMMARY

Key Points

The Federal Budget (pp. 322–327)

- The federal budget is used to achieve macroeconomic objectives.
- Tax revenues can exceed, equal, or fall short of outlays—the budget can be in surplus, balanced, or in deficit.
- Budget deficits create government debt.

Working Problems 1 to 3 will give you a better understanding of the federal budget.

Supply-Side Effects of Fiscal Policy (pp. 328–331)

- Fiscal policy has supply-side effects because taxes weaken the incentive to work and decrease employment and potential GDP.
- The U.S. labor market tax wedge is large, but it is small compared to those of other industrialized countries.
- Fiscal policy has supply-side effects because taxes weaken the incentive to save and invest, which lowers the growth rate of real GDP.
- The Laffer curve shows the relationship between the tax rate and the amount of tax revenue collected.

Working Problems 4 to 7 will give you a better understanding of the supply-side effects of fiscal policy.

Generational Effects of Fiscal Policy (pp. 332–334)

- Generational accounting measures the lifetime tax burden and benefits of each generation.
- A major study estimated the U.S. fiscal imbalance to be $79 trillion—5.8 times the value of one year's production.
- Future generations will pay for 57 percent of the benefits of the current generation.
- About two thirds of U.S. government debt is held by the rest of the world.

Working Problems 8 and 9 will give you a better understanding of the generational effects of fiscal policy.

Fiscal Stimulus (pp. 334–339)

- Fiscal policy can be automatic or discretionary.
- Automatic fiscal policy might moderate the business cycle by stimulating demand in recession and restraining demand in a boom.
- Discretionary fiscal stimulus influences aggregate demand *and* aggregate supply.
- Discretionary changes in government expenditure or taxes have multiplier effects of uncertain magnitude but the tax multiplier is likely the larger one.
- Fiscal stimulus policies are hampered by uncertainty about the multipliers and by time lags (law-making lags and the difficulty of correctly diagnosing and forecasting the state of the economy).

Working Problems 10 to 21 will give you a better understanding of fiscal stimulus.

Key Terms

Automatic fiscal policy, 334
Balanced budget, 324
Budget deficit, 324
Budget surplus, 324
Council of Economic Advisers, 323
Cyclical surplus or deficit, 335
Discretionary fiscal policy, 334
Employment Act of 1946, 322
Federal budget, 322
Fiscal imbalance, 332
Fiscal policy, 322
Fiscal stimulus, 334
Generational accounting, 332
Generational imbalance, 333
Government debt, 326
Government expenditure multiplier, 337
Laffer curve, 331
Present value, 332
Structural surplus or deficit, 335
Tax multiplier, 337
Tax wedge, 329

STUDY PLAN PROBLEMS AND APPLICATIONS

myeconlab You can work Problems 1 to 21 in MyEconLab Chapter 13 Study Plan and get instant feedback.

The Federal Budget (Study Plan 13.1)

Use the following news clip to work Problems 1 and 2.

Economy Needs Treatment

It's the debt, stupid! Only when the government sets out a credible business plan will confidence and hiring rebound.

Source: *The Wall Street Journal*, October 7, 2010

1. How has the U.S. government debt changed since 2006? What are the sources of the change in U.S. government debt?
2. What would be a "credible business plan" for the government to adopt?
3. At the end of 2008, the government of China's debt was ¥4,700 billion. (¥ is yuan, the currency of China). In 2009, the government spent ¥6,000 billion and ended the year with a debt of ¥5,300 billion. How much did the government receive in tax revenue in 2009? How can you tell?

Supply-Side Effects of Fiscal Policy (Study Plan 13.2)

4. The government is considering raising the tax rate on labor income and asks you to report on the supply-side effects of such an action. Answer the following questions using appropriate graphs. You are being asked about *directions* of change, not exact magnitudes. What will happen to
   a. The supply of labor and why?
   b. The demand for labor and why?
   c. The equilibrium level of employment and why?
   d. The equilibrium before-tax wage rate and why?
   e. The equilibrium after-tax wage rate and why?
   f. Potential GDP?
5. What fiscal policy action might increase investment and speed economic growth? Explain how the policy action would work.
6. Suppose that instead of taxing *nominal* capital income, the government taxed *real* capital income. Use appropriate graphs to explain and illustrate the effect that this change would have on
   a. The tax rate on capital income.
   b. The supply of and demand for loanable funds.
   c. Investment and the real interest rate.
7. **What Obama Means for Business**

   The core of Obama's economic plan is (a) more government spending: $65 billion a year for universal health insurance, $15 billion a year on alternative energy, $20 billion to help homeowners, $60 billion to bolster the nation's infrastructure, $10 billion annually to give students college tuition in exchange for public service, and on and on; and (b) ending the Bush tax cuts on families making more than $250,000 and raising payroll taxes on those same higher-income earners. He would increase the 15 percent capital gains tax rate—probably to 25 percent—raise the tax on dividends, and close $1.3 trillion in "corporate tax loopholes."

   Source: *Fortune*, June 23, 2008

   Explain the potential supply-side effects of the various components of Obama's economic plan. How might these policies change potential GDP and its growth rate?

Generational Effects of Fiscal Policy (Study Plan 13.3)

8. The Congressional Budget Office projects that, under current policies, U.S. public debt will reach 233 percent of GDP in 30 years and nearly 500 percent in 50 years.
   a. What is a fiscal imbalance? How might the U.S. government reduce the fiscal imbalance?
   b. How would your answer to part (a) influence the generational imbalance?
9. **Increase in Payroll Taxes Needed for Social Security**

   Social Security faces a $5.3 trillion shortfall over the next 75 years, but a congressional report says the massive gap could be erased by increasing payroll taxes paid by both employees and employers from 6.2 percent to 7.3 percent and by raising the retirement age to 70.

   Source: *USA Today*, May 21, 2010

   a. Why is Social Security facing a $5.3 trillion shortfall over the next 75 years?
   b. Explain how the suggestions in the news clip would reduce the shortfall.
   c. Would the suggestions in the news clip change the generational imbalance?

Fiscal Stimulus (Study Plan 13.4)

10. The economy is in a recession, and the recessionary gap is large.
    a. Describe the discretionary and automatic fiscal policy actions that might occur.
    b. Describe a discretionary fiscal stimulus package that could be used that would *not* bring an increase in the budget deficit.
    c. Explain the risks of discretionary fiscal policy in this situation.

Use the following news clip to work Problems 11 to 13.

Obama's Economic Recovery Plan

If the president is serious about focusing on jobs, a good start would be to freeze all tax rates and cut federal spending back to where it was before all the recent bailouts and stimulus spending.

Source: *USA Today*, September 9, 2010

11. What would be the effect on the budget deficit and real GDP of freezing tax rates and cutting government spending?
12. What would be the effect on jobs of freezing tax rates and cutting government spending?
13. If the government froze its current spending and instead cut taxes, what would be the effect on investment and jobs?
14. The economy is in a recession, the recessionary gap is large, and there is a budget deficit.
    a. Do we know whether the budget deficit is structural or cyclical? Explain your answer.
    b. Do we know whether automatic fiscal policy is increasing or decreasing the output gap? Explain your answer.
    c. If a discretionary increase in government expenditure occurs, what happens to the structural deficit or surplus? Explain.
15. **Comprehensive Tax Code Overhaul Is Overdue**

    Some right-wingers in Congress claim that tax cuts pay for themselves. Despite their insistence, there is ample evidence and general expert agreement that they do not.

    Source: *The Washington Post*, April 24, 2006

    a. Explain what is meant by tax cuts paying for themselves. What does this statement imply about the tax multiplier?
    b. Why would tax cuts not pay for themselves?

Use the following news clip to work Problems 16 and 17.

Summers Calls for Infrastructure Spending

Larry Summers, the outgoing director of the White House National Economic Council, said the United States must ramp up spending on domestic infrastructure to drive the economic recovery. He said that a combination of low borrowing costs, cheap building costs, and high unemployment in the construction industry make this the ideal time to rebuild roads, bridges, and airports.

Source: Ft.com, October 7, 2010

16. Is this infrastructure spending a fiscal stimulus? Would such spending be a discretionary or an automatic fiscal policy?
17. Explain how the rebuilding of roads, bridges, and airports would drive the economic recovery.

Use the following news clip to work Problems 18 to 20.

Stimulus Debate Turns on Rebates

As pressure built up on Washington to juice the economy, a one-time consumer rebate emerged as the likely centerpiece of a $150-billion stimulus program. But who should actually get rebates? Everyone who pays income taxes? Or only lower- and middle-income households because they are more likely to spend more of their rebate than are higher-income households, spend it quickly, and every dollar spent on stimulus could generate a dollar in GDP?

Source: *CNN*, January 22, 2008

18. a. Explain the intended effect of the $150 billion fiscal stimulus package. Draw a graph to illustrate the effect.
    b. Explain why the effect of this fiscal policy depends on who receives the tax rebates.
19. What would have a larger effect on aggregate demand: $150 billion worth of tax rebates or $150 billion worth of government spending?
20. Explain whether a stimulus package centered around a one-time consumer tax rebate is likely to have a small or a large supply-side effect.
21. Compare the impact on equilibrium real GDP of a same-sized decrease in taxes and increase in government expenditure.

ADDITIONAL PROBLEMS AND APPLICATIONS

myeconlab You can work these problems in MyEconLab if assigned by your instructor.

The Federal Budget

22. **U.S. Budget Deficit to Hit $1.3 trillion**

    The Congressional Budget Office said this year's budget gap would be $71 billion less than last year's. The U.S. budget deficit of $1.3 trillion makes it the second largest deficit ever in dollars, trailing only last year's $1.4 trillion. To put those numbers in perspective, the shortfalls for 2009 and 2010 are each three times as big as the government's annual deficit had ever been previously.

    Source: *The Associated Press*, August 19, 2010

    Of the components of government outlays and receipts, which have changed most to contribute to these huge budget gaps in 2009 and 2010?

Supply-Side Effects of Fiscal Policy

Use the following information to work Problems 23 and 24.

Suppose that in the United States, investment is $1,600 billion, saving is $1,400 billion, government expenditure on goods and services is $1,500 billion, exports are $2,000 billion, and imports are $2,500 billion.

23. What is the amount of tax revenue? What is the government budget balance?
24. a. Is the government's budget exerting a positive or negative impact on investment?
    b. What fiscal policy action might increase investment and speed economic growth? Explain how the policy action would work.
25. Suppose that capital income taxes are based (as they are in the United States and most countries) on nominal interest rates. And suppose that the inflation rate increases by 5 percent. Use appropriate diagrams to explain and illustrate the effect that this change would have on
    a. The tax rate on capital income.
    b. The supply of loanable funds.
    c. The demand for loanable funds.
    d. Equilibrium investment.
    e. The equilibrium real interest rate.

Use the following information to work Problems 26 and 27.

Obama: Give Economy $50 Billion Boost

Barack Obama said that lawmakers should inject another $50 billion immediately into the sluggish U.S. economy. "Such relief can't wait until the next president takes office." Obama supports the expansion and extension of unemployment benefits and calls for an additional 13 weeks of benefits to be added to what is typically a 26-week cap on federal payments. At the same time, Obama criticized John McCain for proposing to extend all of President Bush's 2001 and 2003 tax cuts.

Source: CNN, June 9, 2008

26. a. Explain the potential demand-side effect of extending unemployment benefits.
    b. Explain the potential supply-side effect of extending unemployment benefits.
    c. Draw a graph to illustrate the combined demand-side and supply-side effect of extending unemployment benefits.
27. Compare the supply-side effect of Obama's proposal to extend unemployment benefits with McCain's policy to extend Bush's 2001 and 2003 tax cuts.

Use the following news clip to work Problems 28 and 29.

John McCain's Tax Policy

McCain wants to make the Bush tax cuts permanent; then cut taxes further. He would slash the corporate tax, double the child-care tax credit, and allow businesses to write off the full cost of capital investments in one year. Despite these cuts, McCain insists that he can balance the budget within four years with promised savings from running a tighter ship and increased tax revenues as the economy expands.

Source: *Fortune*, July 7, 2008

28. Explain the potential supply-side effects of the various components of McCain's economic plan.
29. Where on the Laffer curve do you think McCain believes the U.S. economy lies? Explain your answer.

Generational Effects of Fiscal Policy

30. **Push to Cut Deficit Collides With Politics as Usual**

    So it goes in Campaign 2010, where cutting the deficit is a big issue, but where support for doing some of the hard things to achieve that is running into politics as usual. Nowhere is that more apparent than in the debate—or lack thereof—on the nation's spending on big entitlement programs. According to the latest projections from the Congressional Budget Office, spending on the big three entitlement programs—Social Security, Medicare, and Medicaid—is to rise by 70 percent, 79 percent, and 99 percent, respectively, over the next 10 years.

Source: *The Wall Street Journal*, October 5, 2010

If politicians continue to avoid debating the projected increases in these three entitlement programs, how do you think the fiscal imbalance will change? If Congress holds the budget deficit at $3.1 trillion, who will pay for the projected increases in expenditure?

Fiscal Stimulus

31. The economy is in a boom and the inflationary gap is large.
    a. Describe the discretionary and automatic fiscal policy actions that might occur.
    b. Describe a discretionary fiscal restraint package that could be used that would not produce serious negative supply-side effects.
    c. Explain the risks of discretionary fiscal policy in this situation.
32. The economy is growing slowly, the inflationary gap is large, and there is a budget deficit.
    a. Do we know whether the budget deficit is structural or cyclical? Explain your answer.
    b. Do we know whether automatic stabilizers are increasing or decreasing aggregate demand? Explain your answer.
    c. If a discretionary decrease in government expenditure occurs, what happens to the structural budget balance? Explain your answer.

Use the following news clip to work Problems 33 to 35.

Juicing the Economy Will Come at a Cost

The $150-billion stimulus plan will bump up the deficit, but not necessarily dollar for dollar. Here's why: If the stimulus works, the increased economic activity will generate federal tax revenue. But it isn't clear what the cost to the economy will be if a stimulus package comes too late—a real concern since legislation could get bogged down by politics.

Source: CNN, January 23, 2008

33. Explain why $150 billion of stimulus won't increase the budget deficit by $150 billion.
34. Is the budget deficit arising from the action described in the news clip structural or cyclical or a combination of the two? Explain.
35. Why might the stimulus package come "too late?" What are the potential consequences of the stimulus package coming "too late?"

Economics in the News

36. After you have studied *Reading Between the Lines* on pp. 340–341 answer the following questions.
    a. What were the key proposals of Republicans in Congress for restoring the U.S. economy to full employment. Describe them.
    b. Explain why holding the line on taxes and cutting government spending might be more effective than increasing government spending. Draw a graph to illustrate your answer.
    c. Explain why an increase in government expenditure could be counterproductive in the economic climate of 2010 and 2011. Draw a graph to illustrate your answer.
37. **U.S. Financial Crisis Over? Not Really**

    Economist Deepak Lal says the U.S. financial crisis is not solved and contains the seeds of a more serious future crisis. For India and China, with no structural deficit, a temporary budget deficit above that resulting from automatic fiscal policy makes sense. But it doesn't make sense for the United States with its large structural deficit.

    Source: rediff.com, October 18, 2010

    More Fiscal Stimulus Needed

    Economist Laura Tyson says there is a strong argument for more fiscal stimulus combined with a multi-year deficit reduction plan.

    Source: marketwatch.com, October 15, 2010

    a. How has the business cycle influenced the U.S. federal budget in the 2008–2009 recession?
    b. With which news clip opinion do you agree and why?
    c. Why might Laura Tyson favor a multi-year deficit reduction plan and would that address the concerns of Deepak Lal?

After studying this chapter, you will be able to:

- Describe the objectives of U.S. monetary policy and the framework for setting and achieving them
- Explain how the Federal Reserve makes its interest rate decision and achieves its interest rate target
- Explain the transmission channels through which the Federal Reserve influences real GDP, jobs, and inflation
- Explain the Fed's extraordinary policy actions

14 MONETARY POLICY

At eight regularly scheduled meetings a year, and in an emergency between regular meetings, the Federal Reserve decides whether to change its interest rate target. And every business day, the Federal Reserve Bank of New York operates in financial markets to implement the Fed's decision and ensure that its target interest rate is achieved. Financial market traders, journalists, and pundits watch the economy for clues about what the Fed will decide at its next meeting.

How does the Fed make its interest rate decision? Can the Fed speed up economic growth and lower unemployment by lowering the interest rate and keep inflation in check by raising the interest rate?

What special measures can the Fed take in a financial crisis like the one that engulfed the U.S. and global economies in 2008?

This chapter combines what you learned about the functions of the Fed in Chapter 8 and about aggregate demand and aggregate supply in Chapter 10. You will learn how the Fed influences the interest rate and how the interest rate influences the economy. You will also review the extraordinary challenge faced by the Fed today. In *Reading Between the Lines* at the end of the chapter, you will see the Fed's dilemma in the face of stubborn recession and massive monetary stimulus.

Monetary Policy Objectives and Framework

A nation's monetary policy objectives and the framework for setting and achieving those objectives stem from the relationship between the central bank and the government.

We'll describe the objectives of U.S. monetary policy and the framework and assignment of responsibility for achieving those objectives.

Monetary Policy Objectives

The objectives of U.S. monetary policy are set out in the mandate of the Board of Governors of the Federal Reserve System, which is defined by the Federal Reserve Act of 1913 and its subsequent amendments, the most recent of which was passed in 2000.

Federal Reserve Act The Fed's mandate was most recently clarified in amendments to the Federal Reserve Act passed by Congress in 2000. The 2000 law states that mandate in the following words:

> The Board of Governors of the Federal Reserve System and the Federal Open Market Committee shall maintain long-run growth of the monetary and credit aggregates commensurate with the economy's long-run potential to increase production, so as to promote effectively the goals of maximum employment, stable prices, and moderate long-term interest rates.

Goals and Means This description of the Fed's monetary policy objectives has two distinct parts: a statement of the goals, or ultimate objectives, and a prescription of the means by which the Fed should pursue its goals.

Goals of Monetary Policy The goals are "maximum employment, stable prices, and moderate long-term interest rates." In the long run, these goals are in harmony and reinforce each other. But in the short run, these goals might come into conflict. Let's examine these goals a bit more closely.

Achieving the goal of "maximum employment" means attaining the maximum sustainable growth rate of potential GDP and keeping real GDP close to potential GDP. It also means keeping the unemployment rate close to the natural unemployment rate.

Achieving the goal of "stable prices" means keeping the inflation rate low (and perhaps close to zero).

Achieving the goal of "moderate long-term interest rates" means keeping long-term *nominal* interest rates close to (or even equal to) long-term *real* interest rates.

Price stability is the key goal. It is the source of maximum employment and moderate long-term interest rates. Price stability provides the best available environment for households and firms to make the saving and investment decisions that bring economic growth. So price stability encourages the maximum sustainable growth rate of potential GDP.

Price stability delivers moderate long-term interest rates because the nominal interest rate reflects the inflation rate. The nominal interest rate equals the real interest rate plus the inflation rate. With stable prices, the nominal interest rate is close to the real interest rate, and most of the time, this rate is likely to be moderate.

In the short run, the Fed faces a tradeoff between inflation and interest rates and between inflation and real GDP, employment, and unemployment. Taking an action that is designed to lower the inflation rate and achieve stable prices might mean raising interest rates, which lowers employment and real GDP and increases the unemployment rate in the short run.

Means for Achieving the Goals The 2000 law instructs the Fed to pursue its goals by "maintain[ing] long-run growth of the monetary and credit aggregates commensurate with the economy's long-run potential to increase production." You perhaps recognize this statement as being consistent with the quantity theory of money that you studied in Chapter 8 (see pp. 200–201). The "economy's long-run potential to increase production" is the growth rate of potential GDP. The "monetary and credit aggregates" are the quantities of money and loans. By keeping the growth rate of the quantity of money in line with the growth rate of potential GDP, the Fed is expected to be able to maintain full employment and keep the price level stable.

To pursue the goals of monetary policy, the Fed must make the general concepts of price stability and maximum employment precise and operational.

Operational "Stable Prices" Goal

The Fed pays attention to two measures of inflation: the Consumer Price Index (CPI) and the personal consumption expenditure (PCE) deflator. But the *core PCE deflator,* which excludes food and fuel prices, is the Fed's operational guide and the Fed defines the rate of increase in the core PCE deflator as the **core inflation rate.**

The Fed focuses on the core inflation rate because it is less volatile than the total CPI inflation rate and the Fed believes that it provides a better indication of whether price stability is being achieved.

Figure 14.1 shows the core inflation rate alongside the total CPI inflation rate since 2000. You can see why the Fed says that the core inflation rate is a better indicator. Its fluctuations are smoother and represent a sort of trend through the wider fluctuations in total CPI inflation.

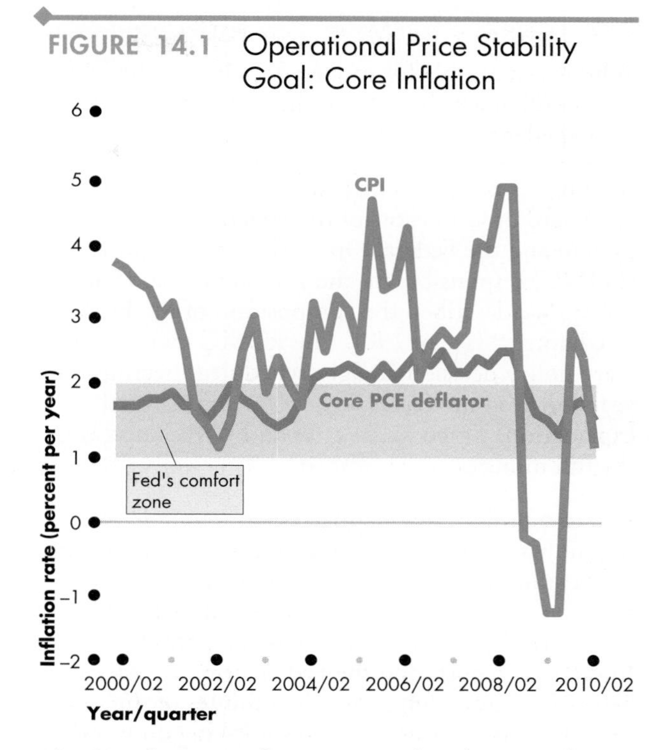

The CPI inflation rate fluctuates more than the core inflation rate. The core inflation rate was inside the Fed's comfort zone between 2000 and 2004 and after 2008 but above the comfort zone upper limit between 2004 and 2008.

Sources of data: Bureau of Labor Statistics and Bureau of Economic Analysis.

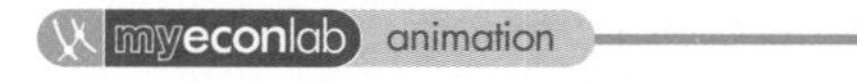

The Fed has not defined price stability, but it almost certainly doesn't regard price stability as meaning a core inflation rate equal to zero. Former Fed Chairman Alan Greenspan suggests that "price stability is best thought of as an environment in which inflation is so low and stable over time that it does not materially enter into the decisions of households and firms." He also believes that a "specific numerical inflation target would represent an unhelpful and false precision."[1]

Ben Bernanke, Alan Greenspan's successor, has been more precise and suggested that a core inflation rate of between 1 and 2 percent a year is the equivalent of price stability. This inflation range might be thought of as the Fed's "comfort zone" for the inflation rate.

Operational "Maximum Employment" Goal

The Fed regards stable prices (a core inflation rate of 1 to 2 percent a year) as the primary goal of monetary policy and as a means to achieving the other two goals. But the Fed also pays attention to the business cycle and tries to steer a steady course between inflation and recession. To gauge the state of output and employment relative to full employment, the Fed looks at a large number of indicators that include the labor force participation rate, the unemployment rate, measures of capacity utilization, activity in the housing market, the stock market, and regional information gathered by the regional Federal Reserve Banks. All these data that describe the current state of the economy are summarized in the Fed's **Beige Book.**

While the Fed considers a vast range of data, one number stands out as a summary of the overall state of aggregate demand relative to potential GDP. That number is the *output gap*—the percentage deviation of real GDP from potential GDP.

When the output gap is positive, it is an inflationary gap that brings an increase in the inflation rate. And when the output gap is negative, it is a recessionary gap that results in lost output and in employment being below its full-employment equilibrium level. So the Fed tries to minimize the output gap.

[1] Alan Greenspan, "Transparency in Monetary Policy," *Federal Reserve of St. Louis Review,* 84(4), 5–6, July/August 2002.

Responsibility for Monetary Policy

Who is responsible for monetary policy in the United States? What are the roles of the Fed, Congress, and the president?

The Role of the Fed The Federal Reserve Act makes the Board of Governors of the Federal Reserve System and the Federal Open Market Committee (FOMC) responsible for the conduct of monetary policy. We described the composition of the FOMC in Chapter 8 (see p. 190). The FOMC makes a monetary policy decision at eight scheduled meetings each year and communicates its decision with a brief explanation. Three weeks after an FOMC meeting, the full minutes are published.

The Role of Congress Congress plays no role in making monetary policy decisions but the Federal Reserve Act requires the Board of Governors to report on monetary policy to Congress. The Fed makes two reports each year, one in February and another in July. These reports and the Fed chairman's testimony before Congress along with the minutes of the FOMC communicate the Fed's thinking on monetary policy to lawmakers and the public.

The Role of the President The formal role of the president of the United States is limited to appointing the members and the chairman of the Board of Governors. But some presidents—Richard Nixon was one—have tried to influence Fed decisions.

You now know the objectives of monetary policy and can describe the framework and assignment of responsibility for achieving those objectives. Your next task is to see how the Federal Reserve conducts its monetary policy.

REVIEW QUIZ

1. What are the objectives of monetary policy?
2. Are the goals of monetary policy in harmony or in conflict (a) in the long run and (b) in the short run?
3. What is the core inflation rate and how does it differ from the overall CPI inflation rate?
4. Who is responsible for U.S. monetary policy?

You can work these questions in Study Plan 14.1 and get instant feedback.

The Conduct of Monetary Policy

How does the Fed conduct its monetary policy? This question has two parts:

- What is the monetary policy instrument?
- How does the Fed make its policy decisions?

The Monetary Policy Instrument

A **monetary policy instrument** is a variable that the Fed can directly control or at least very closely target. The Fed has two possible instruments: the monetary base or the interest rate at which banks borrow and lend monetary base overnight.

The Fed's choice of monetary policy instrument is the interest rate at which the banks make overnight loans to each other. The market in which the banks borrow and lend overnight is called the *federal funds market* and the interest rate in that market is called the **federal funds rate.**

Figure 14.2 shows the federal funds rate since 2000. You can see that the federal funds rate ranges between a high of 6.5 percent a year and a low of 0.2 percent a year. In 2000 and 2006, when the federal funds rate was high, the Fed's actions were aimed at lowering the inflation rate.

Between 2002 and 2004 and again in and since 2008, the federal funds rate was set at historically low levels. During these years, inflation was well anchored at close to or below 2 percent a year, and the Fed was less concerned about inflation than it was about recession and high unemployment. So the Fed set a low interest rate to fight recession.

Although the Fed can change the federal funds rate by any (reasonable) amount that it chooses, it normally changes the federal funds rate by only a quarter of a percentage point.[2]

Having decided the appropriate level for the federal funds rate, how does the Fed move the rate to its target level? The answer is by using open-market operations (see pp. 191–193) to adjust the quantity of monetary base.

To see how an open market operation changes the federal funds rate, we need to examine the federal funds market and the market for bank reserves.

In the federal funds market, the higher the federal funds rate, the greater is the quantity of overnight

[2] A quarter of a percentage point is also called 25 *basis points*. A basis point is one hundredth of one percentage point.

FIGURE 14.2 The Federal Funds Rate

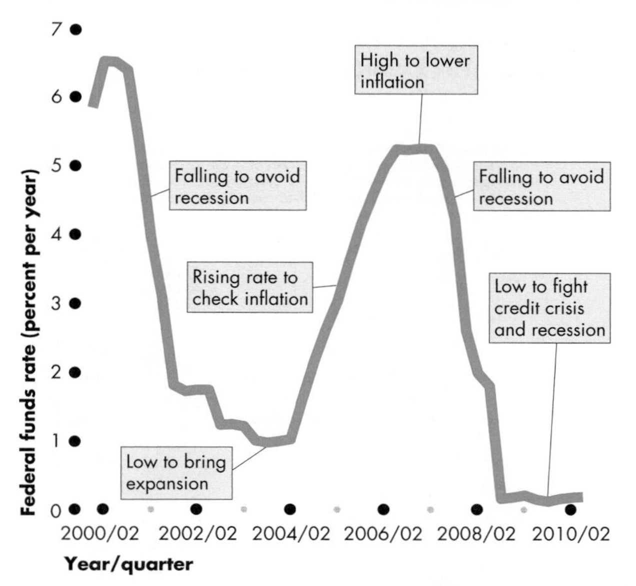

The Fed sets a target for the federal funds rate and then takes actions to keep the rate close to its target. When the Fed wants to slow inflation, it takes actions that raise the federal funds rate. When inflation is low and the Fed wants to avoid recession, it takes actions that lower the federal funds rate.

Source of data: Board of Governors of the Federal Reserve System.

myeconlab animation

FIGURE 14.3 The Market for Reserves

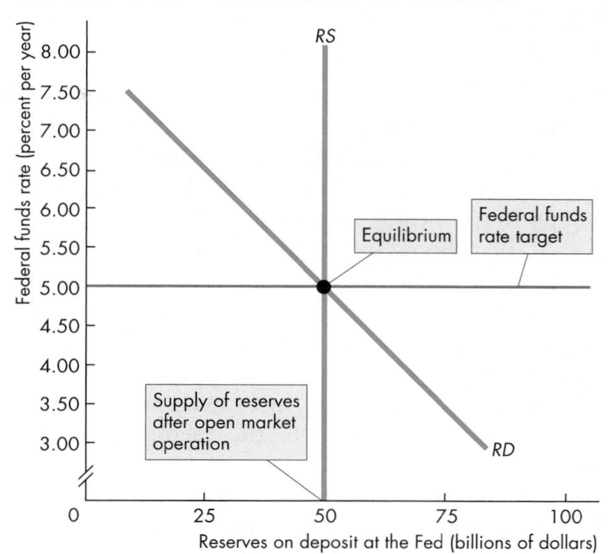

The demand curve for reserves is *RD*. The quantity of reserves demanded decreases as the federal funds rate rises because the federal funds rate is the opportunity cost of holding reserves. The supply curve of reserves is *RS*. The Fed uses open market operations to make the quantity of reserves supplied equal the quantity of reserves demanded ($50 billion in this case) at the federal funds rate target (5 percent a year in this case).

myeconlab animation

loans supplied and the smaller is the quantity of overnight loans demanded. The equilibrium federal funds rate balances the quantities demanded and supplied.

An equivalent way of looking at the forces that determine the federal funds rate is to consider the demand for and supply of bank reserves. Banks hold reserves to meet the required reserve ratio and so that they can make payments. But reserves are costly to hold because they can be loaned in the federal funds market and earn the federal funds rate. So the higher the federal funds rate, the smaller is the quantity of reserves demanded.

Figure 14.3 illustrates the demand for bank reserves. The x-axis measures the quantity of reserves that banks hold on deposit at the Fed, and the y-axis measures the federal funds rate. The demand for reserves is the curve labeled *RD*.

The Fed's open market operations determine the supply of reserves, which is shown by the supply curve *RS*. Equilibrium in the market for bank reserves determines the federal funds rate where the quantity of reserves demanded by the banks equals the quantity of reserves supplied by the Fed. By using open market operations, the Fed adjusts the supply of reserves to keep the federal funds rate on target.

Next, we see how the Fed makes it policy decisions.

The Fed's Decision-Making Strategy

The Fed's decision making begins with the *Beige Book* exercise described in *Economics in Action* on the next page. The Fed then turns to forecasting three key variables: the inflation rate, the unemployment rate, and the output gap.

Inflation Rate The Fed's forecasts of the inflation rate are a crucial ingredient in its interest rate decision. If inflation is above or is expected to move above the top of the comfort zone, the Fed considers raising the

Economics in Action

FOMC Decision Making

The Fed's decision making begins with an intensive assessment of the current state of the economy, which is conducted by the Federal Reserve districts and summarized in the *Beige Book*. Today, the Beige Book is a web posting at http://www.federalreserve.gov/FOMC/BeigeBook/ (see picture opposite).

The FOMC then turns its attention to the likely near-future evolution of the economy and the interest rate change that will keep inflation in check and the economy expanding at close to full employment. In making this assessment, the FOMC pays close attention to the inflation rate, the unemployment rate, and the output gap.

Balancing the signals that it gets from monitoring the three main features of macroeconomic performance, the FOMC meets in its imposing room (see photo opposite) and makes a decision on whether to change is federal funds rate target and if so, what the new target should be.

Having decided on the appropriate target for the federal funds rate, the FOMC instructs the New York Fed to conduct open market operations aimed at hitting the federal funds rate target.

If the goal is to raise the federal funds rate, the New York Fed sells securities in the open market. If the goal is to lower the federal funds rate, the New York Fed buys securities in the open market.

2010

Summary of Commentary on
Current Economic Conditions
by Federal Reserve District

Commonly known as the Beige Book, this report is published eight times per year. Each Federal Reserve Bank gathers anecdotal information on current economic conditions in its District through reports from Bank and Branch directors and interviews with key business contacts, economists, market experts, and other sources. The Beige Book summarizes this information by District and sector. An overall summary of the twelve district reports is prepared by a designated Federal Reserve Bank on a rotating basis.

2010					
January	February	March	April	May	June
13 HTML 273 KB PDF		3 HTML 925 KB PDF	14 HTML 683 KB PDF		9 HTML 225 KB PDF
July	August	September	October	November	December
28 HTML 297 KB PDF		8 HTML 135 KB PDF	20 HTML 187 KB PDF		1

federal funds rate target; and if inflation is below or is expected to move below the bottom of the comfort zone, it considers lowering the interest rate.

Unemployment Rate The Fed monitors and forecasts the unemployment rate and its relation to the natural unemployment rate (see pp. 113–115). If the unemployment rate is below the natural rate, a labor shortage might put upward pressure on wage rates, which might feed through to increase the inflation rate. So a higher interest rate might be called for. If the unemployment rate is above the natural rate, a lower inflation rate is expected, which indicates the need for a lower interest rate.

Output Gap The Fed monitors and forecasts real GDP and potential GDP and the gap between them, the *output gap* (see pp. 252–253). If the output gap is positive, an *inflationary gap*, the inflation rate will most likely accelerate, so a higher interest rate might be required. If the output gap is negative, a *recessionary gap*, inflation might ease, which indicates room to lower the interest rate.

We next look at the transmission of monetary policy and see how it achieves its goals.

REVIEW QUIZ

1. What is the Fed's monetary policy instrument?
2. How is the federal funds rate determined in the market for reserves?
3. What are the main influences on the FOMC federal funds rate decision?

You can work these questions in Study Plan 14.2 and get instant feedback.

Monetary Policy Transmission

You've seen that the Fed's goal is to keep the price level stable (keep the inflation rate around 2 percent a year) and to achieve maximum employment (keep the output gap close to zero). And you've seen how the Fed can use its power to set the federal funds rate at its desired level. We're now going to trace the events that follow a change in the federal funds rate and see how those events lead to the ultimate policy goal. We'll begin with a quick overview of the transmission process and then look at each step a bit more closely.

Quick Overview

When the Fed lowers the federal funds rate, other short-term interest rates and the exchange rate also fall. The quantity of money and the supply of loanable funds increase. The long-term real interest rate falls. The lower real interest rate increases consumption expenditure and investment. And the lower exchange rate makes U.S. exports cheaper and imports more costly, so net exports increase. Easier bank loans reinforce the effect of lower interest rates on aggregate expenditure. Aggregate demand increases, which increases real GDP and the price level relative to what they would have been. Real GDP growth and inflation speed up.

When the Fed raises the federal funds rate, as the sequence of events that we've just reviewed plays out, the effects are in the opposite directions.

Figure 14.4 provides a schematic summary of these ripple effects for both a cut and a rise in the federal funds rate.

These ripple effects stretch out over a period of between one and two years. The interest rate and exchange rate effects are immediate. The effects on money and bank loans follow in a few weeks and run for a few months. Real long-term interest rates change quickly and often in anticipation of the short-term interest rate changes. Spending plans change and real GDP growth changes after about one year. The inflation rate changes between one year and two years after the change in the federal funds rate. But these time lags are not entirely predictable and can be longer or shorter.

We're going to look at each stage in the transmission process, starting with the interest rate effects.

FIGURE 14.4 The Ripple Effects of a Change in the Federal Funds Rate

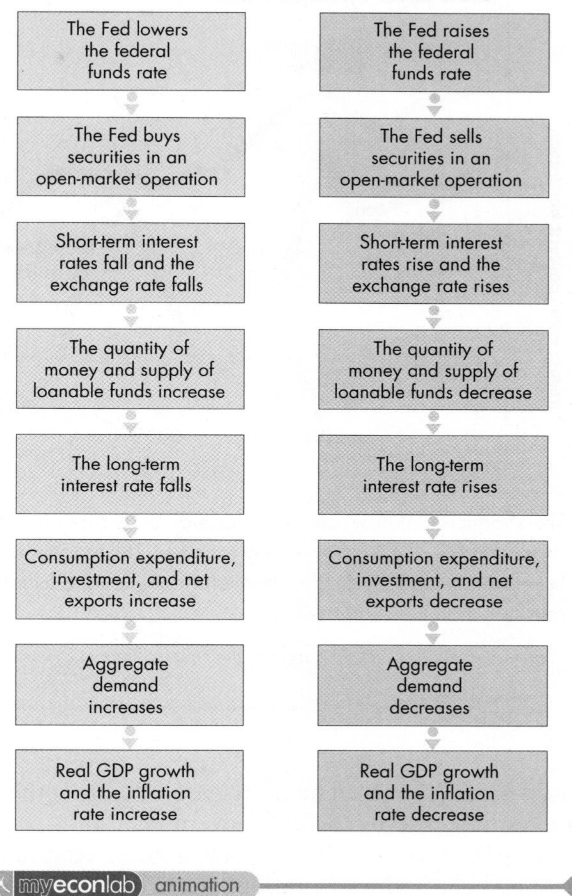

myeconlab animation

Interest Rate Changes

The first effect of a monetary policy decision by the FOMC is a change in the federal funds rate. Other interest rates then change. These interest rate effects occur quickly and relatively predictably.

Figure 14.5 shows the fluctuations in three interest rates: the federal funds rate, the short-term bill rate, and the long-term bond rate.

Federal Funds Rate As soon as the FOMC announces a new setting for the federal funds rate, the New York Fed undertakes the necessary open market operations to hit the target. There is no doubt about where the interest rate changes shown in Fig. 14.5 are generated. They are driven by the Fed's monetary policy.

FIGURE 14.5 Three Interest Rates

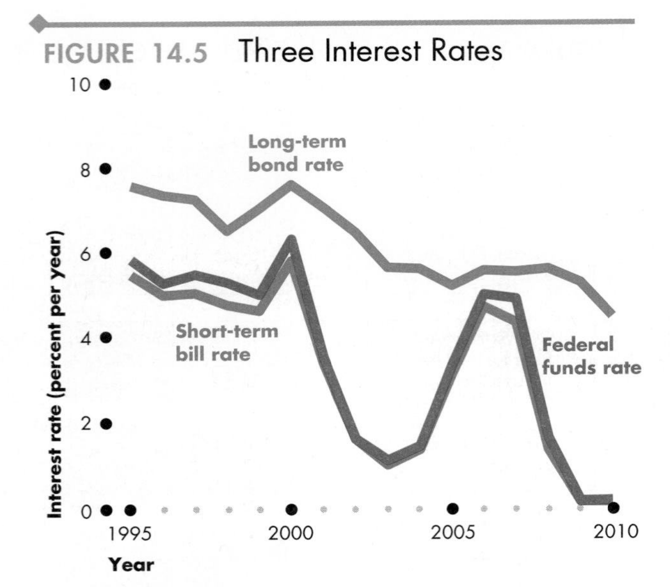

The short-term interest rates—the federal funds rate and the short-term bill rate—move closely together. The long-term bond rate is higher than the short-term rates, and it fluctuates less than the short-term rates.

Source of data: Board of Governors of the Federal Reserve System.

myeconlab animation

Short-Term Bill Rate The short-term bill rate is the interest rate paid by the U.S. government on 3-month Treasury bills. It is similar to the interest rate paid by U.S. businesses on short-term loans. Notice how closely the short-term bill rate follows the federal funds rate. The two rates are almost identical.

A powerful substitution effect keeps these two interest rates close. Commercial banks have a choice about how to hold their short-term liquid assets, and an overnight loan to another bank is a close substitute for short-term securities such as Treasury bills. If the interest rate on Treasury bills is higher than the federal funds rate, the quantity of overnight loans supplied decreases and the demand for Treasury bills increases. The price of Treasury bills rises and the interest rate falls.

Similarly, if the interest rate on Treasury bills is lower than the federal funds rate, the quantity of overnight loans supplied increases and the demand for Treasury bills decreases. The price of Treasury bills falls, and the interest rate rises.

When the interest rate on Treasury bills is close to the federal funds rate, there is no incentive for a bank to switch between making an overnight loan and buying Treasury bills. Both the Treasury bill market and the federal funds market are in equilibrium.

The Long-Term Bond Rate The long-term bond rate is the interest rate paid on bonds issued by large corporations. It is this interest rate that businesses pay on the loans that finance their purchase of new capital and that influences their investment decisions.

Two features of the long-term bond rate stand out: It is higher than the short-term rates, and it fluctuates less than the short-term rates.

The long-term interest rate is higher than the two short-term rates because long-term loans are riskier than short-term loans. To provide the incentive that brings forth a supply of long-term loans, lenders must be compensated for the additional risk. Without compensation for the additional risk, only short-term loans would be supplied.

The long-term interest rate fluctuates less than the short-term rates because it is influenced by expectations about future short-term interest rates as well as current short-term interest rates. The alternative to borrowing or lending long term is to borrow or lend using a sequence of short-term securities. If the long-term interest rate exceeds the expected average of future short-term interest rates, people will lend long term and borrow short term. The long-term interest rate will fall. And if the long-term interest rate is below the expected average of future short-term interest rates, people will borrow long term and lend short term. The long-term interest rate will rise.

These market forces keep the long-term interest rate close to the expected average of future short-term interest rates (plus a premium for the extra risk associated with long-term loans). The expected average future short-term interest rate fluctuates less than the current short-term interest rate.

Exchange Rate Fluctuations

The exchange rate responds to changes in the interest rate in the United States relative to the interest rates in other countries—*the U.S. interest rate differential.* We explain this influence in Chapter 9 (see p. 217).

When the Fed raises the federal funds rate, the U.S. interest rate differential rises and, other things remaining the same, the U.S. dollar appreciates, and when the Fed lowers the federal funds rate, the U.S. interest rate differential falls and, other things remaining the same, the U.S. dollar depreciates.

Many factors other than the U.S. interest rate differential influence the exchange rate, so when the Fed changes the federal funds rate, the exchange rate does not usually change in exactly the way it would with other things remaining the same. So while monetary policy influences the exchange rate, many other factors also make the exchange rate change.

Money and Bank Loans

The quantity of money and bank loans change when the Fed changes the federal funds rate target. A rise in the federal funds rate decreases the quantity of money and bank loans, and a fall in the federal funds rate increases the quantity of money and bank loans. These changes occur for two reasons: The quantity of deposits and loans created by the banking system changes and the quantity of money demanded changes.

You've seen that to change the federal funds rate, the Fed must change the quantity of bank reserves. A change in the quantity of bank reserves changes the monetary base, which in turn changes the quantity of deposits and loans that the banking system can create. A rise in the federal funds rate decreases reserves and decreases the quantity of deposits and bank loans created; and a fall in the federal funds rate increases reserves and increases the quantity of deposits and bank loans created.

The quantity of money created by the banking system must be held by households and firms. The change in the interest rate changes the quantity of money demanded. A fall in the interest rate increases the quantity of money demanded, and a rise in the interest rate decreases the quantity of money demanded.

A change in the quantity of money and the supply of bank loans directly affects consumption and investment plans. With more money and easier access to loans, consumers and firms spend more. With less money and loans harder to get, consumers and firms spend less.

The Long-Term Real Interest Rate

Demand and supply in the market for loanable funds determine the long-term *real interest rate*, which equals the long-term *nominal* interest rate minus the expected inflation rate. The long-term real interest rate influences expenditure decisions.

In the long run, demand and supply in the loanable funds market depend only on real forces—on saving and investment decisions. But in the short run, when the price level is not fully flexible, the supply of loanable funds is influenced by the supply of bank loans. Changes in the federal funds rate change the supply of bank loans, which changes the supply of loanable funds and changes the interest rate in the loanable funds market.

A fall in the federal funds rate that increases the supply of bank loans increases the supply of loanable funds and lowers the equilibrium real interest rate. A rise in the federal funds rate that decreases the supply of bank loans decreases the supply of loanable funds and raises the equilibrium real interest rate.

These changes in the real interest rate, along with the other factors we've just described, change expenditure plans.

Expenditure Plans

The ripple effects that follow a change in the federal funds rate change three components of aggregate expenditure:

- Consumption expenditure
- Investment
- Net exports

Consumption Expenditure Other things remaining the same, the lower the real interest rate, the greater is the amount of consumption expenditure and the smaller is the amount of saving.

Investment Other things remaining the same, the lower the real interest rate, the greater is the amount of investment.

Net Exports Other things remaining the same, the lower the interest rate, the lower is the exchange rate and the greater are exports and the smaller are imports.

So eventually, a cut in the federal funds rate increases aggregate expenditure and a rise in the federal funds rate curtails aggregate expenditure. These changes in aggregate expenditure plans change aggregate demand, real GDP, and the price level.

The Change in Aggregate Demand, Real GDP, and the Price Level

The final link in the transmission chain is a change in aggregate demand and a resulting change in real GDP and the price level. By changing real GDP and the price level relative to what they would have been without a change in the federal funds rate, the Fed influences its ultimate goals: the inflation rate and the output gap.

The Fed Fights Recession

If inflation is low and real GDP is below potential GDP, the Fed takes actions that are designed to restore full employment. Figure 14.6 shows the effects of the Fed's actions, starting in the market for bank reserves and ending in the market for real GDP.

Market for Bank Reserves In Fig. 14.6(a), which shows the market for bank reserves, the FOMC lowers the target federal funds rate from 5 percent to 4 percent a year. To achieve the new target, the New York Fed buys securities and increases the supply of reserves of the banking system from RS_0 to RS_1.

Money Market With increased reserves, the banks create deposits by making loans and the supply of money increases. The short-term interest rate falls and the quantity of money demanded increases. In Fig. 14.6(b), the supply of money increases from MS_0 to MS_1, the interest rate falls from 5 percent to 4 percent a year, and the quantity of money increases from \$3 trillion to \$3.1 trillion. The interest rate in the money market and the federal funds rate are kept close to each other by the powerful substitution effect described on p. 354.

Loanable Funds Market Banks create money by making loans. In the long run, an increase in the supply of bank loans is matched by a rise in the price level and the quantity of *real* loans is unchanged. But in the short run, with a sticky price level, an increase in the supply of bank loans increases the supply of (real) loanable funds.

FIGURE 14.6 The Fed Fights Recession

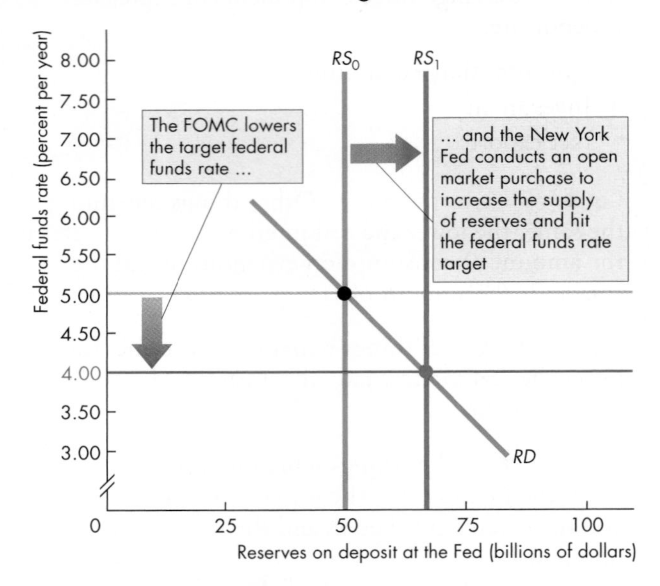

(a) The market for bank reserves

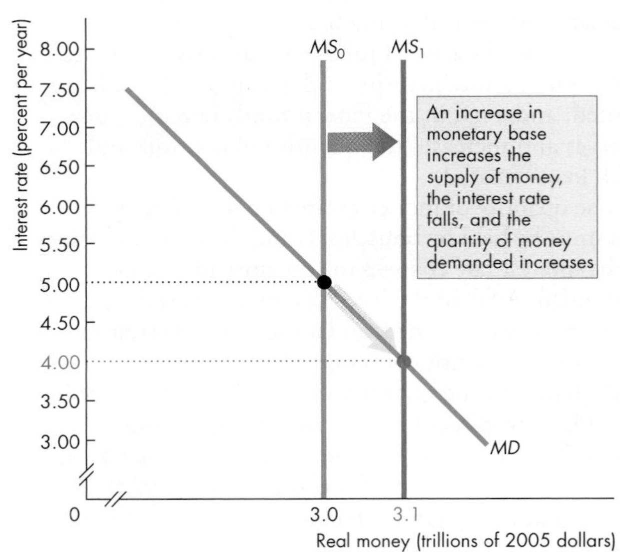

(b) Money market

In part (a), the FOMC lowers the federal funds rate target from 5 percent to 4 percent. The New York Fed buys securities in an open market operation and increases the supply of reserves from RS_0 to RS_1 to hit the new federal funds rate target.

In part (b), the supply of money increases from MS_0 to MS_1, the short-term interest rate falls, and the quantity of money demanded increases. The short-term interest rate and the federal funds rate change by similar amounts.

myeconlab animation

In Fig. 14.6(c), the supply of loanable funds curve shifts rightward from SLF_0 to SLF_1. With the demand for loanable funds at *DLF*, the real interest rate falls from 6 percent to 5.5 percent a year. (We're assuming a zero inflation rate so that the real interest rate equals the nominal interest rate.) The long-term interest rate changes by a smaller amount than the change in the short-term interest rate for the reason explained on p. 760.

The Market for Real GDP Figure 14.6(d) shows aggregate demand and aggregate supply—the demand for and supply of real GDP. Potential GDP is $13 trillion, where *LAS* is located. The short-run aggregate supply curve is *SAS*, and initially, the aggregate demand curve is AD_0. Real GDP is $12.8 trillion, which is less than potential GDP, so there is a recessionary gap. The Fed is reacting to this recessionary gap.

The increase in the supply of loans and the decrease in the real interest rate increase aggregate planned expenditure. (Not shown in the figure, a fall in the interest rate lowers the exchange rate, which increases net exports and aggregate planned expenditure.) The increase in aggregate expenditure, ΔE, increases aggregate demand and shifts the aggregate demand curve rightward to $AD_0 + \Delta E$. A multiplier process begins. The increase in expenditure increases income, which induces an increase in consumption expenditure. Aggregate demand increases further, and the aggregate demand curve eventually shifts rightward to AD_1.

The new equilibrium is at full employment. Real GDP is equal to potential GDP. The price level rises to 120 and then becomes stable at that level. So after a one-time adjustment, there is price stability.

In this example, we have given the Fed a perfect hit at achieving full employment and keeping the price level stable. It is unlikely that the Fed would be able to achieve the precision of this example. If the Fed stimulated demand by too little and too late, the economy would experience a recession. And if the Fed hit the gas pedal too hard, it would push the economy from recession to inflation.

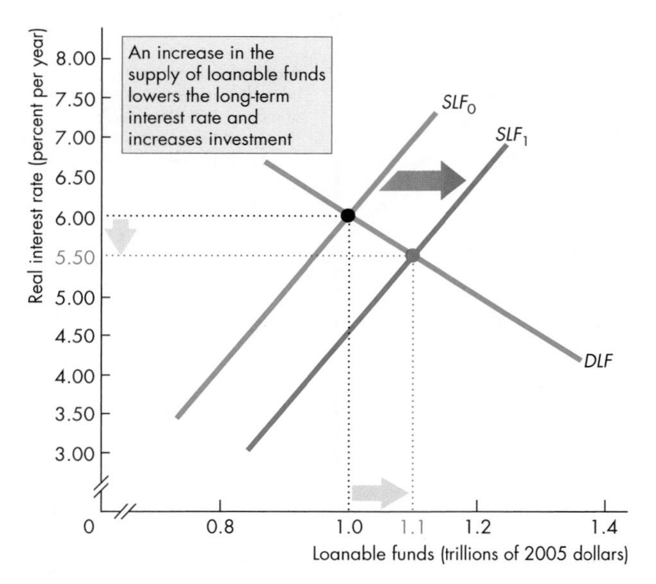

(c) The market for loanable funds

In part (c), an increase in the supply of bank loans increases the supply of loanable funds and shifts the supply curve from SLF_0 to SLF_1. The real interest rate falls and investment increases.

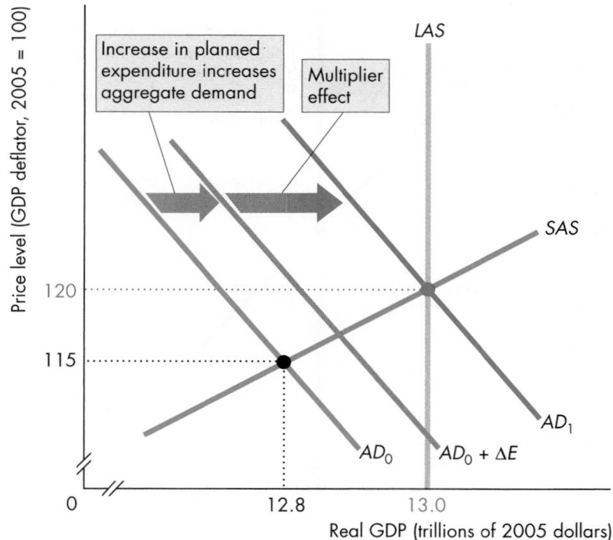

(d) Real GDP and the price level

In part (d), the increase in investment increases aggregate planned expenditure. The aggregate demand curve shifts to $AD_0 + \Delta E$ and eventually it shifts rightward to AD_1. Real GDP increases to potential GDP, and the price level rises.

The Fed Fights Inflation

If the inflation rate is too high and real GDP is above potential GDP, the Fed takes actions that are designed to lower the inflation rate and restore price stability. Figure 14.7 shows the effects of the Fed's actions starting in the market for reserves and ending in the market for real GDP.

Market for Bank Reserves In Fig. 14.7(a), which shows the market for bank reserves, the FOMC raises the target federal funds rate from 5 percent to 6 percent a year. To achieve the new target, the New York Fed sells securities and decreases the supply of reserves of the banking system from RS_0 to RS_1.

Money Market With decreased reserves, the banks shrink deposits by decreasing loans and the supply of money decreases. The short-term interest rate rises and the quantity of money demanded decreases. In Fig. 14.7(b), the supply of money decreases from MS_0 to MS_1, the interest rate rises from 5 percent to 6 percent a year, and the quantity of money decreases from \$3 trillion to \$2.9 trillion.

Loanable Funds Market With a decrease in reserves, banks must decrease the supply of loans. The supply of (real) loanable funds decreases, and the supply of loanable funds curve shifts leftward in Fig. 14.7(c) from SLF_0 to SLF_1. With the demand for loanable funds at *DLF*, the real interest rate rises from 6 percent to 6.5 percent a year. (Again, we're assuming a zero inflation rate so that the real interest rate equals the nominal interest rate.)

The Market for Real GDP Figure 14.7(d) shows aggregate demand and aggregate supply in the market for real GDP. Potential GDP is \$13 trillion where *LAS* is located. The short-run aggregate supply curve is *SAS* and initially the aggregate demand is AD_0. Now, real GDP is \$13.2 trillion, which is greater than potential GDP, so there is an inflationary gap. The Fed is reacting to this inflationary gap.

FIGURE 14.7 The Fed Fights Inflation

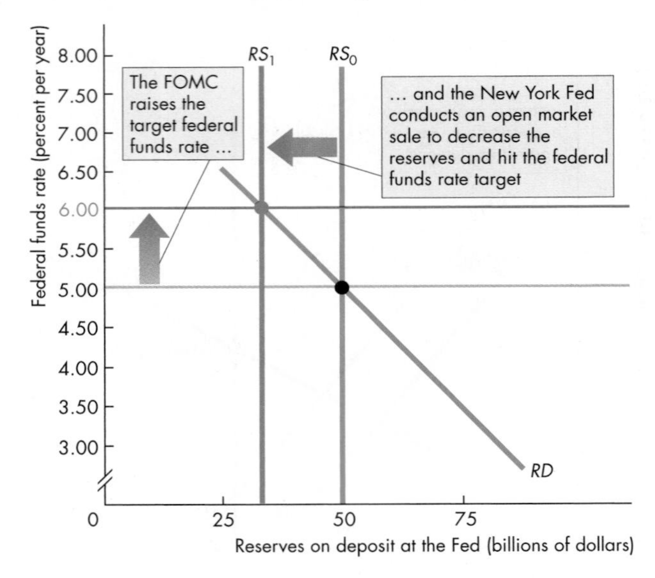

(a) The market for bank reserves

In part (a), the FOMC raises the federal funds rate from 5 percent to 6 percent. The New York Fed sells securities in an open market operation to decrease the supply of reserves from RS_0 to RS_1 and hit the new federal funds rate target.

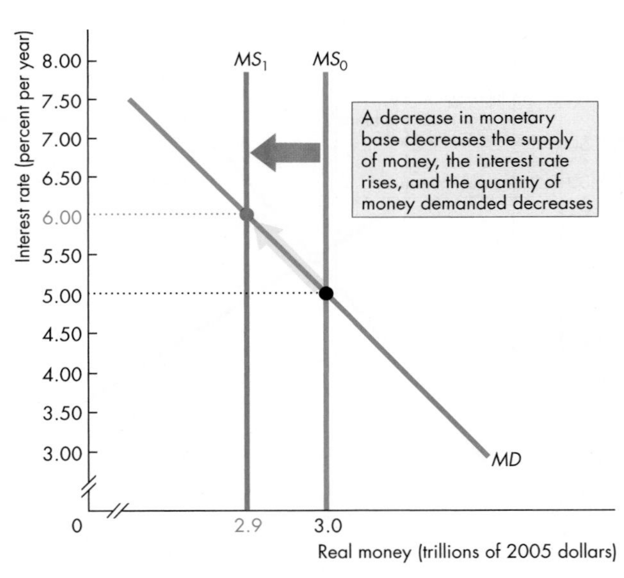

(b) Money market

In part (b), the supply of money decreases from MS_0 to MS_1, the short-term interest rate rises, and the quantity of money demanded decreases. The short-term interest rate and the federal funds rate change by similar amounts.

The increase in the short-term interest rate, the decrease in the supply of bank loans, and the increase in the real interest rate decrease aggregate planned expenditure. (Not shown in the figures, a rise in the interest rate raises the exchange rate, which decreases net exports and aggregate planned expenditure.)

The decrease in aggregate expenditure, ΔE, decreases aggregate demand and shifts the aggregate demand curve to $AD_0 - \Delta E$. A multiplier process begins. The decrease in expenditure decreases income, which induces a decrease in consumption expenditure. Aggregate demand decreases further, and the aggregate demand curve eventually shifts leftward to AD_1.

The economy returns to full employment. Real GDP is equal to potential GDP. The price level falls to 120 and then becomes stable at that level. So after a one-time adjustment, there is price stability.

Again, in this example, we have given the Fed a perfect hit at achieving full employment and keeping the price level stable. If the Fed decreased aggregate demand by too little and too late, the economy would have remained with an inflationary gap and the inflation rate would have moved above the rate that is consistent with price stability. And if the Fed hit the brakes too hard, it would push the economy from inflation to recession.

Loose Links and Long and Variable Lags

The ripple effects of monetary policy that we've just analyzed with the precision of an economic model are, in reality, very hard to predict and anticipate.

To achieve price stability and full employment, the Fed needs a combination of good judgment and good luck. Too large an interest rate cut in an underemployed economy can bring inflation, as it did during the 1970s. And too large an interest rate rise in an inflationary economy can create unemployment, as it did in 1981 and 1991. Loose links between the federal funds rate and the ultimate policy goals make unwanted outcomes inevitable and long and variable time lags add to the Fed's challenges.

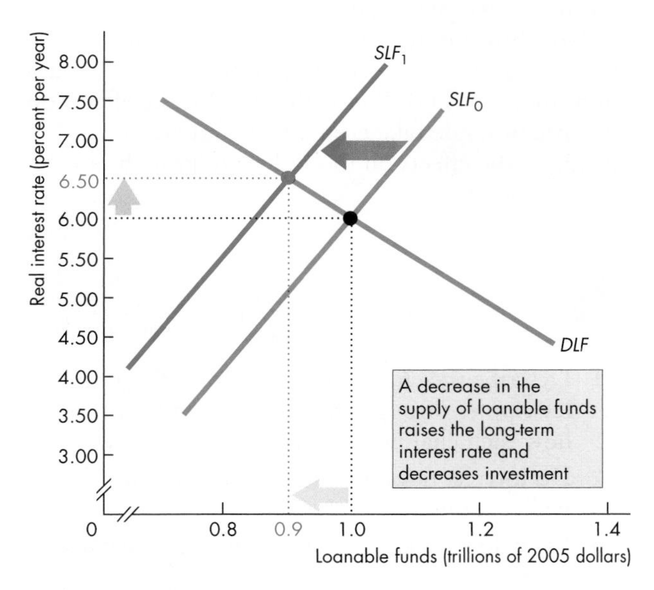

(c) The market for loanable funds

In part (c), a decrease in the supply of bank loans decreases the supply of loanable funds and the supply curve shifts from SLF_0 to SLF_1. The real interest rate rises and investment decreases.

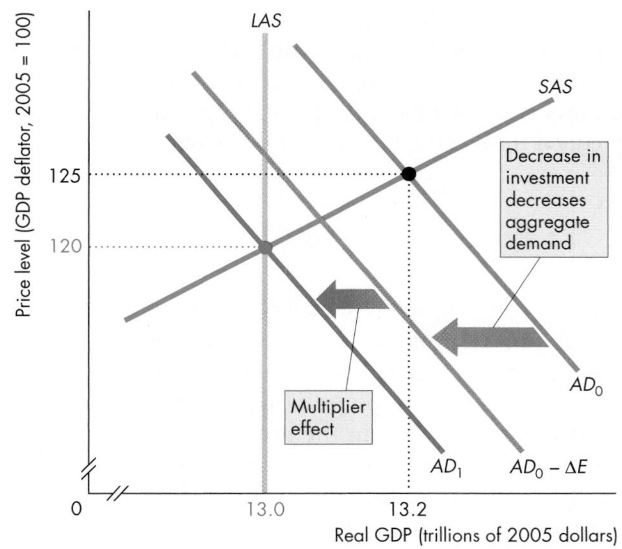

(d) Real GDP and the price level

In part (d), the decrease in investment decreases aggregate planned expenditure. Aggregate demand decreases and the *AD* curve shifts leftward from AD_0 to AD_1. Real GDP decreases to potential GDP, and the price level falls.

Economics in Action

A View of the Long and Variable Lag

You've studied the theory of monetary policy. Does it really work in the way we've described? It does, and the figure opposite provides some evidence to support this claim.

The blue line in the figure is the federal funds rate that the Fed targets *minus* the long-term bond rate. (When the long-term bond rate exceeds the federal funds rate, this gap is negative.)

We can view the gap between the federal funds rate and the long-term bond rate as a measure of how hard the Fed is trying to steer a change in course.

When the Fed is more concerned about recession than inflation and is trying to stimulate real GDP growth, it cuts the federal funds rate target and the gap between the long-term bond rate and the federal funds rate widens.

When the Fed is more concerned about inflation than recession and is trying to restrain real GDP growth, it raises the federal funds rate target and the gap between the long-term bond rate and the federal funds rate narrows.

The red line in the figure is the real GDP growth rate *two years later*. You can see that when the FOMC raises the federal funds rate, the real GDP growth rate slows two years later. And when the Fed lowers the federal funds rate, the real GDP growth rate speeds up two years later.

Not shown in the figure, the inflation rate increases and decreases corresponding to the fluctuations in the real GDP growth rate. But the effects on the inflation rate take even longer and are not as strong as the effects on the real GDP growth rate.

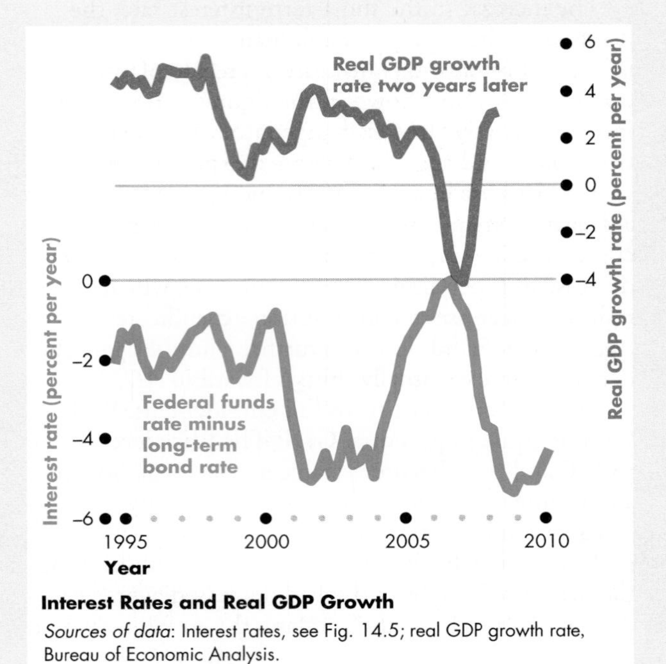

Interest Rates and Real GDP Growth

Sources of data: Interest rates, see Fig. 14.5; real GDP growth rate, Bureau of Economic Analysis.

Loose Link from Federal Funds Rate to Spending The real long-term interest rate that influences spending plans is linked only loosely to the federal funds rate. Also, the response of the *real* long-term interest rate to a change in the nominal interest rate depends on how inflation expectations change. And the response of expenditure plans to changes in the real interest rate depend on many factors that make the response hard to predict.

Time Lags in the Adjustment Process The Fed is especially handicapped by the fact that the monetary policy transmission process is long and drawn out. Also, the economy does not always respond in exactly the same way to a policy change. Further, many factors other than policy are constantly changing and bringing new situations to which policy must respond.

REVIEW QUIZ

1. Describe the channels by which monetary policy ripples through the economy and explain how each channel operates.
2. Do interest rates fluctuate in response to the Fed's actions?
3. How do the Fed's actions change the exchange rate?
4. How do the Fed's actions influence real GDP and how long does it take for real GDP to respond to the Fed's policy changes?
5. How do the Fed's actions influence the inflation rate and how long does it take for inflation to respond to the Fed's policy changes?

You can work these questions in Study Plan 14.3 and get instant feedback.

Extraordinary Monetary Stimulus

During the financial crisis and recession of 2008–2009, the Fed lowered the federal funds rate target to the floor. The rate can't go below zero, so what can the Fed do to stimulate the economy when it can't lower the interest rate any further?

The Fed has answered this question with some extraordinary policy actions. To understand those actions, we need to dig a bit into the anatomy of the financial crisis to which the Fed is responding. That's what we'll now do. We'll look at the key elements in the financial crisis and then look at the Fed's response.

The Key Elements of the Crisis

We can describe the crisis by identifying the events that changed the values of the assets and liabilities of banks and other financial institutions.

Figure 14.8 shows the stylized balance sheet of a bank: deposits plus equity equals reserves plus loans and securities (see Chapter 8, p. 188). Deposits and own capital —equity—are the bank's sources of funds (other borrowing by banks is ignored here). Deposits are the funds loaned to the bank by households and firms. Equity is the capital provided by the bank's stockholders and includes the bank's undistributed profits (and losses). The bank's reserves are currency and its deposit at the Fed. The bank's loans and securities are the loans made by the bank and government bonds, private bonds, asset-backed bonds, and other securities that the bank holds.

Three main events can put a bank under stress:

1. Widespread fall in asset prices
2. A significant currency drain
3. A run on the bank

Figure 14.8 summarizes the problems that each event presents to a bank. A widespread fall in asset prices means that the bank suffers a *capital loss*. It must write down the value of its assets and the value of the bank's equity decreases by the same amount as the fall in the value of its securities. If the fall in asset prices is large enough, the bank's equity might fall to zero, in which case the bank is insolvent. It fails.

A significant currency drain means that depositors withdraw funds and the bank loses reserves. This event puts the bank in a liquidity crisis. It is short of cash reserves.

A run on the bank occurs when depositors lose confidence in the bank and massive withdrawals of deposits occur. The bank loses reserves and must call in loans and sell off securities at unfavorable prices. Its equity shrinks.

The red arrows in Fig. 14.8 summarize the effects of these events and the problems they brought in the 2007–2008 financial crisis. A widespread fall in asset prices was triggered by the bursting of a house-price bubble that saw house prices switch from rapidly rising to falling. With falling house prices, sub-prime mortgage defaults occurred and the prices of mortgage-backed securities and derivatives whose values are based on these securities began to fall.

People with money market mutual fund deposits began to withdraw them, which created a fear of a massive withdrawal of these funds analagous to a run on a bank. In the United Kingdom, one bank, Northern Rock, experienced a bank run.

With low reserves and even lower equity, banks turned their attention to securing their balance sheets and called in loans. The loanable funds market and money market dried up.

Because the loanable funds market is global, the same problems quickly spread to other economies, and foreign exchange markets became highly volatile.

Hard-to-get loans, market volatility, and increased uncertainty transmitted the financial and monetary crisis to real expenditure decisions.

FIGURE 14.8 The Ingredients of a Financial and Banking Crisis

Event	Deposits	+ Equity	= Reserves	+ Loans and securities	*Problem*
Widespread fall in asset prices		▼		▼	Solvency
Currency drain	▼		▼		Liquidity
Run on bank	▼	▼	▼	▼	Liquidity and solvency

myeconlab animation

The Policy Actions

Policy actions in response to the financial crisis dribbled out over a period of more than a year. But by November 2008, eight groups of policies designed to contain the crisis and minimize its impact on the real economy were in place. Figure 14.9 summarizes them, describes their effects on a bank's balance sheet (red and blue arrows), and identifies the problem that each action sought to address.

An open market operation is the classic policy (see pp. 191–192) for providing liquidity and enabling the Fed to hit its interest rate target. With substantial interest rate cuts, open market operations were used on a massive scale to keep the banks well supplied with reserves. This action lowered bank holdings of securities and increased their reserves.

By extending deposit insurance (see p. 188), the FDIC gave depositors greater security and less incentive to withdraw their bank deposits. This action increased both deposits and reserves.

Three actions by the Fed provided additional liquidity in exchange for troubled assets. Term auction credit, primary dealer and broker credit, and the asset-backed commercial paper money market mutual fund liquidity facility enabled institutions to swap troubled assets for reserves or safer assets. All of these actions decreased bank holdings of securities and increased reserves.

The Troubled Asset Relief Program (TARP) was an action by the U.S. Treasury, so technically it isn't a monetary policy action, but it has a direct impact on banks and other financial institutions. The program was funded by $700 billion of national debt.

The original intent (we'll call it TARP 1) was for the U.S. Treasury to buy troubled assets from banks and other holders and replace them with U.S. government securities. Implementing this program proved more difficult than initially anticipated and the benefits of the action came to be questioned.

So instead of buying troubled assets, the Treasury decided to buy equity stakes in troubled institutions (we'll call it TARP 2). This action directly increased the institutions reserves and equity.

The final action was neither monetary policy nor fiscal policy but a change in accounting standards. It relaxed the requirement for institutions to value their assets at current market value—called "mark-to-market"—and permitted them, in rare conditions, to use a model to assess "fair market value."

Taken as a whole, a huge amount of relief was thrown at the financial crisis but the economy continued to perform poorly through 2009 and 2010.

Persistently Slow Recovery

Despite extraordinary monetary (and fiscal) stimulus, at the end of 2010, the U.S. economy remained stuck with slow real GDP growth and an unemployment rate close to 10 percent. Why?

No one knows for sure, but the Fed's critics say that the Fed itself contributed to the problem more than to the solution. That problem is extreme uncertainty about the future that is keeping business investment low. Critics emphasize the need for greater clarity about monetary policy *strategy*. We'll conclude this review of monetary policy by looking at two suggested policy strategies.

FIGURE 14.9 Policy Actions in a Financial and Banking Crisis

Action	**Deposits +**	**Equity =**	**Reserves +**	**Loans and securities**	***Problem addressed***
Open market operation			▲	▼	Liquidity
Extension of deposit insurance	▲		▲		Liquidity
Term auction credit			▲	▼	Liquidity
Primary dealer and other broker credit			▲	▼	Liquidity
Asset-backed commercial paper money market mutual fund liquidity facility			▲	▼	Liquidity
Troubled Asset Relief Program (TARP 1)			▲	▼	Liquidity
Troubled Asset Relief Program (TARP 2)		▲	▲		Solvency
Fair value accounting		▲		▲	Solvency

myeconlab animation

Policy Strategies and Clarity

Two alternative approaches to monetary policy have been suggested and one of them has been used in other countries. They are

- Inflation rate targeting
- Taylor rule

Inflation Rate Targeting A monetary policy strategy in which the central bank makes a public commitment to achieve an explicit inflation target and explain how its policy actions will achieve it is called **inflation rate targeting**. Australia, Canada, New Zealand, Sweden, the United Kingdom, and the European Union have been targeting inflation since the 1990s.

Inflation targeting focuses the public debate on what monetary policy can achieve and the best contribution it can make to attaining full employment and sustained growth. The central fact is that monetary policy is about managing inflation expectations. An explicit inflation target that is taken seriously and toward which policy actions are aimed and explained is a sensible way to manage those expectations.

It is when the going gets tough that inflation targeting has the greatest benefit. It is difficult to imagine a serious inflation-targeting central bank permitting inflation to take off in the way that it did during the 1970s. And it is difficult to imagine deflation and ongoing recession such as Japan has endured for the past 10 years if monetary policy is guided by an explicit inflation target.

Taylor Rule One way to pursue an inflation target is to set the policy interest rate (for the Fed, the federal funds rate) by using a rule or formula. The most famous and most studied interest rate rule is the *Taylor rule* described in *Economics in Action*.

Supporters of the Taylor rule argue that in computer simulations, the rule works well and limits fluctuations in inflation and output. By using such a rule, monetary policy contributes toward lessening uncertainty—the opposite of current monetary policy. In financial markets, labor markets, and markets for goods and services, people make long-term commitments. So markets work best when plans are based on correctly anticipated inflation. A well-understood monetary policy helps to create an environment in which inflation is easier to forecast and manage.

The debates on inflation targeting and the Taylor rule will continue!

Economics in Action

The Taylor Rule

The *Taylor rule* is a formula for setting the federal funds rate. Calling the federal funds rate *FFR*, the inflation rate *INF*, and the output gap *GAP* (all percentages), the Taylor rule formula is

$$FFR = 2 + INF + 0.5(INF - 2) + 0.5GAP.$$

In words, the Taylor rule sets the federal funds rate at 2 percent plus the inflation rate plus one half of the deviation of inflation from 2 percent, plus one half of the output gap.

Stanford University economist John B. Taylor, who devised this rule, says inflation and real GDP would fluctuate much less if the FOMC were to use it—the Taylor rule beats the FOMC's historical performance.

The Taylor rule implies that the Fed caused the boom and bust of the past decade. The federal funds rate was 1.5 percentage points (on average) too low from 2001 through 2005, which fuelled the boom; and the rate was 0.5 percentage points (on average) too high in 2006 and 2007, which triggered the bust.

In the conditions of 2009, the Taylor rule delivered a negative interest rate, a situation that wouldn't have arisen if the rule had been followed.

REVIEW QUIZ

1. What are the three ingredients of a financial and banking crisis?
2. What are the policy actions taken by the Fed and the U.S. Treasury in response to the financial crisis?
3. Why was the recovery from the 2008–2009 recession so slow?
4. How might inflation targeting improve the Fed's monetary policy?
5. How might using the Taylor rule improve the Fed's monetary policy?

You can work these questions in Study Plan 14.4 and get instant feedback.

To complete your study of monetary policy, take a look at *Reading Between the Lines* on pages 364–365, which examines the Fed's aggressive monetary stimulus in 2010.

The Fed's Monetary Policy Dilemma

Poor U.S. Jobs Data Open Way for Stimulus

http://www.ft.com
October 8, 2010

Worse-than-expected September jobs figures underlining the U.S. economy's chronic weakness has removed the last major hurdle to a new stimulus program by the Federal Reserve. ...

A number of Fed officials have said that the U.S. central bank should act soon unless the economic data improve. The September jobs report represented the last opportunity for the data to get better before the Fed's next rate-setting meeting at the start of November.

If the Fed does act, it is likely to buy hundreds of billions of dollars in Treasury bonds—the strategy known as quantitative easing—in an effort to drive down long-term interest rates. Lower interest rates on U.S. assets relative to other countries tend to weaken the dollar.

Stephen Wood, a senior market strategist at Russell Investments, said Friday's jobs data "at a minimum take away the ammunition from the hawks and reinforce the argument of advocates of quantitative easing" on the Federal Open Market Committee.

The main surprise in the report was a 76,000 fall in local government jobs. It suggests that the effects of last year's $787bn fiscal stimulus are starting to fade.

The private sector created a modest 64,000 jobs, most of them in services, well below the 300,000 to 400,000 a month needed to keep up with population growth and tackle rapidly the 9.6 percent unemployment rate.

ESSENCE OF THE STORY

- An increase of 64,000 in private-sector jobs and a fall of 76,000 in local government jobs left the unemployment rate at 9.6 percent.
- Between 300,000 and 400,000 new jobs a month are needed to keep up with population growth.
- The poor jobs figure signals a possible new stimulus by the Fed.
- The Fed would undertake quantitative easing—buy hundreds of billions of dollars of Treasury bonds in an effort to drive down the long-term interest rate.
- Lower U.S. interest rates relative to those in other countries would weaken the dollar.
- Fed "hawks" don't want more quantitative easing.

ECONOMIC ANALYSIS

- Some FOMC members want to use quantitative easing (QE) in a further attempt to boost real GDP and employment.
- Other FOMC members (the "hawks" refered to in the news article) fear inflation and believe that too much QE has already been undertaken.
- The Fed's dilemma is that with unemployment remaining stubbornly high and with inflation subdued, more monetary stimulus seems to be needed, but enormous stimulus is already in place and monetary policy does operate with a long and variable time lag.
- Further, if the dollar starts to depreciate in the foreign exchange market, inflation might take off (the fear of the hawks).
- The figures illustrate the economy in 2010, the possible effects of more stimulus, and the fear of the hawks.
- In Fig. 1, the banks' demand for reserves is *RD*. At a federal funds rate of 0.2 percent a year, the banks are willing to hold any quantity of reserves.
- The Fed's supply of reserves is $2 trillion on the supply curve RS_0. If the Fed undertakes QE and boosts the monetary base by a $0.5 trillion, the supply of reserves increases and the supply curve shifts to RS_1 in Fig. 1, but the interest rate doesn't fall.
- In Fig. 2, the economy real interest rate is 3 percent a year at the intersection of the supply of loanable funds curve SLF_0 and the demand for loanable funds curve *DLF*.
- When the Fed buys government securities to increase reserves, the supply of loanable funds increases and the supply curve in Fig. 2 shifts to SLF_1. But if the dollar is expected to depreciate, speculators move their funds into other currencies. The supply of loanable funds curve reverts to SLF_0, so the interest rate doesn't fall.
- In Fig. 3, real GDP is $13 trillion and the price level is 115 at the intersection of AD_0 and SAS_0. Potential GDP is $14 trillion, so there is a recessionary gap.
- If QE stimulates aggregate demand, the *AD* curve shifts rightward, like the shift to AD_1.
- If the expected depreciation of the dollar brings expected inflation and a higher expected price level, money wage rates rise and the short-run aggregate supply curve shifts to SAS_1. The price level rises and real GDP is stuck at $13 trillion with no change in the output gap. This is the fear of the hawks.

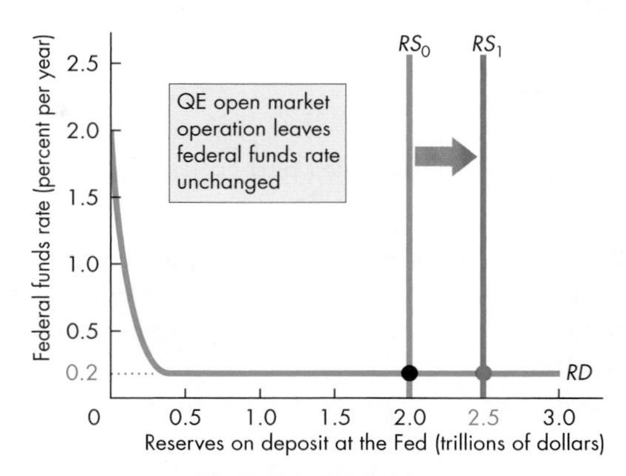

Figure 1 The market for bank reserves

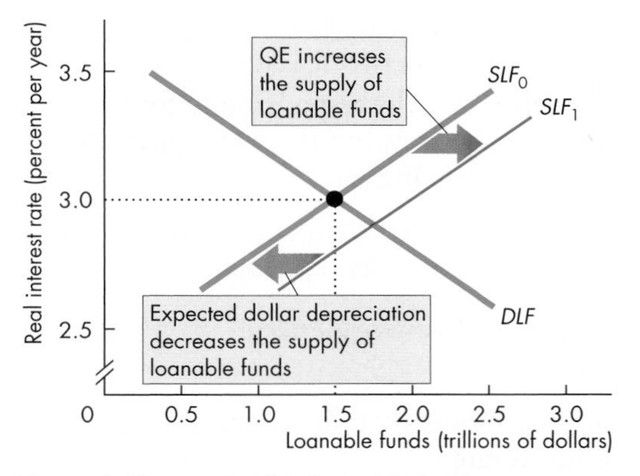

Figure 2 The market for loanable funds

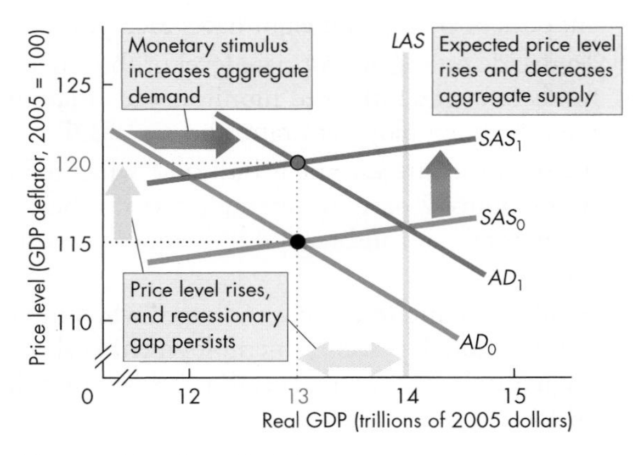

Figure 3 The risk of inflation

SUMMARY

Key Points

Monetary Policy Objectives and Framework

(pp. 348–350)

- The Federal Reserve Act requires the Fed to use monetary policy to achieve maximum employment, stable prices, and moderate long-term interest rates.
- The goal of stable prices delivers maximum employment and low interest rates in the long run but can conflict with the other goals in the short run.
- The Fed translates the goal of stable prices as an inflation rate of between 1 and 2 percent per year.
- The FOMC has the responsibility for the conduct of monetary policy, but the Fed reports to the public and to Congress.

Working Problems 1 to 5 will give you a better understanding of monetary policy objectives and framework.

The Conduct of Monetary Policy

(pp. 350–352)

- The Fed's monetary policy instrument is the federal funds rate.
- The Fed sets the federal funds rate target and announces changes on eight dates each year.
- To decide on the appropriate level of the federal funds rate target, the Fed monitors the inflation rate, the unemployment rate, and real GDP.
- A rise in the interest rate is indicated when inflation is above 2 percent, unemployment is below the natural rate, and real GDP is above potential GDP.
- A fall in the interest rate is indicated when inflation is below 1 percent, unemployment is above the natural rate, and real GDP is below potential GDP.
- The Fed hits its federal funds rate target by using open market operations.
- By buying or selling government securities in the open market, the Fed is able to change bank reserves and change the federal funds rate.

Working Problems 6 to 10 will give you a better understanding of the conduct of monetary policy.

Monetary Policy Transmission

(pp. 353–360)

- A change in the federal funds rate changes other interest rates, the exchange rate, the quantity of money and loans, aggregate demand, and eventually real GDP and the price level.
- Changes in the federal funds rate change real GDP about one year later and change the inflation rate with an even longer time lag.

Working Problems 11 to 20 will give you a better understanding of monetary policy transmission.

Extraordinary Monetary Stimulus

(pp. 361–363)

- A financial crisis has three ingredients: a widespread fall in asset prices, a currency drain, and a run on banks.
- The Fed and U.S. Treasury responded to financial crisis with classic open market operations on a massive scale and by several other unconventional measures.
- Inflation targeting and the Taylor rule are monetary policy strategies designed to enable the central bank to manage inflation expectations and reduce uncertainty.

Working Problems 21 to 26 will give you a better understanding of extraordinary monetary stimulus.

Key Terms

Beige Book, 349
Core inflation rate, 349
Federal funds rate, 350
Inflation rate targeting, 363
Monetary policy instrument, 350

STUDY PLAN PROBLEMS AND APPLICATIONS

myeconlab You can work Problems 1 to 26 in MyEconLab Chapter 14 Study Plan and get instant feedback.

Monetary Policy Objectives and Framework

(Study Plan 14.1)

1. "Unemployment is a more serious economic problem than inflation and it should be the focus of the Fed's monetary policy." Evaluate this statement and explain why the Fed's primary policy goal is price stability.
2. "Because the core inflation rate excludes the prices of food and fuel, the Fed should pay no attention to it and should instead be concerned about the CPI inflation rate." Explain why the Fed regards the core inflation rate as a good measure on which to focus.
3. "Monetary policy is too important to be left to the Fed. The President should be responsible for it." How is responsibility for monetary policy allocated among the Fed, the Congress, and the President?
4. **Bernanke Warns of High Budget Deficits**

   The government must rein in budget deficits in the years ahead, Federal Reserve Chairman Ben S. Bernanke told Congress.

   The Washington Post, October 5, 2010

   a. Does the Fed Chairman have either authority or responsibility for federal budget deficits?

   b. How might a federal budget deficit complicate the Fed's monetary policy? (Hint: Think about the effects of a deficit on interest rates.)

   c. How might the Fed's monetary policy complicate Congress's deficit cutting? (Hint: Think about the effects of monetary policy on interest rates.)
5. **Fed's $2 trillion May Buy Little Improvement in Jobs**

   The Fed has boosted bank reserves and the monetary base by $2 trillion but this action might not have much effect on jobs.

   Source: *Bloomberg*, October 7, 2010

   a. What does the Federal Reserve Act of 2000 say about the Fed's control of the quantity of money?

   b. How can the $2 trillion be reconciled with the Federal Reserve Act of 2000?

The Conduct of Monetary Policy (Study Plan 14.2)

6. What are the two possible monetary policy instruments, which one does the Fed use, and how has its value behaved since 2000?
7. How does the Fed hit its federal funds rate target? Illustrate your answer with an appropriate graph.
8. What does the Fed do to determine whether the federal funds rate should be raised, lowered, or left unchanged?

Use the following news clip to work Problems 9 and 10.

Fed Sees Unemployment and Inflation Rising

It is May 2008 and the Fed is confronted with a rising unemployment rate and rising inflation.

Source: CNN, May 21, 2008

9. Explain the dilemma faced by the Fed in May 2008.
10. a. Why might the Fed decide to cut the interest rate in the months after May 2008?

    b. Why might the Fed have decided to raise the interest rate in the months after May 2008?

Monetary Policy Transmission (Study Plan 14.3)

Use the following news clip to work Problems 11 and 12.

Sorry Ben, You Don't Control Long-Term Rates

Perhaps Ben Bernanke didn't learn in school that long-term interest rates are set by the market, but he is about to learn this lesson. Long-term interest rates cannot be manipulated lower by the central bank for a great length of time.

Source: safehaven.com, May 5, 2009

11. What is the role of the long-term interest rate in the monetary policy transmission process?
12. a. Is it the long-term nominal interest rate or the long-term real interest rate that influences spending decisions? Explain why.

    b. How does the market determine the long-term nominal interest rate and why doesn't it move as much as the short-term interest rates?

Use the following news clip to work Problems 13 and 14.

Dollar Down Slightly on Unabated Fed Concern

Worse-than-expected U.S. employment numbers created an expectation of further easing by the Fed and a fall in the exchange rate.

Source: *The Wall Street Journal*, October 11, 2010

13. How does further easing lower the exchange rate? How does a fall in the exchange rate influence monetary policy transmission?
14. Would a fall in the exchange rate mainly influence unemployment or inflation?

Use the following news clip to work Problems 15 to 17.

Economists' Growth Forecasts Through 2011

Economists surveyed boosted their forecasts for business investment in 2011.

Source: *Bloomberg*, October 11, 2010

15. Explain the effects of the Fed's low interest rates on business investment. Draw a graph to illustrate your explanation.
16. Explain the effects of business investment on aggregate demand. Would you expect it to have a multiplier effect? Why or why not?
17. What actions might the Fed take to stimulate business investment further?

Use the following news clip to work Problems 18 to 20.

IMF Forecasts a Slowdown in U.S. Growth

For the year 2010 the IMF reduced its U.S. real GDP growth forecast from 3.3 percent down to 2.6 percent. The IMF also lowered its growth forecast for 2011 from 2.9 percent to 2.3 percent.

Source: bloggingstocks.com, October 5, 2010

18. If the IMF forecasts turn out to be correct, what would most likely happen to the output gap and unemployment in 2011?
19. a. What actions that the Fed had taken in 2009 and 2010 would you expect to influence U.S. real GDP growth in 2011? Explain how those policy actions would transmit to real GDP.
    b. Draw a graph of aggregate demand and aggregate supply to illustrate your answer to part (a).
20. What further actions might the Fed take in 2011 to influence the real GDP growth rate in 2011? (Remember the time lags in the operation of monetary policy.)

Extraordinary Monetary Stimulus (Study Plan 14.4)

Use the following news clip to work Problems 21 to 23.

Dollar Under Pressure Amid QE2 Speculation

Persistent speculation that the Federal Reserve would soon embark on a fresh program of long-term asset purchases—a second round of quantitative easing or QE2—kept the dollar under pressure in the foreign exchange market ahead of crucial U.S. employment data.

Source: ft.com, October 7, 2010

21. What is the connection between actions that the Fed might take and U.S. employment data?
22. What does the news clip mean by "the dollar under pressure"?
23. Why was the Fed contemplating QE2? What were the arguments for and against further quantitative easing in the fall of 2010?
24. **Prospects Rise for Fed Easing Policy**

    William Dudley, president of the New York Fed, raised the prospect of the Fed becoming more explicit about its inflation goal to "help anchor inflation expectations at the desired rate."

    Source: ft.com, October 1, 2010

    a. What monetary policy strategy is Mr Dudley raising?
    b. How does inflation rate targeting work and why might it "help anchor inflation expectations at the desired rate"?
25. Suppose that the Bank of England decides to follow the Taylor rule. In 2005, the United Kingdom has an inflation rate of 2.1 percent a year and its output gap is –0.3 percent. At what level does the Bank of England set the repo rate (the U.K. equivalent of the federal funds rate)?
26. Suppose that the FOMC had followed the Taylor rule starting in 2000.
    a. How would the federal funds rate have differed from its actual path?
    b. How would real GDP and the inflation rate have been different?

ADDITIONAL PROBLEMS AND APPLICATIONS

myeconlab You can work these problems in MyEconLab if assigned by your instructor.

Monetary Policy Objectives and Framework

Use the following information to work Problems 27 to 29.

The Fed's mandated policy goals are "maximum employment, stable prices, and moderate long-term interest rates."

27. Explain the harmony among these goals in the long run.
28. Explain the conflict among these goals in the short run.
29. Based on the performance of U.S. inflation and unemployment, which of the Fed's goals appears to have taken priority since 2000?
30. What is the core inflation rate and why does the Fed regard it as a better measure than the CPI on which to focus?
31. Suppose Congress decided to strip the Fed of its monetary policy independence and legislate interest rate changes. How would you expect the policy choices to change? Which arrangement would most likely provide price stability?

Use the following news clip to work Problems 32 to 34.

Fiscal 2010 Deficit Seen Slightly Below $1.3 trillion

The federal government recorded a budget deficit of just slightly less than $1.3 trillion in fiscal 2010, the second-worst mark since 1945, the Congressional Budget Office said Thursday.

Source: *The Wall Street Journal*, October 7, 2010

32. How does the federal government get funds to cover its budget deficit? How does financing the budget deficit affect the Fed's monetary policy?
33. How was the budget deficit of 2010 influenced by the Fed's low interest rate policy?
34. a. How would the budget deficit change in 2011 and 2012 if the Fed moved interest rates up?
    b. How would the budget deficit change in 2011 and 2012 if the Fed's monetary policy led to a rapid depreciation of the dollar?
35. The Federal Reserve Act of 2000 instructs the Fed to pursue its goals by "maintain[ing] long-run growth of the monetary and credit aggregates commensurate with the economy's long-run potential to increase production."
    a. Has the Fed followed this instruction?
    b. Why might the Fed increase money by more than the potential to increase production?

The Conduct of Monetary Policy

36. Looking at the federal funds rate since 2000, identify periods during which, with the benefit of hindsight, the rate might have been kept too low. Identify periods during which it might have been too high.
37. Now that the Fed has created $2 trillion of bank reserves, how would you expect a further open market purchase of securities to influence the federal funds rate? Why? Illustrate your answer with an appropriate graph.
38. What is the Beige Book and what role does it play in the Fed's monetary policy decision-making process?

Use the information that during 2009 and 2010 both the inflation rate and the unemployment rate increased to work Problems 39 to 41.

39. Explain the dilemma that rising inflation and rising unemployment poses for the Fed.
40. Why might the Fed decide to try to lower interest rates in this situation?
41. Why might the Fed decide to raise interest rates in this situation?

Monetary Policy Transmission

Use the following information to work Problems 42 to 44.

From 2001 through 2005, the long-term *real* interest rate paid by the safest U.S. corporations fell from 5.5 percent to 2.5 percent. During that same period, the federal funds rate fell from 5.25 percent to 2.5 percent a year.

42. What role does the long-term real interest rate play in the monetary policy transmission process?
43. How does the federal funds rate influence the long-term real interest rate?
44. What do you think happened to inflation expectations between 2001 and 2005 and why?

45. **Dollar Tumbles to 15-year Low Against Yen**

    The dollar tumbled to a fresh 15-year low on persistent fears over the U.S. economic outlook.

    Source: yahoo.com, October 7, 2010

    a. How do "fears over the U.S. economic outlook" influence the exchange rate?
    b. How does monetary policy influence the exchange rate?

Use the following news clip to work Problems 46 and 47.

Top Economist says America Could Plunge into Recession

Robert Shiller, Professor of Economics at Yale University, predicted that there was a very real possibility that the United States would be plunged into a Japan-style slump, with house prices declining for years.

Source: timesonline.co.uk, December 31, 2007

46. If the Fed had agreed with Robert Shiller in December 2007, what actions might it have taken differently from those it did take? How could monetary policy prevent house prices from falling?
47. Describe the time lags in the response of output and inflation to the policy actions you have prescribed.

Use the following news clip to work Problems 48 and 49.

Greenspan Says Economy Strong

The central bank chairman said inflation was low, consumer spending had held up well through the downturn, housing-market strength was likely to continue, and businesses appeared to have unloaded their glut of inventories, setting the stage for a rebound in production.

Source: cnn.com, July 16, 2002

48. What monetary policy actions had the Fed taken in the year before Alan Greenspan's optimistic assessment?
49. What monetary policy actions would you expect the Fed to take in the situation described by Alan Greenspan?

Extraordinary Monetary Stimulus

50. **Fed's Plosser: Doesn't Currently Support Further Asset Buying**

    Further Federal Reserve asset purchases will not speed up the labor market recovery and could damage the Fed's credibility, said Federal Reserve Bank of Philadelphia President Charles Plosser, who is opposed to further asset buying of any size at this time.

    Source: nasdaq.com, October 12, 2010

    a. Describe the asset purchases that are causing Charles Plosser concern.
    b. How might asset purchases damage the Fed's credibility?

51. Suppose that the Reserve Bank of New Zealand is following the Taylor rule. In 2009, it sets the official cash rate (its equivalent of the federal funds rate) at 4 percent a year. If the inflation rate in New Zealand is 2.0 percent a year, what is its output gap?

Economics in the News

52. After you have studied *Reading Between the Lines* on pp. 364–365 answer the following questions.
    a. What was particularly unusual about the state of the economy in 2010?
    b. What was the Fed's expectation about future employment, real GDP growth, and inflation at the time of the news article?
    c. How would quantitative easing influence the market for bank reserves, the market for loanable funds, and aggregate demand and aggregate supply?
    d. How would you expect the exchange rate to feature in the transmission of monetary policy to real GDP and the price level?

53. **Fed Official Issues Call for Aggressive Action**

    Charles Evans, president of the Federal Reserve Bank of Chicago, wants the Fed to do much more to stimulate the economy. He wants the Fed to buy U.S. Treasury bonds and commit to raising the inflation rate above its informal 2 percent target.

    Source: *The Wall Street Journal*, October 5, 2010

    a. Why, in the economic conditions of October 2010, did Charles Evans want to see the Fed stimulating more?
    b. What would be the effects of the Fed buying U.S. Treasury bonds? Explain the immediate effects and the ripple effects.
    c. What would be the effects of the Fed committing to an inflation rate greater than 2 percent?
    d. What are the risks arising from greater monetary stimulus?

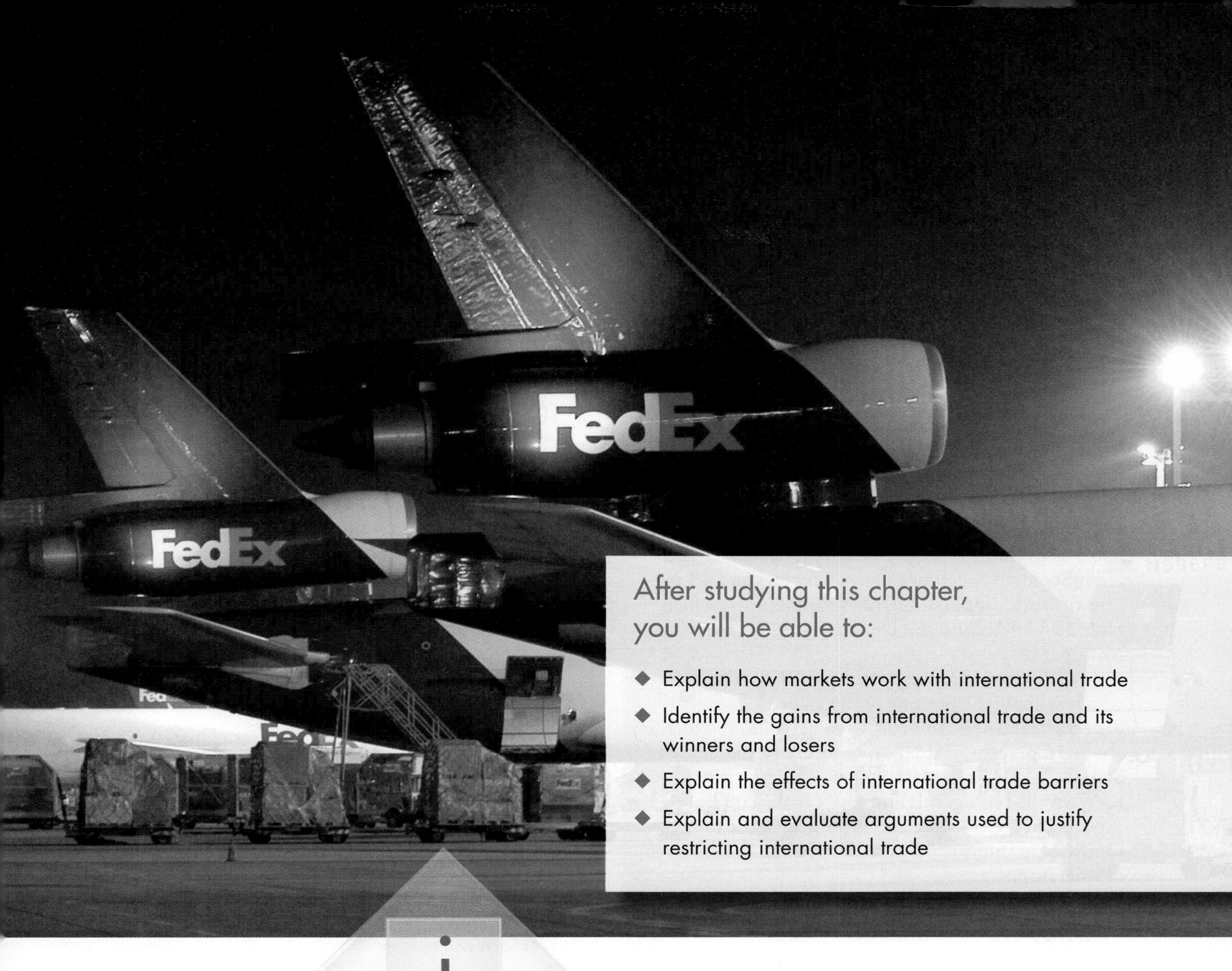

After studying this chapter, you will be able to:

- Explain how markets work with international trade
- Identify the gains from international trade and its winners and losers
- Explain the effects of international trade barriers
- Explain and evaluate arguments used to justify restricting international trade

15 INTERNATIONAL TRADE POLICY

iPods, Wii games, and Nike shoes are just three of the items you might buy that are not produced in the United States. In fact, most of the goods that you buy are produced abroad, often in Asia, and transported here in container ships and FedEx cargo jets. And it's not just goods produced abroad that you buy—it is services too. When you make a technical support call, most likely you'll be talking with someone in India, or to a voice recognition system that was programmed in India. Satellites or fiber cables will carry your conversation along with huge amounts of other voice messages, video images, and data.

All these activities are part of the globalization process that is having a profound effect on our lives. Globalization is controversial and generates heated debate. Many Americans want to know how we can compete with people whose wages are a fraction of our own.

Why do we go to such lengths to trade and communicate with others in faraway places? You will find some answers in this chapter. And in *Reading Between the Lines* at the end of the chapter, you can apply what you've learned and examine the effects of a tariff that the Obama government has put on tires imported from China.

How Global Markets Work

Because we trade with people in other countries, the goods and services that we can buy and consume are not limited by what we can produce. The goods and services that we buy from other countries are our **imports**; and the goods and services that we sell to people in other countries are our **exports**.

International Trade Today

Global trade today is enormous. In 2009, global exports and imports were $31 trillion, which is one half of the value of global production. The United States is the world's largest international trader and accounts for 10 percent of world exports and 13 percent of world imports. Germany and China, which rank 2 and 3 behind the United States, lag by a large margin.

In 2009, total U.S. exports were $1.6 trillion, which is about 11 percent of the value of U.S. production. Total U.S. imports were $2 trillion, which is about 14 percent of total expenditure in the United States.

We trade both goods and services. In 2009, exports of services were about 33 percent of total exports and imports of services were about 19 percent of total imports.

What Drives International Trade?

Comparative advantage is the fundamental force that drives international trade. Comparative advantage (see Chapter 2, p. 38) is a situation in which a person can perform an activity or produce a good or service at a lower opportunity cost than anyone else. This same idea applies to nations. We can define *national comparative advantage* as a situation in which a nation can perform an activity or produce a good or service at a lower opportunity cost than any other nation.

The opportunity cost of producing a T-shirt is lower in China than in the United States, so China has a comparative advantage in producing T-shirts. The opportunity cost of producing an airplane is lower in the United States than in China, so the United States has a comparative advantage in producing airplanes.

You saw in Chapter 2 how Liz and Joe reap gains from trade by specializing in the production of the good at which they have a comparative advantage and then trading with each other. Both are better off.

Economics in Action

Trading Services for Oil

Services top the list of U.S. exports and oil is the nation's largest import by a large margin.

The services that we export are business, professional, and technical services and transportation services. Chemicals were the largest category of goods that we exported in 2009.

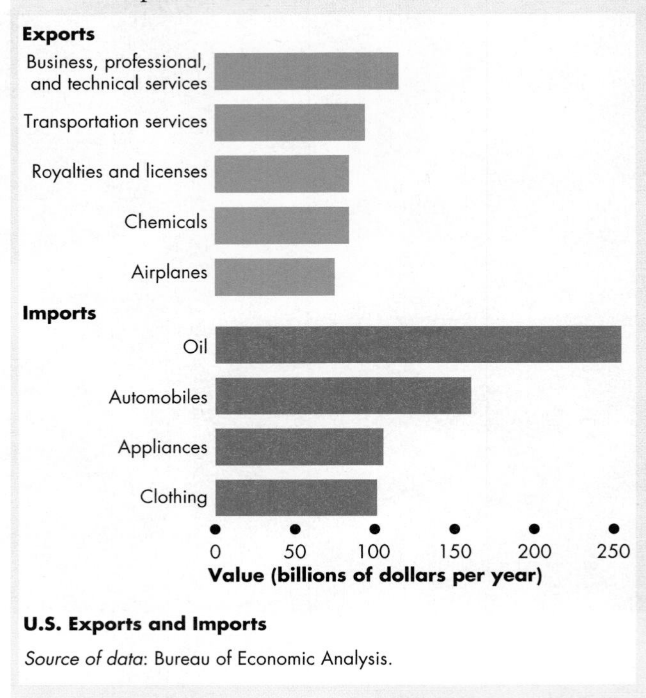

U.S. Exports and Imports

Source of data: Bureau of Economic Analysis.

This same principle applies to trade among nations. Because China has a comparative advantage at producing T-shirts and the United States has a comparative advantage at producing airplanes, the people of both countries can gain from specialization and trade. China can buy airplanes from the United States at a lower opportunity cost than that at which Chinese firms can produce them. And Americans can buy T-shirts from China for a lower opportunity cost than that at which U.S. firms can produce them. Also, through international trade, Chinese producers can get higher prices for their T-shirts and Boeing can sell airplanes for a higher price. Both countries gain from international trade.

Let's now illustrate the gains from trade that we've just described by studying demand and supply in the global markets for T-shirts and airplanes.

Why the United States Imports T-Shirts

The United States imports T-shirts because the rest of the world has a comparative advantage in producing T-shirts. Figure 15.1 illustrates how this comparative advantage generates international trade and how trade affects the price of a T-shirt and the quantities produced and bought.

The demand curve D_{US} and the supply curve S_{US} show the demand and supply in the U.S. domestic market only. The demand curve tells us the quantity of T-shirts that Americans are willing to buy at various prices. The supply curve tells us the quantity of T-shirts that U.S. garment makers are willing to sell at various prices—that is, the quantity supplied at each price when all T-shirts sold in the United States are produced in the United States.

Figure 15.1(a) shows what the U.S. T-shirt market would be like with no international trade. The price of a shirt would be $8 and 40 million shirts a year would be produced by U.S. garment makers and bought by U.S. consumers.

Figure 15.1(b) shows the market for T-shirts with international trade. Now the price of a T-shirt is determined in the world market, not the U.S. domestic market. The world price is less than $8 a T-shirt, which means that the rest of the world has a comparative advantage in producing T-shirts. The world price line shows the world price at $5 a shirt.

The U.S. demand curve, D_{US}, tells us that at $5 a shirt, Americans buy 60 million shirts a year. The U.S. supply curve, S_{US}, tells us that at $5 a shirt, U.S. garment makers produce 20 million T-shirts a year. To buy 60 million T-shirts when only 20 million are produced in the United States, we must import T-shirts from the rest of the world. The quantity of T-shirts imported is 40 million a year.

FIGURE 15.1 A Market With Imports

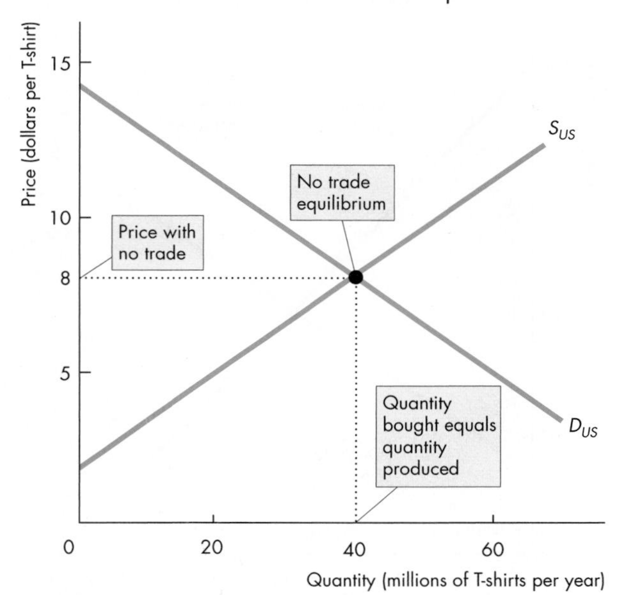

(a) Equilibrium with no international trade

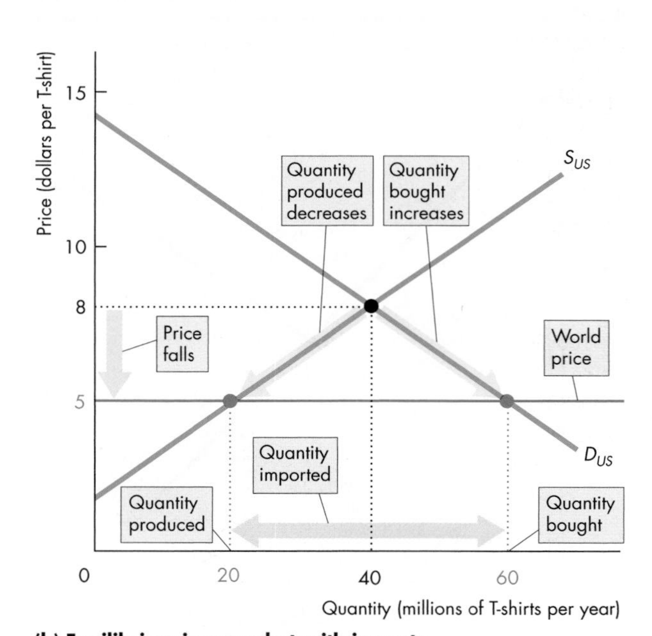

(b) Equilibrium in a market with imports

Part (a) shows the U.S. market for T-shirts with no international trade. The U.S. domestic demand curve D_{US} and U.S. domestic supply curve S_{US} determine the price of a T-shirt at $8 and the quantity of T- shirts produced and bought in the United States at 40 million a year.

Part (b) shows the U.S. market for T-shirts with international trade. World demand and world supply determine the world price, which is $5 per T-shirt. The price in the U.S. market falls to $5 a shirt. U.S. purchases of T-shirts increase to 60 million a year, and U.S. production of T-shirts decreases to 20 million a year. The United States imports 40 million T-shirts a year.

myeconlab animation

Why the United States Exports Airplanes

The United States exports airplanes because it has a comparative advantage in producing them. Figure 15.2 illustrates how this comparative advantage generates international trade in airplanes and how this trade affects the price of an airplane and the quantities produced and bought.

The demand curve D_{US} and the supply curve S_{US} show the demand and supply in the U.S. domestic market only. The demand curve tells us the quantity of airplanes that U.S. airlines are willing to buy at various prices. This demand curve tells us the quantity demanded at each price when all airplanes produced in the United States are bought in the United States. The supply curve tells us the quantity of airplanes that U.S. aircraft makers are willing to sell at various prices.

Figure 15.2(a) shows what the U.S. airplane market would be like with no international trade. The price of an airplane would be \$100 million and 400 airplanes a year would be produced by U.S. aircraft makers and bought by U.S. airlines.

Figure 15.2(b) shows the U.S. airplane market with international trade. Now the price of an airplane is determined in the world market and the world price is higher than \$100 million. Because the world price exceeds the U.S. price with no international trade, the United States has a comparative advantage in producing airplanes. The world price line shows the world price at \$150 million.

The U.S. demand curve, D_{US}, tells us that at \$150 million an airplane, U.S. airlines buy 200 airplanes a year. The U.S. supply curve, S_{US}, tells us that at \$150 million an airplane, U.S. aircraft makers produce 700 airplanes a year. The quantity produced in the United States (700 a year) minus the quantity purchased by U.S. airlines (200 a year) is the quantity of airplanes exported, which is 500 airplanes a year.

FIGURE 15.2 A Market with Exports

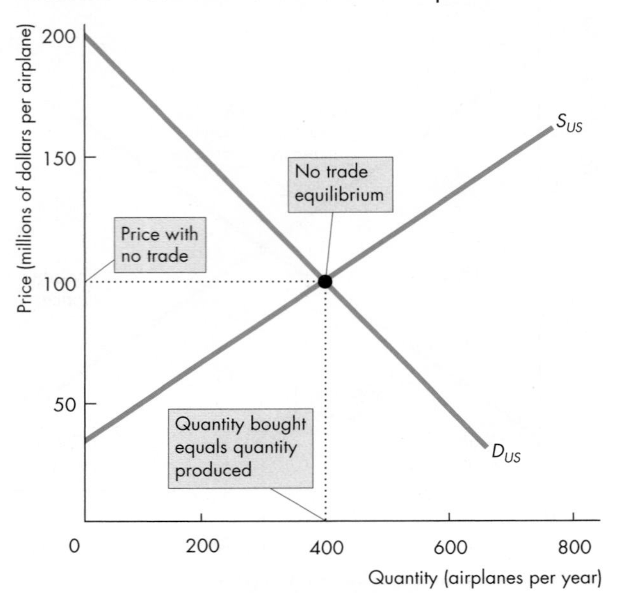

(a) Equilibrium without international trade

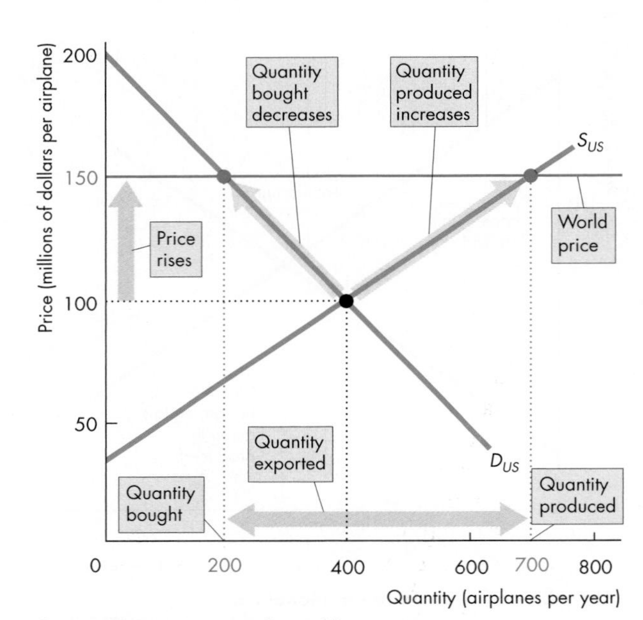

(b) Equilibrium in a market with exports

In part (a), the U.S. market with no international trade, the U.S. domestic demand curve D_{US} and the U.S. domestic supply curve S_{US} determine the price of an airplane at \$100 million and 400 airplanes are produced and bought each year.

In part (b), the U.S. market with international trade, world demand and world supply determine the world price, which is \$150 million per airplane. The price in the U.S. market rises. U.S. airplane production increases to 700 a year, and U.S. purchases of airplanes decrease to 200 a year. The United States exports 500 airplanes a year.

myeconlab animation

Winners and Losers from International Trade

International trade has winners, and it has losers. It is because some people lose that we often hear complaints about international competition. We're now going to see who wins and who loses from international trade. Then you will be able to understand who complains about international competition and why. You will learn why we hear producers complaining about cheap foreign imports. You will also see why we never hear consumers of imported goods and services complaining and why we never hear exporters complaining except when they want greater access to foreign markets.

Gains and Losses from Imports We can measure the gains and losses from imports by examining their effect on the price paid and quantity consumed by domestic consumers and their effect on the price received and quantity sold by domestic producers.

Consumers Gain from Imports When a country freely imports something from the rest of the world, it is because the rest of the world has a comparative advantage at producing that item. Compared to a situation with no international trade, the price paid by the consumer falls and the quantity consumed increases. It is clear that the consumer gains. The greater the fall in price and increase in quantity consumed, the greater is the gain to the consumer.

Domestic Producers Lose from Imports Compared to a situation with no international trade, the price received by a domestic producer of an item that is imported falls. Also, the quantity sold by the domestic producer of a good or service that is also imported decreases. Because the domestic producer of an item that is imported sells a smaller quantity and for a lower price, this producer loses from international trade. Import-competing industries shrink in the face of competition from cheaper foreign-produced goods.

The profits of firms that produce import-competing goods and services fall, these firms cut their workforce, unemployment in these industries increases and wages fall. When these industries have a geographical concentration, such as steel production around Gary, Indiana, an entire region can suffer economic decline.

Gains and Losses from Exports Just as we did for imports, we can measure the gains and losses from exports by looking at their effect on the price paid and quantity consumed by domestic consumers and their effect on the price received and quantity sold by domestic producers.

Domestic Consumers Lose from Exports When a country exports something to the rest of the world, it is because the country has a comparative advantage at producing that item. Compared to a situation with no international trade, the price paid by the consumer rises and the quantity consumed in the domestic economy decreases. The domestic consumer loses. The greater the rise in price and decrease in quantity consumed, the greater is the loss to the consumer.

Domestic Producers Gain from Exports Compared to a situation with no international trade, the price received by a domestic producer of an item that is exported rises. Also, the quantity sold by the domestic producer of a good or service that is also exported increases. Because the domestic producer of an item that is exported sells a larger quantity and for a higher price, this producer gains from international trade. Export industries expand in the face of global demand for their product.

The profits of firms that produce exports rise, these firms expand their workforce, unemployment in these industries decreases and wages rise. When these industries have a geographical concentration, such as software production in Silicon Valley, an entire region can boom.

Net Gain Export producers and import consumers gain, export consumers and import producers lose, but the gains are greater than the losses. In the case of imports, the consumer gains what the producer loses and then gains even more on the cheaper imports. In the case of exports, the producer gains what the consumer loses and then gains even more on the items it exports. So international trade provides a net gain for a country.

REVIEW QUIZ

1. Explain the effects of imports on the domestic price and quantity, and the gains and losses of consumers and producers.
2. Explain the effects of exports on the domestic price and quantity, and the gains and losses of consumers and producers.

You can work these questions in Study Plan 15.1 and get instant feedback.

International Trade Restrictions

Governments use four sets of tools to influence international trade and protect domestic industries from foreign competition. They are

- Tariffs
- Import quotas
- Other import barriers
- Export subsidies

Tariffs

A **tariff** is a tax on a good that is imposed by the importing country when an imported good crosses its international boundary. For example, the government of India imposes a 100 percent tariff on wine imported from California. So when an Indian imports a $10 bottle of Californian wine, he pays the Indian government a $10 import duty.

Tariffs raise revenue for the government and enable the government to satisfy the self-interest of the people who earn their incomes in the import-competing industries. But as you will see, tariffs and other restrictions on free international trade decrease the gains from trade and are not in the social interest. Let's see why.

The Effects of a Tariff To see the effects of a tariff, let's return to the example in which the United States imports T-shirts. With free trade, the T-shirts are imported and sold at the world price. Then, under pressure from U.S. garment makers, the U.S. government imposes a tariff on imported T-shirts. Buyers of T-shirts must now pay the world price plus the tariff. Several consequences follow and Fig. 15.3 illustrates them.

Figure 15.3(a) shows the situation with free international trade. The United States produces 20 million T-shirts a year and imports 40 million a year at the world price of $5 a shirt. Figure 15.3(b) shows

FIGURE 15.3 The Effects of a Tariff

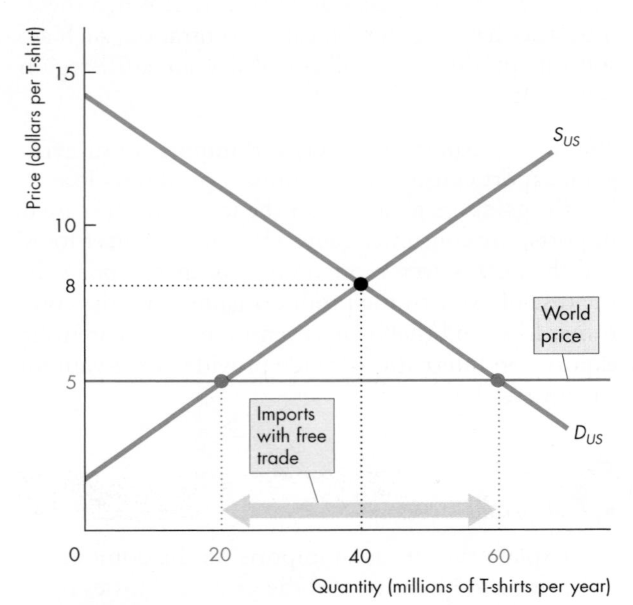

(a) Free trade

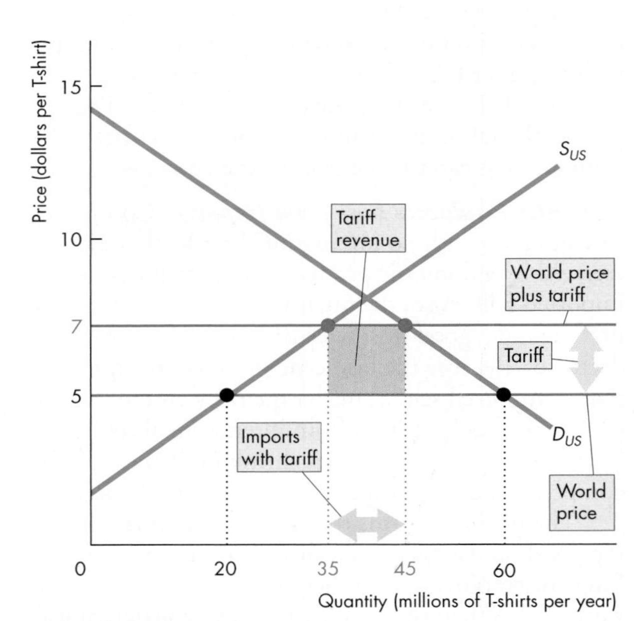

(b) Market with tariff

The world price of a T-shirt is $5. With free trade in part (a), Americans buy 60 million T-shirts a year. U.S. garment makers produce 20 million T-shirts a year and the United States imports 40 million a year.

With a tariff of $2 per T-shirt in part (b), the price in the U.S. market rises to $7 a T-shirt. U.S. production increases, U.S. purchases decrease, and the quantity imported decreases. The U.S. government collects a tariff revenue of $2 on each T-shirt imported, which is shown by the purple rectangle.

myeconlab animation

what happens with a tariff set at $2 per T-shirt. The following changes occur in the market for T-shirts:

- The price of a T-shirt in the United States rises by $2.
- The quantity of T-shirts bought in the United States decreases.
- The quantity of T-shirts produced in the United States increases.
- The quantity of T-shirts imported into the United States decreases.
- The U.S. government collects a tariff revenue.

Rise in Price of a T-Shirt To buy a T-shirt, Americans must pay the world price plus the tariff, so the price of a T-shirt rises by the $2 tariff to $7. Figure 15.3(b) shows the new domestic price line, which lies $2 above the world price line

Decrease in Purchases The higher price of a T-shirt brings a decrease in the quantity demanded along the demand curve. Figure 15.3(b) shows the decrease from 60 million T-shirts a year at $5 a shirt to 45 million a year at $7 a shirt.

Increase in Domestic Production The higher price of a T-shirt stimulates domestic production, and U.S. garment makers increase the quantity supplied along the supply curve. Figure 15.3(b) shows the increase from 20 million T-shirts at $5 a shirt to 35 million a year at $7 a shirt.

Decrease in Imports T-shirt imports decrease by 30 million, from 40 million to 10 million a year. Both the decrease in purchases and the increase in domestic production contribute to this decrease in imports.

Tariff Revenue The government's tariff revenue is $20 million—$2 per shirt on 10 million imported shirts—shown by the purple rectangle.

Winners, Losers, and the Social Loss from a Tariff A tariff on an imported good creates winners and losers and we're now going to identify the winners and losers. When the U.S. government imposes a tariff on an imported good,

- U.S. consumers of the good lose.
- U.S. producers of the good gain.
- U.S. consumers lose more than U.S. producers gain: society loses.

U.S. Consumers of the Good Lose Because the price of a T-shirt in the United States rises, the quantity of T-shirts demanded decreases. The combination of a higher price and smaller quantity bought makes the U.S. consumers worse off when a tariff is imposed.

Economics in Action

U.S. Tariffs Almost Gone

The Smoot-Hawley Act, which was passed in 1930, took U.S. tariffs to a peak average rate of 20 percent in 1933. (One third of imports was subject to a 60 percent tariff.) The **General Agreement on Tariffs and Trade (GATT)** was established in 1947. Since then tariffs have fallen in a series of negotiating rounds, the most significant of which are identified in the figure. Tariffs are now as low as they have ever been but import quotas and other trade barriers persist.

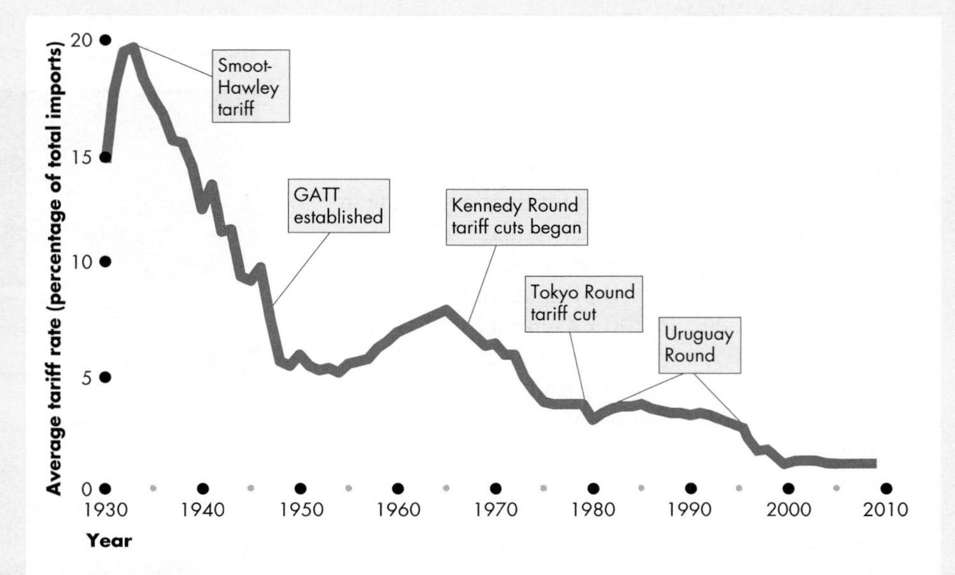

Tariffs: 1930–2009

Sources of data: U.S. Bureau of the Census, *Historical Statistics of the United States, Colonial Times to 1970,* Bicentennial Edition, Part 1 (Washington, D.C., 1975); Series U-212: updated from *Statistical Abstract of the United States:* various editions.

U.S. Producers of the Good Gain Because the price of an imported T-shirt rises by the amount of the tariff, U.S. T-shirt producers are now able to sell their T-shirts for the world price plus the tariff. At the higher price, the quantity of T-shirts supplied by U.S. producers increases. The combination of a higher price and larger quantity produced increases the producers' profits. So U.S. producers gain from the tariff.

U.S. Consumers Lose More Than U.S. Producers Gain: Society Loses Consumers lose from a tariff for three reasons:

1. They pay a higher price to domestic producers
2. They consume a smaller quantity of the good
3. They pay tariff revenue to the government

The tariff revenue is a loss to consumers but is not a social loss. The government can use the tax revenue to buy public services that consumers value. But the other two sources of consumer loss include some social losses.

There is a social loss because part of the higher price paid to domestic producers pays the higher cost of domestic production. The increased domestic production could have been obtained at lower cost as an import. There is also a social loss from the decreased quantity of the good consumed at the higher price.

Import Quotas

We now look at the second tool for restricting trade: import quotas. An **import quota** is a restriction that limits the maximum quantity of a good that may be imported in a given period. Most countries impose import quotas on a wide range of items. The United States imposes them on sugar, bananas, beef, and manufactured goods such as textiles, paper, and tires.

Import quotas enable the government to satisfy the self-interest of the people who earn their incomes in the import-competing industries. But you will discover that like a tariff, an import quota decreases the gains from trade and is not in the social interest.

Economics in Action

Self-Interest Beats the Social Interest

The **World Trade Organization (WTO)** is an international body established by the world's major trading nations for the purpose of supervising international trade and lowering the barriers to trade.

In 2001, at a meeting of trade ministers from all the WTO member-countries held in Doha, Qatar, an agreement was made to begin negotiations to lower tariff barriers and quotas that restrict international trade in farm products and services. These negotiations are called the **Doha Development Agenda** or the **Doha Round**.

In the period since 2001, thousands of hours of conferences in Cancún in 2003, Geneva in 2004, and Hong Kong in 2005, and ongoing meetings at WTO headquarters in Geneva, costing millions of taxpayers' dollars, have made disappointing progress.

Rich nations, led by the United States, the European Union, and Japan, want greater access to the markets of developing nations in exchange for allowing those nations greater access to the rich world's markets, especially for farm products.

Developing nations, led by Brazil, China, India, and South Africa, want access to the farm product markets of the rich world, but they also want to protect their infant industries.

With two incompatible positions, these negotiations are stalled and show no signs of a breakthrough. The self-interest of rich and developing nations is preventing the achievement of the social interest.

The Effects of an Import Quota The effects of an import quota are similar to those of a tariff. The price rises, the quantity bought decreases, and the quantity produced in the United States increases. Figure 15.4 illustrates the effects.

Figure 15.4(a) shows the situation with free international trade. Figure 15.4(b) shows what happens with an import quota of 10 million T-shirts a year. The U.S. supply curve of T-shirts becomes the domestic supply curve, S_{US}, plus the quantity that the import quota permits. So the supply curve becomes S_{US} + *quota*. The price of a T-shirt rises to $7, the quantity of T-shirts bought in the United States decreases to 45 million a year, the quantity of T-shirts produced in the United States increases to 35 million a year, and the quantity of T-shirts imported into the United States decreases to the quota quantity of 10 million a year. All the effects of this quota are identical to the effects of a $2 per shirt tariff, as you can check in Fig. 15.3(b).

Winners, Losers, and the Social Loss from an Import Quota An import quota creates winners and losers that are similar to those of a tariff but with an interesting difference.

When the government imposes an import quota,

- U.S. consumers of the good lose.
- U.S. producers of the good gain.
- Importers of the good gain.
- Society loses.

U.S. Consumers of the Good Lose Because the price of a T-shirt in the United States rises, the quantity of T-shirts demanded decreases. The combination of a higher price and smaller quantity bought makes the U.S. consumers worse off. So U.S. consumers lose when an import quota is imposed.

U.S. Producers of the Good Gain Because the price of an imported T-shirt rises, U.S. T-shirt producers increase production. The combination of a higher

FIGURE 15.4 The Effects of an Import Quota

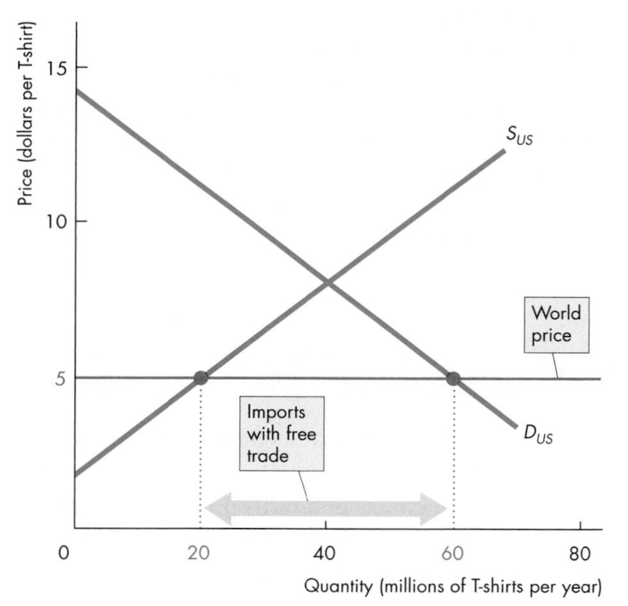

(a) Free trade

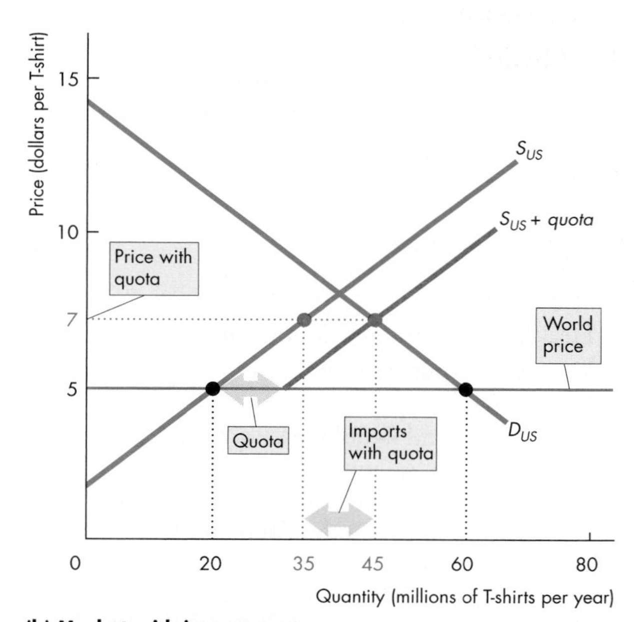

(b) Market with import quota

With free international trade, in part (a), Americans buy 60 million T-shirts at the world price. The United States produces 20 million T-shirts and imports 40 million a year. With an import quota of 10 million T-shirts a year, in part (b), the supply of T-shirts in the United States is shown by the curve S_{US} + *quota*. The price in the United States rises to $7 a T-shirt. U.S. production increases, U.S. purchases decrease, and the quantity of T-shirts imported decreases.

myeconlab animation

price and larger quantity produced increases producers' profit. So U.S. producers gain from the quota.

Importers of the Good Gain The importer is able to buy the good on the world market at the world market price, and sell the good in the domestic market at the domestic price. Because the domestic price exceeds the world price, the importer gains.

Society Loses Society loses because the loss to consumers exceeds the gains of domestic producers and importers. Just like the social losses from a tariff, there is a social loss from the quota because part of the higher price paid to domestic producers pays the higher cost of domestic production. There is a social loss from the decreased quantity of the good consumed at the higher price.

Tariff and Quota Compared You've looked at the effects of a tariff and a quota and can now see the essential differences between them. A tariff brings in revenue for the government while a quota brings a profit for the importers. All the other effects of a quota are the same as the effects of a tariff, provided the quota is set at the same quantity of imports that results from the tariff.

Tariffs and quotas are equivalent ways of restricting imports, benefiting domestic producers, and harming domestic consumers.

Let's now look at some other import barriers.

Other Import Barriers

Two sets of policies that influence imports are

- Health, safety, and regulation barriers
- Voluntary export restraints

Health, Safety, and Regulation Barriers Thousands of detailed health, safety, and other regulations restrict international trade. For example, U.S. food imports are examined by the Food and Drug Administration to determine whether the food is "pure, wholesome, safe to eat, and produced under sanitary conditions." The discovery of BSE (mad cow disease) in just one U.S. cow in 2003 was enough to close down international trade in U.S. beef. The European Union bans imports of most genetically modified foods, such as U.S.-produced soybeans. Although regulations of the type we've just described are not designed to limit international trade, they have that effect.

Voluntary Export Restraints A *voluntary export restraint* is like a quota allocated to a foreign exporter of a good. This type of trade barrier isn't common. It was initially used during the 1980s when Japan voluntarily limited its exports of car parts to the United States.

Export Subsidies

A *subsidy* is a payment by the government to a producer. When the government pays a subsidy, the cost of production falls by the amount of the subsidy so supply increases. An **export subsidy** is a payment by the government to the producer of an exported good so it increases the supply of exports. Export subsidies are illegal under a number of international agreements including the North American Free Trade Agreement (NAFTA) and the rules of the World Trade Organization (WTO).

Although export subsidies are illegal, the subsidies that the U.S. and European Union governments pay to farmers end up increasing domestic production, some of which gets exported. These exports of subsidized farm products make it harder for producers in other countries, notably in Africa and Central and South America, to compete in global markets.

Export subsidies bring gains to domestic producers, but they result in inefficient overproduction of some food products in the rich industrial countries, underproduction in the rest of the world, and create a social loss for the world as a whole.

REVIEW QUIZ

1. What are the tools that a country can use to restrict international trade?
2. Explain the effects of a tariff on domestic production, the quantity bought, and the price.
3. Explain who gains and who loses from a tariff and why the losses exceed the gains.
4. Explain the effects of an import quota on domestic production, consumption, and price.
5. Explain who gains and who loses from an import quota and why the losses exceed the gains.

You can work these questions in Study Plan 15.2 and get instant feedback.

The Case Against Protection

For as long as nations and international trade have existed, people have debated whether a country is better off with free international trade or with protection from foreign competition. The debate continues, but for most economists, a verdict has been delivered and is the one you have just seen. Free trade promotes prosperity for all countries; protection is inefficient. We've seen the most powerful case for free trade—it brings gains for consumers that exceed any losses incurred by producers, so there is a net gain for society.

But there is a broader range of issues in the free trade versus protection debate. Let's review these issues.

Two classical arguments for restricting international trade are

- The infant-industry argument
- The dumping argument

The Infant-Industry Argument

The **infant-industry argument** for protection is that it is necessary to protect a new industry to enable it to grow into a mature industry that can compete in world markets. The argument is based on the idea of *dynamic comparative advantage*, which can arise from *learning-by-doing*.

Learning-by-doing, a powerful engine of productivity growth, and on-the-job experience can change comparative advantage. But these facts do not justify protection.

First, the infant-industry argument is valid only if the benefits of learning-by-doing *not only* accrue to the owners and workers of the firms in the infant industry but also *spill over* to other industries and parts of the economy. For example, there are huge productivity gains from learning-by-doing in the manufacture of aircraft.

But almost all of these gains benefit the stockholders and workers of Boeing and other aircraft producers. Because the people making the decisions, bearing the risk, and doing the work are the ones who benefit, they take the dynamic gains into account when they decide on the scale of their activities. In this case, almost no benefits spill over to other parts of the economy, so there is no need for government assistance to achieve an efficient outcome.

Second, even if the case is made for protecting an infant industry, it is more efficient to do so by giving the firms in the industry a subsidy, which is financed out of taxes. Such a subsidy would encourage the industry to mature and to compete with efficient world producers and keep the price faced by consumers at the world price.

The Dumping Argument

Dumping occurs when a foreign firm sells its exports at a lower price than its cost of production. Dumping might be used by a firm that wants to gain a global monopoly. In this case, the foreign firm sells its output at a price below its cost to drive domestic firms out of business. When the domestic firms have gone, the foreign firm takes advantage of its monopoly position and charges a higher price for its product. Dumping is illegal under the rules of the WTO and is usually regarded as a justification for temporary tariffs, which are called *countervailing duties*.

But there are powerful reasons to resist the dumping argument for protection. First, it is virtually impossible to detect dumping because it is hard to determine a firm's costs. As a result, the test for dumping is whether a firm's export price is below its domestic price. But this test is a weak one because it can be rational for a firm to charge a low price in a market in which the quantity demanded is highly sensitive to price and a higher price in a market in which demand is less price-sensitive.

Second, it is hard to think of a good that is produced by a *global* monopoly. So even if all the domestic firms in some industry were driven out of business, it would always be possible to find alternative foreign sources of supply and to buy the good at a price determined in a competitive market.

Third, if a good or service were a truly global monopoly, the best way of dealing with it would be by regulation—just as in the case of domestic monopolies. Such regulation would require international cooperation.

The two arguments for protection that we've just examined have an element of credibility. The counterarguments are in general stronger, however, so these arguments do not make the case for protection. But they are not the only arguments that you might encounter. There are many other new arguments against globalization and for protection. The most common ones are that protection

- Saves jobs
- Allows us to compete with cheap foreign labor
- Penalizes lax environmental standards
- Prevents rich countries from exploiting developing countries

Saves Jobs

First, free trade does cost some jobs, but it also creates other jobs. It brings about a global rationalization of labor and allocates labor resources to their highest-valued activities. International trade in textiles has cost tens of thousands of jobs in the United States as textile mills and other factories closed. But tens of thousands of jobs have been created in other countries as textile mills opened. And tens of thousands of U.S. workers got better-paying jobs than as textile workers because U.S. export industries expanded and created new jobs. More jobs have been created than destroyed.

Although protection does save particular jobs, it does so at a high cost. For example, until 2005, U.S. textile jobs were protected by an international agreement called the Multifiber Arrangement. The U.S. International Trade Commission (ITC) has estimated that because of import quotas, 72,000 jobs existed in the textile industry that would otherwise have disappeared and that the annual clothing expenditure in the United States was $15.9 billion ($160 per family) higher than it would have been with free trade. Equivalently, the ITC estimated that it cost $221,000 a year to save each textile job.

Imports don't only destroy jobs. They create jobs for retailers that sell imported goods and for firms that service those goods. Imports also create jobs by creating income in the rest of the world, some of which is spent on U.S.-made goods and services.

Allows Us to Compete with Cheap Foreign Labor

With the removal of tariffs on trade between the United States and Mexico, people said we would hear a "giant sucking sound" as jobs rushed to Mexico. Let's see what's wrong with this view.

The labor cost of a unit of output equals the wage rate divided by labor productivity. For example, if a U.S. autoworker earns $30 an hour and produces 15 units of output an hour, the average labor cost of a unit of output is $2. If a Mexican auto assembly worker earns $3 an hour and produces 1 unit of output an hour, the average labor cost of a unit of output is $3. Other things remaining the same, the higher a worker's productivity, the higher is the worker's wage rate. High-wage workers have high productivity; low-wage workers have low productivity.

Although high-wage U.S. workers are more productive, on average, than low-wage Mexican workers, there are differences across industries. U.S. labor is relatively more productive in some activities than in others. For example, the productivity of U.S. workers in producing movies, financial services, and customized computer chips is relatively higher than their productivity in the production of metals and some standardized machine parts. The activities in which U.S. workers are relatively more productive than their Mexican counterparts are those in which the United States has a *comparative advantage*. By engaging in free trade, increasing our production and exports of the goods and services in which we have a comparative advantage and decreasing our production and increasing our imports of the goods and services in which our trading partners have a comparative advantage, we can make ourselves and the citizens of other countries better off.

Penalizes Lax Environmental Standards

Another argument for protection is that many poorer countries, such as China and Mexico, do not have the same environmental policies that we have and, because they are willing to pollute and we are not, we cannot compete with them without tariffs. So if poorer countries want free trade with the richer and "greener" countries, they must raise their environmental standards.

This argument for protection is weak. First, a poor country cannot afford to be as concerned about its environmental standards as a rich country can. Today, some of the worst pollution of air and water is found in China, Mexico, and the former communist countries of Eastern Europe. But only a few decades ago, London and Los Angeles topped the pollution chart. The best hope for cleaner air in Beijing and Mexico City is rapid income growth. And free trade contributes to that growth. As incomes in developing countries grow, they will have the *means* to match their desires to improve their environment. Second, a poor country may have a comparative advantage at doing "dirty" work, which helps it to raise its income and at the same time enables the global economy to achieve higher environmental standards than would otherwise be possible.

Prevents Rich Countries from Exploiting Developing Countries

Another argument for protection is that international trade must be restricted to prevent the people of the rich industrial world from exploiting the poorer people of the developing countries and forcing them to work for slave wages.

Child labor and near-slave labor are serious problems that are rightly condemned. But by trading with poor countries, we increase the demand for the goods that these countries produce and, more significantly, we increase the demand for their labor. When the demand for labor in developing countries increases, the wage rate also increases. So, rather than exploiting people in developing countries, trade can improve their opportunities and increase their incomes.

The arguments for protection that we've reviewed leave free-trade unscathed. But a new phenomenon is at work in our economy: *offshore outsourcing*. Surely we need protection from this new source of foreign competition. Let's investigate.

Offshore Outsourcing

Citibank, the Bank of America, Apple, Nike, Wal-Mart: What do these U.S. icons have in common? They all send jobs that could be done in America to China, India, Thailand, or even Canada—they are offshoring. What exactly is offshoring?

What Is Offshoring? A firm in the United States can obtain the things that it sells in any of four ways:

1. Hire American labor and produce in the United States.
2. Hire foreign labor and produce in other countries.
3. Buy finished goods, components, or services from other firms in the United States.
4. Buy finished goods, components, or services from other firms in other countries.

Activities 3 and 4 are **outsourcing**, and activities 2 and 4 are **offshoring**. Activity 4 is **offshore outsourcing**. Notice that offshoring includes activities that take place inside U.S. firms. If a U.S. firm opens its own facilities in another country, then it is offshoring.

Offshoring has been going on for hundreds of years, but it expanded rapidly and became a source of concern during the 1990s as many U.S. firms moved information technology services and general office services such as finance, accounting, and human resources management, overseas.

Why Did Offshoring of Services Boom During the 1990s? The gains from specialization and trade that you saw in the previous section must be large enough to make it worth incurring the costs of communication and transportation. If the cost of producing a T-shirt in China isn't lower than the cost of producing the T-shirt in the United States by more than the cost of transporting the shirt from China to America, then it is more efficient to produce shirts in the United States and avoid the transportation costs.

The same considerations apply to trade in services. If services are to be produced offshore, then the cost of delivering those services must be low enough to leave the buyer with an overall lower cost. Before the 1990s, the cost of communicating across large distances was too high to make the offshoring of business services efficient. But during the 1990s, when satellites, fiber-optic cables, and computers cut the cost of a phone call between America and India to less than a dollar an hour, a huge base of offshore resources became competitive with similar resources in the United States.

What Are the Benefits of Offshoring? Offshoring brings gains from trade identical to those of any other type of trade. We could easily change the names of the items traded from T-shirts and airplanes (the examples in the previous sections of this chapter) to banking services and call center services (or any other pair of services). An American bank might export banking services to Indian firms, and Indians might provide call center services to U.S. firms. This type of trade would benefit both Americans and Indians provided the United States has a comparative advantage in banking services and India has a comparative advantage in call center services.

Comparative advantages like these emerged during the 1990s. India has the world's largest educated English-speaking population and is located in a time zone half a day ahead of the U.S. east coast and midway between Asia and Europe, which facilitates 24/7 operations. When the cost of communicating with a worker in India was several dollars a minute, as it was before the 1990s, tapping these vast resources was just too costly. But at today's cost of a long-distance telephone call or Internet connection, resources in India can be used to produce services in the United States at a lower cost than those services can be produced by using resources located in the United States. And with the incomes that Indians earn from exporting services, some of the services (and goods) that Indians buy are produced in the United States.

Why Is Offshoring a Concern? Despite the gain from specialization and trade that offshoring brings, many people believe that it also brings costs that eat up the gains. Why?

A major reason is that offshoring is taking jobs in services. The loss of manufacturing jobs to other countries has been going on for decades, but the U.S. service sector has always expanded by enough to create new jobs to replace the lost manufacturing jobs. Now that service jobs are also going overseas, the fear is that there will not be enough jobs for Americans. This fear is misplaced.

Some service jobs are going overseas, while others are expanding at home. The United States imports call center services, but it exports education, health care, legal, financial, and a host of other types of services. Jobs in these sectors are expanding and will continue to expand.

The exact number of jobs that have moved to lower-cost offshore locations is not known, and estimates vary. But even the highest estimate is a tiny number compared to the normal rate of job creation.

Winners and Losers Gains from trade do not bring gains for every single person. Americans, on average, gain from offshore outsourcing, but some people lose. The losers are those who have invested in the human capital to do a specific job that has now gone offshore.

Unemployment benefits provide short-term temporary relief for these displaced workers. But the long-term solution requires retraining and the acquisition of new skills.

Beyond providing short-term relief through unemployment benefits, there is a large role for government in the provision of education and training to enable the labor force of the twenty-first century to be capable of ongoing learning and rapid retooling to take on new jobs that today we can't foresee.

Schools, colleges, and universities will expand and get better at doing their jobs of producing a highly educated and flexible labor force.

Avoiding Trade Wars

We have reviewed the arguments commonly heard in favor of protection and the counterarguments against it. There is one counterargument to protection that is general and quite overwhelming: Protection invites retaliation and can trigger a trade war.

The best example of a trade war occurred during the Great Depression of the 1930s when the United States introduced the Smoot-Hawley tariff. Country after country retaliated with its own tariff, and in a short period, world trade had almost disappeared. The costs to all countries were large and led to a renewed international resolve to avoid such self-defeating moves in the future. The costs also led to the creation of the General Agreement on Tariffs and Trade (GATT) and are the impetus behind current attempts to liberalize trade.

Why Is International Trade Restricted?

Why, despite all the arguments against protection, is trade restricted? There are two key reasons:

- Tariff revenue
- Rent seeking

Tariff Revenue Government revenue is costly to collect. In developed countries such as the United States, a well-organized tax collection system is in place that can generate billions of dollars of income tax and sales tax revenues. This tax collection system is made possible by the fact that most economic transactions are done by firms that must keep properly audited financial records. Without such records, revenue collection agencies (the Internal Revenue Service in the United States) would be severely hampered in their work. Even with audited financial accounts, some potential tax revenue is lost. Nonetheless, for industrialized countries, the income tax and sales taxes are the major sources of revenue and tariffs play a very small role.

But governments in developing countries have a difficult time collecting taxes from their citizens. Much economic activity takes place in an informal economy with few financial records, so only a small amount of revenue is collected from income taxes and sales taxes. The one area in which economic transactions are well recorded and audited is international trade. So this activity is an attractive base for tax collection in these countries and is used much more extensively than it is in developed countries.

Rent Seeking Rent seeking is the major reason why international trade is restricted. **Rent seeking** is lobbying for special treatment by the government to create economic profit or to divert the gains from international trade away from others. Free trade increases consumption possibilities *on average*, but not everyone shares in the gain and some people even lose. Free trade brings benefits to some and imposes costs on others, with total benefits exceeding total costs. The uneven distribution of costs and benefits is the principal obstacle to achieving more liberal international trade.

Returning to the example of trade in T-shirts and airplanes, the benefits from free trade accrue to all the producers of airplanes and to those producers of T-shirts that do not bear the costs of adjusting to a smaller garment industry. These costs are transition costs, not permanent costs. The costs of moving to free trade are borne by the garment producers and their employees who must become producers of other goods and services in which the United States has a comparative advantage.

The number of winners from free trade is large, but because the gains are spread thinly over a large number of people, the gain per person is small. The winners could organize and become a political force lobbying for free trade. But political activity is costly. It uses time and other scarce resources and the gains per person are too small to make the cost of political activity worth bearing.

In contrast, the number of losers from free trade is small, but the loss per person is large. Because the loss per person is large, the people who lose *are* willing to incur considerable expense to lobby against free trade.

Both the winners and losers weigh benefits and costs. Those who gain from free trade weigh the benefits it brings against the cost of achieving it. Those who lose from free trade and gain from protection weigh the benefit of protection against the cost of maintaining it. The protectionists undertake a larger quantity of political lobbying than the free traders.

Compensating Losers

If, in total, the gains from free international trade exceed the losses, why don't those who gain compensate those who lose so that everyone is in favor of free trade?

Some compensation does take place. When Congress approved the North American Free Trade Agreement (NAFTA) with Canada and Mexico, it set up a $56 million fund to support and retrain workers who lost their jobs as a result of the new trade agreement. During NAFTA's first six months, only 5,000 workers applied for benefits under this scheme. The losers from international trade are also compensated indirectly through the normal unemployment compensation arrangements. But only limited attempts are made to compensate those who lose.

The main reason why full compensation is not attempted is that the costs of identifying all the losers and estimating the value of their losses would be enormous. Also, it would never be clear whether a person who has fallen on hard times is suffering because of free trade or for other reasons that might be largely under her or his control. Furthermore, some people who look like losers at one point in time might, in fact, end up gaining. The young autoworker who loses his job in Michigan and becomes a computer assembly worker in Minneapolis might resent the loss of work and the need to move. But a year later, looking back on events, he counts himself fortunate.

Because we do not, in general, compensate the losers from free international trade, protectionism is a popular and permanent feature of our national economic and political life.

REVIEW QUIZ

1. What are the infant industry and dumping arguments for protection? Are they correct?
2. Can protection save jobs and the environment and prevent workers in developing countries from being exploited?
3. What is offshore outsourcing? Who benefits from it and who loses from it?
4. What are the main reasons for imposing a tariff?
5. Why don't the winners from free trade win the political argument?

You can work these questions in Study Plan 15.3 and get instant feedback.

We end this chapter on international trade policy with *Reading Between the Lines* on pp. 386–387. It applies what you've learned by looking at the effects of a U.S. tariff on imports of tires from China.

A Tariff on Tires

China: Tire trade penalties will hurt relations with U.S.

USAToday
September 12 2009

WASHINGTON—President Obama's decision to impose trade penalties on Chinese tires has infuriated Beijing. ...

The federal trade panel recommended a 55% tariff in the first year, 45% in the second year, and 35% in the third year. Obama settled on 35% the first year, 30% in the second, and 25% in the third, [White House Press Secretary Robert] Gibbs said.

"For trade to work for everybody, it has to be based on fairness and rules. We're simply enforcing those rules and would expect the Chinese to understand those rules," Gibbs said. ...

The steelworkers union ... says more than 5,000 tire workers have lost jobs since 2004, as Chinese tires overwhelmed the U.S. market.

The U.S. trade representative's office said four tire plants closed in 2006 and 2007 and three more are closing this year. During that time, just one new plant opened. U.S. imports of Chinese tires more than tripled from 2004 to 2008 and China's market share in the United States went from 4.7% of tires purchased in 2004 to 16.7% in 2008, the office said. ...

China said the tariffs do not square with the facts, ... citing a 2.2% increase in 2008 from 2007, and a 16% fall in exports in the first half of 2009 compared with the first half of 2008.

The new tariffs, on top of an existing 4% tariff on all tire imports, take effect Sept. 26. ...

ESSENCE OF THE STORY

- The United States is imposing a tariff on tires imported from China of 35 percent in 2009 and falling after two years to 25 percent.
- The steelworkers union says that more than 5,000 U.S. tire workers have lost jobs since 2004.
- Four U.S. tire plants closed in 2006 and 2007 and three were closing in 2009.
- Between 2004 and 2008, U.S. imports of Chinese tires more than tripled and China's share of the U.S. tire market increased from 4.7 percent of tires purchased in 2004 to 16.7 percent in 2008.
- China said that the rate of increase in 2008 was 2.2 percent and in the first half of 2009 its tire exports to the United States fell by 16 percent compared with the first half of 2008.

ECONOMIC ANALYSIS

- In the global economy, 450 firms produce more than 1 billion tires a year.
- The United States produces tires and imports tires from other countries.
- In 2004, the wholesale price of a tire, on average, was $40. The United States produced 235 million tires and imported 15 million.
- Figure 1 shows this situation. The demand curve is D_{US} and the supply curve is S_{US04}. The world price is $40 a tire and the gap between the quantity demanded and quantity supplied is filled by tire imports.
- Between 2004 and 2008, the price of rubber, one of the main inputs into a tire, doubled. With this rise in the price of a resource used to produce tires, the supply of tires in the United States decreased and the supply curve shifted leftward to S_{US08}.
- Tire producers in China felt the same rise in the price of rubber, but by installing the latest technology machines and with low-cost labor, they were able to prevent the cost of producing a tire from rising. The world price didn't rise.
- The decrease in U.S. supply with no change in the world price brought a surge of tire imports, especially from China.
- U.S. tire producers scaled back production and fired workers. In Fig. 1, U.S. production fell to 200 million tires a year and tire imports rose to 50 million a year.
- In this situation, the United States imposed a 35 percent tariff on Chinese-made tires. Figure 2 illustrates. The world price plus tariff raised the wholesale price in the United States to $55 a tire.
- U.S. supply is S_{US09} and at the higher price, U.S. firms increase the quantity of tires supplied to 215 million a year. The quantity demanded decreases to 240 million a year and U.S. imports shrink.
- The U.S. government collects tariff revenue (the purple rectangle).
- U.S. consumers pay a higher price and buy fewer tires. U.S. consumers lose from the tariff. U.S. producers sell more tires and receive a higher price. Producers gain from the tariff.

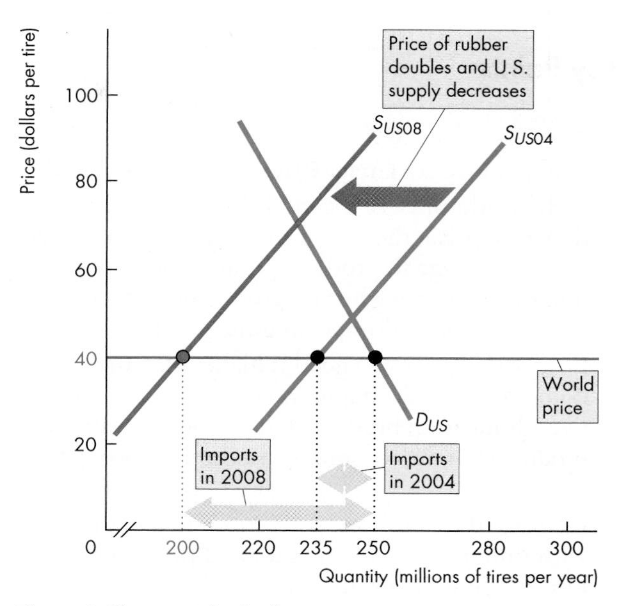

Figure 1 The surge in tire imports

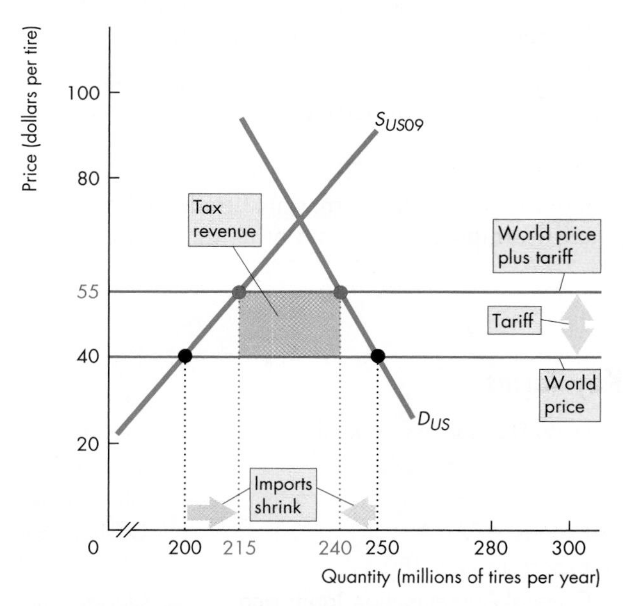

Figure 2 The effects of the tariff on tire imports

SUMMARY

Key Points

How Global Markets Work (pp. 372–375)

- Comparative advantage drives international trade.
- If the world price of a good is lower than the domestic price, the rest of the world has a comparative advantage in producing that good and the domestic country gains by producing less, consuming more, and importing the good.
- If the world price of a good is higher than the domestic price, the domestic country has a comparative advantage in producing that good and gains by producing more, consuming less, and exporting the good.
- Compared to a no-trade situation, in a market with imports, consumers gain and producers lose but the gains are greater than the losses.
- Compared to a no-trade situation, in a market with exports, producers gain and consumers lose but the gains are greater than the losses.

Working Problems 1 to 8 will give you a better understanding of how global markets work.

International Trade Restrictions (pp. 376–380)

- Countries restrict international trade by imposing tariffs, import quotas, and other import barriers.
- Trade restrictions raise the domestic price of imported goods, decrease the quantity imported, make consumers worse off, make producers better off, and damage the social interest.

Working Problems 9 to 20 will give you a better understanding of international trade restrictions.

The Case Against Protection (pp. 381–385)

- Arguments that protection is necessary for infant industries and to prevent dumping are weak.
- Arguments that protection saves jobs, allows us to compete with cheap foreign labor, is needed to penalize lax environmental standards, and prevents exploitation of developing countries are flawed.
- Offshore outsourcing is just a new way of reaping gains from trade and does not justify protection.
- Trade restrictions are popular because protection brings a small loss per person to a large number of people and a large gain per person to a small number of people. Those who gain have a stronger political voice than those who lose and it is too costly to identify and compensate losers.

Working Problem 21 will give you a better understanding of the case against protection.

Key Terms

STUDY PLAN PROBLEMS AND APPLICATIONS

myeconlab You can work Problems 1 to 21 in MyEconLab Chapter 15 Study Plan and get instant feedback.

How Global Markets Work (Study Plan 15.1)

Use the following information to work Problems 1 to 3.

Wholesalers of roses (the firms that supply your local flower shop with roses for Valentine's Day) buy and sell roses in containers that hold 120 stems. The table provides information about the wholesale market for roses in the United States. The demand schedule is the wholesalers' demand and the supply schedule is the U.S. rose growers' supply.

Price (dollars per container)	Quantity demanded	Quantity supplied
	(millions of containers per year)	
100	15	0
125	12	2
150	9	4
175	6	6
200	3	8
225	0	10

Wholesalers can buy roses at auction in Aalsmeer, Holland, for $125 per container.

1. a. Without international trade, what would be the price of a container of roses and how many containers of roses a year would be bought and sold in the United States?
   b. At the price in your answer to part (a), does the United States or the rest of the world have a comparative advantage in producing roses?
2. If U.S. wholesalers buy roses at the lowest possible price, how many do they buy from U.S. growers and how many do they import?
3. Draw a graph to illustrate the U.S. wholesale market for roses. Show the equilibrium in that market with no international trade and the equilibrium with free trade. Mark the quantity of roses produced in the United States, the quantity imported, and the total quantity bought.

Use the following news clip to work Problems 4 and 5.

Underwater Oil Discovery to Transform Brazil into a Major Exporter

A huge underwater oil field discovered late last year has the potential to transform Brazil into a sizable exporter. Fifty years ago, Petrobras was formed as a trading company to import oil to support Brazil's growing economy. Two years ago, Brazil reached its long-sought goal of energy self-sufficiency.

Source: *International Herald Tribune*, January 11, 2008

4. Describe Brazil's comparative advantage in producing oil and explain why its comparative advantage has changed.
5. a. Draw a graph to illustrate the Brazilian market for oil and explain why Brazil was an importer of oil until a few years ago.
   b. Draw a graph to illustrate the Brazilian market for oil and explain why Brazil may become an exporter of oil in the near future.

Use the following news clip to work Problems 6 and 7.

Postcard: Bangalore. Hearts Set on Joining the Global Economy, Indian IT Workers are Brushing up on Their Interpersonal Skills

The huge number of Indian workers staffing the world's tech firms and call centers possess cutting-edge technical knowledge, but their interpersonal and communication skills lag far behind. Enter Bangalore's finishing schools.

Source: *Time*, May 5, 2008

6. a. What comparative advantages does this news clip identify?
   b. Using the information in this news clip, what services do you predict Bangalore (India) exports and what services do you predict it imports?
7. Who will gain and who will lose from the trade in services predicted in the news clip?
8. Use the information on the U.S. wholesale market for roses in Problem 1 to
   a. Explain who gains and who loses from free international trade in roses compared to a situation in which Americans buy only roses grown in the United States.
   b. Draw a graph to illustrate the gains and losses from free trade.
   c. Calculate the gain from international trade.

International Trade Restrictions (Study Plan 15.2)

Use the following news clip to work Problems 9 and 10.

Steel Tariffs Appear to Have Backfired on Bush

President Bush set aside his free-trade principles last year and imposed heavy tariffs on imported steel to help out struggling mills in Pennsylvania and West Virginia. Some economists say the tariffs may have cost more jobs than they saved, by driving up costs for automakers and other steel users.

Source: *The Washington Post*, September 19, 2003

9. a. Explain how a high tariff on steel imports can help domestic steel producers.
   b. Explain how a high tariff on steel imports can harm steel users.
10. Draw a graph of the U.S. market for steel to show how a high tariff on steel imports
    i. Helps U.S. steel producers.
    ii. Harms U.S. steel users.

Use the information on the U.S. wholesale market for roses in Problem 1 to work Problems 11 to 16.

11. If the United States puts a tariff of $25 per container on imports of roses, what happens to the U.S. price of roses, the quantity of roses bought, the quantity produced in the United States, and the quantity imported?
12. Who gains and who loses from this tariff?
13. Draw a graph to illustrate the gains and losses from the tariff and on the graph identify the gains and losses and the tariff revenue.
14. If the United States puts an import quota on roses of 5 million containers, what happens to the U.S. price of roses, the quantity of roses bought, the quantity produced in the United States, and the quantity imported?
15. Who gains and who loses from this quota?
16. Draw a graph to illustrate the gains and losses from the import quota and on the graph identify the gains and losses, and the importers' profit.

Use the following news clip to work Problems 17 and 18.

Car Sales Go Up as Prices Tumble

Car affordability in Australia is now at its best in 20 years, fueling a surge in sales as prices tumble. In 2000, Australia cut the tariff to 15 percent and on January 1, 2005, it cut the tariff to 10 percent.

Source: *Courier Mail*, February 26, 2005

17. Explain who gains and who loses from the lower tariff on imported cars.
18. Draw a graph to show how the price of a car, the quantity of cars bought, the quantity of cars produced in Australia, and the quantity of cars imported into Australia changed.

Use the following news clip to work Problems 19 and 20.

Why the World Can't Afford Food

As [food] stocks dwindled, some countries placed export restrictions on food to protect their own supplies. This in turn drove up prices, punishing countries—especially poor ones—that depend on imports for much of their food.

Source: *Time*, May 19, 2008

19. a. What are the benefits to a country from importing food?
    b. What costs might arise from relying on imported food?
20. If a country restricts food exports, what effect does this restriction have in that country on the price of food, the quantity of food it produces, the quantity of food it consumes, and the quantity of food it exports?

The Case Against Protection (Study Plan 15.3)

21. **Chinese Tire Maker Rejects U.S. Charge of Defects**

    U.S. regulators ordered the recall of more than 450,000 faulty tires. The Chinese producer of the tires disputed the allegations and hinted that the recall might be an effort by foreign competitors to hamper Chinese exports to the United States. Mounting scrutiny of Chinese-made goods has become a source of new trade frictions between the United States and China and fueled worries among regulators, corporations, and consumers about the risks associated with many products imported from China.

    Source: *International Herald Tribune*, June 26, 2007

    a. What does the information in the news clip imply about the comparative advantage of producing tires in the United States and China?
    b. Could product quality be a valid argument against free trade?
    c. How would the product-quality argument against free trade be open to abuse by domestic producers of the imported good?

ADDITIONAL PROBLEMS AND APPLICATIONS

myeconlab You can work these problems in MyEconLab if assigned by your instructor.

How Global Markets Work

22. Suppose that the world price of sugar is 10 cents a pound, the United States does not trade internationally, and the equilibrium price of sugar in the United States is 20 cents a pound. The United States then begins to trade internationally.
    a. How does the price of sugar in the United States change?
    b. Do U.S. consumers buy more or less sugar?
    c. Do U.S. sugar growers produce more or less sugar?
    d. Does the United States export or import sugar and why?
23. Suppose that the world price of steel is $100 a ton, India does not trade internationally, and the equilibrium price of steel in India is $60 a ton. India then begins to trade internationally.
    a. How does the price of steel in India change?
    b. How does the quantity of steel produced in India change?
    c. How does the quantity of steel bought by India change?
    d. Does India export or import steel and why?
24. A semiconductor is a key component in your laptop, cell phone, and iPod. The table provides information about the market for semiconductors in the United States.

Price (dollars per unit)	Quantity demanded (billions of units per year)	Quantity supplied (billions of units per year)
10	25	0
12	20	20
14	15	40
16	10	60
18	5	80
20	0	100

Producers of semiconductors can get $18 a unit on the world market.

a. With no international trade, what would be the price of a semiconductor and how many semiconductors a year would be bought and sold in the United States?
b. Does the United States have a comparative advantage in producing semiconductors?

Use the following news clip to work Problems 25 and 26.

Act Now, Eat Later

The hunger crisis in poor countries has its roots in U.S. and European policies of subsidizing the diversion of food crops to produce biofuels like corn-based ethanol. That is, doling out subsidies to put the world's dinner into the gas tank.

Source: *Time*, May 5, 2008

25. a. What is the effect on the world price of corn of the increased use of corn to produce ethanol in the United States and Europe?
    b. How does the change in the world price of corn affect the quantity of corn produced in a poor developing country that has a comparative advantage in producing corn? What happens to the quantity it consumes and the quantity that it either exports or imports?
26. Explain why the U.S. and European policies of subsidizing the production of corn creates a social loss for a poor developing country that has a comparative advantage in producing corn.

Use the following news clip to work Problems 27 and 28.

South Korea to Resume U.S. Beef Imports

South Korea will reopen its market to most U.S. beef. South Korea banned imports of U.S. beef in 2003 amid concerns over a case of mad cow disease in the United States. The ban closed what was then the third-largest market for U.S. beef exporters.

Source: CNN, May 29, 2008

27. a. Explain how South Korea's import ban on U.S. beef affected beef producers and consumers in South Korea.
    b. Draw a graph of the market for beef in South Korea to illustrate your answer to part (a). Identify the Korean winners and losers from this policy. Is this policy in Korea's social interest?
28. a. Assuming that South Korea is the only importer of U.S. beef, explain how South Korea's import ban on U.S. beef affected beef producers and consumers in the United States.
    b. Draw a graph of the market for beef in the United States to illustrate your answer to part (a). Does anyone in the United States gain from Korea's policy?

International Trade Restrictions

Use the following information to work Problems 29 to 31.

Before 1995, trade between the United States and Mexico was subject to tariffs. In 1995, Mexico joined NAFTA and all U.S. and Mexican tariffs have gradually been removed.

29. Explain how the price that U.S. consumers pay for goods from Mexico and the quantity of U.S. imports from Mexico have changed. Who are the winners and who are the losers from this free trade?
30. Explain how the quantity of U.S. exports to Mexico and the U.S. government's tariff revenue from trade with Mexico have changed.
31. Suppose that in 2008, tomato growers in Florida lobby the U.S. government to impose an import quota on Mexican tomatoes. Explain who in the United States would gain and who would lose from such a quota.

Use the following information to work Problems 32 and 33.

Suppose that in response to huge job losses in the U.S. textile industry, Congress imposes a 100 percent tariff on imports of textiles from China.

32. Explain how the tariff on textiles will change the price that U.S. buyers pay for textiles, the quantity of textiles imported, and the quantity of textiles produced in the United States.
33. Explain how the U.S. and Chinese gains from trade will change. Who in the United States will lose and who will gain?

Use the following information to work Problems 34 and 35.

With free trade between Australia and the United States, Australia would export beef to the United States. But the United States imposes an import quota on Australian beef.

34. Explain how this quota influences the price that U.S. consumers pay for beef, the quantity of beef produced in the United States, and the U.S. and the Australian gains from trade.
35. Explain who in the United States gains from the quota on beef imports and who loses.

The Case Against Protection

36. **Trading Up**

    The cost of protecting jobs in uncompetitive sectors through tariffs is high: Saving a job in the sugar industry costs American consumers $826,000 in higher prices a year; saving a dairy industry job costs $685,000 per year; and saving a job in the manufacturing of women's handbags costs $263,000.

    Source: *The New York Times*, June 26, 2006

    a. What are the arguments for saving the jobs mentioned in this news clip?
    b. Explain why these arguments are faulty.
    c. Is there any merit to saving these jobs?

Economics in the News

37. After you have studied *Reading Between the Lines* on pp. 386–387, answer the following questions.
    a. What events put U.S. tire producers under pressure and caused some to go out of business?
    b. Explain how a tariff on tire imports changes domestic production, consumption, and imports of tires.
    c. Illustrate your answer to part (b) with an appropriate graphical analysis.
    d. Explain how a tariff on tire imports creates winners and losers and why the losses exceed the gains.
38. **Aid May Grow for Laid-Off Workers**

    Expansion of the Trade Adjustment Assistance (TAA) program would improve the social safety net for the 21st century, as advances permit more industries to take advantage of cheap foreign labor—even for skilled, white-collar work. By providing special compensation to more of globalization's losers and retraining them for stable jobs at home, an expanded program could begin to ease the resentment and insecurity arising from the new economy.

    Source: *The Washington Post*, July 23, 2007

    a. Why does the United States engage in international trade if it causes U.S. workers to lose their jobs?
    b. Explain how an expansion of the TAA program will make it easier for the United States to move toward freer international trade.

PART FIVE

UNDERSTANDING MACROECONOMIC POLICY

Tradeoffs and Free Lunches

A policy tradeoff arises if, in taking an action to achieve one goal, some other goal must be forgone. The Fed wants to avoid a rise in the inflation rate and a rise in the unemployment rate. But if the Fed raises the interest rate to curb inflation, it might lower expenditure and increase unemployment. The Fed faces a short-run tradeoff between inflation and unemployment.

A policy free lunch arises if in taking actions to pursue one goal, some other (intended or unintended) goal is also achieved. The Fed wants to keep inflation in check and, at the same time, to boost the economic growth rate. If lower inflation brings greater certainty about the future and stimulates saving and investment, the Fed gets both lower inflation and faster real GDP growth. It enjoys a free lunch.

The two chapters in this part have described the institutional framework in which fiscal policy (Chapter 13) and monetary policy (Chapter 14) are made, described the instruments of policy, and analyzed the effects of policy. This exploration of economic policy draws on almost everything that you learned in previous chapters.

These policy chapters serve as a capstone on your knowledge of macroeconomics and draw together all the strands in your study of the previous chapters.

Milton Friedman, whom you meet below, has profoundly influenced our understanding of macroeconomic policy, especially monetary policy.

Milton Friedman *was born into a poor immigrant family in New York City in 1912. He was an undergraduate at Rutgers and a graduate student at Columbia University during the Great Depression. From 1977 until his death in 2006, Professor Friedman was a Senior Fellow at the Hoover Institution at Stanford University. But his reputation was built between 1946 and 1983, when he was a leading member of the "Chicago School," an approach to economics developed at the University of Chicago and based on the views that free markets allocate resources efficiently and that stable and low money supply growth delivers macroeconomic stability.*

Friedman has advanced our understanding of the forces that determine macroeconomic performance and clarified the effects of the quantity of money. For this work, he was awarded the 1977 Nobel Prize for Economic Science.

By reasoning from basic economic principles, Friedman (along with Edmund S. Phelps, the 2006 Economics Nobel Laureate) predicted that persistent demand stimulation would not increase output but would cause inflation.

When output growth slowed and inflation broke out in the 1970s, Friedman seemed like a prophet, and for a time, his policy prescription, known as monetarism, *was embraced around the world.*

"Inflation is always and everywhere a monetary phenomenon."

MILTON FRIEDMAN
The Counter-Revolution in Monetary Theory

TALKING WITH **Stephanie Schmitt-Grohé**

What attracted you to economics?

When I graduated from high school, I was interested in both chemistry and economics but I wasn't sure which I wanted to study, so I enrolled in both programs. Within the first year of study, I realized that I wanted to pursue a career in economics. I took a class in which we learned how fiat money can have value and how the central bank can control the inflation rate. This seemed very important to me at the time—and still does after so many years.

What led you to focus your research on monetary and fiscal stabilization policy?

I always was very interested in economic policy and both monetary and fiscal stabilization policy have large and clear effects on a society's well-being. The same is certainly true for other areas of economics, but the benefits of macroeconomic stabilization policy are particularly easy to see; and it isn't difficult to find historical examples where bad monetary and fiscal policies unnecessarily lowered the standard of living.

What was your first job as a professional economist? How did you get started?

My first job out of graduate school was at the Board of Governors of the Federal Reserve System in Washington. This was a fabulous experience. Watching the policy-making process, I became motivated to work on having a more consistent and compelling theoretical framework on which to base monetary policy advice, and in particular, learning to develop tools to perform evaluation of alternative monetary policy proposals.

Only a few years out of graduate school, you and your economist husband, Martin Uribe, accepted a challenge to contribute to an assessment of "dollarization" for Mexico. First, would you explain what dollarization is?

When a country dollarizes, the U.S. dollar becomes legal tender, replacing the domestic currency. Ecuador, for example, is dollarized. In the case of Mexico in 1999, there were proposals, mainly coming from the business community, to replace the peso with the U.S. dollar.

Why might dollarization be a good idea?

Such proposals are typically motivated by the desire to avoid excessive inflation and excessive exchange rate volatility. Dollarization also makes inflationary finance of the Treasury Department impossible.

And what are the costs of dollarization?

One cost is that the country loses the revenues it gains from issuing money. A second cost is that the country loses the ability to conduct monetary stabilization policy. In effect, the domestic central bank can no longer influence the business cycle through interest rate or exchange rate policy. The question that Martin and I wanted to answer was "how costly is it for a country to give up the ability to conduct monetary stabilization policy?" We quickly realized that we didn't have the tools to answer this question in a way that we regarded as satisfying.

Briefly, what did you have to do to enable you to say whether dollarization is a good or bad idea?

STEPHANIE SCHMITT-GROHÉ is Professor of Economics at Columbia University. Born in Germany, she received her first economics degree at Westfälische Wilhelms-Universität Münster in 1987, her M.B.A in Finance at Baruch College, City University of New York in 1989, and her Ph.D. in economics at the University of Chicago in 1994.

Professor Schmitt-Grohé's research covers a wide range of fiscal policy and monetary policy issues that are especially relevant in today's economy as the consequences of the 2007 mortgage crisis play out.

Working with her husband, Martin Uribe, also a Professor of Economics at Columbia University, she has published papers in leading economics journals on how best to conduct monetary policy and fiscal policy and how to avoid problems that might arise from the inappropriate use of a simple policy rule for setting the federal funds rate. She has also contributed to the debate on inflation targeting.

In 2004, Professor Schmitt-Grohé was awarded the Bernácer Prize, awarded annually to a European economist under the age of 40 who has made outstanding contributions in the fields of macroeconomics and finance.

Michael Parkin talked with Stephanie Schmitt-Grohé about her work and the challenges of conducting stabilization policy.

We wanted to be able to quantify the loss in economic welfare that comes from not being able to target monetary policy at stabilizing the domestic economy. To do this, we needed to compute two measures of economic welfare, one arising from Mexican monetary policy and another under dollarization. But we wanted our measures to be based on an empirically compelling and sufficiently detailed model of the Mexican business cycle.

At that time there were no measurement techniques available that allowed us to perform this task. So over the course of the next five years we developed the tools that we needed. One tool is an algorithm that computes (approximately but with sufficient accuracy) economic welfare under any given monetary policy, including the two of interest to us: Mexican dollarization and actual Mexican monetary policy. A second tool that we developed is another algorithm to compute optimal monetary policy—the best available monetary policy.

. . . if the central bank responds to the output gap, economic welfare suffers.

Knowing the highest level of economic welfare that can be achieved allows us to judge how close practical policy proposals come to optimal policy.

And what was your biggest surprise?

I think our biggest surprise in this research program was how small the welfare costs of some very simple policy rules are vis-à-vis the optimal policy. Martin and I have shown in a number of papers that simple interest rate rules are very close to the best that can be achieved.

How would you describe the best stabilization policy for smoothing the business cycle and keeping inflation in check?

Good stabilization policy is not necessarily a policy that smoothes the business cycle, in the sense that it minimizes output fluctuations. On the contrary, it might be that trying to avoid cyclical fluctuations lowers economic welfare. Suppose, for example, that business-cycle fluctuations arise from fluctuations in the growth rate of productivity—as real business cycle theory suggests. Then economic welfare decreases if we limit the cyclical increase in output that comes from the increase in productivity.

Good stabilization policy is not necessarily a policy that smoothes the business cycle

The findings of my work with Martin suggest that a simple and highly effective monetary policy is one whereby the central bank raises the short-term interest rate by more than one-for-one when inflation exceeds the targeted level of inflation. Interest rate feedback rules of this type are similar to the Taylor rule, but contrary to Taylor's rule, our results suggest that the central bank should not respond to output variations in setting the short-term nominal interest rate. We find that if the central bank responds to the output gap, economic welfare suffers.

Regarding fiscal policies, the results of several of our papers strongly suggest smoothing out distortionary tax rates and using variations in the level of government debt to address cyclical budget shortfalls.

You've done some recent research with Martin on the optimal or best inflation rate. What is the optimal rate?

Many central banks have an inflation target. In developed economies it is about 2 percent per year and in emerging market economies it is about 4 percent per year. Martin and I are trying to answer the seemingly simple and innocent question: Which level of the inflation rate should a central bank target? Is it the observed values of 2 percent and 4 percent? Or should it be zero, or 6 percent, or why not aim for a negative inflation rate—a falling price level?

Three costs of inflation are relevant for determining the best inflation rate. The first is the burden of inflation as a tax—a tax on money holdings that decreases the quantity of money that people want to hold and increases transactions costs. To avoid the inflation tax and minimize transactions costs, it would be best if money had the same rate of return as a bond. This outcome is achieved if the nominal interest rate is zero and the inflation rate is negative and equal to minus the real of interest. This result regarding the best level of inflation is known as the Friedman rule.

... the optimal inflation rate is well below the two percent or more that we observe.

The second is the cost of changing nominal prices. If inflation is, say 5 percent per year and firms cannot freely adjust their prices, then the firms which for some reason have not adjusted their prices in a long time will be charging an inefficient price. So with sluggish price adjustment, inflation distorts relative prices and thus leads to inefficient resource allocations in the economy. The best way to avoid such inefficiencies is to target zero inflation.

Avoiding these two costs require different inflation rates, one negative and one zero, but neither is close to the positive inflation targets that we observe almost every central pursuing.

The third cost is one that arises if the nominal prices of goods and the nominal wages of workers are rigid downward, meaning that nominal prices and nominal wages can only go up but never down. If this is a valid description of the world, then any relative price change between two goods or any fall in the real wage can only be brought about by a rise in the price level. So in principle, nominal downward rigidities can explain why we see positive inflation targets. However, in a realistic model of the economy that incorporates this idea, the best inflation rate is at most half a percent per year. So the optimal inflation rate is well below the two percent or more that we observe.

What are the implications of your work for avoiding and living with the credit market conditions that emerged in August 2007 and dominated the economy through 2008?

Over the past decade, financial institutions that act like banks have developed. They are not, however, required by law to be under the regulations and supervision of the government in the same way as regular banks are. Going forward, I believe that it is desirable to have an overhaul of the existing regulatory system in order to ensure equal regulation and supervision for all financial institutions.

What advice do you have for a student who is just starting to study economics? Is it a good choice of major? What subjects go well with it?

If you are just starting studying economics, be patient. Economics can be more formal than other social sciences, and because of this, it may take a little while before you can apply what you learn in your economics classes to enhance your understanding of the economy around you. Subjects that are nice complements with economics are statistics and applied math.

Do you have any special advice for young women who might be contemplating a career in economics?

About one third of newly minted economics Ph.Ds are women, but only about 8 percent of full professors in a Ph.D.-granting economics department are women. Looking at statistics like this can be discouraging. However, from my fifteen years of experience of working in this field, I don't see any reason why young women who are about to start a career in economics will not be able to change these statistics.

Above full-employment equilibrium A macroeconomic equilibrium in which real GDP exceeds potential GDP. (p. 252)

Absolute advantage A person has an absolute advantage if that person is more productive than another person. (p. 38)

Aggregate demand The relationship between the quantity of real GDP demanded and the price level. (p. 246)

Aggregate planned expenditure The sum of planned consumption expenditure, planned investment, planned government expenditure on goods and services, and planned exports minus planned imports. (p. 266)

Aggregate production function The relationship between real GDP and the quantity of labor when all other influences on production remain the same. (p. 139)

Allocative efficiency A situation in which goods and services are produced at the lowest possible cost and in the quantities that provide the greatest possible benefit. We cannot produce more of any good without giving up some of another good that we *value more highly*. (p. 33)

Automatic fiscal policy A fiscal policy action that is triggered by the state of the economy with no action by the government. (p. 334)

Autonomous expenditure The sum of those components of aggregate planned expenditure that are not influenced by real GDP. Autonomous expenditure equals the sum of investment, government expenditure, exports, and the autonomous parts of consumption expenditure and imports. (p. 270)

Autonomous tax multiplier The change in equilibrium expenditure that results from a change in autonomous taxes divdied by the change in autonomous taxes. (p. 288)

Balanced budget A government budget in which receipts and outlays are equal. (p. 324)

Balanced budget multiplier The change in equilibrium expenditure that results from equal changes in government expenditure and lump-sum taxes tdivided by the change in government expenditure. (p. 289)

Balance of payments accounts A country's record of international trading, borrowing, and lending. (p. 225)

Beige book The Fed's publication that summarizes all the data that it gathers and that describes the current state of the economy. (p. 349)

Below full-employment equilibrium A macroeconomic equilibrium in which potential GDP exceeds real GDP. (p. 253)

Benefit The benefit of something is the gain of pleasure that it brings and is determined by preferences. (p. 8)

Bond A promise to make specified payments on specified dates. (p. 161)

Bond market The market in which bonds issued by firms and governments are traded. (p. 161)

Budget deficit A government's budget balance that is negative—outlays exceed receipts. (p. 324)

Budget surplus A government's budget balance that is positive—receipts exceed outlays. (p. 324)

Business cycle The periodic but irregular up-and-down movement in production. (p. 91)

Capital The tools, equipment, buildings, and other constructions that businesses use to produce goods and services. (p. 4)

Capital and financial account A record of foreign investment in a country minus its investment abroad. (p. 225)

Capital accumulation The growth of capital resources, including *human capital.* (p. 36)

Central bank A bank's bank and a public authority that regulates the nation's depository institutions and conducts monetary policy, which means it adjusts the quantity of money in circulation and influences interest rates. (p. 190)

Ceteris paribus Other things being equal—all other relevant things remaining the same. (p. 22)

Chained-dollar real GDP A measure of real GDP derived by valuing production at the prices of both the current year and previous year and linking (chaining) those prices back to the prices of the reference base year. (p. 100)

Change in demand A change in buyers' plans that occurs when some influence on those plans other than the price of the good changes. It is illustrated by a shift of the demand curve. (p. 54)

Change in supply A change in sellers' plans that occurs when some influence on those plans other than the price of the good changes. It is illustrated by a shift of the supply curve. (p. 59)

Change in the quantity demanded A change in buyers' plans that occurs when the price of a good changes but all other influences on buyers' plans remain unchanged. It is illustrated by a movement along the demand curve. (p. 57)

Change in the quantity supplied A change in sellers' plans that occurs when the price of a good changes but all other influences on sellers' plans remain unchanged. It is illustrated by a movement along the supply curve. (p. 60)

Classical A macroeconomist who believes that the economy is self-regulating and that it is always at full employment. (p. 256)

Classical growth theory A theory of economic growth based on the view that the growth of real GDP per person is temporary and that when it rises above subsistence level, a population explosion eventually brings it back to subsistence level. (p. 147)

Comparative advantage A person or country has a comparative advantage in an activity if that person or country can perform the activity at a lower opportunity cost than anyone else or any other country. (p. 38)

Competitive market A market that has many buyers and many sellers, so no single buyer or seller can influence the price. (p. 52)

Complement A good that is used in conjunction with another good. (p. 55)

Consumer Price Index (CPI) An index that measures the average of the prices paid by urban consumers for a fixed basket of the consumer goods and services. (p. 117)

Consumption expenditure The total payment for consumer goods and services. (p. 85)

Consumption function The relationship between consumption expenditure and disposable income, other things remaining the same. (p. 266)

Core inflation rate The Fed's operational guide is the rate of increase in the core PCE deflator, which is the PCE deflator excluding food and fuel prices. (p. 349)

Core CPI inflation rate The CPI inflation rate excluding volatile elements (food and fuel). (p. 121)

Cost-push inflation An inflation that results from an initial increase in costs. (p. 298)

Council of Economic Advisers The President's council whose main work is to monitor the economy and keep the President and the public well informed about the current state of the economy and the best available forecasts of where it is heading. (p. 323)

Crawling peg An exchange rate that follows a path determined by a decision of the government or the central bank and is achieved in a similar way to a fixed exchange rate. (p. 223)

Creditor nation A country that during its entire history has invested more in the rest of the world than other countries have invested in it. (p. 227)

Crowding-out effect The tendency for a government budget deficit to raise the real interest rate and decrease investment. (p. 172)

Currency The notes and coins held by individuals and businesses. (p. 185)

Currency drain ratio The ratio of currency to deposits. (p. 194)

Current account A record of receipts from exports of goods and services, payments for imports of goods and services, net interest income paid abroad and net transfers received from abroad. (p. 225)

Cycle The tendency for a variable to alternative between upward and downward movements. (p. 99)

Cyclical surplus or deficit The actual surplus or deficit minus the structural surplus or deficit. (p. 335)

Cyclical unemployment The higher than normal unemployment at a business cycle trough and the lower than normal unemployment at a business cycle peak. (p. 113)

Debtor nation A country that during its entire history has borrowed more in the rest of the world than other countries have lent in it. (p. 227)

Deflation A persistently falling price level. (p. 116)

Demand The entire relationship between the price of the good and the quantity demanded of it when all other influences on buyers' plans remain the same. It is illustrated by a demand curve and described by a demand schedule. (p. 53)

Demand curve A curve that shows the relationship between the quantity demanded of a good and its price when all other influences on consumers' planned purchases remain the same. (p. 54)

Demand for loanable funds The relationship between the quantity of loanable funds demanded and the real interest rate when all other influences on borrowing plans remain the same. (p. 166)

Demand for money The relationship between the quantity of money demanded and the nominal interest rate when all other influences on the amount of money that people wish to hold remain the same. (p. 197)

Demand-pull inflation An inflation that starts because aggregate demand increases. (p. 296)

Depository institution A financial firm that takes deposits from households and firms. (p. 187)

Depreciation The decrease in the value of a firm's capital that results from wear and tear and obsolescence. (p. 86)

Desired reserve ratio The ratio of reserves to deposits that banks *plan* to hold. (p. 194)

Direct relationship A relationship between two variables that move in the same direction. (p. 16)

Discouraged worker A marginally attached worker who has stopped looking for a job because of repeated failure to find one. (p. 111)

Discretionary fiscal policy A fiscal action that is initiated by an act of Congress. (p. 334)

Disposable income Aggregate income minus taxes plus transfer payments. (pp. 248, 266)

Doha Development Agenda (Doha Round) Negotiations held in Doha, Qatar, to lower tariff barriers and quotas that restrict international trade in farm products and services. (p. 378)

Dumping The sale by a foreign firm of exports at a lower price than the cost of production. (p. 381)

Economic growth The expansion of production possibilities. (p. 36)

Economic growth rate The annual percentage change in real GDP. (p. 134)

Economic model A description of some aspect of the economic world that includes only those features of the world that are needed for the purpose at hand. (p. 10)

Economics The social science that studies the *choices* that individuals, businesses, governments, and entire societies make as they cope with *scarcity* and the *incentives* that influence and reconcile those choices. (p. 2)

Efficiency A situation in which the available resources are used to produce goods and services at the lowest possible cost and in quantities that give the greatest value or benefit. (p. 5)

Employment Act of 1946 A landmark Congressional act that recognizes a role for government actions to keep unemployment low, the economy expanding, and inflation in check. (p. 322)

Employment-to-population ratio The percentage of people of working age who have jobs. (p. 110)

Entrepreneurship The human resource that organizes the other three factors of production: labor, land, and capital. (p. 4)

Equilibrium expenditure The level of aggregate expenditure that occurs when aggregate *planned* expenditure equals real GDP. (p. 272)

Equilibrium price The price at which the quantity demanded equals the quantity supplied. (p. 62)

Equilibrium quantity The quantity bought and sold at the equilibrium price. (p. 62)

Excess reserves A bank's actual reserves minus its desired reserves. (p. 194)

Exchange rate The price at which one currency exchanges for another in the foreign exchange market. (p. 212)

Expansion A business cycle phase between a trough and a peak—a period in which real GDP increases. (p. 91)

Exports The goods and services that we sell to people in other countries. (pp. 86, 372)

Export subsidy A payment by the government to the producer of an exported good. (p. 380)

Factors of production The productive resources used to produce goods and services. (p. 3)

Federal budget The annual statement of the outlays and receipts of the government of the United States, together with the laws and regulations that approve and support those outlays and taxes. (p. 322)

Federal funds rate The interest rate that the banks charge each other on overnight loans. (pp. 187, 350)

Federal Open Market Committee The main policy-making organ of the Federal Reserve System. (p. 190)

Federal Reserve System (the Fed) The central bank of the United States. (p. 190)

Final good An item that is bought by its final user during the specified time period. (p. 84)

Financial capital The funds that firms use to buy physical capital. (p. 160)

Financial institution A firm that operates on both sides of the market for financial capital. It borrows in one market and lends in another. (p. 162)

Firm An economic unit that hires factors of production and organizes those factors to produce and sell goods and services. (p. 41)

Fiscal imbalance The present value of the government's commitments to pay benefits minus the present value of its tax revenues. (p. 332)

Fiscal policy The use of the federal budget, by setting and changing tax rates, making transfer payments, and purchasing goods and services, to achieve macroeconomic objectives such as full employment, sustained economic growth, and price level stability. (pp. 248, 322)

Fiscal stimulus The the use of fiscal policy to increase production and employment. (p. 334)

Fixed exchange rate An exchange rate the value of which is determined by a decision of the government or the central bank and is achieved by central bank intervention in the foreign exchange market to block the unregulated forces of demand and supply. (p. 222)

Flexible exchange rate An exchange rate that is determined by demand and supply in the foreign exchange market with no direct intervention by the central bank. (p. 222)

Foreign currency The money of other countries regardless of whether that money is in the form of notes, coins, or bank deposits. (p. 212)

Foreign exchange market The market in which the currency of one country is exchanged for the currency of another. (p. 212)

Frictional unemployment The unemployment that arises from normal labor turnover—from people entering and leaving the labor force and from the ongoing creation and destruction of jobs. (p. 113)

Full employment A situation in which the the unemployment rate equals the natural unemployment rate. At full employment, there is no cyclical unemployment—all unemployment is frictional and structural. (p. 113)

Full-employment equilibrium A macroeconomic equilibrium in which real GDP equals potential GDP. (p. 253)

General Agreement on Tariffs and Trade (GATT) An international agreement signed in 1947 to reduce tariffs on international trade. (p. 377)

Generational accounting An accounting system that measures the lifetime tax burden and benefits of each generation. (p. 332)

Generational imbalance The division of the fiscal imbalance between the current and future generations, assuming that the current generation will enjoy the existing levels of taxes and benefits. (p. 333)

Goods and services The objects that people value and produce to satisfy human wants. (p. 3)

Government debt The total amount that the government has borrowed. It equals the sum of past budget deficits minus the sum of past budget surpluses. (p. 326)

Government expenditure Goods and services bought by government. (p. 86)

Government expenditure multiplier The quantitative effect of a change in government expenditure on real GDP. It equals the change in real GDP that results from a change in government expenditure on goods and services divided by the change in government expenditure. (pp. 288, 337)

Government sector balance An amount equal to net taxes minus government expenditure on goods and services. (p. 228)

Gross domestic product (GDP) The market value of all final goods and services produced within a country during a given time period. (p. 84)

Gross investment The total amount spent on purchases of new capital and on replacing depreciated capital. (pp. 86, 160)

Human capital The knowledge and skill that people obtain from education, on-the-job training, and work experience. (p. 3)

Hyperinflation An inflation rate of 50 percent a month or higher that grinds the economy to a halt and causes a society to collapse. (p. 116)

Import quota A restriction that limits the maximum quantity of a good that may be imported in a given period. (p. 378)

Imports The goods and services that we buy from people in other countries. (pp. 86, 372)

Incentive A reward that encourages an action or a penalty that discourages one. (p. 2)

Induced expenditure The sum of the components of aggregate planned expenditure that vary with real GDP. Induced expenditure equals consumption expenditure minus imports. (p. 270)

Infant-industry argument The argument that it is necessary to protect a new industry to enable it to grow into a mature industry that can compete in world markets. (p. 381)

Inferior good A good for which demand decreases as income increases. (p. 56)

Inflation A persistently rising price level. (p. 116)

Inflationary gap An output gap in which real GDP exceeds potential GDP. (p. 252)

Inflation rate targeting A monetary policy strategy in which the central bank makes a public commitment to achieve an explicit inflation rate and to explain how its policy actions will achieve that target. (p. 363)

Interest The income that capital earns. (p. 4)

Interest rate parity A situation in which the rates of return on assets in different currencies are equal. (p. 220)

Intermediate good An item that is produced by one firm, bought by another firm, and used as a component of a final good or service. (p. 84)

Inverse relationship A relationship between variables that move in opposite directions. (p. 17)

Investment The purchase of new plant, equipment, and buildings, and additions to inventories. (p. 86)

Keynesian A macroeconomist who believes that left alone, the economy would rarely operate at full employment and that to achieve full employment, active help from fiscal policy and monetary policy is required. (p. 256)

Keynesian cycle theory A theory that fluctuations in investment driven by fluctuations in business confidence—summarized in the phase "animal spirits"—are the main source of fluctuations in aggregate demand. (p. 306)

Labor The work time and work effort that people devote to producing goods and services. (p. 3)

Labor force The sum of the people who are employed and who are unemployed. (p. 109)

Labor force participation rate The percentage of the working-age population who are members of the labor force. (p. 111)

Labor productivity The quantity of real GDP produced by an hour of labor. (p. 143)

Laffer curve The relationship between the tax rate and the amount of tax revenue collected. (p. 331)

Land The "gifts of nature" that we use to produce goods and services. (p. 3)

Law of demand Other things remaining the same, the higher the price of a good, the smaller is the quantity demanded of it; the lower the price of a good, the larger is the quantity demanded of it. (p. 53)

Law of supply Other things remaining the same, the higher the price of a good, the greater is the quantity supplied of it. (p. 58)

Lender of last resort The Fed is the lender of last resort—depository institutions that are short of reserves can borrow from the Fed. (p. 193)

Linear relationship A relationship between two variables that is illustrated by a straight line. (p. 16)

Loanable funds market The aggregate of all the individual markets in which households, firms, governments, banks, and other financial institutions borrow and lend. (p. 164)

Long-run aggregate supply The relationship between the quantity of real GDP supplied and the price level when the money wage rate changes in step with the price level to achieve full employment. (p. 242)

Long-run macroeconomic equilibrium A situation that occurs when real GDP equals potential GDP—the economy is on its long-run aggregate supply curve. (p. 250)

Long-run Phillips curve A curve that shows the relationship between inflation and unemployment when the actual inflation rate equals the expected inflation rate. (p. 303)

M1 A measure of money that consists of currency and traveler's checks plus checking deposits owned by individuals and businesses. (p. 185)

M2 A measure of money that consists of M1 plus time deposits, savings deposits, money market mutual funds, and other deposits. (p. 185)

Macroeconomics The study of the performance of the national economy and the global economy. (p. 2)

Margin When a choice is made by comparing a little more of something with its cost, the choice is made at the margin. (p. 9)

Marginal benefit The benefit that a person receives from consuming one more unit of a good or service. It is measured as the maximum amount that a person is willing to pay for one more unit of the good or service. (pp. 9, 34)

Marginal benefit curve A curve that shows the relationship between the marginal benefit of a good and the quantity of that good consumed. (p. 34)

Marginal cost The *opportunity cost* of producing *one* more unit of a good or service. It is the best alternative forgone. It is calculated as the increase in total cost divided by the increase in output. (pp. 9, 33)

Marginal propensity to consume The fraction of a *change* in disposable income that is consumed. It is calculated as the *change* in consumption expenditure divided by the *change* in disposable income. (p. 268)

Marginal propensity to import The fraction of an increase in real GDP that is spent on imports. It is calculated as the *change* in imports divided by the *change* in disposable income. (p. 269)

Marginal propensity to save The fraction of a *change* in disposable income that is saved. It is calculated as the *change* in saving divided by the *change* in disposable income. (p. 268)

Marginally attached worker A person who currently is neither working nor looking for work but has indicated that he or she wants and is available for a job. (p. 111)

Market Any arrangement that enables buyers and sellers to get information and to do business with each other. (p. 42)

Means of payment A method of settling a debt. (p. 184)

Microeconomics The study of the choices that individuals and businesses make, the way these choices interact in markets, and the influence of governments. (p. 2)

Monetarist A macroeconomist who believes that the economy is self-regulating and that it will normally operate at full employment, provided that monetary policy is not erratic and that the pace of money growth is kept steady. (p. 257)

Monetarist cycle theory A theory that fluctuations in both investment and consumption expenditure, driven by fluctuations in the growth rate of the quantity of money, are the main source of fluctuations in aggregate demand. (p. 306)

Monetary base The sum of Federal Reserve notes, coins and depository institution deposits at the Fed. (p. 191)

Monetary policy The Fed conducts the nation's monetary policy by changing interest rates and adjusting the quantity of money. (p. 248)

Monetary policy instrument A variable that the Fed can directly control directly or at least very closely target. (p. 350)

Money Any commodity or token that is generally acceptable as the means of payment. (pp. 42, 184)

Money multiplier The ratio of the change in the quantity of money to the change in the monetary base. (p. 195)

Money price The number of dollars that must be given up in exchange for a good or service. (p. 52)

Mortgage A legal contract that gives ownership of a home to the lender in the event that the borrower fails to meet the agreed loan payments (repayments and interest). (p. 161)

Mortgage-backed security A type of bond that entitles its holder to the income from a package of mortgages. (p. 162)

Multiplier The amount by which a change in autonomous expenditure is magnified or multiplied to determine the change in equilibrium expenditure and real GDP. (p. 274)

National saving The sum of private saving (saving by households and businesses) and government saving. (p. 165)

Natural unemployment rate The unemployment rate when the economy is at full employment—natural unemployment as a percentage of the labor force. (p. 113)

Negative relationship A relationship between variables that move in opposite directions. (p. 17)

Neoclassical growth theory A theory of economic growth that proposes that real GDP per person grows because technological change induces an amount of saving and investment that makes capital per hour of labor grow. (p. 147)

Net borrower A country that is borrowing more from the rest of the world than it is lending to it. (p. 227)

Net exports The value of exports of goods and services minus the value of imports of goods and services. (pp. 86, 228)

Net investment The amount by which the value of capital increases—gross investment minus depreciation. (pp. 86, 160)

Net lender A country that is lending more to the rest of the world than it is borrowing from it. (p. 227)

Net taxes Taxes paid to governments minus cash transfers received from governments. (p. 164)

Net worth The market value of what a financial institution has lent minus the market value of what it has borrowed. (p. 163)

New classical A macroeconomist who holds the view that business cycle fluctuations are the efficient responses of a well-functioning market economy bombarded by shocks that arise from the uneven pace of technological change. (p. 256)

New classical cycle theory A rational expectations theory of the business cycle in which the rational expectation of the price level, which is determined by potential GDP and *expected* aggregate demand, determines the money wage rate and the position of the *SAS* curve. (p. 306)

New growth theory A theory of economic growth based on the idea that real GDP per person grows because of the choices that people make in the pursuit of profit and that growth will persist indefinitely. (p. 148)

New Keynesian A macroeconomist who holds the view that not only is the money wage rate sticky but also that the prices of goods and services are sticky. (p. 257)

New Keynesian cycle theory A rational expectations theory of the business cycle that emphasizes the fact that today's money wage rates were negotiated at many past dates, which means that *past* rational expectations of the current price level influence the money wage rate and the position of the *SAS* curve. (p. 306)

Nominal GDP The value of the final goods and services produced in a given year valued at the prices that prevailed in that same year. It is a more precise name for GDP. (p. 89)

Nominal interest rate The number of dollars that a borrower pays and a lender receives in a year expressed as a percentage of the number of dollars borrowed and lent. (p. 165)

Normal good A good for which demand increases as income increases. (p. 56)

Official settlements account A record of the change in official reserves, which are the government's holdings of foreign currency. (p. 225)

Offshore outsourcing A U.S. firm buys finished goods, components, or services from other firms in other countries. (p. 383)

Offshoring A U.S. firm hires foreign labor and produces in a foreign country or a U.S. firm buys finished goods, components, or services from firms in other countries. (p. 383)

Open market operation The purchase or sale of government securities—U.S. Treasury bills and bonds—by the Federal Reserve in the loanable funds market. (p. 191)

Opportunity cost The highest-valued alternative that we must give up to get something. (pp. 8, 31)

Output gap The gap between real GDP and potential GDP. (pp. 114, 252)

Outsourcing A U.S. firm buys finished goods, components, or services from other firms in the United States or from firms in other countries. (p. 383)

Phillips curve A curve that shows a relationship between inflation and unemployment. (p. 302)

Positive relationship A relationship between two variables that move in the same direction. (p. 16)

Potential GDP The value of production when all the economy's labor, capital, land, and entrepreneurial ability are fully employed; the quantity of real GDP at full employment. (p. 90)

Preferences A description of a person's likes and dislikes and the intensity of those feelings. (pp. 8, 34)

Present value The amount of money that, if invested today, will grow to be as large as a given future amount when the interest that it will earn is taken into account. (p. 332)

Price level The average level of prices. (p. 116)

Private sector balance An amount equal to saving minus investment. (p. 228)

Production efficiency A situation in which goods and services are produced at the lowest possible cost. (p. 31)

Production possibilities frontier The boundary between the combinations of goods and services that can be produced and the combinations that cannot. (p. 30)

Profit The income earned by entrepreneurship. (p. 4)

Property rights The social arrangements that govern the ownership, use, and disposal of anything that people value.Property rights are enforceable in the courts. (p. 42)

Purchasing power parity A situation in which the prices in two countries are equal when converted at the exchange rate. (p. 220)

Quantity demanded The amount of a good or service that consumers plan to buy during a given time period at a particular price. (p. 53)

Quantity supplied The amount of a good or service that producers plan to sell during a given time period at a particular price. (p. 58)

Quantity theory of money The proposition that in the long run, an increase in the quantity of money brings an equal percentage increase in the price level. (p. 200)

Rational choice A choice that compares costs and benefits and achieves the greatest benefit over cost for the person making the choice. (p. 8)

Rational expectation The best forecast possible, a forecast that uses all the available information. (p. 301)

Real business cycle theory A theory of the business cycle that regards random fluctuations in productivity as the main source of economic fluctuations. (p. 306)

Real exchange rate The relative price of U.S.-produced goods and services to foreign-produced goods and services. (pp. 221)

Real GDP The value of final goods and services produced in a given year when valued at the prices of a reference base year. (p. 89)

Real GDP per person Real GDP divided by the population. (pp. 90, 134)

Real interest rate The nominal interest rate adjusted to remove the effects of inflation on the buying power of money. It is approximately equal to the nominal interest rate minus the inflation rate. (p. 165)

Real wage rate The money (or nominal) wage rate divided by the price level. The real wage rate is the quantity of goods and services that an hour of labor earns. (p. 140)

Recession A business cycle phase in which real GDP decreases for at least two successive quarters. (p. 91)

Recessionary gap An output gap in which potential GDP exceeds real GDP. (p. 253)

Relative price The ratio of the price of one good or service to the price of another good or service. A relative price is an opportunity cost. (p. 52)

Rent The income that land earns. (p. 4)

Rent seeking The lobbying for special treatment by the government to create economic profit or to divert the gains from international trade away from others. (p. 385)

Required reserve ratio The minimum percentage of deposits that depository institutions are required to hold as reserves. (p. 193)

Reserves A bank's reserves consist of notes and coins in its vaults plus its deposit at the Federal Reserve. (p. 187)

Rule of 70 A rule that states that the number of years it takes for the level of a variable to double is approximately 70 divided by the annual percentage growth rate of the variable. (p. 134)

Saving The amount of income that is not paid in taxes or spent on consumption goods and services. (p. 160)

Saving function The relationship between saving and disposable income, other things remaining the same. (p. 266)

Scarcity Our inability to satisfy all our wants. (p. 2)

Scatter diagram A graph that plots the value of one variable against the value of another variable for a number of different values of each variable. (p. 14)

Self-interest The choices that you think are the best ones available for you are choices made in your self-interest. (p. 5)

Short-run aggregate supply The relationship between the quantity of real GDP supplied and the price level when the money wage rate, the prices of other resources, and potential GDP remain constant. (p. 243)

Short-run macroeconomic equilibrium A situation that occurs when the quantity of real GDP demanded equals the quantity of real GDP supplied—at the point of intersection of the *AD* curve and the *SAS* curve. (p. 250)

Short-run Phillips curve A curve that shows the tradeoff between inflation and unemployment, when the expected inflation rate and the natural unemployment rate remain the same. (p. 302)

Slope The change in the value of the variable measured on the y-axis divided by the change in the value of the variable measured on the x-axis. (p. 20)

Social interest Choices that are the best ones for society as a whole. (p. 5)

Stagflation The combination of inflation and recession. (pp. 255, 299)

Stock A certificate of ownership and claim to the firm's profits. (p. 162)

Stock market A financial market in which shares of stocks of corporations are traded. (p. 162)

Structural surplus or deficit The budget balance that would occur if the economy were at full employment and real GDP were equal to potential GDP. (p. 335)

Structural unemployment The unemployment that arises when changes in technology or international competition change the skills needed to perform jobs or change the locations of jobs. (p. 113)

Substitute A good that can be used in place of another good. (p. 55)

Supply The entire relationship between the price of a good and the quantity supplied of it when all other influences on producers' planned sales remain the same. It is described by a supply schedule and illustrated by a supply curve. (p. 58)

Supply curve A curve that shows the relationship between the quantity supplied of a good and its price when all other influences on producers' planned sales remain the same. (p. 58)

Supply of loanable funds The relationship between the quantity of loanable funds supplied and the real interest rate when all other influences on lending plans remain the same. (p. 167)

Tariff A tax that is imposed by the importing country when an imported good crosses its international boundary. (p. 376)

Tax multiplier The quantitative effect of a change in taxes on real GDP. (p. 337)

Tax wedge The gap between the before-tax and after-tax wage rates. (p. 329)

Technological change The development of new goods and of better ways of producing goods and services. (p. 36)

Time-series graph A graph that measures time (for example, years, quarter, or months) on the *x*-axis and the variable or variables in which we are interested on the *y*-axis. (p. 98)

Tradeoff A constraint that involves giving up one thing to get something else. (p. 8)

Trend The tendency for a variable to move in one general direction. (p. 99)

Unemployment rate The percentage of the people in the labor force who are unemployed. (p. 110)

U.S. interest rate differential The U.S. interest rate minus the foreign interest rate. (p. 217)

U.S. official reserves The government's holding of foreign currency. (p. 225)

Velocity of circulation The average number of times a dollar of money is used annually to buy the goods and services that make up GDP. (p. 200)

Wages The income that labor earns. (p. 4)

Wealth The value of all the things that people own—the market value of their assets—at a point in time. (p. 160)

Working-age population The total number of people aged 16 years and over who are not in jail, hospital, or some other form of institutional care. (p. 109)

World Trade Organization (WTO) An international organization that places greater obligations on its member countries to observe the GATT rules. (p. 378)

PHOTO CREDITS

Michael Parkin (page vii) John Tamblyn

College campus (page 1) Image Source/Getty Images

Parrot cartoon (page 2) Copyright © 1985 The New Yorker Collection/Frank Modell from cartoonbank.com. All Rights Reserved.

Sneaker factory (page 5) Adek Berry/Getty Images

Intel Chip (page 6) Imagebroker/Alamy

Pollution (page 6) Digital Vision

Lehman Brothers (page 7) Kurt Brady/Alamy

Corn (page 29) MNPhoto/Alamy

Ethanol gasoline pump (page 29) Alex Farnsworth/The Image Works

Boeing (page 41) Randy Duchaine/Alamy

Clothing factory (page 41) INSADCO Photography/Alamy

Gas prices (page 51) Justin Sullivan/Staff/Getty Images

Oil drill (page 65) Alberto Incrocci/Getty Images

Strawberry picking (page 67) Chris O'Meara/AP Images

Smith (page 79) Bettmann/Corbis

Bhagwati (page 80) Michael Parkin

Man at Computer (page 83) OJO Images Ltd/Alamy

American McDonalds (page 92) Scott Olson/Staff/ Getty Images

Asian McDonalds (page 92) Bloomberg via Getty Images

Chefs (page 93) AFP/Getty Images

Mother (page 93) AFP/Getty Images

Interview (page 107) Alexander Raths/Shutterstock

Great Depression (page 108) Library of Congress Prints and Photographs Division [LC-USZ62-63966]

Workers at Machine (page 114) Bloomberg/Getty Images

Hume (page 129) Print Collector/HIP/The Image Works

Clarida (page 130) Courtesy of author

Shangai (page 133) Image Source/Getty Images

The Rocket (page 145) National Railway Museum/SSPL/The Image Works

Outdoor market (page 146) Jose Silva Pinto/AP Images

Stock exchange (page 159) Richard Drew/AP Images

Fannie Mae (page 163) Frontpage/Shutterstock

Freddie Mac (page 163) Frontpage/Shutterstock

Greenspan (page 175) Scott J. Ferrell/Congressional Quarterly/Getty Image

Credit card (page 183) VladKol/Shutterstock

Exchange desk (page 211) Greg Balfour Evans/Alamy

Schumpeter (page 237) Bettmann/Corbis

Sala-i-Martin (page 238) Courtesy of author

Construction worker (page 241) Joe Gough/Shutterstock

Harry Reid, et all (page 248) Evan Vucci/AP Images

Bernanke (page 248) Susan Walsh/AP Images

Trichet (page 248) Bernd Kammerer/AP Images

King (page 248) Martin Rickett/AP Images

Carney (page 248) Adrian Wyld/The Canadian Press/AP Images

Seattle port (page 265) Gabe Palmer/Alamy

Couple paying bills (page 295) Jose Luis Pelaez Inc/Getty Images

Maynard Keyes (page 317) Stock Montage

Caballero (page 318) Courtesy of author

Capitol Building (page 321) Jonathan Larsen/Shutterstock

Obama signing Fiscal Act (page 336) Pete Souza/The White House

Romer (page 339) Photo by Peg Skorpinski

Barro (page 339) Courtesy of Robert J. Barro, Harvard University

Uhlig (page 339) Courtesy of Harlad Uhlig

Federal Reserve (page 347) Jonathan Larsen/Shutterstock

Beige Book (page 352) US Federal Reserve

Fed board meeting (page 352) Courtesy of the Federal Reserve Bank of Philadelphia

FedEx planes (page 371) Oliver Berg/DPA/Corbis

WTO meeting in Doha (page 378) Denis Balibouse/Reuters/Corbis.

Freidman (page 393) Marshall Heinrichs/Addison Wesley

Schmitt Grohe (page 394) Courtesy of author

Quincy Market in Boston, Massachusetts, USA (cover) Medioimages/Photodisc

The Pearson Series in Economics

Abel/Bernanke/Croushore
*Macroeconomics**

Bade/Parkin
*Foundations of Economics**

Berck/Helfand
The Economics of the Environment

Bierman/Fernandez
Game Theory with Economic Applications

Blanchard
*Macroeconomics**

Blau/Ferber/Winkler
The Economics of Women, Men and Work

Boardman/Greenberg/Vining/ Weimer
Cost-Benefit Analysis

Boyer
Principles of Transportation Economics

Branson
Macroeconomic Theory and Policy

Brock/Adams
The Structure of American Industry

Bruce
Public Finance and the American Economy

Carlton/Perloff
Modern Industrial Organization

Case/Fair/Oster
*Principles of Economics**

Caves/Frankel/Jones
World Trade and Payments: An Introduction

Chapman
Environmental Economics: Theory, Application, and Policy

Cooter/Ulen
Law & Economics

Downs
An Economic Theory of Democracy

Ehrenberg/Smith
Modern Labor Economics

Ekelund/Ressler/Tollison
*Economics**

Farnham
Economics for Managers

Folland/Goodman/Stano
The Economics of Health and Health Care

Fort
Sports Economics

Froyen
Macroeconomics

Fusfeld
The Age of the Economist

Gerber
*International Economics**

Gordon
*Macroeconomics**

Greene
Econometric Analysis

Gregory
Essentials of Economics

Gregory/Stuart
Russian and Soviet Economic Performance and Structure

Hartwick/Olewiler
The Economics of Natural Resource Use

Heilbroner/Milberg
The Making of the Economic Society

Heyne/Boettke/Prychitko
The Economic Way of Thinking

Hoffman/Averett
Women and the Economy: Family, Work, and Pay

Holt
Markets, Games and Strategic Behavior

Hubbard/O'Brien
*Economics**
*Money and Banking**

Hughes/Cain
American Economic History

Husted/Melvin
International Economics

Jehle/Reny
Advanced Microeconomic Theory

Johnson-Lans
A Health Economics Primer

Keat/Young
Managerial Economics

Klein
Mathematical Methods for Economics

Krugman/Obstfeld/Melitz
*International Economics: Theory & Policy**

Laidler
The Demand for Money

Leeds/von Allmen
The Economics of Sports

Leeds/von Allmen/Schiming
*Economics**

Lipsey/Ragan/Storer
*Economics**

Lynn
Economic Development: Theory and Practice for a Divided World

Miller
*Economics Today**
Understanding Modern Economics

Miller/Benjamin
The Economics of Macro Issues

Miller/Benjamin/North
The Economics of Public Issues

Mills/Hamilton
Urban Economics

Mishkin
*The Economics of Money, Banking, and Financial Markets**
*The Economics of Money, Banking, and Financial Markets, Business School Edition**
*Macroeconomics: Policy and Practice**

Murray
Econometrics: A ModernIntroduction

Nafziger
The Economics of Developing Countries

O'Sullivan/Sheffrin/Perez
*Economics: Principles, Applications and Tools**

Parkin
*Economics**

Perloff
*Microeconomics**
*Microeconomics: Theory and Applications with Calculus**

Perman/Common/ McGilvray/Ma
Natural Resources and Environmental Economics

Phelps
Health Economics

Pindyck/Rubinfeld
*Microeconomics**

Riddell/Shackelford/Stamos/ Schneider
Economics: A Tool for Critically Understanding Society

Ritter/Silber/Udell
*Principles of Money, Banking & Financial Markets**

Roberts
The Choice: A Fable of Free Trade and Protection

Rohlf
Introduction to Economic Reasoning

Ruffin/Gregory
Principles of Economics

Sargent
Rational Expectations and Inflation

Sawyer/Sprinkle
International Economics

Scherer
Industry Structure, Strategy, and Public Policy

Schiller
The Economics of Poverty and Discrimination

Sherman
Market Regulation

Silberberg
Principles of Microeconomics

Stock/Watson
Introduction to Econometrics
Introduction to Econometrics, Brief Edition

Studenmund
Using Econometrics: A Practical Guide

Tietenberg/Lewis
Environmental and Natural Resource Economics
Environmental Economics and Policy

Todaro/Smith
Economic Development

Waldman
Microeconomics

Waldman/Jensen
Industrial Organization: Theory and Practice

Weil
Economic Growth

Williamson
Macroeconomics

READING BETWEEN THE LINES

Reading Between the Lines, which appears at the end of each chapter, helps students think like economists by connecting chapter tools and concepts to the world around them.

Macroeconomic Data

These macroeconomic data series show some of the trends in GDP and its components, the price level, and other variables that provide information about changes in the standard of living and the cost of living—the central questions of macroeconomics. You will find these data in a spreadsheet that you can download from your MyEconLab Web site.

	NATIONAL INCOME AND PRODUCT ACCOUNTS	1964	1965	1966	1967	1968	1969	1970	1971	1972	1973
	EXPENDITURE APPROACH										
the sum of	1 Personal consumption expenditures	411.5	443.8	480.9	507.8	558.0	605.1	648.3	701.6	770.2	852.0
	2 Gross private domestic investment	102.1	118.2	131.3	128.6	141.2	156.4	152.4	178.2	207.6	244.5
	3 Government expenditure	143.2	151.4	171.6	192.5	209.3	221.4	233.7	246.4	263.4	281.7
	4 Exports	35.0	37.1	40.9	43.5	47.9	51.9	59.7	63.0	70.8	95.3
less	5 Imports	28.1	31.5	37.1	39.9	46.6	50.5	55.8	62.3	74.2	91.2
equals	6 Gross domestic product	663.6	719.1	787.7	832.4	909.8	984.4	1,038.3	1,126.8	1,237.9	1,382.3
	INCOME APPROACH										
	7 Compensation of employees	370.7	399.5	442.6	475.1	524.3	577.6	617.2	658.9	725.1	811.2
plus	8 Net operating surplus	171.2	189.7	203.2	205.8	218.6	225.5	219.3	243.3	275.4	310.2
equals	9 Net domestic income at factor cost	541.9	589.2	645.8	680.9	742.9	803.1	836.5	902.2	1,000.5	1,121.4
plus	10 Indirect taxes less subsidies	54.6	57.7	59.3	64.1	72.2	79.4	86.6	95.8	101.3	112.0
	11 Depreciation (capital consumption)	66.4	70.7	76.5	82.9	90.4	99.2	108.3	117.8	127.2	140.8
equals	12 GDP (income approach)	662.9	717.6	781.6	827.9	905.5	981.7	1,031.4	1,115.8	1,229.0	1,374.2
plus	13 Statistical discrepancy	0.8	1.5	6.2	4.5	4.3	2.9	6.9	11.0	8.9	8.[illegible]
equals	14 GDP (expenditure approach)	663.7	719.1	787.8	832.4	909.8	984.6	1,038.3	1,126.8	1,237.9	1,382.2
	15 Real GDP (billions of 2005 dollars)	3,392.3	3,610.1	3,845.3	3,942.5	4,133.4	4,261.8	4,269.9	4,413.3	4,647.7	4,917.0
	16 Real GDP growth rate (percent per year)	5.8	6.4	6.5	2.5	4.8	3.1	0.2	3.4	5.3	5.8
	OTHER DATA										
	17 Population (millions)	191.9	194.3	196.6	198.8	200.7	202.7	205.1	207.7	209.9	211.9
	18 Labor force (millions)	73.1	74.4	75.7	77.3	78.7	80.7	82.8	84.4	87.0	89.4
	19 Employment (millions)	69.3	71.1	72.9	74.4	75.9	77.9	78.7	79.4	82.1	85.1
	20 Unemployment (millions)	3.8	3.4	2.9	3.0	2.8	2.8	4.1	5.0	4.9	4.4
	21 Labor force participation rate (percent of working-age population)	58.7	58.9	59.2	59.6	59.6	60.1	60.4	60.2	60.4	60.8
	22 Unemployment rate (percent of labor force)	5.2	4.5	3.8	3.8	3.5	3.5	5.0	6.0	5.6	4.9
	23 Real GDP per person (2005 dollars per year)	17,675	18,576	19,559	19,836	20,590	21,021	20,820	21,249	22,140	23,200
	24 Growth rate of real GDP per person (percent per year)	4.3	5.1	5.3	1.4	3.8	2.1	–1.0	2.1	4.2	4.8
	25 Quantity of money (M2, billions of dollars)	424.7	459.2	480.2	524.8	566.8	587.9	626.5	710.3	802.3	855.5
	26 GDP deflator (2005 = 100)	19.6	19.9	20.5	21.1	22.0	23.1	24.3	25.5	26.6	28.1
	27 GDP deflator inflation rate (percent per year)	1.6	1.8	2.9	3.1	4.3	5.0	5.3	5.0	4.3	5.5
	28 Price index (1982–1984 = 100)	31.0	31.5	32.4	33.4	34.8	36.7	38.8	40.5	41.8	44.4
	29 CPI inflation rate (percent per year)	1.3	1.6	2.9	3.1	4.2	5.5	5.7	4.4	3.2	6.2
	30 Current account balance (billions of dollars)	6.8	5.4	3.0	2.6	0.6	0.4	2.3	–1.4	–5.8	7.1

1974	1975	1976	1977	1978	1979	1980	1981	1982	1983	1984	1985	1986
932.9	1,033.8	1,151.3	1,277.8	1,427.6	1,591.2	1,755.8	1,939.5	2,075.5	2,288.6	2,501.1	2,717.6	2,896.7
249.4	230.2	292.0	361.3	438.0	492.9	479.3	572.4	517.2	564.3	735.6	736.2	746.5
317.9	357.7	383.0	414.1	453.6	500.7	566.1	627.5	680.4	733.4	796.9	878.9	949.3
126.7	138.7	149.5	159.4	186.9	230.1	280.8	305.2	283.2	277.0	302.4	302.0	320.3
127.5	122.7	151.1	182.4	212.3	252.7	293.8	317.8	303.2	328.6	405.1	417.2	452.9
1,499.5	1,637.7	1,824.6	2,030.1	2,293.8	2,562.2	2,788.1	3,126.8	3,253.2	3,534.6	3,930.9	4,217.5	4,460.1
890.3	949.2	1,059.4	1,180.6	1,335.6	1,498.4	1,647.7	1,819.8	1,919.8	2,035.7	2,245.7	2,412.0	2,559.4
314.1	351.0	392.3	444.0	508.8	546.4	560.6	652.9	669.2	756.1	910.6	971.0	995.9
1,204.4	1,300.2	1,451.7	1,624.6	1,844.4	2,044.8	2,208.3	2,472.7	2,589.0	2,791.8	3,156.3	3,383.0	3,555.3
121.6	130.8	141.3	152.6	162.0	171.6	190.5	224.1	225.9	242.0	268.7	286.7	298.5
163.7	190.4	208.2	231.8	261.4	298.9	344.1	393.3	433.5	451.1	474.3	505.4	538.5
1,489.7	1,621.4	1,801.2	2,009.0	2,267.8	2,515.3	2,742.9	3,090.1	3,248.4	3,484.9	3,899.3	4,175.1	4,392.3
[illegible].8	16.3	23.5	21.2	26.1	47.0	45.3	36.6	4.8	49.7	31.5	42.3	67.7
[illegible]9.5	1,637.7	1,824.7	2,030.2	2,293.9	2,562.3	2,788.2	3,126.7	3,253.2	3,534.6	3,930.8	4,217.4	4,460.0
[illegible]9.9	4,879.5	5,141.3	5,377.7	5,677.6	5,855.0	5,839.0	5,987.2	5,870.9	6,136.2	6,577.1	6,849.3	7,086.5
–0.6	–0.2	5.4	4.6	5.6	3.1	–0.3	2.5	–1.9	4.5	7.2	4.1	3.5
213.9	216.0	218.1	220.3	222.6	225.1	227.7	230.0	232.2	234.3	236.4	238.5	240.7
92.0	93.8	96.2	99.0	102.2	105.0	107.0	108.7	110.2	111.5	113.5	115.5	117.8
86.8	85.8	88.8	92.0	96.0	98.8	99.3	100.4	99.5	100.8	105.0	107.2	109.6
5.2	7.9	7.4	7.0	6.2	6.1	7.7	8.3	10.7	10.7	8.5	8.3	8.2
61.3	61.2	61.6	62.2	63.2	63.7	63.8	63.9	64.0	64.0	64.4	64.8	65.3
5.6	8.5	7.7	7.0	6.1	5.9	7.2	7.6	9.7	9.6	7.5	7.2	7.0
22,861	22,592	23,575	24,412	25,503	26,010	25,640	26,030	25,282	26,186	27,823	28,718	29,443
–1.5	–1.2	4.3	3.6	4.5	2.0	–1.4	1.5	–2.9	3.6	6.3	3.2	2[illegible]
902.1	1,016.2	1,152.0	1,270.3	1,366.0	1,473.7	1,599.8	1,755.5	1,909.3	2,125.7	2,308.8	2,494.6	2,7[illegible]
30.7	33.6	35.5	37.8	40.4	43.8	47.8	52.2	55.4	57.6	59.8	61.6	[illegible]
9.1	9.4	5.7	6.4	7.0	8.3	9.1	9.4	6.1	4.0	3.8	3.0	[illegible].9
49.3	53.8	56.9	60.6	65.2	72.6	82.4	90.9	96.5	99.6	103.9	107.6	[illegible]4.5
11.0	9.1	5.8	6.5	7.6	11.3	13.5	10.3	6.2	3.2	4.3	3.6	–0.4
2.0	18.1	4.3	–14.3	–15.1	–0.3	2.3	5.0	–5.5	–38.7	–94.3	–118.2	[illegible]78.4